"Whether journeying to Key West, Fla., Humboldt County, Calif., Ireland or Istanbul, Mr. Cockburn is a warrior/freethinker, armed with courage and gifted prose to cut down the hypocrisies of tyrants. He is a Marxist Mencken—a composite of comic-poet Andrei Codrescu, the erudite Christopher Hitchens and the gonzo journalist Hunter S. Thompson."

New York Times

"Always surprising, outrageous, brilliant and yet strangely compassionate. He weaves together the public and the private with a sustained comic ingenuity that is matchless."

Edward Said

"The example Alexander set retains full force … With an inexpugnable refusal of any paltering or temporization, Alexander put politics in command. *A Colossal Wreck* stands as an inspiration to do likewise."

Perry Anderson, *New Left Review*

"Cockburn's radicalism remained a fixed red star in the political firmament … According to conventional wisdom such predictability must result in tedium, yet even a casual skim through *A Colossal Wreck* reveals ample occasion for delight as well as outrage."

Times Literary Supplement

"Between the malevolence of the Republicans and the mediocrity of the Democrats, the last four decades have been a pretty dismal time to be a left-wing radical in the United States. Few of us have stayed scrappy; still fewer have kept a sense of humor. Cockburn—hedonist, populist, brawler, dandy—made it a little easier. I wish the next generation one of him."

George Scialabba, *Los Angeles Review of Books*

"It's alive on every page, this thing; its feisty sentences wriggle … *A Colossal Wreck* will have a long life among those who care about the crackling deployment of the English language, partly because Mr. Cockburn had such a wide-ranging mind … His book is a stay against boredom."

Dwight Garner, *New York Times*

"A fine trip through a rambunctious, productive, provocative and well-lived life."

Kirkus Reviews

"Cockburn's stylish prose is full of erudition, ribald gossip, and pithy insight … [his] gleefully contrarian punditry makes for an entertaining read."

Publishers Weekly

"This is a book that exhales life and comes with that brio which is characteristic of Alexander Cockburn."

Vijay Prashad, *CounterPunch*

"Alex struck American journalism like lightning."

Michael Tomasky, *Daily Beast*

"*A Colossal Wreck* provides ample evidence for Cockburn's standing as one of the left's most perceptive and entertaining commentators."

Guardian

"Alexander Cockburn set a high standard of crusading journalism for fifty years … With his Wildean wit, love of elegant women, penchant for hunting and fondness for P. G. Wodehouse, Cockburn defied the stereotype of the disgruntled left-wing scribe."

Independent

"Cockburn essentially pioneered the modern persona for which Christopher Hitchens became much better known: the fancily Oxford-educated leftie Brit littérateur/journalist who would say all the outrageous things his bland Yank counterparts lacked the wit, courage, erudition, or *épater*-spirit to utter on their own … Cockburn was far more committed and purposeful in his outrageousness."

James Fallows, *Atlantic*

"Cockburn … renders a broad perspective on political corruption and American culture."

Booklist

"An overflowing goodie basket of wit, expert deprecation, intellectual comradeship … and incisive ramble."

James Wolcott, *Vanity Fair*

A COLOSSAL WRECK

A Road Trip Through Scandal, Political Corruption and American Culture

Alexander Cockburn

VERSO
London • New York

This paperback edition first published by Verso 2014

1 3 5 7 9 10 8 6 4 2

Verso
UK: 6 Meard Street, London W1F 0EG
US: 20 Jay Street, Suite 1010, Brooklyn, NY 11201
www.versobooks.com

Verso is the imprint of New Left Books

ISBN-13: 978-1-78168-295-1 (PB)
eISBN-13: 978-1-78168-182-4 (US)
eISBN-13: 978-1-78168-493-1 (UK)

British Library Cataloguing in Publication Data
A catalogue record for this book is available from the British Library

The Library of Congress has cataloged the hardback edition as follows

Cockburn, Alexander.
[Essays. Selections]
A colossal wreck : a road trip through political scandal, corruption, and American culture / Alexander Cockburn. — First edition.

pages cm

Summary: "Alexander Cockburn was one of the most influential journalists of his generation. As the Atlantic noted, he was a towering figure who 'would say all the outrageous things his bland counterparts lacked the wit, courage, erudition, or epater-spirit to utter on their own.' In A Colossal Wreck, written prior to his death in July 2012, Cockburn reveals his great literary spirit, incisive reading of the situation, and campaigning vim into a single volume that will undoubtedly be seen as his masterpiece. Whether ruthlessly exposing the hypocrisy of Washington from Clinton to Obama, pricking the pomposity of those in power, or tirelessly defending the rights of the oppressed or silenced, Cockburn was the most gifted contrarian of his generation"— Provided by publisher.

ISBN 978-1-78168-119-0 (hardback)

1. United States—Politics and government—1993-2001. 2. United States—Politics and government—2001-2009. 3. United States—Politics and government—2009- 4. Politics, Practical—United States. 5. Political culture—United States. 6. Political corruption—United States. 7. United States—Social conditions—1980- 8. World politics—20th century. 9. World politics—21st century. 10. Cockburn, Alexander. I. Title.

E885.C625 2013

320.0973'0905—dc23

2013018400

Typeset in Minion Pro by MJ & N Gavan, Truro, Cornwall
Printed in the US by Maple Press

I met a traveller from an antique land
Who said: Two vast and trunkless legs of stone
Stand in the desert. Near them, on the sand,
Half sunk, a shattered visage lies, whose frown,
And wrinkled lip, and sneer of cold command,
Tell that its sculptor well those passions read
Which yet survive, stamped on these lifeless things,
The hand that mocked them, and the heart that fed;
And on the pedestal these words appear:
"My name is Ozymandias, king of kings:
Look on my works, ye Mighty, and despair!"
Nothing beside remains. Round the decay
Of that colossal wreck, boundless and bare
The lone and level sands stretch far away.

Shelley, "Ozymandias"

Contents

Introduction

By Andrew Cockburn

Some fool back in the '90s excoriated Alexander in the leftish English weekly the *New Statesman* for being "anti-American." The context, as I recall, was a paean to the supposedly radical initiatives of the Clinton administration, as contrasted with the moribund conservative regime in Britain. My brother, as readers of the present volume will shortly be reminded, never had any illusions about Clinton (or Hillary, "one of nature's bluestockings"), his reports on that theme thus exciting the indignation of this transatlantic Clintonista. It may have been the very stupidest of all the insults hurled over the years at Alexander. From the moment he landed here in 1972 (following the Mysterious Affair of the Balham Parrot, see page 351), he embraced with arms flung wide what he called "the vastness, the richness, the beauty and the grotesqueries of America in all its thousand landscapes."

His knowledge of those landscapes was profound, deepened over decades by wide-ranging and meticulously planned voyages of exploration into the hinterland, in which disparate samples of historical, biological, cultural, anthropological, and political interest were eagerly scanned and evaluated. See for example his description of Midland, Texas, as surveyed in July 2001. In a scant 900 or so words we learn about the incredible heat of the place; its economic position relative to neighboring Odessa; Audubon's condition (sedentary) at the time he painted his electrifying series on viviparous quadrupeds (look it up, Alexander always believed people should use the dictionary); the vulgar gossip that Laura Bush, wife of George W., had a "racy twenties" before settling down; a review of the Permian Basin Petroleum Museum—"does for hydrocarbons what the Uffizi does for Renaissance Italy"—segueing into a history of oil in west Texas; the Bush family's unsuccessful efforts to make a big pile of money in same; a telling reminder that while grimier Odessa has been a contender for Murder Capital USA, the more upscale Midland is the rape capital of Texas. A few days later he has moved on to a knowledgeable analysis of the political and journalistic trajectory of Katherine Graham, erstwhile proprietor of the *Washington Post*. (She had just died.) Many of us will never go to Midland and didn't know Mrs. Graham, but as with so much of the landscape that fell under Alexander's enthusiastic inspection, we need feel no loss. We can go there with him.

He could get interested in anything or anyone, which is why he got on so well with children. Rarely did he encounter someone for whom he had no kind word whatsoever, though exceptions included Barbara Bush, wife of forty-one, mother of forty-three—"one of the meaner women I'd met in a long time"—and various highway patrolmen insistent that some ancient vehicle had managed to exceed the speed limit: "His ferrety little eyes swivel around the back of the station wagon, linger on some cactuses I've picked up in a nursery in Truth or Consequences, linger further on my Coleman ice chest and then came back to my car papers …" The station wagon in question, a 1964 Newport, had spent the previous six years sitting in a field. A wood rat had built a nest in the glove compartment, and three of the four door locks were frozen. This was just one of the fleet of classics whose mechanical shortfalls were guaranteed to supply the necessary elements of chance and serendipity on his expeditions, connecting him to an archipelago of AAA tow-truck operators, garage mechanics, motel desk clerks, barbeque chefs and other denizens of the hinterland he loved. It was a better way than most of connecting with various emotional wellsprings in the American psyche, as on the day we pulled into a gas station in eastern Oklahoma in a newly acquired '59 Chrysler Imperial convertible sometime in the early 1980s and a fellow customer broke down in tears at the sight of the proud machine, exclaiming "that was when America was worth something; you ought to take that thing to Detroit and park it outside Chrysler headquarters so they'd be ashamed of themselves." (Later, Alexander did just that, tracing the actual car's precise heritage via its Vehicle Identification Number and the UAW to the production line that birthed it, manned at the time by middle-class Trotskyites from Long Island who had migrated to Detroit years before in confident but misplaced anticipation of the proletarian revolution.)

Traversing landscapes both beautiful and grotesque ("Martha's Vineyard … that hateful island"), Alexander's last book in no way stints on the scandal—those vulgar rumors about Laura B., for example—and political corruption as promised in his subtitle. In fact it delivers far more, presenting future generations with a high-resolution view of the great pileup, the colossal wreck, of the system as it careened off the end of the twentieth century and into the rocky landscape of the twenty-first. As such, it should be on the reading list of all school and college contemporary history courses, an honest chronicle from one who followed faithfully the injunction of the nineteenth-century London *Times* editor quoted on page five regarding the role of the press and its prime duty of disclosure: "whatever passes into its keeping becomes a part of the knowledge and the history of our times."

So, fortunately, future students puzzled by the Gadarene rush of America's economic overseers into the credit bubble and consequent financial smash-up may note his reaction to Treasury Secretary Robert Rubin's February 1995 statement of intent to repeal the Glass-Steagall Act that had kept Wall Street vaguely honest since the New Deal: "The Clinton administration, dominated in economic and financial matters by Wall Street's man Rubin, is now aiming to give banks and the securities firms everything they have yearned for." What followed, therefore, should not have come as a surprise. If in the future Mrs. Clinton is accorded treatment even more reverent than she receives today, it will be bracing to discover his trenchant comparison, early in 1996, between the then First Lady and the British Fabian reformer Beatrice Webb: "There's the same imperious gleam, the same lust to improve the human condition until it conforms to the wretchedly constricted vision of freedom which gave us social-worker liberalism, otherwise known as therapeutic policing. The Clintonite passion for talking about children as 'investments' tells the whole story."

That was before Monica Lewinsky came along to entertain us all and, as Alexander never tired of pointing out, save Social Security. In thrall to Wall Street, Clinton had been well on the way to privatizing the system, but dependence on congressional liberal democrats, necessary for avoidance of impeachment, meant the bankers and gougers were balked of their promised booty. Normally harsh on Clinton, the ubiquitous hypocrisies of the affair elicited Alexander's militant support for the embattled president, not least in his savage condemnation of his former friend Christopher Hitchens following the latter's betrayal of *his* old friend Sidney Blumenthal. While the press reveled in Pecksniffian admonitions of the chief executive, Alexander was there to strike a more sympathetic, sadder note: "Bill Clinton, leader of the free world, couldn't engage in a furtive embrace of a woman not his wife in the Oval office because he thought the gardener would peer in the windows. For the pitifully few moments of semi-gratification he and Monica Lewinsky were able to indulge each other, the two had to seclude themselves in a windowless corridor, a love site without even the close excitement of a broom closet."

Sympathy gave way to outrage when Clinton took to bombing people. "This was the Cowards' War," he wrote in June 1999 of the aerial war on Yugoslavia, "bombing a country for two and a half months from 30,000 feet. It was the Liberals' War waged by social democracy's best and brightest, intent on proving once again that wars can be fought with the best and most virtuous of intentions: the companion volume to Hillary Clinton's *It Takes a Village* turns out to be *It Takes an Air Force*."

Derision of such manifestations of hypocrisy was a recurrent theme in his writing, leading him now and then into interesting associations (not least his veneration for Jerry Ford, "our greatest president"), and thereby inducing casual observers to label him a "contrarian." This silly term, proudly adopted by some as self-description, denotes in reality a discard of principle in favor of reflexive posturing. That was emphatically not Alexander's course. Whether it was the Fully

Informed Jury Association, a cause normally associated with the right, or the fashion for hate crime legislation, or the ethnic cleansing of 150,000 Serbs from Krajina in 1995, Alexander was always stimulated by his unerring scent for an injustice. Our father Claud used to say that his own lifelong radicalism was no less inspired by regular doses of the *Magnificat* ("He hath put down the mighty from their seats") in his public school chapel as from Marx, and my brother was no different, never really shifting his aim-point from deserving targets. "There was indeed a vast criminal class coming to its full vicious potential in the 1990s," he observed in 2002, "a group utterly vacant of the most elementary instincts of social propriety, devoid of moral fiber, selfish to an almost unfathomable degree. The class comes in the form of our corporate elite."

Such forthright talk became commonplace after Wall Street's collapse brought said elite into disrepute, but was not so fashionable in 2002. His contemporary musings on the inauguration of Bush-era monstrosities have a similarly percipient snap. Bush's initial post-9/11 speech to Congress, for example, was "a declaration of lawlessness, with the concept of 'justice' being reduced to that of the freedom to shoot the other guy on whatever terms America may find convenient." Two administrations and twelve years of drone killings later, we can see how right he was.

Anyone commenting on the contemporary political scene, as Alexander did with unflagging energy for forty years, might possibly sound a little depressing at times. The wonder of his long road trip, ending in a cancer clinic in a small German town (whose history he immediately researched on arrival, unearthing many intriguing details), is that we never want to get off the ride.

PART 1

1995

January 1

To: Daisy Cockburn

Last year a Mexican muralist with nothing to do was here, and so I got him to do an 18-foot-by-8-foot ceiling mural on the roof of my garage become library. Roof meaning ceiling. I said it should more or less address the theme of the meaning of the universe. So there were horses on the vault of heaven and then—being Mexican—he had a peasant crucified to a corncob and lower down a great big skull and lower down Adam and Eve looking really bummed-out. Then some nice birds and an owl with wings extended.

After a year looking at this, I bumped into Daniel the painter back from Mexico and said that I was Anglo-Irish, not Mexican, and so I wanted everything more bushy-tailed. The peasant not crucified but waving a machete; no skull; and Adam and Eve looking excited as though they were off on a lovely picnic. He digested all this with relatively good grace and his (American) wife wagged her head in strong agreement. I felt like Pope Julius telling Michelangelo to give up this idea of god handing Adam a formal note of contract and just have the hands reaching out, know what I mean, Mike. Then what about instead of the skull, THE SPIRIT OF THE ETERNAL FEMININE. Daniel immediately wanted a Mayan-type woman crouching in eternal toil and suffering so I said No and dug up a painting by Dante

Gabriel Rosetti, *Prosperia*, one of those pre-Raph girls, all eyes and raised shoulder and haunted mien, and said try this one for the pose.

Then he needed a face so I think you are going to end up on the ceiling of the library holding a Humboldt lily which he's made the size of a gladiolus. The lily will have to be curbed, and the eternal feminine is a bit at odds with everything else, so we'll have to see. I hope you survive the final cut, as they say in Hollywood.

January 2

Dear Mr. Cockburn,

You ask where Bill Clinton was during the Vietnam War and I can tell you; he was spying on the anti-war movement. I was told this by an acquaintance of David Druiding, whose wife learned this from Hoyt Purvis. Hoyt Purvis was the Chief of Staff for Senator Fulbright during the Vietnam War. Bill Clinton worked for Senator Fulbright during the war and was found out to be spying on him. Mr. Purvis is currently the director of the Fulbright Institute of International Relations at the University of Arkansas in Fayetteville.

Unclassified has speculated that Bill Clinton may have been working for the CIA while he was at Oxford since other Rhodes scholars are known to have done this.

Edward G. Qubain, Austin, Texas

January 5

The world has become a sadder and more boring place. On 1 January Gary Larson hung up his sketch pad, which means the end of the universe as Larson has successfully managed to reconstruct it in the past decade and a half. Larson is not the first satirist to tell parables through beasts. But, before him, cows never had the sensitivities of Proust, nor dogs the wisdom of Solomon. There have been great painters of nature, but none with that exquisite precision which catches the taut excitement of an anteater as it sits in its burrow watching television and shouting, "Vera, come quick. Some nature show has a hidden camera in the Ericksons' burrow. We're going to see their entire courtship behavior."

Often the before-and-after narrative is obscure, as in the great cartoon showing a duck and one of Larson's patented mad scientists on a desert island, sinking ship in background, with the duck quacking triumphantly, "So, Professor Jenkins! ... My old nemesis ... We meet again, but this time the advantage is mine! Ha! Ha! Ha!" The joke comes out of the linking of the line from old kitsch thrillerdom to the abashed Jenkins–triumphant duck confrontation. But what were those past circumstances? And what will the duck do?

There was an uproar in 1984 when Larson drew a cartoon of a woman shouting out of the window, "Here, Fifi! C'mon! ... faster, Fifi!" The eager little hound is dashing up the path, aquiver with doggie trust, but we can see that the dog door is stoutly barred on the inside and that Fifi is going to fetch up against it with a tremendous wallop, a wallop that was as nothing to the torrent of complaint from the sort of citizens you meet in the newsagent's, buying birthday cards for their pets. Brooding on the fuss, Larson wrote: "The key element in any attempt at humor is conflict. Our brain is suddenly jolted into trying to accept something that is unacceptable."

In one of his collections, *The PreHistory of the Far Side*, Larson offers what are purportedly childhood sketches saved by his mother from the kindergarten period of his career. These feature prison bars on the windows, slavering hellhounds, a father holding him above a crocodile's jaws and other fun scenes from the dark vale of infancy.

In *PreHistory*, Larson offers some cartoons he never even bothered to send out for syndication. "Jesus rises from the grave," says the caption under a picture of a rather haggard Redeemer frying up some breakfast next to an open coffin and thinking: "I wonder what time it is ... I feel like I've been dead for three days."

January 11

The duty of the press—an over-roasted chestnut. For uplift we may turn to the editorials written by Robert Lowe for the London *Times* in 1851. He had been instructed by his editor to refute the claim of a government minister that if the press hoped to share the influence of statesmen, it "must also share in the responsibilities of statesmen."

"The first duty of the press," Lowe wrote, "is to obtain the earliest and most correct intelligence of the events of the time, and instantly, by disclosing them, to make them the common property of the nation. The statesman collects his information secretly and by secret means; he keeps back even the current intelligence of the day with ludicrous precautions, until diplomacy is beaten in the race with publicity. The Press lives by disclosures; whatever passes into its keeping becomes a part of the knowledge and the history of our times; it is daily and forever appealing to the enlightened force of public opinion—standing upon the breach between the present and the future, and extending its survey to the horizon of the world … For us, with whom publicity and truth are the air and light of existence, there can be no greater disgrace than to recoil from the frank and accurate disclosure of facts as they are. We are bound to tell the truth as we find it, without fear of consequences—to lend no convenient shelter to acts of injustice and oppression, but to consign them at once to the judgment of the world."

From which high-minded sentiments we may turn to the views expressed by Sir Melford Stevenson, who was a British high court judge from 1957 to 1979. To a group of journalists discussing ethical procedures he remarked: "I think you're all much too high-minded. I believe that newsworthiness is a firm realization of the fact that there's nothing so much the average Englishman enjoys on a Sunday morning—particularly on a Sunday morning—as to read a bit of dirt. And that would be my test of newsworthiness … There is a curious synthetic halo around these people who are called 'investigative' journalists. Now so far as most courts are concerned—and I think most jurors—the concept of a journalist driven by moral fervor to investigate a public scandal is a lot of nonsense. He enjoys the comforting thought that he has a bit of moral fervor which is filling his pocket as well. And there are few more desirable positions in life than that."

January 15

The Polish director Andrzej Wajda writes in his little memoir about movie-making, *Double Vision*, that once he started directing *Hamlet* and realized the whimsical, arbitrary quality of the plot, the hardest thing was to relate onstage the sequence of the events in proper order, from Hamlet's first meeting with his mother and the king to Fortinbras's victorious entrance in the final scene. That sequence of events could have been different if:

1. Hamlet had come to terms with his uncle, the king.
2. He had refused to believe in his father's ghost.
3. He had not succumbed to Ophelia's charms.
4. He had succeeded in killing the king while he was at prayer.
5. He had not killed Polonius by mistake, thinking he was the king.

Plus a whole lot of other "ifs."

And yet, Wajda goes on, "we have to admit that *Hamlet* has a steel-like logic." One thing just inevitably leads to another.

Wajda also tells a good story about something that happened the day the French left Algiers. People took to the streets and, in the course of events, still in a state of euphoria, arrived at the television studios. The gaping, empty studios, the television cameras and equipment scattered here and there, did not in the minds of the surging crowd seem to have any connection with what they conceived as television—that is, at least until the moment that someone in the know plugged in the cameras. Suddenly the blank screens of the monitors lit up, and the demonstrators saw their own bodies and faces on-screen. At first they were amused. Then they were emboldened. Hey, we're on TV! They realized if they could see themselves on the monitors, the rest of the population could also see them on TV sets throughout the city. Maybe even further. They began to sing, dance, recite. The result was an uninterrupted television show that for once was completely authentic. It finally ended, as do all such spontaneous demonstrations, with the arrival of the police and armed officers.

January 18

Being without electricity for four days here in storm-lashed Petrolia gives one a keen admiration for gas-fired water heaters (to which

I will be converting shortly). I enjoyed the recovered memory of living by lamplight, which I did for a number of years when I was growing up in Ireland. After 6:00 in the evening until about 7:00 in the morning, life becomes a matter of moving through a darkened house from one small pool of warm light to another. I have two lamps. Unlike the hard-edged world of the light bulb, everything is imprecise in outline. Everything looks like one of the those dark seventeenth- or eighteenth-century paintings. Most of my friends look better by lamplight too. Cooking becomes a different enterprise, based much more on smell or on the noise of a sizzle or a rolling boil. I'm fairly short-sighted, but in lamplight, it doesn't matter, because you can't see much anyway.

This situation reminds me of a story I once read about endemic trachoma in the Egyptian village of Gamileya. Trachoma is an infection that causes the inner surface of the eyelids to become chronically inflamed. In Gamileya, people do not require conventionally "normal" vision to conduct their daily activities. Plowing, sowing seed and harvesting don't require much vision. If there is some small task they are unable to do, their extended family does it for them, thus they do not perceive themselves as disabled.

Early last Wednesday morning, as I felt my way around the house, falling over the cats, listening to hear if the water was boiling, Petrolia played a final joke. Amid the violent thunderstorm that was raging, with the waters roiling not far from my window, the earth decided to heave in a fairly modest—4.3—earthquake.

February 10

I was astonished to see Robert Hughes confess in the *New York Review of Books* that he and his wife watch the MacNeil-Lehrer show every night. Imagine, day after day, week after week, year after year. "Good night, Jim. Good night, Robin."

I parodied MacNeil and Lehrer once in *Harper's* and that was it for Lewis Lapham. They never forgave him or me.

ROBIN MACNEIL (voice-over): Should one man own another?

MACNEIL: Good evening. The problem is as old as man himself. Do property rights extend to the absolute ownership of one man by another? Tonight, the slavery problem. Jim?

LEHRER: Robin, advocates of the continuing system of slavery argue that the practice has brought unparalleled benefits to the economy. They fear that new regulations being urged by reformers would undercut America's economic effectiveness abroad. Reformers, on the other hand, call for legally binding standards and even a phased reduction in the slave force to something like 75 percent of its present size. Charlayne Hunter-Gault is in Charleston. Charlayne?

And so on.

Bob is an old friend. We've fished together. We've even done that most intimate, secret of things—we went to a tax accountant together. Back in the mid-1970s we formed a mutual support group of two, forcing ourselves to get abreast of the federal tax situation. At Jason Epstein's instigation, Mr. Hoffman of Garlick and Hoffman agreed to see us. We arrived at the appointed hour with our shoeboxes filled with bus receipts and other records. Mr. Hoffman looked over the fine red velvet suit Bob had donned for the occasion. "Filing a joint return?" he asked cautiously.

March 1

On Monday, February 27, as Wall Street was digesting morning headlines about the Barings disaster, Treasury Secretary Rubin rose to address New York securities traders at a savings bond lunch. His chosen theme was "modernization," which in Wall Street parlance—and Rubin, former chief of Goldman Sachs, is a Wall Street man par excellence—usually means the sweeping away of any regulatory inhibition on the power to make as much money as possible, as fast as possible.

And thus it turned out. Rubin announced that the Clinton administration plans to overturn the Glass-Steagall Act which separates commercial and investment banking. Separate legislation will allow banking–insurance ties.

Glass-Steagall was signed on June 16, 1933. It was designed to restore confidence in the nation's banking system, reeling after a series of runs and panics. It established the Federal Deposit Insurance Corporation. In return for federal support for their liabilities the banks were required to submit to regulation. Glass-Steagall forbade banks from short-term trading of most securities and from underwriting corporate offerings. Issuance of stocks and bonds was left to the securities industry.

It's the aim of every captain of finance to preside over a universal financial institution where the velocity of capital can approach the speed of light.

Banks want to get into the securities industry because there's extra money to be picked up in handling stocks, bonds and kindred short-term IOUs. Securities firms want to get into the banking business because it gets them access to the Federal Reserve payments mechanism, whereby the Fed stands behind banks as their lender of the last resort.

The Clinton administration, dominated in economic and financial matters by Wall Street's man Rubin, is now aiming to give banks and the securities firms everything they have yearned for.

March 3

Dear Mr. Cockburn,

On March 29, 1994, my friend and associate, June Weinstrock, was severely beaten by a mob in San Cristobal, Guatemala. Her attackers were fired to hysteria by rumors that Americans were abducting Guatemalan children and selling their organs. Apparently unaware of the rumors, she approached and/or spoke with children at a bus stop in town. Meanwhile, nearby, a distraught mother called out for her child who had become separated from her in a crowd. A street vendor joked that "The Gringa took him ... for body parts." June is presently hospitalized in Anchorage, slowly convalescing from major brain damage—at present unable to walk, but beginning to recover speech.

I have been investigating the background of this event concerning child abductions and the so-called organ trade. I have read several journalistic accounts of the event and its surrounding circumstances.

Do you know any of the documented cases that are trackable to a source? In particular, autopsy evidence would be compelling.

Sincerely,

Coert Olmstead

The body-part story has been circulating for years. In the early 1980s the CIA even said that it was disinformation put out by the KGB to discredit America. At one time or another many investigators from TV documentary programs and newspapers have tried to follow the body-parts trail but haven't come up with much. The best discussion of the whole subject I've come across is in the Nancy Scheper-Hughes's book about the Brazilian northeast, *Death Without Weeping*, where she discusses the not baseless fear of poor women there that their children will be kidnapped by middle-class women without off-spring of their own. The body-parts fear surfaces there too. There are genuine accounts from all over the world—most recently India—of people selling one of their kidneys and so forth. Asset transfer …

March 23

It turns out that the directors of Barings Bank knew perfectly well that Nick Leeson, their man in Singapore, was staking their future on some bets on the movement of the Japanese Nikkei index. Since Leeson had made them a lot of money the previous year they thought he was going to repeat his achievement.

Then, in the hour of emergency, the Barings directors turned to the Bank of England to bail them out. The Bank's top man was away skiing in Switzerland, so the decision fell on the shoulders of his number two, whose interest that Sunday evening lay not in saving one of the oldest private investment houses in England, but in advancing his adulterous liaison with an Irish girl with whom he was enjoying intimacies on the carpet of the governor's office.

So the second in command said No to Barings, which promptly went belly up, though its directors still voted themselves enormous bonuses. The Irish girl decamped to her native sod, whence she communicated details of the adultery to the British press, much to the discomfiture of the second-in-command's wife, Helen Jay, who said she would stand by him, though not to the extent of appearing in photographs with her treacherous spouse.

I went out with the very nice Helen briefly in the mid-1960s. She and her twin sister Catherine were once taken as symbolic of a youthful Labour Party, poised to snatch control of the nation's destinies from the palsied Conservatives who had been in power for fourteen years, until they met in defeat in 1964 at the hands of Harold Wilson and his Labour cohorts.

The pretty Jay twins attended the Buckingham Palace Garden party that year dressed in the Mondrianesque clothes of the French designer Courrèges and were thought to be striking exemplars of the new, go-ahead age of social democracy that was about to unfold.

Meanwhile their father, Douglas Jay, became President of the Board of Trade in the Wilson cabinet. Owing to his nympholeptic tastes he was known as Mucky Doug. I remember having enjoyable late night drinks with Gareth Stedman Jones and the twins in their father's Hampstead Heath house when suddenly the door of the living room was flung open and there stood the cabinet minister, resplendent in his pajamas and flourishing one of those red dispatch boxes—like a small suitcase—in which cabinet members proudly carry home their papers. I hoped he was going to invoke the nation's business and he did, bellowing that he had "the nation's business to attend to" and would we "please leave," which we duly did.

Later Helen took up with Nicholas Tomalin, a well-known journalist who hired me as number two when he became literary editor of the *New Statesman*. The editor was Paul Johnson. Tomalin's adulteries with Helen tended to be the topic of his tipsy lunch-time reveries as we sat in some pub in Lincoln's Inn of the sort later immortalized in fiction by my sister Sarah Caudwell. "Everything's good if the fucking is good," Tomalin would mumble as he slurped his way through his staple lunch-time bottle of white wine.

His literary editorship was meant to spell a new life instead of the "investigative journalism" by which he had made his name, exposing French shippers for mislabeling their vintages. But soon he wearied of the kingdom of letters and went off to cover the 1973 Yom Kippur war, and was killed by the wire-guided missile of what Paul Johnson described in his memorial speech as a "Syrian savage." Now Helen is with the assistant head of the Bank of England which shows you the trend of events in Blighty.

March 29

"Here and there in the midst of American society you meet with men full of a fanatical and almost wild spiritualism, which hardly exists in Europe. From time to time strange sects arise which endeavor to strike out extraordinary paths to eternal happiness. Religious insanity is very common in the United States ...

"The soul has wants that must be satisfied; and whatever pains are taken to divert it from itself, it soon grows weary, restless and disquieted amid the enjoyments of sense. If ever the faculties of the great majority of mankind were exclusively bent upon the pursuit of material objects, it might be anticipated that an amazing reaction would take place in the souls of some men. They would drift at large in the world of spirits, for fear of remaining shackled by the close bondage of the body.

"It is not, then, wonderful if in the midst of a community whose thoughts tend earthward a small number of individuals are found who turn their looks to heaven. I should be surprised if mysticism did not soon make some advance among a people solely engaged in promoting their own worldly welfare."—from "Why some Americans manifest a sort of fanatical Spiritualism." Chapter XII of de Tocqueville's *Democracy in America.*

April 12

An astoundingly silly quote from Antonio Gramsci, arguing that dumb toil can be liberating: "Once the process of adaptation has been completed, what really happens is that the brain of the worker, far from being mummified, reaches a state of complete freedom. The only thing that is completely mechanized is the physical gesture: the memory, reduced to simple gestures repeated at an intense rhythm, 'nestles' in the muscular and nervous centers and leaves the brain free and unencumbered for other occupations."

Read that to the next person who complains about carpal tunnel syndrome. I knew Lenin was a fanatic Taylorist, but it turns out AG was the same way. Gramsci came to this idiotic conclusion after considering type compositors whom he arrogantly supposed to be mechanistically transcribing without considering the text's "often fascinating intellectual content." He wrote this about the same time the British type compositors at the London *Daily Mail* prompted the General Strike of 1926 by refusing to typeset an article they regarded as anti-labor.

April 14

In a significant shift in its admissions policy, Harvard University apparently no longer regards murder as a useful, even decisively impressive credential.

When she was fourteen, Gina Grant killed her alcoholic mother, admitting to a South Carolina court that she struck her thirteen times with a lead crystal candle holder. This was back in 1990. Grant pleaded no contest to voluntary manslaughter and spent six years in juvenile detention. Then a judge agreed that she could go north to Massachusetts and try for a fresh start under the supervision of her (deceased) father's aunt and her husband.

At first living with her relatives and then alone, Grant did extraordinarily well at Cambridge Rindge and Latin high school, getting straight As, tutoring poor children, flourishing in the school's overall social life. Harvard offered her early admission.

But now Grant's very achievements have turned back on her. The *Boston Globe* ran a story on Grant. The high school had recommended her as demonstrating unusual determination in overcoming obstacles. (Such obstacles did not, in the school's mind, include Grant's matricide, of which it was ignorant.) Publication brought a slew of newspaper clippings about the murder case, which had been widely publicized in South Carolina at the time. These clippings were sent anonymously to the *Globe*, and also to Harvard, which lost no time in snatching back the invitation of early admission.

A spokesman for the university, Joe Wrinn, says that such an offer had been made under the Early Action program for exceptional applicants but had been rescinded "after careful consideration of new information that was not disclosed at the time of the application." Grant's lawyer says Gina thought the records of the case were sealed. When the *Globe*'s reporter asked her about her mother, she'd answered that her death was a very painful matter she didn't want to discuss.

Thus the new Harvard rule. Murderers—even those who've passed through the legal system and emerged the other end—need not apply.

Now consider the case of Héctor Gramajo. At the time Grant was having that terminal confrontation with her mother, Gramajo was defense minister of Guatemala. He has superintended the counterinsurgency program of the early 1980s, during the presidency of Rios Montt, in which many thousands of Mayan Indians were slaughtered. Indeed, Gramajo was key in designing the entire program to eliminate all opposition, using tactics including massacres, selective murders, disappearances and torture.

Nor was he ashamed of his role. In a 1991 article in a Harvard journal called *International Review* Gramajo was quoted by Wellesley professor Schirmer as telling her that he was personally "in charge of" a commission that devised the 70%/30% civil affairs program. "You don't need to kill everyone to complete the job," Gramajo confided. "We instituted civil affairs which provide development for 70% of the population while we kill 30%." Schirmer asked him how he came up with the numbers and Gramajo answered, "One said 30% just for the sake of saying it. We said 30% so that the repression would be less."

As he once told another interviewer, "I consider myself a product of the American educational system … since the beginning of my basic training." And indeed he had been part of a US Early Action program to pick out young comers, shuttling them north to attend military schools.

Gramajo's final year as defense minister did nothing to diminish his blood-spattered reputation. A dozen or so university students were kidnapped and tortured and their bodies dumped in various parts of Guatemala City. In November Sister Dianna Ortiz was kidnapped, tortured, raped and thrown into a pit with dead bodies and rats. Her life was only spared when it was discovered she was an American.

By now Gramajo's name had figured in innumerable human rights reports, no doubt part of the "General Gramajo file" considered by Harvard, when its Kennedy School granted him a Mason fellowship. It is not known whether Gramajo made full disclosure of his past on the entry form. Harvard had been advised of Gramajo's suitability by the US Agency for International Development. Gramajo was clearly being groomed as a presidential candidate in the 1995 elections.

He stayed a year at Harvard, studying public policy and graduating in 1991 in a ceremony marred only by the serving on him of a civil suit brought by the Center for Constitutional Rights (CCR), seeking millions in damages for the torture and killing of nine Mayan Indians. A separate suit served a week later stated he was responsible for the abduction of Sister Ortiz.

A federal judge in Boston is now considering a motion for a default judgment, brought by the CCR.

April 20

Guilford—Here I am in the middle of the southern Vermont countryside, in a friend's farmhouse. No one around, and not a sound. Makes you realize how busy the Northern California country is. No matter where you are, there's always a chainsaw, some four-wheeler stuck, a dope grower peering at you from behind a tree. Something.

Here, it's as if everyone's at work in town—which they are, or down in New York—and the countryside has been put away in mothballs till the summer. Very odd. Of course I may be more than usually sensitive to this because it's the empty farmhouse of my pal Andrew Kopkind who died last year and I haven't been here in ten years.

I began my tour for my new book, *The Golden Age Is in Us*, last night in Amherst with a crowd of 200. A young man came up and informed me that when the Pentagon wished to summon its "secret strategic reserve" (I suppose them to be the elite commandos) it would get NPR to play the opening bars of Beethoven's Fifth Symphony.

"Doesn't this allow the possibility of confusion?" I said to the young man. "I mean, there are many people at NPR who might play the opening bars of Beethoven's Fifth not knowing it's a secret code. Are there standing orders at NPR *not* to play Beethoven's Fifth until they get an order from the Pentagon? And are the people in the elite reserve commandos the sort of people likely to listen to NPR, or are they ordered to listen by the Pentagon, which means the NPR's audience consists of commandos, which means the conservatives should support it." The young man looked depressed, so I felt sorry for him and said maybe there was something in it. He looked at me pityingly and said perhaps it was better for my peace of mind that I didn't know certain things.

April 23

I drive to Storrs, in western Connecticut, where there's a big state campus and a good bookstore. After a talk and some book signing I have dinner with a jolly crew which includes a funny woman named Leslie Brody who recounts her time as deputy minister of education in the White Panther Party. At one point she traveled to Paris to confer with the North Vietnamese, but misread the map of the metro and was late for her appointment. The North Vietnamese seemed put out, and would only talk in general terms about art and gardening.

Also at the dinner was Mary Gallucci, whose grandfather won the triple jump—hop, skip and jump—at the Intercalated Olympic Games of 1906. He was Irish, but since Ireland was still a colony, the British flag was raised during the medal-giving ceremony. He then swarmed up the flagpole and substituted the Irish flag, which was a pretty heavy thing to do in 1906.

April 24

Hartford—Visited Mark Twain's house. The old boy lived in great, albeit rather heavy Victorian style. In the bookshop is the Paige compositor, the linotype machine in which he invested heavily and which bankrupted him. This—the last extant example—is a colossal piece of equipment, about fifteen feet long.

Twain loved type, having started hand-setting when he was thirteen. By the 1890s a skilled compositor could handset and justify about 1,500 characters per hour. The Paige compositor could manage 12,000. But the inventor mimed the human hand-setting, and the Paige was mechanically baroque. The Mergenthaler Linotype appeared on the market at almost the same time and finished off the Paige in no time. Twain declared bankruptcy in 1894, and wrote *Tom Sawyer* and *Pudd'nhead Wilson* to start working off the debts, which he finished doing in 1898.

Declining industrial cities always do well in terms of affordable spaces and reasonable cheap housing. I give a talk in a former typewriter factory, now called Real Artways, run by my friend Will Wilkins and devoted to avant-garde events. I remember a story Forest, the chap who fixes my manual typewriters in Eureka, once told me. The Underwood factory in Hartford had a metal pressing shop where ropes affixed to the workers' elbows dragged their arms back as the press came down, ensuring they wouldn't be mangled. The factory had visitor tours. Then someone took a photo and in the end a Soviet newspaper printed it with the caption, "American workers chained to their work bench." Tours were canceled forthwith.

May 10

It was when the *Challenger* blew up on national television in 1986 that the idea of counseling children in the wake of such disasters seems to have caught on.

Of course it must have been horrifying for the students of Christa McAuliffe to see the explosion and know their teacher had died. Maybe they needed a quiet word. But children across the country? And what did the shrinks tell them? That O-rings freeze, presidential schedules require timely lift-off, accidents happen, it's time to move on? In my experience kids are pretty realistic and most times rather enjoy a good disaster. They can take it.

Maybe these occasional lapses into child counseling at moments of high national drama occur as substitutes for all the times children face mundane evil, and learn to accept it as part of the normal order of things, with no counselor at hand.

Take the case of eight-year-old Marisa Means. Her dad Bill had been encouraged by his company, Structural Dynamics Research Corp., to bring her to the office as part of "Take Our Daughters to Work Day" celebrated on April 27 last. So Bill and Marisa arrived at company premises some fifteen miles east of Cincinnati, Ohio, and went to his office. Not long thereafter Bill, a systems engineering manager who had been with the company for two years, was called in by his supervisor and fired. Next thing they knew, Bill was clearing his office in front of his daughter and then the two were escorted off the premises.

Later, a company flack, Donald Newman, said the timing had been "regrettable."

What Marisa saw was not the work of a paranoid mass murderer as in Oklahoma, nor the frailty of equipment and judgment as with the *Challenger*. She saw a banal evil: the company that had invited her to bring a pack lunch and spend the day with her dad at work kicked him out. She saw her father humiliated and she'll probably carry the memory for the rest of her days.

May 17

Detroit—The "Gun Stock '95" rally held at Freedom Hill, in Macomb County, on a gusty Saturday in mid-May had been advertised to me by local leftists as a potential mini-Nuremberg of a far-right crowd. I drove north from Detroit expecting to find grim-jawed Patriots toting awesome armament and mustered in their camos in defense of the Second Amendment.

The right of the people to bear arms most certainly was upheld with lusty cascades of rhetoric, but the mood was amiable and the crowd of some 2,500 keenly enjoyed the speeches. No guns were visible and camo was forbidden. Discreet ribbons identified Patriots. The most bellicose-looking creature was a rather weary Doberman Pinscher, Brutus, wearing a collar of M-60 bullets. Photographers from as far afield as France, hungering for images of Angry White Rightists, fell upon Brutus with cries of joy.

As I came in, a man from Putting People First was lashing away at Jeremy Bentham, the English utilitarian, as part of a multi-pronged assault on environmentalists. The environmentalists, the speaker shouted, "make no moral distinction between a rat and a human being." The blame for this appalling down-grading in the status of the "the most magnificent of all creatures ever to walk the face of the planet, MAN" was duly traced to Bentham who—though the speaker did not quote him directly—declared about animals in 1780 that "The question is not, Can they reason? Nor, Can they talk? But, Can they suffer?" Bentham said that as with human slaves, animals should not be tormented.

As the crowd—many of them young autoworkers from the plants around the region—followed with commendable attention, the speaker showed how Benthamite thought led to Nazism: "Among civilized states the Germans were the first to end vivisection. Hitler treated his dog better than the Jews. And they call *us* Nazis!"

Of course if anyone in that crowd had kicked poor old Brutus, the Doberman, on the grounds that Bentham was wrong and dogs don't suffer, he would have been torn limb from limb.

I toured the book and pamphlet tables. They contained a variety of alluring material, starting with a thick, spiral bound volume, entitled *Lethal Laws*, subtitle, *Documentary Proof: Enforcement of "Gun Control" Laws Clears the Way for Governments to Commit Genocides*. This extremely interesting history ($25.00 list price, knocked down for yours truly to $15 because "the press needs to know") of attempted and actual genocides, starting with assaults on Japanese Americans in World War II, had as its tightly argued premise the proposition that " 'gun control' is the key to genocide … genocides occur when leaders with 'sure cures' for 'national problems' ram new ideas down the citizens' throats … ordinary technologies expand government power over citizens." The three authors, Jay Simkin, Aaron Zelman and Alan Rice, identify themselves as members of Jews for the Preservation of Firearms Ownership (America's Aggressive Civil Rights Organization), headquartered in Milwaukee.

On the main stage, the organizer of the event, Michael Sessa, an intense man in his forties, tried to abbreviate the lengthy speech he had, he told me later, sat up all night preparing. He was kind enough to hand it over. Most of it could have been delivered by a leftist in the late '60s without changing a comma. The name Martin Luther King, mentioned at the Gun Stock rally by one of the speakers, got a cheer. (So, it should be added, did the names of Detroit policemen involved in the fatal beating of a black man.)

Back in Detroit leftist friends berated me for taking too friendly an attitude to the afternoon's proceedings. I told them we should have had our booths and literature up at the event, assuming the organizers would have let us. What's always missing from the populist-right analysis is who actually runs the world. They say "the Masons," or the "the Jews," or some other preferred candidate. But they always miss out on the corporations. Show them the Fortune 500 and they look blank.

But these young workers should be getting decent radical analysis and some respectful attention. Tell someone he's a Nazi long enough, and he may just become one, just for the hell of it and as a way of saying F— you to the powers-that-be.

June 21

A few years ago, my daughter and I visited the Huntington Library near Pasadena, California. Halfway down the spacious public gallery, replete with its Gutenberg Bible, Shakespeare folios, early maps, and other testaments to the rise of capitalism, there is a case containing a scrap of paper on which is a letter written by Andrew Jackson. The note is an injunction to massacre. He commands General John Coffee to destroy the Creek Indians in Tallahatchie, in the Mississippi Territory, and "under a discreet officer … to envelop any Indians that may be spying on the south east bank … you will in performing this service keep the greatest order and observe the greatest circumspection." Coffee descended upon the Creek Indians, murdered the braves, 186 in all, and captured eighty-four women and children. President Jackson adopted one of the orphans. There, in the case in the Huntington Library, is the order, with deletions and rephrasings scored on it by Jackson. Down the years it has carried the testament of individual responsibility and, though the author did not see it that way, individual guilt. It is not a record that, in the age of electronic, industrialized consciousness, would have survived.

June 28

This year is the 325th anniversary of the day when the jurors in the trial of William Penn refused to convict him of violating England's Conventicle Act (which declared as seditious any religious meeting outside the sanction of the Church of England) despite clear evidence that he had openly preached a Quaker sermon. The judge promptly incarcerated four of these jurors and they spent nine weeks in jail, after which their release and exoneration established forever as English and American legal doctrine that it is the right and responsibility of the trial jury to decide both on matters of fact and the validity of the law in the specific case before it. These rights are enshrined in the Fifth, Sixth and Seventh Amendments, along with other rights enumerated in or implied by the Constitution.

Since I started to write about the Fully Informed Jury Association (FIJA), it's been somewhat demoralizing to discover how many liberals and leftists actually fear juries, and think our affairs would be better conducted without them, preferring panels of "experts" or "qualified" persons passed through all the usual filtration systems to produce people of conventional thought and moral posture.

I'm just about ready to junk the whole left/right taxonomy as useless and indeed an active impediment to thought and action. Why should we be dominated by a political labeling system based on where people sat in the Constituent Assembly in Versailles in 1789 with factions gathered to the right and to the left of the President's desk?

July 5

I talked today to M. I. "Red" Beckman, who once wrote a little book, *The Church Deceived*, which contains anti-Semitic passages. A reporter in the *Wall Street Journal*, Wade Lambert, charged that such writings by Beckman somehow compromised FIJA, of which he is an active member.

I talked with Beckman on the phone at some length. His central focus seemed to be the government's abuse of power via the IRS, which he termed a "terrorist" organization. A Christian, he thinks all organized religions and governments use people ruthlessly. He says many adherents of Judaism are slaves of Satan, but he says the same of adherents to other religions, particularly those assenting to a 501(c)(3) relationship with the state. He was against the Vietnam War. He says the pendulum swung too far to the left and people like him are working to stop it swinging too far to the right. He says Hitler was a criminal, Reagan was a criminal. He thinks … But, so far as FIJA is concerned, what Beckman thinks and says is not the point. To denounce FIJA because Beckman supports jury nullification is like denouncing the Fifth Amendment because Communists used it in the '50s.

All over America constituencies written off as hopelessly uneducable have been abandoned to their own resources to deal with American capital moving abroad. The "farm crisis," "oil politics," NAFTA, the IMF and the World Bank can produce simultaneously militias in America and Chiapas. The "left" should get off its high horse and re-examine the real-life grass-roots' resourcefulness in America; to acknowledge that abandoned constituencies have fallen back on the Bill of Rights, and that this turns out to be a pretty good compass; and to think about joining in the defense of the jury.

July 12

The "shadowy one-world government" the militias worry about is the Fed and the big banks both here and abroad, plus the IMF and the World Bank and other multinational financial institutions reaching broad agreement on tight money and "favorable business conditions," meaning enough unemployment to ensure that employers have the upper hand.

These days banker-bashing or Fed-bashing, which used to be a decent national sport, is taken to be uncouth in respectable circles—as though one was somehow ranting about the Freemasons. Rep. Jim Leach of Iowa, chairman of the House Banking Committee, recently suggested that such attacks were tantamount to anti-Semitism. So now it's anti-Semitic to attack banks and bond houses?

When I lived in England back in the 1960s one could hear Prime Minister Harold Wilson denounce the "gnomes of Zurich" on an almost daily basis. He was talking about the international bankers who made life difficult for his Labour government. No one accused Wilson of being anti-Semitic. People knew he was talking about the behavior of bankers, not the behavior of Jews.

July 14

Dear Bruce,

Remember that fellow I warned you about from the *San Francisco Chronicle*? I think his name was Jerry Carroll (not Jon). Back at the end of the 1980s this Carroll invited me to have lunch at what he described as a "good place to eat." This turned out to be one of the most expensive restaurants—The Campton Grill—in San Francisco. When the bill came he asked me to put up $50, on the grounds that he didn't have enough money and the newspaper would never stand for it. Then, when he wrote up the interview, he derided me for eating in costly places.

I swore never to eat another lunch with an interviewer. Of course I forgot and agreed on a rendezvous with Jack Shafer, the new editor of the *San Francisco Weekly*. We had what I thought was a perfectly amiable lunch at a place of his choosing—pleasant and by no means pretentious—called George's Global Kitchen, somewhere south of Market in San Francisco.

I knew almost from the moment I sat down that Shafer had already written most of the story in his head, that he'd figured out his angle and it didn't much matter what I said. But everything passed off calmly enough and he even faxed me a friendly note a few days later saying he'd enjoyed it.

Then the actual piece comes through the fax machine from the

AVA [*Anderson Valley Advertiser*]. Here's how it began: "If you've ever handled a venomous snake you already know what it's like to chat with Alexander Cockburn." (The piece, by the way, was headed "The Tale of an Asp.") "Not just your average poisonous Marxist reptile, Cockburn is all grins and hisses and eye contact and bared Irish fangs as he chomps his soft-shell-crab sandwich at George's Global Kitchen. It's a giddy thrill to be inside the kill zone of the greatest living exponent of bilious journalism and in my reverie I ponder the original Irish diaspora in which St. Patrick chased the serpents from the island and for a moment fantasize that Cockburn himself is descended from a race of socialistic bogtrotting snake people who escaped Ireland to sting and paralyze capitalists such as myself ..."

How can you win? I smile at the man and this becomes "all grins and hisses and eye contact." Suppose I'd given him a more somber greeting. Then we'd have had "all sullen stares and shifty glances and pursed lips as he self-righteously declined all nourishment."

July 19

The marketing director of Verso, my publisher, calls. It is Wednesday. He has in his hand the *New York Times Book Review* for the following Sunday. The *Book Review* goes out early to subscribers in the book trade.

He begins to read. I hear phrases like "self-proclaimed Leninist," and await paragraphs about my addiction to Stalin, my forgiving posture toward the Purges, my determination to evict all Jews in Israel into the sea. This is, after all, the *New York Times.*

But no. It seems the reviewer, a fellow called Douglas Brinkley, billed as an historian at the University of New Orleans, actually likes my book, *The Golden Age Is in Us.*

"Whether journeying to Key West, Fla., Humboldt County, Calif., Ireland or Istanbul, Mr. Cockburn is a warrior/freethinker, armed with courage and gifted prose to cut down the hypocrisies of tyrants. He is a Marxist Mencken—a composite of comic-poet Andrei Condrescu (minus the Transylvanian sarcasm), the erudite Christopher Hitchens (minus the radical chic impulse) and the gonzo journalist Hunter S. Thompson (minus the drugs, guns and rock-and-roll)."

The marketing director tells me this is worth 500 book sales. I think to myself maybe it's worth another $5,000 on the next book contract.

By the last paragraph the review is calling me "a life-loving anarchist," presumably having abandoned the self-proclaimed Leninism of the reviewer's beginning. I'm a quick learner! "Still," the review concludes, "many readers will be astonished to discover that the 'irrelevant' left still has much to offer as we search for a utopian resolution to your tangled social problems. *The Golden Age Is in Us* is a delightful reminder that the New Left, which blossomed in the 1960s, has not completely withered and died."

Better than waking up in bed with a dead policeman or a wet umbrella, as my father used to say.

July 26

"When I began work on this biography, I intended it to be a very favorable portrait ..." Thus Shelden, in the opening chapter of his new book, *Graham Greene: The Enemy Within*. Shelden goes on to say that examination of Greene disclosed unsavory aspects of his character. So he reversed track and wrote a character assassination.

This is an old rhetorical trick, in which the biographer sadly announces that in mid-investigation the scales fell from his eyes. In Shelden's case the truth is more likely that with Greene dead and thus incapable of suing for libel, the time was ripe for a demolition job running counter to the official biography being slowly released in three volumes by Norman Sherry.

Shelden's book is substantively thin and pretty silly. Poor Greene can't do anything without being assailed for low motives and possible misbehavior. A trip to Africa in the company of his cousin Barbara adds up to inferences by Shelden about Greene's conduct merely because the cousin wore shorts, thus displaying bare legs to her putatively ravenous relative who, as Shelden prissily emphasizes, had a wife and child back in England.

I have an interest in all this because my father, Claud, was a lifelong pal of Greene's, going to the same school (of which the headmaster was Greene's father, Charles) and sharing in many escapades into their twenties and beyond. In his introduction to my father's final collection of his memoirs, *Claud Cockburn Sums Up*, Greene wrote, "If I were asked who are the greatest journalists of the twentieth century, my answer would be G. K. Chesterton and Claud Cockburn. Both are more than journalists: both produced at least one novel which will be rediscovered with delight, I believe, in every generation: *The Man Who Was Thursday* and *Ballantyne's Folly*." Knowing of this friendship, biographers would beat a path to my father's door. I once heard a television interviewer solemnly ask him about Greene's assertion that he—Graham that is—had been "dead drunk every day" of his first term at Oxford.

"Well, I didn't notice," my father replied.

"You mean, he wasn't?"

"No, Greene is a very truthful man and if he said he was dead drunk every day, he was and the fact that I didn't notice it must have meant I was equally drunk."

The transcript of this conversation turns up in Sherry's first volume, plus my father's gloss to the assiduous biographer on what heavy drinking meant at Oxford in the mid-1920s.

"I got up fairly early, 8 a.m. I would then drink a large sherry glass of neat whiskey before breakfast and drank heavily throughout the day. I drank approximately a bottle and a half of whiskey every day, exclusive of wines and beers. God the amount of liquor one took on board! How the hell could I notice how much Greene had. I suppose I was two-thirds stewed the whole time. It seems to me I remembered everything—perfectly alert and so on. In those days it was alright."

Evelyn Waugh, my father's cousin and also at Oxford at that time, added helpfully that drinking is the "greatest thing Oxford has to teach."

Shelden roots about, coming up with supposed dirt about Greene's deviousness, penchant for dirty tricks and double crosses of a wife, mistresses and friends.

Under this sort of earnestly malicious scrutiny most people

wouldn't look too good, and it takes an effort of will to turn aside from Shelden's litany of presumptive encounters with women and young things of both sexes (scant evidence offered in the latter two instances) to remember that Greene essentially had three serious relationships with women in his life: his wife, Vivien; Catherine Walston, the American heiress with whom he had a tortured life in the '40s and with whom he planned to have sexual congress behind every altar in Italy; and Yvonne Cloetta, in whose company he spent much of the last quarter century of his life. This is scarcely the helter-skelter progress of a committed Don Juan.

Greene's Catholicism is another irresistible opportunity for biographers to turn out page after page on guilt, the bite of conscience, the nature of evil and so forth. My father regarded Greene's conversion in a more mundane light: "I knew him before Vivien. Quite early on, Graham said to me that he had fallen madly in love with this girl, but she wouldn't go to bed with him unless he married her. So I said, 'Well, there are lots of other girls in the world, but still if that's the way you feel, well go ahead and marry her. What difference does it make?' And then he came back and said (this went on over quite a number of weeks), 'The trouble is that she won't marry me unless I become a Catholic.' I said, 'Why not? If you're really so obsessed with this girl, you've got to get it out of your system.' He was rather shocked, because he said, 'You of all people, a noted atheist.' I said, 'Yes, because you're the one that's superstitious, because I don't think it matters. If you worry about becoming a Catholic, it means you take it seriously, and you think there is something there.' I said, 'Go right ahead—take instruction or what ever balderdash they want you to go through, if you need this for your fuck, go ahead and do it, and as we both know the whole thing is a bloody nonsense. It's like Central Africa—some witch doctor says you must do this before you can lay the girl.' And then to my amazement the whole thing suddenly took off and became serious and he became a Catholic convert. So I felt perhaps I'd done the wrong thing."

Greene wasn't that complicated a fellow, though the biographers have a vested interest in making him so. He loved elaborate practical jokes and often these were designed to cock a snook at authority, "throw grit in the State machinery," as he once put it. What more estimable course for a writer?

August 9

The Unabomber got several thousand words of his prose published at the start of August in the *New York Times* and *Washington Post.* Price of his admission: Three murdered people, plus maimings, with threats of more to come. Of course you can find people with a much higher career body count—Henry Kissinger for example—in the Op-Ed columns. Bombing one's way onto the front pages is usually the last recourse of a president heading down in the polls. At all events it's not a practice to be encouraged.

September 23

Most of the time people don't really read things, particularly opinion pieces by politicians. They see a couple of predictable phrases bowing and scraping at them, register a small blip on the brainscan and move on. I doubt whether anyone has ever read a piece by Henry Kissinger from start to finish. You see words like "resolve," "statesmanship" and so forth and avert your eyes. The samc is true of most TV punditry too.

When my father was working in the Berlin office of the London *Times*, back in the late 1920s, he became irritated by the complacent obtuseness of the bureau chief and put a satiric report from "Our Correspondent in Jerusalem" on his desk. "Small disposition here," cabled the correspondent, "attach undue importance raised certain quarters result recent arrest and trial leading revolutionary agitator followed by what is known locally as 'the Calvary incident.'" The piece was obviously based on an off-the-record interview with Pontius Pilate. The bureau chief glanced through the dispatch, saw all the usual phrases and passed it on to London, where only the vigilance of a telex operator prevented it from appearing in the *Times* the following morning.

September 27

When Bosnian Muslims are shelled, driven from their homes or murdered, the world weeps. When Serbs are driven from their homes or are discovered with their throats cut, eyes stay dry. When Serbs do the cleansing, it's "genocide." When Serbs are cleansed, it's either silence, or an exultant cry that they had it coming to them.

The largest ethnic cleansing of the entire war—the expulsion of the Serbs from the Krajina region now overrun by the Croats—is a topic virtually unmentioned in any news forum in the United States.

At least 150,000 Serbs have now fled the Krajina, abandoning the homes in which they and their ancestors have lived since the seventeenth century. President Franjo Tudjman of Croatia bellowed coarsely from this "freedom train" that the refugees left so fast they didn't have time to take "their dirty hard currency and their dirty underwear"—language somewhat similar in timbre to Tudjman's diatribes about the Jews in his professorial writings.

October 4

OJ innocent! We the jury, to judge by most of the people I spoke to at the Petrolia store, at the post office and on the phone after the verdict, thought OJ was guilty. Of course they, the real jury, found otherwise. The word "nullification" is now being wrongly thrown around for what the jury did.

Don Doig of the Fully Informed Jury Association—which campaigns for the constitutional right of jurors to "nullify," that is, to disregard law and the instructions of the judge, and to be told in advance of that right—put it thus: "I believe that this verdict does not represent a nullification of the law against murder, but it may reflect the jury's distrust of the testimony of police and other prosecution witnesses. If the police are demonstrably racist, or if they routinely violate the rights of defendants, particularly if they're black, then there could well be legitimate doubts that the guilt of the defendant had been established beyond a reasonable doubt."

So the guilty verdict went, not against Simpson, but against the Los Angeles Police Department, which has been on more or less continual trial since the beating of Rodney King. No juror has yet said so publically, but I suspect that this decision against the police would include counts ranging from sloppiness, careless handling of evidence and botched procedures, to racism, as symbolized by Detective Mark Fuhrman's vicious reminiscences overshadowing all. Given Fuhrman, but much else besides, the evidence against the cops was at least strong as the evidence against Simpson.

November 29

Here comes the "Comprehensive Antiterrorism Act of 1995," otherwise known as HR-1710. Under its provisions, many of them sought for years by the FBI, the state will accumulate further vast powers abusive of privacy and due process.

HR-1710 defines terrorism in terms so broad that offenses now treated as vandalism under state law would in federal law become "terrorism." The use of a .22 caliber rifle to inflict "substantial damage" on a stop sign would become "terrorism." Planning with one's friends—i.e., partaking in a "conspiracy"—to shoot at the aforementioned stop sign would become "terrorism." Shooting at the stop sign and missing would similarly be "terrorism," with all the fearsome sanctions attaching to any offense burdened with that description.

Privacy, already severely eroded by predations upon the Fourth Amendment, would take another beating. Sections 302–304 and 310 of the bill would give the FBI access to an individual's bank accounts, credit cards, employment and travel records, without a court order and without evidence of criminal activity. The target of such secret enquiries might never know of the FBI's scrutiny, or of the reasons that prompted it. The FBI could get data on an individual from a credit bureau merely by telling a judge that the target individual may "be in contact with" an agent of a foreign power.

December 20

People are getting loonier all the time. Robin Cembalist, a columnist from *Jewish Forward* in New York, called me a couple of weeks ago to ask what I thought about the attack on me in the *Voice Literary Supplement*. The *VLS* isn't big in Humboldt County. Maybe nowhere else either west of the Hudson, since no one from anywhere in the country has called to exult or commiserate or even say they'd seen it.

Soon a very, very long article by Michael Tolkin, the fellow who wrote Altman's *The Player*, came churning through the fax, courtesy of Cembalist. It was mostly about *The Turner Diaries*, with lunges at yours truly when the mood took him. Among my achievements: I'd driven him back to Judaism. Among my deficits: by quoting Bruce Cockburn's line, "If I had a rocket launcher ..." I'd expressed the unspoken impotence and hypocrisy of the left. I apparently hate liberalism because of its Judaism. Mostly Tolkin was ruminating sourly on the fact that if the Jews hadn't rejected the concubine Timna, she wouldn't have ended up with Esau's son Eliphaz "who had grown up with his father's resentment" and given birth to Amalek. You'll recall the Amalekites whom the Lord God enjoined the children of Israel (as relayed by the prophet Samuel to Saul) to smite and "utterly destroy all that they have and spare them not; but slay both man and woman, infant and sucking ox and sheep, camel and ass." The divinely mandated genocide was duly performed, with Samuel himself finally hewing King Agag in pieces before the Lord in Gilgal.

Apparently Tolkin feels all this could have been avoided if the Timna crisis had been better handled. As things are, "The Book is the Book of the Order of Amalek. We cast them off, set them in motion, and wherever we're weak, there they are."

So like the hound of heaven which pursued Francis Thompson to the Catholic Church, I have pursued Tolkin back into the synagogue he had abandoned. ("I came back to Judaism because of a few columns by Alexander Cockburn.")

Most of what Tolkin wrote was either mad or incomprehensible but he got furious when Cembalist told him she'd faxed me his ravings. "I think a Jew sending it is a betrayal," she reported him in the *Forward* as saying. "It's theoretically wrong for a Jewish paper to send it." He went on, "If I'm trying to say something to fellow Jews—saying it in a language that may be difficult for non-Jews to understand—to bring it to the attention of non-Jews may be dangerous to the Jews."

The effrontery and demented self-righteousness! Imagine, if I publicly berated a columnist for faxing one of my articles to a Jew.

1996

January 4

Animal rights people in Arcata, the buckle of the PC belt here in northern California, are buying lobsters out of restaurant tanks and shipping them back up to Maine to resume their submarine existence, at least until the next bit of rotted herring in the next lobster trap attracts their attention. The Maine lobstermen say that the do-gooders should watch a lobster tearing up a crab before getting so worked up.

The big scandal in the lobster world remains that of Ralph, the thirty-seven-pounder being weighed some years back in the Boston Aquarium when he supposedly made "a convulsive leap" from the weighing tray and cracked his shell on the floor. Tears streaming down their faces, the Aquarium folk broiled up Ralph on the grill the next day, which just happened to be July 4. Avenge Ralph! All power to the Soviets!

In April 1933, soon after they came to power, the Nazis preoccupied themselves with determining the most merciful way to dispatch crabs and lobsters. In 1936 a law was promulgated decreeing that they were to be thrown into rapidly boiling water. Scientists at the Nazi ministry of the interior had produced learned research papers on the kindest method of killing.

January 5

Troglodytes have been on my mind since I found in Breasted's *History of Egypt* that King Sesostris III (twelfth dynasty) was a devoted fort builder and named one such structure on the island of Uronarti, "Repulse of the Troglodytes." According to the *Britannica* (11th edition), "Their burial rites were peculiar. The dead body, its neck and legs bound together with withies of the shrub called *paliurus*, was set up on a mound, and pelted with stones amidst the jeers of the onlookers, until its face was completely covered with them. A goat's horn was then placed above it, and the crowd dispersed with manifestations of joy."

January 12

In Humboldt County, where I live, in the Mattole Valley, a couple of hours drive south of Eureka, the ranchers here run cattle on the hills, or the river bottom or the King Range, which is controlled by the Bureau of Land Management. The sheep have come and mostly gone. Here it's cattle, raised and grazed and shipped off to the feedlots. I suppose my house goes through a couple of sheep, a pig and a hindquarter of a cow each year. The pig would be one raised by a 4-H kid—Cisco Benemann's was the best so far—from around Ferndale, an hour over the hills, and killed and cut up by a local butcher. The cow for the last two years was called Mochie, raised by Michael Evenson.

At a Christmas party last year I ate a good piece of beef, said so, and Michael told me it was from Mochie and sold me a hindquarter. He gave me this little piece of Homeric history about her origins, which go back to the early 1970s, when a number of counterculture folk headed north from the Bay Area and settled in southern Humboldt. Michael bought Mochie's grandmother as a day-old calf in a Fortuna auction in 1972. She gave good milk in Michael's three-cow dairy. At the age of sixteen or seventeen, she'd had fourteen calves and earned retirement. She died in the pasture of natural causes at the age of twenty-two. Her last calf was a heifer, who herself had fourteen calves. Michael sold her to a couple that wanted a milk cow, and he got back the calf she was about to have:

So the animal you had part of was that calf that came to me. I was out of milking and dairy by then. I had very few animals and the pasture was in perfect condition. About sixty acres. When I first got there we figured about fifteen acres a cow but after we reseeded it, this dropped down to ten. When you reseed, you reseed a balanced diet, with perennial and annual grasses, so the soil is always alive with something. A lot of variety. It was a mix Fred Hurlbutt, a rancher in Garberville, developed. My animals were slaughtered in winter and the butcher thought they'd been on grain. I don't grain feed animals. Too concentrated and unbalanced. My animals always had choices, in the kind of grasses to eat and where to sleep. I had cross fencing but they were generous enough pastures and choice. I had goats in the 1960s and they really taught me animals like choices. They let you know when they're not happy. There have never been any diseases on my place.

Bullocks I'd slaughter after about two years. I don't lie to my animals. I tell them the only way I know, using English, that I'm going to slaughter them. I give them as much love and care as I can. Then, when they're slaughtered they will be part of my body, part of your body. You do the same in your garden.

The couple I sold Mochie's mother to are hippies living east of the Eel River. She's a midwife and he grows lettuce. They're new settlers, and they were the ones who called the calf Mochie. I never sent any animal to a commercial slaughterhouse. Mochie was four and she was breaking fences and wandering. I used a 30.30 and shot her behind the ear, out through the eye.

Michael is off red meat now. A friend of his, the late John Iris, who started the Wild Iris Institute for Sustainable Forestry, got bone cancer when he was fairly young. In the military he'd worked in missile silos in Europe, and with nuclear warheads in Vietnam. He lived in Briceland and went on a macrobiotic diet. Michael joined him, eating fish and chicken, but nothing from the nightshade family, for example tomatoes or potatoes. No milk, no red meat, "even though I had a freezer full of beef and a cow I was milking. I felt better. I'm realizing now my life has changed because I no longer have twice daily contact with cows. I wouldn't say life is more peaceful. It became more turbulent."

So much for versions of pastoral in the Mattole Valley. Most people don't have the option of getting Greg Smith to kill them a lamb.

Probably most people wouldn't want to cut it up. Someone in the supermarket in Garberville the other day went to the manager and complained because the meat-counter man had some bloodstains on his apron. But even so, there are options. If you don't like the thought of debeaked chickens sitting in a wire box all their lives, don't buy them. Figure out if you can have a meal that squares with ethical standards you can live with, or even vaguely aspire to. If you don't want to eat a piece of an animal tortured by hog barons, then cut up by prisoners, aside from campaigning against such cruelties and conditions, ask yourself, is there a way out, at a level that goes beyond eating the pre-Fall diet.

January 17

I was sad to see ROTC being kicked around the paddock as "targeting poor minority students, the Armed Forces' favorite cannon fodder these days." Come on, fellows! Where else is the reserve army of the unemployed supposed to end up?

There's nothing wrong with a bit of military training, particularly if it might open up some avenue of employment, not to mention self-esteem, among people otherwise destined to be hamburger flippers, crack runners or whatever. I'm for a citizen army. Abolish Annapolis Naval Academy, the Air Force Academy, and West Point, and install a draft, no exemptions.

The Pentagon is the US economy's last line of defense, never forget it, and probably the only way that any money will get redistributed to the deserving. Ninety-nine percent to Lockheed and the other big firms, one percent to basic training, ROTC and so forth.

The only way many kids can get anywhere near college is on military scholarships. As in many other societies in history the armed forces do offer an avenue for advancement when all else seems closed.

January 24

Hillary Clinton is one of nature's blue-stockings. The prime do-gooder blue-stocking of all time was probably Beatrice Webb, who with her husband Sydney fostered the political tendency known as Fabianism, very influential in the evolution of the British Labour Party. The Fabian view was that under the expert guidance of enlightened intellectuals such as the Webbs, society would gradually evolve toward maximum efficiency—good drains, good trains, sound economic management, with the state judiciously presiding over all.

Beatrice was a stringent supervisor. As a child I used to listen to Malcolm Muggeridge, a close friend of my father, describe his visits to the Webb household, where he was courting Beatrice's niece, Kitty. Beatrice would order Sydney to go for a jog before lunch. The wretched man would trot off down the driveway, with Malcolm lumbering after him. No longer under the scrutiny of Beatrice, he would dodge in behind the barn, invite Malcolm to recline on a bale of hay and spend the next hour talking about the future of the world.

Then they would have to sprint back up the driveway to where Beatrice would lay her hand on Sydney's brow, ascertaining from the perspiration that improvement—in this case physical—had indeed taken place.

Time and again, reading Hillary Rodham Clinton's *It Takes a Village*, I was reminded of Beatrice Webb. There's the same imperious gleam, the same lust to improve the human condition until it conforms to the wretchedly constricted vision of freedom which gave us social-worker liberalism, otherwise known as therapeutic policing.

The Clintonite passion for talking about children as "investments" tells the whole story. Managed capitalism (progressivism's ideal, minted in the Teddy Roosevelt era) needs regulation, and just as the stock market requires—somewhat theoretically these days—the Securities and Exchange Commission, so too does the social investment (a child) require social workers, shrinks, guidance counselors and the whole vast army of the helping professions, to make sure the investment yields a respectable rate of return.

The do-good progressives at the start of the century saw the family—particularly the immigrant family—as a conservative institution, obstructive to the progressive goals of society and the state. So, they attacked it. Then their preferred economic system—consumer capitalism—began to sunder the social fabric, and so today's do-gooders say that the family and the children, our "investment," must be saved by any means necessary. When the FBI was getting ready to incinerate the Branch Davidians they told Janet Reno the group's children were being abused. Save them, she cried. They went at it and all, including the children, were burned alive.

January 25

The best review of HRC's book is written by a man now dead, Christopher Lasch, in his *Haven in a Heartless World: The Family Besieged*, published in 1977.

The lesson Lasch draws in all his books is that radicalism did triumph in the United States. But it was not the radicalism of Marx or any kind of socialism. Instead, what triumphed was the radicalism of the helping professions, transforming the state into the engine of therapy "because the no longer surprising fact is that therapy and bureaucracy have considerable affinity; each seeks rationalization, each is hierarchical and, above all, each is authoritarian."

Hillary the helper: self-disclosure is anathema to her. The reticence that has landed her in the present troubles with the special prosecutor may well stem as much from childhood as from the prudence of a power broker from Arkansas. Early in her book she writes with elegiac warmth about playing softball and kindred sports, "all under the watchful eyes of parents." Then, a couple of pages later, she remarks sharply that "in reality, our past was not so picture-perfect … Ask those who grew up in the picture-perfect houses about the secrets and desperation they sometimes concealed." That's as near as she gets to saying anything interesting about herself.

January 31

Lady Olga Maitland, member of parliament for Sutton and Cheam, visits the proud nation of Turkey. She and her husband are sitting at a sumptuous outdoor banquet when the Turk next to her unzips his trousers. "Robin," she hisses to her husband, a phlegmatic barrister, "He's produced Mr. Mouse." Robin motions for her to be quiet and—the Englishman's great fear—to avoid making a scene. "But Robin," Lady Olga whispers, "Mr. Mouse is standing at attention!" "Just ignore it, dear," her husband advises, "and it will go away." "And do you know," Lady Olga later reports to her friends with great excitement, "When we finished lunch two hours later, Mr. Mouse was still standing at attention!"

February 7

Suddenly it's the "trust" crisis. Important national institutions like Harvard, the *Washington Post* and the Kaiser Family Foundation began collectively sinking their teeth into the matter sometime last year and at the end of January the *Post* fired off a six-part series decked out with doleful front-page headlines such as "In America, Loss of Confidence Seeps into All Institutions" and graphs about "public trust" with the trend lines all pointing down.

Cut your way through the thick underbrush of graphs and pizza-slice graphics in the *Post*'s series (Harvard and Kaiser will be firing off their independent summaries later on) and you find something simple: It's as if P. T. Barnum set forth across the country to see if one was still being born each minute, got to the edge of the Midwest, looked around and then muttered to himself with drawn features, "No suckers!"

The *Post* rests its whole "waning trust" thesis on a couple of vignettes in part one of its series. In the opening paragraph Janice Drake, mother of three in Detroit, doesn't trust the neighborhood teenager who fails to pull his pants up properly. In paragraph two, eighteen-year-old Lori Miller of Madison, Wisconsin, says she never knows who the next Jeffrey Dahmer might turn out to be.

Drawing on this database, paragraph three says we've become "a nation of suspicious strangers" and this is why we've lost confidence in the federal government.

If Janice Drake had told the *Post* she puts in three hours a week running errands for old folk and young Lori said she relied on her friends for emotional back-up we wouldn't have had a crisis.

The one thing the *Post*, Harvard, the Kaiser Family Foundation and all the hired professors can't face is that the correct premise for an independent citizenry is *not* to trust government—not Pericles in ancient Athens, not Bill Clinton now. And, across the last thirty years, government has willfully forfeited such scant reservoirs of trust as might have remained.

During the Civil War thirteen states announced drastic "no confidence" in federal government. The people in these thirteen states simultaneously exhibited great trust and confidence in each other.

There is one group the American people most definitely don't trust: namely the people who survey them, usually at 6.30 p.m. when they're sitting down to eat. People perform for surveys. They pretend to be Roseanne, or Archie Bunker or Eddie Murphy or Beavis and Butthead. They don't trust professors and pundits, who repay them by claiming they trust no one.

February 12

To: Daisy Cockburn; Chloe Cockburn; Patrick Cockburn; Olivia Ruspoli Wilde; Andrew

Subject: Dr. William Cockburn

Bill Cockburn seems to have had a sound view on causes of scurvy. The citrus fruit "cure" was obviously a cover story put out by Seamen's Union.

From a book about the search for a cure for scurvy by David Harvie: "Cockburn, who trained at Edinburgh and Leyden, was a very influential, conservative snob who had been physician to the fleet and who had made a great deal of money in private practice, largely by promoting his 'Electuary'—a doubtful cure for dysentery. This potion, which he kept secret, had been obtained in Italy. He claimed it had been used to cure Pope Clement XI in 1731, and despite complaints from Admiralty Commissioners, his patron, Admiral Sir Cloudesley Shovell promoted its widespread use in the Navy. Despite his influence, his dull, inflexible approach resulted in a lack of conspicuous medical progress during his career. He was described as 'an old, very rich quack' and is ironically the only naval physician to be buried in

Westminster Abbey. Cockburn's big contribution to the processional discussion of scurvy was that it was caused by congenital laziness among the sailors. He did admit that fresh vegetables might help those already sick, and had even witnessed the efficacy of lemons, but on serious preventative measures he had nothing new to say."

February 14

Here's a little parable from Oregon about the Lesser-of-Two-Evils. At one point in the US Senate race between Ron Wyden and Gordon Smith, there was a Green candidate called Lou Gold. Then, as the race came down to the wire, the green establishment in Oregon told Gold that every vote counted and, if he stayed in, his third-party candidacy could throw the race to the man of darkness, Smith. So Gold stood down.

The Oregon green establishment took out ads saying it was a choice between the Despoilers and Protectors and that a vote for Wyden was a vote for the temple of Nature. Wyden rewarded these expressions of support with stentorian speeches to the effect that the Clinton logging plan—under whose auspices old growth is falling and the spotted owl going to its long home—wasn't cutting enough. In the end Wyden beat Smith by 1.5 percent. The green vote put him over the top. Now he's saying that since he represents all the people of Oregon, including the chainsaw faction who voted for Smith, he wants to lay Oregon waste, the same way Smith promised.

February 21

For my harsh remarks about Hillary Rodham Clinton's book *It Takes a Village* I am taken to task by Ruth Rosen, prof of history at UC Davis. According to Rosen, writing angrily in the *Los Angeles Times*, anyone who is publicly savaged by William Safire and yours truly "must be doing something right."

Rosen thinks that attacks on HRC are not "simply politics as usual" and that HRC "is the kind of strong woman that weak men love to hate, a brilliant woman who makes mediocre men feel incompetent."

The left's attacks on HRC "stem from a more visceral misogyny" and that "even today, there are still some liberal men who cannot grasp the radical nature of what they call 'women's issues.' "

Rosen says that "like Jane Addams and Eleanor Roosevelt, Hillary Clinton believes that a truly humane society places children, not corporations at the center of its economic agenda" and that she's "the perfect scapegoat because she has a moral compass and is not afraid to follow it."

The one thing Dr. Rosen couldn't bring herself to do was read HRC's book. Admiring Hillary usually depends on such omissions. Look at her book, or her commodity trades, or her membership on the board of an incinerator company or her treatment of the employees of the White House travel office and you like her less.

HRC's résumé, it seems to me, contains the bankruptcy of a certain strain of feminism, the same way her husband's résumé, in this single person, encapsulates the bankruptcy of the Democratic Party.

February 22

Last week it was Peter McKay's turn to be on the losing end of the libel wars. In the London *Evening Standard* he wrote up a much discussed recent event in which Gore Vidal had been lunching at the River Café in Hammersmith. These modish restaurants feature flagons of olive oil. Mistaking such a vessel for a beaker of wine, Vidal took a swig, and then did a predictable amount of spluttering and gasping. Recovering himself, Vidal finally snarled to the wide-eyed company, "You let me do that! You want me to die because then Edmund White will be King Fag!"

White went round Paris and later Key West telling this story with great delight, but Vidal was not pleased with a slightly florid account of the episode that appeared in McKay's column. He duly instructed his legal representatives in London, Biddle & Co., to threaten savage litigation on the grounds that this defamatory story made him look ridiculous and shamefully rude about the excellent White; that in fact the amount of olive oil had been trifling, the discomfort transitory and the occasion lunch, not dinner, as McKay's item had inferred.

McKay offered to fly to Ravello and do a long and flattering profile of Vidal, with disclaimers of the episode cunningly inserted into the text. But Vidal declined. He has been holding out for a public retraction in the *Standard*, plus an appropriate sum to mitigate the usual intense pain and suffering, probably around three or four thousand dollars worth.

February 26

Dear Sir,

In a highly misleading piece in the last issue of your review (25.02.96), Gerald Clarke, the biographer of Truman Capote, pays pious homage to the film of *Beat the Devil* as a "small comic masterpiece, as original now as it was in 1953." In the excerpt you publish from *Capote: The Shooting Script* Clarke gives the impression that the script was all the work of Capote. He graphically describes his hero on the Amalfi coast "wearing an overcoat that fell almost to his ankles, with a long lavender scarf flapping behind it, rushing down to the set every morning with dialogue he had spent the night writing." In reality *Beat the Devil*, the cast of which included Humphrey Bogart, Gina Lollobrigida, Peter Lorre and Robert Morley, is a faithful rendition of a novel written by my father Claud Cockburn and published in Britain in 1953. I do not know what Capote was doing with his nights but writing an original script for *Beat the Devil* was not one of them. In reality my father had sold the film rights to the book to John Huston, an old friend of his, for sterling 3,000 at a moment when he was living in Ireland and in serious need of money. Claud had been denounced by Senator McCarthy as the 84th most dangerous Red in the world and had therefore considered it prudent to publish his novel under the nom de plume James Helvick.

The credits for the film when it appeared announced that the screenplay was by Truman Capote from a novel by James Helvick. Since nobody had heard of Helvick—and Huston did not want to rush round in the America of the early 1950s publicizing the fact he was in fact the notorious ex-Communist Claud Cockburn—this has led to subsequent confusion. *Beat the Devil* was later republished twice under my father's real name but the belief that Capote had written it has never died.

It has been amusing, if somewhat irritating over the years, to watch admirers of Capote see evidence of his literary skills pulsating in every word of the dialogue in Huston's film. For admirers like Mr. Clarke Capote provided "words that were completely fresh." In reality Capote's contribution was limited to a few concluding scenes which had to be altered at the last moment. My father was in Ireland and Capote, who happened to be available in Italy, was pressed into service. In subsequent years, as the film acquired a cult following, Capote did nothing to contradict exaggerated accounts of his own connection with the movie.

Sincerely,
Patrick Cockburn

To: Patrick Cockburn

Subject: Re: piece on beat the devil in guardian

Very good. Gore Vidal, who of course loathed Truman C., told me about a year ago that the lines not taken from BTD were supplied by Robert Morley.

February 28
The love of our newspapers for free trade surely has something to do with the fact that although there has been fearsome attrition in the journalistic profession, at least the lost jobs here aren't reappearing south of the border at a fraction of the cost. The day that column-writing is subcontracted to high school students in Guatemala I expect to see a turn around on the trade issue among the opinion-forming classes.

Free trade is a class issue. The better-off like it. Their stocks go up as the out-sourcing company heading south lays off its work force. The worse-off see the jobs disappear. You don't have to be an economist with a Ph.D. to figure out what is happening. At the start of this year Walmart reported its first loss in ninety-nine quarterly earnings reports. It seems Walmart's customers were unable to afford the "luxury" items on which the store makes its best margins. As long as people can't afford to shop at Walmart for anything more than the bare essentials of existence, Pat Buchanan will find people ready to vote for him.

March 6

In 1922, in the wake of the 1921 treaty by which the British ceded the bulk of Ireland, assassins killed General Sir Henry Wilson, one of Britain's top military commanders, as he was entering his house in Belgravia, London. My mother, walking to school at the age of eight, was an eyewitness.

The British took the assassination as a Hamas-type attempt by Irish Republicans to undermine the treaty. They conveyed their view to the infant Irish Free State government, which then unleashed an artillery barrage upon Republicans holed up in the Four Courts, destroying the building which housed the national archive, including every Irish certificate of birth and death.

Coincidence (Long Arm of): My mother having watched General Sir Henry fall to Fenian bullets, went home and reported the episode to her parents. It turned out well for her. She had been in London against her will, removed from Myrtle Grove, formerly Walter Raleigh's house, in the town of Youghal in Ireland. Here she was enjoying a happy childhood under the supervision of her grandmother, Edith Blake, a woman with nationalist sympathies. But her parents wanted her to come to London and go to school. With Wilson's murder they were now terrified that as a witness she might attract unwholesome attentions, of the police, Republicans and so on. She was sent back to Myrtle Grove.

Fifty years later she was telling the story to a new friend, Veronica Anderson, mother of Perry, who grew up in Waterford, forty-five miles to the east. Veronica listened and then said, "Did you see a milkman?" "No," replied my mother, very surprised. "Neither did I," Veronica agreed. Newspaper accounts of Wilson's shooting had featured a plucky, but imaginary, milkman who chased the assassins.

As a little girl Veronica had also been walking to school in Belgravia that day, at that time. I suppose the vulgar Marxists would merely murmur, Class is destiny.

March 21

Plain English: At Bodmin Assizes, in the 1930s, Mr. Justice Wright had to pass sentence upon an elderly agricultural laborer who had been found guilty of deplorable bestiality. In somewhat indistinct tones his Lordship announced: "Prisoner at the Bar, the jury have convicted you, on the clearest evidence, of disgusting and degrading offenses. Your conduct is viewed by all right-minded men with abhorrence. The sentence of the court is that you be kept in penal servitude for seven years."

It was obvious that this diatribe had not been audible to the prisoner, who had stood with his hand cupping his ear, straining to learn his fate. Therefore, the judge said: "Warder, repeat to the prisoner the sentence of the court."

The task was beyond the warder's powers, but he did his best, shouting at the condemned felon: "His lordship says you are a dirty old bastard, and he's put you away for seventeen years."

Whereupon His Lordship observed, "Warder, I have no objection to your paraphrasing my sentence, but you have no power to increase it."

Michael Gilbert tells this story in his *Legal Anecdotes*.

A Scotch friend tells me of a man in Dumfries who somehow became a magistrate for a day in the local court. A shoplifter was brought before him and the evidence of guilt was clear. The magistrate-for-a-day assumed a grave face, leaned forward and addressed the prisoner: "Hamish McTavish, you have been found guilty of the crime of shoplifting. It is my duty to inform you that on a set day you shall be taken from this place to another place and there hanged by the neck until you are dead, and may God have mercy on your soul."

McTavish fainted dead away and the clerk whispered incredulously to the magistrate-of-the-day that he had no right to impose such a sentence.

"I know, I know," he said, "but I've always wanted to say that."

March 27
Ralph Nader put up a good performance on *Meet the Press* last Sunday.

TIM RUSSERT: But people are going to say, Ralph Nader, in the end this is a real world. Would you prefer to have Bill Clinton or Bob Dole sitting in the Oval Office, because one of those two men are going to be the President?

NADER: I would prefer neither in the real world.

RUSSERT: It wouldn't bother you if you woke up in November and said, "Bill Clinton was not re-elected today because he lost the state of California to Bob Dole and the reason was that Ralph Nader siphoned off 6 percent of the voters who would have voted for Bill Clinton"?

NADER: If that happens to Clinton because he refuses to adopt a very important campaign finance reform, he deserves it …

RUSSERT: And if he embraced some of your issues that you're talking about this morning, you would be, then, reluctant to challenge him all the way through to November?

NADER: Not at all. Politicians always need an opposition that stays to its convictions and holds them to their promises …

March 28
Just because the Nazis were keen on animal rights, this doesn't mean that all animals rights activists are Nazis. The Nazis were keen on alternative medicine too, but this doesn't mean that the homeopathy and alternative medicine crowd are Nazis. See Robert Jay Lifton's interesting paragraphs in *The Nazi Doctors*:

> Perhaps the most severe conflict between the Nazi bio-medical vision and the traditional medical profession was in relation to nonmedical healers, known as "healing practitioners" (*heilpraktikers*) and "healers" (*heilkundiger*). These groups generally stress the outdoor life, natural foods, and overall re-orientation in living; they often flouted established

medical practice and sometimes treated serious diseases with dubious therapies. Long active in Germany, these healers appealed to the regime's biological romanticism and mysticism and found their strongest supporter in deputy party leader Rudolf Hess, the most intense biological mystic in the Nazi inner circle.

In 1939, as a lasting expression of its relationship to the "nature movement," the Nazis opened a new hospital outside Munich that was to epitomize many of the principles of the "new German Medicine": for example, common dining halls, outdoor bathing pools, special indoor physical-therapy centers, and recreation centers. These features would aid physical and mental rehabilitation, prevent "diseases of civilization," and strengthen "natural forces of resistance" to disease that were both physical and psychological. Not a "hospital," it was a "house of health" (*Gesundungshaus*).

May 2

"A loan-at-interest is the only known thing in the entire universe that does not suffer entropy. It grows with time. All other things, ourselves included, fade and die." Those of you maxed out on your credit cards but still making those monthly payments at some outrageous rate know this as well as I (who have learned by dint of bitter experience not to have credit cards at all).

Those first three sentences came from an informative letter that Stan Lusby of Otago, New Zealand, sent to one of my favorite newspapers, *Catholic Worker*, a while back. Lusby commenced his discussion of capitalism with some personal disclosures. He had, Lusby confided, known all his life that lending money at interest was intrinsically wrong. "I came late in life to Christianity, and it was a great source of comfort to verify my intuition through scripture, although I am now deeply enmeshed in debt, having listened to my peers and not the word of God."

Lusby then supplied a succinct history of the origins of the very word "capitalism":

> The word "capitalism" comes from "caput tally" or head-count of the slaves. I followed the line of word discovery further, after reading the *New English Bible*, for it referred to Nebuchadnezzar "investing" Jerusalem

> with his troops. "Vestment" means clothing that one puts on, but "investment" implies that one has been cloaked-in. It was the Roman word for a military operation for the taking of slaves. Clearly, such a military operation called for a minimum physical injury to a salable commodity and what we now call siege tactics were deployed.
>
> The military word "captain" refers to the one who counts the heads of slaves. It is used in both the land and marine branches of military. Out of starvation, the defenders "capitulated" (Latin, *caput*, head). On the long march back to Rome, the captain carved the daily head-count into a horizontal component of the scaffolding of the tent in which the captives were housed at night. Even today, such a piece of scaffolding is still known as a "ledger." To prevent the slaves breaking away, they were tied with a piece of leather called a "bond" to a long pole termed a "bank." That word survives to this day in the expression "a bank of oars," coming, as it does, from the galleys which were powered by slaves.

Lusby should have added that the word also survives as "the bank," to which we are held captive by the long thong of debt.

May 8

On April 18 Israeli shells crashed into a United Nations compound, manned by Fijian soldiers, at Qana in southern Lebanon. They were 155mm shells with M-732 proximity fuses which detonated each round seven meters above the ground, causing maximum casualties and what the military calls "amputation wounds." They were fired from new American-made M109A1 howitzers, which need a forward "spotter" for precise targeting.

Inside the compound—itself the approximate area of a city block—there were two buildings crammed with Lebanese villagers fleeing Israeli bombardment. Only these two structures, a chapel and a meeting hall, were destroyed. Nothing else in the compound was seriously damaged. No UN people were hurt. Estimates of the dead have edged up to around 105, but no one really knows. Did the Israelis know that refugees were in the compound? Yes. Some forty-eight hours before the massacre a senior member of the UN staff in southern Lebanon had told an Israeli general that the UN was protecting 5,000 refugees in all its compounds, including Qana.

May 9

The *Nation* magazine held a meeting on "The Fifties" last week, at Town Hall in New York. A decent number of people, many of them of mature vintage, showed up. The last time I visited Town Hall was back in 1983, and that was another *Nation* event about the 1950s, in the form of an evening about the Rosenbergs. By the third millennium maybe we'll hit the '60s?

The big news about the recent evening was a strong attack on rock 'n' roll. The onslaught was made by Fred Hellerman of the Weavers, a group temporarily put out of business by the 1950s blacklist. Hellerman, advanced in years but spry, denounced rock 'n' roll as "mindless and devoid of content," and held it no accident that it coincided with the worst years of the cultural blacklist. He singled out Bill Haley and "Rock Around the Clock" for specific abuse, and even essayed a kind of "shabbadooba" cry. In response, Allen Ginsberg, also on the platform, cried out in apparent solidarity with Little Richard, "a-wap-bam-boom."

I was at school when the film of *Rock Around the Clock* was banned in Britain as being liable to madden youth and cause attrition of moral fiber. In 1975 my brother Andrew was working in London for a TV program on the year 1955. The film revolved around the memories of two men, George Melly and Derek Taylor, of 1950s Liverpool. George, very sensibly, was rather reticent on specific details of his own experiences. Derek, later press agent for the Beatles and a very nice man all round, had met his wife to be, Joan, at a dance in New Brighton, the leisure destination across the Mersey from Liverpool. Andrew thought he would recreate the occasion and rented the relevant dancehall for the occasion asking the Vintage Rock 'n' Roll Appreciation Society to furnish Teddy Boys, for a *quid pro quo* of beer plus the screening.

Gratifying numbers of Teddy Boys turned out in their thick crepe soles, drainpipe trousers, drape jackets and greased hair with Duck's Arse capillary deployment. Many of them were now mature in years themselves, with young 'uns—three generations in one case—also garbed in proper '50s style. Andrew and his team screened *Rock Around the Clock*.

The crowd rose to the occasion, dancing in the aisles during the screening and then doing what was to be expected of any audience in such circumstances, viz., they destroyed the movie theater and then moved down the main street smashing every window. The next day Andrew had to put about £2,000 worth of bank notes into a paper bag and walk down the same street, paying off the shopkeepers.

May 22

The hysteria about teen violence is more than matched by the alarums about a pubescent rutting boom, with "children having children" and children giving one another AIDS. Bill and Hillary seldom stop sermonizing on this. Adults listen agog to the boastful lies of teenage boys and then rush to judgment. In 1970, 20 percent of boys and 4 percent of girls in junior high schools claimed on self-reporting surveys to have had sex. In 1992 the figure had risen to 27 percent of boys and 20 percent of girls.

And if rising legions of pubescents were "sexually active," how come the pregnancy rate among ten to fourteen year olds hasn't similarly skyrocketed? In 1976, 3.2 babies, abortions, and miscarriages per 100 junior high school girls; in 1988 3.3. Amid this supposed "junior high sexual revolution," 98 percent of the girls arrived at age fifteen never having been pregnant. Junior high students must be America's most skilled condom deployers. Seventh graders should be enlisted to hold seminars for US grownups, who sport the industrial world's highest rates of unplanned pregnancy.

Just 1 percent of all births in the United States each year and 8 percent of all teenage births involve partners under eighteen. From the point of view of both pregnancy and AIDS, the riskiest option for teenagers (for both girls and boys in the latter instance) is to have sex with adults. Prudent teenagers should stick to their own cohort.

Responsible for these misrepresentations have been core liberal nonprofit groups such as Planed Parenthood, the Children's Defense Fund, and the Urban Institute, all massaging the Clinton Administration's Blame Kids First strategy. In the small print of its technical reports you'll find Marian Wright Edelman's Children's

Defense Fund—of which Hillary used to be a board member—mentioning the role of adult misbehavior, abuse and/or impregnation in connection with teenage mothers, but not in the fund's PR campaigns. Similarly, Planned Parenthood and the Alan Guttmacher Institute hype the "epidemic of 1 million teenage pregnancies every year," ignoring seventy years of birth statistics showing that, in the main, teenage mothers have adult partners.

On the bottom line here is *sotto voce* Malthusianism. Much of the screaming at teenagers about condoms, pregnancy and AIDS risk is a way of saying don't ever have children if you're poor (and of course, don't have fun).

May 29

The liberal prostration before Clinton is unprecedented. When Jimmy Carter veered right in the late 1970s, the unions put together the Progressive Alliance and Teddy Kennedy ran as the radical challenger (itself somewhat of an irony considering that Ted has probably damaged more worker's livelihoods than almost anyone in the US Senate by leading the charge on deregulation of trucking and airlines).

The only challenge now is from Ralph Nader, and he doesn't seem to be putting much heart into his run in California under the Green Party label. Former California governor Jerry Brown, who now has a talk show on Pacifica, is saying that when he interviewed Nader recently, the latter didn't even mention he was running for President.

Meanwhile the *New York Times Magazine* gave Clinton a warm kiss in the form of a profile by its White House correspondent, Todd Purdum. Specimens from the hero-gram: "He is charming, informal, PC-profane as he sips ice water and searches face to face for approval, his beefy hands and long, oddly delicate fingers cutting the air. Even after announcing that he is losing his voice, he talks for thirty more minutes. The performance is, in the end, overwhelming."

White House correspondents tend to find almost any President overwhelming. The late John Hersey even managed to be overwhelmed by the executive majesty of my favorite Commander-in-Chief, Jerry Ford. The *New York Times Magazine* ran the Hersey piece almost exactly twenty years ago. Nothing much changes in the relation between press and power.

Probably the greatest fawner has been *Time*'s Hugh Sidey. Back in the early '60s he had a piece in *Life* about JFK headlined, "He Eats Up News, Books at 1,200 Words a Minute." All over America people rushed to sign up in speed-reading classes. Fatalities were recorded as word sprinters blew their cerebral cortices. In 1994 Sidey admitted to the *Washington Post*, "I haven't any idea how fast he read. The figure was kind of hoked up."

July 17

News just in from England: it turns out George Orwell was a police nark. In 1949 he supplied a Secret Service unit based in the British Foreign Office with just the sort of list Senator Joe McCarthy flourished a few years later. Orwell, then dying of TB, gave Celia Kirwan of the covert Information Research Department eighty-six names of people he regarded as "crypto-communist" or "fellow travellers." One of the names was former Labour Party leader Michael Foot. Orwell's biographer, Bernard Crick, is quoted in the *Guardian* for July 12 as saying Orwell had kept a notebook of "suspects," in which "many were plausible, a few were far-fetched and unlikely." Of course, once Orwell had played the informer, Big Brother opened files on them, however "far-fetched" or "unlikely" they may have been as Commie collaborators. Let's see what Orwell lovers have to say about this.

The revelations about Orwell's blacklist came in the form of documents released at the British Public Records Office last week. The papers show that the Information Research Department was particularly keen to promote *Animal Farm*. One Foreign Office official in Cairo remarked that "the idea is particularly good for Arabic in view of the fact that both pigs and dogs are unclean animals to Muslims."

July 28

At least in the old days Bob Dole used to have suavity and aplomb. He flicked insults at his enemies with a caddish leer. Now his barbs have all the force of marshmallows, and he whines just like another loser, Mondale, a dozen years ago.

He got into trouble for trying to claim that cigarettes aren't addictive. Now it's true that the word "addiction" is seriously overworked. The trouble really took off when the twelve-steppers took the stupid position that even one teensy sip made you an alcoholic, as debased on the ladder of self-indulgence as the man who puts down half a bottle of gin before breakfast.

The AA crowd didn't invent "alcoholism." That came somewhere in the 1890s when the self-respecting "drunkard" or "sot" was transmuted into the pitiful, helpless "alcoholic." Throughout most of its etymological and semantic career "addict" had a judicial connotation, as in "to deliver over formally by sentence of a judge," which is the first definition in the *Oxford English Dictionary*, published in the early 1930s, but depending on work done fifty years earlier.

Morphine was what brought "addict" to its modern, pejorative meaning. The supplement to the 1930s *OED*, published at the same time, has "addict" defined as "one who is addicted to the habitual and excessive use of a drug ... as in morphia addict." People like Sherlock Holmes, shooting up his 7 percent solution, brought the word to its new, low station, though Orientalists would probably claim that after the opium wars of the mid-nineteenth century in which the British forced the Chinese to accept imports of opium, the imperial power developed the notion of the addicted Chinese masses to excuse their own low behavior.

August 7

A Democratic President has just destroyed a big chunk of the New Deal and not one major Democratic figure has defected because this President destroyed the tiny protections for those down on their luck, for children, for single mothers, for immigrants between jobs, who have been paying taxes for maybe ten or twenty years. Donna Shalala didn't quit. Robert Reich didn't quit. Peter Edelman of HHS did quit. Marion Wright Edelman cancelled a demonstration before Clinton's decision "because I didn't want to be Sister Souljah," then issued a bitter statement, but she didn't say she was shifting her support to Ralph Nader. Ron Dellums's office was saying that he understood Clinton's need to "hold the center." Barney Frank said that Clinton had done more for the poor than Ralph Nader. (There may be a personal edge there since Nader once said publically it was disgusting of Frank to run a homosexual prostitution ring out of his congressional office.)

Here, for the third time in thirty years, we have a historic opportunity for the rallying of left forces beyond the Democratic Party. It happened in 1968 with Eugene McCarthy; and in 1984 and 1988 with Jesse Jackson. Now we have another chance. And who steps forward as our public champions? Bernie Sanders, the "independent" hot-air factory from Vermont, requests everyone to vote for Bill Clinton. The Labor Party, born in Cleveland a month ago, insisted that no labor candidates be fielded for the foreseeable future, and further stipulates that no labor-affiliate field independent candidates. Prominent Labor Party folk are simultaneously on the Democratic National Committee. Unions active in promoting the Labor Party have made a deal with the Democrats that the Labor Party will do nothing impertinent or subversive, such as actually run candidates against Democrats. From day one, with all that nonsense about doing nothing till 100,000 advocates are signed up, the entire Labor Party effort has been an exercise in demobilization, achieving the miracle of a Third Party that is the wholly owned subsidiary of the party it is challenging.

This leaves us with Ralph Nader, who has the public status, the knowledge and the right political instincts.

August 21

Back in 1980, I spent a day on Senator Ted Kennedy's campaign plane amid his futile effort to wrest the Democratic Party nomination from Jimmy Carter. We flew to South Bend, Indiana, to get a photo op of Kennedy with some steel workers in front of a smokestack. Then we rushed to Nebraska to get another shot of the Senator in front of a grain elevator, with farmers. Back then to New York to line up the next day's opening shot, which would be the Senator eyeballing urban devastation in the South Bronx.

I suggested to Kennedy's press man that it would surely be more a rational use of everyone's time and money to have a central campaign studio in the Washington suburbs, entrusted to one of the big Theme companies. Here the essential "theme rides" of American electioneering could be permanently installed, under appropriate corporate logos. Campaigning politicians would be able to use the facility, getting the corporations to pick up some of the tab and collecting the balance from the press corps.

The "Conventionworld" theme exhibit mounted by the Republicans last week found its home most appropriately in San Diego, where techniques of theming and artful manipulation of space find expression at the famous zoo. Old-fashioned zoos had animals pacing about in cages, with labels giving information about their origins and the Linnaean category of the denizens. The human visitors gazed from a safe distance. It was thus with political conventions, where informed commentators would discuss the social anthropology of state delegations which would in turn often defiantly display themselves in vulgar shows.

These days zoo staging has transmuted from older modes of confinement, whether the cages or moated enclosures—derivative from romantic painting—designed by the German Carl Hagenback at the start of the century. The trend now—pioneered by Jon Coe and Grant Jones, who constructed the Woodland Park gorilla exhibit in Seattle in the mid-1980s—is called "landscape immersion," with visitors enveloped in the appropriate habitat of the exhibit. As Mellissa Greene put it in an interesting article for the *Atlantic* for December 1987, describing Woodland Park, "There are no fences or walls against which to calculate depth, and the visitor's peripheral vision is deliberately limited … Wider vision might allow a visitor to calculate his position and give him an inappropriate glimpse" of something at odds with the affecting gorilla experience.

Conventionworld this month in San Diego showed that the Republican impresarios have taken all this to heart. There was no moat between podium and audience. Landscape immersion was so complete that when, for example, Republican Asian-Americans were being "themed," TV onlookers were allowed no peripheral vision of the white human landscape surrounding the relatively few Asian-Americans present.

SeaWorld, owned by the Anheuser-Busch Corp. and host to about four million visitors a year—same as the zoo—was a favored venue for convention events, nourished by the kitsch atmospherics of purity and *la mer*, with dolphins and orca recruited with behavioral techniques to exhibit the fundamental harmony of creation, under corporate auspices.

SeaWorld is non-union, with minimum wage levels for the attendants. (At least the zoo is Teamster-organized, through there should be more interspecies union work. Why leave it all to the human society?) In the polar bear exhibit (a big new pool with enhanced underwater availability) three of the bears had salmonella poisoning and were confined to what the guide brightly termed their "bedrooms." This meant compulsory overtime for eighteen-month-old Chinook, who was putting in thirteen-hour days. I thought Chinook looked frayed and angry, but the guide insisted the cub was doing "a real good job" in exhibiting polarbearishness to the audience. Chinook could do with a union rep same way poor Dunda the elephant needed one a few years back when it was discovered she was being savagely beaten for disciplinary infractions. Don't snarl, organize!

Every now and again orangutans organize an *intifada*. The last was in 1990, when the Bornean apes carefully built up reserves of rocks and caused $570,000 worth of damage to the 1.5″ glass.

September 11

When I was sixteen I developed a passion for the baroque and in my enthusiasm hitch-hiked part of the way by barge up the Rhine—price of the ride, playing chess with the captain—to Würzburg to admire the Bishop's *Residenz* with its ceilings by Tiepolo, which supposedly prompted Napoleon to say that if he could not be emperor of France he would want to be bishop of Würzburg.

I made my journey in 1957 and now find from his very fine article in the *Catholic Worker* of June–July 1996, that Gordon Zahn was there at the same time. Zahn recalls how, at 9.20 p.m. on March 16, all the bells of Wurzburg began to ring, a reminder of the time, twelve years earlier, when British bombs hurtled down, destroying 85 percent of Wurzburg in twenty minutes and killing 3,000 men, women and children now buried in a common grave in Wurzburg cemetery. The Bishop's palace was heavily damaged, though the Tiepolo ceilings were spared.

Wurzburg had no military significance. There was no reason for the raid, beyond the desire to exterminate and destroy. Like myself, Zahn had walked about Wurzburg back in that 1957 spring, brooding on the Apocalypse twelve years before. He'd been a wartime conscientious objector, and reflected on his Wurzburg visit that the bombing "must be described … as a work of calculated barbarism and the slaughter of its inhabitants as calculated murder." But this piece in the *Catholic Worker* discusses a new memoir, *The Withered Garland*, by the RAF commander Peter Johnson, who led that raid. After reading *The Withered Garland*, Zahn now confesses that "impossible though it may have seemed then, I believe that, were Peter Johnson and I ever to meet, we could be good friends."

Johnson's father was a captain in the British Navy, killed in 1914, at the very start of World War I, in a German submarine attack. Young Peter grew up with a great hatred of Germans. World War II found him in the Royal Air Force. In 1942 he applied to join Bomber Command. Here he was soon furnished with vivid evidence of the moral context for his activities. Soon after he had assumed active command of his squadron, a visiting high-up from London was inspecting photographs of the results of a raid on Dusseldorf. The VIP woofed with satisfaction: "Capital, capital. This is really getting somewhere. I do congratulate you." Johnson looked over his shoulder and got a glimpse of the photos.

"I had never seen anything like them. Seen through the stereoscopic glass, the detail was staggeringly clear, showing just rows and rows of apparently empty boxes which had been houses. They had no roofs or content. This had been a crowded residential area, long streets of terraced houses in an orderly right-angled arrangement, covering virtually the whole of the six-inch square photograph. There were one or two open spaces, but the chief impression was just those rows and rows of empty shells, a huge dead area where once thousands of people had lived. There were no craters, simply those burnt out houses."

Johnson began to have "reflections and doubts." He wondered why incendiaries were necessary in the raids on the Krupp's munitions works at Essen and Kiel. "Nothing but the end of the war," he wrote in an undelivered letter intended for a girlfriend killed in a German raid on London, "can stop the destruction of practically every city in Germany." Johnson was beginning to fathom the fact, as Zahn writes, that "though Hitler may have proclaimed and boasted of the Third Reich's commitment to *Totaller Krieg* [Total War] … it remained for British and American airpower to develop, perfect and practice it without moral restraint."

Johnson evokes British bombing policy, in particular "de-housing," introduced by Lord Cherwell, scientific advisor to Prime Minister Winston Churchill. It was reckoned that a ton—2,000 pounds—of bombs dropped on a town center would destroy forty buildings and de-house one to two hundred people. Factoring in rates of warplane production it was happily computed by Cherwell and his men that soon a third of the entire German population would be "turned out" of house and home.

In February 1942 Lord Portal, Chief of the Air Staff, declared that "operations should now be focused on the morale of the enemy civil population and, in particular, of industrial workers," adding later "I suppose it is clear that the aiming points are to be the built-up areas, not for instance the dockyards or aircraft factories." Churchill, with his usual bluntness, called upon the Minister of Aircraft Production for "an absolutely devastating extermination attack by very heavy bombers."

Assigned, on the morning of March 16, 1945, the target of Wurzburg, Johnson did ask, "Why?" "Bit of railway junction," he was told. Johnson wondered what to do. He could refuse to order his squadron into this mission, which would mean court martial and maybe execution. It would not prevent the raid and, Johnson reflected, would mean his wife and children would get no pension. He enquired again about the merits of the target, and was told by the intelligence officer with great irritation, "I've said it's an important railway center [which Johnson knew was not so] and also there are thousands of houses totally undamaged, sheltering tens of thousands of Germans. I hope that will not be the case tomorrow, which will be another nail in the enemy's coffin."

Johnson led the raid. Three thousand died and Wurzburg was almost completely destroyed. There were too many bodies for nails and coffins. Just a big hole for all in the cemetery and, later, a chronicle of the raid with eighty-seven pages listing the victims by name and former address. Zahn remembers his verdict of 1957, about the bombers being "barbarian murderers." After reading Johnson's memoir (published by New European Publications, in London, with the subtitle *Reflections and Doubts of a Bomber*) Zahn writes now of the officer in charge:

> A barbarian? After reading his memoir I can no longer make that judgment. The sensitivity of the undelivered letter, the struggling with his conscience growing ever more intense as the nature of the air war became clearer—these reveal a concern about, and respect for, moral considerations and limits meriting credit, even admiration.
>
> A murderer? Harsh though the judgment may be, it is hard to see what other term would be appropriate for the action itself, the slaughter of three thousand civilians, including women and children, in a war already won. Obedience to orders, even seen as a sworn duty cannot justify engaging in what he believed—worse still, what he knew—to be an action contrary to the Law of War: the murder of an entire city and its population.

Zahn takes Johnson's book as an act of contrition that could awake other consciences. "In any event, the final judgment is not ours to make, but we can pray with some confidence that the Heavenly Bookkeeper will take full account of the sincerity and, in His boundless mercy, forgive."

September 25

Sioux Falls—Here I am, in South Dakota with the express and only purpose of covering Republican Senator Larry Pressler with the slime of innuendo, aimed at providing just that marginal twitch in public opinion which will ensure the victory of his Democratic opponent, a conservative Midwest Democrat named Tim Johnson. And who knows? Johnson's eviction of two-term incumbent Pressler could, at only a modest level of unlikelihood, mean the recapture of the Senate by the Democrats, a return to the best we can hope for—gridlock in the US Congress.

I'm here to hurl slurs at Pressler at the request of my old friend Jim Abourezk, who served as US Senator for South Dakota between 1972 and 1978 before quitting in disgust because he couldn't get anything done. Jim, Lebanese by family origin, was born on the Rosebud Indian Reservation where his father and mother ran a store, and in course of time became a populist politician and certainly one of the most radical denizens of Congress in this century. In the mid-1970s his bill proposing vertical divestiture of the oil companies—meaning they couldn't simultaneously own oil wells, tanker fleets, refineries and gas stations—failed in the Senate by only three votes, marking the high-water point in post-Watergate legislative exuberance. The oil companies, led by Texaco, promptly doubled their purchase orders on Congress.

Jim, now practicing law in Sioux Falls, mostly on behalf of a Yankton Indian tribe, has one failing: a loyalty to the Democratic Party that is invulnerable to the repeated rebukes of history. He's a lesser-of-two-evils man and when driven into a corner starts the traditional keening about appointments to the federal bench.

Jim nourishes a particular contempt for Pressler, partly because this nincompoop took over the Senate seat Abourezk had held throughout the 1970s. Mentally frail and morally inert, Pressler is a man long and widely derided in Washington as an imbecile of fantastic proportions. Jokes about Pressler have haunted him from the beginning of his congressional career, when he bucked the Watergate crash for Republicans and won a House seat in 1974.

All the above facts about Pressler—ranging from his incredible stupidity to speculation about his supposedly meandering sexual preferences—have for many years been a source of ribaldry and gossip in Washington and South Dakota. Only the ordinary voters have been spared the truth, with newspapers, radio and television respectfully displaying the words and deeds of their senior Senator.

Hence Jim Abourezk's plea that I hurry east.

I did his bidding. On the appointed day in Sioux Falls, September 19, I faced a grueling schedule of two morning radio shows, an address to the City Club, a speech at the University of South Dakota's Vermillion campus, addresses at two bookstores—Zanbros and Barnes and Noble—plus sidewalk encounters. At each opportunity I derided Pressler. On one radio show a listener called in to ask whether the fact that my father Claud had once written for the English *Daily Worker* might perhaps have affected my view of the Senator.

At the City Club Mrs. Pressler's daughter by a previous marriage rose to denounce my treatment of her stepfather. The local newspaper reported that she quavered words of denunciation of my brutality before sitting down "amid stifled sobs." That may be but she was seen ten minutes later clambering into her car with a Pressler supporter, roaring with laughter. Kevin Schieffer, Pressler's former Chief of Staff, exhibited the imbecility of his boss by insisting on a lengthy exchange—carried on public radio—about the substantive evidence for my allegations. Pressler rushed out a statement saying that I was trying to ruin his life and that I was a tool of the Johnson campaign.

When it was all over, the local Gannett paper, the *Argus Leader*, carried the charges and editorialized that I had failed to prove them. But perhaps … out there my words will have found their mark, sufficient to make the difference. Jim Abourezk pronounced himself satisfied.

October 2

Like a death ship, its sails hanging limply off the spars, Campaign Dole drifts ever deeper into a Sargasso Sea of disaster. Dole campaigns on the crime issue and the Justice Department reports that violent crime is down 10 percent. He hammers the Clinton economy and the Bureau of the Census announces that real income for the average American went up for the first time in six years, and that the number of Americans living in poverty dropped from 36.4 million—a tidy total, to be sure—by 1.6 million.

Things are so bad for Campaign Dole that the columnist Mary McGrory reckons its shining moment came when Bob fell off a platform in California.

October 4

Ever since leaving South Dakota, I've been moving westward in the '72 Imperial, noting the effects of political campaigning on the landscape. Bad. Driving into Yellowstone from Cody, the road was ripped for sixty miles, with several hundred bulldozers, loaders, oilers, dump trucks and graders massed along terrain that looked like the Plain of Jars after four years of American bombing in Laos. This is Senator Alan Simpson's annual contribution to the economy of Wyoming, with millions poured into the effort to build something resembling the New Jersey Turnpike from Cody through to Old Faithful, then out the other side to West Yellowstone.

After a night under canvas in sub-freezing temperatures in Yellowstone, never my favorite park, I turned southward into the Tetons, finally entering the town of Jackson Hole, a horrible spot now favored by President Bill who told Vernon Jordan not so long ago that he much preferred it to Martha's Vineyard, since it was impossible to get "pussy" in the stuffy Massachusetts resort. Jackson Hole probably reminds Clinton of Hot Springs.

October 9

Back in 1991, when outing was a hot topic, I wrote about the matter and got the opinions of my friend John Scagliotti, maker of the famous historical documentary *Before Stonewall*. The test for outing, John said, should be:

> Has the person benefited from being in the closet in careerist terms, in the sense of actively pretending to be something he or she is not?

> There's a difference between a passive closet, in which you simply survive and hope for the best, and the active closet, which involves putting on a heterosexual mask and promoting yourself as such, which is in ethical contradiction to your actual life. You've made the choice. You're living an actual lie, bringing girls to the company ball and so on.
>
> So, think about a gay actor who has made the decision to advance his career by pretending to be heterosexual. But by doing that he is insulting and oppressing all those who are already out. Take Barry Diller, who is in a position of enormous power at Fox. Why doesn't he push for a gay and lesbian TV show, which I could produce, which would be a gay version of *In Living Color*? Now, no one wants to out little people, gay teachers and so on—unless gay teachers are publicly anti-gay—but I would out people who are gay and yet are promoting heterosexuality.
>
> I believe as a general proposition that people should come out. It would be better for them. But at the same time I understand that such a public coming out might hurt or confuse children, parents, etc. But just as there's a difference between being passively and actively in the closet, you can be actively or passively out. In the former, you are publicly espousing a case, and in the latter, passive case, you are attempting to live a gay or lesbian life within the limits of what's possible for you and not too hurtful to parents, children, etc. One of the reasons straight people don't understand outing is that they don't understand what it's like to be gay. It's all more complicated than they think.

J. Edgar Hoover used the gossip columnist Walter Winchell to out Commies. Gossip usually has a repressive function in the mainstream press, which is why outing has to remain a subterranean, countercultural activity. Yet even in the counterculture, or at the level of the off-beat and unofficial, gossip always has the twin function of being liberating—letting the sunlight in—and repressive, in the sense of exposing the personal and the private, naming names and hurting people. Gossip represents visible fault lines at the social surface, reflecting subterranean, gradual shifts in our social attitudes. Although the liberating and repressive functions are both at work, given the structure of media ownership and control, the repressive function is usually dominant.

November 6

It's all over, thank God. The American People took one last lingering look at the options, breathed the deepest of sighs, and mostly decided to stay at home. The stay-at-homes always win.

One big factor militating in Clinton's favor was something virtually unmentioned: the end of the cold war. For almost half a century this was all-important. A president had to demonstrate he could defend the Republic by all means necessary, including nuclear obliteration of the planet. If the Soviet Union had existed in 1992 George Bush would have been reelected.

By 1991 it was all over and America was ready for a draft-dodger in the White House. Dickie Morris's genius was to stick the Republicans with all their truly unpopular causes (assault weapons, abortion ban, end to affirmative action) and co-opt all the rest for Bill Clinton. It worked like a dream. As for Bill, I along with thirty million Americans of Irish descent liked what he did for Gerry Adams.

November 13

It's just like the man said: vote for the lesser of two evils and you get both. Or, vote for Clinton and you get the other one free. Hardly had the polls closed before Clinton was saying that he's likely to appoint the man—Dole—he'd spent the previous six months reviling to be in charge of a bipartisan commission to re-evaluate Medicare—a program he'd spent the previous six months hollering that Dole would destroy. And people wonder why the citizenry is cynical! The whole point of democracy is *not* to have bipartisan government.

Goodbye to the "soccer moms," altogether the silliest confection of the entire campaign. In the end the soccer moms, deemed Clinton's secret weapon, voted for him *less* than other female cohorts. Biggest enthusiasts for the man from Hope were elderly widows and young single mothers, far too frazzled to care about soccer. Judging from the ones I know, the soccer moms voted for Nader. What next? Across the past three elections the press has given us Joe Sixpack, the Reagan Democrat, the Angry White Male and most recently, the Soccer Mom. Aging Boomers?

In Humboldt County about 20 percent of the voters went either for Perot or Nader. In Mendocino the percentage was a bit higher. In a straw poll of 2,000 high school kids in Humboldt, over 25 percent went for a third party candidate, which is a comfort.

There's not much to console oneself with otherwise. Large portions of the nation's affairs are now being run by three men from Alaska. Appropriations, the powerful committee that Hatfield used to run, will now be under the sway of Ted Stevens, who really would drill through his mother if he thought there was oil in substrates below her coffin. Energy policy is under the sway of Alaska's junior Senator, Frank Murkowski. In the House natural resources are overseen by Rep. Don Young, a former trapper and riverboat captain whose congressional office resembles a cheap Ketchikan taxidermy, its wall covered with the skins of Alaskan grizzlies, the lacquered corpses of king salmon and severed heads of Roosevelt elk and Sitka black-tailed deer.

Young does have a certain charm. Animal rights advocate Mary Tyler Moore once read a poem about the cruelty of steeljaw leghold traps before the Merchant Marine subcommittee, on which Young was serving. Accompanying Moore was Cleveland Amory, who periodically inserted a pencil into a trap, causing it to snap shut. The moment was highly charged and Young, as a hunter, trapper and taxidermist, realized dramatic action was required to turn the tide. His solution was to place his hand in a trap he had brought along and then begin calmly to question a witness as though nothing unusual had occurred. "I never told anyone, but it hurt like hell," Young later confided to a congressional aide.

November 14

Goodbye, Larry. The only incumbent US Senator turned out of office was … yes, you've guessed it, Larry Pressler of South Dakota. I claim the victory. He went down by about 5,000 votes, against the trend in the state, where Republicans mostly carried the day. Before I traveled to Sioux Falls at the invitation of Jim Abourezk (Pressler's predecessor in the Senate), Larry was running even with Tim Johnson.

After my slurs on his character his standing briefly rose, as Dakotans made a show of standing by their man, then sank steadily as solidarity was overwhelmed by rank prejudice. I am responsible for the Democratic majority in the Senate. Take that, you work-within-the-system types!

November 20

In the early 1970s Mobil decided to fight back against the consumer lobby denouncing it for price gouging in the wake of the oil shocks of 1973. The company's boss, William Tavoulareas, and his Vice-President for public relationships, Herb Schmertz, decided to capture just the sort of middle and upper income support sought by Texaco thirty years earlier with opera sponsorship.

Schmertz did this by successfully placing Mobil commercials on public television, while simultaneously winning for himself the reputation of being the most munificent patron of culture since Lorenzo de' Medici. He managed this amazing feat by getting Mobil to sponsor Masterpiece Theater on PBS. Schmertz, the patron, and Stan Calderwood of the PBS station WGBH in Boston, the original object of his patronage, deserve credit for turning public television into the prime corporate showcase.

Indeed, many of America's cultural furbishments turn out to be the gifts of oilmen deeming it necessary to daub perfume on their profit statements.

After minions of John D. Rockefeller caused state troopers in Colorado to incinerate striking miners, their wives and children in the Ludlow massacre of 1914, Rockefeller hired a journalist, Ivy Lee, to improve his abysmal public standing. Lee threw himself inventively into the task. Young John D. Rockefeller Jr. was dispatched to Colorado to mix with the miners and project concern. Soon the press was praising the common touch of this plutocrat mingling with the ordinary folk. Meanwhile Lee told John D. Sr. to lavish a few of his millions on charitable projects and to give dimes to children. Soon the old robber's name was practically synonymous with the philanthropic impulse.

It seems to work … and then it all falls apart. Just when a gratified citizenry is listening to Texaco's operas or goggling at Mobil's Masterpiece Theater or rambling through some Rockefeller-endowed museum, it all goes wrong. A tanker runs aground. The price of gas shoots up. And then the people remember what they never really forgot: they hate Big Oil.

November 21

As Warren Christopher packs his files and prepares to quit the State Department, one man in particular exults and cries Good Riddance. He is Kinsey Marable, purveyor of rare books at an excellent bookstore by that name situated at 1525 Wisconsin Avenue, in Washington, DC.

When Christopher became Secretary of State in the far-off dawn of the Clinton era, he was granted a Secret Service bodyguard. Christopher's Georgetown house stands on Volta Place, which runs off Wisconsin. From Marable's bookstore one can look up Volta Place, though the view is partially obscured by a fine old maple tree directly outside Marable's premises.

Reviewing security arrangements for Christopher the Secret Service concluded that a potential assassin could clamber up into the leafy maple, seclude himself amidst its foliage and then, at leisure, take a potshot at the Secretary of State as he emerged from his house. So they mutilated the tree, sawing off its branches. The maple promptly began to die, and with each leaf it shed the fury of Kinsey Marable waxed ever more fierce.

He phoned the State Department. He wrote harsh letters to Christopher, pointing out the needless amputation of the maple. Finally, last Hallowe'en, he dressed up in a short skirt, applied make-up, clapped a blousy wig on his head and teetered up to Christopher's front door on high heels. He rang the bell and the bodyguard opened the door.

"I'm here," shrilled Marable. "Mr. Christopher sent for me because his wife is out of town." "Mr. Christopher is out," the bodyguard snarled, and slammed the door. It's Marable's hope that stories of

Christopher's closet queendom will soon circulate inside the Beltway, doing harm to the reputation of the pinstriped lawyer.

December 2

Sir James Goldsmith made millions by getting out of the stock market in 1987 because he thought it was going to be announced that mosquitoes could carry AIDS. He thought this would cause worldwide panic and the stock market would collapse. Many a tycoon's reputation for omniscience rest on faulty data.

Back in the fall of 1987, there were indeed fears on this score. I wrote on August 22 of that year, a time when I was living in Key West: "People are worried about getting AIDS from mosquitoes. I've not heard of any authoritative conclusion either way. Watching the possibly lethal bugs buzz about makes one realize how people felt about mosquito noises in the heyday of yellow fever. I read somewhere recently that between 1819 and 1839 the British army had a death rate of 483 per thousand men on station in Sierra Leone." Those lucky enough to possess a copy of *The Golden Age Is in Us* will find this entry on page five. I phoned my old friend Edward Jay Epstein that same day in August 1987 and told him the fears of Key West. Since Ed was a boon companion of Goldsmith's he passed the word along and the tycoon acted with all due dispatch.

1997

January 3

I see the word "underclass" a lot. On the issue of poverty here's a bracing quote from Thomas Carlyle:

> One of the ominous characteristics of this reforming age, the Custom of addressing "*The Poor*," as a permanent Class, assumed to consist ordinarily of the same individuals. Just as in Jamaica I might address myself to "*the Negroes*." Now if this have a sound foundation in the fact, it assuredly marks a most deplorable State of Society. The Ideal of a Government is that which under the existing circumstances most effectually affords Security of the Possessors, Facility to the Acquirers, and *Hope* to all. Poverty, whatever can justify the designation of "the Poor" ought to be a transitional state—a state to which no man ought to admit himself to belong, tho' he may find himself *in* it because he is passing *thro'* it, in the effort to leave it. Poor men we must always have, till the Redemption is fulfilled, but *The Poor*, as consisting of the *same* individuals! O this is a sore accusation against any society! And to address an Individual as having *his* interest merged in his character as one of *the Poor*, his *abiding* interest! … The Poor can have, ought to have, one interest only—*viz*, to cease to be *poor*. But to call the man who by labor maintains himself under *human* conditions and comforts, who by labor procures himself what is needful for him and his essential affections a Pauper—to *designate* the sum total of such Laborers *the Poor*! O if this be not a foul misuse of words, if there be a ground in fact for it, it is in the same proportion a dire impeachment of both Church and State, such as would warrant a Revolution. For that Country must have a Canker at the Core.

January 15

Day of Repentance: The Salem witch trials took place in the spring of 1692. Ten girls, aged nine to seventeen, had met that winter in the house of Samuel Parris, pastor of the Salem Village Church. After learning palmistry and other crafts from Tituba, Parris's West Indian slave, they accused Tituba and two old women of bewitching them.

Hysteria spread rapidly. The trials began and when they were done, nineteen had been hanged and one pressed to death for refusing to plead.

Four years passed, then the colonial legislative body of Massachusetts adopted a resolution calling for a Day of Repentance and fasting in memory of the victims. The bill was drafted by Judge Samuel Sewall, who had presided in the Salem trials, and who invoked "the late tragedy raised among us by Satan and his instruments."

This week there's an echo ceremony in Salem, exactly 300 years after the first Day of Repentance. It's been organized by Carol Hopkins of San Diego, who sat on a grand jury in that city a few years ago and realized the dreadful injustices being inflicted on innocent people in the "Satanic abuse hysteria" sweeping the country in the 1980s and the 1990s. Present in Salem this week are many of the people thrown into prison on the say-so of tots whose testimony was coerced and perverted by "therapists," social workers and mountebanks.

Bobby Fijnje will be there. He was held without bail in Florida for over a year when he was in his early teens, on the say-so of Janet Reno, at that time the state attorney of Dade County. Fijnje was ultimately acquitted as were others railroaded by Reno in her "crusade" against child abusers which gave her a national reputation. Kelly Michaels will be there. So will Peggy and Ray Buckey, victims of the infamous McMartin proceeding, the longest and most expensive trial in US history.

On the night of January 13 a candlelit walk proceeds to Salem's memorial to the witch trial victims. The 14th is the 300th anniversary of the Day of Repentance. These days, Hopkins says, the Salem-style persecutors don't talk much about Satanic abuse in day-care centers, in fact, they're keen not to raise it. They've moved on, to the "recovered memory" nonsense, and to "facilitated communication" (persuading autistic children they've been abused).

January 22
I've long since learned to expect little or nothing from an inaugural speech. It's like looking for good prose on an insurance form. But Clinton's bathos oozing from my radio last Monday was so oleose that I began to sit up and pay attention. It was useless. When I tried to take notes, my pen slithered off the page, as if it had grease on it. All I could inscribe was a formula phrase about hope and civility not being in government but in ourselves.

We don't need civility. We need civilization, which is something far different. The ancient Greeks were civilized. They had fiery debates, which were far from civil. The Melian dialogue, put by the historian Thucydides in the mouths of the Melians and the Athenians about to overwhelm them is one of the glories of the world. It is also an uncivil, harsh evocation of the political realities of imperial power.

Bipartisanship is another fraud word, which reminds me of the anthropologist Laura Nader's brilliant phrase which skewers both civility and bipartisanship: "coercive harmony," meaning the notion that if you don't button your lip, don't fall in behind the limp standard of "bipartisanship" you are a nutty exceptionalist, best ignored or put onto a daily dose of Thorazine or Haldol.

And how cozening a word is this "community," with its agreeable intimations of the village, the meeting hall and the amiable ethic of all-for-one and one-for-all. But America is not a community. It is a nation encompassing faction, partisan interest, the powerful, the weak, the rich, the poor—with a future to be brokered out of the crucible of fierce antagonisms.

Clinton's sloppy, tired phrases limp through the reality of America like an obese Sunday jogger waddling down the road. He talks of challenges and of bridges, but the challenge of *what*, a bridge to *where*?

A couple of days before the inaugural I was one of the speakers at a fund-raiser for Bear Lincoln, an Indian from the Round Valley reservation in Mendocino County, northern California, who is now facing death penalty charges brought by the Mendocino district attorney, arising out of a lethal exchange of gun fire on April 14, 1995, which left two Indians and one sheriff's deputy dead. The circumstances are hazy in the extreme and the capital charges against Bear Lincoln outrageous.

At the fund-raiser Tony Serra, Lincoln's defense attorney, talked uncivilly, rudely, about the constitutional realities in America in 1997, which make it harder and harder for ordinary folk to be confident they will find any justice in the courtroom.

Serra began with the separation of powers. Gone. No longer do judges have discretion in sentencing. The mandatory guidelines tie their hands, and force them to put someone away for ten years who they know deserves a year at most. With prosecutors framing charges to fit the guidelines, denying bail and then recruiting an army of snitches rewarded with cash or reduced charges or reduced prison time, what chance have accused persons got if they have the rashness to plead innocent?

The last best hope of the accused, Serra went on, is the jury, and here too constitutional rights are on their way to the scrap heap. In California Governor Pete Wilson, malign in this as in all his political instincts, pushes for majority verdicts. The cornerstone of the jury system is firstly the right to nullify—i.e., set the law aside if the jurors' consciences require it—and second, the right of one juror to stand alone and prevail. Bring in majority verdicts: 10–2, 9–3, and it's all over.

The Fourth Amendment, protecting citizens against unreasonable searches and seizures? Virtually a dead letter, Serra said. I know this well enough, since every fall the California Highway Patrol men in Humboldt and Mendocino counties regard it as their right to stop and search every car or truck driven by persons they conceive, after a couple of glances, to be possibly involved in the marijuana business.

Step by step we head into the police state, the most recent milestone being the incredible US Supreme Court decision that when imposing sentences judges can take into consideration charges on which the jury has found the accused innocent.

These are the uncivil realities of our time.

March 12

Katharine Graham, empress of the Washington Post company, has had the pleasure of seeing her *Personal History* reviewed in grossly flattering terms by normally clear-eyed types such as Julia Reed and Nora Ephron. And even if Nora Ephron felt ties of friendship precluded anything but warm praise she could at least have hinted in her *New York Times* review that KG has moved rightward across the political spectrum over the years. Someone who was on good terms with Harry Bridges—the famous red dockworker union leader in San Francisco—in her youth and with Warren Buffett and Nancy Reagan in her mature years has most surely headed somewhere.

The thing about the book that irked me was her cavalier treatment of Larry Stern, who gets a couple of brief mentions as a *Post* reporter. In fact Larry, who died at the age of fifty while jogging on Martha's Vineyard, was a marvelous reporter and editor at the *Post* and contributed immensely to its strength in the 1980s when the *Post* made its reputation. These days, under the deadly editorship of Len Downey, it's hidebound and dreary, which is exactly what I remember Larry predicting would happen, not long before he took that fatal jog in the late summer of 1979.

The last noise linking Larry to the *Washington Post* building was that of breaking glass. After his death there was a big and emotional memorial up on the roof of the *Post* building. At its climax Ben Bradlee, still the editor, took his glass and threw it violently against the wall in a grand gesture of farewell. Hundreds of other people promptly did the same, and I remember KG looking on sourly as the mound of glass shards grew higher.

At that same memorial I learned some new facts. Larry had once been on a boat with another *Post* reporter, George Lardner, and two girls, and had successfully proved that the ferry crossing between Edgartown and Chappaquiddick could be swum in darkness by journalists as well as Senators. And he invented the term "credibility gap."

I made some post-mortem trouble for him by writing an obit in which I said he "was not one of those pallidly objective souls who need a route map to get from a gas shortage to Exxon headquarters" and that he had been a Trotskyist in his hot youth. The reds-under-the-bed crowd seized on this as fresh evidence for their nutty theory that the *Washington Post* really was a radical conspiracy.

March 19

> Hall's wife patted the bed and instructed me to display the mutilation. Hillary exclaimed, "God!" and immediately began performing oral sex on me. Apparently aroused by the carving in my vagina, Hillary stood up and quickly peeled out her matronly nylon panties and pantyhose. Uninhibited despite a long day in the hot sun, she gasped, "Eat me, oh, god, eat me now." I had no choice but to comply with her orders, and Bill Hall's wife made no move to join me in my distasteful task. Hillary had resumed examining my hideous mutilation and performing oral sex on me when Bill Clinton walked in. Hillary lifted her head to ask, "How'd it go?"
>
> Clinton appeared totally unaffected by what he walked into, tossed his jacket on a chair and said, "It's official. I'm exhausted. I'm going to bed."

This excerpt is from what was billed late last year by its disseminators as "the hot book of the season," *Trance Formation of America through Mind Control*, which lacks the simple punch of the old Olympia Press titles eager sixteen-year-olds like myself used to buy in Paris back in the late 1950s. Some were written by Akbar del Piombo, who was in fact a jolly New York Jew whose last name was Rubin, a good artist who needed to make ends meet.

Trance Formation is—according to the bibliographic details on the fax—by Cathy O'Brien "with" Mark Phillips. As can be seen from the excerpt above, the authors have diligently conflated conspiracy and porn in a manner that is highly entertaining. You'll also note that the aim is not to arouse the reader, but to make a political point about the Clintons, and this takes us back to the glory years of political pornography, which were during the French Revolution. There's a good account by Lynn Hunt in the concluding chapter of the 1993 book she edited for Zone, called *The Invention of Pornography: Obscenity and the Origins of Modernity, 1500–1800.*

Between 1774 and 1788—the eve of the Revolution—the number of titles in the genre of political pornography rose steadily and, according to Hunt, took off after the Revolution burst in 1789. *Les aristos* were portrayed as impotent, diseased and of course debauched. The central figure was Marie Antoinette. Hunt describes one "very pornographic" pamphlet called *L'Autrichienne en goguettes*, i.e., the Austrian's frolics. Marie is portrayed in embraces with her brother-in-law, the Comte d'Artois, and with her favorite, the Duchesse de Polignac.

Hunt says that in these pornographic pamphlets the Queen was often depicted as a lesbian and that in them "sexual degeneration went hand in hand with political corruption. Counterpoised, most often only implicitly, to the degenerate aristocrat and the sodomitic priest of the ancient regime was the healthy love of the new patriots."

In my cousin's house in Ireland there's a portrait of Marie Antoinette done by an elderly Frenchman from memory, for my great grandmother. He'd been a pageboy at Versailles. Maybe he was Cherubin, though the portrait is dignified.

I wonder if there was a spasm of political porn in England in the Thatcher years. Certainly many cherished sexual fantasies about her, mostly of an S/M variety. The late Pablo Escobar, of the Medellin cartel, once told his friend Mario Arango, who passed it on to my brother Andrew, that he thought Thatcher the most desirable woman in the world.

March 26

One of the more radical minds in America left us last week. Colonel John Boyd died in Florida at the age of seventy, and though the US Air Force honored him Thursday, March 20, with a funeral in Arlington, complete with guard and fly-past, there are doubtless many souls in the Pentagon relieved that so troublesome an intellect is no longer on active service.

When people want to make a gesture toward military strategic thinking they usually come up with a couple of quotes from Sun Tzu or Von Clausewitz. Boyd's was not a widely known name among the general public, but among theorists of conflict he was unrivalled. It is no exaggeration to set him on the plinth next to Sun Tzu.

No one challenges received ideas without being an incendiary soul, and Boyd's first sign of mutiny against the militarist tradition came in late 1945 in Japan. As an enlisted man in the occupying US forces Boyd became irked at the fact that his fellow conscripts had to sleep without blankets on the freezing floors of abandoned Japanese hangers, while their officers luxuriated in pleasant circumstances, indifferent to the condition of their men.

With the tactical daring that was to characterize his career, Boyd led his fellows in burning down the hangars. Threatened with disciplinary retribution, he held up a copy of the Uniform Military Code, which he had taken the time to study, and pointed out that though he might be guilty of arson, the officers had breached one of the fundamental tenets of the Code, that they had to take care of their men. An embarrassed silence was followed by the dropping of all charges against Boyd and the subsequent provision of warm blankets.

Boyd flew missions over Korea and here is where his ideas first began to take form. As he pondered the reason for the better kill ratio of the American F-86 fighter plane over the theoretically superior Soviet MIG-15, it occurred to Boyd that the US plane's advantage lay in the fact that the pilot had a far better field of vision from his cockpit, and that though the MIG-15 could perform discrete maneuvers more efficiently, the F-86 was superior in transitioning from one maneuver to the next.

Thus germinated Boyd's concept of the underlying patterns of conflict, and how the upper hand in any conflict could be obtained. Boyd summarized this in a mnemonic: OODA—or as he called it, the OODA loop, with the letters standing for Observation, Orientation, Decision, and Action. Key here is the ability to run through the OODA loop, or a series of these, quicker than your foe.

Boyd had noticed that as an opponent is continually outlooped he becomes progressively disoriented and eventually loses all ability to respond rationally. This loss was most vividly demonstrated by the fact that outlooped fighter pilots sometimes simply flew into the ground. When he was a fighter pilot instructor at Nellis Air Force

Base in Nevada in the 1950s, Boyd, applying his own principles, became known as "40-Second Boyd," by reason of the standing bet he had with any pilot that he could beat them in a mock dog fight in forty seconds or pay $40. He never lost.

Put in these schematic terms, Boyd's OODA loop might seem to be simply a commonsense precept, like many a military mnemonic. But the radical implications became apparent when Boyd applied the concept to the design of aircraft, which is where he began to tread on some sensitive toes. The military and its prime partners, the defense contractors, were mighty happy with the orthodoxy that a plane that was a faster, more heavily armed and more freighted with complex gadgetry was the proper weapon to procure. The more complex the plane, of course, the more contented were the arms builders, as they pocketed the taxpayers' dollars.

Boyd conceived of a simple lightweight fighter plane appropriate to his doctrine of OODA loop maneuverability. The Pentagon high brass and their business allies resisted bitterly. Boyd deployed his strategic and tactical ideas in a brilliant campaign of bureaucratic warfare. With allies in what became known as the Fighter Mafia, Boyd captured the attention of James Schlesinger, Secretary of Defense, in the early 1970s, and persuaded him to back their vision, which ultimately took the form of the F-16.

All through the 1980s the Boyd reformers fought their battles through the Armed Services Committees and through thousands of patient explanations to sympathetic journalists who were furnished with the headline-making exposés about faked tests and kindred lies of the arms lobby. Boyd, by now out of uniform, became an underground hero in Washington, delivering his ideas in what was known as the Boyd Briefing.

In its ultimate form this briefing took thirteen hours to deliver, as Boyd gave enthralled audiences—often military officers—what amounted to a unified field theory of human activity, ranging from the tactics of fighter combat to the rivalries of economic and political systems. The briefings were open to anyone interested. Among the keenest students of Boyd were a bunch of young Republicans including Newt Gingrich, who lost no time in inviting Boyd to lecture at the Republican Campaign Academy, Gingrich's staff college. Though Boyd would have been equally willing to instruct Democrats in the art of war and maneuver, not a single one ever bothered to show up at his talks. Boydians would say that they certainly paid a price as the Democrats were consistently outmaneuvered in the early 1990s.

Boyd had that rare talent: relentless intellectual focus on the task at hand. To hear him dissect tactics employed at the battle of Leuctra, when the Thebans beat the Spartans in 371 BC, was as overwhelming as to hear him discuss the relevance of Gödel, Heisenberg and the Second Law of thermodynamics to human behavior. Beyond all that, Boyd was an honest, modest, populist who never lost his humanity amid a life devoted to the consideration of war.

April 9

Maddened by what she regarded as my insufficiently alarmed posture on the "population crisis" and my censorious remarks about coercive family planning, a woman from the Santa Cruz area on California's Central Coast accuses me of ignorance, prejudice and hypocrisy. Reading further into her letter I find Carol Fuller's final defiant charge: "I don't know anything about Mr. Cockburn personally other than he is an aging Marxist, British aristocrat, but I would bet he has numerous children raised by a variety of wives while he gave us the benefit of this thoughtful political analysis ..." So much for Santa Cruz.

"Aging," I grant you. None of us, Carol Fuller included, has figured how to get round that one. "Marxist"? These days I'd say Marx*ish,* the way Jonathan Miller used to joke in *Beyond the Fringe* when someone asked him if was a Jew and he'd say, "Hmm, well, Jew*ish.*" "British"? Not so. Irish by nationality, Irish-Scottish by blood. Just two wives, which is probably well below the average, and one daughter. So there are my credentials for talking about population. I'm a mongrel underbreeder.

The best and brightest have always been the most assiduous advocates of population control. The gung-ho, can-do spirit of these fanatics was embodied by Reimert Ravenholt, a director of

USAID's population program. "Like a spring torrent after a long, cold winter, the United States has moved with crescendo strength during recent years to provide assistance for population and family planning throughout the developing world," he wrote in 1973. In a 1977 interview—in which he said that his agency's goal was to sterilize one-quarter of the world's women—Ravenholt warned that a population explosion, by supposedly causing a fall in living standards in the South, could spark revolt "against the strong US commercial presence" in the Third World.

The policy underlying Ravenholt's exuberance was National Security Study Memorandum 200, commissioned and prepared in 1974 when Henry Kissinger was head of the NSC. In a prefiguring of the present "empowerment" nonsense HK's planners stressed that the US should "help minimize charges of imperialist motivation behind its support of population activities by repeatedly asserting that such support derives from a concern with the right of the individual to determine freely and responsibly the number and spacing of children."

The true concern of the study's authors was maintaining access to Third World resources (the document was prepared during the height of the "commodity crisis"). NSSM-200 worried that the "political consequences" of population growth could produce internal instability in nations "in whose advancement the US is interested." In extreme cases where population pressures "lead to endemic famine, food riots and breakdown of social order ... the smooth flow of needed materials will be jeopardized."

April 16

Zoyd lives! The Place: The Joyce Theater, New York. The Date: Monday, April 7, 1997. The Occasion: A fund-raiser for Dance Theater Workshop, honoring the Jerome Foundation of Minneapolis.

The Big Event: After an hour of fiddle-faddle the stage darkens. Slowly from the ceiling lowers a yellow window frame, which comes to rest about thirty inches above a blood-red mat. From stage right enters my dear friend Elizabeth Streb, in blood-red spandex. She is wearing swimming goggles and a mien of high purpose. She takes several long strides to upstage center, sixteen feet from the frame.

The audience is now looking through the dangling frame at Elizabeth, who executes a pop turn to the left, now facing the crowd. After a lengthy period of spiritual preparation, in which a profound silence falls upon the perplexed audience, she starts her run toward the frame, issues a sharp war cry and dives headfirst through what turns out to be glass. There is an explosion of shards, a perfect hole and Elizabeth lands safely in a perfect line on the mat, her Movement Moment triumphantly achieved. The new "dance" is called Breakthrough. Meanwhile the wealthy donors mustered in the front two rows delicately and nervously dust the glass from their prosperous bodies.

June 18

Down in Los Angeles a couple of weeks ago I passed swarm after swarm of bicyclists whizzing down the Pacific Coast Highway and it wasn't long before I realized this was an AIDS charity ride, all the way from San Francisco. Later I met someone who'd been to the triumphal concluding ceremonies. Mayor Riordan was there, and when someone wheeled in the riderless bicycle—reprising the riderless horse at big-time national obsequies with boots of the departed one shoved backwards in the stirrups—there wasn't a dry eye in the house.

The kitsch thing with the riderless bike sent me straight back to a chapter, "The kitschification of AIDS," in Daniel Harris's *The Rise and Fall of Gay Culture*, just published by Hyperion. Starting with the famous Benetton ad of a man obviously dying of AIDS under a cheap print of Jesus calling from the Other Side while his parents clutch and sob, Harris observes accurately that "in a little over a decade AIDS has become so thoroughly commercialized that the marketing of compassion now sustains a number of flourishing cottage industries, such as those represented in Under One Roof, the gift store housed in the San Francisco headquarters of the Quilt."

Those in charge of marketing the disease have attempted to place its primary commemorative monument within the context of a wholesome tradition of American history, to turn it into a kind of faux antique, an artifact from a phantasmal Arcadia. In this mythic, prelapsarian America, AIDS is stripped of its stigma as the scourge of depraved homosexuals and endowed instead with the integrity of a bucolic community in which good-natured rustics of unspoiled simplicity produced their handicrafts in a utopic atmosphere of democracy and cooperation.

July 16

In the old days of not-so-long ago, there was no mistaking about the transition from poor to rich when you traveled from Cork to London. The roads around Cork were full of Ford Escorts and low-end Toyotas. A BMW in the smaller towns was a rarity. These days the square in my old hometown of Youghal, thirty miles east of Cork, is choc-a-block with BMWs, Audis and Mercedes. There's money around. In 1996 the Irish Republic produced more wealth per head of population than the UK. Only a quarter of a century ago, by the same measure, gross domestic product in Ireland was half that of England.

The natural instinct of an Irish person with title to a field and $50,000 spare in the pocket is to build a bungalow, preferably faced off with pebble dash or concrete or raw, liverish sandstone. Something, in fact, whose prime esthetic function is that of *not*—at any price—resembling an old Irish thatched cottage.

The result, particularly in the west of Ireland, has been the imposition of ribbons of these ugly buildings along the coast and inland rural roads, while simultaneously the country towns are being abandoned by those with the money to build and the patience to commute, usually at lethal speeds.

In another decade or so, the Irish countryside will no longer exist and the place will have transmuted into a sort of suburbia *in rure.*

Concrete is the outward and visible manifestation of affluence. My village of Ardmore, at the west end of county Waterford, has its Business Development Council busy devising ways of showing that the place is on the cutting edge of progress. The beautiful cliffs now sport dreary guideposts, benches, concrete steps. Public lavatories and then perhaps a heritage center will soon finish off one of the loveliest vistas in Europe.

People are better off than they used to be, but in many ways the place has gone downhill. In the late 1950s you could walk clear across Dublin in the middle of the night and be reasonably confident nothing untoward would occur. I did so many times. Not any more. Dublin is in the midst of a heroin plague, and desperate addicts hold up shopkeepers, brandishing syringes of blood they claim to be AIDS-infected, threatening a lethal jab at the slightest sign of resistance. There are plenty of thieves in the countryside, too, many of them very violent.

I can remember my friend Gareth Browne developing an appetite for traditional Irish music that led him to found Claddagh Records, which first showcased the Chieftains. In the late '50s he'd come to stay and drag round his vast reel-to-reel tape recorder to one cottage after another, while old ladies droned their way through all ninety-six verses of "The Walls of Limerick." These days much of this tradition of music has degenerated into awful Celtic kitsch, a new-age O'Muzak stew.

July 23

It pains me to say it, but English food—at least in London—has truly improved. I took my daughter to a restaurant in Knightsbridge. It was pretty fancy, with a bizarre mix of distressed green walls, Balthus-type art and big plates done in the Constructivist manner with Russian words on them. I ordered fish soup and pig's foot, and felt a father's burst of pride when my daughter ordered oysters and the pig's foot too.

When they arrived, the pig's feet lay starkly, one on each plate next to a little cloud of mashed potato. I sliced in, and there was no resistance. A normal pig's foot has about thirty pieces of bone and cartilage. This had none. Instead it had braised sweetbreads and a chicken stuffing. The only piggish thing left in our feet was the braised skin.

They were very good. The *maitre d'*, in an accent that veered oddly between Parisian French and East End Cockney, swore he ate them for breakfast every day.

July 30

My brother Patrick phones from Israel. Patrick is the London *Independent*'s correspondent in Jerusalem, having spent much of the last quarter century working first for the *Financial Times* and then for his present employer throughout the Middle East.

What was irking Patrick was the utter predictability of most press photographers. He'd been out covering a confrontation in Hebron between Israeli soldiers, fundamentalist settlers and Palestinian kids throwing rocks. "The sole ambition of these photographers," Patrick said, "is to get behind the kids throwing the rocks, and get their shot at the precise moment the rock leaves the kid's hand and arcs toward the soldiers." And it's true. We've all seen that shot a thousand times.

"Meanwhile," Patrick went on, "not far from these kids is the school where the girls come out and walk down the steps and there are settler women screaming at them and spitting at them, guarded by Israeli soldiers in case one of the Palestinian schoolgirls tries to retaliate. Not a photographer to be seen, even though it was a wonderful opportunity for a dramatic photograph that told a story. Since I was writing about this scene I went over to the photographers massed behind the rock-throwing kids and told them that if one of them photographed the scene at the school they would be assured of a sale of that photograph to my newspaper. Not one of them would do it. Not one of them wanted to leave off taking exactly the same photograph that they have all taken thousands and thousands of times."

August 1
To: Daisy Cockburn
Cc: Patrick Cockburn

Subject: Dark Days for Nigel

JAIL TIME FOR SCIENTIST GUILTY OF TRAP-MAKING

By Court Reporter

A former MoD scientist who set a mantrap in his garage has been given an 18-month jail term. The judge also ruled there should be an extended licence period in respect of the sentence as he thought 53-year-old Nigel Cockburn was "potentially very dangerous."

Earlier this month, Cockburn, of Cloonmore Avenue, Orpington, was convicted at Maidstone Crown Court of setting lethal booby traps at the garage in Wood Street, Swanley. He had set the traps after suffering a spate of burglaries.

The trap was found after police were called to a garage fire on July 10 last year at a row of three dilapidated cottages Cockburn owned in Wood Street.

One of the traps injured an Army explosives expert called in to investigate after a quantity of ammunition was found there by police and fire crews.

Captain Iain Swan of the Royal Logistics Corps suffered arm injuries when he opened the door to a shed and had to raise his arm to block the device as it swung at his head.

The judge sentencing Cockburn said Capt Swan could have been blinded. The Recorder Mr Christopher Wilson told Cockburn: "The nature of your former occupation makes you potentially very dangerous. You are an expert in counter-terrorism and have considerable experience in dealing with explosive devices."

A microwave oven which had its door removed and had been wired at the back to be permanently on was also found in the shed. And the court was told in 2004 Cockburn had also wired up a door to the mains in order to shock intruders.

He claimed he had been burgled 20 times in 14 years and the police had not done anything about it. Cockburn was said to have told police he would kill burglars if he had the chance.

He was sentenced to twelve months for assault causing actual bodily harm, eighteen months for setting a mantrap, and three months for possessing ammunition without a certificate, to run concurrently.

Cockburn, who worked for the MoD for 36 years, had denied the charges but was found guilty.

He was cleared of wounding with intent.

September 3

The short century of the common man begins and ends with a royal passing: in 1914, the murder of the Archduke Franz Ferdinand at Sarajevo, and now, three years shy of the millennium, the death of Princess Diana. The Diana cult—for what else can we call it?—offers her as the people's princess, but this is merely the sleight of hand of the old fairy tales, where the prince most admirably displayed his royal essence by moving among his subjects as a commoner.

The British wanted a love story, and it began well, before turning into vulgar soap opera as so many love stories do. Too bad a good fairy wasn't on hand to warn young Diana about the future that fateful day when Prince Charming came and knocked on her door. In the end she only truly seemed to come into her own when in the company of people in worse shape than herself. She would glow, as though the proximity of imminent death and suffering lent a steadying hand, a comfort to her fraught existence. No wonder she took such an interest in minefields.

As she bent down to embrace a little boy, oblong handbag elegantly raised to shield her cleavage from the photographers, it was obvious that she did not mind the paparazzi, in fact needed their constant attention, but on terms she hoped to be hers. That's how everyone in show business wants it. Probably Dodi snapped, "Lose them," to the chauffeur, who obediently ran the car up to the fatal 121 mph. Di surely knew, far better than Dodi, that paparazzi were inescapably part of the terms of her trade and gave her comfort and meaning, as surely as did her encounters with the dying and the maimed.

September 5

This time around President Bill spent his time on Martha's Vineyard in the house of real-estate developer Richard Friedman. I'm unclear whether this is what was once the proud home of Robert McNamara where Clinton stayed back in the year of the Somali fiasco, and from which redoubt he ordered the attempts to murder Mohammed Aidid, the late capo of Mogadishu.

I remember visiting in the early 1980s. The house had a commanding view of Great Beach, a stretch of sand usually covered with lawyers and wreathed in fog. As he led our party down the cliff path and onto this bleak expanse, McNamara's face darkened. He had, he said, "tried everything." He'd sought relief in the courts and from the most resourceful fixers of Edgartown. Every stratagem had failed. We wondered what he was talking about. As we gained the beach itself McNamara stretched out a hand, shielding his eyes in eloquent despair. All around us was a pride of nudists, cocks and tits akimbo. It turned out that McNamara had taken these nudists below his house as a personal affront, with a depth of passion equaling his attempts to wipe Vietnam from the face of the earth. But the nudists had held their ground, had indeed prevailed. Eventually McNamara sold the house and moved away. John Belushi moved in.

September 10

My daughter called last week from London, saying that the entire nation had gone insane. I faxed her a couple of pieces I'd written about Diana and she said that if this sort of cold-eyed commentary were read out on the streets of London, the author would be torn apart by the crowd. She also said she was grateful, and glad to see the old man had a spark of radicalism left in his bones.

As he dandled me on his knee, my father used to tell me the story of how he and some trusty comrades sabotaged King George V's jubilee back in the 1930s. They ascertained that the route of the procession ran down Fleet Street. Three days before the parade they dressed as workmen and told newspaper offices on both sides of the street that they were city employees stringing up banners. They slung one across the street with "God Bless Our King" written on it.

On the day of the actual parade, they returned and found the crowd so great they could scarcely get near the string they had run down from the banner and around the corner into an alley. Eventually a partner in crime got on my father's shoulders and pulled the string. The banner fell open, to reveal the words, "Twenty-five years of hunger, misery, and war." They heard a gasp and great bay of rage from the crowd on Fleet Street, and took to their heels.

When they saw the newsreels, everything had gone even better than they had dreamed. The news cameras were right behind the King's coach and caught the banner perfectly as it fell open. I saw it myself about a decade ago, and it was odd to see the jerky horses in the old footage, and the commotion, and remember Claud's role. Down the years it's been easy to forget—until the Diana insanity—how reverent the British were about royalty not so long ago.

In the 1950s, my family was very friendly with the late Malcolm Muggeridge, who wrote a piece about the royal family for an American magazine. I think it might have been the old *Saturday Evening Post*, or perhaps *Look*. By today's standards Mug's piece was tame to the point of invisibility. He wrote things like, "Even her friends say Queen Elizabeth can be dowdy and a frump." But the roof fell in. At the time Muggeridge had a big job at the BBC. He was promptly dropped. People traveled great distances to daub horseshit on his country house in Robertsbridge, Sussex. His son John had just been killed in a skiing accident and Malcolm's wife Kitty got plenty of letters from people saying how glad they were this had happened.

September 11

A photograph is by definition a moment seized from time, and the seizure can remove context in a way that might not exactly be unethical, but does damage the truth. Photographers tend, alas, to think in clichés. Refugees must never laugh. Hungry children must never smile. Someone once told me that Walker Evans's famous black-and-white photographs of the Okies fleeing the dust bowl, printed in

James Agee's *Let Us Now Praise Famous Men*, didn't exactly do justice to the humanity of these Okies, shown by Evans as invariably grim. The contact sheets apparently showed laughter as well as tears, exuberance as well as despair.

The patron saints of photojournalism all manipulated grossly. Photography is, almost always, manipulation. Take the famous photo of young love in Paris, the boy and his girl kissing with abandon. Turns out it was set up. Or take Henri Cartier-Bresson's equally famous picture of the batty old woman wagging a flag somewhere in the American Northeast on July 4. Turns out Henri set her up with the flag. So the picture was a lie. Unethical? Most assuredly. That's the nature of the beast.

September 17

First one friend of mine and then a second developed arrhythmia last week. One of them told me that what with the irregular heart beat he was worried about having sex on the ground he might croak on the job. It's a fear that often besets the older man with any sort of pain between Adam's apple and belly button. I referred my pal to a study by M. Ueno cited in an essay by Hackett and Rosenbaum called "Emotion, Psychiatric Disorders, and the Heart," published in *Heart Disease*, edited by Eugene Braunwald, published in 1980. The Ueno essay is alluringly titled "The So-called Coition Death," published in something abbreviated as Jap. J. Leg. Med. 17:330.1962, though why the Japanese should be so interested in this I'm not sure, since their rates of heart disease are remarkably low owing to the huge intake of sashimi and seaweed. On the other hand, Japanese executives are in the habit of dropping dead from overwork.

Coital death is unusual. Ueno's study showed that coition accounted for 0.6 percent of endogenous sudden deaths. Most of these occurred in the context of extramarital screwing. Males in that situation were on average thirteen years older than their companions and one-third were drunk at the time.

Of course this fear of dying while fucking is connected to the notion that the latter activity involved a great expenditure of physical effort. Not really. One study by Hellerstein and Piedman reckoned that the equivalent cost in oxygen of maximal activity during intercourse approximates six calories per minute. During "foreplay" and "afterplay" about 4.5 calories are consumed. I'm not sure what "afterplay" involves now. In the good old days it meant lighting a cigarette, puffing on it and blowing lazy smoke rings in the air, sort of, while trying to persuade the love partner to get up and mix a gin and tonic.

Hellerstein and Friedman conclude that the demand placed on the heart by sexual intercourse is equal to that of "a brisk walk around the block or climbing a flight of stairs." No big deal really. We should all try it more often. At least that's what I told my arrhythmic friend.

October 8

My favorite forger is still the amiable German who did the Hitler diaries in the early 1980s, though the old ladies who managed to sell their forged Mussolini diaries *twice* run him a close second. When he finished dashing off the Fuehrer's daily reflections into a series of cheap notebooks, he decided their authenticity would be improved if Hitler's initial were embossed on the cover. So he hastened off to the stationary store to buy some Letraset, only to discover that the letter A had run out. He decided to use F instead. So each notebook had FH. Not a single one of the experts noticed.

One of Princess Di's ancestors fell for a forgery by an Italian called Joseph Vella, who claimed in 1794 he'd unearthed the seventeen lost books of the Roman historian Livy. His story was that he'd got them from a Frenchman who'd stolen them off a shelf in Santa Sophia in Constantinople. They were, Vella said, in Arabic, which was not implausible, since the Arabs translated classical works, which is how many were saved.

Vella persuaded Di's ancestor, Lady Spencer, to put up the money for a translation into Italian, and quickly made a specimen page, which he claimed was the whole of the sixteenth book of Livy's history. Now Vella got the bit between his teeth and reported another great find, the ancient history of Sicily in the Arabic period, across 200 years, plus all the correspondence between the Arab governors of Sicily and their superiors in Africa. The king of Naples showered Vella with medals and other gratuities, including a pension. There was a problem. The only Arab text he had was a book about Mohammed. But though his knowledge of Arab orthography was scant, he inserted dots, curlicues and similar flourishes that looked like Arab script. When he published a facsimile, further praise was heaped upon him for translating these illegible scribbles. Vella said he'd almost lost an eye after poring over the manuscript and the view was he should get a higher pension.

Vella's work was published throughout Europe, until finally an Orientalist examined the manuscript, declared it to be the history of Mohammed and family, and Vella went to prison.

October 15

I've been following the gastronomic excursions of *Vogue*'s Jeffrey Steingarten with increasing concern. The man is out of control. October's *Vogue* features him in an excursion to Rome as the climax of an obsessive three-year quest to make pizza bianco and pane Genazo. The former is a kind of bread, a bit like focaccia, and pane G is a wholemeal bread.

Steingarten's approach evokes the single-mindedness of a Mars shot as prepared by the Jet Propulsion Lab in Pasadena. He notes his arrival time in Rome. He scuttles to his target bakeries to measure and collate, oblivious to the charms of the city, or indeed of his companion soon—one surmises—bored to distraction by her employer.

It's all a bit reminiscent of someone engaged in sex with eyes fixed not on the beloved but on some Masters and Johnson diagram of neural responses. Steingarten represents the ultimate triumph of positivism. He races to collect samples of Italian flour, malt and water for later analysis in US labs. He reports excitedly that one Italian manufacturer had overestimated the protein content of its flour by *nearly 3 percent*. Enraptured by such triumphs of US lab analysis, Steingarten has nothing to say about the vital gluten levels in the flour that are both a feature of the flour and a consequence of the way in which the dough is kneaded.

Such omission is emblematic of Steingarten's approach, which sees breadmaking as an activity akin to manufacturing rocket fuel, rather than as the outcome of an interaction among domestic yeasts, wild yeasts and variabilities in wheat strains and water. Fermentation involves not just the introduction of domesticated yeasts, but also the chance invasion of wild ones. Bread is a living thing that involves both. As anyone who regularly bakes bread well knows, bread becomes better not purely as a function of technique or careful measurement and proper ingredients, but rather because the kitchen becomes progressively colonized by wild yeasts. This is why European bakeries, somewhat messier than the sterile kitchens of this country's commercial US bakers, produce better, tastier bread. The dough-encrusted towel, the unsterile bowl all play their part in providing a haven for wild yeasts.

Steingarten describes how his researcher, Martina, begins to pale as he outlines his scientific endeavor: "By the time my oration has finished, Martina's nutty skin has turned a ghostly white. At least she has grasped the heavy responsibility that now weighs upon her handsome shoulders." Actually, Martina was grasping the dreadful truth that she had to spend the next several days with an idiot thinking that science alone can capture the ineffable.

November 5

One of the Republicans' problems is they've always overstated the case against Clinton, so they've devalued the currency of abuse. Now no one pays any attention and Bill's popularity ratings remain high, whatever dirt laps about his knees. The thing to do is wait until he's dead and then let him have it. This is what happened to the Roman Emperor Nero. The sweaty plebes of Rome liked him. He was populist in political tilt, snooted the upper-crust Senators and threw terrific parties, to which the ordinary folks were invited.

But history took its revenge, in the form of the denunciations of Nero by Tacitus, Suetonius and the rest, propagandists for the Roman upper crust. But the Christians hated him too, for obvious reasons. Then after nearly 2,000 years of maltreatment by these mythographers, poor Nero got chewed up again by the French religious mythographer Ernest Renan, who depicted him in pitiless terms as the Antichrist. Eagerly reading Renan was a Polish nationalist, Henryk Sienkiewicz, who wrote *Quo Vadis*, serialized in *Gazeta Polska* between 1894 and 1896, earning him the Nobel Prize in 1905. Nero got excoriated once more, not only as the Great Beast, but also as somehow the proto-foe of Polish nationalism.

The first *Quo Vadis* came in 1901, and by 1912 Enrico Guazzoni produced the third adaptation, running for a full two hours and blessed with incredible success, including a premiere at the Royal Albert Hall in the presence of King George V, and in New York, where it was the first film ever to play in a Broadway theater. With Guazzoni's *Quo Vadis* the new medium reveled in long shots and pans around crowds (sweaty plebs) enjoying the martyrdom of Christians, under the supervision of Nero.

By now, *Quo Vadis* was becoming a weapon of the Catholic Church in Italy in its battles with the new secular state, and once again Nero proved useful in his beastliness. Next came DeMille's *The Sign of the Cross* in 1932, once again offering the easy contrast between the depravity of Charles Laughton and the Christian purity of Mercia. Nero's doom was sealed in 1951 with the released of Mervyn LeRoy's *Quo Vadis*, when he was represented by Peter Ustinov in all his foreign decadence, set against the manly strength of Robert Taylor and the American way. So Nero stood for Stalinism and everything foul. The voiceover at the start of the movie talks about AD 64 as a period when "the individual is at the mercy of the state … and rulers surrender their subjects to bondage." But simultaneously the hounding and suicide of the novelist Petronius is taken by Maria Wyke as an allegory of Hollywood blacklists.

November 19

Nanny-gate is winding down. At its height it represented the fiercest stress to Anglo-American relations since the war of 1812, when my ancestor Admiral Sir George Cockburn burned down the White House, then hastened along to the *National Intelligencer* to avenge himself on the press which had treated him roughly. Sir George told his men to destroy the newspaper's type fonts saying, "Be sure that all the C's are destroyed so the rascals cannot any longer abuse my name."

Woodward wasn't a nanny but an au pair. Back in the 1950s in Britain the au pair was usually a Swedish girl. The headmaster of my boarding school had two—the only females under the age of thirty in our fastness in Perthshire. Fitzpayne and I faced expulsion for having tea with them in the headmaster's study at a time we thought the man was safely absent on some official function.

The nanny was the pivotal figure in male upper-class character formation. Mothers were seen once a day for about thirty minutes, when the youngster was brought down from the nursery quarters to be displayed in the drawing room. After the onset of boarding school at the age of eight, these contacts between mother and offspring shrank to the four months' vacation time. The son and heir's maternal substitute was of course the nanny, in Churchill's case (Mrs. Everest) along with many others the only woman such men loved. Heirs to large estates would get their own back on Mummy by booting her out into the "dower house," a structure—sometimes converted stables—detached from the main house.

Among the many anguishing *rites de passage* was the transition from care by nanny to supervision at the boarding school by Matron, in my case an austere figure in starched white who would line all us little boys up and then, one by one, have us come forward so she could briefly cup our testicles in her chill hand. There might be useful employment for Amirault prosecutors here. There was a successful restaurant in London in the 1980s in which waitresses were dressed as nannies and matrons and barked fierce commands like "Eat up your carrots, young man!" at a clientele whimpering with pleasure at this *temps retrouvé*.

After Matron's ministrations we would head off to chapel and once a term have the pleasure of hearing the headmaster announce that we would "now sing the one hundred and thirty-sixth psalm, verses one to six." We would naturally look at the omitted verses which concluded with the psalmist's delighted cry, "Blessed be he who taketh the little children and dasheth them against the stones."

I should note that in my case contact with Mama was extended far beyond the half hour display at cocktail time, since she bred horses and we all rode a lot though we feared the dangers of the chase. How we yearned for snow and ice in the winter months which meant riding was off, instead of which we would hear the exuberant, ominous cry, "Lovely day for hunting."

November 23

Behind every fortune lies a crime, Balzac wrote, and no doubt that was true in the case of the steel dynasty of Jones and Laughlin, in Pittsburgh. But the Laughlin side of that enterprise produced James Laughlin, who shunned the family business in favor of publishing and launched New Directions—the most sustained presentation of good writers in the history of one publishing company: Pound, William Carlos Williams on down.

I said to my friend Ben Sonnenberg, the day after Laughlin died last week, that it was probably one of the most culturally productive uses of surplus extraction in the history of American capitalism. Ben suggested the Mellons, but that's because Ben is an Anglophile and loves those eighteenth-century paintings of horses the Mellon family purchased out of Gulf Oil loot. Think of what some of the other American fortunes have produced: from Singer sewing machines to ... the *New Republic*. I asked Ben—who used his patrimony to found *Grand Street* (now the property of Jean Stein)—whether he thought crime lay behind his dough and he said that alas, it wasn't a fortune. I suppose "tidy sum" would better describe it. Ben Sonnenberg Sr., the famous publicist, wanted to have written on his gravestone, "At least I never took a cent from Joe Kennedy or Howard Hughes." His house was number 19 Gramercy Park South, and Ben Jr. once told me his father's butler sneaked out late one night after his master's death and planted the urn under some bush in the Square itself.

We turned to discussion of another productive fortune, that of Pirandello's father who was in the sulfur business on Elba, enabling young Luigi to get on with his writing. Last week I saw Pirandello's final play, *The Mountain Giants*, at the La Jolla theater, well acted and staged by students in the theater department of the University of California at San Diego. It is a wonderful piece of work and not, so far as I could see, particularly "unfinished" as it is usually described. Ben Jr. said that in the years when he'd been active in New York theater he'd tried endlessly to get *The Mountain Giants* produced there, but without success.

Then he told me a good joke. Grasshopper goes into bar. Bartender: "Good lord, we've got a drink named after you." Grasshopper: "Why would you call a drink Bob?"

November 26

OSWALD'S TALE

Dear Mr. Anderson,
Alexander Cockburn, ever obstinate, is of the opinion that JFK's "assassin, Lee Harvey Oswald, shot the President because he believed, not without reason, that this deed would help save the Cuban Revolution." Oswald disagreed.

From his arrest until his summary execution, Oswald spent almost 48 hours in police custody. Reportedly, 12 of those hours were spent in interrogation by state and federal police. There are no stenographic or taped records of these interrogations, and Oswald was denied legal representation. However, memoranda by some of the investigating officials were published in the Warren Commission Report. These officials report that Oswald vehemently denied shooting either the President or officer J. D. Tippit, and two of these officials also report that Oswald expected Cuban policy to remain unchanged with the death of JFK.

According to Inspector Thomas J. Kelly of the Secret Service: "[Oswald] said there would be no change in the attitude of the American people toward Cuba with President Johnson becoming President because they both belonged to the same political party and the one would follow pretty generally the policies of the other."

Also present, Capt. J. W. Fritz, of the Dallas Police Department writes: "Someone of the federal officers asked Oswald if he thought Cuba would be better off since the President was assassinated. To this he replied that he felt that since the President was killed that someone else would take his place, perhaps Vice-President Johnson, and that his views would probably be largely the same as those of President Kennedy."

Sincerely yours,
Jock Penn, Petaluma

P.S. Alexander Cockburn urges Alex (*Repo Man*) Cox to "concentrate on making a decent movie for once," instead of uttering Malthusian heresies. Cox's latest movie is more than decent. *The Winner*, now on video, appears at first to be a lame neo-noir *Pulp Fiction* knockoff, but hang in there and Cox's nihilistic apocalyptic allegory will get to you. If you liked *Dr. Strangelove*, *Grosse Point Blank*, *Natural Born Killers*, and *King of Kings*, *The Winner* is your meat.

Alexander Cockburn replies:
If we proceed with my view that Oswald was a rational assassin, it's not likely that he would have told the authorities cited by Penn that he killed Kennedy to save the Cuban Revolution. He would have said—as he did—that he didn't kill the President and that it would make no difference to US policy toward Cuba that JFK was dead. A pro-Cuba Oswald would certainly not wish suspicion to be directed toward Cuba.

But in fact with the death of Kennedy, the efforts to kill Castro so hotly promoted by Jack and Bobby diminished. Oswald was right in his calculation.

December 3

One area in which British journalism is indubitably superior is in the writing of obituaries. Sometimes the *New York Times* will produce something readable, even piquant, but jaunty frankness about the departed one is not tolerated. Every now and again, down the years,

I've shouted a few insults at some freshly tamped grave, and the disrespect invariably provokes outrage.

The quality English newspapers, by contrast, have turned obituaries into an important sector of their coverage. In this respect the *Independent* (which pioneered the obit renaissance) and the *Daily Telegraph* are particularly well edited. Before me this Friday, November 28, is the *Telegraph*'s obituary of Dan Farson, covering two-thirds of a page of this respectable broadsheet, read mostly by an upper and middle-class conservative audience.

Farson was a famous homosexual drunk, emblem of London's old Soho, whose pubs and restaurants my father took me to in the early 1950s. I suppose an equivalent in terms of *mise-en-scène* and boozy louch-ness, would have been the old Lion's Head in the Village which I never knew. Dan was the son of Negley Farson, a famous US correspondent who wrote for the *Chicago Daily News* in the early 1930s, reporting from Europe. His memoirs, *Way of a Transgressor*, often turn up in the second-hand bookshops. Dan made his living as a photographer and journalist. The *Telegraph*'s obituarist evoked his life with humor and bracing honesty. The obit begins in traditional style and then rapidly changes tempo. "Daniel Farson, who has died aged 70, was a talented television journalist, writer and photographer; he was also a nightmare drunk." I doubt you'd get such a lead in the *New York Times*.

From that opening the anonymous obituary keeps up an ebullient tempo of reminiscence: "He never lost his hair, which was fair; in old age he presumably dyed it … He would go off at nights to such places as a pub nicknamed The Elephants' Graveyard. It was some surprise that, with his alarmingly risky sex life, he had not been murdered … Over and over again Farson's assaults on London meant drinking all day, picking up a rent boy and very often being robbed by him at his hotel. He was barred from several hotels for trivial offenses such as being found with his trousers round his ankles in the corridor. One Sunday afternoon in the Coach and Horses [a bar in Greek St., later HQ for the satirical weekly *Private Eye*] an angry rent boy (aged about 30) came into the pub and tried to shame Farson into paying for his afternoon services. Farson was shameless: 'But you didn't bloody do anything,' he shouted back. 'And I bought all the drinks.'"

With such anecdotes the obituarist not only offers good entertainment but draws a vivid picture of the old Soho, frequented by painters such as Lucien Freud and Francis Bacon, about whom Farson wrote a book called *The Gilded Gutter Life of Francis Bacon*. The old Soho, where Karl Marx also lived his Soho life in terms once excitedly described by a Prussian spy, is certainly dead and gone. Farson's obit concludes: "On the day of the funeral of Diana, Princess of Wales, Farson went to the Coach and Horses in Soho, straight from a trip to Sweden. He stood at the bar, noisily impersonating a friend, Sandy Fawkes, bursting into tears. Behind him young people told him to shut up because they were trying to hear the speech of Earl Spencer on television. Such had become the bohemia that he was shortly to leave for the last time."

December 4

The British Public Records Office is releasing seventy-year-old material, including Home Office files on Lord Alfred Douglas, aka Bosie, Oscar Wilde's young lover. In 1923 Douglas was jailed for criminal libel of Winston Churchill, having alleged in a pamphlet that Churchill had accepted a bribe from a German-born financier named Sir Ernest Cassels, to publish a misleading report about the battle of Jutland. For this Bosie pulled six months.

While languishing in Wormwood Scrubs prison, Douglas wrote *De Excelsis*, a reprise on Wilde's *De Profundis*, written in Reading Jail. The jailers confiscated this and never gave it back, on grounds that it repeated the libels Douglas had been imprisoned for. Douglas bitterly contrasted his treatment with the more generous attitude toward Wilde: "When Oscar Wilde wrote in prison a filthy and blasphemous screed entitled *De Profundis* which consisted largely of abuse of myself and others then living, and contained an apology for every kind of vice and abomination, the Home Office made no difficultly at all about allowing him to take out his MS."

While it was denying Lord Alfred Douglas's request the Home

Office was also upholding a ban on Radclyffe Hall's pioneering lesbian novel, *The Well of Loneliness*. The Home Secretary, Chuter Ede, was sympathetic, noting carefully that "the perversion which it [i.e., the novel] is supposed to celebrate is more widespread than commonly thought." But the ban lasted until 1968.

And after sixty years the Home Office has released papers showing that David Lloyd George, Prime Minister in 1917, successfully sought the release of Alice Wheeldon, a suffragette who had tried to poison him on the grounds that World War I, for which she apparently held Lloyd George partly responsible, had slowed the cause of women's rights. Wheeldon had engaged in arson and sabotage in the feminist cause. She was a former postmistress who ran a second-hand clothes shop in Derby, fighting her battles with her daughter Hettie at her side. Alice got ten years for trying to poison the PM, a lenient sentence by modern standards. But Lloyd George had her released after a brief period on the grounds that her incarceration was a PR disaster and she was unwell and might die in prison.

December 17

Edward Said, passing through London on his way to India, gave a talk at an event sponsored by the *New Left Review* and the *London Review of Books* on "Co-existence." Edward's point was that after the wreckage of Oslo and the poison of Netanyahu and the "into-the-sea-with-them" irreconcilables, it behooves intellectuals in the Jewish and Arab diaspora to talk about coexistence inside Israel/Palestine. The intellectuals mustered for the occasion, such as George Steiner, agreed, though one can ask, Why just allocate the great task to Jews and Arabs? What about the rest of us, mongrels though we mostly are?

Later, everyone gathered at one of those functions the liberal/left excel in organizing: in the narrow, noisy basement of an indifferent restaurant, offering dank meatballs to be eaten with one's fingers. I sat down next to Edward to say hello and almost immediately a man I'd never previously met and didn't recognize rose up and addressed me directly. "Allow me to say I think you are a fucking asshole." Before I could ask for clarifying evidence, he dashed from the restaurant.

It turned out to be Salman Rushdie. Rushdie was presumably still simmering from criticisms, richly deserved, that I made about him for his disgusting behavior after the Sivas massacre. Some Turkish secularists had gathered in the town of Sivas to make a public reading from Rushdie's *Satanic Verses*. The same sort of Islamic fanatics as support the fatwa against Rushdie then set fire to the hotel in which the secularists were staying, and more than thirty were burned to death. Rushdie promptly denounced the secularists as acting in a manner he had not authorized. It was a chicken-hearted display. This happened a few years ago. The Islamic arsonists have just been convicted.

December 29
To: Patrick Cockburn

Subject: Bad King John, proto-Islamo-Fascist

Did you know he seriously considered becoming a Muslim? I'm reading R. W. Southern's *Western Society and the Church in The Middle Ages*, vol. 2 of the Pelican History of the Church. In it Southern notes that King John of England while excommunicated by the Pope for nearly four years, gave serious thought to becoming a Muslim. The steps King John took in this direction were recounted in detail by a contemporary chronicler, Matthew Paris, laid out in *Chronica Majora*, ed. H. R. Luard, in R.S. (Rolls Series—Chronicles and Memorials of Great Britain and Ireland during the Middle Ages), 1874, ii, 559–64. I'm getting hold of this vital text which will no doubt be in Latin, unless Luard translated it.

1998

January 7

The Kennedys never go quietly, do they? Somehow it's beyond their powers. And if you had to define an *echt* Kennedy manner of passing, Michael's would surely be it. Here we had a phalanx of Kennedys, plus entourage, skiing downhill in mass formation, a menace to all others on the slope and for good measure tossing a football between them, with Michael video-taping with his other hand.

The assassination buffs are agog. For them, the question is: Who moved the tree? A home video taken by a German tourist the day before the fatal encounter shows the tree at least fifteen feet east of its final rendezvous with the speeding Michael.

January 9

How frail a thing is human memory! On New Year's Day the *New York Times* ran an AP story about a settlement between the Quaker Oats Co., MIT and some former students. The students were among 100 boys, many of them wards of the state, who were the unwitting objects of research in the 1940s and 1950s when they were fed cereal containing radioactive materials. In the last week of 1997, Quaker and MIT agreed to pay over $1.85 million to the plaintiffs.

The way AP reported the story, Quaker and MIT had lured the

boys from Fernald School in order to "prove that the nutrients in Quaker oatmeal travel throughout the body." Quaker's aim was supposedly to match the advertising claim of its deadly corporate rival, Cream of Wheat.

This is by no means the whole story. In 1949 the parents of boys at the Fernald School, some of them mentally retarded, were asked to give consent for the children to join the Fernald science club. (The wards of the state presumably got the go-ahead from some Rep. of the Commonwealth of Massachusetts.) The boys were then the unwitting objects of experiments, supervised by the Atomic Energy Commission (AEC), in partnership with Quaker Oats, in which they were given radioactive oatmeal. The researchers wanted to see if the chemical preservatives in cereal prevented the body from absorbing vitamins and minerals, with the radioactive materials acting as tracers. They also wanted to assess the effects of radioactive materials on the kids.

The AP story missed the AEC's role altogether, which is just how the AEC—now the Department of Energy—would have liked it. There are many experiments from that era that sound like a continuation of the Nazis' researches in the labs at Dachau, which is scarcely a coincidence since the CIA spirited out many of those same Nazi scientists, bringing them to work for the AEC and other bodies in the "Paperclip" program, as the CIA codenamed it.

To give just one other of these experiments: in 1963, 131 prisoners in Oregon and Washington had their scrotums and testicles exposed to 600 roentgens of radioactivity. They had given consent, but were not warned of the cancer risk. Later almost all of the prisoners were given vasectomies or were surgically castrated. The doctor who performed the sterilization operations said they were conducted to "keep from contaminating the general population with radiation-induced mutants." In defending the sterilization experiments, Dr. Victor Bond—a physician at the Brookhaven nuclear lab—said, "It's useful to know what dose of radiation sterilizes. It's useful to know what different doses of radiation will do to human beings." One of Bond's colleagues, Dr. Joseph Hamilton of the University of California Medical School in San Francisco, said more candidly that the radiation experiments which he had helped oversee "had a little of the Buchenwald touch."

January 12

A fellow I know recently shared a sports box with President Bill and mentioned they had a friend in common. This friend was a woman—now an academic—Bill had had a big thing with many years ago, before he met HRC. Bill launched into fond reminiscence, misty-eyed and affectionate. As he listened, the fellow realized that Bill had absolutely no self-consciousness in his nostalgic reverie. He felt, the fellow said later, that if he'd asked Bill whether he had a kink in his cock, the President would have launched off on this topic with equal enthusiasm and lack of restraint.

All the while Bill was rambling on about his former girlfriend, members of Bill's entourage were sticking their heads into the sports box, asking the Pres did he want to talk to this fat cat or that fat cat who were offering huge sums to the DNC. This is the man's life. No wonder he didn't want to stop talking about his old flame.

January 14

Girls love to talk dirty, given half a chance. Two days after Representative Bono had his last and positively final encounter with that tree in the Tahoe basin, California newspapers were full of ominous stuff about mandatory helmets for skiers. I read this in the *San Francisco Chronicle* in our local store and remarked to R. and A., the two women behind the counter, that in any given twenty-four hours in America there must be at least a dozen fatalities involving people falling out of bed while screwing, bashing their heads on the floor, etc., etc., and that the way things were going we'd soon all have to wear helmets before getting it on.

The girls lit up.

"And mandatory knee pads against carpet burn," cried A.

"And mandatory pads against tile burn in the shower," shouted R. merrily.

A couple of minutes later they were laughing about doing it in airplanes. Racy stuff. I headed for the door, ears a-tingle.

January 15

The big New Year's resolution is the same one I always make. Really good tax records. This time, for $15 I bought a diary which has a whole page for each day. January 1 was a snap. I put the miles I drove in my car, plus charitable dispensations ($2 to a man standing in the rain at a street corner with a sign saying he'd work for food), plus cost of meals and brief reason why they could be counted as business-related entertainment. Then I put down the cost of all my newspapers. I entered check numbers, totals and deductible disbursements. I spent several minutes thinking how easy tax preparation will be in February 1998, and about the chagrin of the IRS auditor when he realizes that this time he's met his match. I even called my brother and handed him a short lecture on the importance of proper record-keeping.

It took a whole day—January 2—for reality to creep back into my life. The virtuous, one-page-per-day diary is grim to behold, so I bought a nice little Mexican diary, with plenty of demotic iconography and almost no space for anything except for a couple of phone numbers a day. A spiral wire holds the flimsy pages and if 1997 is anything to go by, somewhere in July 1998, I'll lose the first three months of the year. I'll fall behind in my estimated quarterly payments. I'll have to guess the miles driven. So, 1998 will be a year when, as with other years, I pay enough in interest and penalties to hold the B-2 bomber program together single-handed. All the same, the Air Force has come to rely on me and I'd hate to let them down.

February 17

Many people go through life rehearsing a role they feel that the fates have in store for them, and I've long thought that Christopher Hitchens has been asking himself for years how it would feel to plant the Judas kiss.

And now, as a Judas and a snitch, Hitchens has made the big time. On February 5, amid the embers of the impeachment trial, he trotted along to Congress and swore out an affidavit that he and his wife, Carol Blue, had lunch with White House aide Sidney Blumenthal last March 19 and that Blumenthal had described Monica Lewinsky as a stalker. Since Blumenthal had just claimed in his deposition to the House impeachment managers that he had no idea how this linking of the White House stalker stories had started, Hitchens's affidavit was about as flat a statement as anyone could want that Blumenthal has perjured himself, thus exposing himself to a sentence of up to five years in prison. At the very least, Hitchens has probably cost Blumenthal about $100,000 in fresh legal expenses on top of the $200,000 tab he's already facing. Some friend.

And we are indeed talking about friendship here. They've been pals for years and Hitchens has not been shy about trumpeting the fact. Last spring, when it looked as though Blumenthal was going to be subpoenaed by prosecutor Starr for his journalistic contacts, Hitchens blared his readiness to stand shoulder to shoulder with his comrade: "together we have soldiered against the neoconservative ratbags," Hitchens wrote in the *Nation* last spring. "Our life à deux has been, and remains an open book. Do your worst. Nothing will prevent me from gnawing a future bone at his table or, I trust, him from gnawing in return." This was in an edition of the *Nation* dated March 30, 1998, a fact which means—given the *Nation*'s scheduling practices—that Hitchens just writing these loyal lines immediately before the lunch—Hitchens now says he thinks it was on March 19, at the Occidental Restaurant near the White House—whose conversational menu Hitchens would be sharing with these same neoconservative, right-wing ratbags ten months later.

The surest way to get a secret into mass circulation is to tell it to Hitchens, swearing him to silence as one does so. His friends have known this for years. As a compulsive tattler and gossip Hitchens gets a frisson I'd guess to be quasi-sexual in psychological orientation out of the act of tattling or betrayal.

This brings us to Hitchens's snitch psychology, and the years of psychic preparation that launched him into the affidavit against his friend Blumenthal. Like those who question themselves about the imagined future role—"would I really leap through fire to save my friend," "would I stay silent if threatened with torture"—Hitchens has, I feel certain, brooded constantly about the conditions under which he might snitch, or inform. A good many years ago we were discussing the German Baader-Meinhof gang, some of whose members were on the run at the time. Hitchens, as is his wont, stirred himself into a grand little typhoon of moral outrage against the gang, whose reckless ultra-leftism was, he said, only doing good to the right. "If one of them came to my front door seeking shelter," Hitchens cried, "I would call the police in an instant and turn him in!" Wouldn't you just, I remember thinking at the time. I've often thought about that outburst since, and whether in fact Christopher was at some level already in the snitch business.

Over the past couple of years the matter of George Orwell's snitching has been a public issue. Orwell, in the dawn days of the cold war and not long before his own death, compiled a snitch list of Commies and fellow travelers and turned them over to Cynthia Kirwan, a woman for whom he had the hots and who worked for the British secret police. Now, Orwell is Hitchens's idol, and he lost no time in defending Orwell's snitch list in *Vanity Fair* and the *Nation*. Finally, I wrote a *Nation* column giving the anti-Orwell point of view, taking the line that the list was mostly idle gossip, patently racist and anti-Semitic, part and parcel of McCarthyism. Bottom line, snitching to the secret police wouldn't do. Hitchens seemed genuinely surprised by my basic position that snitching is a dirty business, to be shunned by all decent people.

Then, in the middle of last week, he snitched on Sidney. Why did he do it? I didn't see him with Tim Russert on *Meet the Press*, but apparently he looked ratty, his physical demeanor not enhanced by a new beard. I have read the transcript where, as I anticipated, Hitchens says he simply couldn't let the Clinton White House get away with denials that they had been in the business of slandering women dangerous to them, like Monica, or Kathleen Willey.

There were couple of moments of pure Hitchens. Only Hitchens could charge someone with perjury and then sneer that the object of his accusations was contemptible for having a legal representative. And only Hitchens could publicly declare Blumenthal to have lied to Congress and then with his next breath affirm in a voice quivering with all the gallantry of loyal friendship that "I would rather be held in contempt of court" than testify in any separate court action brought against Blumenthal.

Did Hitchens really think things through when he told the House impeachment people toward the end of last week he was willing to swear out an affidavit on the matter of the famous March lunch? Does he think that with this affidavit he will "reverse the whole impeachment tide" and bring Clinton down? Or is he, as Joan Bingham told Lloyd Grove of the *Washington Post*, merely trying to promote a forthcoming book? A woman who knows Hitchens well, and who is inclined to forgive, has suggested that the booze has finally got to him and that his behavior exhibits all the symptoms of chronic alcoholism: an impulsive act, dramatically embarked upon and, in the aftermath, only vaguely apprehended by the perp.

It's true, Hitchens does drink a staggering amount with, as all acquaintances will agree, a truly amazing capacity to pull himself together and declaim in a coherent manner while pints of alcohol and gallons of wine are coursing through his bloodstream. But he does indeed seem only vaguely to understand what he has done to Sidney. On Sunday February 7, he was telling one journalist that he still thought his friendship with Sidney could be saved. By Tuesday, he was filing a *Nation* column, once again reiterating his friendship for Blumenthal, intimating he'd done him a big favor, blaming Clinton for everything he, Hitchens, was doing to Blumenthal and concluding with a whine of self-pity that the whole affair would probably end with him, Hitchens, being cited for contempt of court.

Perhaps more zealously than most, Hitchens has always liked to have it both ways, identifying himself as a man of the left while in fact being, as was his hero Orwell particularly toward the end of his life, a man of the right.

There is the final question: is Hitchens making it all up, about the March 19 lunch? Blumenthal says he has no recollection, and adds, as all agree, that there had already been hundreds of references in the press to Monica being a stalker, and he may just have repeated to Hitchens and Blue what he'd read in the papers. It was a month, remember, when the White House was being very careful in what it was saying about Monica because they were uncertain which way she would jump and didn't want to anger her.

Joe Conason, of the *New York Observer*, certainly an eager recipient of White House slants at the time, says he spoke to Blumenthal in that period and Blumenthal refused to talk about Lewinsky at all. It's true, Hitchens can be a terrific fibber, but, short of willful misrepresentation, maybe, amid this insensate hatred for Clinton he remembered the conversation the way he deemed it to have taken place rather than the way it actually happened.

In his own affidavit Hitchens did not say that Blumenthal had directly cited Clinton as describing Lewinsky as a stalker and on CNN he tagged only Blumenthal as describing Monica thus. Yet, in her affidavit, filed after her husband's from the west coast where she has been staying, Carol Blue said that Blumenthal had indeed cited Clinton as describing Lewinsky as a stalker and also as crazy. It seems extraordinary that Hitchens and Blue couldn't get their affidavits straight, and it seems that Blue's affidavit was filed purely with the intention of further damaging Blumenthal—which indeed it has.

Hitchens has done something despicable. It wasn't so long ago that he was confiding to a *Nation* colleague, in solemn tones, that for him the most disgusting aspect of the White House's overall disgusting behavior was "what they have done to my friend Sidney." He's probably still saying it. Hitchens always could cobble up a moral posture out of the most unpromising material.

March 4

"As far as chemical and biological weapons are concerned, Saddam Hussein is a repeat offender. He has used them against his neighbors and on his own people."—Madeleine Albright, Secretary of State.

By Albright's criteria, Saddam has a way to go to catch up with the United States. In 1942, US Army and Navy doctors infected 400 prisoners in Chicago with malaria in experiments designed to get "a profile of the disease and develop a treatment for it." Most of the inmates were black, none were informed of the risks of the experiment. Nazi doctors on trial at Nuremberg cited the Chicago malaria experiments as part of their defense.

In 1947, the US Army put on its payroll Dr. Shiro Ishii, the head of the Imperial Army of Japan's bio-warfare unit. During World War II, Dr. Ishii had deployed a wide range of biological and chemical agents against Chinese and Allied troops. He also operated a large research center in Manchuria, where he conducted bio-weapons experiments on Chinese, Russian and American prisoners of war. Ishii infected prisoners with tetanus; gave them typhoid-laced tomatoes; developed plague-infected fleas; infected women with syphilis; performed dissections on live prisoners; and exploded germ bombs over dozens of men tied to stakes. In a deal hatched by Gen. Douglas MacArthur, Ishii turned over more than 10,000 pages of his "research findings" to the US Army, avoided prosecution for war crimes and was invited to lecture at Ft. Detrick, the US Army bio-weapons center in Frederick, Maryland.

In 1950 the US Navy sprayed large quantities of *Serratia marcescens*, a bacteriological agent, over San Francisco, promoting an outbreak of pneumonia-like illnesses and causing the death of at least one man, Ed Nevins.

A year later, Chinese Premier Zhou Enlai charged that the US military and the CIA had used bio-agents against North Korea and China. Zhou produced statements from twenty-five US prisoners of war backing his claims that the US had dropped anthrax-contaminated feathers, mosquitoes and fleas carrying yellow fever and propaganda leaflets spiked with cholera over Manchuria and North Korea. Secretary of State Dean Acheson dismissed Zhou's accusations as being based on the "coerced confessions of brainwashed POWs." Acheson blamed the outbreaks of disease in northern China and Korea on the "Communists' inability to care for the health of the people under their control." But in the fall of 1952 an International Commission looking into the matter produced a 700-page report supporting Zhou's claims. The report noted that the insects found in the vicinity of the US "leaflet drops" were not native to the region. The Commission noted a "striking similarity" with the techniques perfected by Dr. Ishii during the Japanese occupation of Manchuria.

From 1950 through 1953, the US Army released chemical clouds over six US and Canadian cities. The experiments were designed to test dispersal patterns of chemical weapons. Army records noted that the compounds were used over Winnipeg, Canada, where there were numerous reports of respiratory illnesses, involving cadmium, a highly toxic chemical.

In 1951 the US Army secretly contaminated the Norfolk Naval Supply Center in Virginia with infectious bacteria. One type was chosen because blacks were believed to be more susceptible than whites. A similar experiment was undertaken later that year at Washington, DC's National Airport. The bacteria was later linked to food and blood poisoning and respiratory problems.

Savannah, Georgia, and Avon Park, Florida, were the targets of repeated Army bio-weapons experiments in 1956 and 1957. Army CBW researchers released millions of mosquitoes on the two towns in order to test the ability of insects to carry and deliver yellow fever and dengue fever. Hundreds of residents fell ill, suffering from fevers, respiratory distress, stillbirths, encephalitis and typhoid. Army researchers disguised themselves as public health workers in order photograph and test the victims. Several deaths were reported.

In 1981, Fidel Castro blamed an outbreak of dengue fever in Cuba on the CIA. The fever killed 188 people, including eighty-eight children. In 1988, a Cuban exile leader named Eduardo Arocena admitted "bringing some germs" into Cuba in 1980.

Four years later an epidemic of dengue fever struck Managua, Nicaragua. Nearly 50,000 people came down with the fever and dozens died. This was the first outbreak of the disease in Nicaragua. It occurred at the height of the CIA's war against the Sandinista government and followed a series of low-level "reconnaissance" flights over the capital city.

This is not to mention atmospheric nuclear testing.

May 20

Ron Ridenhour died on Sunday, May 10, at the age of fifty-two. He'd been playing handball, having told friends he'd probably had a few too many margaritas the night before. Then he sat down against a wall, turned blue and died. It reminds me too sharply of another journalist, my friend Larry Stern, whom Ron also knew, who went jogging at about the same age and keeled over. Journalists should take an arm's-length attitude toward immoderate physical exercise.

I met Ron in New Orleans back in 1988. We talked about My Lai and how he'd heard about it, investigated it, and finally brought the massacre into the light of day. Ron's point was always that My Lai was an operation, "an act of policy, not an aberration. Above My Lai that day were helicopters filled with the entire command staff of the brigade, division and task force, from 7.30 a.m. to 11.30 a.m. It takes a long time to kill over 600 people."

Then on the thirtieth anniversary of My Lai, this last March, I talked to him again, about Hugh Thompson, Lawrence Colburn and Glenn Andreotta getting Soldier's Medals for their action in saving some civilians that day. I asked him how he'd feel if someone offered him the medal. "I didn't save any lives," he said dryly. Ron was far too well-mannered to say it, but I knew he must have felt that there was something altogether too symmetrical and phony about the sudden discovery of Thompson as My Lai's Lone American Hero, matching the prosecution of Rusty Calley as My Lai's Lone American Villain.

May 27

I called my publisher, Verso Books, the other day and found its executive director, Colin Robinson, agog over the success of Verso's 150th anniversary edition of Marx and Engels's *Communist Manifesto*. He'd already sent me the sleek little book with its introduction by the British historian Eric Hobsbawm. I told Colin waspishly it looked like an espresso, or maybe latte table book, with its somber, stylish cover design of a red flag by the Russian émigré artists Komar and Melamid flapping over a black background: Marxism without hope.

Robinson wasn't irked at all. He said Verso had printed 25,000 copies and they were selling like hot cakes. The publicity had been gratifying. He'd nearly persuaded Barney's to do a window display of fashionable models, all with copies of the *Manifesto* poking from their handbags or pockets. On his desk, he boasted, were great piles of excited articles that had run in the US press, all touting the new Marx craze.

I don't like Verso's edition. It looks like a memento rather than a manifesto. The old Moscow publishing house booklet which I read back in the late 1950s looked like it meant business. It was aimed at people who wanted to overthrow capitalism, and said so right away.

Hobsbawm says the proletariat is a failure and maintains that these days the prime countervailing force is environmentalism. Not the environmental movement, please note. The movement, which springs in part from utopian socialism, implies action and struggle. Hobsbawm seems to see environmentalism as prudently managed capitalism on a global scale, with social engineers nicely equipped with the appropriate degrees in charge.

Back in 1958 the American sociologist Lewis Feuer introduced his edition of the *Manifesto*, writing that the revolutionary intellectual of the '30s has been replaced by the managerial intellectual of the '50s, and with this change in social temper the philosophy of Karl Marx would be consigned by many persons to the museum of their youthful indiscretions. In 1998 these same managerial intellectuals want to manage the entire planet, and Hobsbawm, who had a few youthful indiscretions of his own, sees barbarism as the only alternative to such planetary supervision by credentialed, scientific professionals (presumably financed by George Soros and the Nature Conservancy). So Verso's is a manifesto without class struggle, without revolution.

How different an attitude to history than Marx's. In his last edition of the *Manifesto*, in 1882, he excitedly used news of the class struggle in Russia and America to adjust his revolutionary gunsights. His aim remained true, as did his commitment.

But to divorce the *Manifesto* from revolution, as does Hobsbawm, is indeed to produce a Marxism without hope. Marx merely becomes a preface to the great German sociologist Max Weber who once described capitalism as mechanized petrification embellished with a sort of convulsive self-importance.

Many reviewers of Verso's *Manifesto* have tended to see it as a celebration—admittedly acerbic—of global capitalism, sweeping away all hindrances to the basic task of accumulation. Both the neo-liberal *New Yorker* and conservative *Times Literary Supplement* have praised Marx for his perspicacity and overall up-to-dateness in seeing which way capitalism was headed, while saying that where he truly messed up was in his revolutionary politics. Marx gets whacked with words like promethean or utopian, to show how he sent Communism off down a blind alley.

September 16

The more minutely we are able to examine the private side of vastly powerful public persons, the more pity we should feel for their condition. For many years the Emperor Franz Joseph, leader of the Austro-Hungarian Empire, used to try to get an extra kettle of hot water brought along miles of corridors in his palace to warm his bath. His orders were given a respectful hearing, then ignored.

Bill Clinton, leader of the free world, couldn't engage in a furtive embrace of a woman not his wife in the Oval Office because he thought the gardener would peer in the windows. For the pitifully few moments of semi-gratification he and Monica Lewinsky were able to indulge each other, the two had to seclude themselves in a windowless corridor, a love site without even the close excitement of a broom closet.

The Starr report, released on September 11, on the intimacies of the President and the White House intern, must surely rank as one of the most bizarre documents about the sex life of a public person ever given to the world. A thousand years from now, cultural anthropologists will marvel at the insensate detail of its portrait of what happened when a president in his late forties was seduced by a rich girl from Beverly Hills. The Starr report is Clinton's legacy, as striking a symbol of our time as was the scaffold of Louis XVI to the late eighteenth century.

This is not to undercut the demented nature of the Starr report, which has as eerie a feel to it as a proceeding from the Spanish Inquisition or one of those court sessions from the Middle Ages when animals were placed on trial for heresy. To us, in the late twentieth century, it is unfathomable that serious people should have considered putting a pig or a goose through the rigors of the judicial process. A century from now our descendants will surely marvel at an age—ours—when millions and millions of dollars were spent to determine that the President and Ms Lewinsky enjoyed ten bouts of oral sex in two years, attended by two orgasms per partner across that entire time.

Even adding in the bouts of phone sex it certainly doesn't add up to a fulfilling relationship. The sparsity of sexual fulfillment makes a previous White House incumbent, Warren Harding, look like Casanova by comparison. Nor was Bill Clinton's comportment entirely gross. He was tempted; infatuated. He told Monica he'd had hundreds of affairs in his youth but that now, after forty, he had been trying to commit himself more strongly to his marriage.

They exchanged gifts. In the words of the report, "He told her he enjoyed talking to her. She recalled him saying that the two of them were emotive and full of fire and she made him feel young." In the end she turns into the spoiled girl from hell, storms the White House, spurns jobs secured for her by the President and Vernon Jordan. And of course she led him badly astray by swearing that she'd never, ever told a soul.

Editorial moralists have sprung to their high horses. The *New York Times* spoke of reading the Starr report with "a heavy heart and churning emotions." This is like saying one reads Judith Krantz with a heavy heart and churning emotions. The dalliance—"affair" is far too serious a word—between Clinton and Lewinsky simply won't sustain the burden of moral reproof being placed upon it. It's like treating Edward Lear as if he was Homer.

It's clear enough now that Kenneth Starr did Clinton a huge favor by confining himself so relentlessly to the President's sex life. Not even a whiff from the stagnant marsh of Whitewater riffles his pages. A report which is designed to evict a president by means of impeachment surely has to have some urgency to it—some sense of great misdeeds of state, the boding darkness of *Macbeth*. You can't send round to Congress a report in the style of *Midsummer Night's Dream* and expect those folks in Congress to muster the seriousness of statesmen and stateswomen pondering high crimes and misdemeanors. It just won't wash.

As things are, the American people once again seem to be displaying themselves as mature adults, endowed with a sense of realism, unlike the opinion-formers who have been howling as though the President molested a child in its pram.

On February 19, 1996, so Independent Counsel Starr discloses to us, the President was closeted with Monica in the Oval Office, telling her they could still meet but that there could be no more canoodling. In the midst of this tête-à-tête he took a call from one of the Fanjul family, powerful Florida sugar barons who at the time were battling the idea that they should have to pay any money to compensate for the damage to the Everglades attendant upon their sugar-growing activities in Florida. Even as Clinton was talking to Fanjul, Al Gore was agitating for such a levy. By the end of the conversation we know there was one, and can surmise there were two, satisfied parties. The Sugar Baron and the President, each man efficiently serviced.

But Ken Starr wasn't writing about this happily consummated relationship, which is why Americans won't take this report seriously. They understand the difference between petty moral dereliction and political corruption.

October 7

Driving through Indiana, Ohio, Illinois, Wisconsin and out across the Northern Plains, it's clear enough, in jokes and derision at the blue noses, that the cavortings of Bill and Monica and the maneuvers of the Republicans and Democrats have been good for America. It's been marvelously cathartic for people to have had to talk so long and so loudly about blowjobs, orgasms, infidelity and privacy. Nothing has been more ridiculous than the whinings of parents about how to talk to the kids about it all. Kids who've watched forty-five deaths a day on American TV their whole lives are experiencing a marked elevation in the quality of their cultural consumption by listening to accounts of Bill and Monica's sexual encounters, such as they were. (Ironically, it's always been Hillary-think that kids need special counseling when some big untoward event occurs, like an eleven-year-old blowing away some classmates.)

One thing is certain, as the network correspondents like to say at the wrap-up point. The car mechanics of America are for Bill. The '64 Chrysler New Yorker I'm driving developed serious gas feed and overheating problems at 5 p.m. in central Indiana the afternoon I was due to give a talk about my and Jeffrey St. Clair's book *Whiteout*, in a bookstore in Chicago, at 7 p.m. Rodney Sheets, owner and manager of One Stop Auto in Columbia City, flung himself into the emergency, but still had time to deride at some length Henry Hyde. This was Quayle country and at intervals Rodney would chat with several of his children who were running in and out of the shop. So here was a devoted parent and advocate of family values, possibly a former Quayle voter, but still thinking the uproar is ridiculous.

It was the same in Milwaukee, where Peggy and Dennis of Lake Shore Mobil took up the work Rodney had not had time to finish. If Bill's future was in their hands, Bill would be safe. A word about mechanics. In the late 1940s and early 1950s many Americans got screwed around by car salesmen. The odium carried over to mechanics. Theirs is not the most trusted profession in the charts, albeit not nearly so low as journalists and politicians. But as the owner of ten old cars from the 1950s and 1960s, all of which at various times I've driven around or across the country, and in all of which I've been beleaguered by various grave setbacks and crises, I've only had about four unsatisfactory encounters with mechanics in which I could say I've been seriously hard done by. This yields an "I-was-screwed" statistic of a fraction of one percent. Set this against the risk factor associated with encounters with academic people and the entertainment industry and you will agree, mechanics are as honest a bunch as the unpaid staffers of the *Catholic Worker*, which is saying a great deal.

October 10

Fall is always the best time to meander around the country. Across the Midwest the corn is being harvested. The browns and golds of stubble and still-standing stalks warm those vast flat or slightly undulating vistas. In Chicago, we stayed in Danny Postell's and Tom Petralis's nice apartment in Rodgers Park—$600 a month, a pleasant mixed ethnic neighborhood, small lakeside park and public beach available for dips in Lake Michigan, which I took. We looked at the map. The decision, as always, is whether to head southwest along old 66, or straight west through Iowa and Nebraska, or take the northerly routes through the Dakotas. This time we aim to go along upper Missouri, right under the Canadian border, maybe go through Glacier National Park. The old Lewis and Clark route, more or less. (One of the local papers had a story about new efforts to find their camp sites. It seems that some of the men on the Lewis and Clark expedition had syphilis, which they treated with mercury. The mercury hangs around in the soil, and so now the researchers run around with sensors and locate the sites.)

About 100 miles along 94 from Minneapolis we came to Sauk Centre, and espied a sign for the Sinclair Lewis Interpretive Center. Lewis was born in Sauk Centre, which he offered to the world as Gopher Prairie in *Main Street*, the novel published in 1920 that made his name.

Fortunately the Info Center has not yet found the money to transform itself into an interactive learning experience in the modern manner, replete with audio-visual aids and the indispensable computers. In fact, the "center" is an old-fashioned small museum with fading photographs and photostats of Lewis's working manuscripts. Some of these were detailed plans Lewis drew of his fictional towns, plus his real-estate maps of the inhabitants' precise locations and their family histories. Every time he visited a graveyard, he'd take down names for future use.

The Center, unsurprisingly, presented Lewis as a Man of Letters, gravely posed in tweeds. The only indication that he might have been somewhat of a rip-snorter was a photograph of Marcella Powers, the young aspiring actress with whom Lewis began a five-year relationship in 1939, when she was eighteen and he was 54 and still married to Dorothy Thompson. From her later letters, Marcella, who died in 1975, seems to have been a lively and intelligent person. My father, who met Lewis in Berlin in the late 1920s, recalled "Red" Lewis as a boozer of formidable proportions.

I'd forgotten how good a writer Lewis was. "This is America," he wrote in the epigraph to *Main Street*. "Main Street is the climax of civilization. That this Ford car might stand in front of the Bon Ton Store, Hannibal invaded Rome and Erasmus wrote in Oxford cloisters. What Ole Jenson the grocer says to Ezra Stowbody the banker is the new law for London, Prague, and the unprofitable isles of the sea; whatsoever Ezra does not know and sanction, that thing is heresy, worthless for knowing and wicked to consider."

To give some longer sense of perspective, the Interpretive Center also has an interesting photograph of a Viking Altar stone into which Norsemen, wandering across the prairie, drilled four holes to support a canopy under which a priest had celebrated mass in 1362. Bishop George Spettz rededicated the stone in 1975.

We left the Interpretive Center and headed for Sauk Centre's greatest pride, Main Street, though the citizens were naturally furious when the novel was first published. Now the banner on Main Street says, "A View of the Past, A Vision of the Future."

October 15

ORWELL'S SHITLIST

Dear Mr. Anderson,
In Alexander Cockburn's recent frenzied attack on George Orwell and his now infamous shitlist, he quotes Peter Davison as saying that Cockburn's father was Orwell's "political foe." The following might be of interest to those fans of the deadly ideological wars of the 1930s and 1940s.

Cockburn's father, Claud Cockburn, was a Communist who Graham Greene called one of "the two greatest journalists of the twentieth century." Unfortunately, the one collection of his work that

I've seen, *Cockburn in Spain*, doesn't live up to this accolade. The book is a collection of Cockburn's Spanish Civil War dispatches to the Communist *Daily Worker*. Here's a taste:

"The POUM, acting in cooperation with well-known criminal elements, and with certain other deluded persons in the anarchist organizations, planned, organized and led the attack in the rearguard, accurately timed to coincide with the attack on the front at Bilbao.

"In the past, the leaders of the POUM have frequently sought to deny their complicity as agents of a Fascist cause against the People's Front. This time they are convicted out of their own mouths as clearly as their allies, operating in the Soviet Union, who confessed to the crimes of espionage, sabotage, and attempted murder against the government of the Soviet Union."

Note Claud Cockburn's party line reference to the Moscow show trials.

Orwell, of course, fought with the POUM. In his vivid and moving memoir of the Spanish Civil War, *Homage to Catalonia*, Orwell responds to the Communist propaganda attacks, including some produced by Cockburn, directed against the POUM. Ironically, Orwell went to Spain with the intention of enlisting with a Communist unit. He still planned to join one until the POUM, which had been labeled Trotskyist by the Communists, was attacked in Barcelona and its leaders purged. Anyone interested in the details should read *Homage to Catalonia* in which Orwell refers to Claud Cockburn by his *Daily Worker* pseudonym, Frank Pitcairn.

Interestingly, Alexander Cockburn, in *The Golden Age Is in Us*, quotes a section of a review of a book about Roger Hollis in which his father, Claud, figures prominently. Roger Hollis, if memory serves, was the head of MI5, roughly the British equivalent of the FBI, and is now suspected of being a long time Soviet mole. It appears, according to the review, that Claud Cockburn was under the protection of Hollis. Cockburn and Hollis were at Oxford together, but Hollis concealed their association and kept Cockburn's file in his personal safe. And Hollis has been accused of refusing to provide evidence to wartime witch-hunters who wanted to prosecute. Hollis is also accused with involvement in furthering Cockburn's "activities."

Was Claud Cockburn a Soviet agent? Did he dutifully name names to his superiors? If so, what happened to their sorry asses? Perhaps, when Claud Cockburn's Russian, American and British Intelligence files are released, it may be time for another round of righteous indignation.

As far as I know, Orwell never had a secret agenda. His political views and his political loyalties were out in the open. I suspect that Orwell would have given the same assessments of the same people to anyone who asked.

Also, according to Cockburn, "the list displays Orwell as suspicious of Jews, homosexuals, and blacks ..." This is an interesting statement coming from a journalist whose Mossad file is probably as thick as Noam Chomsky's.

Moreover, when I sent an earlier version of this letter to the AVA in September, 1996, it wasn't printed because Alexander Cockburn was unable to respond. Cockburn, it seems, was busy fag-baiting in the Dakotas. As I recall, Cockburn outed some Senatorial candidate who Cockburn later took partial credit for defeating. But, of course, Cockburn was only battling hypocrisy.

Sincerely yours,

Jock Penn, San Rafael

Alexander Cockburn replies: Anyone who wants to test Graham Greene's high estimate of my father's work should read his memoirs, issued under various titles including *A Discord of Trumpets*, *I Claud*, *In Time of Trouble*, and *Cockburn Sums Up*. *A Discord of Trumpets* shows up from time to time in second-hand bookstores here, or on internet sites. *Cockburn in Spain* was a reissue of *Reporter in Spain*, my father's dispatches from the Spanish Civil War for the *Daily Worker*, written under the name Frank Pitcairn. There were good things in that collection, and stuff that reads badly now. It was done at great speed during the Spanish Civil War to rally popular support for the Loyalists, and sold in great numbers and translations around the world. He believed in the "treason trials" then. So did a lot of other people. Later, he ceased to believe in them. In 1946 he stopped working for the party. Unlike Orwell, he didn't rush to squeal, secretly squeal, on his comrades to the British Secret Service.

There's enormous mythmaking about POUM and Spanish anarchism today. I don't think my father, in hindsight, would particularly modify his views.

Penn uses a passage from *Golden Age* very disingenuously. A friend of my father is describing, and deriding, the views of a right-wing nut, to the effect that Roger Hollis was a Soviet agent. Penn alludes to the views of the nut, views which were held by a particularly nasty bunch of ultra-right-wingers in the British intelligence establishment, but doesn't disclose the context.

I dimly remember some earlier, even more stupid letter from Penn. Perhaps I said it was too stupid to publish—not that this warning infallibly deters the mighty editor. I do remember with pride my excursion to South Dakota in 1996 to point out to the citizenry that Senator Larry Pressler was a hypocrite. The citizenry evidently agreed, in the only upset of a Republican Senator that year.

I don't understand the paragraph about the Mossad. Orwell certainly was suspicious of Jews, blacks and homosexuals. My father was a Communist agitator. No, he didn't send Orwell-type lists to Moscow.

October 16

Hucksterism in the name of "good causes" is now as embedded in the liberal life and mindstyle as hookworm in the foot of an African child. Today, at the level of symbolic action, a person of progressive temperament can live in a bubble-bath of moral self-satisfaction from dawn to dusk.

Take that morning cup of coffee. Maybe it comes courtesy of the self-congratulatory Thanksgiving Coffee, or Equal Exchange, an outfit in Boston which, as its name suggests, claims it has smoothed out the inequitable wrinkles in the coffee trade between the Third World and the First.

The coffee is perhaps consumed at a table made of choice hardwood certified as having been harvested under "sustainable" forest practices. The coffee machine is powered by "green electricity" offered by Working Assets. And who knows? The coffee pot was perhaps acquired with a *Nation* credit card.

Take Equal Exchange. Here is a nonprofit in Massachusetts that makes the very big claim that it is rectifying the iniquities of First/Third World trade in coffee beans. "Feed your soul as well as your body," the outfit's ad proclaims in the *New Yorker*, raising the battle-standard of fairness. They buy "direct" from small farmers, they say, thus eliminating the middle man.

No they haven't. They've taken over the function of "conscience" middle man from the ordinary First World coffee brokers and there's really very little evidence that the Third World growers, as opposed to the soul-fed coffee drinkers at First World tables, do better because Equal Exchange is doing the brokering. They buy from grower co-ops, Equal Exchange boasts. But so do ordinary First World coffee brokers, paying the same prices.

But if Equal Exchange is having little or no impact on conditions of production in the Third World, it certainly is having an effect, a baneful one, on small local businesses across America. Equal Exchange flies a buyer from a First World co-op grocery store on a two-week jaunt to Costa Rica, courtesy of the American taxpayer. The group tours the coffee *fincas* and a good time is had by all. On return, the buyer might expand the coffee rack of Equal Exchange, with bins provided by Equal Exchange.

This means less business for the small local roaster, local sales people, local distributors. Lo and behold, what do we have but the Conscience Industry's equivalent of General Foods or Proctor and Gamble, with the nonprofit's executives scarcely paying themselves starvation salaries.

Start with the word "sustainable." These days fund-raisers and grant-writers string it round each sentence like an adjectival fannypack, bulging with self-congratulation. Mostly, the term is meaningless or a vague expression of hope. In the case of timber, it's a haphazard and often highly debatable designation that amounts to little more than a vague pledge that the timber is not virgin old growth.

Working Assets' offer of "green" power has been an astounding piece of effrontery, since the consumer has not the slightest way of knowing whether the electricity thus provided comes from solar or nuclear, or hydro or coal-burning generating stations. The *Nation*'s credit card offers a low interest charge, to be sure, but you'd better not be late with your payments.

Imagine singling out a major oil company as morally in good standing! It's far less rational than pumping Amoco's gas because Johnny Cash stands behind the product. At least that's an aesthetic decision. World Wildlife thus singled out Shell for praise last year, the same oil company in whose interests, absent any bleat of protest by Shell, the Nigerian generals hanged Ken Saro-Wiwa and his companions. And imagine giving Mitsubishi, as Rainforest Action Network did, the opportunity for this prime destroyer of Asian forests the chance to hang a "good behavior" sign around its neck.

The problem here is that because there's barely a left and certainly no politically left party, fake politics have taken over. Morris Dees of the Southern Poverty Law Center has raised an endowment of almost $100 million with which he's done very little, meanwhile frightening elderly liberals into ponying up contributions with the fantasy that the heirs to Adolf Hitler are about to come marching down Main Street, lynching blacks and putting the Jews into gas ovens. The fund-raising of Dees offers a banefully distorted view of the American political landscape. There isn't a public school in any county in the United States which doesn't represent a menace to blacks a thousand times more potent than what remains of the KKK.

As for B. Sanders, whose fund-raising letters this election time have once again been touting Congress's only "independent progressive socialist," his latest achievement has been to give the cold shoulder to delegations traveling all the way from Texas to Vermont to challenge the Conscience Complex in one of its most self-satisfied redoubts.

Sanders has been prominent among those in the North East congressional delegation on trying to export the region's nuclear waste to a poor, largely Hispanic community in Texas, Sierra Blanca. The only merit in dumping the waste there as opposed to, say, Burlington, is that the people in Burlington are richer and have more clout. When the Sierra Blancans turned up in Vermont, Sanders put out the word that he would quit any platform graced by any of their members. If you truly like "independents" in Congress, better by far to send your money to Ron Paul, who acts upon his proclaimed beliefs, unlike Sanders.

November 18

"So it turns out Koestler was a rapist. I can't say I'm surprised." It's bracing to have one's dislikes confirmed, and since I've always thought Arthur Koestler was a shit, I hastened to get back to my sister-in-law, Janet Montefiore, who had phoned me with the news.

Why wasn't she surprised? Jan, a prof of English lit with a prodigious memory, quoted something a disobliging Koestler had written about a woman in his essay in *The God That Failed*. "She was a puny, plain girl whom I had never seen before, but the deliberately slatternly way in which she was dressed and her provocative air in walking in betrayed her at once as a comrade … She was the neurotic, Cinderella type—the frustrated bourgeois girl turned voluntary proletarian—which abounded in the German Party."

The disclosures about Koestler as a rapist come from David Cesarani's new book, *Arthur Koestler: The Homeless Mind*, excerpted recently in the London *Daily Telegraph*. The most graphic description is of Koestler's attack on Jill Craigie, a filmmaker and wife of Michael Foot, well-known socialist and, for a brief period, leader of the Labour Party.

It was 1951. Koestler was still married to the Englishwoman Mamaine Paget. On May 4, Koestler called up and said he wanted to go to a pub. Craigie said Michael was away but finally agreed to take Koestler on a little tour of Hampstead, at the conclusion of which Koestler insisted she give him lunch.

Craigie recalls that while he was helping her wash up, Koestler "suddenly grasped my hair, he pulled me down and banged my head on the floor. A lot." Koestler was "very, very violent," but Craigie managed to struggle free and rush outside. She thought of going to the police station nearby but, in Cesarani's words, "she was scared that such a recourse would lead to awful publicity for her and

Michael. She would be accusing a world famous novelist of rape; they had been on a pub crawl and she had admitted him into her home by herself. It didn't look good."

She hoped that Koestler would leave, but he didn't. Having no money and no exact idea of what she should do, she went back inside. It was a move that was, as she recalled, "rather stupid of me." Koestler attacked her again, gripping her by the throat. Craigie was frightened he would kill her. "In the end I was overborne. I was terribly tired and weakened. There's a limit to how much strength one has and he was a very strong man. And that was it."

As he was leaving, Koestler said, "I thought you always had a bit of a yen for me." Craigie insists she had given Koestler not a bit of encouragement, but reckons that the practiced way he embarked on his assault suggested it was part of "a pattern." Richard Crossman, another prominent member of the Labour Party, later told Craigie and Foot that Koestler "was a hell of a raper, Zita [Crossman's wife] had a terrible time with him." Cesarani writes that "Koestler had beaten and raped women before; over the next few years it would be almost a hallmark of his conduct."

Koestler's enthusiasm for rape was matched by his aversion to abortion. In *The Lotus and the Robot*, he deplored "the slaughter of the unborn with its concomitant ill-effects on women," the supposed effect of Western decadence on Japan. As Cesarani remarks, "his comment on abortion is a grotesque example of hypocrisy."

Cesarani was alluding to Koestler's refusal of Elizabeth Jane Howard's request that he use a condom while making love in a canoe. She became pregnant, and Koestler went into "a state of panic," she said. The "idea of having children was anathema to him." She had an abortion, and afterward called Koestler because she had no food and was too weak to shop. He came over, exhibited scant sympathy and told her, "You'll get over it."

Remembering the bit about the "neurotic, Cinderella type," we find Cesarani quoting Koestler on his taste in women: "I always picked one type: beautiful Cinderellas, infantile and inhibited, prone to be subdued by bullying." Just so, he seems to have bullied his third wife into a suicide pact with him, which included dispatch of the family dog. He was seventy-seven with leukemia and Parkinson's; she was twenty-one years younger.

There's a thread between Koestler's tastes, rapes and passage with Communism. JoAnn Wypijewski sent me a few other quotes from his essay: "I was running after the Party, thirsting to throw myself completely into her arms, and the more breathlessly I struggled to possess and be possessed by her, the more elusive and unattainable she became." Maybe post-Communist Koestler wrote those words, then went off and raped a "Cinderella type," just to feel better and get his own back on the party.

1999

January 13
Listening to someone on CNN the other day describe the ceremony surrounding day one of the impeachment process, I realized that at last America has its answer to British royal coronations. Wolf Blitzer, or one of his CNN colleagues, had exactly the same hushed intonation that Richard Dimbleby used to describe proceedings in Westminster Abbey: "And here comes Black Rod, carrying the ewer of holy oil, in a tradition that has continued unbroken since Richard II." "And now the group of thirteen Republicans presenting the charges against President Clinton is entering the Senate chamber in a tradition unbroken since Andrew Johnson …"

As I've always maintained, every presidency should have its impeachment, to begin on the Thursday following the first weekend of every third year in each presidential term. Under this practice Bill Clinton would have already survived his first impeachment back in 1995. It's wonderful to see how Clinton of all people has reinvested the presidency with historical dimension. The other day at the post office I actually heard two people arguing about Reconstruction.

January 20
Bill Clinton's most torrid love affair has always been with the twenty-first century and with his own role in ushering it in. And as so often in

the past the Republicans showed at Tuesday night's State of the Union that they have no coherent strategy for dealing with the relationship. The President said that it was his hope that in the new millennium no older American would live in fear of penury or hunger. The Democrats applauded and the cameras turned to Republican house majority leader Dick Armey, who sat grimly with arms folded. The President hailed America's fighting men and women and looked forward to a more peaceful world. The camera picked up the empty seats of Republican legislators like Henry Hyde, who'd chosen to stay away.

One could see the Republicans' desperation not only in Armey's graceless pose and in Hyde's contemptuous absence, but also in the formal party response to Clinton's address by House Republicans Jennifer Dunn and Steve Largent. In the old days they would have showered any Democratic President with ribald invective about tax-and-spend liberalism, but Clinton spiked those guns long ago. So Dunn and Largent used most of their allotted spans prattling about their normalcy, their children. Perhaps the idea was to strike a contrast with the satyr of 1600 Pennsylvania Avenue, but if so, it didn't work. To beat Bill Clinton at the game of launching America into an even more prosperous future you need an orator of equivalent effrontery and political hucksterism, like Newt Gingrich.

But Newt, who loves gassing about the twenty-first century as much as Bill, is gone, and the Republicans are clearly in dire straits. To watch them these days is like watching a gambler mortgaging everything to one rash bet. In the Republicans' case it's the hope that after a year of steadily mounting evidence to the contrary, some new disclosure, some toxic affidavit from Jane Doe, an appearance by Monica Lewinsky as witness at the Senate impeachment hearings, will turn the tide.

Maybe it will happen but the chances seem dim. Meanwhile Clinton's speech Tuesday night shows the political mess they're in, quite aside from the unpopularity of their attempts to kick Clinton out of office. If there's a president who has managed to touch more political buttons in one speech, it's hard to recall him.

For the liberals and the AFL-CIO there was the President's call for the minimum wage to go up by a dollar. For Wall Street there was a gesture to the great goal of privatizing Social Security and handing it over to the mutual funds industry (something that Clinton had been on the verge of doing, when the Lewinsky scandal broke and he decided he need every friend in Congress he could muster). Law and order types got the pledge to keep people in prison till they are drug free and the military got its promise of a hike in defense spending. Women heard language about an ending of discrimination and a female President, and gays got a pledge on hate crimes.

To be sure, Clinton's speech was ripe with brazen affronts to reason and justice. His proposed "reform" of Medicare included an injunction to sick old people to be smart shoppers. He permitted himself a populist sneer at international trade agreements and then threw in a plea for presidential fast-track authority to make them. The man who spoke in emotional tones about "humanizing" international trade agreements is the same Bill Clinton who once helped to push through the inhuman Multilateral Agreement on Investments.

One could go on like this, with a radical riposte to every second paragraph in Clinton's lengthy address. America's precious heritage? This is the administration that's throwing the rest of Alaska's arctic plain to the oil industry. But here again the Republicans have saved Bill Clinton from the insistent criticism from the left he deserves. Who—among liberals and leftists—wants to be on the same side as the Republican house managers?

Rhetorically speaking, the President does well when he is in peril. It was the same last year, just after the Lewinsky scandal broke. One simply has to admire his resilience. After all the narrow shaves and premature political death notices down the years, Clinton clearly believes in a visceral sense, far more profound than balanced political assessment, that he's going to make it. This brash life force shines through and to judge by the polls most Americans admire such determination to survive on the political stage. And here again is the Republican's problem. Clinton's greatest love, for the future, is one beyond the scope of Ken Starr's investigations. And since they have bet all on Starr, what can they do?

February 17
There are two ways to look at Bill Clinton's persecution, both of them valid, one inspiriting and the other dismal. The inspiriting truth about the long scandal, terminated by Senatorial acquittal of the President last Friday by a simple majority on both counts, is that puritanism was vanquished. This is truly a glorious victory. Puritanism runs through America with as dark a trail of misery as in other societies cursed with its oppressive shadow.

Clinton was truly saved by the ordinary people. The elites would have finished him off months ago. And what the ordinary people have been saying is that they do not accept the premise (and all the hypocrisies that premise engenders) that presidents and politicians have to be moral exemplars. The ordinary people have stated clearly life is messy, but that getting in that sort of mess is not an impeachable offense.

The dismal aspect to Clinton's travails concerns the rise of the prosecutorial state, whose shadow ordinary people dislike as much as they do puritans.

I stand to receive $1,000 from an east coast publisher, Russ Smith, who bet Bill would go, though I shall have to wait until Clinton steps down at the end of his term. That publisher has conceded that if Clinton is struck dead by a meteorite or run over by a car, my victory will stand, since our bet is about the President's survival of the scandal, not any bolt from heaven. I also stand to get another $250 from an unwise associate of this publisher. Even in the final week of impeachment there were offers to wager even more money, coming from right-wing conspiratorialists with the devout belief that a fresh wave of scandals will lay Bill low.

March 15

WHOSE INDEPENDENCE?

Dear Bruce,
During the recent Senate "trial" of Bill Clinton, few journalists invested so many words in the defense of Bill Clinton than Cockburn.

Yet, now that Clinton—under cover of NATO—has taken small baby steps toward stopping an ongoing genocide, Cockburn wants Clinton impeached. What gives?

In his despicably titled "Sieg Hiel, NATO," Cockburn asserts that Kosovo is an integral part of Serbia. He also asserts that whatever is happening in Kosovo is an "internal affair" of "sovereign Serbia" and therefore nobody else's business. So NATO's military actions against Serbia (NATO being a front group for US imperialists) are "illegal." Another example of "shameless" American "gangsterism."

What's funny is that Cockburn's idea of what constitutes international law and order matches Henry Kissinger's. It is a view shared by that old drunk running Russia and by the bent-over little Stalinists running China. In fact, about every blood-soaked dictator in the world agrees that "national sovereignty" is a licence to kill off whatever "restless ethnic minority" that happens to be plaguing them.

Then Cockburn departs from such company to blame Clinton and the US for failing to stop the recent genocides in east Africa. Cockburn can blame us if he wants to, but why doesn't he blame the Organization of African Unity or the United Nations? And if some sinister western power is behind all of the bad things that happen in this world, then Cockburn should blame the massacres on the French and not us.

Cockburn assails NATO for usurping the rightful authority of the UN. Yet, given the UN's disgraceful record as peace keepers and abject inability to mount any type of military action, why would NATO want the UN's "help"? If you were trying to work out a will with your family, why would you invite your deranged distant cousin?

I respectfully decline to dip my beard into the intricate goulash of Balkan politics. But I do know genocide when I see it. When I was in Vietnam I developed a grudging respect for the Viet Cong. Soldier to soldier, I had to admire their courage, discipline and willingness to sacrifice. I've been watching the Serbian army operate for years, first in Slovenia, then in Croatia, then in Bosnia and now in Kosovo. What I see is a ragtag bunch of neo-Nazis whose depravity is matched only by their cowardice (and the cowardice of NATO and the UN).

In this sorry human catastrophe there is plenty of blame to go around. But for this war—and war it will be—we can put the blame squarely on the Serbs. In their attempt to exterminate a people so they can take over their land they have forfeited their claim to the land. The "end game" for the Serb invaders of Kosovo should be: disband and disperse, be killed or be captured. For the regime of Milošević and his butchers, there should be extinction. For the Kosovars, whose blood now waters their ancestral lands, Independence.

B. Patterson
Boonville

Alexander Cockburn replies: This is the true yawp and blare of the demented, power-mad assholes who got us into Vietnam, and ended up killing over two million people. Invincible ignorance married to overweening arrogance. Start with Patterson's concept of sovereign rights. I assume, on his "first-come" theory, that he will raise no objection when an Indian kicks him out of his house in Boonville. Next move to Patterson's theory of foreign relations, which owes everything to the ethos that exterminated Indians here: namely an "end game" brusquely characterized as "disband and disperse, be killed or be captured." And behind that, the even brusquer and indubitably final solution: "extinction."

Of course Patterson apes the CNN brigade which relentlessly devalues the word "genocide." The Serbs aren't committing genocide. If they were, there would be no refugees. The common estimate of deaths in Kosovo before the NATO bombing started is 2,000. Genocide? Give me a break.

The UN's role as peace-keeper will always be only as good as the dominant powers permit it to be. There have been some successes and many failures. That doesn't vitiate the infinite superiority of the UN as, at least in outline, a world forum, as opposed to NATO which is an aggressive, regional military alliance. And as for the UN's "abject inability to mount any type of military action," the eviction of Iraq from Kuwait in 1991 was a UN action. Bush spent months cementing a UN alliance against Saddam. It's a mark of the accelerated trend of the US toward international gangsterism that the NATO bombardiers have steered clear of any UN forum.

Before calling the Serbs "neo-Nazis" Patterson should read a little history. Hitler invaded Serbia in World War II and more than a million Serbs lost their lives, many of them in Jasenovac, a concentration camp run by the Croats. And the Serb fighters for whom Patterson displays such contempt still managed to tie down several Nazi divisions for years.

March 29

It was Jeff Frieden, some time in the mid-1980s, who urged me to call Lynn Turgeon for advice and counsel on Eastern European economies. Lynn, he explained, was a prof of economics at Hofstra and an original thinker. I talked to Lynn—the first in hundreds of such conversations—and swiftly realized he had the quality, so admired by harried columnists, of expressing ideas in clear, unpatronizing terms. Lynn was a passionate Keynesian, which sometimes lent an unguarded edge to his discussion of Hitler's economic policies or Reagan's military deficits. Across a decade or so of phone calls, he gave me an education in the economic history of the twentieth century that was always bracing.

Lynn wasn't a lively writer and surely his many friends learned to dread his mimeographed accounts of his journeys through Eastern Europe and the Soviet Union. He was relentless in reporting the price of potatoes in the local markets. In conversation he was often droll, rendering history as both drama and parable. A conversation could slide from myths about the consequences of Weimar inflation, Britain's policy on the gold standard, to Hitler's Keynesianism, to Bretton Woods, to Marriner Eccles, to Leon Keyserling's evolving of military Keynesianism in the Truman era, to the Kennedy arms spending spree, to Volcker's spell at the Fed, to the factors that finally did in the Soviet Union. Even if, down the years, one got to know Lynn's themes and peeves (as a farm boy, he had no love for the rural condition), there was always something to be learned. His books, among them *The Advanced Capitalist System* and *Bastard Keynesianism*—were tonic too.

Lynn was polite in disposition and manner, a radical. His mother lived to be 100, and I thought he'd be around for years, but cancer took him off at the age of seventy-six in early March. He navigated an intellectual and analytic course that, over the years, left him far more often right than wrong.

March 31

It's bracing to see the Germans taking part in NATO's bombing. It lends moral tone to an operation to have the grandsons of the Third Reich willing, able and eager to drop high explosive again, in this instance on the Serbs. To add symmetry to the affair, the last time Serbs in Belgrade had high explosive dropped on them was in 1941 by the sons of the Third Reich. To bring even deeper symmetry, the German political party whose leader, Schroeder, ordered German participation in the bombing is that of the Social Democrats, whose great grandfathers enthusiastically voted credits to wage war in 1914, to the enormous disgust of Lenin, who never felt quite the same way about social democrats ever after. Whether in Germany or England or France, all social democratic parties in 1914 tossed aside previous pledges against war, thus helping produce the first great bloodletting of our century.

Today, with social democrats leading governments across Europe—Schroeder, Blair, Jospin, Prodi—all fall in behind Clinton. This is, largely, a war most earnestly supported by liberals and many so-called leftists. Bernie Sanders has voted Aye, and in London Vanessa Redgrave cheers on the NATO bombers. There's been some patronizing talk here about the Serbs' deep sense of "grievance" at the way history has treated them, with the implication that the Serbs are irrational in this regard. But it's scarcely irrational to remember that Nazi Germany bombed Belgrade in World War II, or that Germany's prime ally in the region, Croatia, ran a concentration camp at Jasenovac where tens of thousands of Serbs—along with Jews and gypsies—were liquidated. Nor is it irrational to recall that Germany in more recent years has been an unrelenting assailant of the former Yugoslav federation, encouraging Slovenia to secede and lending determined support to Croatia, in gratitude for which Croatia adopted, on independence in 1991, the German hymn, "Danke Deutschland."

So much for Serb feelings about Germany. Serbia has some reason to feel similar resentment toward the United States. The biggest single ethnic cleansing of the mid-1990s in the former Yugoslavia was conducted by Croatia under the supervision of the United States, whose military generals and CIA officers issued targeting instructions to Croatian artillery for the ethnic clearing. The targets were Serbs, living in Serbian territory, in the Krajina. Heading the Croatian cleansers was President Franjo Tudjman, who has rehabbed Nazi war criminals. Yet somehow it is Serbia's Milošević who is demonized here as Hitler.

April 14

Just like the blacks and Hispanics we've been reading about lately I get pulled over once in a while by the cops and it's clear they think I'm a possible drug transporter. I make a distinction here between the pretext stops and the speeding offenses. Drive over 75 miles an hour regularly and you'll get a ticket once in a while. And since everyone in America except people carrying high explosives drives at some point over 75 mph, everyone in America at some point gets a ticket.

I commute fairly regularly between Petrolia in Humboldt County and Berkeley, a distance of about 350 miles. The other day I was driving a 1964 Newport station wagon north and was astounded suddenly to see a red light go on behind me, somewhere near Ukiah, and a pissy young CHP officer, on the short side, come around to the passenger door, hand on holster.

By the time a police officer reaches the passenger door any prudent driver should already have license, registration and proof of insurance held between finger and thumb, with both hands high on the driving wheel and no sudden movements, thus hopefully averting what we may term the Diallo Effect. I did everything wrong, the reason being that the ziplock bag holding my papers was under the driver's seat and so, contrary to procedures just outlined, I was bowed down with my head under the steering wheel trying to find the bag.

The officer stared tensely as I finally surfaced with the bag and leaned over to try and get the passenger door open. This is a station wagon that had been sitting in a field for the preceding six years. All the door locks, except for the driver's side, had frozen. There had been a wood rat nest in the glove compartment, which was why the papers were under the seat. The passenger door handle broke when I tried to wrench it open.

Finally I got the passenger window down. The cop said, as though already testifying in court, that he had been heading south, rounding a bend and had seen me come the other way, overtaking a car as I did so, in the outside lane.

At this point a CHP officer will usually have sized you up, figured you are no major menace to civilization, not drunk and—computer check on license pending—maybe not the big catch of the evening. Courteous behavior by the driver usually yields rewards, with the ticket written up for 72 mph instead of a reckless driving citation for going over 90. I was polite, peppering my remarks with "officer."

It got me nowhere.

"I'm going to my car to write the citation," he snapped. His costume was the blue fatigue jumpsuit that the French riot police used to wear back in the 1960s. He had a particularly large gun. Off he trotted to run my license and after five minutes came back with a ticket accusing me of driving at seventy-eight miles an hour, a speed which, he remarked, he would have thought "this old car" incapable. "Did you just eyeball the car or get me on the radar?" I asked, and he, rather too quickly, said "radar." This seemed to me intrinsically unlikely, given the circumstances.

The problem here is that the California Highway Patrol has organized things so that now local counties get a larger cut of the fine. If no one drove over the limit in California there would be an immediate cash crunch in the administration of the state. Speeding here is a civic duty.

The fines are getting higher and higher too, with add-ons and extra penalties and special taxes and fines of one sort and other, so that running an amber light (not my particular specialty) can see the offender writing out a check for $150 by the time it's all over.

The pretext stops, as related to the drug war, are of a different order. Three years ago I was taking a 1972 Imperial two-door hardtop, known to the cognoscenti at the time as a hardtop convertible, across the country and was driving along Interstate 90 through Montana. Not far out of Butte I could see the state trooper behind me. He kept his car just to my left rear so that my natural reaction, looking to keep an eye on him in my left side mirror, was to run a little further right to the edge of the inside lane. Suddenly his light went on. The trooper, a trim twenty-eight-year-old with a slightly less trim twenty-six-year-old trainee beside him, said that I had driven across the inside white line of the Interstate verge. This was the pretext.

If possible—though these days they tell you urgently to stay in your car—get out and stand at an equal setting with the cop. This I did. He hemmed and hawed a bit and after a while asked if I was carrying large sums of money. I laughed and said "I wish." By this time we'd gravitated to the back end of the car and he was looking hopefully at the trunk. Was I carrying arms? Absolutely not. Truth be told, I remember I had half a bottle of gin in the trunk and wondered whether it was illegal in the state of Montana.

Now, there are a million ways he could have got me to open the trunk, even without a search warrant, starting with a simple statement that he feared for his life. But instead he blurted out hopefully, "Are you carrying large amounts of drugs?" "No." Well, though I was unshaven, wearing dark glasses, beautiful Daria in the passenger seat and driving a boat, he didn't order me to open up. Maybe it's because I'd told him I was a writer. He saw a red stain on my ringers and cried out, "Is that blood?" I said no, it was ink and showed him the fountain pen and that broke his spirit.

April 21

Strange are the ways of men! It feels like only yesterday that the *New York Times* was denouncing President Bill as a moral midget, deserving of the harshest reprobation for fondling Monica Lewinsky's breasts. And today here's the *New York Times* doling out measured praise to the same President for blowing little children in pieces.

The *Times* last Thursday had pictures of those dead refugees on its cover, bombed by NATO's aviators. Editorial page editor Howell Raines staked out the *Times'* official view that "For now, NATO must sustain and intensify the bombing." What a weird guy Raines must be. Kiss Monica's tits and he goes crazy. Bomb peasants and he shouts for more.

Maybe some corner of Clinton's brain reckons that bombs on Serbia will extinguish Monica Lewinsky from popular memory. But what man of mature judgment and compassion would not prefer to be remembered by the Starr report than by bomb craters and dead bodies? Many people thought Clinton would be the first President who would somehow prefer Starr's volume as his epitaph, however embarrassing. But no. Like all the others he wants craters and corpses as his requiem. Memoirs: "I took the grave decision to request punitive …," NOT "I took the delightful decision to reach for her magnificent breasts …" What a puritan culture we live in.

April 28

Now concerts of Marilyn Manson and KMFDM have been canceled. President Clinton will probably propose laws soon banning long black coats and making it an indictable offense to use the word "gothic." In his radio broadcast last Saturday Clinton said piously—amid celebrations of the violent NATO alliance—that "every one of us must take responsibility to counter the culture of violence. The government must take responsibility to counter the culture of violence." In terms of hypocrisy, this is on par with Clinton telling little kids in a school in Anacostia to conduct themselves in an upright moral fashion not long before he was unzipping his pants for Monica L. There'll be further vindictive assaults on the rights of young people, who as usual will incur collective guilt. Meanwhile the obvious lesson that war breeds violence will be carefully ignored.

By now mandatory apologies for what happened at Columbine High are incumbent on Marilyn Manson, video-game manufacturers, Hollywood, publishers of *Mein Kampf*, and the internet. The only people who apparently don't have to apologize are the US military and their civilian overseers who trained and paid the pilot dad of one of the teen killers; who sent F-16s over the funerals in Littleton; who are now pounding the Serbs each day and night; who mint the currency of violence.

No so far from Columbine High School in Littleton is Fort Carson Army base, where they practice invading countries like Serbia. One of the families of the killers (two-parent, suburban) had a breadwinner retired from the military. This is Harris's dad. His mother works at a gourmet food shop. Mr. Klebold is a geophysicst and Mrs. Klebold works with the disabled. Klebold Jr. drove a BMW. If the parents had been single mothers on welfare, or hippies, or in a small religious sect, we surely would have been inundated with preachments against single mothers, hippies and religious sects as trainers for mass murder. But there's been a certain embarrassment about the parents of Eric Harris and Dylan Klebold, who appear to have embodied the suburban American dream.

Commentators have fastened onto the fact that one of the two youths had a personal website "espousing an addled philosophy of violence." Those were the words of the *New York Times*' editorial writer, either Howell Raines or one of his stable. Yes, the same editorial team that espoused an addled philosophy of violence a few days earlier, suggesting that NATO "intensify the bombing" of Serbia. Perhaps nytimes.com was the website the kid had on his computer.

May 26

In mid-May the British government moved with frantic speed to disable the website on which a former disgruntled MI6 officer posted the names of British intelligence agents. Too late. On May 14, the LaRouchies posted the list, heading it with the statement "'The MI6 factor' in the murder of Princess Diana," and announcing that the LaRouchies's *Executive Intelligence Review* had already identified three MI6 agents as "suspected culprits acting on behalf of the House of Windsor, under the personal order of Prince Philip." The LaRouchies claim that Sir David Speeding, head of MI6, was ordered—presumably by Prince Philip and his consort—to murder

Diana and her consort; toward this end he sent his assistant to Paris, along with other MI6 personnel.

May 30

It seems that Bill Clinton's staff schedules three hours each day for the Commander in Chief to read books and make phone calls. Michael Kaufman disclosed this in the *New York Times* last Saturday. At least these days Clinton is getting a bit more honest in describing his reading habits. In 1992, he tried to pretend that he liked nothing better than to curl up with the infinitely tedious *Meditations* of Marcus Aurelius. Now he admits straightforwardly that he likes Walter Mosely, Sue Grafton and Jonathan Kellerman.

June 2

In the final months of World War II the Nazis tried to delay the advance of the Allies by opening the dikes in Holland. The man issuing this order was the German high commissioner in Holland, Seyss-Inquart. By the end of 1944 about 500,000 acres of land had been flooded, leading to what historian Gabriel Kolko called "the most precipitous decline in food consumption any West European country suffered during the war." Of the 195 Nazis indicted at Nuremberg, Seyss-Inquart was one of twenty-four sentenced to death.

Seyss-Inquart merely opened dikes in Holland. Kolko, who commented on that consequent fall in Dutch food consumption, was testifying about this German war criminal at the Vietnam tribunal, convened by Bertrand Russell in 1967 to hold hearings into US war crimes in Indochina. Kolko told the tribunal how the US Air Force had bombed the Toksan dam near Pyongyan. The plan was to destroy the irrigation system supplying 75 percent of North Korea's rice farms. A subsequent USAF study of the bombing of the Toksan and Chasan dams noted, "These strikes, largely passed over by the press, military observers and news commentators … constituted one of the most significant air operations of the Korean war." Of these deeds, the USAF historian remarked equably that the timing was aimed to be devastating in its psychological effect, when the exhausting labor of rice transplanting had been completed, but before the roots had become firmly embedded.

The bombing of the North Korean dams was a rousing success. Water bursting through the holes in the Toksan dam made by US bombs "scooped clean" miles of valley below, with the added bonus of not only wiping out the rice paddies but also drowning Korean civilians in underground shelters. The USAF study exulted that "to the Communists the smashing of the dams meant primarily the destruction of their chief sustenance—rice. The Westerner can little conceive the awesome meaning that the loss of this staple food commodity has for the Asian—starvation and slow death." Another study detected "oriental fatalism" in the way the North Koreans carried on desperate repair efforts without regard for the delayed-action bombs also dropped around the target area.

Similar successful assaults were made on dams in Vietnam. In 1969 Henry Kamm, a *New York Times* reporter, recounted how there had been a dam south of Hue "blasted by American jets to deprive the North Vietnamese of a food supply." Kamm returned later to find that the paddies had then been destroyed by salt water encroaching from the South China Sea.

June 9

The sole purpose of the bombing was to demonstrate to Serbia and to the world NATO's capacity to bomb, thus killing nearly 2,000 civilians, destroying much of Serbia's infrastructure, and prompting the forced expulsion and flight of around a million Kosovars. Wars have been triggered by the frailest of excuses and prolonged on the slightest of rationales.

This was the Cowards' War, bombing a country for two and a half months from 30,000 feet. It was the Liberals' War waged by social democracy's best and brightest, intent on proving once again that wars can be fought with the best and most virtuous of intentions: the companion volume to Hillary Clinton's *It Takes a Village* turns out to be *It Takes an Air Force.*

Americans who had supported Bill's right to remain President even though he had kissed Monica Lewinsky began to turn sharply against him when he bombed Serbian schools.

Here in the US the war found almost all Democrats in Congress marshaled for war. The heroic exceptions were twenty-six Democrats in the House, led by Dennis Kucinich of Ohio—himself of Irish-Croat ancestry—who leagued with a majority of House Republicans twice to deny Clinton legitimization for his war. Most liberals favored the bombing. Gross was the spectacle of Susan Sontag brigading herself with Zbigniew Brzezinski and Madeleine Albright in terming this bombing campaign "a just war."

June 30

A fifteen-year-old girl attending a very ritzy liberal arts school in the Northeast told me last week that 80 percent of the kids in her class were on Prozac, Dexedrine or Ritalin, either separately or in combo. The pretext used by the school authorities for the legal prescription of these drugs is Attention Deficit Disorder (ADD), or ADHD, Attention Deficit Hyperactivity Disorder. The student is asked three questions along the lines of "Do you find yourself daydreaming or looking out the window during the school?" Say yes, as 100 percent of all kids around the world throughout all human history will obviously do if they are truthful, and the kids' parents are urged to give the school a go-ahead to pump in the brew of uppers and anti-depressants.

At this particular school, my informant told me, there's also a flourishing under-the-counter market in the same drugs. She herself had resisted the school's urgings to take Ritalin, but said that there is heavy pressure to do so, not least because a student on Ritalin or Dexedrine can, according to one theory, get perked for the brief period of an exam to perform better than a student who is drug free. She gave a heartrending description of a friend who had, by dint of the usual preposterous questions, had been diagnosed as having ADD, and who had been pushed into taking Ritalin and Prozac by the school and her parents, much against her will. Previously a vivacious and jolly young thing, she is now strung-out, morose, thoroughly dispirited and probably on the way to expulsion.

Eric Harris, one of the Columbine killers, was on Luvox. Like Prozac, Zoloft and Paxil, Luvox is a selective serotonin reuptake inhibitor or SSRI. The idea is to change the amount of serotonin reaching the brain and thus prevent depression. Kip Kinkel, the kid from Springfield, OR, who shot his parents and two students to death, was on Prozac.

One particularly gloomy view of Ritalin comes from the Drug Enforcement Agency, which issued this statement after a 1996 conference on ADHD and Ritalin: "The use of stimulants [such as Ritalin] for the short-term improvement of behavior and under-achievement may be thwarting efforts to address the children's real issues, both on an individual and societal level. The lack of long-term positive results with the use of stimulants and the specter of previous and potential stimulant abuse epidemics, give cause to worry about the future. The dramatic increase in the use of [Ritalin] in the 1990s should be viewed as a marker or warning to society about the problems children are having and how we view and address them."

July 7

Back in the age of innocence, in the 1950s, kids ordered up their firepower out of catalogues and you'd see students heading to school on bus or subway, toting guns they'd be using later that day in the ROTC drills. Back then parents fretted over the horror of comics and switchblades. Let little Albert dip his nose too deeply into the blood-drenched comics being put out by publishers such as William Gaines of *Mad* magazine fame, and he'd surely be set on the slippery slope of crime and slaughter.

In fact Gaines was hauled before a committee run by that tireless grandstander, Senator Estes Kefauver of Tennessee, who also held famous hearings at the time into racketeering and the Mob. Here's an extract from the transcript of the committee's encounter with Gaines, as it appears in Frank Jacobs's very funny *The Mad World of William*

M. Gaines, published by Bantam in 1972. Gaines is being questioned by Hebert Beaser, one of the committee's counsels:

BEASER: Is that the sole test of what you put in your magazines, whether it sells? Is there any limit of what you wouldn't put in your magazine because you thought a child shouldn't see or read about it?

GAINES: No, I wouldn't say there is any limit for the reason you outlined. My only limits are bounds of good taste. What I consider good taste.

BEASER (probing): Then you think a child cannot in any way, shape or manner, be hurt by anything that the child reads or sees?

GAINES: I do not believe so.

BEASER (still probing): There would be no limit actually to what you'd put in magazines.

GAINES: Only within the bounds of good taste.

KEFAUVER (doubtful): Here is your May issue. This seems to be an arm with a bloody ax holding a woman's head up which has been severed from her body. Do you think that's in good taste?

GAINES: Yes, sir. I do, for the cover of a horror comic. A cover in bad taste, for example, might be defined as holding the head a little higher, so that the blood could be seen dripping from it, and moving the body over a little so that the neck of the body could be seen to be bloody.

(Murmurs, stirrings among spectators.)

KEFAUVER (still doubtful): You've got blood coming out of her mouth.

GAINES: A little.

KEFAUVER: And here's blood on the ax. I think most adults are shocked by that. Now here's a man with a woman in a boat and he's choking her to death with a crowbar. Is that in good taste?

GAINES: I think so.

HANCOCK: How could it be worse?

HENNINGS (coming to the rescue): Mr. Chairman, I don't think it is really the function of our committee to argue with this gentleman.

Jacobs reports that Gaines more than held his own in the initial hours of testimony, but then faded abruptly, seeming harassed and defensive. The reason was that he'd ingested a bracing dose of Dexedrine, thinking he'd ride through the session on its coattails only to find that the drug's effects had worn off abruptly, leaving him high and dry.

July 9

One of the joys of talking to Larry Pratt, President of the Gun Owners of America, is that one can hear Charlton Heston denounced as a cocktail-swilling, brie-nibbling Hollywood sellout, only too delighted to betray the Second Amendment if it means he gets his face on network TV and taken seriously on Capitol Hill.

And it's true. Heston's NRA collapsed in the wake of the Columbine killings in Colorado. Only a combo of House conservatives and liberals was able to beat back the recent gun bill. Even so Pratt still fears that another house bill could get conferenced with New Jersey Senator Frank Lautenberg's Senate Bill 254, which could introduce laws making it all but impossible for gun shows to continue to operate. Liberals hate gun shows, regarding them as the seedbeds of all that's wrong with America. This is nonsense. Gun shows do of course attract people eager to exercise their Second Amendment rights, collect or exchange various types of firearms and so forth. They are also vibrant rendezvous for important elements of popular American culture. They are anti-government, genuinely populist and lots of fun. Which is why the better element, Lautenberg in the lead, wants to do them in.

Pratt's solution to the schoolyard killings: let the teachers bear arms, just like they do in South Africa, where one instructor recently gunned down a bellicose student. Pratt also faxed me an interesting recent study on urban delinquency, put out by the Office of Juvenile Justice and Delinquency Prevention (part of the Justice Department) in 1994. This was a survey of delinquency in Rochester, Pittsburgh, and Denver, tracking delinquency "pathways," as affected by drugs, school attendance, parental oversight, gang membership and so forth. The study shows clearly enough that one way of keeping kids out of trouble is to let them carry legal guns. Out of 1,000 boys and girls surveyed in Rochester in the early 1980s, some 7 percent of the boys owned illegal guns by the ninth and tenth grades. Legal guns are held by 3 percent. There is a strong correlation between illegal guns and delinquency and drug use. Seventy-four percent of the illegal gun owners commit street crimes, 24 percent commit gun crimes and 41 percent use drugs. Then the Justice Department study continues, "Boys who own legal firearms, however, have much lower rates of delinquency and drug use and are even *slightly less delinquent than nonowners of guns*" (my italics).

July 14

Gore and George W. are alike as two peas, right down to the same slightly dazed look that comes of having big-time politicians as fathers and interesting encounters with powerful drugs in their formative years. I don't know anything about Gore's mother, but Barbara Bush was one of the nastier women I've ever interviewed (a half-hour session in 1979, when George Sr. was fighting Ronald Reagan for the nomination). Maybe there's a difference here.

In fact a debate between Al and George W. on the subject of parents—*their* parents—might be the sole means of putting together an exciting debate in 2000. Imaginatively staged, with both men injected with sodium pentothal, and moderated by Geraldo Rivera and Gail Sheehy, such an encounter might scrape off the dreadful rime of banality that cakes their public personae and reveal the wounded egos beneath.

As a force capable of reinvigorating our political DNA the left is in terrible shape. The radical right—which has contributed 80 percent of the political energy in the country for the past twenty years—is almost as impotent although more healthily endowed with a hostility to state power. The left will never break away from the Democratic Party to any important degree, since the institutional ties between labor and Democrats will never allow it. Who else might precipitate a reinvigoration of the system?

July 21

You would have thought that after Chappaquiddick the Kennedy clan would have imposed a permanent ban on any visits, or attempted visits, to Martha's Vineyard. The problem in that family seems to be an incapacity to assess odds properly or absorb the lessons of the past. So here we have John, arriving late with his wife and sister-in-law at that airport in New Jersey, calling it wrong. He must have known he would have to land at dusk or after. He knew he would have to rely on his eyes, since he didn't know how to fly on instruments. At this point a prudent person would have thought twice. A prudent person wouldn't have skied down a slope, playing a ball game and holding a video camera. A prudent person …

It's a miracle half the ruling class isn't wiped out around Martha's Vineyard every year. That hateful island is often shrouded in fog; normal commercial flights are canceled and the rich then whistle up charter flights, often with pilots either weary or half drunk. Even the ferry from Woods Hole isn't entirely safe for the big-wigs. Back in the Vietnam era Defense Secretary Robert McNamara was nearly wrestled over the side by an anti-war zealot.

I'm not sure what the exact averages are, per person mile flown, but small planes are unwise forms of conveyance. Helicopters are even more lethal. Even so, the last time, back in the early 1980s, I was on Martha's Vineyard I was desperate for escape, so much so I declined even to wait for the ferry. Instead I chartered a small plane, instructing the pilot to fly myself and my daughter to Keene, NH. That's the sort of effect the island has on one.

August 11
Steve Levitt, an economist at the University of Chicago, and John Donohue III, a law prof at Stanford, have been circulating a paper—reported in the *Chicago Tribune* on August 8—arguing that the legalizing of abortion in the early 1970s has contributed to the falling crime rate in the 1990s. Indeed they claim that legalized abortion may account for as much as half the overall crime drop between 1991 and 1997. Levitt says abortion "provides a way for the would-be mothers of those kids who are going to lead really tough lives to avoid bringing them into the world." The authors cite statistics from five states that legalized abortion before the *Roe v. Wade* decision of 1973. These five states with high abortion rates in the early 1970s had greater crime drops in the 1990s.

The *Trib*'s story quotes Cory Richards, a policy wonk at the Guttmacher Institute, as saying, "This is an argument for women not being forced to have children they don't want to have. This is making the point that it's not only bad for the women, but for children and society."

So, from the social-engineering, crime-fighting point of view the reintroduction of the death penalty in 1977 had the legalization of abortion in 1975—the *Roe v. Wade* decision—as its logical precursor and concomitant. And the death penalty for undesired embryos has had the advantage of being a lot more certain, and cheaper to administer, than the death penalty for undesired adults. I don't think it's the way the women's movement put the choice issue back in the early 1970s, but I can certainly imagine Hillary arguing for abortion as socially therapeutic.

August 20
Nabbed back in March for speeding in my 1964 station wagon I finally made it to traffic school last week. Under California law you can thus shield your rashness from the insurance companies, provided there's at least an eighteenth-month interval from your last citation.

Down the years, here in the Golden State, I've been to a few such sessions, which have to last eight hours. My first such school, back in the late 1980s, was in Riverside, on the eastern margin of the greater Los Angeles area. The composition of the thirty-odd people was 50 percent white, 50 percent black. At all classes the initial routine is for each person to divulge name and cause of citation. In the Riverside class almost all the blacks said they'd been cited for going a few miles over the limit, in urban areas: 30 mph instead of 25. So reasonably enough, all the blacks thought they'd been framed. Almost all the whites had been caught speeding on the highway, doing 70 and over. They all thought they'd been breaking the law.

My next class, in Santa Cruz, was run by a California Highway Patrol officer who spent most of the session giving us useful hints on how to avoid being caught speeding. In Berkeley a couple years ago, our class was run by a former alcoholic who underwent visible nervous breakdown throughout the eight-hour session, saying the breakdown was prompted by his daughter's driving skills and her indifference to her father. As he issued our certificates he tearfully thanked us for sharing.

The class in Eureka last week was run by a former cop from San Diego, who divides his time between running a driving school and representing tax deadbeats before the IRS. He offered a torrent of statistics. The most dangerous time to drive: Friday evening, closely followed by Saturday night, closely followed by Sunday night. The safest day is Tuesday. The last twenty-four-hour period in California in which no one was killed on the roads was on May 1, 1991 (which turns out to have been a Wednesday).

Amid this deluge of numbers he paused to review the best way to deal with the officer as he approaches your car. It's best, he said, to have your hands up on the wheel. The instructor plunged into cop's-eye view about what it was like to approach a car. Death could be waiting. There was no job, he told us, more perilous than that of the police officer.

I told him I didn't think this claim was true; that in fact police work is among the safer occupations, that the likelihood of being killed in the line of duty was exceedingly slim. He held his ground, but the figures support my view. If you tot up the numbers of local police, sheriff's deputies, state police, special police (a mysterious category in the US Statistical Abstract) and all sworn officers both full- and part-time, the total in 1992 was 661,103. The total of police killed accidentally and feloniously in that year across the country was 129, which seems to be about average in any year. This gives a death rate per 100,000 cops of twenty, most of whom are probably killed in car crashes. The rate of death per 100,000 in coal mining was thirty-eight in 1995, making it the riskiest job, followed by other forms of mining (twenty-five), oil and gas extraction (twenty-three), agriculture, forestry and fishing (twenty-two). If cops walked more and drove less, they'd probably halve their death rate, putting them on par with people in the electrical, gas and sanitary services, at eight or so per 100,000.

That wasn't my only tussle of the evening in the traffic class. We tangled again on the subject of drunk driving. After reciting the savage penalties meted out to those caught driving under the influence of alcohol, the instructor gave an impassioned speech in favor of the pillory of public ridicule and contempt, meaning in this instance that convicted drunks would have to display an orange license tag. I told the class I thought penalties for drunk driving were already out of hand, at least for those who had caused no harm. This intervention was badly timed, because the instructor completed the class by showing a half-hour movie about a teenage drunk who killed a young woman, and his consequent remorse. I felt as though I had somehow argued that the teen drunk killer should have been levied a $10 fine and then handed back his driver's license. The big disclosure of the evening is that the American Psychiatric Association is putting road rage into its next edition of the *Diagnostic and Statistical Manual of Mental Disorders*, meaning that this nebulous category has now been okayed by shrinks as a bona fide condition, amenable to insured treatment by anti-depressants and kindred potions. Having made road rage official, the shrinks can now begin to coin money off it.

September 22

Now it turns out that the greatest writer of the twentieth century, with the possible exception of Flann O'Brien, was nearly put on trial as a traitor after World War II. No, not Ezra Pound, but P. G. Wodehouse. Last week the British Public Records office released files showing that the director of public prosecutions, Sir Theobald Matthew, thought that a trial of Wodehouse would be a tricky prospect, but said that "If Wodehouse ever comes to this country, he should be prosecuted." In the event, Wodehouse lived in the US continuously from 1944 on.

Wodehouse broadcast from Germany in 1941, having been marched off to an internment camp in Upper Silesia after the Nazis invaded France and came across the writer working away in his house at Le Touquet, writing one of his very best novels, *Joy in the Morning*. After he'd spent eleven months in the internment camp, American friends saw a photograph of him and worried about his somewhat emaciated appearance. Wodehouse was soon released and taken to Berlin, where he accepted the request of Werner Plack, a German foreign ministry official he'd known slightly before the war, that he do some broadcasts to America about his experience in the internment camp. The five talks were sequestered by the British authorities for many years. When they were finally released they turned out to be slightly labored, knockabout reminiscences in a jocular vein. Wodehouse evidently enjoyed internment life, as did many Englishmen who, like Wodehouse, regarded public school as the high point of their lives.

Wodehouse could conceivably be faulted for poor judgment but he certainly didn't deserve the vicious campaign launched against him in the British press.

Of course Wodehouse was saying nothing that wasn't also entertained by many in the Western governing elites who had always yearned for Hitler to invade the Soviet Union, and who had been pro-fascist in the 1930s, at a time Wodehouse was making fun of British fascists with his portrait of Oswald Mosley, memorably satirized in the form of Sir Roderick Spode in another of Wodehouse's best books, *The Code of the Woosters*. Many years ago I wrote an intro to a Random House reissue of this novel. Wodehouse wrote his best stuff in the late 1930s and 1940s. Bertie Wooster remains his greatest creation. Wodehouse was an extraordinary technician. His public school, Dulwich, also gave us Raymond Chandler. Both of them emigrated here, and forged prose styles that made use of a highly formalized mannerism, while remaining a supple and fluid language, like Shakespearean English.

October 13

From the typographical clamor raised in the *New York Daily News*, you'd have thought *New York Press* columnist George Szamuely had been caught committing satanic abuse in a day-care center. But it turned out that Szamuely's great crime was to have taken too many books—580 is a number that shows up in the press reports—out of the New York University library, and been remiss in giving them back. The *News* and other newspapers have exultantly noted that Szamuely faces an overdue fine of $31,000, plus charges of grand larceny and possible jail time. John Beckman, described as a university spokesman, strutted through the news stories like some frontier sheriff twirling his six-gun: "Don't mess with NYU librarians."

Some of the news stories noted that among the books held by Szamuely was Hegel's *Phenomenology of Spirit*. It's well-known that only Hungarians have the fortitude to grapple with this exhausting work. The last person I know to have read it thoroughly was my dear friend Nicholas Krasso, a student of Lukács who fled Budapest for England in 1956. We spent a lot of time together in the mid-1960s, and Nicholas was forever quoting from the *Phenomenology*, which he said was best studied under the influence of LSD. Poor Nicholas fell asleep reading one night, and died in the smoke caused by the cigarette that fell from his drooping hand. Hegel was probably on the bed somewhere, probably the London Library's copy. What a fitting way for a copy of the *Phenomenology* to go!

Another of the books cited by the news stories—this particular one was on the AP wire—was *Thoughts on Machiavelli*. So, how many other NYU students have any interest in Leo Strauss? A simple test. If Szamuely pleads innocent and opts for a jury trial, as I very much hope he will, let his attorney make a pile of the books in the courtroom, and then, let the jurors note how many times these books had been checked out before the erudite Szamuely got his hands on them. Probably most of them sat ignored, awaiting the moment NYU decided to sell them off to a book broker.

NYU should be glad and thank Szamuely for freeing up its shelf space.

Szamuely may be charged with grand larceny. Two or three centuries ago, the standard was simple: Stealing books is not a crime unless the books are sold. There's no evidence Szamuely was popping along to the Strand to flog off editions of Hobbes. He held those books for admirable reasons, such that a jury would understand. He needed them for the same reasons my shelves groan with volumes (Hegel's *Phenomenology* included) I may never get to, may never re-read. To surrender them is to confess that, yes, I may die before I get around to reading Hegel properly, or all the dialogues of Plato, or all Balzac's novels, or all the volumes of Motley's *Rise of the Dutch Republic*; I may die before I write the column or the essay or the book that requires absolutely that these books be instantly to hand.

November 1

Riding the BART across to San Francisco, I heard two young black women who'd presumably got on the train at North Richmond, deep in conversation.

Girl #1: When I first heard something, my baby started to wake up, so I was patting him on his back, and we were talking for a few more minutes, and then I heard, "No, no, I ain't got nothing, I ain't got nothing. Stop!" Then I said, "Don't that sound like Tony?" and my brother said, "Naw, girl," and I said, "Yes, it does," so I jumped off the couch and by this time they were already by my front door. Then I heard, "Oh man, come on, I ain't got nothing." Then I said, "Rich, get out there and help." So I opened the door and he was laid down on my front doorstep.

Girl #2: Was he on his knees?

Girl #1: No, on his butt, kinda to the side with one of them on him with a shotgun pointed him and the other one was in front of him with a gun, so when I opened the door he put the gun in my face and I said, "Oh shit" and shut the door.

Girl #2: You looked at him and he looked at you?

Girl #1: Yes, I looked right at him. Then I shut the door back, and I got stuck. I was stuck. I didn't know what to do. I said, "Oh my god, oh my god, shit." Then I locked my door and heard someone say, "Take off you coat, punk, what yo got in yo pockets?" and Tony said, "I ain't got nothing," and they were hitting him. Then I don't know if he got up by hisself or if they pulled him up and they keep saying, "Give me what you got, punk." Tony said, "I ain't got nothing, please don't kill me, don't shoot me." Then they said, "Stop crying like a little bitch," two times, then "What the fuck is you looking at?" two times too, and then Tony said, "Please, don't kill me, don't shoot me," and one said, "Shut the fuck up." Bop, Bop.

Girl #2: What's bop bop?

Girl #1: A gun was fired and I didn't hear Tony no more.

November 3

The Day of the Dead, aka Hallowe'en, posed the usual dilemma: What to wear?

For many years, back in my New York days, I would rent an alligator's head from a store called—I think—Animals into People. It was heavy, but striking. Low types thought it amusing to stub out their cigarettes in my paper maché jaws. My brother Andrew used to caper on the dance floor as a penguin and his wife Leslie as a bear. Up in Petrolia, in the backwoods of northern California, alligator jaws are hard to come by, so for the past few years I've been hauling out black tie, tails and top hat.

But this year I was down in Berkeley and tails seemed too normal for dancing at Ashkenaz to the California Cajun Orchestra. In the end Barbara and I went as a pair of gypsies, two of seven I spotted in the course of the evening. Also popular were Arab sheikhs (three), nondescript Dracula look-alikes, earth goddesses too numerous to count, plus a dazzling cocktail waitress in fishnet tights, gripped all too firmly by a fellow in cut-price monster rig. Lucky brute. Those habituated to the baroque turnouts of the West Village or of the Castro, across the bay in San Francisco, will say this was pretty tame, and so it was. Half the point of the fancy dress is its comforting predictability: pirates, gypsies, Marie Antoinette, a couple of Abe Lincolns, a quartet of fortune tellers and the usual coven of witches. As a boy I was seldom out of skirts, either my school kilt or at home, a Victorian evening dress of which I was extremely fond, though my parents never evinced quite the same enthusiasm. Great was their relief when I laid aside the petticoats and bustle and pulled on the drainpipe pants and drape jacket of a mid-'50s rocker.

November 24

Amid the latest batch of Nixon tapes there's a ripe one from May 13, 1971, recently described by James Warren in the *Chicago Tribune*. Discussing welfare reform with Haldeman and Ehrlichman the President snarls about the little Negro bastards, before remarking indulgently that "I have the greatest affection for them but I know they're not going to make it for 500 years." The leader of the Free World and his senior advisors then drift into a chat about homosexuality, occasioned by the President's viewing of an "All in the Family" episode featuring Archie's son-in-law, described by the Prez as "obviously queer, wears an ascot, but not offensively so."

Nixon: "I don't mind the homosexuality, I understand it. Nevertheless, goddamn, I don't think you glorify it on public television, homosexuality, even more than you glorify whores. We all know we have weaknesses. But goddammit, what do you think that does to kids. You know what happened to the Greeks! Homosexuality destroyed them. Sure, Aristotle was a homo. We all know that. So was Socrates."

Nixon: "You know what happened to the Romans? The last six Roman emperors were fags. Let's look at the strong societies. The Russians. Goddamn, they root them out."

Mention of the morally robust Soviet Union prompts Nixon to contemplate its decadent antithesis, Northern California. He tells Ehrlichman, "San Francisco has just gone clean over." (It's unclear what they are referring to. Nixon would have been reading news reports about big anti-war demonstrations the day before. The President may have equated attacks on him with homosexual decadence.)

Nixon: "It's not just the ratty part of town. The upper class in San Francisco is that way. The Bohemian Grove, which I attend from time to time. It is the most faggy goddamned thing you could ever imagine, with that San Francisco crowd. I can't shake hands with anyone from San Francisco." It's funny to think of Nixon at the Bohemian Grove's summer bash on the Russian River, brooding about the fall of Greece and Rome, aghast at the annual revue in the which the flower of California's ruling class lumbers on stage in tutus and melon-stuffed bras. Imagine his apocalyptic ravings to Ehrlichman if he could have foreseen the most exciting political race in this pre-millennial season, in which a black man and a homosexual are battling it out in a runoff for the mayoralty of San Francisco, a contest in which neither skin color nor sexual orientation is the paramount issue.

December 1

If a few thousand *New York Times* readers found themselves munching turkey with an extremely high salt content, it was surely the fault of that swag-bellied gormandizer, R. W. Apple Jr. A few days before Thanksgiving the *Times* ran a long piece by Apple describing a private dinner prepared for himself and his wife by Alice Waters, owner of the famous Berkeley restaurant Chez Panisse. The meal in question—a promo for Waters—was a Thanksgiving menu, and, as so often in the case of Apple's food essays, left one amazed at the fact that his liver is still working. He should certainly bequeath it to the Smithsonian.

What caught my eye in the Waters recipe as relayed by Apple was the stipulation that the turkey be brined for seventy-two hours. Now, I brine meat from time to time, meaning one submerges the piece of beef or pork in a solution of salt, sugar and a few spices. One can also add sodium nitrite, to add a pleasing pink color to the meat, though health nuts say this saltpeter is a no-no. A week or so in the brine will give a four-pound chunk of meat a thoroughly salty taste, and even three days will definitely tilt it over into the "well-salted" category. But one can also brine pork just for twenty-four hours to give the meat an almost imperceptible zing, and this is surely what Waters had in mind with her turkey.

I brined a twenty-pound turkey raised by one of my neighbors, and was lifting it out of the crock, preparatory to spit-roasting it, when guests arrived from the Bay Area. I told them my suspicions about Apple's seventy-two-hour edict, and they immediately reported that they'd been reading a recipe by Waters in one of the San Francisco papers, advising a twenty-four-hour turkey brining period. I've not yet run across a cookbook that advises a longer time.

The spit-roasting, incidentally, was a great success. The turkey revolved over its bed of coals and, even though the chestnut stuffing all fell out through the truss stings, the brined bird (which took only two and a half hours to cook to an internal temperature of 165 degrees at the deepest point of its splendid bosom) was hailed by our party of thirteen as the finest they'd ever consumed. It could have been the brine, or the spit-roasting, or the turkey's pleasant circumstances—a wild hillside rich in seeds, summer grasshoppers and fall apples—or of course a mixture of all three.

December 8

Beyond the wildest hopes of the street warriors, five days in Seattle brought us one victory after another. The protesters—initially shunned and denounced by the respectable "inside strategists," despised by the press, gassed and bloodied by the cops and national guard—shut down the opening ceremony, prevented Clinton from addressing the WTO delegates at the Wednesday night gala, turned the corporate press from prim denunciations of "mindless anarchy" to bitter criticisms of police brutality, and forced the WTO to cancel its closing ceremonies and to adjourn in disorder and confusion, without an agenda for the next round.

In the annals of popular protest in America, these were shining hours, achieved entirely outside the conventional arena of orderly protest and white paper activism and the timid bleats of professional leadership of big labor and environmentalists. This truly was an insurgency from below in which all those who strove to moderate and deflect the turbulent flood of popular outrage managed to humiliate themselves.

December 29

People wearied of millennial summings-up even earlier than they got bored with Y2K. Jeffrey St. Clair and I did put together our *CounterPunch* list of what we reckoned to be the best, or most influential, non-fiction books of the twentieth century first published in English. Adamic's *Dynamite*, *Architectural Standards*, *A Potter's Manual*, Gertrude Jekyll on gardening, *Learning from Las Vegas*, *Fear and Loathing in Las Vegas*, *Desert Solitaire*, *I Claud* ... All in all, about 120 books, at least half of which are out of print.

Probably the ones on our list I look at most frequently are the eleventh edition of the *Encyclopaedia Britannica* and the *Oxford English Dictionary*. Those who imagine the OED to be a nineteenth-century publication should know that by 1900 only the volumes covering A, B, C, D, E, F and H had been published. As a reader has already pointed out to us, the thirteenth edition of the *Britannica* is even better than the eleventh, containing all the material in the earlier one, plus useful stuff on World War I. I'd like to say that a century producing the eleventh edition and the OED can't be all bad, but then again in both cases the animating force behind these vast projects was nineteenth-century energy and intellectual style.

People deploring the twentieth century usually imagine themselves in some more leisured epoch, maybe chatting with Dr. Johnson in a Fleet St. tavern or attending one of Sophocles' plays in classical Athens. But on the law of averages one would more likely have been a half-starved peasant, then and now.

I thank my own stars I was presented to the world in the twentieth century, in 1941, by a Scottish doctor in a kilt angered at having his fishing interrupted by my mother's labor. This was near Inverness and my father was in London, pondering how to get us out of that era's version of Y2K, which was Hitler's impending invasion. But Hitler never did make it, even though one of his rockets did for our house. The century has been good to me. So let's wave out the millennium gracefully with a hearty adieu. Onward!

2000

January 15

Back in 1979 Tim Hermach, now fearless leader of the Native Forest Council and breathing the righteous air of Eugene, Oregon, was a businessman seeking commercial advantage. In 1979 this search took him to Little Rock, Arkansas, where his associate Tookie McDaniel said the swiftest way of getting a certificate of origin necessary for a rebar (reinforcing steel for construction) deal was by conferring personally with the new governor of the state.

In short order a dinner was arranged with young Governor Bill at the Little Rock Hilton. Tim recalls that they were scarcely seated before Bill was greeting a pretty young waitress in friendly fashion, putting his hand up her dress while announcing genially to the assembled company, "This woman has the sweetest cunt in Little Rock."

Tim, an Oregon boy by origin, tells us he listened with burning ears and mouth agape as Bill talked of womanhood in terms of astounding crudity. Badinage notwithstanding, some business was transacted. Hermach tells us that Governor Bill "very openly, nothing shy about it, said words to the effect that our end use certificate would cost about $10,000," said transaction being of a personal, informal nature. "Since ours was a $2 million deal, we didn't care," Tim recalls.

Governor Bill also informed Hermach that they should go to the Stephens Bank the following day to complete all necessary arrangements.

These tractations concluded, Governor Bill repaired to the Hilton's nightclub with boon companions, where they cavorted lewdly with sundry flowers of Little Rock before repairing to bedrooms in the upper regions of the hotel.

January 26

Before his election as state attorney general in 1976, Bill and Hillary had lived in Fayetteville, instructing youth at the University of Arkansas. To celebrate his marriage Bill had bought a small house, much disliked by his bride. Great was her relief when the voters' nod compelled their removal to Little Rock.

Now the small house on California Boulevard had to be rented to supplement the modest income of Arkansas' chief legal officer. Here's an account of Bill as landlord from a woman who, back in those years, was the best friend of one of the first tenants to pay, in person, the monthly check to the state attorney general.

In his self-appointed role as property manager Bill Clinton personally set the qualifications required to rent the property. Chief among them was the requirement to be young, attractive and blonde. Landlord Bill would show up regularly at 9 a.m. Saturday mornings, the day of any home Razorback football game. He would invite one of the young renters to attend the game with him, then spend the rest of the afternoon and evening with them, exploring matters of mutual interest.

Bill developed a particularly keen interest in our source's friend, who happened to be from Dallas, of striking appearance and a cheerleader for the Razorbacks. Bill's Saturday morning arrivals at the house on California Boulevard were not welcome to the cheerleader. Nor were what she described as his incessant "gropings." Despite her reproofs Bill persisted, with such obstinate pertinacity that eventually she transferred to Texas A&M and men of greater subtlety and refinement such as College Station is deservedly famous for.

Now we're in 1983 and Bill is back in the governor's mansion in Little Rock, following the awful interregnum, after the voters had banished him from office at the end of his first term. The bearer of our story here is the son of an Arkansas Democrat state legislator who passed his formative years in the Dog Patch state, and at the period we are now discussing, in the town of Fayetteville, where he was an officer in the university's student government.

In this capacity he helped plan a conference of student government officers throughout the state college and university system. Among the invitees were many of the big names in Arkansas' political life, including Governor Bill and also Jim Guy Tucker (whose political career came to an abrupt halt in the mid-1990s, courtesy of special prosecutor K. Starr).

What's a student conference without a party? Our friend tells us he had taken particular care to invite Governor Bill since he was notorious throughout Fayetteville as being a devotee of marijuana and our friend was eager to get stoned in such illustrious company. Both Clinton and Tucker signaled that they would gladly attend the gathering.

The conference opened with a formal speech by Governor Bill, and our friend noted that the attention of Arkansas' chief executive wandered somewhat during his oration, his eyes seeming to drift with increasing frequency to a nice-looking young woman sitting in the front row. Our friend left to make preparations for the party, which indeed turned out to be a most genial occasion. Joints were fired up, Jim Guy Tucker gracefully declined the offer of Ozark homegrown and responded to enquiries about Governor Bill's whereabouts with the news that Bill would assuredly not pass up revelry such as this. But the hours flew by and Bill didn't show.

Then our friend encountered a young woman from the University of Arkansas at Little Rock who asked if she could get a ride home to the hotel, confiding, "I don't know how to say this, but my roommate's not here. I think she's with the governor." Our chivalrous friend drove her to the hotel and then, next morning, met her at a conference panel and asked how things had gone. She said her friend had not shown that night. An hour later who should appear but the attractive young thing our friend had seen the previous day drinking in the governor's honeyed words in the front row. She was wearing the same clothes. Her roommate greeted her with welcoming cries and in the girlish glow of confidence that followed, she boasted of prolonged and intimate tractations with the governor.

Some liberals take the odd view that Bill has let down the '60s. Robert Scheer, now a syndicated columnist based at the *Los Angeles Times*, opted for this line. Scheer wrote at the end of January that if the allegations about Lewinsky were true, then it was yet more evidence that Clinton "persists in letting his generation down by betraying the sexual revolution that contained its greatest promise." Sex in the countercultural '60s, according to the brazen Scheer, "aspired to be a union of equals recognizing the sensual needs of women as well as of men and shunning the privileges of male power that had dominated the sexual history of this country."

Wrong. The big complaint of the countercultural women in the '60s was that the radical males, particularly leaders like Bob Scheer, were sexist pigs. That's why we got the women's movement that cranked up in 1969 (and peaked in 1974).

Against this sentimental evocation of caring '60s males "recognizing the sensual needs of women" Scheer pilloried Bill as an "unimaginative and indeed mechanical" exponent of "vintage retro redneck sex." Scheer should go back and read Gennifer Flowers's delightful tell-all memoir, *Passion and Betrayal*, before he gets so snooty.

February 7

A cop would probably say it's unfair, just coincidence, but the news stories are coming over the brow of the hill, shoulder to shoulder, and they do spell out a larger message. The police chief of Los Angeles, Bernard C. Parks, announces his department's reckoning that ninety-nine people were framed by disgraced ex-officer-turned-informant Rafael Perez and partners. Parks is calling on DA Gil Garcetti to dismiss the cases "en masse."

Illinois governor George Ryan suspends his state's imposition of the death penalty, declaring that he "cannot support a system which has proven so fraught with error." Since 1977 Illinois has executed twelve and freed thirteen from death row after their innocence had been conclusively established.

In New York, four officers are going on trial for fatally riddling an unarmed man, Amadou Diallo, with forty-one bullets.

A generation's worth of "wars on crime" and of glorification of the men and women in blue have engendered a culture of law enforcement that is all too often viciously violent, contemptuous of the law, morally corrupt and confident of the credulity or complicity of the courts.

Those endless wars on crime and drugs have engendered not merely our two million prisoners but a vindictive hysteria that pulses on the threshold of homicide in the bosoms of many of our uniformed law enforcers. A lot of cops are walking time bombs. Even soothing words spoken to them in a calm voice can spark a red gleam in their eyes. God help you if you're black. The other day a black man in LA described the time he spent each day figuring out routes across the city to reduce his chances of getting pulled over, maybe beaten, maybe framed, maybe imprisoned.

Police work is far from being one of America's more dangerous occupations, but cops assiduously cultivate that impression. Police funerals are getting to be on a par with the obsequies of European royalty fifty years ago. Recently two San Francisco policemen crashed in their helicopter during a routine maintenance flight. Their funeral was attended by a huge throng of police from across California, state officials and the mayor of San Francisco. Would a city engineer or maintenance woman get this kind of send-off, even if their jobs demonstrated a higher statistical risk?

The press feeds obsessively on these "fallen hero" rituals. On January 12 in Unity, Maine, six-year-old triplets died in a house fire. County Sheriff Robert Jones, also a part-time fireman, was filling a tanker with water a couple of blocks from the blaze when he collapsed and died. It was his forty-eighth birthday. He got a hero's send-off, with massed ranks of state cops in attendance. True, Sheriff Jones might have been on the brink of bold deeds, possibly even entailing the supreme sacrifice, but that seems a frail peg on which to hang a state funeral. These ceremonies have always been demonstration rituals designed to protect the cops' budgetary appropriations and boost their overall image.

At least some of this often lethal cop edginess surely comes from a fractured sense of class status and function. After all, most police come from the working class and the vast majority shift class loyalty in the course of duty. Historically, this switch was recognized and fostered, especially during the time of police union organizing. In the early industrial period police wages began to run at about double those of similarly unskilled workers, and this doesn't even take into account bonuses for strikebreaking. Better working conditions meant greater allegiance to semi-military organization. Yet despite such job perks for cops, morale often lagged. One of the grander ideas for the necessary morale boosting came from big-city mayors, elevating cop death to the status of near sainthood by flying the flag at half-mast and cajoling entire city staffs to turn out for a blue funeral.

March 6

In Monroe, Louisiana, Kathy Looney, twenty-nine, convicted of abusing three of her eight children, was ordered at the end of February to undergo medical sterilization or face lengthy jail time. District Judge Carl V. Sharp issued a ten-year suspended sentence and placed Looney on five years of probation. "I don't want to have to lock you up to keep you from having any more children, so some kind of medical procedure is needed to make sure you don't." Looney's lawyer asked the judge to reconsider.

The eugenic impulse is always lurking. These days it's surfacing once again, not only in old-fashioned coercive sterilization such as that imposed by the Louisiana judge but in programs of genetic improvement, using all the new splicing technologies.

During the years when Americans were being involuntarily sterilized as part of a multi-state eugenics program dating back to 1907, what did the leading medical journals here have to say on the topic in their editorials?

The editorial record of the *New England Journal of Medicine* in the early 1930s was awful. Editorials lamented the supposed increase in the rate of American feeble-mindedness as dangerous and the economic burden of supporting the mentally feeble as "appalling."

In 1934 the *Journal*'s editor, Morris Fishbein, wrote that "Germany is perhaps the most progressive nation in restricting fecundity among the unfit," and argued that the "individual must give way to the greater good."

But by the mid-1930s, particularly after the report from the Neurological Association and energetic interventions by the chairman of its special committee, Abraham Myerson, the *New England Journal* had a change of heart and declared that sterilization laws to prevent propagation were "unwise" and sterilization should not be mandatory. The *Journal of the American Medical Association* followed the same curve.

In 1974 US District Court Judge Gerhard Gesell said that "Over the last few years, an estimated 100,000 to 150,000 low-income persons have been sterilized annually in federally funded programs." The late Allan Chase quoted this in his great book *The Legacy of Malthus*, and noted that the US rate equaled that of Nazi Germany where the twelve-year career of the Third Reich after the German Sterilization Act of 1933 (in part inspired by US laws) saw two million Germans sterilized as social inadequates.

Gesell pointed out that though Congress had decreed that family planning programs function on a voluntary basis "an indefinite number of poor people have been improperly coerced into accepting a sterilization operation under the threat that various federally funded benefits would be withdrawn. Patients receiving Medicaid assistance at childbirth are evidently the most frequent targets of this pressure."

Starting in the early 1990s poor women were allowed by Medicaid funding to have Norplant inserted into their arms, then when they complained of pain and other unwelcome side effects they were told no funding was available to have the Norplant rods taken out.

April 14

I got an invitation to speak a couple of months ago from an outfit called antiwar.com, which is run by a young fellow called Justin Raimundo. "Antiwar.com is having its second annual national conference March

24 and 25, and we'd like you to be the luncheon speaker," Raimundo wrote. "The conference will be held at the Villa Hotel, in San Mateo (near the airport). The theme of the conference is 'Beyond Left and Right: The New Face of the Antiwar Movement.' We have invited a number of speakers spanning the political spectrum. Confirmed so far: Patrick J. Buchanan, Tom Fleming (of *Chronicles* magazine), Justin Raimondo (Antiwar.com), Kathy Kelly (Iraq Aid), Alan Bock (Orange County Register), Rep. Ron Paul (R-Texas), representatives of the Serbian Unity Congress, and a host of others."

Raimundo seasoned his invite with a burnt offering, in the form of flattery, always pleasing to the nostrils: "All of us here at Antiwar.com are big fans of your writing: we met, once, at a meeting during the Kosovo war where you bravely took up the fight for the united front left-right alliance against imperialist war. We can promise you a small honorarium, a lunch, free admission to all conference events—and a good time."

As a seasoned analyst of such communications, my eye of course fell sadly upon the words "small honorarium," a phrase that in my case usually means somewhere between $150 and $350. Being a libertarian Justin had boldly added the prospect of a "good time." Leftist invitations rarely admit this possibility in formal political communications, even in the distant days when the left supposedly had a lock on drugs and sex.

I said I'd be happy to join in such an enterprise, and in due course got some angry e-mails from lefties who seem to feel that any proximity to Buchanan is a crime, even if the subject was gardening.

I chose the '67 convertible as properly defiant of the auto-safety lobby and headed south from Berkeley. This was most emphatically a shirt-and-tie, skirt-and-nice-shoes crowd. Justin Raimundo was draped in the sort of gray pinstripe favored by London gents when they want a holiday from blue. But all the same the folks were unmistakably libertarians, not Democrats or Republicans. Democrats would have been more casual, Republicans far more assertive. From the podium I gazed out at white faces, seeing only two black countenances, one of them unmistakably that of yet another liberal bête-to-hate, Lenora Fulani.

Their amiable hilarity at my sallies reminded me of Goldsmith's lines in "The Deserted Village" about the pupils of the country schoolmaster: "Full well they laughed with counterfeited glee / At all his jokes, and many a joke had he." (How many people have read the whole of that wonderful poem, one of the most savage denunciations of free trade ever written?)

"Can we unite," I asked the crowd, "on the anti-war platform? We have already, in the case of Kosovo for example. But where would you as libertarians want to get off the leftist bus? A leftist says 'Capitalism leads to war. Capitalism needs war.' But you libertarians are pro-capitalism, so you presumably have a view of capitalism as a system not inevitably producing or needing war. Lefties have always said capitalism has to maximize its profits and the only way you can maximize profits in the end is by imperial war, which was the old Lenin thesis …

"I think the old categories are gone. I see no virtue to them. I see Bernie Sanders listed as an Independent Socialist in the US Congress. I see what Bernie Sanders has supported, starting with the war in Kosovo. And then I see Ron Paul, on the other hand, writing stuff against war which could have been written by Tom Hayden in 1967."

Driving back to Berkeley with $300 in cash in my pocket, I mentally toasted antiwar.com. Alas, not many leftists will ever want to have much to do with them.

April 18

At the end of April we'll have arrived at the twenty-fifth anniversary of the end of the Vietnam War, when the last fugitives clambered into helicopters at the US Embassy compound in Saigon.

For years the anti-war left was told to be embarrassed about the '60s, put through re-education rites designed to elicit the confession that "excesses" were committed, mistakes made. Of course mistakes were made, starting with the failure to stop the war eight years earlier, in 1967. We misread the larger calendar. After Tet, after the May–June events in Paris, we thought revolution was around the corner. The Tet Offensive of 1968 remains one of the great moments of the twentieth century, even though one can see in retrospect that General Giap's desperate throw signaled the fact that the Americans had indeed been successful in exterminating the National Liberation Front in South Vietnam. We make mistakes all the time, again and again, however much we try to "draw the correct lessons." Big deal. History isn't like a bus, conveniently carrying a destination sign above the windshield. Every time I go to a political gathering on the left, it's filled with people, self included, who have made mistakes about the way history was headed, about the vulnerability of capitalism, but who were on the right track all the same. The most mistaken people of all are those so frightened of making mistakes they end up missing the right bus when it finally comes round the corner.

May 9

Barbara had that coy, breathless, somewhat defiant way of coming into the house that told me the whole story. I knew she was about to tell me she'd just found a dog, just caught sight of the One and Only. Actually Barbara, aka Barbara Yaley, was good about it. She said she was about to get a dog and that my inevitably favorable opinion would be duly taken into account. Jasper was at that point in time on display by the Milo Foundation of likely dogs rescued from the shelters before they get the needle. In Berkeley the Milo Foundation musters the dogs on Fourth St. a couple of blocks north of University Avenue every other weekend.

We headed off to Fourth St., and in short order headed back with forty pounds of dog, a stray from up north in Laytonville where the ranchers dump whole litters of border collies by the side of the road. By the look of him Jasper was part border, part lab, plus those self-important whiskers that tell you that terrier is in the genetic splice. Okay, I think he's a terrific dog, and, well aware that he'd been nose to nose with the Reaper, Jasper thinks we're terrific too. Who says endless gratitude becomes cloying?

These days, when we're in Berkeley, we load up Jasper and head down University, over I-80 and onto what was once a proud garbage dump, then North Waterfront Park and now César Chávez Park. It's one of the most beautiful vantage points in the Bay Area. Due west across the water is the Golden Gate Bridge, then swinging one's gaze south, the towers of downtown San Francisco, the Bay Bridge and due east the Berkeley hills.

Seventeen acres of this pleasing expanse are available to off-leash dogs, an incredible achievement of Berkeley dog lovers who spent about seven years of delicate political maneuvering to secure, last year, "pilot project status" for the off-leash area. To win it they had to surmount fierce opposition from the Audubon Society, the Sierra Club and the Citizens for an East Shore State Park, eager to seize the acreage of César Chávez Park and add it to their domain. State parks in California have never yet held off-leash areas.

The whole off-leash thing cranked up nationally about five years ago. I can't verify my instinct here, but I think it has been at least in part the consequence of organizing work of mid-life radicals bringing the war home, discovering that winning a little leg room for Fido is one cause whose fruition is something we might see in our own lifetimes.

The usual gripes of the anti-off-leash forces? They try to seize the high moral ground by giving us the old Either/Or. Why should we be seeking playgrounds for dogs when we aren't giving them to children? Answer: Civilization is not a zero sum game. Let's have both. Kids and dogs. Dog poop? Dogs on leashes do it as much as dogs running free, and surveys show that, once they win their off-leash area, dog lovers self-police with all the vigilance of a neighborhood committee of public safety in the Paris of Robespierre and Saint-Just. The off-leash area in César Chávez is probably the cleanest acreage in the East Bay.

A dog that can run free is a happy dog, uplifter of domestic morale. Owners are healthier too, dashing along after dogs like Jasper.

May 16

Now it's Al Gore, crime fighter, outlining his plans in a recent speech in Atlanta. The erstwhile dope smoker from Tennessee fears the erstwhile cocaine user from Texas has the edge on the crime issue. Hence his dash for the low ground. Among the Atlanta pledges: The minute he's settled into the Oval Office and signed a pardon for the former incumbent, President Gore will be calling for 50,000 more cops (more half-trained recruits like the ones who shot Amadou Diallo) and for allowing off-duty cops to carry concealed weapons (which almost all of them do anyway).

No, it's unlikely President Gore will endorse medical marijuana, despite his erstwhile post-Vietnam therapy with opium-laced marijuana in the days when he worked for the *Tennessean*. In the words of his friend John Warnecke (who imported the Thai sticks from the West Coast), Al "smoked as much as anybody I knew down there, and loved it."

Among Gore's other big plans to combat crime: He wants to target telemarketers who prey on seniors. What about telemarketers who prey on people sitting down to dinner?

Gore knows all about addiction. His sister Nancy, as he reminds us from time to time, was killed by cigarettes, unable to kick the habit even as she was breathing with one cancerous lung. He also knows about congenital dispositions. His wife, Tipper, is a depressive. He knows about therapy too, having communed with shrinks when he was having the midlife sag that partly prompted his 1992 book *Earth in the Balance*.

June 18

We're just about thirty-one years away from the great Stonewall riot, which set the tone for years of defiant gay insurgency. So where's this spirit of defiance today?

Here's a clue. In early June, we were able to read in our national newspapers that about sixty gay employees of the CIA were joined by a busload of intelligence workers from the National Security Agency for an event designed to evince gay pride. Present were top officials, including George J. Tenet, the Director of Central Intelligence. Addressing the gay spooks was Barney Frank, the noted gay Rep. from Massachusetts.

Taste the ironies. The gay spooks, albeit proud, were still unidentifiable, and then returned to their tasks of planning the sabotage of the Cuban economy, the undermining of Libya, and other staples of the Agency's daily fare. How would the Stonewall rioters of the late '60s have reacted to that?

Gays have always had an uneasy relationship with the state and with the authorities, for sound reasons. Down the decades they've been hunted, entrapped, arrested, sentenced, persecuted. With increasing vigor and effect since Stonewall they've fought back. But now we have the repugnant spectacle of many prominent gays and gay groups oblivious to this long history. Take the death penalty. There's no more glaring expression of the inequities of race and class than the manner in which the death penalty is operated in our society, yet many gay rights groups have been silent on capital punishment, including the richest and biggest of them all, the Human Rights Campaign. They're mute as the state hauls off the poor and the black to die, and save their lungs for "hate crime" laws, for longer prison terms, for more repression by the state.

Listen to Richard Hymes, of the New York City Gay and Lesbian Anti-Violence Project: "Hate crimes legislation would remove the decision making process regarding plea bargaining and reduced or dismissed sentences out of the judges' hands because they set a benchmark of punishment for each offense which cannot be pleaded, bargained away or dismissed." In other words, the zeal to deal with anti-gay violence now leads to advocacy of laws which threaten justice, due process and civil liberties.

Years ago a great criminal court judge in Detroit—Justin Ravitz—explained the criminal justice system as America's "only working railroad." And now many gays are toiling to make sure that the railroad runs on time, even on overtime. About half the states now have hate-crime laws that include language on sexual bias. Not a word in any of those laws in any of those states will stop a gay person being attacked, not a word will reduce discrimination in our society, not a word will erode the repression against which those Stonewallers fought thirty-one years ago.

July 18

A Democrat in the White House is no guarantee of a liberal on the Court. Gerald Ford picked John Stevens, one of the Court's current liberal champions and indeed the only justice to rule against two oil companies in one of the recent batch of Supreme Court decisions. Nixon's nominee, Harold Blackmun, wrote the *Roe v. Wade* decision. Twenty years later Bush Sr.'s nominee, Souter, probably the most liberal justice today, wrote the *Planned Parenthood v. Casey* decision in 1992 reaffirming the "essential holding" of *Roe v. Wade*, and arguing that "choice" was now installed in the national culture. The Court echoed that view in its recent upholding of the *Miranda* rule.

And why had choice become thus installed, why was the "essential holding" being reaffirmed? Through the activity of social movements, through the political pressure of millions of people. The idea that our moral fabric, the tenor of our culture, the texture of our freedoms derive from the US Supreme Court, and therefore somehow depend on whom Gore or Bush may or may not nominate, is ludicrous. The US Supreme Court, like all ruling state institutions, bends in a benign direction only under the impulse of powerful social movements.

Throughout the nation's history the US Supreme Court has generally been a reactionary force and it will no doubt be so whether Gore or Bush is elected in November, or whether the Democrats or Republicans control the Senate. A partial exception was the Warren court, which had the coincidence of three great justices, Black, Douglas, and the Eisenhower-appointed William Brennan, and which was prompted by the rise of the civil rights movement and the political assertion of black people to try and head off more drastic social explosions. In so doing it buttressed a federal government that was unflinchingly hostile to the interest of working people, minorities and the environment. *Reynolds v. Sims*, in 1966, turned many rural counties into Third World latifundia.

August 30

In AD 193 the Roman Praetorian Guard murdered the Emperor Pertinax and proceeded to auction off the imperial throne to the highest bidder. Until this year the most strenuous emulation of this feat by the US military came in 1980, when the Joint Chiefs of Staff took bids on the White House from the ramparts of the Pentagon. Despite fierce bidding by Jimmy Carter, the Chiefs had no hesitation in accepting Republican pledges and in proclaiming that only Ronald Reagan would keep the Empire strong.

We are in the climactic moments of the 2000 auction.

September 22

The collapse of the government's case against Wen Ho Lee last week represents one of the greatest humiliations of a national newspaper in the history of journalism. One has to go back to the publication by the London *Times* of the Pigott forgeries in 1887 libeling Charles Stewart Parnell, the Irish nationalist hero, to find an equivalent debacle.

Yet not a whisper of contrition, not a murmur of remorse, has as yet agitated the editorial pages of the *New York Times*, which now righteously urge the appointment of a "politically independent person of national standing to review the entire case."

No such review is required to determine the decisive role of the *New York Times* in sparking the persecution of Wen Ho Lee, his solitary confinement under threat of execution, his denial of bail, his shackling, the loss of his job, the anguish and terror endured by this scientist and his family. On March 6, 1999, the *Times* carried a report by James Risen and Jeff Gerth entitled "Breach at Los Alamos" charging an unnamed scientist with stealing nuclear secrets from the government lab and giving them to the People's Republic of China. The espionage, according to a security official cited by Risen and Gerth, was "going to be just as bad as the Rosenbergs."

Two days later Wen Ho Lee, an American of Taiwanese descent, was fired from his job. Ahead of him lay months of further pillorying in a racist witch hunt led by the *Times*, whose news columns were replete with further mendacious bulletins from Risen and Gerth, and whose Op Ed page featured William Safire using their stories to launch his own calumnies against Wen Ho Lee and the Clinton administration.

Guided by Safire, the Republicans in Congress pounced upon the Wen Ho Lee case with an ardor approaching ecstasy. By the spring of 1999 their effort to evict Bill Clinton from office for the Lewinsky affair had collapsed. They needed a new stick with which to beat the administration and the *New York Times* handed it to them.

In Safire's insinuations, the Clinton White House was an annex of the Middle Kingdom, and the transfer of US nuclear secrets merely one episode in a long, dark narrative of treachery to the American flag. Former US Senator Warren Rudman went on NBC's "Meet the Press" and declared flatly, "The agenda for the body politic is often set by the media. Had it not been for the *New York Times* breaking the story of Chinese espionage all over the front pages, I'm not sure I would be here this morning."

The most preposterous expression of the Republican spy crusade against the Clinton administration came with the release of the 900-page report named after California Rep. Christopher Cox, filled with one demented assertion after another, including the memorable though absolutely false claim that "the stolen information includes classified information on seven US thermonuclear warheads, including every currently deployed thermonuclear warhead in the US ballistic missile arsenal."

Yet Risen and Gerth's stories had been profuse with errors from the outset. Their prime source had been Notra Trulock, an embittered security official in the Department of Energy intent upon his own vendettas within the DoE. Risen and Gerth eagerly swallowed his assertions. From him and other self-interested officials they relayed one falsehood after another: that Wen Ho Lee had failed a lie-detector test; that the Los Alamos lab was the undoubted source of the security breach; that it was from Los Alamos that the Chinese had acquired the blueprint of the miniaturized W-88 nuclear warhead.

Had the *New York Times* launched its campaign of terror against Wen Ho Lee at the height of the cold war, it is quite likely that Wen Ho Lee would have been swept to his doom, most likely with a sentence of life imprisonment amid vain efforts of his defenders to get the scientist a fair hearing. It is doubtful that US District Judge James Parker in New Mexico would have had the courage to denounce the

Justice Department for a shabby case and to order the release of Wen Ho Lee after harshly criticizing the fifty-nine-count government indictment and the "demeaning, unnecessarily punitive conditions" in which Wen Ho Lee had been held.

But we are no longer amidst the fevers of the cold war. And though the Pentagon has wanly tried to foment a budget-boosting campaign to suggest that China represents a fearsome military threat, it has not been taken with any great seriousness. The exaggerations of Chinese might are simply too egregious.

So, in these post-cold war years, Wen Ho Lee did have his sturdy defenders. Some were government officials evidently appalled by the *Times*' campaign. Some commentators, most notably Lars-Erik Nelson of the *New York Daily News*, were scathing about the case against Wen Ho Lee. In July of 1999 the *New York Review of Books* published a long piece by Nelson which explicitly criticized the witch-hunt and noted the malign role of the *New York Times*. Nelson pointed out how many of the supposedly filched "secrets" had been publicly available for years. By September of 1999 the *New York Times* had evidently entertained sufficient disquiet to publish a long piece by William Broad which decorously—though without any explicit finger-pointing—undermined the premises of Risen and Gerth's articles.

None of this helped Wen Ho Lee escape terrifying FBI interrogations in which an agent flourished the threat of execution. He was kept in solitary, allowed to exercise one hour a day while shackled, kept in a constantly lit cell.

Even near the end, when it was plain that the government's case was falling apart, US Attorney General Janet Reno's prosecutors successfully contested efforts to have Wen Ho Lee released on bail. And when Judge Parker finally threw out almost the entire case the prosecutors continued to insist, as has Reno, that their conduct had been appropriate throughout.

The *New York Times*, without whose agency Wen Ho Lee would never have spent a day in a prison cell, perhaps not even have lost his job, is now with consummate effrontery urging an investigation of the bungled prosecution.

In an extraordinary breach of conventional decorum the President of the United States has criticized his own Attorney General for the way Wen Ho Lee has been maltreated. Yet the editors of the *New York Times* can admit no wrong. Risen and Gerth are not required to offer reflections on the outcome of the affair.

When the forgeries of Richard Pigott, described in the 1911 edition of the *Encyclopedia Britannica* as "a needy and disreputable Irish journalist," against Parnell were exposed, he fled to Madrid and there blew out his brains. The London *Times* required years to efface the shame of its gullibility. Would that the *New York Times* was required to admit equivalent error. But it won't. Next year it will no doubt preen amid whatever Pulitzer awards are put its way by the jury of its friends. This is no-fault journalism.

September 24

Newt Gingrich had the first take on George W.'s pick for veep: "Dick Cheney is even more conservative than me." Leave it to the Bush crowd to allow the Democrats to resurrect Gingrich once more in their campaign ads. Of course, Newt has always been misclassified by the political taxonomists as a conservative. Underneath the bluster, Gingrich is a closet neoliberal and a technophile, fully marinated in the argot of third-wavism and cyberspeak. It's not surprising that he and Al Gore (frequent dining companions during their days in the House) are both disciples of Alvin Toffler and Carl Sagan and share the belief that getting urban America wired up to the internet is a fast-track out of poverty.

November 2

A political culture is under siege. Hear the panic as the waters pour into Atlantis.

Jesse Jackson cries out that "Our very lives are at stake." Paul Wellstone quavers that George W. Bush will "repeal the twentieth century." Martin Peretz, owner of the Gore-loving *New Republic*, writes furiously that "Naderism represents the emotional satisfaction of the American left at the expense of the social and economic satisfaction of women, blacks, gays, and poor people in America."

Somewhere in the third week of October the Gore crowd woke up to the clear and awful thought that they might not make it, that maybe it wasn't their time any more and that the man to blame is Ralph Nader. Gore had bombed in the debates. The Greens had organized a whole string of Nader super-rallies across the northern half of the country from Seattle and Portland, through the upper Midwest to New York. In Minnesota Nader was polling over ten percent on some counts. In Washington, Oregon, Minnesota, Wisconsin, Michigan and Maine, maybe even California, Nader could make enough of a dent to put Bush over the top.

And so the Get-Ralph campaign began in earnest.

I've always seen Ralph as our Robespierre, having to make do with class-action suits instead of the guillotine. Years ago the late Jim Goode, at that time editor of *Penthouse*, used to look across the piles of pin-ups with a shudder of distaste (he was gay) and snarl at me, "Alex, is your hate pure?" "Yes, Jim." Ralph's hate is pure. He'd no doubt prefer to be running at over 30 percent, but short of that, the privilege of being able to influence the race in at least six states is exactly what Nader had been waiting for all along: the power to remind the Democratic Party it can't take for granted the progressive slice of the country.

Even if the Nader/Green run vanishes off the margin of history by the end of the year it still will have given many young folk a taste for the excitements of radical political organizing. People carry such hours and days with them for the rest of their lives, as the inspiring leaven in our business-as-usual loaf.

November 9

Yes, Nader didn't break 5 percent nationally, but he should feel great, and so should the Greens who voted for him. Their message to the Democrats is clear. Address our issues, or you'll pay the same penalty next time around. Nader should draw up a short list of Green non-negotiable issues and nail it to the doors of the Democratic National Committee.

By all means credit Nader, but of course Gore has only himself to blame. He's a product of the Democratic Leadership Council, whose pro-business stance was designed to regain the South for the Democrats. Look at the map. Bush swept the entire South, with the possible exception of Florida. Gore's electoral votes came from the two coasts and the old industrial Midwest. The states Gore did win mostly came courtesy of labor and blacks.

Take Tennessee, where voters know Gore best. He would have won the election if he'd carried his home state. Gore is good with liberals earning $100,000–$200,000. He can barely talk to rural people, and he made another fatal somersault, reversing his position on handguns after telling Tennessee voters for years that he was solid on the gun issue. Guns were a big factor in Ohio and West Virginia too. As for Nader holding the country to ransom, what's wrong with a hostage taker with a national backing of 2.7 million people? The election came alive because of Nader.

December 13

On the one hand the calls for "closure," "finality" and national unity. On the other, Justice John Paul Stevens's bitter summation: "In the interest of finality, however, the majority [of the US Supreme Court] effectively orders the disenfranchisement of an unknown number of voters whose ballots reveal their intent, and are therefore legal votes under [Florida] state law, but were for some reason rejected by the ballot-counting machines … Although we may never know with complete certainty the identity of the winner of this year's presidential election the identity of the loser is perfectly clear. It is the nation's confidence in the judge as an impartial guardian of the law."

Part 2

2001

January 18
JoAnn was recently traveling in a limo from Baltimore to a town in West Virginia and fell into conversation with the driver, who related some of his ferryings to and fro of various bigwigs. One of these was Hillary Clinton. "An ornery woman," the driver commented. "And what a mouth on her!"

The driver went on to describe an occasion on which he was driving the First Lady and a couple of her female friends through a poor area of Washington, DC. They passed a beggar, and as they did so the First Lady expressed her disgust for the mendicant, adding "He wouldn't be a bum if he had a piece of ass." The driver was able to shed no light on how or why she had arrived at this conclusion, stunned as he was by the coarse nature of her observations. Then they passed two young black women with babies. "There go two welfare cases. They make me sick. They're too lazy to work," said Senator Clinton, champion of mothers and children everywhere.

January 28
Attending the annual *Texas Monthly* bash, George W. was asked what he and Bill Clinton had talked about in their White House photo op. George W. described how he had asked Clinton why Al Gore was taking his defeat with such poor grace. "It's been eight years," Clinton

genially replied, "and we still haven't figured out Al." Bill added hastily: "But he's been a great Vice-President."

February 5

Oklahomans are selective in their grief after a mass killing. They took about eighty years even to make official acknowledgement of the scores of dead blacks slaughtered in the Tulsa race riots, while fiercely denying reparations. Nor is the Oklahoma City site a simple memorial. Funded by us taxpayers it offers an Institute for the Prevention of Terrorism. But if Oklahomans refuse to confront McVeigh's motives and rationale, what credentials can their Institute have for any preventive strategies?

There's something ghoulish about the way Oklahomans are remembering their 168, from the repellent architecture and commemorative furniture of the site, to the icky blather about "survivors" and "closure," to the nature of this supposed "closure," focused on killing more people (whether those on death row for whose denial of habeas corpus rights they fiercely lobbied in the passage of the Effective Death Penalty Act), or McVeigh, whose jury they entertained as though it was a victorious football team, and whose execution they have been drawing lots to attend.

There are plenty of references in the Memorial literature to Oklahoma City as part of the American heartland. From that heartland have gone forth across the world Oklahoma lads who have, in government service, dropped bombs, gone on terror missions like Bob Kerrey's, participated in dreadful campaigns of extermination. Now, if they were to visit the Memorial, would not a survivor of one of those missions, a Vietnamese or a Salvadoran say, perhaps feel that some expression of empathy with other acts of terror was in order? Face it, there are plenty of "survivors" around the world, bereft of their parents, brothers, sisters, kids, because some Oklahoman kitted out in one of the national uniforms pressed the button, pulled the trigger, lit the fuse.

But no, the Memorial specifically offers a definition derived from USC Title II Section 265 F(A) of terrorism as "politically motivated violence perpetrated against non-combatant targets by subnational groups … Note definition excludes irrational acts, purely criminal and economic activities or acts committed by nation states."

McVeigh made some of these points, and to say that he has the better of the argument with the Oklahoma Memorial is not in the least to apologize for what I described as his evil act, it's to say that the Memorial offered me kitsch rather than dignified and considered sorrow.

February 15

Bill Clinton now proposes to establish an office in Harlem, on 125th Street, scarce more than a few stone throws away from where Gore delivers homilies to journalism students in Columbia University. Each has found his appropriate setting: the defeated veep pouring banalities about journalism and politics into the ears of ambitious high fliers already sending their résumés and clips to the *New York Times*; Clinton the moral reprobate fleeing a blizzard of criticism for auctioning a pardon to a billionaire crook by setting up shop among the poorer folk, rolling out a real-estate boom in the area.

February 18

Late last week a senior pollster in Clinton's inner circle spotted a journalistic acquaintance in a Georgetown supermarket and pinned him against his shopping cart with a vibrant diatribe against Gore.

How, the pollster hissed, can we explain that Gore was unable to run on the Clinton economy, unable to mention millions of jobs created through the Clinton '90s? She answered her own question. Because to do so would have meant mentioning Clinton's name and Gore couldn't bring himself to do that.

Why not? The answer, the pollster said, went far back before the Lewinsky affair that so troubled Al and Tipper. It seems that Al has always felt that it was he who actually won the 1992 election, bailing Bill out of all his problems over draft-dodging and Gennifer Flowers. Through Clinton's two terms Al's conviction that he rather than Bill should by rights by sitting in the Oval Office throbbed painfully in his psyche. Result: he never spoke to the boss and couldn't bear to ask him to help in those last desperate campaign days.

March 3

A few weeks ago I found myself at a small theater in SoHo, attending what had been billed to me as a recreation of Weimar and the world of Sally Bowles. This same Sally Bowles, as first created in a short story by Christopher Isherwood, then in *I Am a Camera*, a stage version that transmuted into *Cabaret*, was based on Jean Ross, my father's second wife, a charming woman. Naturally, I've always taken an interest in the fictional versions of her time in Berlin.

The production in SoHo turned out to have nothing to do with Berlin and everything to do with Giuliani, since the strippers ousted from gainful employment in their usual premises were regrouping under the banner of Art. In fact it was a big relief not to listen to pastiche songs in the manner of Kurt Weill. It was the occasion of the much-heralded snow storm that menaced New York the day of George Bush's inauguration, so the audience of six was heavily outnumbered by the strippers. The acts were okay, though not particularly rousing. The star of the evening didn't take off so much as a petticoat, being a magician who, since we're on the subject of Weill, looked slightly like Lotte Lenya in her cameo appearance as the KGB officer in *From Russia With Love*. She ogled the sparse audience gloriously as she bumbled her way through her tricks.

Jean Ross was a gentle, cultivated and very beautiful woman, not a bit like the vulgar vamp displayed by Lisa Minnelli. Jean died before her time at the age of sixty-two. Her daughter Sarah, my half sister, wrote wonderful detective stories under the name Sarah Caudwell: among them *The Shortest Way to Hades*, *The Sirens Sang of Murder*, *Thus Was Adonis Murdered*, and, posthumously published, *The Sibyl in Her Grave*. Before she turned to crime Sarah was a barrister, and a very good one. She used to negotiate my contracts with Verso and I'd pay her by taking her to lunch at the Ritz. As in any other venue she'd light up her pipe, then when waiters rushed up to protest, fling the thing into her handbag, from which smoke would soon begin to wreathe our table.

Sarah felt strongly about Isherwood's use of her mother, and wrote a piece about it in the British weekly, the *New Statesman*, in the mid-1980s. Her mother Jean, she wrote, "never liked *Goodbye to Berlin*, nor felt a sense of identity with the character of Sally Bowles, which in many respects she thought more closely modeled on one of Isherwood's male friends. (His homosexuality could not at that time be openly admitted.)" Sarah's point was that Isherwood, supposedly so *avant-garde*, was actually very conventional:

> The convention does not permit an attractive young woman to have much in the way of intellectual accomplishments, and Isherwood follows it loyally. There is nothing in his portrait of Sally to suggest that she might have had any genuine ability as an actress, still less as a writer. My mother, on the other hand, was at least talented enough as an actress to be cast as Anitra in Max Reinhardt's production of *Peer Gynt* and competent enough as a writer to earn her living, not long afterwards, as a scenario-writer and journalist.
>
> Above all, the convention requires that a woman must be either virtuous (in the sexual sense) or a tart. So Sally, who is plainly not virtuous, must be a tart. To depend for a living on providing sexual pleasure, whether or not in the context of marriage, seemed to [Jean] the ultimate denial of freedom and emancipation. The idea so deeply repelled her that she simply could not, I think, have been attracted to a man who was rich, or allied herself permanently to anyone less incorrigibly impecunious than my father. She did not see the question as one of personal morality, but as a political one.

The pipe smoking did in Sarah in the end, presumably causing the cancer in her esophagus that killed her at the age of sixty, last year. I knew her best at Oxford in the early '60s where she intrigued successfully to have women admitted to the Oxford Union. She was always exclaiming about so-and-so's "wonderful profile," pursuing dons with this particular asset. One don was known for watching television and Sarah, amid the ashes of her love, sent him this verse:

I cast aside my modesty, I laid aside my shame
And on my knees I offered love—Or something much the same.
You brushed my powder from your sleeve, with elegant precision
And murmured: "Conversation is killing television."

March 8

In intelligence committee rooms on Capitol Hill and in briefing sessions in the FBI, CIA, and other redoubts of the national security establishment, the air now quivers with gloomy assessments of the secrets "compromised" by the FBI's Robert Hanssen, a senior official who stands accused of working for the Russians since 1985.

If you believe the FBI affidavit against him filed in federal court, Hanssen betrayed spies working for the US, some of whom were then executed. Among many other feats he allegedly ratted on "an entire technical program of enormous value, expense and importance to the United States" which turns out to have been the construction of a tunnel under the new Soviet Embassy in Washington, DC. He trundled documents by the cartload to "dead drops" in various suburbs around Washington, DC, often within a few minutes' walk from his house.

It's amusing to listen to the US counter-intelligence officials now scorning Hanssen for lack of "tradecraft" in using the same drop week after week. These are the same counter-intelligence officials who remained incurious across the decades about the tinny clang of empty drawers in their TOP SECRET filing cabinets, all contents removed on a daily basis by Ames and Hanssen who deemed the use of copying machines too laborious. In just one assignment, the CIA later calculated, Ames gave the KGB a stack of documents estimated to be fifteen to twenty feet high. Hanssen was slack about "tradecraft" because he knew just how remote the possibility of discovery was. The only risk he couldn't accurately assess was the one that brought him down, betrayal by a Russian official privy to the material he was sending to Moscow.

April 5

Gallup, NM—Drive across the United States, mostly on Interstate 40, and you have plenty of time to listen to the radio. Even more time than usual if, to take my own situation, you're in a 1976 Ford 350 one-ton, plowing along at 50 mph. By day I listen to FM.

Bunked down at night, there's some choice on the motels' cable systems, all the way from C-SPAN to pay-as-you-snooze filth, though there's much less of that than there used to be, or maybe you have to go to a Marriott or kindred high-end place to get it. By contrast the choice on daytime radio, FM or AM, is indeed a vast wasteland, far more bleak than the high plains of Texas and New Mexico I've been looking at for the past couple of days.

It's awful. Even the religious stuff has gone to the dogs. I remember twenty years ago making the same drive through the bible belt and you'd hear crazed preachers raving in tongues. These days hell has gone to love. Christian radio is so warm and fuzzy you'd think you were listening to Terry Gross. By any measure, and you don't need to drive along I-40 to find this out, radio in this country is in ghastly shape.

Since the 1996 Telecommunications "Reform" Act, conceived in darkness and signed in stealth, the situation has got even worse. Twenty, thirty years ago broadcasters could own only a dozen stations nationwide and no more than two in any single market. Today the company Clear Channel alone owns more than 800 stations pumping out identical muck in all states. Since 1996 there's been a colossal shake-out. Small broadcasters can no longer hack it. Two or three companies with eight stations each control each market. Bob McChesney cites an industry publication as saying that the amount of advertising is up to eighteen minutes per hour, with these commercials separated by the same endless, golden oldies. On I-40 in Tennessee alone I listened to "Help!" at least sixteen times.

April 10

So far as rape is concerned, because of the rape factories more conventionally known as the US prison system, there are estimates that twice as many men as women are raped in the US each year. A Human Rights Watch report in April of this year cited a December 2000 *Prison Journal* study based on a survey of inmates in seven men's prison facilities in four states.

The results showed that 21 percent of the inmates had experienced at least one episode of pressured or forced sexual contact since being incarcerated, and at least 7 percent had been raped in their facilities. A 1996 study of the Nebraska prison system produced similar findings, with 22 percent of male inmates reporting that they had been pressured or forced to have sexual contact against their will while incarcerated. Of these, more than 50 percent had submitted to forced anal sex at least once. Extrapolating these findings to the national level gives a total of at least 140,000 inmates who have been raped.

May 8

Liberals have massed to defend Bob Kerrey, usually by saying that he was just a grunt following orders. In the *Los Angeles Times*, Bob Scheer announced that Kerrey is "a good man" and that the fellow who should be in the dock is Robert McNamara, who wasn't even Secretary of Defense when Kerrey lined up those women and babies in Thanh Phong and had his unit of SEALs machine-gun them at a range of ten feet.

On Fox, Christopher Hitchens, implacable foe of the war criminal Kissinger, had similar kind words for Kerrey:

COLMES: What's your view on Bob Kerrey?

HITCHENS: Of Bob Kerrey? Well, he's my president, in fact, since I teach at the New School, and I think he wouldn't—he wouldn't have made that bad a president. I know him slightly. I like him very much. But look, none of the people he killed were raped. None of them were dismembered. None of them were tortured. None of them were mutilated, had their ears cut off. He never referred to them as gooks or slopes or afterwards. So … for one day's work in a free-fire zone in the Mekong Delta, it was nothing like as bad as most days.

Why does Scheer say Kerrey is a "good" man and Hitchens confide to the Fox audience that "I like him very much"? There's far more evidence to say "Bob Kerrey is an evil man." His political career offers meager evidence to back any plea that Kerrey improved the human condition and if we are to say that he is a good man solely because he voted against the war on Iraq, then we have to call Sam Nunn "good" too, and we doubt that even Scheer would want to do that.

Kerrey's an admitted war criminal.

Just listen to his disgusting disclosures to Dan Rather in *60 Minutes II*, Monday night:

RATHER: If in fact it did happen. If there was an old man, an old woman and three children being killed. Was it or was it not within the rules of engagement for you and your men as you understood it, if necessary, to kill those people?

KERREY: Yes, again, I don't know how you're gonna cut this tape, but I don't have any doubt that the people that we killed were at the very least sympathetic to the Viet Cong. And at the very most, were supporting their efforts to kill us.

RATHER: Old men, women and children.

KERREY: Yes, I mean, the Viet Cong, in a guerrilla war, the people that get caught in the middle are the civilians. And the Viet Cong were a thousand percent more ruthless than any standard operating procedure that any American GI or Navy SEAL had.

Last month you didn't know that Kerrey had left a ditchful of civilians behind him and accepted a medal for an action that read—officially phrased—21 VC KIA (BC). That means twenty-one Viet Cong, killed in action (body count). So—a liar as well as a killer, since he knew the figures were falsified. This month you do know. So perhaps by the watercooler or in the corridor we hear: "Oh hi Bob! Shit happens, right?"

June 10

What happened to trout? Of all the farm fed fish they're the most tasteless. Order one in a restaurant these days and you get something tasting like blotting paper. It was different once.

Listen to the French writer, Jean Giono in *La France à Table*:

> Never with butter, never with almonds; that is not cooking, it is packaging. (It is, of course, understood that my recipes are not for all comers.) With the exception of *truite en bleu* nobody knows how to cook a trout. It is the most unfortunate fish on earth. If an atomic bomb destroyed the world tomorrow, the human race would vanish without ever having known the taste of a trout. Of course, I am no more talking of tank-bred trout than I would give a recipe for cooking a dog or a cat.
>
> So, a fine fat, or several fine fat, trout from the river, fresh (that goes without saying), gutted, scaled, etc.... A frying-pan previously rinsed out with flaming wine vinegar. Make this empty pan very hot. Into this very hot pan, a mixture of water and virgin olive oil (a claret glass of olive oil to 3 of water). Let it boil fast. Add a bouquet of thyme and nothing else whatsoever except 2 crushed juniper berries and some pepper.
>
> Reduce the mixture, and when there is nothing but a centimeter of fast boiling liquid left in the pan, put your fine fat, or several fine fat, trout gently into the liquid. Do not turn the fish over. Cover the pan and boil 1 minute, then 3 minutes very gently, and serve.

This rapid boiling of oil and water is the way to make bouillabaisse, which is fast food, the way fish should always be. Get the mix boiling, just like Giono says, then throw in your firm fleshed fish like bass or snapper with the smaller stuff five minutes later. Take it all off after another three minutes, put a slice of bread in each soup plate, a dish of aioli (garlic mayonnaise) in the center and go to it.

When I was a schoolboy in Scotland I used to catch little, pink-fleshed burn trout, roll them in oatmeal, then fry them. Hard to forget. A couple of years ago, on a pack trip in the Golden Trout Wilderness in the California Sierra, I moodily noted the lack of any trout in a stream of high repute and was told that biologists from the state's Fish and Game Department had decided the resident trout were alien and poisoned them with rotenone. If they'd introduced trout with the correct birth certificates, they hadn't survived.

Fishwise, the stream was dead for the next year and we're now told by our friends Tim and Odette Larson, who regularly pack mules into the Wilderness, there are trout back seemingly identical to the ones purged by Fish and Game.

July 20

I love scrubby old state highways, warm with commercial life. Highway 90 runs from Florida through Alabama and Louisiana, then on across Texas. I got onto it at Mobile and trundled westward into New Orleans, in time to go along and pay my respects to John Sinclair, formerly of the MC5 and now one of the city's prime musical figures, notably on his radio show. The night I got into town Sinclair was presiding over a benefit at the House of Blues, on Decatur St. for Coco Robicheaux to whom some disaster has befallen. Robicheaux was wearing a bright purple suit. Sinclair is tall and has a goatee beard, which juts out, a bit like Don Quixote's.

Sinclair told the crowd that a year earlier he and his wife had been grateful recipients of the proceeds of a similar benefit. Later he told me that the Coco Robicheaux benefit was the third in a recent series of "fire recovery events," starting with Eddie Bo's fire in what Sinclair thought to be 1999.

> Jerry Brock, my wife Penny and some other people organized a benefit for Eddie and his sister Veronica which brought a lot of people together and helped raise money so Eddie could get back on his feet. Then our own house burned up in January 2000 while we were out of town and we would have been completely devastated if Jerry Brock and Bill Taylor hadn't quickly put together a benefit concert at the House of Blues with music by Eddie Bo, Snooks Eaglin, Deacon John, Wild Magnolias, Treme Brass Band, Jon Cleary, Kermit Ruffins & the Barbecue Swingers, James Andrews, John Mooney, Coco Robicheaux and others. The show raised $12,500 at the door and another $7,500 in donations and sales of donated items that night, which allowed us to replace all our equipment, furniture and household essentials and get back on our feet after the fire.
>
> Then Coco's apartment caught fire just before JazzFest this year and Dell Long put together this benefit at the House of Blues to help him recover. The musicians in New Orleans also play at benefits for people

> who need help with their medical bills and other catastrophes, and generally everybody helps take care of each other when trouble strikes. There are very few of us in the New Orleans musical community who have any resources outside of what we're hustling up to get through the week or the present month. Few have insurance of any kind, let alone medical or fire insurance, so there's what I call the "people's insurance" when your friends get together and raise money to help you out. It's a beautiful thing.

It is indeed. I listened for a while, then went off to the Hotel Richelieu, and listened to a couple of new arrivals speculating on the career of the wily cardinal. I've never had time to explore the bayou country southwest of New Orleans and resolved to spend a day doing that. 90 took me west towards the turn off to Abbeville. Encouraged by its sign I stopped at a roadside café, Badeaux's in Des Allemands, Louisiana. For its soups the menu featured crab stew, shrimp stew, seafood gumbo and chicken and sausage gumbo, all at $5.50 a bowl or $3.50 for a cup. Plus soft-shell crab when in season for $10.95.

Heartened by seafood gumbo and soft-shell crab and a bill under $20, I continued along 14 and soon saw a pick-up, with a sign saying "live crab at 4 p.m." A jolly Cajun fisherman showed me two boxes, "big ones in the right go for $7 and the smaller ones $4". I asked for three large ones, figuring I could boil them up in my motel room on an electric plate stowed in the Plymouth Belvedere for just such purposes. "That'll be $2," said the fisherman, looking a bit scornful. It turns out it's $7 a dozen. So I bought a dozen and cooked them in my room in the Sunrise Motel on 90 on the edge of Lake Charles, letting them cool overnight and keeping them in my Coleman ice chest for dinner the next evening.

But that last night in Louisiana I had crawfish étouffée in a diner at Creole, which is the intersection of 82 and 27. This was after a beautiful back-road drive through sugarcane, sudden surprising vistas of shipyards, more cane, endless bayous, with the sun tilting down over the vast panorama of wetlands. I only had one really inedible meal between Landrum, SC, and Petrolia, northern California—a horrible plate of supposedly Mexican food in Truth or Consequences, NM. In that place in Creole, everything turned out right. Amidst Cajun oil riggers or fishermen belching and cursing over their Budweisers I had a great plate of crawfish in peppery rice for $10 and got back on the road with an optimistic outlook on the human condition. I stopped in the Sunrise Motel and fell asleep amidst the fragrance of the boiled crabs.

July 22

In Columbus, Texas, Jerry Mikeska's Bar-B-Q sign announces SEVEN DAYS WITHOUT BARBQ MAKES ONE WEAK. In the old days that probably would have read Makes A Man Weak. Not any more; and there were plenty of sisters chowing down. Mikeska's walls were profuse with the relicts of innumerable hunting excursions: mountain sheep, bear, moose, deer, bobcat. Mr. Mikeska himself, elderly and formally attired, moved from table to table, thanking the truckers, commuters and tourists for coming by. Old world courtesy and we all felt the better for it.

I headed northwest again, planning to spend the night in Abilene but suddenly saw a sign for Midland, and resolved to pay my respects to the childhood home of George W. Bush, not least memorable as the place where he later lived with his bride, the divine Laura.

You can see why George Bush doesn't believe in global warming. Having grown up in West Texas summers he doubtless believes it can never get any hotter. It was 101F at 8.30 p.m. as I stopped to ask directions to motel row from the inhabitants of a Dairy Queen, two girls on an outing from Odessa (the grimier oil town down the Interstate a few miles) and a solitary Goth in traditional black garb.

Since Laura is the nation's First Librarian I thought it only right to visit Midland's library and was searching for it when I passed a building labeled Museum of the South West and stopped for a look. The first room had Audubon's prints of Texas animals from his last book, *Viviparous Quadrupeds of North America*, published between 1845 and 1848. Audubon died three years later. They are marvelous, and some of them, such as the ocelot and jaguar (now extinct in Texas), so lively looking that you'd swear the artist had sketched them from life. But by that time in his life Audubon rarely moved from his house on the Hudson, to which specimens arrived in various stages of putrefaction, sometimes pickled in rum.

There are two other splendid special collections in the Midland library, devoted to genealogy and petroleum. In a break from poring over Roemer's Texas I chatted with the curator of these collections, to be told that Laura Bush, née Welch, had worked as a librarian in Austin. In Midland she'd been a teacher. I've heard vulgar gossip about Laura's racy twenties before she settled down, and I thought there perhaps a tinge of disapproval in the voices of two ladies in the genealogy section when they discussed local history with me and made mention of "the Welch girl."

I rounded out the Midland visit with an excursion to the truly tremendous Permian Basin Petroleum Museum on Interstate 20, which does for hydrocarbons what the Uffizi does for the art of Renaissance Italy. The museum's entry is framed by two oil pumps, like triumphal gryphons. Here is to be found the famous map by O. C. Harper, done in 1924 and reckoned to be one of the most outstanding feats of reconnaissance geology in history. Harper accurately deduced the whereabouts of the vast oil resources of the Permian basin of West Texas and eastern New Mexico.

A year later other geologists, scouts and land speculators were rushing to Midland and had soon, as an oilman later recalled in a news story of the 1950s displayed in the museum, "married all but a few of the single girls who had finished high school and a few who had not. Whirlwind courtships of two weeks to a month prior to the wedding were not uncommon. The few remaining eligible single young girls had but to decide with whom and how many dates they would have each evening. The young women were outnumbered about six to one by the single young men."

By 1928 just one oil field, the 1,100-foot-deep Yates, was rated as having a daily production potential of 2.2 million barrels a day, just under the daily national consumption at that time of 2.6 million a day.

George Bush Sr. arrived in 1948, later recalling that "We all just wanted to make a lot of money quick." The time I interviewed her back in 1980 I thought Barbara Bush one of the meaner women I'd met in a long time, and looking at the photos in the oil museum you could see why she might have been bitter. To ship out from the East Coast first to broiling, oil-sodden Odessa and then in 1950 to broiling, oil-sodden Midland must have been a jarring experience. George Sr. never did make a big pile out of oil and neither did George W., who spent the '50s in Midland as a boy and returned there between 1975 and 1986 to try to make his pile.

It was hard to tear myself away, but the placed closed and I drove down the Interstate to seedy and depressed looking Odessa which one year edged Miami to become Murder Capital of the USA. The notorious aggressions of a slice of Odessa's citizenry probably accounts for the fact that the nearby, more prosperous and classy Midland county is Texas's rape capital on a per capita basis, according to Ms. Betty Dickerson of the Midland Rape Crisis Center. So much for the timeless values Bush claims to have imbibed in West Texas. Leaving Odessa I passed a sign for the Harvest Time Church: "Jesus Knows That Life Can Be Hard As Nails," then, to the right, black on gold and red, the more urgent, "ETERNITY, IT'S HELL WITHOUT JESUS."

July 25

Joe Pulitzer famously said, "A newspaper has no friends." Looking at the massed ranks of America's elites attending Katharine Graham's funeral in Washington last Monday, it's maybe churlish to recall that phrase, but it's true. At least in political terms Mrs. Graham had way too many friends. Her newspaper had its hour when she had real enemies, when Nixon's Attorney General was screaming his famous threat, and when Nixon was threatening to pull her company's Florida TV licenses.

The twin decisions, concerning the Pentagon Papers and Watergate, that made Mrs. Graham's name as a courageous publisher, came at precisely the moment when, in biographical terms, she was best equipped to handle pressure. She'd had eight years to overcome the initial timidities that bore down on her after Phil Graham's suicide left her with a newspaper she resolved to run herself. Yet the amiable but essentially conservative bipartisanship that had the notables of each incoming administration palavering happily in her dining room hadn't yet numbed the spinal nerve of the *Post* as any sort of spirited journalistic enterprise.

In late 1974, after Nixon had been tumbled, Mrs. Graham addressed the Magazine Publishers' Association and issued a warning: "The press these days should be rather careful about its role. We may have acquired some tendencies about over-involvement that we had better overcome. We had better not yield to the temptation to go on refighting the next war and see conspiracy and cover-up where they do not exist." She called for a return to basics. Journalists should "stop trying to be sleuths." In other words: The party's over, boys and girls! It's not our business to rock the boat. Did Mrs. Graham privately strong-arm her staff to follow her line? But editors and reporters are not slow to pick up clues as to the disposition of the person who pays the wages, and Mrs. Graham sent out plenty of those.

Mrs. Graham had plenty of reasons, material and spiritual, to find excessive boat-rocking distasteful. The family fortune, and the capital that bought and nourished the *Post*, was founded in part on Allied Chemical, the company run by her father Eugene Meyer. Perhaps because rabble-rousers had derisively taunted her as "Kepone Kate" after a bad Allied Chemical spill in the James River, we remember a hard edge in her voice when she deplored "those fucking environmentalists." Privately her language was salty.

In the early 1980s she associated increasingly with Warren Buffett, the Nebraska investor who bought 13 percent of the *Post*'s B stock and who was then riding high as America's most venerated stock player. Graham became a big-picture mogul, pickling herself in the sonorous platitudes of the Brandt Commission, on which she served. I do remember a very strange evening in a Washington nightclub with Lally Weymouth in the late 1970s in which Mrs. Buffett formally displayed her arts as a torch singer, followed with almost overconspicuous attention by Mrs. Graham and Mr. B.

Former mayor Marion Barry had some pro-forma kindly words for Katharine Graham after her death, but I've always thought that one decisive verdict on the *Post*'s performance in a city with a major black population came with that jury verdict acquitting Barry on a cocaine bust. Those jurors knew that the *Post*, along with the other

Powers That Be, was on the other side from Barry, and we've no doubt that firmed up their assessment of the evidence. In that quarter, for sure, neither the *Post* nor Mrs. Graham had an excessive amount of friends.

September 12

Did Osama bin Laden outwit US intelligence agencies in a deadly game of decoy or double bluff? Three weeks before the attack of September 11, security at the World Trade Center was abruptly heightened; six weeks before the attack a US Army base in New Jersey was placed on top security alert.

As regards the heightened security at the Trade Center, we are told that according to a businessman working in World Trade Building number 7 (the forty-one-story structure that collapsed after having been evacuated) "security was heightened three weeks ago, including the introduction for the first time of sniffer dogs and the physical search of all trucks prior to their being waved into the entrance from the street."

The US Army base in New Jersey is the Arsenal at Picatinny. At the start of July the Arsenal was placed at a very high state of alert, with some staff locked in their offices for a period.

Set this information against the fact that Osama bin Laden, now prime suspect, said in an interview three weeks ago with Abdel-Bari Atwan, the editor of the London-based *Al-Quds Al-Arabi* newspaper, that he planned "very, very big attacks against American interests."

So, was there an attempted attack some time in August, or was it merely a feint by the bin Laden units, to prompt an alert, then a relaxation of US security procedures?

The Pearl Harbor base containing America's naval might was thought to be invulnerable, yet in half an hour 2,000 were dead, and the cream of the fleet destroyed. This week, within an hour on the morning of September 11, security at three different airports was successfully breached, the crews of four large passenger jets efficiently overpowered, their cockpits commandeered, and navigation coordinates reset.

In three of the four missions the assailants succeeded probably far beyond the expectations of the planners. As a feat of suicidal aviation the Pentagon kamikaze assault was particularly audacious, with eyewitness accounts describing the Boeing 767 skimming the Potomac before driving right through the low-lying Pentagon perimeter, in a sector housing Planning and Logistics.

The two Trade Center buildings were struck at what structural engineers say were the points of maximum vulnerability.

The phrases "faceless coward" and "faceless enemy" have been bandied about. The lust for retaliation traditionally outstrips precision in identifying the actual assailant. The targets abroad will be all the usual suspects: rogue states (most of which, like the Taliban or Saddam Hussein, started off as creatures of US intelligence). The target at home will be the Bill of Rights.

The explosions were not an hour old before terror pundits like Anthony Cordesman, Wesley Clark, Robert Gates, and Lawrence Eagleburger were saying that these attacks had been possible "because America is a democracy," adding that now some democratic perquisites might have to be abandoned. What might this mean? Increased domestic snooping by US law enforcement and intelligence agencies; ethnic profiling; another drive for a national ID card system.

The aftermath of the attacks did not offer a flattering exhibition of America's leaders. For most of the day the only Bush who looked composed and in control was Laura, who happened to be waiting to testify on Capitol Hill. Her husband gave a timid and stilted initial reaction in Sarasota, Florida, then disappeared for an hour before resurfacing at Barksdale airbase in Shreveport, Louisiana, where he gave another flaccid address with every appearance of bring on tranquilizers. He was then flown to a bunker in Nebraska, before someone finally had the wit to suggest that the best place for an American President at a time of national emergency is the Oval Office.

Defense Secretary Donald Rumsfeld remained invisible most of the day, even though it would have taken him only a few short steps to get to the Pentagon pressroom and make some encouraging remarks. When he did finally appear the substance of his remarks and his demeanor were even more banal and unprepossessing than those of his commander in chief. At no point did Vice-President Cheney appear in public.

Absent national political leadership, the burden of rallying the nation fell as usual upon the TV anchors, all of whom seem to have resolved early on to lower the emotional temper, though Tom Brokaw did lisp a declaration of War against Terror. One of the more ironic sights was Dan Rather talking about retaliation against bin Laden. It was Rather, wrapped in a turban, who voyaged to the Hindu Kush in the early 1980s to send back paeans to the Mujahedeen (trained and supplied by the CIA in its largest ever operation), which ushered onto the world stage such well-trained cadres as those now deployed against America.

The eyewitness reports of the collapse of the two Trade Center buildings were not inspired, at least for those who have heard the famous eyewitness radio reportage of the crash of the Hindenberg Zeppelin in Lakehurst, New Jersey, in 1937 with the anguished cry of the reporter, "Oh the humanity, the humanity." Radio and TV reporters these days seem incapable of narrating an ongoing event with any sense of vivid language or dramatic emotive power.

The commentators were similarly incapable of explaining with any depth the likely context of the attacks. It was possible to watch the cream of the nation's political analysts and commentating classes, hour after hour, without ever hearing the word "Israel," unless in the context of a salutary teacher in how to deal with Muslims. One could watch hour after hour without hearing any intimation that these attacks might be the consequence of the recent Israeli rampages in the Occupied Territories that have included assassinations of Palestinian leaders and the slaughter of Palestinian civilians with the use of American aircraft; that these attacks might also stem from the sanctions against Iraq that have seen upward of a million children die; that these attacks might in part be a response to US cruise missile attacks on the Sudanese factories that had been loosely fingered by US intelligence as connected to bin Laden.

September 21

Faced with the great challenge of his speech to the joint session of Congress on Thursday night, the President managed the task capably enough. The speech was a declaration of lawlessness, with the concept of "justice" being reduced to that of the freedom to shoot the other guy on whatever terms America may find convenient. How else are we to interpret the much quoted line that "whether we bring our enemies to justice or bring justice to our enemies, justice will be done." This is the language of terrorism.

"Every nation in every region now has a decision to make," Bush declared. "Either you are with us or you are with the terrorists." Thus has the founding charter of the United Nations been finally discarded, even as a fig leaf, and the founding charter of NATO been reduced to a line from a western.

In terms of substance Bush has committed America and its allies to the overthrow of the Afghan Taliban, with occupation of Afghanistan apparently part of the schedule. Bush pronounces the forthcoming war as one between freedom and fear, with God most definitely on America's side. We are now witnessing the opening volleys of an assault on constitutional freedoms in this country by a government in which opposition has effectively been suspended.

As Bush talked about unified national purpose, the news cameras lingered on Rep. Barbara Lee of Berkeley, everlastingly to her credit the only member of Congress to vote against authorization of open-ended retaliation. Aside from Lee, there were few independent voices in Congress. Among them was the Texas libertarian Republican, Ron Paul, who told his colleagues, "Demanding domestic security in times of war invites carelessness in preserving civil liberties and the right of privacy. Frequently the people are only too anxious for their freedoms to be sacrificed on the altar of authoritarianism thought to be necessary to remain safe and secure."

Of great concern is Attorney General John Ashcroft's agenda, now being rushed to Congress. There are three components to what has been described as "the mother of all anti-terrorism bills": immigration; wiretapping and domestic intelligence surveillance; search and seizure. The bill sought by Ashcroft vests virtually unlimited authority in the US Attorney General to target non-citizens with arrest, indefinite incarceration, and deportation. The arrests can be made on the basis of secret evidence with little or no opportunity for meaningful judicial review.

Ashcroft is seeking expanded wiretapping power, plus enhanced ability to snoop on e-sites. The bill seeks roving wiretap ability, meaning that the police could tap any phone used by their target, no matter to whom that phone might belong. As usual, an emergency is being used as the pretext for a far wider assault on basic constitutional rights.

Absent dropping a Big One, how can the necessary revenge be exacted? Cruise missiles, used by Bill Clinton as a way of expressing his displeasure at Sudan, may be useful for destroying pharmaceutical factories, hospitals, even defense ministries, but the body counts are not dramatic. But who or what is there to bomb in Afghanistan? A land invasion in force, a blitzkrieg sparing nothing and no one? Afghanistan is famously the graveyard of punitive missions embarked upon by the Great Powers, as the British discovered in the nineteenth century and the Soviets in the 1980s.

One familiar way extricating oneself from confrontation with an unsuitable foe is to substitute a more satisfactory one. Already there's a lobby, the most conspicuous of whom is former CIA chief James Woolsey, pressing the case for Iraq as possible sponsor or co-sponsor of the World Trade Center attacks. So sanctions against Iraq could be strengthened, its cities bombed and perhaps even another invasion attempted.

Bush's entourage have been talking in Mao-like terms about "protracted war," or a "war in the shadows." The purely nominal ban against US government-sponsored assassination (there have been numerous CIA-backed attempts against Castro since the mid-1970s ban, if you believe the Cubans) will be lifted.

On the morning of September 11 Judge Henry Wood was trying, of all things, an American Airlines crash-damage case in the Federal District court in Little Rock, Arkansas. In the wake of the attacks there were orders to close the courthouse. All obeyed, except Judge Wood, aged eighty-three, who insisted that jury and lawyers and attendants remain in place. Turning down a plea for mistrial by the defendant, Wood said, "This looks like an intelligent jury to me and I didn't want the judicial system interrupted by a terrorist act, no matter how horrible."

Wood's was the proper reaction. America could do with more of what used to be called the Roman virtues. A monstrous thing happened in New York, but should this be a cause for a change in national consciousness? Is America so frail? People talk of the trauma of another Pearl Harbor, but truth to say, the trauma in the aftermath of the Day of Infamy in 1941 was far in excess of what the circumstances warranted, and assiduously fanned by the government for reasons of state. Ask the Japanese Americans who were interned.

Why, for that matter, ground all air traffic and semi-paralyze the economy, with further interminable and useless inconveniences promised to travelers in the months and possibly years to come? Could any terrorist have hoped not only to bring down the Trade Center towers but also destroy the airline industry? It would have been far better to ask passengers to form popular defense committees on every plane, bring their own food and drink, keep alert for trouble and look after themselves. A properly vigilant democracy of the air. Remember, even if there were no X-ray machines, no searches, no passenger checks, it would still be far more dangerous to drive to the airport than to get on a plane.

What sort of accommodation should America make right now? How about one with the history of the past hundred years, in an effort to improve the moral world climate of the next hundred years? We use the word accommodation in the sense of an effort to get to grips with history, as inflicted by the powerful upon the weak. We have been miserably failed by our national media here, as Jude Wanniski, political economist and agitator of conventional thinking, remarked in the course of a well-merited attack on "bipartisanship," which almost always means the obdurate determination to pursue a course of collective folly without debate: "It is because of this bipartisanship that our press corps has become blind to the evil acts we commit as a nation."

America has its enemies circling the campfires and threatening the public good. They were rampant the day before the September

11 attacks, with the prospect of deflation, sated world markets, idled capacity, shrinking social services. Is ranting about Kabul and throwing money at the Pentagon going to solve those national emergencies?

There is no compelling reason to accept that bin Laden is the Master Terror Mind of the World. On some fairly persuasive accounts, his resources have dwindled, both in terms of money and equipment. He lives in a cave without phone or fax or email, hungrily devouring long-outdated editions of newspapers brought by visitors. He may be an inspirational force to the terrorist cadres, but we strongly doubt that he is the hands-on master of terror portrayed by the administration, manipulating world financial markets.

A great nation does not respond to a single hour of terrible mayhem in two cities by hog-tying itself with new repressive laws and abuses of constitutional freedoms, like Gulliver doing the work of the Lilliputians and lashing himself to the ground with a thousand cords.

September 22

Deliberating on a back road whether to make a detour and visit the Gila Cliff Dwellings, I finally decide it's too late and swing back onto a larger road. Red lights promptly go on and I see a state patrol car with two cops in it. After a long interval during which they check me out, a young cop comes over and leans through the passenger window. He alleges I rolled past a red stop sign and then asks me what I'm doing in this part of New Mexico.

His ferrety little eyes swivel around the back of the station wagon, linger on some cactuses I've picked up in a nursery in Truth or Consequences, linger further on my Coleman ice chest and then come back to my car papers. Either this is a training session for Ferret Eyes or a pretext stop to see if I'm carrying drugs. Armed with my license and car papers the two spend another twenty minutes on their radio. Finally Ferret Eyes comes back and lays a $49 citation on me, inquiring as to whether I plead guilty as charged or want to fight it out in the courts. This all seems hurried and devoid of due process, but I tell him I won't fight it. I roll on my way, soured on New Mexico.

In contrast to the carefree posture of the Baptists, leaving God to sort it all out, the signs outside the high schools mostly flaunt the worry-ridden "Have a Safe Summer," until I get to Globe, NM, a mining town on State Highway 70, whose high-school sign dares to say, "Have a Happy Summer."

September 24

Along State Highway 70 I rolled through Globe. And later on route 60 I was afforded a definitive vignette of the role of environmental regulation, in the form of a vast, awful mine, like a cross between something out of Caspar Friedrich and a Fritz Lang nightmare. A mountain of shale, its base oozing green puss, topped by a mining building, the whole thing a thousand feet high, and right at the bottom, next to the highway, a tiny shack labeled "Environmental Compliance" and next to this the cryptic sign, "Zero and Beyond."

Then came more mines and astounding red-rock sandstone formations, before, ten minutes later, on the other side of the range, a sign for the Boyce Thompson Arboretum. I rolled right past it and then, always a sucker for gardens and arboreta, made a U and went in. So glad I did, since these 1,075 acres of the Sonoran desert nestling at the base of Picketpost mountain now comprise one of the premier horticultural attractions of the country, for which we can thank William Boyce Thompson and, no doubt, Mrs. Thompson.

Thompson was a mining engineer from Montana, who made his pile figuring out where to dig some of the big holes I had been gazing at a few minutes earlier. Flush with income from the Inspiration Consolidated Copper Company at Globe-Miami, Thompson won his honorary title of "Colonel" by leading a Red Cross expedition to Russia in 1917.

As he marched across the arid Asian steppes towards St. Petersburg, the Colonel became mightily impressed not only by the extreme hunger he witnessed on all sides but also by the fact that what little food the locals had often came from plants. All foods, the Colonel suddenly appreciated, come originally from plants. Back in Arizona he swiftly laid plans for an arid land arboretum where plants from the world's deserts could be brought together, their uses assayed and their seeds distributed.

Work began in 1923 and by 1929 it was up and running as a joint project of the arboretum, the Forest Service, the Bureau of Indian Affairs, and the Civilian Conservation Corps. These days there are over 3,000 different plants flourishing at Boyce Thompson, and among the beneficiaries of the Colonel are sperm whales, a substitute for whose oil is the oil pressed from seeds of the desert jojoba bush, now planted on a large scale in Arizona.

I wandered about in the 105 degree heat and soon saw in the distance the tapering trunk, some thirty-five feet high, of an *Idria columnaris*, otherwise known as the Boojum, whose erroneous identification proved so fatal to the baker in Lewis Carroll's masterpiece, *The Hunting of the Snark*. All around were marvelous cacti and kindred succulents such as euphorbias and agaves.

September 26

I had been planning to head straight across Texas to El Paso with a detour south to Big Bend Ranch State Park which sits on the north bank of the Rio Grande, also passing through Marfa which used to, maybe still does, feature Rock Hudson's house in *Giant*, then coming north again to the Balmorhea springs, with beautiful stone work done by the Civilian Conservation Corps (CCC) in the 1930s. I was there years ago, in 1988, while driving a 1960 Plymouth Valiant across country. But this July it was ferociously hot and though the '62 Plymouth station wagon was running well, its venerable air conditioning more than satisfactory, I didn't fancy the thought of breaking down in the middle of the Cuesta de Burro mountains.

So, prior to the visit to Midland, I headed northwest for the Texas hill country, the region of the Pedernales often associated with the ranch and memory of LBJ, and an hour later found myself in Fredericksburg, which offers the curious traveler not only the Admiral Nimitz museum of the Pacific War, plus the George H. Bush Gallery, but also a profusion of German restaurants, each displaying meat-heavy, schlag-strewn menus in the broiling Texan forenoon.

Consulting the copy of *Roemer's Texas* I'd found in the public library in Midland I found out why. This same Friedrich von Roemer is noted as the father of Texan geology, hence grandfather of the delighted cries of Texan oilmen whenever the geology of Texas yielded its proper bounty. In 1845 Roemer visited Texas and published an excellent account of his explorations four years later, correctly deprecating most previous writings on the state as "crude untruths and fabulous exaggerations."

Across the Guadeloupe mountain range and down into Alamogordo, sixty miles south of the Trinity site, I found point zero for the explosion of America's first nuclear device. It's hard to drive far across the American West without passing a military base or a prison. I drive into White Sands National Monument, which is surrounded by the White Sands Missile Range, some 4,000 square miles of desert which hosted America's first efforts to adapt German rockets, with Nazi scientists toiling happily in their new homes, spirited westward by the same US intelligence services that extricated Klaus Barbie and sent him to Bolivia.

One such scientist was Georg Richkey, who was the supervisor at the Mettelwerk missile complex that used slave labor from the Dora concentration camp. In retaliation against sabotage to the plant—prisoners would piss on electrical equipment, causing spectacular malfunctions—Richkey would hang them twelve at a time from factory cranes, with wooden sticks shoved into their mouths to muffle their cries. Later US intelligence officers obstructed efforts by the Allies, and the US State Department, to try Richkey as a war criminal, and brought him to the US where he resumed his missile work at Wright AFB.

I drove for a while through the white gypsum dunes that constitute the prime allurement of the Monument, whose best feature is actually the adobe reception and office buildings designed and put up by Hispanic laborers under the supervision of a Kansas journalist who had successfully campaigned for the Monument in the 1930s. The buildings are now deservedly on the register of historic structures. That evening I drive along the main street of Truth or Consequences. I notice that the South West Pharmacy has a sign below it, "Ask Us

About Free Prozac." Below is another sign for the Wellness Store, "A Neural Pharmacy." Across the street I see the Hot Springs Health Center. I pick the Trail motel ($24, good wide front court, nice sign, Christians, no phone in the room).

As for the town's name, I'd always imagined it came from some cowboy bet in the 1880s. Not a bit of it. In 1950, so the Chaparral Guide in my motel told me, NBC TV and radio producer Ralph Edwards took the occasion of the tenth anniversary of his program "Truth or Consequences" to put out the word that he wished "some town in the US liked and respected our show so much that it would like to change its name to Truth or Consequences." The Mexico State Bureau of tourism promptly relayed his hope to the manager of the Hot Springs Chamber of Commerce—at long last an opportunity to shake off the town's status of second-best to Hot Springs Arkansas, playpen of Boy Clinton. In a special election, 1,294 of the citizenry voted for the change with 294 opposed. Amid cries from the vanquished traditionalists there was soon a second poll with the same result. The people were asked to vote again on the matter in 1964 and yet again in 1967, which suggests the diehards were still fighting.

September 28

Drive through the interior of California and you drive past prisons. In Adelanto the mother and daughter who ran the local Days Inn told me that they already had two in town, one state and one federal, and were scheduled for three more. Higher up Interstate 5 you pass Avenal and Coalinga, with others over the horizon. In San Jose the headlines spoke of further implosion in the e-markets. Hewlett Packard was set to lay off thousands worldwide.

I chugged up through the wine country and into Humboldt County and in mid-afternoon, 4,000 miles, and ten days after I left Landrum, SC, having needed only one quart of oil and having established an average of 17 mpg, the '62 Plymouth Belvedere swung into my yard in Petrolia. Five minutes later two F-14s, or maybe F-18s, flew down the tiny valley at 500 feet, amid a deafening roar. "The sound of freedom," they used to call it. These were pilots being assholes. I watched my horses jump about four feet in the air. A mile down river, Margie Smith's old horse jumped too, wounded itself on a fence post and bled to death.

November 9

Open the November 5 edition of *Newsweek* and here's Jonathan Alter, munching coyly on the week's hot topic, namely the propriety of the FBI torturing obdurate September 11 suspects in the Bureau's custody here in the United States. Alter says no to cattleprods, but continues the sentence with the observation that something is needed to "jump start" the stalled investigation. The tone is lightly facetious, as in "Couldn't we at least subject them to psychological torture, like tapes of dying rabbits or high-decibel rap?" There are respectful references to Alan Dershowitz (who is running around the country promoting the idea of "torture warrants" issued by judges) and to Israel, where, "until 1999 an interrogation technique called 'shaking' was legal. It entailed holding a smelly bag over a suspect's head in a dark room, then applying scary psychological torment … Even now, Israeli law leaves a little room for 'moderate physical pressure' in what are called 'ticking time bomb' cases."

As so often with unappealing labor, Alter arrives at the usual American solution: outsource the job: "we'll have to think about transferring some suspects to our less squeamish allies, even if that's hypocritical."

What's striking about Alter's commentary and others in the same idiom is the abstraction from reality, as if torture is so indisputably a dirty business that all painful data had best be avoided. One would have thought it hard to be frivolous about the subject of torture, but Alter managed it.

2002

February 22

The hoof prints of Lucifer are everywhere. And since this is America, eternally at war with the darker forces, the foremost Enemy Within is sex, no quarter given. Here are some bulletins from the battlefront, drawn from a smart essay on "Sex and Empire" in the March issue of *The Guide*, a Boston-based monthly travel magazine, whose features and editorials have "about the best gay sex politics around," according to Bill Dobbs of Queerwatch, whom I take as my advisor in these matters.

In February 2000, eighteen-year-old Matthew Limon had oral sex with a fourteen-year-old male schoolmate. A Kansas court sentenced him to seventeen years in prison, a punishment upheld by a federal court in February.

Last July, Ohio sentenced twenty-two-year-old Brian Dalton to seven years in prison because of sex fantasies he wrote in his diary. A woman teacher in Arizona up on trial last month for a relationship with a seventeen-year-old boy faces 100 years in prison.

Apropos the triumph of identity politics across the last thirty years, Bill Andriette, the author of "Sex and Empire," remarks wittily that "In America, your clout as identity group depends how much of an enhanced sentence someone gets for dissing you" and then observes that "The same PR machinery that produces all these feel-good identities naturally segues into manufacturing demonic ones, indeed, creates a demand for them. The ascription of demonic sexual identities onto people helps drive repression, from attacks on Internet freedom to sex-predator laws. Identity politics works gear-in-gear with a fetishization of children, because the young represent one class of persons free of identity, the last stand of unbranded humanity, precious and rare as virgin prairie."

This brings us into an Olympian quadruple axis of evil: sexually violent predators (familiarly known as SVPs) preying on minors of the same sex. There's no quarrelling between prosecutor and judge, jury and governor, Supreme Court and shrinks. Lock 'em up and throw away the key.

I went to a Bar Mitzvah in Berkeley the other day, and after listening to passages from the Torah transmitting Yahweh's extremely rigorous prescriptions for his temple, right down to the use of acacia wood and dolphin skins, heard Marita Mayer, an attorney in the public defender's office in Contra Costa county, describe the truly harrowing business of trying to save her clients—SVPs—from indeterminate confinement in Atascadero, the state's prime psychiatric bin within its prison system.

Among Mayer's clients are men who pleaded guilty to sex crimes in the mid-1980s, mostly rape of an adult woman, getting a fixed term of anywhere from ten to fifteen years. In the good old days, if you worked and behaved yourself, you'd be up for parole after serving half the sentence.

In California, as in many other states, SVP laws took effect in the mid-1990s, on the crest of the repressive wave of hysteria over child sex abuse and crime generally: mandatory minimum sentences, reduction or elimination of statutes of limitation, erosion of the right to confront witnesses, community notification of released sex offenders, surgical and chemical castration, prohibition of mere possession of certain printed materials, this last an indignity previously only accorded atomic energy secrets.

So California passes its SVP law in January of 1996, decreeing that those falling into the category of SVP have a sickness that requires treatment and cannot be freed, until a jury agrees unanimously that they are no longer a danger to the community. The adjudicators vary from state to state. Sometimes it's a jury, or merely a majority of jurors, sometimes a judge, sometimes a panel, sometimes an (unlicensed) "multidisciplinary team."

Mayer's clients, serving out their years in Pelican Bay or Vacaville or San Quentin, counting the months down to parole date, suddenly find themselves back to jail in Contra Costa county, told they've got a mental disorder and can't be released till a jury decides they're no danger to the community. Off to Atascadero they go for a two-year term, at the end of which they get a hearing, and almost always another two-year term.

"Many of them refuse treatment," Mayer says. "They refuse to sign a piece of paper saying they have a mental disease." Of course they do. Why sign a document saying that for all practical purposes you may well be beyond reform or redemption, that you are Evil by nature, not just a guy who did something bad and paid the penalty?

It's the AA model of boozing as sin, having to say you are an alcoholic and will always be in that condition, one lurch away from perdition. Soon everything begins to hinge on someone's assessment of your state of mind, your future intentions. As with the damnable liberal obsession with hate-crime laws, it's a nosedive into the category of "thought crimes."

There the SVPs sit in Atascadero surrounded by psych techs eager to test all sorts of statistical and behavioral models, phallometric devices designed to assist in the persuasion of judge and jury that yes, the prisoner has a more than 50 percent likelihood of exercising his criminal sexual impulses, should he be released.

Thus, by the circuitous route of "civil commitment" (confining persons deemed to be a danger to themselves or others) we have ended up with a situation that, from the constitutional point of view, is indeed absolutely Evil: that of being held in preventive detention or locked up twice for the same crime.

"It's using psychiatry, like religion, to put people away," Mayer concludes. "Why not hire an astrologer or a goat-entrail reader to predict what the person might do? Why not the same for robbers as for rapists? What's happening is double jeopardy. If we don't watch it, it will come back to haunt us. People don't care about child rapists, but the Constitution is about protections. I think it's shredding the Constitution. I get into trouble because they say I'm into jury nullification and that's not allowed. Most of my clients tell me it's worse in Atascadero than in the regular prisons. How do I feel about these guys? When I talk to my clients I don't presume to think what they'll do in future. I believe in redemption. I don't look at them as sexually violent predators, I see them as sad sacks, they have to register. They could be hounded from county to county. Even for a tiny crime they'll be put away. Their lives are in ruin. I pity them."

But not goat entrails, surely. The animal rights crowd would never stand for it.

February 28

Chalk up another milestone for sex ed. The University of California at Berkeley has put a "male sexuality" class on ice after the campus newspaper, the *Daily Californian*, published allegations that as part of their course students were taken to a strip club where they watched their instructor have sex, and also participated in an "orgy" at an party. A female sexuality course is also under review.

As news of the Berkeley ban came in I happened to be leafing through the analysis of a man code-named "Beta," the foot fetishist in *Sexual Aberrations*, written by Freud's sometime pal Wilhelm Stekel. "I must mention," Stekel writes with perhaps excessive enthusiasm, "Beta wasn't in the least animated by women's ankles, legs or lovely shoes." No, the dirty beast "wanted to see the shoe fit tightly" and "is promptly enlivened by the sight of corns and envies every chiropodist he sees. He likes only male feet: red, swollen, dirty, sweaty and inflamed feet."

Beta craved to view and smell only the feet of the poor, not out of class solidarity but because their economic condition meant they had badly fitting shoes in which they worked hard all day: "On warm days, he goes to the Danube where poor working men may be found in droves, bathing their sweaty, swollen feet. It is the sight of these large, red feet that then gives him a thrill. He rushes home to masturbate."

March 2

Life is returning to normalcy in Kandahar after the grim supervision of the Taliban clerics. Joyful sons of Sodom are to be seen driving along the boulevards of the ancient city, their catamites demurely installed in the passenger seat. Kandahar has long been fabled as the San Francisco of South Asia.

It seems that the rape of young boys by warlords was one of the key factors behind Mullah Omar's mobilizing of the Taliban. There was a famous fracas in 1994 when two warlords faced off in a dispute over which of them would have the right to rape an attractive young fellow who had fallen into their clutches. There was gunplay in which civilians were killed. Eventually the lad was freed by Mullah Omar's group and the one-eyed zealot was promptly inundated with requests to help in other such disputes.

The inhabitants of Kabul, who had seen their city devastated and thousands killed in the war between muj warlords, similarly yearned for the security, albeit puritanical, offered by the Taliban. Farmers and poor city dwellers who had seen mass rapes of their daughters by the warlords' armed rabbles also strongly supported the Taliban, reckoning that the compulsory burkas were no bad thing if it meant the safety of women going out in public.

One of Omar's first decrees when the Taliban took power in 1994 was the suppression of homosexuality. Accused sodomites endured Trial by Wall Push. In one such trial in February of 1998, "three men sentenced to death for sodomy in Kandahar were taken to the base of a huge mud and brick wall, which was pushed over by tank." Two of them died, but in an instructive example of how the Taliban tempered its stern ways with an acknowledgement of the capricious workings of Allah, one crawled away to live and love another day.

But now that pre-Taliban normalcy is returning to Kandahar, just as it is to the rest of Afghanistan, tens of thousands are fleeing to Pakistan to escape banditry and starvation. "One can see the pairs returning," Tim Reid reports in the London *Times*. "Usually a heavily bearded man, seated next to, or walking with, a clean-shaven, fresh faced youth." He adds that "it is usually a terrible fate for the boys concerned" but they get out of poverty. "Once the boy falls into the man's clutches—nearly always men with a wife and family—he is marked for life, although the Kandaharis accept these relationships as part of their culture."

March 12

Back in April 1989, a Billy Graham memo to Nixon was made public. It took the form of a secret letter from Graham, dated April 15, 1969, drafted after he had met with Graham in Bangkok with missionaries from Vietnam. These men of God said that if the peace talks in Paris were to fail, Nixon should step up the war and bomb the dikes. Such an act, Graham wrote excitedly, "could overnight destroy the economy of North Vietnam."

Graham lent his imprimatur to this recommendation. Thus the preacher was advocating a policy to the US Commander in Chief that on Nixon's own estimate would have killed a million people. The disclosure of Graham as an aspirant war criminal did not excite any commotion when it became public in 1989, twenty years after it was written. I recall finding a small story in the *Syracuse Herald-Journal*. No one thought to chide Graham or even question him on the matter.

Very different has been the reception of a new tape revealing Graham, Nixon and Haldeman palavering about what Graham refers to as the Jewish "stranglehold" on Hollywood and the media. In this 1972 Oval Office session Nixon raises the topic, saying "we can't talk about it publicly." The President cites Paul Keyes, a political conservative who was executive producer of the NBC hit *Rowan and Martin's Laugh-In*, as telling him that "eleven of the twelve writers are Jewish." "That right?" says Graham, prompting Nixon to claim that *Life* magazine, *Newsweek*, the *New York Times*, the *Los Angeles Times*, and others, are "totally dominated by the Jews." Nixon says network TV anchors Howard K. Smith, David Brinkley, and Walter Cronkite are "front men who may not be of that persuasion," but that their writers are "95 percent Jewish."

"This stranglehold has got to be broken or the country's going down the drain," the nation's best-known preacher declares. "You believe that?" Nixon asks. "Yes, sir," Graham says. "Oh, boy," replies Nixon. "So do I. I can't ever say that but I believe it." "No, but if you get elected a second time, then we might be able to do something," Graham replies.

Magnanimously Nixon concedes that this does not mean "that all the Jews are bad" but that most are left-wing radicals who want "peace at any price except where support for Israel is concerned. The best Jews are actually the Israeli Jews." "That's right," agrees Graham, who later concurs with a Nixon assertion that a "powerful bloc" of Jews confronts Nixon in the media. "And they're the ones putting out the pornographic stuff," Graham adds.

Later Graham says that "a lot of the Jews are great friends of mine. They swarm around me and are friendly to me. Because they know I am friendly to Israel and so forth. They don't know how I really feel about what they're doing to this country." After Graham's departure Nixon says to Haldeman, "You know it was good we got this point about the Jews across." "It's a shocking point," Haldeman replies. "Well," says Nixon, "it's also, the Jews are an irreligious, atheistic, immoral bunch of bastards."

Within days of these exchanges becoming public the eighty-three-year old Graham was hauled from his semi-dotage, and impelled to express public contrition. "Experts" on Graham were duly cited as expressing their "shock" at Graham's White House table talk.

Why the shock? Don't they know that this sort of stuff is consonant with the standard conversational bill of fare at 75 percent of the country clubs in America, not to mention many a Baptist soiree? Nixon thought American Jews were lefty peaceniks who dominated the Democratic Party and were behind the attacks on him. Graham reckoned it was Hollywood Jews who had sunk the nation in porn. Haldeman agreed with both of them. At whatever level of fantasy they were all acknowledging power. But they didn't say they wanted to kill a million Jews. That's what Graham said about the Vietnamese and no one raised a bleat.

April 23

Late in the evening in back-road America you tend to pick the motels with a few cars parked in front of the rooms. There's nothing less appealing than an empty courtyard, with maybe Jeffrey Dahmer or Norman Bates waiting to greet you in the Reception office. The all-night clerk at the Lincoln Motel (three cars out front) in Austin, Nevada, who checked me in at around 11.30 p.m. a few nights ago, told me she was eighty-one, and putting in two part-time jobs, the other at the library, to help her pay her heating bills since she couldn't make it on her Social Security.

She imparted this info without self-pity as she took my $29.50, saying that business in Austin last fall had been brisk and that the fifty-seven motel beds available in the old mining town had been filled with crews laying fiber-optic cable along the side of the road, which in the case of Austin meant putting it twenty feet under the graveyard that skirts the road just west of town.

Earlier that day, driving from Utah through the Great Basin along US-50, billed as "the loneliest road," I'd seen these cables, blue and green and maybe two inches in diameter, sticking out of the ground on the outskirts of Ely, as if despairing at the prospect of the Great Salt Lake desert stretching ahead, through league after league of sagebrush.

So we can run fiber-optic cable through the western deserts but not put enough money in the hands of eighty-one-year-olds so they don't have to pull all-night shifts clerking in motels. At least the lady in Austin was spry and interested in life, refreshed by her intermittent naps on the couch in the sitting room off the reception office, dipping into her book, with the motel cat to keep her company, across the road from the International Café, which serves good breakfasts and decent drinks from a magnificent wooden bar that came round the Horn from Europe back in Austin's mining heyday in the 1870s.

People who drive or lecture their way through the American interior usually notice the same thing, which is that you can have rational conversations with people about the Middle East, about George W. Bush, and other topics certain to arouse unreasoning passion among sophisticates on either coast.

April 24

The ripe tones of Archbishop Mahony of Los Angeles filled my house last week, courtesy of National Public Radio. Mahoney spoke of his horror, his shame, at the stories of priestly abuse. He apologized to the victims. The mellifluous sanctimony of his penitence filled the room with such unction that I burst out laughing. What a surprise it all is! Priests hitting on altar boys! Priests molesting children. We're shocked, shocked!

When Oscar Wilde was packed off to Reading Jail in 1895 for sodomy, the railway trains to Brighton and Dover were soon replete with panicked gays fleeing England to Paris. Hundreds of Catholic priests here, many of them in retirement, must be asking themselves whether it might be prudent to remove themselves from the jurisdiction until the heat dies down.

It was bound to happen. Five years ago a senior dignitary in the Roman Catholic hierarchy confided that over the previous decade the Church had paid out over a billion dollars in out-of-court settlements as well as court fights on priest abuse cases.

Anyone with any knowledge of these cases knows perfectly well that this is no matter of a few rotten apples in the barrel. Sometimes, hearing about one priestly molester after another, one has the impression that not only has the Catholic Church been the prime sanctuary for repressed gays for the past several hundred years but that there isn't a priest alive that hasn't at some point made advances to an altar boy or boy scout. At least in the Middle Ages they got off with the nuns, or in the nineteenth century when they could afford domestics, the maid.

And certainly the Church has protected these priests, moved them around the country, away from an area where their activities had become known. The Church has some very dingy closets to clean out.

May 15

THE ROOTS OF WAR RHETORIC

Dear Sir,
I was amused to learn from Alexander Cockburn that the Vietnam War was caused by Ian Fleming, the creator of James Bond. It is tempting to classify this as a fine example of the Mendocino School of deductive logic. In fact, Mr. Cockburn joins a respected group of American social critics with his claim.

In *Life on the Mississippi*, Mark Twain suggests that Sir Walter Scott caused the American Civil War. It seems that the romantic tales of chivalry so imbued the antebellum Southern culture that military conflict was widely supported throughout years of unbelievable destruction. There is a modicum of truth in each claim.

I would suggest a more likely literary trigger to the Vietnam War is *Profiles in Courage*. The author of that work, John F. Kennedy, was certain to believe in the ideals he portrayed, and in fact lived. Sadly, he was also in a position to act on those beliefs.

Sincerely,
Edwin Shelby, Fountain Hills, Arizona

Alexander Cockburn replies: Of all rhetorical modes, irony and hyperbole are the most perilous. There were people who believed Swift's *Modest Proposal* was for real, Shelby among them no doubt.

May 16

Over the past twenty years I've learned there's a quick way of figuring just how badly Israel is behaving. There's a brisk uptick in the number of articles here accusing "the left" of anti-Semitism. Of course the rhetorical trick is to conflate "Israel" or "the State of Israel" with "Jews" and argue that they are synonymous. Ergo, to criticize Israel is to be anti-Semitic.

These days you can't even say that the *New York Times* is owned by a Jewish family without risking charges that you stand in Goebbels's shoes. I even got accused of anti-Semitism the other day for mentioning that the Jews founded Hollywood, which they most certainly did, as recounted in a funny and informative book published in 1988, *An Empire of Their Own: How the Jews Invented Hollywood* by Neal Gabler.

The encouraging fact is that despite the efforts of the Southern Poverty Law Center to drum up funds by hollering that the Nazis are about to march down Main Street, there's remarkably little anti-Semitism in the US, and almost none that I've ever been able to detect on the American left, which is of course amply stocked with non-self-hating Jews.

It's comical to find the left's assailants trudging all the way back to Leroi Jones and the '60s to dig up the necessary anti-Semitic jibes. The less encouraging fact is that there's not nearly enough criticism of Israel's ghastly conduct towards Palestinians, which in its present phase is testing the waters for reaction here to a major ethnic cleansing of Palestinians, just as Rep. Dick Armey called for.

It's not anti-Semitic to denounce ethnic cleansing, a strategy which, according to recent polls, around half of all Israeli Jews now heartily endorse. In this instance the left really has nothing to apologize for, but those who accuse of it of anti-Semitism certainly do. They're apologists for policies put into practice by racists, ethnic cleansers, and in Sharon's case, an unquestioned war criminal who should be in the dock for his conduct.

July 19

Last week *Sight and Sound* released its list of "the top 10 films of all time." My list:

1. *The Girl Can't Help It*, 1956, written and directed by Frank Tashlin. (Also author of the incomparable *Bear That Wasn't*, very influential on my childhood.)

2. *Invasion of the Body Snatchers*, 1956, based on a story by Jack Finney, screenplay by Daniel Mainwaring, maybe with input from Sam Peckinpah; directed by Don Siegel.

3. *Sweet Smell of Success*, 1957, written by Clifford Odets and Ernest Lehman; directed by Alexander Mackendrick. Best thing ever done on the press.

4. *Some Like It Hot*, 1959, written by Billy Wilder and I.A.L. Diamond; directed by Billy Wilder. The perfect movie.

5. *La Dolce Vita*, 1960, written by Fellini and Flaiano; directed by Federico Fellini. (I know, I know. What about all the other Italians? But this one did have Anita Ekberg dancing in the fountain.)

6. *Jason and the Argonauts*, 1963, written by Beverley Cross and Jan Read; directed by Don Chaffey. Peplums are my great love.

7. *Pierrot Le Fou*, 1965, written and directed by Jean-Luc Godard, with Anna Karina. Wonderful color.

8. *The Fantastic Voyage*, 1966, adapted by David Duncan from an Otto Klement–Jay Lewis Bixby story; directed by Richard Fleischer. With Raquel Welch and a terrific scene of Donald Pleasance being eaten by white antibodies. I think it prefigures the AIDS epidemic.

9. *Life of Brian*, 1979, written by Terry Jones, Graham Chapman, John Cleese, Terry Gilliam, Eric Idle, Michael Palin; directed by Terry Jones. World's greatest political movie. About the sectarian left, made when the awful Trot Gerry Healy was wooing the Redgrave family.

10. *Eating Raoul*, 1982, written and directed by Paul Bartel. Perfect Happy Enders film.

Haven't seen too many movies since then, though I watched a funny parody of teen girl films the other day in a motel in Los Angeles. I loved *Homeward Bound: The Incredible Journey*, watched without headphones on a plane between NYC and LAX and wept when the Golden Retriever came over the hill at the end. The tough A&R chick in the window seat stared at my tear-stained cheeks, revolted. It came as a big shock when they told me there was voice-over.

As can be seen, movies aren't a big thing in my life. I'd like to have included Bergman's *Smiles of a Summer's Night* (another from that amazing cultural year of 1955), if only because I took Judith Oakley to the Headington Classic in Oxford to watch it in 1962 and held the door open for her. She slammed it on my fingers as a reproof to my male chauvinist profession of "manners," which was my introduction to the Women's Movement.

September 7

Amid the elegies for the dead and the ceremonies of remembrance, seditious questions intrude: Is there really a war on terror; and if one is indeed being waged, what are its objectives?

The Taliban are out of power. *Papaver somniferum*, the opium poppy, blooms once more in Afghan pastures. The military budget is up. The bluster war on Iraq blares from every headline. On the home front the war on the Bill of Rights is set at full throttle.

On this latter point we can turn to Merle Haggard, the bard of blue-collar America, the man who saluted the American flag more than a generation ago in songs such as the "Fighting Side of Me" and "Okie from Muskogee." Haggard addressed a concert crowd in Kansas City a few days ago in the following terms: "I think we should give John Ashcroft a big hand ... (pause) ... right in the mouth!" Haggard went on to say, "the way things are going I'll probably be thrown in jail tomorrow for saying that, so I hope y'all will bail me out."

It will take generations to roll back the constitutional damage done in the wake of the September 11 attacks. Emergency laws lie around for decades like rattlesnakes in summer grass. As Joanne Mariner of Human Rights Watch points out to me, one of the main legal precedents that the government is using to justify detaining "enemy combatants" without trial or access to a lawyer is an old strike-breaking decision. The government's August 27 legal brief in the Padilla "enemy combatant" case relies heavily on *Moyer v. Peabody*, a Supreme Court case that dates back to 1909.

The case involved Charles Moyer, President of the Western Federation of Miners, a Colorado trade union that fought for such radical reforms as safe working conditions, an end to child labor, and payment in money rather than in company scrip. As part of a concerted effort to crush the union, the governor of Colorado had declared a state of insurrection, called out the state militia, and detained Moyer for two and half months without probable cause or due process of law.

In an opinion that deferred obsequiously to executive power (using the "captain of the ship" metaphor), the US Supreme Court upheld Moyer's detention. It reasoned that since the militia could even have fired upon the strikers (or, in the Court's words, the "mob in insurrection"), how could Moyer complain of a mere detention? The government now cites the case in its Padilla brief to argue that whatever a state governor can do, the President can do better. As Mariner remarks, next thing you know they'll be citing the Japanese internment precedents.

September 21

When the young basketball star Len Bias died of a cocaine overdose back in 1986 Tip O'Neill and Ronald Reagan raced each other to show the world who could punish the poor quickest and hardest. The White House urged the DEA to take ABC News along to raids on crack houses in South Central LA. O'Neill drove through the Anti-Drug Abuse Act, with its twenty-nine new mandatory minimum sentences, and the 100-to-1 disparity in sentencing for crack/powder cocaine dealers. We were on our way to lockup time for the poor, mostly young blacks and Hispanics. At present rates, the chances of a black man being behind bars sometime in his life are one in four.

All through the 1980s and '90s professorial mountebanks like James Q. Wilson, John DiIulio, and Charles Murray grew sleek from bestsellers about the criminal, probably innate propensities of the "underclass," about the pathology of poverty, the teen predators, the collapse of morals, the irresponsibility of teen moms.

Now, there was indeed a vast criminal class coming to its full vicious potential in the 1990s: a group utterly vacant of the most elementary instincts of social propriety, devoid of moral fiber, selfish to an almost unfathomable degree. The class comes in the form of our corporate elite.

Given a green light in the late 1970s by the deregulatory binge urged by corporate-funded think tanks and launched legislatively by Jimmy Carter and Ted Kennedy, by the 1990s America's corporate leadership had evolved a simple strategy for criminal self-enrichment.

Step one: lie about your performance, in a manner calculated to deceive investors. This was engineered by the production of a "pro-forma" balance sheet freighted with accounting chicanery of every stripe and hue, willingly supplied by Arthur Andersen and others. Losses were labeled "capital expenditures"; losing assets were "sold" to co-conspirators in the large banks for the relevant accounting period. Later, using Generally Accepted Accounting Principles, slightly more realistic balance sheets would be presented to the SEC and the IRS.

Flaunting the "pro-forma" numbers, corporations would issue more stock, borrow more money from some co-conspiratorial bank, buy back the stock for the chief executives, who would further inflate its value by dint of bogus accountancy, sell the stock to the chumps and bail out with their millions before the roof fell in, leaving pension funds like CalPERS holding the bag.

The scale of looting? Prodigious. This orgy of thievery, without parallel in the history of capitalism, was condoned and abetted year after year by the archbishop of our economy, Alan Greenspan, a man with a finely honed sense of distinction between the scale of reproof merited by the very rich and those less powerful. When Ron Carey led the Teamsters to victory in 1997, Greenspan rushed to denounce the "inflationary" potential of modestly improved wage packets. Even though declared innocent by a jury of his peers, Carey, who had actually led a union to victory, was forbidden ever to run in a union election again.

Where are the sermons from Greenspan about the inflationary potential of stock-option fortunes lofted on the hot air of crooked accountancy and kindred conspiracies?

Let someone die in gangbanger crossfire on a slum corner, and William Bennett indicts an entire generation, an entire race. Where are the sermons from Bennett, Murray and the "Sunday Show" moralists about the CEOs scuttling off with their swag, leaving their employees to founder amid wrecked pensions and destroyed prospects? A street kid in South Central is in the computer by the time he's ten. No "criminal propensity" profiles for grads of the Wharton or Harvard business schools.

You have to go back to Marx and Balzac to get a truly vivid sense of the rich as a criminal elite. These giants did bequeath a tradition of joyful dissection of the morals and ethics of the rich, carried on by Veblen, Moody, Wright Mills, Domhoff, Lundberg, and others. But by the mid-1960s disruptive political science was not a paying proposition if you were aiming for tenure. A student studying Mills would be working nights at the soda fountain while the kid flourishing Robert Dahl and writing rubbish about pluralism would get the grad fellowship.

Back in the 1950s we were reading stuff about the moral vacuum in affluent suburbia by people like Vance Packard and David Riesman. I guess inner loneliness soon became inner joy. There was nothing wrong about putting one's boot on a colleague's neck and cashing in. Where are the books now about these forcing grounds for the great corporate criminal cohort of the 1990s, coming of age in the Reagan years?

In fact, it's nearly impossible to locate books that examine the class of corporate executives through the lens of cool, scientific contempt. As Charles Derber, professor of sociology at Boston College, explains, much of the current writing on CEO culture is published in magazines like *Fortune* or *BusinessWeek*. And though there are a few authors—like Robert Monks—who focus their attention on executive culture, nowhere will you find empirical studies on the sociobiological roots of the criminal tendencies of the executive class.

Why? The rich bought out the opposition. Back in the mists of antiquity, you had Communists and Socialists and populists who'd read Marx and who had a pretty fair notion of what the rich were up to. Even Democrats had a grasp of the true situation. Then came the witch-hunts and the buyouts, hand in hand. Result, an Enron exec could come to maturity without ever once hearing an admonitory word about it being wrong to lie, cheat, and steal, sell out your co-workers, defraud your customers.

The finest schools in America produced a criminal elite that stole the store in less than a decade. Was it all the fault of Ayn Rand, of Carter and Kennedy, of the Chicago School, of Hollywood, of God's demise? You'd think there's at least a *Time* cover in it.

October 13

Here's why I'm against the UN as promoter of federalism and world guv'mint. This just in from Geneva, Switzerland, via Reuter's wire: "UN upholds French ban on 'dwarf throwing.'" It turns out that a diminutive stuntman who had protested against a French ban on the practice of "dwarf throwing" has lost his case before some sort of UN human rights judicial body. The tribunal issued some typically pious UN claptrap about the need to protect human dignity being paramount.

The dwarf, a fellow called Manuel Wackenheim, argued that a 1995 ban by France's highest administrative court was discriminatory and deprived him of a job being tossed around in discos and similar venues.

The UN Human Rights Committee said it was satisfied "the ban on dwarf-tossing was not abusive but necessary in order to protect public order, including considerations of human dignity." It also said the ban "did not amount to prohibited discrimination."

Dwarfs and their throwers will have to search out venues, like prize fighters in eighteenth-century England. Soon some place like Slovakia will be the only venue. No doubt a UN embargo will then ensue, with draconian sanctions, appointment of inspectors/spies, followed by the inevitable intervention, NATO bombing and occupation.

So here's a bunch of UN administrators, each of them probably hauling down an annual salary hefty enough to keep a troupe of dwarfs in caviar for life, dooming poor little Wackenheim to the unemployment lines, before going home to scream at their underpaid Romanian maidservants or to get a blowjob from a thirteen-year-old girl from Kiev in the local whorehouse. In the old days dwarfs could stand proud, strutting down the boulevards, around circus rings, or forming part of some amusing display, or matching themselves against pitbulls (a popular nineteenth-century English pastime).

I can remember dwarfs from my childhood in Ireland, along with other bodies remote from conventional anatomy. Walking down the main street of any Irish town reminded one of Breughel. Not any more. I guess even in Catholic Ireland the doc takes a look and chokes nature's sports before they've got out of the starting gate.

If the UN had been around at the time, the hunchbacks of Philip IV of Spain would have been forbidden to pose for Velazquez, and Jeffrey Hudson (eighteen inches at the age of nine, gracefully proportioned) would never have been permitted to step out of a pie on the dining room table of his boss, George Villiers, the first Duke of Buckingham. Having emerged from the pastry, Hudson saluted Villiers's guests, King Charles I and his Queen, Henrietta Maria, who promptly adopted him.

Spared a UN sponsored abortion to save him from an existence incompatible with human dignity, Hudson led an adventurous life and survived two duels, one against a turkey cock and the other in combat with a certain Mr. Crofts. The arrogant Crofts turned up for the duel with a water pistol, but Hudson stood on his dignity and insisted that the engagement be for real. They put Hudson up on a horse to get him level with Crofts and he promptly shot the man dead. Captured by Turkish pirates, Hudson said his tribulations made him grow, and having held steady at eighteen inches from nine to thirty, he shot up to 3 foot 9.

Another dwarf, Charles Stratton (aka General Tom Thumb) killed one of my favorite painters, Benjamin Haydon, who was exhibiting his vast work "The Banishment of Aristides," in the Egyptian Hall in London. But the crowds preferred to gawp at General Thumb, on display in the same Hall. Thumb drew 600 pounds sterling in his first week, while Haydon got only a measly seven pounds, thirteen shillings. Haydon went off home to his studio and killed himself.

Dwarf tossing? The job came with the stature. William Beckford, the eccentric millionaire who wrote *Vathek* and built the famous folly at Fonthill, was one of the last to have a dwarf in private service, though E. J. Woods, author of the useful *Giants and Dwarfs* (1860), says Beckford's dwarf was "rather too big to be flung from one guest to another, as was the custom at dinners in earlier days."

October 15

The Earth Charter is the spawn of Steven C. Rockefeller, Canadian eco-mogul Maurice Strong, and Mikhail Gorbachev, who has said of it, "My hope is that this charter will be a kind of Ten Commandments, a Sermon on the Mount, that provides a guide for human behavior toward the environment in the next century and beyond."

The portage of the Charter at the end of last year began at an Earth Ceremony in Vermont, where Rockefeller (chairman of the Rockefeller Brothers Fund and the Earth Charter International Drafting Committee) is professor emeritus of religion at Middlebury College. Present was Jane Goodall, of chimpanzee fame, one of whose thumb tips was once nipped off by a chimp asserting its dignity when Goodall tried to cosy up to it at the Laboratory for Experimental Medicine and Surgery in Primates, part of NYU and located in Sterling Forest. (Goodall tried to cover it up by saying she'd caught her thumb in a car door.)

The Charter, which finally puffed into Johannesburg in time for last month's Earth Summit, is housed and transported in the cheesy Ark of Hope, furiously described on the New American Patriot website as "a blasphemous mimicry of the biblical Ark of the Covenant, which held the two tablets containing the Ten Commandments that God gave to Moses." Accompanying the Charter and the Ark are the "Temenos Books," containing aboriginal Earth Masks and "visual prayers/affirmations for global healing, peace, and gratitude," created by 3,000 artists, teachers, students, and mystics.

"Temenos" is the word for the precincts of a temple, and accurately reflects the ersatz religiosity of UN ritualism.

According to the Charter, we must: "Recognize that all beings are interdependent and every form of life has value ..." (except of course for human fetuses, which are not included in the UN's definition of "every form of life," merely as disposable protoplasm). There's the predictable affirmation of faith in the "inherent dignity of all human beings," excluding those who are finished off by euthanasia or haled before the ICC or required to clean the bathrooms of overpaid UN bureaucrats.

Now comes the jackboot: the earth must "adopt at all levels

sustainable development plans and regulations; prevent pollution of any part of the environment; internalize the full environmental and social costs of goods and services in the selling price; ensure universal access to health care that fosters reproductive health and responsible reproduction." In other words, population control, as promoted through the century by the Rockefellers, who of course assigned the Manhattan real estate to the UN for its HQ.

December 16

We've been without power for a week now. As the storm winds rattled the window panes and the lamps guttered low, warming the room to the tints of a La Tour painting, and as Becky Grant's youngest, Oliver, gamboled with Jasper, I sang of the ancient times of *7 Days*, a weekly I was involved with at the end of the '60s in London. There were about twenty people in the collective, with all decisions, down to the refinements of punctuation and the proper use of the semi-colon, settled by debate and democratic vote, 50 percent men, 50 percent women. Democracy at that level is very tiring.

Late one night as I labored over the photographs with our design team, I heard a crackling on the aged stairs of the old building on Shavers Place, a hundred yards from Piccadilly Circus, where we were perched on the top floor. I pulled open the door, to be confronted by a sheet of flame. It later turned out that some group of Ulster-based Orangemen had taken exception to our measured posture on the Irish question and had decided to torch the building.

We decided to abandon ship. Carrying boxes of valuable prints from Magnum we walked the narrow catwalk that led to the next building, and kicked in the window. There was a screech of alarm as a couple of Palestinians who were working late on their magazine saw the window burst in and thought the Israeli commandos were about to follow. By dawn we had the pages made up and then it was a rush to the train station, then an hour down to the printers. So different now; so much easier, so much cheaper. Who says there isn't progress in human affairs, though I do miss the inky excitement of those old hot type days.

December 18

It's one of the staple and indeed few remaining pleasures of American political life. A Republican taken with drink, speaking unguardedly near a live microphone—or in Trent Lott's case coasting through a ritual farewell speech on automatic pilot—drops a racist gibe or fond salute to America's dark past. The rituals of outrage, apology, self-abasement, renewed outrage, deeper self-abasement, forgiveness or rejection, duly follow.

Sometimes the sinner is ceremoniously booted into oblivion, as happened with Richard Nixon's Secretary of Agriculture, Earl Butz, or Reagan's Secretary of the Interior, James Watt. Sometimes, as is now happening in Lott's case, the Democrats give him a thumping while hoping that in the end Lott will hold on to his post as Senate Majority whip, the better to remind black voters that this is the true face of the Republican Party, featuring the Klansman's robe, the burning cross and the lynching tree. Better Lott than some oily substitute like Frist of Tennessee solemnly declaring that the Republican Party has finally put the past behind it and that the healing should now begin.

One of Bill Clinton's many offenses was that he devalued the public apology. He had to make so many of them that they ceased to be valid as currency, like bank notes in the German inflation of the early 1920s when people had to take a wheelbarrow of cash to buy a sausage for lunch.

These days, post-Clinton, a manly mumble of contrition is no good. Unless a politician comes out with a truckload of apologies and keeps sending them round the track for a week, people claim he's refusing to climb down, and keep insisting, Does Lott really and truly mean it? And for that matter, why stop with Lott? What about the four Dixiecrat states that voted for Strom Thurmond back in 1948? Shouldn't their governors today issue formal apologies, and make available "apology bins" in every neighborhood wherein those who actually voted for Strom, or their descendants, can deposit personal expressions of remorse?

Another factor in this inflation is the fact that sometimes the apology is rejected, no matter how often repeated. The Democrats and the press did this to Jesse Jackson—columnists like the late James

Reston, who defiled the editorial pages of the *New York Times* on a weekly basis with racist diatribes about Jackson's effrontery as a black man in presuming to seek the Democratic presidential nomination in 1984 and 1988, then whacked him again for inadequate demonstrations of remorse for his crack about Hymietown. Senator Joe Lieberman even managed to bracket Jackson and Lott together, saying that neither of them were sincere in covering themselves with sackcloth and ashes.

December 29

America has lost one of its senior weapons inspectors, one of its most ardent would-be dismantlers of weapons of mass destruction. Phil Berrigan died in the evening on December 6, at Jonah House, the community in Baltimore he co-founded in 1973, surrounded by family and friends. For forty years he campaigned against war and violence, most of all against nuclear weapons. Challenge America's weapons of mass destruction, and the state locks you up. Phil Berrigan spent about eleven years in prison in the cause of peace and disarmament.

Berrigan wrote a final statement in the days before his death. His final comments included this: "I die with the conviction, held since 1968 and Catonsville, that nuclear weapons are the scourge of the earth; to mine for them, manufacture them, deploy them, use them, is a curse against God, the human family, and the earth itself."

Blessed are the peacemakers, Jesus told the crowd in the Sermon on the Mount, and Lo, Ronald Reagan named the MX nuclear missile the Peacemaker.

The Berrigans and their brave comrades shed their blood on a nuclear warhead being manufactured at the GE plant in King of Prussia, Pennsylvania, recalling the blood that Jesus shed for sinful humanity, and Lo, they named a ballistic missile submarine USS *City of Corpus Christi*, the city of the body of Christ, and they probably knew not what they did, aside from honoring the home port of some Texan pork dispenser on Capitol Hill.

The word from Jonah House is that those who mourn for Berrigan and wish to honor his memory may make donations in Berrigan's name to Citizens for Peace in Space, Global Network Against Nuclear Weapons, Nukewatch, Voices in the Wilderness, the Nuclear Resister, or any Catholic Worker house.

Philip Berrigan was born in 1923 in the Minnesota Iron Range, in the town of Two Harbors, about thirty miles east of the birthplace of the man who wrote *Masters of War*. He was the first priest to ride in a civil rights movement Freedom Ride.

In 1967 he poured blood on draft files in Baltimore with three others, known as the "Baltimore Four." A year later he burned draft files in Catonsville, MD, with eight others, including his brother, Fr. Daniel Berrigan. That action was known as the "Catonsville Nine." He was convicted of destruction of US property, destruction of Selective Service records, and interference with the Selective Service Act of 1967.

In 1971, while in prison, he was named co-conspirator by J. Edgar Hoover and a Harrisburg grand jury, charged with plotting to kidnap Henry Kissinger and blow up the utility tunnels of US Capitol buildings. In the event he was convicted only of violating prison rules for smuggling out letters. On September 9, 1980, he poured blood and hammered with seven others on Mark 12A warheads at a GE nuclear missile plant, King of Prussia, PA. He was charged with conspiracy, burglary, and criminal mischief; convicted and imprisoned. The action became known as the "Plowshares Eight," and began the international Plowshares movement. He participated in five more Plowshares actions, resulting in seven years of imprisonment.

December 30

Many years ago my father visited the secretary of a British society that used certain measurements in the Grand Pyramid in Egypt to predict the future. After running through the basic mathematical drill the secretary murmured that in his estimation the predictive power of the Grand Pyramid was over-estimated. Scenting a possible recantation my father pressed him. What sort of "over-estimation," he asked. Well, said the secretary, many people believe that the calculations to make current predictions based on the pyramid can be done "in five minutes." Not so. "Serious predictions involve math that requires at least three weeks to complete."

Nuts are never more impressive than when admitting just a measure of uncertainty into the precision of their mad interpretations. And yes, the same can be said of economic forecasters.

2003

January 10

CITATION SWIPING

Editor,
I was amazed at the effrontery of the Cockburn, and, presumably, Norman Finkelstein charge of plagiarism against Alan Dershowitz. The fact that the Ottoman-ruled Palestinian town of Safed was a center of rabbinical activities and mystical Judaism in the sixteenth century is a commonplace of Jewish studies as well as tourist guidebooks, in addition to Ottoman history.

To claim that remarking upon it in a sentence that reworks an earlier statement of this fact is plagiarism is as ridiculous as arguing that one could plagiarize the statement "Washington, DC is the capital of the United States." Further, the argument that in recycling citations, even with identical ellipses, Dershowitz committed plagiarism is intellectual dishonesty on the part of Cockburn, at its most extreme. Reusing citations is not plagiarism even when the wording is identical. Every serious working journalist and author knows this.

Stephen Schwartz,
Washington, DC

Cockburn replies: How piquant that the portly messenger of the Prophet should rise in defense of theft. The last time I saw him, it was on C-SPAN whining to a small crowd in a bookstore that Hitchens had plagiarized his patented keyword "Islamofascism." God forbid that I should ever be compelled to read his books, but I've no doubt that if I swiped his citations without acknowledgement he would hasten to alert the world to my crimes. The only outstanding question: why does Schwartz want to kiss Dershowitz's ass?

January 14

For sale: Rare 1985 Ford Escort diesel station wagon, which of course you won't have to smog. Acquired by Alex Cockburn in South Carolina two years ago. Driven reliably hither and yon, until fuel feed problems developed from broken off sending unit in the tank. Tank was cleaned out, new sending unit installed, but there's still a feed glitch. This is the car's only problem so far as Cockburn knows, but now he's got other fish ('62 Belvedere SW, '60 Valiant, '67 300 convertible, etc.) to fry. New clutch assembly; new rotors and pads on front brakes; new battery; nice upscale paint job. Newish tires. Does about forty miles to the gallon. Odo probably accurate at about 68,500 miles. $1,800. Car's in Boonville.

April 7

One house I stayed in for a few days was in Thornhill Square, three quarters of a mile or so north of King's Cross. The neighborhood is on the way up in the world, but still agreeably humble along Caledonian Road itself. Each morning I would walk along, enjoying the simple dramas of the shop fronts, the hopes and despairs of small retail entrepreneurs. The tasteful element always hate them and dream of bulldozers, but I love streets like this, such as the old Main in Montreal twenty years ago, or Lincoln Boulevard today south of I-10 in Los Angeles.

Running north on the east side of the street, from the corner of Caledonian Road and Richmond Street we have: a smart pub called the Tarmon, with a fine display of hanging floral baskets; Caly Gents Hairdresser (wash and cut £8, dry cut £6, child's cut £5, OAP £4), a smart-looking place; Skaters take-away, with pictures of a chicken and a fish; Uncle Eric Kebab House; Pleasure Garden (grimy, shuttered, broken signage advertising SAU, SPA and UB); Kings Pizza; double frontage of "Kaim Todner, solicitor, crime, prisoners' rights, mental health, family"; print and copy shop; Caledonian supermarket (a small store with good vegetables on display); Austin Daniel Property; Guzel Café and Restaurant; smart double front of Istanbul Social Club; Dental Surgeon (shuttered and barred, with note, "Dr Kylahs would be pleased to attend Dr Mean's patients, or any other patients, at his surgery at 2 Biddland Road)"; four more shuttered stores and bags of rubble, including Logman Ltd, "specializing in watermelons"; William Hill, betting shop (Ladbroke's across the road); E&A Drycleaner; Leonard Villa, picture framer; Somal Hair and Beauty Center ("stand-up sunbeds, hair extension, nail extension"); post office (also newsagent); KIG café and restaurant, with sign in window, "Full breakfast, bacon, bubble, eggs, beans, sausage, mushroom, tomato, black pudding, 2 slices of bread, tea or coffee, £4.50"; chemist; two shuttered stores; smart double façade of Rigpa Tibetan Buddhist Center; drear frontage of London Taxi Club; Wear-2-Rave, selling trendy gear; Parker Sales and Lettings; Islington Bar, under repair; then Bridgeman Road.

Round the corner was Islington Council's West Branch library, with comfortable reading room, nicely stocked shelves, and a big children's library across the hall. The rack by the entrance featured helpful pamphlets for owners of missing cats and dogs (contact the Lost Dogs Line, run by the Metropolitan Police and Battersea Dogs Home); for male victims of sexual assault ("research shows that the majority of sexual assaults against men are committed by heterosexual males"); for frustrated litigators ("Have You Been Injured? Was Someone Else to Blame?"), issued by the Law Society; for the worried, a detailed pamphlet titled "NHS Abortion (termination of pregnancy services in Camden and Islington)." Denizens of hysterical America, note the tranquil, confident tone: "Having An Abortion: This section describes how the NHS abortion service is organized, and how to access it. If you have decided that abortion is the right option for you, your GP or local family planning clinic can refer you. If your GP has a conscientious objection to abortion, he/she should say so and refer you to another doctor who does not hold these views."

On the back of the pamphlet a paragraph calmly explains that it has been produced "for any woman living in the boroughs of Camden or Islington who is thinking about ending her pregnancy." This paragraph is reproduced in Turkish, Bengali, Chinese and Greek.

The bookcases carried good selections of fiction, biography, politics, and so on. I picked out a volume of *The Lyttelton Hart-Davis Letters*, exchanged in the 1950s between two cultured gents, one a teacher, the other a publisher. Indeed, Rupert Hart-Davis published the first volume of my father's autobiography, *In Time of Trouble*, in 1956. My eye falls on a quote from William Johnson who, under the name Cory, instructed upper-class youth at Eton between 1834 and 1872: One of the faculties a good education develops, Cory wrote, is to "express assent or dissent in graduated terms." I was still laughing over this as I ate a plate of chicken kebab and fresh salad, in the Guzel Café round the corner, cost £4.50.

April 21

Walmart's planning to move strongly into organic food. The company's CEO, Lee Scott, said at Walmart's last annual general meeting, "We know that customers at all ends of the income spectrum want organic and natural food. But, frankly, most of them just can't afford the high prices the specialty stores charge. Well, we don't think you should have to have a lot of money to feed your family organic foods."

It's a far cry from the 1970s, when organic food meant a bin of expensive potatoes looking like something out of Hieronymus Bosch, in the local hippy co-op. Wait a decade or two and every potato coming out of the state of Idaho will be labeled "organic," a word already under very serious stress. The process will be entirely predictable. The big food companies will buy federal and state legislation designed to put the small producers out of business, same way the meat companies finished off the small packers and processors years ago, by insisting on hundreds of thousands of dollars' worth of stainless steel and other "sanitary" equipment, all intended to bankrupt the local sausage or ham maker.

Repositioning of the definition of "organic" is already proceeding apace. Again according to *BusinessWeek*, "Last fall, the Organic Trade Assn., which represents corporations like Kraft, Dole, and Dean Foods, lobbied to attach a rider to the 2006 Agricultural Appropriations Bill that would weaken the nation's organic food standards by allowing certain synthetic food substances in the preparation, processing, and packaging of organic foods. That sparked outrage from organic activists. Nevertheless, the bill passed into law in November, and the new standards will go into effect later this year."

It's true, of course, that organic food—in any acceptable use of the term—is better for us and good that consumer demand is prompting this huge shift. But the priorities of corporate farming are not those of the small organic producer. The bottom line will be premised on large-scale production, relentless lowering of costs and attrition of standards.

July 1

Perry Anderson and his wife, Chaohua Wang, came to stay. Chaohua left me this poem:

> Jasper
> Blue sky, white clouds
> familiar from elementary school textbook
> Jasper leaping into the water
> a black sword through the silence
> Tidal sound of pine grove, unchanged
> a countryside summer dream
>
> Wars break suddenly, gunfire coming from afar
> Mid-East conflict, Nagasaki, Governor's recall …
>
> A dagger, a javelin, a counterpunch,
> A Lu Xun secluded in his Wang River estate
> Has "fair play" been postponed?

Second stanza refers to the rifle-practice in distance, the topic of your book on Palestine-Israel, and the conversations of the evening.

Third stanza links the two images which Lu Xun—our Brecht—used to describe the thrust of his essays, and your magazine; then refers to the lyrical poetry of Wang Wei (seventh-century Tang poet), about his rural idyll by the river of the same name.

Last line alludes to the title of Lu Xun's famous piece of 1925, attacking compromisers with the established order, rejecting their calls for fair play with the authorities.

September 24

A mighty and a passionate heart has ceased to beat.

Edward Said, the greatest Arab of his generation, died in hospital in New York City Wednesday, September 24 at 6.30 pm, felled at last by complications arising from the leukemia he fought so gamely ever since the early 1990s.

We march through life buoyed by those comrades-in-arms we know to be marching with us, under the same banners, flying the same colors, sustained by the same hopes and convictions. They can be a thousand miles away; we may not have spoken to them in months; but their companionship is burned into our souls and we are sustained by the knowledge that they are with us in the world.

Few more than Edward Said, for me and so many others beside. How many times, after a week, a month or more, I have reached him on the phone and within a second been lofted in my spirits, as we pressed through our updates: his trips; his triumphs; the insults sustained; the enemies rebuked and put to flight. Even in his pettiness he was magnificent, and as I would laugh at his fury at some squalid gibe hurled at him by an eighth-rate scrivener, he would clamber from the pedestal of martyrdom and laugh at himself.

He never lost his fire, even as the leukemia pressed, was routed, pressed again. He lived at a rate that would have felled a man half his age and ten times as healthy: a plane to London, an honorary degree, on to Lebanon, on to the West Bank, on to Cairo, to Madrid, back to New York. And all the while he was pouring out the Said prose that I most enjoyed, the fiery diatribes he distributed to *CounterPunch* and to a vast world audience. At the top of his form his prose has the pitiless, relentless clarity of Swift.

The Palestinians will never know a greater polemical champion. A few weeks ago I was, with his genial permission, putting together from three of his essays the concluding piece in our forthcoming *CounterPunch* collection, *The Politics of Anti-Semitism*. I was seized, as so often before, by the power of the prose: how could anyone read those searing sentences and not boil with rage, while simultaneously admiring Edward's generosity of soul: that with the imperative of justice and nationhood for his people came the humanity that called for reconciliation between Palestinians and Israeli Jews.

His literary energy was prodigious. Memoir, criticism, homily, fiction poured from his pen, a fountain pen that reminded one that Edward was very much an intellectual in the nineteenth-century tradition of a Zola or a Victor Hugo, who once remarked that genius is a promontory in the infinite. I read that line as a schoolboy, wrote it in my notebook and though I laugh now a little at the pretension of the line, I do think of Edward as a promontory, a physical bulk on the intellectual and political landscape that forced people, however disinclined they may have been, to confront the Palestinian experience.

Years ago his wife Mariam asked me if I would make available my apartment in New York, where I lived at that time, as the site for a surprise fortieth birthday for Edward. I dislike surprise parties but of course agreed. The evening arrived; guests assembled on my sitting room on the eleventh floor of 333 Central Park West. The dining-room table groaned under Middle Eastern delicacies. Then came the word from the front door. Edward and Mariam had arrived! They were ascending in the elevator. Now we could all hear Edward's furious bellow: "But I don't want to go to dinner with ******* Alex!" They entered at last and the shout went up from seventy throats, Happy Birthday! He reeled back in surprise and then recovered, and then saw about the room all those friends who had traveled thousands of miles to shake his hand. I could see him slowly expand with joy at each new unexpected face and salutation.

He never became blasé in the face of friendship and admiration, or indeed honorary degrees, just as he never grew a thick skin. Each insult was as fresh and as wounding as the first he ever received. A quarter of century ago he would call, with mock heroic English intonation, "Alex-and-er, have you seen the latest *New Republic*? Have you read this filthy, this utterly disgusting diatribe? You haven't? Oh, I know, you don't care about the feelings of a mere black man such as myself." I'd start laughing, and say I had better things to do than read Martin Peretz, or Edward Alexander or whoever the assailant was, but for half an hour he would brood, rehearse fiery rebuttals and listen moodily as I told him to pay no attention.

He never lost the capacity to be wounded by the treachery and opportunism of supposed friends. A few weeks ago he called to ask whether I had read a particularly stupid attack on him by his very old friend Christopher Hitchens in the *Atlantic Monthly*. He described with pained sarcasm a phone call in which Hitchens had presumably tried to square his own conscience by advertising to Edward the impending assault. I asked Edward why he was surprised, and indeed why he cared. But he was surprised and he did care. His skin was so, so thin, I think because he knew that as long as he lived, as long as he marched onward as a proud, unapologetic and vociferous Palestinian, there would be some enemy on the next housetop down the street eager to dump sewage on his head.

Edward, dear friend, I wave adieu to you across the abyss. I don't even have to close my eyes to savor your presence, your caustic or merry laughter, your elegance, your spirit as vivid as that of d'Artagnan, the fiery Gascon. You will burn like the brightest of flames in my memory, as you will in the memories of all who knew and admired and loved you.

September 25

As one who once wrote a book titled *The Golden Age Is in Us*, I took myself off on a Saturday to look at an exhibition in the National Galley on Trafalgar Square, called "Paradise," a traveling show which had already been shown in Bristol and Newcastle, attracting 160,000 people, apparently double what they would have expected normally in those galleries. People want to know the lineaments of paradise, whose earthly possibilities utopians used to spend much time usefully describing, though not much anymore.

The exhibition turned out to be patchy, with the curator scraping together a show from available ingredients, such as a Boucher, a Gauguin, a Constable, a Monet, a Rothko, a couple of Renaissance paintings and so forth. But making my visit entirely worthwhile there was one marvelous painting, one of Stanley Spencer's Cookham paintings about the Last Judgment, done in 1934. It shows a dustman resurrected in his beefy wife's arms, she in "ecstatic communion with the dustman's corduroy trousers" as Spencer put it. Other dustmen and women, plus a cat, surround the couple.

"I feel in this Dustman picture," Spencer wrote,

> that it is like watching and experiencing the inside of a sexual experience. They are all in a state of anticipation and gratitude to each other. They are each to the other, and all to any one of them, as peaceful as the privacy of a lavatory. I cannot feel anything is Heaven where there is any forced exclusion of any sexual desire …
>
> The picture is to express a joy of life through intimacy. All the signs and tokens of home life, such as the cabbage leaves and teapot which I have so much loved that I have had them resurrected from the dustbin because they are reminders of home life and peace, and are worthy of being adored as the dustman is. I only like to paint what makes me feel happy. As a child I was always looking on rubbish heaps and dustbins with a feeling of wonder. I like to feel that, while in life things like pots and brushes and clothes etc may cease to be used, they will in some way be reinstated, and in this Dustman picture I try to express something of this wish and need I feel for things to be restored. That is the feeling that makes the children take out the broken teapot and empty jam tin.

Small things these, but there was also a big new thing in Spencer's life, namely his attraction to a new arrival in Cookham, Patricia Preece and her companion Hilda. Patricia was famous as having been the cause of the death of W. S. Gilbert, the librettist of the noted team of Gilbert and Sullivan. Aged seventeen in 1911 and under her birth name of Ruby, she caught the eye of randy old Gilbert, who invited her to come for a swim in the lake at his Harrow home. As she splashed about he conceived, or professed to conceive, the notion that she was out of her depth and might drown. Swimming out, no doubt planning to clasp her in a savior's embrace, he had a heart attack and died in front of her. The press had a fine time describing her as a "fair-haired seventeen-year-old schoolgirl."

It's the presence of Patricia, though not her image, that suffuses the painting with sexual ecstasy, even though it's the ample Hilda, who'd fled from Cookham to her mother in Hampstead, who is in ecstatic communion with the corduroy trousers. It's as earthy and beautiful an expression of the paradise of carnal passion as Joyce's pages in *Ulysses* about Bloom looking at Gertie. Though Spencer was a member of the Royal Academy and had the right to hang four paintings in the annual show, it was rejected, prompting his furious resignation. This great painting was without a purchaser till a Liverpool gallery bought it in 1947.

Whoever thought to put Spencer into the Paradise exhibit got it right. In ancient times death in the Golden Age was always incorporated into life as a sensate pleasure, followed immediately by an improved life, the way most folks including all those flocking to the show in Bristol and Newcastle would like it. In those earlier times they had Saturnalia which meant not so much drunken sex sprees as subversion of the conventional moral order.

October 7

People on the left spend a lot more time than they should complaining about the mainstream papers, most particularly the *New York Times*. They fume at the breakfast table, and often in print, or on the airwaves, bitterly decrying falsities in the "newspaper of record." What do they expect? In fact, they should rejoice when the *Times* gets things wrong, which it mostly does, and take it as a singular event when it blunders into accuracy.

The dreariest place on any campus is the J-school, and whenever any young person comes to me to write a testimonial for them to get into journalism school I rail bitterly at their decision, though I concede that these days a diploma from one of these feedlots for mediocrity is pretty much mandatory for anyone who wants to get into mainstream journalism.

Now the *Times* is nursing its bruises from the Jayson Blair affair. There are so many smellier corpses in the *New York Times*'s mausoleum, not to mention that larger graveyard of truth known as the American Fourth Estate, that it's hard to get too upset about what Blair did. This same Blair was a young black reporter on the *New York Times*, exposed and denounced at colossal length on May 11 by a team of reporters from his own paper. The guy is now in hiding, his career in ruins.

From all the editorial hand-wringing you'd think he'd undermined the very foundations of the Republic. It reminds me of a *New York Times* editorial back in 1982, commenting on what began with my own exposé of Christopher Jones, a young man who had written an article in the *New York Times* magazine about a visit to Cambodia during which he claimed to have seen Pol Pot through binoculars.

In this same piece Jones made the mistake of plagiarizing an entire paragraph from André Malraux's novel *La Voie Royale*, and I pointed this out in a column in the *Village Voice*, adding the obvious point that Jones's binoculars must have been extremely powerful to have allowed him to recognize Pol Pot, let alone describe his eyes as "dead and stony."

My item stirred the *Washington Post* to point an accusing finger. Then the *Times* itself unleashed a huge investigation of the wretched Jones and ran a pompous editorial proclaiming, "It may not be too much to say that, ultimately, it debases democracy."

I remember thinking at the time that as a democracy-debaser Jones looked like pretty small potatoes, and it's the same way with Jayson Blair now. He made up quotes, invented scenes, and plagiarized the work of other reporters, and if senior *Times* editors had not been as optimistically forgiving as, say, the Catholic hierarchy in dealing with a peccant priest, Blair would, and should, have been promptly fired after his second major screw-up.

But in the larger scale of things Blair's improprieties are of no great consequence. The people into whose mouths he put imaginary words, and from whose imagined front porch he pretended to see tobacco fields instead of tract homes are not notably put out. Ordinary Americans reckon that since you shouldn't believe a word of anything you read in a newspaper or hear over the airwaves, what's so different about Jayson Blair.

The Jayson Blair scandal comes on the heels of what was one of the most intensive bouts of botched reporting, wild speculation and straightforward disingenuous lying in the history of American journalism, a bout which prompted an invasion, many deaths and now—given the way things are currently headed—the likelihood of mass starvation. In other words, the lousy reporting really had consequences.

The invasion of Iraq was premised on the existence of weapons of mass destruction. None has yet been found and most of the US detective teams are now wanly returning home. Did the *New York Times* assist in this process of deception? Very much so. Just look through the clips file of one of its better known reporters, Judith Miller.

It was Miller who first launched the supposedly knowledgeable Iraqi nuclear scientist Khidir Hamza on the world, crucial to the US government's effort to portray a nuclear-capable Saddam. Miller it was who most recently wrote a story about a supposed discovery of a chemical WMD site, based entirely on the say-so of a US military unit about an Iraqi scientist whom Miller was not permitted to identify, let alone meet and interview.

Thus far there's been no agonized reprise from the *New York Times* on its faulty estimate of the credibility of Hamza. And though Blair's fabrications about the homecoming of Jessica Lynch were minutely dissected neither the *Times* nor any other US paper that I've read has had anything to say about the charges made in the London *Times* that the "heroic" rescue of Lynch was from an undefended hospital in circumstances very different and less creditable than those heralded by a Pentagon desperate for good publicity during a time when the invasion seemed to have faltered amid unexpectedly stiff resistance.

December 15

The last time I saw pictures of a man with long hair being displayed as a trophy of the American Empire it was Che Guevara, stretched out dead on a table in a morgue in Valle Grande in the eastern Bolivian mountains. In those edgier days, in late 1967, the Bolivian Army high command wanted him dead, the quicker the better, though the CIA wanted him alive for interrogation in Panama.

After a last chat with the CIA's Félix Rodriguez, George Bush Sr.'s pal, a Bolivian sergeant called Terran shot Che in the throat and Rodriguez got to keep his watch. They chopped off Guevara's hands for later checking to make sure the ID was correct. Years later, his skeleton, sans hands, was located and flown back to Havana for proper burial.

"It is better this way," Guevara told Rodriguez at the end. "I should never have been captured alive," he said, showing that even the bravest weaken at times. At the moment of his capture by the Bolivian Army unit, a wounded Guevara had identified himself, telling the soldiers he was Che and worth more to them alive than dead.

Back in 1967 most of the world mourned when Che's capture and death seized the headlines. A million turned out in Havana to listen to Fidel Castro's farewell speech. It's been downhill all the way since then. The revolutionary cause has mostly gone to hell in a handcart and the next time America's Most Wanted came out with his hands up, badly in need of a haircut, it was a mass murderer called Saddam Hussein, helped into power by the CIA a year after Guevara's death. "I'm the President of Iraq," he said, and then tried to cut a deal.

I went straight from the Monday morning news clips of the US Army's film of Saddam having his teeth checked to have my own teeth cleaned by Tom, an oral hygienist in Santa Rosa, northern California. To try to deflect Tom from his stern rebukes for my own flossing failures I mentioned the footage of Saddam with his mouth open, while someone checked out his teeth.

Though he gave no professional opinions on the state of Saddam's gums, it turned out Tom had spent a couple of years in Basra, in southern Iraq, imparting the elements of oral hygiene to the locals. "I'd point out to them that their gums were bleeding, and they'd sigh, and say it was Allah's will." Then, like millions round the world that morning we (though, of necessity, I did most of the listening) reviewed the various options awaiting Saddam.

There were plenty of pieties in the opinion columns that Monday morning about the need for a manifestly independent tribunal where Saddam could be accorded every legal courtesy and the administration of justice would be scrupulous.

It was impossible to read this claptrap without laughing since that same morning Wesley Clark was testifying in the International Criminal Tribunal for the former Yugoslavia (ICTY), a body conjured into existence by the UN Security Council. As for it being anything other than a US puppet, ICTY was looking pretty slutty that morning, since the US government had successfully bullied the court into allowing Clark to testify in the absence of public or press, in what the ICTY demurely termed a "temporary closed session" with delayed transmission of the transcript, to allow the US government to "review the transcript and make representations as to whether evidence given in open session [*sic*] should be redacted in order to protect the national interests of the US." To further protect the interests of General Clark, he would only have to endure limited cross examination by Milošević, a feisty cross-examiner.

All the US wants is for Saddam to be hauled into some kangaroo court and after a brisk procedure—in which Saddam will no doubt be denied opportunities to interrogate old pals from happier days, like Donald Rumsfeld—be dropped through a trap door with a rope tied around his neck, maybe with an Iraqi, or at least a son of the Prophet, pulling the lever.

These pretenses at judicial propriety are absurd. I prefer the posture of the Arab-American woman who said Saddam should be put in a cage and drowned with spit.

December 27

It has been astounding that a world-scale monster such as Rupert Murdoch has thus far fared well at the hands of his various profilers and biographers. Criticisms of him have either been too broad-brush to be useful, or too tempered with Waugh-derived facetiousness about press barons. Murdoch is far too fearsome an affront to any civilized values to escape with mere facetiousness.

Now at last Murdoch is properly burdened with the chronicler he deserves. *The Murdoch Archipelago* (just published by Simon & Schuster in the UK) is written by Bruce Page, a distinguished, Australian-raised journalist who has lived and worked in England for many years, perhaps best known for his work in leading one of the great investigative enterprises of twentieth-century journalism, the Insight team at the (pre-Murdoch) London *Sunday Times*.

As an essay in understanding what the function of the press should be in a democratic society, Page's book is an important one, focused on the world's leading villains.

I had some brief and vivid personal encounters with Murdoch in the late 1970s at the *Village Voice* and I've known Page for many years. In the late 1960s I shared billing with him as one of the four helmsmen of the London-based Free Communications Group, whose manifesto about the media and democracy was set forth in the first issue of our very occasional periodical, *The Open Secret*. (The other two helmsmen were Gus McDonald, latterly a Blair-ennobled Labour enforcer in the House of Lords, and Neal Ascherson, a very good writer.)

I talked to Page about his book in London in mid-November in the midst of the twin invasions of Bush and Murdoch, the latter briefly alighting in London to crush a rising by some shareholders in British Sky Broadcasting who had been claiming that the company was being run by Murdoch as a private fiefdom in a manner injurious to their interests.

It was a characteristic Murdoch performance, marked by his usual arrogance, thuggery and deception. In one particularly spectacular act of corporate contempt he first told the shareholders at the AGM that Tony Ball, moved over to make way for Murdoch's son James, had received no severance payment, and then revealed briefly thereafter that £10 million was being paid to Ball to make sure he would not compete with Sky's now non-existent rivals. The true function of the $10 million is more likely to ensure Ball's future discretion, since the latter knows the whereabouts of many bodies whose disinterment might inconvenience Murdoch, throwing an unpleasing light on Sky's unfettered (by Blair's regulators) use of its Thatcher-derived monopoly.

Amid his rampages at BSkyB Murdoch gave an interview to the BBC in which he placed Tony Blair on notice that the loyalty of Murdoch's newspapers was not to be taken for granted. Referring to himself respectfully in the first person plural, Murdoch was kind enough to intimate that "we will not quickly forget the courage of Tony Blair" but then made haste to emphasize that he also enjoys friendly relations with the new Tory leader Michael Howard.

On the mind of this global pirate is a topic in which one would have thought he would have had scant interest, namely national sovereignty. Murdoch professed himself exercised by the matter of the EU Constitution. Slipping on the mantle of Britishness, Murdoch pronounced that "I don't like the idea of any more abdication of our sovereignty in economic affairs or anything else."

The *Guardian* found this altogether too brazen and editorialized the following Monday that "Rupert Murdoch is no more British than George W. Bush. Once upon a time, it's true, he was an Australian with Scottish antecedents. But some time ago he came to the view that his citizenship was an inconvenience and resolved to change it for an American passport. He does not live in this country and it is not clear that he is entitled to use 'we' in any meaningful sense of shared endeavour. To be lectured on sovereignty by someone who junked his own citizenship for commercial advantage is an irony to which Mr Murdoch is evidently blind."

Then the *Guardian* got a bit rougher: "Readers have to be put on notice that the views expressed in Murdoch titles have not been freely arrived at on the basis of normal journalistic considerations."

Page's core thesis is that Murdoch offers his target governments a privatized version of a state propaganda service, manipulated without scruple and with no regard for truth. His price takes the form of vast government favors such as tax breaks, regulatory relief (as with the recent FCC ruling on the acquisition of Direct TV), monopoly markets, and so forth. The propaganda is undertaken with the utmost cynicism, whether it's the stentorian fake populism and soft porn in the UK's *Sun* and *News of the World*, or shameless bootlicking of the butchers of Tiananmen Square.

I asked Page if he thought this a fair summary.

PAGE: Your précis of my argument is exact. It may be worth noting that reviewers of *Archipelago* drawn from the still-persistent Old Fleetstrasse culture have (in the words of my old colleague Lew Chester) produced "innumerable contortions devised to miss its main argument." Peter Preston stated that "Bruce" (we are *not* on first-name terms) failed to offer any thesis of how it was all done. Similarly Anthony Howard, who of course has worked many years under the Murdoch banner. You may recall the first three paragraphs of the book:

> Rupert Murdoch denies quite flatly that he seeks or deals in political favours. "Give me an example!" he cried in 1999 when William Shawcross interviewed him for *Vanity Fair*. "When have we ever asked for anything?"
>
> Shawcross didn't take up the challenge. Rather, he endorsed Murdoch's denial, by saying that Rupert had never lied to him.
>
> We can show that Murdoch was untruthful—and Shawcross far too tolerant, both in the interview and in his weighty biography of Murdoch. Not only has Murdoch sought and received political favours: most of the critical steps in the transmutation of News Limited, his inherited business, into present-day News Corp. were dependent on such things. Nor is there essential change in his operations as the new century gets under way, and he prepares his sons to extend the dynasty.

I worked quite hard with the Simon & Schuster lawyers to make this so blunt as to show that anyone missing the point was practicing voluntary astigmatism.

On one radio show I was put up with a certain Teresa Wise of Accenture (formerly Andersen Consulting, limb of Rupert's defunct auditors). She purported to knot her brow over the question of News Corp.'s governance, and produced one of the true standard lines: "It's very easy to demonize Mister Murdoch …" Into the sagacious pause which would clearly have been followed by a laissez-passer, I managed to insert: "Can we have a little less of this? It is actually very difficult, and very hard work, to demonize Rupert. This is because he is in fact demonic, and he frightens a great many people in and around the media industries. Nobody should say how easy it is to demonize unless they have some working experience of the process."

We then had a period of silence from her.

Murdoch often denies he is the world's most powerful media boss. There's a natural discretion in those who have unelected political influence: as their power lacks legitimacy, they prefer it to pass unnoticed. But it goes somewhat further in Murdoch's case. Though his Australian-based News Corporation controls newspapers and broadcasting networks to a unique extent, and the governments of America, Australia, Britain and China treat him with great solicitude, Murdoch considers himself a simple entrepreneur ringed by relentless opponents.

He is in reality the man for whom Margaret Thatcher set aside British monopoly law so that he could buy the *Times* and the *Sunday Times*, and to whom she later handed monopoly control of British satellite television. His newspapers supported Thatcher with ferocious zeal—but switched eagerly to Tony Blair's side once it was clear that New Labour would leave Murdoch in possession of the marketplace advantages bequeathed by Conservative predecessors. But Murdoch (who likes a royal plural) says: "We are … not about protectionism through legislation and cronyism …"

In similar transactions, Ronald Reagan's right-wing administration let Murdoch dynamite US media laws and set up the Fox network, and a left-wing Australian administration let him take monopoly control of the country's newspaper market. But to Murdoch, who thinks himself a victim of "liberal totalitarians," this is no less than he deserves. He observes no connection between the business concessions governments award to News Corp. and the support News Corp. affords to such benefactors—deep subservience in the case of China's totalitarian elite: "We are about daring and doing for ourselves" he believes.

COCKBURN: But surely he retains some sense of irony, of cynicism, when he professes such nonsense?

PAGE: In *Alice in Wonderland* the White Queen says she can believe "six impossible things before breakfast," but Murdoch easily outdoes her. Sigmund Freud's grandson Matthew, a celebrated London public-relations man, is married to Rupert's daughter Elisabeth and has said with surprise that his father-in-law actually believes the stuff in his own newspapers.

We may be sure Mr. Freud is not so credulous. Nor are most people who know News Corp.'s publications. The London *Sun* coins money. But opinion-surveys show less than one in seven readers trust what it says (however diverting).

In legend Murdoch has an infallible popular touch, displayed in escalating circulations. But the legend misleads somewhat: Murdoch is not commercially invincible in areas where governments can't help. The plinth of his British empire, the rigorously prurient *News of the World*, was selling more than six million copies when he bought it: since, half its sales have vanished, while other papers have gained. The *New York Post* consistently loses money, and most companies would close it.

There are many curiosities—political, editorial, financial, fiscal—about News Corp.'s media ascendancy. But central to it is the psychology of the Murdoch family, and the credulousness Matthew Freud diagnosed. Murdoch is the man who promoted the "diaries" of Adolf Hitler, and today believes in Saddam Hussein's Weapons of Mass Destruction—scarcely more real, though the two dictators indeed share attributes.

For politicians in Beijing, Washington and London this psychology makes Mr. Murdoch an ideal media ally. They have illusions to peddle: Murdoch may be relied on to believe, and try to persuade others. Beijing, for instance, asserts that China cannot prosper except by accepting totalitarian Communist rule—ignoring, therefore, the party's matchless record of criminal incompetence. Rupert's achievements here are notorious, but those of his son James hardly less. James's speech celebrating in Rupert's presence the "strong stomach" which enables them both to admire Chinese repressive techniques shocked even the rugged investors hearing it.

It appears that Rupert considers James his successor, planning to give him command of BSkyB, the British satellite-TV broadcaster which News Corp. wants to link into a worldwide system. Such an advance in media power will require much political aid—that of the Bush administration particularly, and there is no supporter of Mr. Bush and his wars that can outdo Rupert's enthusiasm.

COCKBURN: It's awful to think that we have younger Murdochs on hand to plague the planet for a few more decades.

PAGE: Such psychology is a family tradition. Rupert inherited the basis of News Corp. from his Australian father Sir Keith Murdoch, a great propagandist in 1914–18 (the "golden age of lying"). Purportedly an independent war-correspondent, Keith Murdoch acted in fact as political agent to Billy Hughes, his country's wartime prime minister: plotting with him to conscript thousands of young men into a bloodbath supervised by incompetent British generals.

The plot narrowly failed—as did an anti-Semitic intrigue against the Australian general John Monash, whose volunteer divisions broke the German line. Details are an Australian concern, but we should note the success with which Rupert's father later posed as an heroic rebel rescuing young men from ruthless generals: a pioneer feat of spin-doctoring and truth-inversion. Rupert's media still sustain his father Keith's mythology ("the journalist who stopped a war"). The son, born in 1931, has always lived in the shadow of a spurious hero, uncritically promoted.

Just such narratives characterize the "authoritarian personality," identified by Theodor Adorno, and refined by later psychologists. Growth requires us all to make terms with our parents' real qualities—good or bad—and where that process fails, authoritarian qualities appear: intolerance of relationships other than dominion or submission, and intolerance of the ambiguity which equal standing implies. Such characteristics in Murdoch are shown by the testimony of many News Corp. veterans. Executives—editors specially—are ejected, regardless of quality, at a flicker of independence. Murdoch demands internally the same subservience he offers to outside power.

Conformity is enforced by mind-games like Murdoch's notorious telephone calls—coming to his executives at random moments, and consisting on his own part chiefly of brooding silence. The technique generates fear, and those who rebel against it are swiftly removed.

Authoritarians often possess charm—or skill in flattery. But a strong component is swift, apparently decisive judgment: "premature closure," or jumping to conclusions. This explains the credulousness Adorno found in authoritarians, for penetrating complex truths usually demands some endurance of ambiguity.

COCKBURN: If the authoritarian personality is unsuited to realistic news-gathering, how has Murdoch achieved media pre-eminence?

PAGE: Journalists are insecure, because they must trade in the unknown. Their profession, said the sociologist Max Weber, is uniquely "accident-prone." Good management may reduce this insecurity—but the News Corp. style actually uses insecurity as a disciplinary tool. And the seeming assurance of the authoritarian has tactical benefits: Murdoch can swap one attitude for another with zero embarrassment, and it enables him to "deliver" newspapers to any power he approves of. Readers naturally grow skeptical. But this does not yet harm News Corp.'s business model.

It would have been remarkable for Rupert to develop in non-authoritarian fashion, given his inheritance. When his father died he had neither graduated from university, nor gained any real newspaper tradecraft. In order to take control of what was then News Limited, under the trust Sir Keith established, Rupert had to accept his father as a paragon of journalistic integrity: to convince the trustees, believers in that myth, of his desire to emulate it. Exactly when independence is essential for personal and professional development, a spurious parental image descended on him. And he has emulated the political propagandist, not the mythological paragon.

The outcome attracts today's politicians because a sickness afflicts them. In all developed societies trust in politics has declined: while democracy advances in the developing world, it finds itself ailing in its homelands. Finding themselves distrusted, politicians turn for a cure to tabloid journalism—Murdoch's especially—which they realize is distrusted still more than themselves. They do so just as victims of a slow, fatal disease use quack medicines if the real cure still seems too strenuous.

The real problem of politics is the increasingly complex, and therefore occult nature of advanced society. We fancy it has become more open, and it somewhat has. But progress has fallen behind the needs of better-educated, less deferential citizens whose problems grow more daunting intellectually. The state for which politicians are responsible cannot explain itself to its citizens.

It might reverse this by opening itself far more freely to scrutiny. But against this the bureaucrats—public and private—on whom politicians rely for administrative convenience conduct a relentless guerrilla attack. Should politicians choose to fight back, they will not lack allies, for most Western societies still have some competent, independent news media and the demand exists among citizens. In Britain real newspapers, and broadcasters like the BBC, continue to be trusted as Murdoch's tabloids will never be. But quack remedies still appeal to governments: and all Murdoch asks in return is a little help in extending his monopolies.

Of course if the process goes far enough, only the quack remedy will be available, and democracy's ailment would then be terminal.

December 31

Count our blessings, an act the eternally pessimistic American left usually shuns.

2003 was a pretty good year. Who can complain about a span of time in which both William Bennett and Rush Limbaugh—exposed as, respectively, a compulsive gambler and a drug addict—were installed in the public stocks amid the derision of the citizenry? Some say that they've both winched themselves out of the mud, with Bennett's sessions in Las Vegas and Limbaugh's steady diet of OxyContin already faded in the public mind. Maybe so. But still, there's nothing so enjoyable as the plight of a professional moralizer caught in the wrong part of town.

For a vivid account of just how bad the *New York Times* has been for many, many years, I strongly recommend John L. Hess's vivid memoir *My Times: A Memoir of Dissent*, published by Seven Stories Press, that came out in September. Hess—cranky, heterodox, cultured, and irreverent—is the Ideal type of what any member of our profession should be, but who is usually leached out of the system in the dawn of their careers. He was a brilliant Paris correspondent in the '60s and early '70s, before he returned to New York and promptly wrote memorable exposés of the Metropolitan Museum (notably the incredible antics of its director Thomas Hoving) and of New York's nursing homes. Then he and his wife Karen briefly took charge of the food and restaurant column and caused turmoil in that back-scratching sector. Real journalists don't end up teaching ethics (aka kissing corporate ass) in journalism schools. They write till they drop. John Hess is a real journalist, virtually an extinct breed. Long may he write.

Hess writes the *Times*' obituary as America's supposedly greatest paper. In his caustic pages there is nothing more savage, and contrite, than his account of what the *New York Times* did not report about the Vietnam War in the late 1960s. Every journalism student, and every reporter, should have this book in their backpacks.

Of course 2003 was a year in which the governments, the intelligence services, the military bureaucracies, the intellectual whoremongers and whores of two countries, America and Britain, displayed themselves as brazen and incompetent liars as they maneuvered towards war on Iraq.

So why did the US want to invade Iraq and finish off Saddam? There are as many rationales as there were murderers on Christie's Orient Express. In the end my mind goes back to something my friend the political scientist Doug Lummis wrote from his home in another outpost of the Empire, in Okinawa at the time of the first onslaught on Iraq at the start of the '90s. Iraq, Lummis wrote, had been in the '80s a model of an oil-producing country thrusting its way out of the Third World, with a good health system and an efficient bureaucracy cowed from corrupt practices by a brutal regime. The fundamental intent of the US in 1991 was to thrust Iraq back, deeper, ever deeper into Third World indigence.

In the fall I was in London and across a weekend enjoyed the hospitality of the first-class journalist Richard Gott, also of his wife Vivienne. At one point our conversation turned to the question of motive, and I was interested to hear Gott make the same point as Lummis, only about the attack of 2003. I asked him why he thought this, and Gott recalled a visit he'd made to Baghdad last year.

This was a time when the natural and political inclination of most opponents of the impending war was to stress the fearful toll of the sanctions imposed from 1990 on. Gott had a rather different observation, in part, because of his experience in Latin America. Baghdad, he said, looked a lot more prosperous than Havana. "It was clear today," Gott wrote after his visit, "from the quantity of goods in the shops, and the heavy traffic jams in the urban motorways, that the sanctions menace has been effectively defeated. Iraq is awakening from a long and depressing sleep, and its economy is clearly beginning to function once more. No wonder it is in the firing line."

Eyes other than Gott's no doubt observed the same signs of economic recovery. Iraq was rising from the ashes, and so, it had to be thrust down once more. The only "recovery" permitted would be on Uncle Sam's terms. Or so Uncle Sam, in his arrogance, supposed.

2004

January 6
My problem with the Hitler–Bush pairing is not so much the comparison per se, which is solidly in the respectable mainstream of political abuse, but in the strange hysteria of Democrats about Bush as a leader of such consummate evil, so vile that any Democrat would be preferable. Any Democrat? George Bush is by definition a warmonger, but Wesley Clark, one of the contenders for the Democratic nomination, actually issued an order that could have sparked Armageddon. Back in the war on Yugoslavia, in his capacity as NATO's Supreme Commander, Clark ordered the British general, Sir Michael Jackson, to block Russian planes about to land at Pristina airport. Jackson refused to obey, declaring in one furious exchange quoted in *Newsweek*, "I'm not going to start the Third World War for you."

The central political issue this year is the absolute corruption of the political system and of the two parties that share the spoils. Wherever one looks, at the gerrymandered districts, the balloting methods, the fund-raising, corruption steams like vapor from a vast swamp. To rail about Bush as Hitler is to blur what should be the proper focus. If you want to hear an American answer to Hitler-as-warmonger at full tilt go and read the speeches John F. Kennedy was making and planning to make when he was shot.

Hitler, genocidal monster that he was, was also the first practicing Keynesian leader. When he came to power in 1933 unemployment stood at 40 percent. Economic recovery came without the stimulus of arms spending. Hitler wanted a larger population, so construction subsidies produced a housing boom. There were vast public works such as the autobahns. He paid little attention to the deficit or to the protests of the bankers about his policies. Interest rates were kept low and though wages were pegged, family income increased by reason of full employment. By 1936 unemployment had sunk to one percent. German military spending remained low until 1939.

Not just Bush but Howard Dean and the Democrats could learn a few lessons in economic policy from that early, Keynesian Hitler, whose hostility to unions they also echo. As for warmongering, American presidents and would-be presidents don't need lessons from anyone. As Hitler freely acknowledged in his campaign bio, *Mein Kampf*, the debt was the other way round.

January 28

My dear friend and late *Nation* colleague Andrew Kopkind liked to tell how, skiing in Aspen at the height of the Vietnam War, he came round a bend and saw another skier, Defense Secretary Robert McNamara, alone near the edge of a precipice. This was during the period of Rolling Thunder, which ultimately saw three times as many bombs dropped on Vietnam as the Allies dropped on Europe in World War II. "I could have reached out with my ski pole," Andy would say wistfully, "and pushed him over."

Alas, Andy shirked this chance to get into the history books and McNamara survived the 1960s, when, as US Secretary of Defense, he contributed more than most to the slaughter of 3.4 million Vietnamese (his own estimate). He went on to run the World Bank, where he presided over the impoverishment, eviction from their lands, and death of many millions more round the world. And now here he is, the star of Errol Morris's much-praised, in my view wildly overpraised, documentary *The Fog of War*, talking comfortably about the millions of people he's helped to kill. It reminded me of films of Albert Speer, Hitler's architect and then head of war production. Speer loved to admit to an overall guilt. But when he was pressed on specific nastiness, like working Jews or Russians to death in arms factories, he would insist, eyes ablaze with forthrightness, that he knew nothing of such infamies.

The "fog of war" is a tag usually attributed to von Clausewitz, though the German philosopher and theorist of war never actually used the phrase. Eugenia Kiesling argued a couple of years ago in *Military Review* that the idea of fog—unreliable information—wasn't a central preoccupation of Clausewitz. "Eliminating fog," Kiesling wrote, "gives us a clearer and more useful understanding of Clausewitz's friction. It restores uncertainty and the intangible stresses of military command to their rightful centrality in *On War*. It allows us to replace the simplistic message that war intelligence is important with the reminder that Clausewitz constantly emphasizes moral forces in war."

As presented by McNamara, through Morris, "the fog of war" usefully deflects attention from clear and unpleasant facts entirely unobscured by fog. McNamara can talk about confusions, fog, about what actually happened on August 2 or 4, 1964, thus detouring unfogged daylight, of which there was plenty, about the moral failures of US commanders, including McNamara, waging war on the Vietnamese. Roberta Wohlstetter was a pioneer in this fogging technique back in the 1950s, with her heavily subsidized *Pearl Harbor: Warning and Decision*, which deployed the idea of distracting "noise" as the phenomenon that prevented US commanders, ultimately Roosevelt, from comprehending the information that the Japanese were about to launch a surprise attack. Wohlstetterian "noise" thus obscured the fact that FDR wanted a Japanese provocation, and knew the attack was coming, though probably not its scale and destructiveness.

When McNamara looks back down memory lane there are no real shadows, just the sunlight of moral self-satisfaction: "I don't fault Truman for dropping the bombs"; "I never saw Kennedy more shocked" (after the murder of Ngo Dinh Diem); "never would I have authorized an illegal action" (after the Tonkin Gulf fakery); "I'm very proud of my accomplishments and I'm very sorry I made errors" (his life). Slabs of instructive history are missing from Morris's film.

McNamara rode into the Pentagon on one of the biggest of big lies, the bogus "missile gap" touted by Kennedy in his 1960 campaign against Nixon. It was all nonsense. As Defense Secretary, McNamara ordered the production of 1,000 Minuteman strategic nukes, this at a time when he was looking at US intelligence reports showing that the Soviets had one silo with one untested missile.

To Morris now he offers homilies about the menace of nuclear Armageddon. It's cost-free to say such things, grazing peacefully on the tranquil mountain pastures of his eighty-seven years.

Back in 1994 (you can find the remarks on page 409 of my *The Golden Age Is in Us*) I had a conversation with Noam Chomsky, where McNamara's name cropped up. "If you look at the modern intelligentsia over the past century or so," Chomsky said,

> they're pretty much a managerial class, a secular priesthood. They've gone in basically two directions. One is essentially Leninist. Leninism is the ideology of a radical intelligentsia that says, "We have the right to rule." Alternatively, they have joined the decision-making sector of state capitalist society, as managers in the political, economic and ideological institutions.
>
> The ideologies are very similar. I've sometimes compared Robert McNamara to Lenin, and you only have to change a few words for them to say virtually the same thing.

"Management," McNamara declared in 1967, "is the gate through which social and economic and political change, indeed change in every direction, is diffused through society." Substitute "party organization" for "management" and you have Lenin.

Of course the managerial ideal for McNamara was a managerial dictatorship. World Bank loans surged to Pinochet's Chile after Allende's overthrow, to Uruguay, to Argentina, to Brazil after the military coup, to the Philippines, to Suharto after the 1965 coup in Indonesia. And to the Romania of Ceauşescu. McNamara poured money—$2.36 billion between 1974 and 1982—into the tyrant's hands. In 1980 Romania was the Bank's eighth biggest borrower. McNamara crowed delightedly as Ceauşescu razed whole villages, turned hundreds of square miles of prime farm land into open-pit mines, polluted the air with coal and lignite, turned Romania into one vast prison, applauded by the Bank in an amazing 1979 economic study cited by Rich as tokening the "Importance of Centralized Economic Control."

So the McNamara of the World Bank evolved naturally, organically, from the McNamara of Vietnam. The one was prolegomenon to the other, the horrors perhaps on a narrower and more vivid scale, but ultimately lesser in dimension and consequence.

As displayed by Morris, McNamara never offers any reflection on the social system that produced and promoted him, a perfectly nice, well-spoken war criminal. As his inflation of his role in the foe-bombing of Japan shows, he can go so far as to falsely though complacently indict himself, while still shirking bigger, more terrifying and certainly more useful reflections on the system that blessed him and mercilessly killed millions upon millions under FDR, Truman, Eisenhower, JFK, LBJ, and Nixon.

I don't think Morris laid a glove on McNamara, who should be feeling well pleased. Like Speer, he got away with it yet again. In the weeks after the film was launched he scurried to Washington to participate in forums on the menace of nuclear destruction with the same self-assurance that he went to Vietnam and Cuba to review the record. If Morris had done a decent job, McNamara would not have dared to appear in any public place.

March 4

"When all seems dark," my father, Claud, used to say when I was a teenager, "try reading a little Marx. It puts things in perspective." As I'd mope over the defection of some girlfriend he'd thrust a copy of the *Eighteenth Brumaire* into my hand and tell me to cheer up. I remembered Claud's advice last weekend, when news that one of the world's great Marxist economists, Paul Sweezy, had died at the age of ninety-three.

Sweezy wasn't at all like Marx in personal demeanor. Karl was hairy, bohemian, cantankerous whereas Paul, godlike in his good looks, radiated an amiable and dignified calm, as least in my limited personal experience. Reading Marx, you feel you're getting to the truth of the matter and it was the same way with Sweezy. He wrote and taught with extraordinary clarity.

After Sweezy's death, I asked Robert Pollin, once a student of Sweezy's, for his thoughts on Sweezy. Bob remembered the excitement of Sweezy's lectures at the New School back in the day, and he swiftly furnished many interesting paragraphs about Sweezy's great contributions, in the big books and in *Monthly Review*, which he founded with Leo Huberman in 1949.

At Harvard in the 1930s Sweezy was the star grad student of Joseph Schumpeter. Pollin reckons that Schumpeter was thinking of Sweezy, whom he greatly admired, when he wrote in *Capitalism, Socialism, Democracy* that capitalism would not survive because capitalism breeds intellectual freedom, hence people with critical faculties, and it's inevitable that this spirit breeds powerful minds who will turn their guns on the deficiencies of capitalism itself. Then Schumpeter, conservative himself, wrote that socialism would succeed, maybe unwieldy, but more egalitarian nonetheless, in part because the brilliant thinkers grown dissatisfied with the crassness and injustices of capitalism would also rise to the top in a socialist society, and make it function decently. "And again," Bob writes, "who else could he have had in mind here but Paul, his student and protégé?"

Different times, brighter hopes. These days we're looking at a lot of socialist rubble, but simultaneously at a capitalist architecture whose stresses and failures Sweezy, in accessible terms, decade after decade, in his books and in the *Monthly Review*, which he founded with Leo Huberman in 1949, trenchantly detected and explained: the reasons for the New Deal's failure, until World War II bailed out the system; military Keynesianism and the Korean War as the prime factors in US recovery after that war; underdevelopment in the Third World, consequence of dependency that was created by imperialism; as well as the increasing role of finance in the operations of capitalism.

Way ahead of most, Sweezy was clear-eyed about the trends: the capture of more and more of society's wealth by the rich, the threat this pyramid of purchasing power poses to the stability of the whole system, the need for the left to bolster what defenses working people can muster against the predators. Sweezy, Bob Pollin writes,

> was the most powerful Marxist exponent of under-consumptionism since Rosa Luxemburg. Keynes himself later embraced this as his analysis of the 1930s depression. Under-consumptionism is the tendency in capitalist economies for the capitalists to produce more things than the people can afford to buy. Capitalism could solve this problem through more income equality, and more social control over investment spending. But capitalists don't like that solution. Therefore, as Sweezy and Baran argued in *Monopoly Capital*, they come up with alternative means of getting buyers for the things monopolist firms decide to produce: they get the military to spend, they induce spending through advertising, and they ride the wave of epoch-making innovations like the automobile (which brought public highway construction and government subsidized construction of the suburbs).

Read Sweezy's books and you can understand why we have US Marines presiding over the continuing enslavement of Haiti, why we have John Kerry proclaiming his doctrine of progressive interventionism, why we have Alan Greenspan calling for a renewed onslaught on Social Security. Sweezy taught generations how to understand these things, how not to be surprised. Like all great teachers he gave us the consolations as well as the burden of such knowledge. If you know what's happening you're in a position to figure out how to do something about it, and that's always uplifting.

March 31

Michael Newdow, a California doctor with a law degree, has been arguing to the US Supreme Court that the reference to God in the Pledge of Allegiance uttered daily by millions of school children is unconstitutional. The Pledge was originally written by a former Baptist minister, Francis Bellamy, in 1892 to promote the 400th anniversary of Columbus's discovery of the Americas.

In 1954, amid the freezing gusts of the cold war, the Rev. George M. Docherty, pastor at the New York Avenue Presbyterian Church in Washington, DC, preached to a distinguished congregation including President Dwight D. Eisenhower that the Pledge should contain a reference to God, thus distinguishing it from kindred pledges by "little Muscovites" similarly pledging their loyalty to the hammer and sickle. Living "under God," Docherty thundered, was "a definitive fact of the American way of life." He conceded that "honest atheists" might disagree, but added that in his opinion the First Amendment's guarantee of freedom of expression "is not, and was never meant to be, a separation of religion and life," and that, honesty notwithstanding, "an atheistic American is a contradiction in terms."

America was in the midst of a tumid uptick in religious pietism at the time, powered in part by the need to display America's Biggest Ally in the fight against Communism. In fact the tremendously popular Eisenhower had had an unconventional spiritual upbringing, with his father's faith stemming from the Mennonite Baptist River Brethren, who had moved from Pennsylvania to Kansas. His mother Ida was a Jehovah's Witness. Eisenhower was the first President to join a church (Presbyterian) after being elected President. (Lincoln is the only American President to have steered clear of churches altogether.)

Eisenhower and Congress rushed to implement Docherty's call. Congress was unanimous and the only religious group that objected was that of the Boston Unitarians. "One Nation Under God" was added to the Pledge, and when the federal Ninth Circuit Court of Appeals ruled it unconstitutional last year and that school children didn't have to recite it if they didn't want to, Congress once again exhibited unanimity in reproving the uppity judges.

April 12

Today brings us the hundredth anniversary of the birth of Claud Cockburn, father of other Cockburns—the brothers Alexander, Andrew, and Patrick; Claudia Flanders, Sarah Caudwell; grandfather of Daisy Cockburn, Chloe Cockburn-Scheff, Olivia Wilde, Charlie Cockburn, Henry Cockburn, Alexander Cockburn, Laura Flanders, Stephanie Flanders.

Claud was the greatest radical journalist of his age, an inspiring influence not only on *CounterPunch*, but on many other seditious journalistic enterprises, such as the UK's *Private Eye*, the fortnightly at whose helm he stood at a crucial moment in the early 1960s, or the

National Guardian founded by Cedric Belfrage, James Aronson, and John McManus.

Claud was a child of empire, born in the British legation in Peking, son of Harry Cockburn, the British minister there during the Boxer rising, who had spent twenty years in Chungking and was on friendly terms with the Empress Dowager of the Middle Kingdom. Claud grew up mostly in Budapest, and went to Berkhamsted school, run by his friend Graham Greene's father. Just young enough to escape slaughter in the Great War, he went to Oxford, lived in Paris, wrote for Ezra Pound's *Dial*, worked for the London *Times* in Berlin, saw the rise of Hitler, and went to New York to describe the Crash.

He turned left, quit the *Times*, joined the *Daily Worker*, the newspaper of the British Communist Party, founded his famous anti-fascist newsletter *The Week*, and fought for the Republic in the Spanish Civil War, joining the Republic militia before the International Brigades were formed. His superiors ordered him back from the front lines to assume the propaganda duties alluded to in the piece below. 1947 saw him quit *The Worker* and the CP, move to Ireland, and start a whole new life as a novelist and freelance commentator. His first book, *Beat the Devil*, written under the name James Helvick, was turned into Huston's well-known film of the same name. He wrote other novels, including *Ballantyne's Folly* and *Jericho Road*, and three volumes of masterly memoirs, collected in *I, Claud.*

He wrote fast, with a beautifully easy style. His prose could be light, ironic, also savage. He was learned but never overbearing, cultivated but never patronizing. He respected and enjoyed people at all social levels and ages. He loved dogs. Under the force of his example who could resist the lure of journalism? None of his sons did, to the initial gloom of our mother Patricia, who knew first-hand that freelance journalism doesn't always bring home regular slabs of bacon.

His body simply wore out when he was seventy-seven though his mind stayed sharp till his last breath.

The day before he died in St. Finbarr's hospital in Cork he dictated a column for the *Irish Times* to Patricia. He never soured on his ideals, never lost faith in humanity's nobler instincts, never failed to see the humor in life.

Shortly before Claud died, amid one of the periodic uproars about upper-class British spies, my friend Ben Sonnenberg asked him to write a piece for Ben's literary quarterly *Grand Street*. Claud turned in a masterly essay, full of astute observations about Guy Burgess and spy mania, but also with a wonderfully tragic-comic memoir about the strange death of Basil Murray in Valencia. I include it here because *Grand Street* is not easily available.

Spies and Two Deaths in Spain
by Claud Cockburn
Before he was revealed as a central figure—perhaps the mastermind—of the Burgess-Maclean-Philby spy scandal, the rapscallion Guy Burgess used sometimes to join me at a table in one of the bars of the House of Commons and, in the course of conversation, proclaim that he was an agent of the Soviet government. This would come out in a drink-slurred roar, clearly audible to, for example, Ernest Bevin, Foreign Secretary, towering massively at the bar, as well as to any other politician or newspaperman in the place.

He would usually, somewhere in the talk, make another emphatic assertion. This was to the effect that he was the illegitimate son of the then Lady Rothschild. It was, he implied, a fact which accounted for his expert knowledge of international finance.

The claim about his illegitimacy was entirely false and quite a number of people who ought to have known better believed it. And his claim to be an agent of the KGB was true and no one believed it. It was a crude and entirely successful example of the double bluff. If anyone—and I suppose there were some such in British counter-intelligence—were to report a suspicion about Burgess's role, his superior was likely to reply with weary contempt, "I know, I know, he keeps saying so himself."

The ploy about Lady Rothschild appealed to people as a fairly titillating piece of gossip. It was useful to Burgess and he employed it for the same reason that his contemporary Brendan Bracken, Britain's Information Minister throughout the war and an immensely successful political and financial pirate, used to claim that he was the illegitimate son of Winston Churchill. Reading the excitingly simplistic accounts of successive spy scandals in British publications, I find it useful to recall these facts about Burgess, which indicate in their own simple way how complex the detection of spies in our midst can be. We have had spy scares every few years, and I have no doubt, are going to have more of them. In the same way, scares about terrorism—together with more or less fraudulent analyses of the supposed activities and motivations of terrorists—will certainly proliferate as the nervous system of the general public increasingly demands sedation in the face of horrifying phenomena.

The public nervous system may be soothed by false explanations. But unless people are encouraged to look rather more coolly and deeply into these same phenomena of espionage and terrorism, they will make no progress towards any genuine self-defense against either.

At this point, it may be wise to remember that there are those whose hysteria on these subjects leads them to believe that any cool analysis amounts almost to a condonation. Such hysteria is of obvious help to spies and terrorists. Let us also note that nobody in any country can truly and totally evaluate the harm an enemy's spies may have done. The real experts in anti-espionage are a great deal more ready to admit this than the horrified public. Even the outstanding Russian dissident, Andrei Sakharov, "father" of their hydrogen bomb, is reported as saying that the secrets betrayed by Klaus Fuchs were of minimal importance in the development of the weapons in the Soviet Union.

A constant element among the facts and fiction about espionage is what we may call "Belief in the Spy as Superman." All intelligence agencies have a vested interest in convincing the world of their machinelike efficiency. Particularly in wartime, but at other times too, the notion of the spy successfully uprooting our secrets, like a pig uprooting truffles, is alarming in itself, and also because it fits and extends the idea which almost everybody has, that the enemy is not only wickeder but also cleverer than we are. Malcolm Muggeridge once told me how, while working for MI6 during the war, he became for a time profoundly depressed by what appeared to him the ineptitude and even clownish folly of some of our intelligence procedures.

His gloom lifted when, after the Allied landings in Italy, his German opposite numbers scampered out of Naples without even burning their vital documents. To his relief he saw from them that the Germans had been proceeding with an ineptitude and folly at least equal to our own.

A frequent element in spy-alarm, notably in Britain and France, is the belief that spies belong to, and are protected by, a higher social and financial class than the common citizenry of the country on which they are spying. An awkward bit of this last element is that it often chances to be true, as is apparent to students of the relationships between certain members of the German and British nobility not only before the outbreak of World War II, but in the intrigues directed particularly against Churchill during the autumn and winter of 1939–1940.

The most insidious of the bases for fear of spies is subtler than the others, yet quite as dangerous. It is rarely formulated but runs roughly, and often subconsciously, like this: if some of our best educated citizens who have had every advantage our society can offer are nonetheless prepared to dedicate themselves to an ideology destructive to that society, may it not be just possible that there is something dangerously wrong with our own philosophy of life?

It is exactly this element that accounts for the extraordinary outburst of outraged surprise with which the British public greeted the exposure of Anthony Blunt as a KGB agent. As in the case of Philby and Maclean, here was a young man of good family who had enjoyed to the full the educational, cultural, and social advantages of a reasonably affluent student at one of Britain's two senior universities. He was as far from deprivation as anyone could get. There was no visible cause for him to turn against society. The thought that, despite all this, some extraordinary power of attraction in Communism's alien and hostile doctrines had seduced him was terrifying. To judge by the tone of many British commentators, it was as alarming as a discovery that a witch-doctor had been secretly at large, exercising black-magical powers over the citizenry.

Such thoughts paralyze the capacity to see and deal rationally with the problem. The true explanation is a great deal simpler. Blunt and the other young men concerned were at Cambridge during the Great Depression. About three million were unemployed, and at that time to be on the dole or in low-paid employment in Britain meant poverty that was often near the starvation line.

John Gunther, in his book *Inside Britain*, notes the astonishment of American visitors at the docility of the British working class under such conditions and the absence of revolutionary outbursts. In this desert of misery, Cambridge was an ostentatious oasis of civilized comfort. It is not at all surprising that Blunt and others should have, with some deep feelings of guilt, questioned the justification for such a state of affairs. On the contrary, it would have been surprising had any sensitive and informed young man coolly accepted his position as though by divine right. The Communists did not require secret recruiting sergeants; the economics of the time were doing the job quite well enough. By contrast, only a few years earlier at Oxford, when the economic situation was less spectacularly dire, the majority of the student population was almost entirely apolitical. If, as some recent publications have suggested, there were Soviet recruiters at the Oxford of that day, they should have been fired for incompetence. Politics was in the main a replay, more or less histrionic, of the Liberal–Conservative struggles of the years before World War I, with Labour adding no more than flavoring to a familiar stew.

Some who delve needlessly deep into the motivations of international spies, and double and triple agents, have made much of the fact that many of what may be called "The Cambridge Group" of distinguished Soviet agents can be shown to have been homosexual or to have had homosexual connections. But let us note that at Oxford in the mid-twenties, homosexuality was as fashionable and obtrusive as Communism was not. From the London press, which liked to paint lurid pictures of goings-on at the university, you could have gathered that the undergraduates were about evenly divided between flaunting and artistically outré homosexuals and sturdy British "hearties" upholding the values for which the preceding generation had died in the war.

Such nonsense apart, it is certainly true that in the most flamboyant and "trend-setting" intellectual circles homosexuality was in some cases so nearly de rigueur that aspiring writers, artists, and above all actors, actually felt compelled to pretend to be homosexual. The slang word for it was "so." In reply to the greeting "How are you?" a common reply was: "So so, but not quite so so as sometimes." A friend of mine who had the most "normal" sexual tastes started a literary magazine which, it was immediately suggested, should have been called *Just So Stories*. When an undergraduate was actually sent down for homosexual practices, astounded observers held competitions to suggest what amazingly spectacular misbehavior he must have indulged in to merit this extraordinary action by the authorities.

Another odd fact is that at that time "womanizer" was a term of abuse. I knew a normally lusty American Rhodes Scholar who could hardly believe that even among those who vigorously deplored the existence of homosexuality, "womanizing" was worse than immoral; it was unspeakably vulgar. This must have had its historical roots in the long ages when Oxford was so successfully isolated by lack of transport from the outside world that prostitutes were the only women available during term time to all but the richest students who could afford gigs and other horse-drawn vehicles to get them at least as far as Reading. By my day the majority of heterosexual people were able to find ways and means of satisfaction, even in term time, but always under the still somewhat inhibiting fear of being dubbed "womanizers."

It is a pity that so many who write of Oxford and Cambridge in the relevant years are so crassly ignorant of the prevailing atmosphere. They remind me of Mr. Vladimir, the Imperial Russian diplomat in Conrad's *The Secret Agent*, as he lectures the title character:

> And Mr. Vladimir developed his idea from on high, with scorn and condescension, displaying at the same time an amount of ignorance as to the real aims, thoughts, and methods of the revolutionary world which filled the silent Mr. Verloc with inward consternation. He confounded causes with effects more than was excusable; the most distinguished propagandists with impulsive bomb throwers; assumed organization where in the nature of things it could not exist; spoke of the social revolutionary party one moment as of a perfectly disciplined army, where the word of chiefs

was supreme, and at another as if it had been the loosest association of desperate brigands that ever camped in a mountain gorge.

We find a Mr. Vladimir at every corner today, spouting his confident but dangerously misleading lectures.

Still, in the areas of spying and terrorism, even the best are inclined to leave out from their sapient and (so far as they go) truthful analyses the factor of unpredictability. Or nonsense, if you prefer. Brooding on this situation, I constantly keep in mind my own experience in the field of espionage, or rather, counter-espionage.

Early in the Spanish Civil War I was what, if one were inclined to pomposity, might be called a section leader of the counter-espionage department of the Spanish Republican government dealing with Anglo-Saxon personalities. My job was principally to vet applications by British and Americans for visas to enter Republican Spain.

It was, as I realized rather late, a "no win" situation for me. Either I allowed in some supposed friend of the Republic who turned out to be a secret enemy, in which case I could very well be shot as a saboteur. Or, overcautiously avoiding this risk, I might exclude some character suspect to me who would later turn out to be a loyal friend of the Republic and a potentially powerful propagandist in its cause. Saboteur again.

It was under these circumstances that I had to consider the application for a visa for Basil Murray, son of Professor Gilbert Murray, whose family and connections were luminaries of the British liberal academic and political world. I was astonished, and more than a little suspicious, when Basil, in making his application, explained that having hitherto lived the life of a roustabout at Oxford and layabout in London, he had suddenly seen the light and wished to dedicate himself to the cause of the Republic. Specifically, he wanted to give radio talks from Valencia, where the government was now established.

Knowing and liking Basil, but still not quite convinced of the strength of his new resolutions, I discussed his application with the Foreign Minister, who thought that I was mad even to consider rejecting the son of so distinguished a figure in Britain who was as well the cousin of the British Foreign Secretary. (This last was untrue, a detail invented by Basil to help in obtaining his visa.)

Basil came to Valencia, and with much sweat and dedication produced several excellent broadcasts. Then he suddenly fell in love with a girl of whom one may say that had she had the words “I am a Nazi spy” printed on her hat, that could hardly have made her position clearer than it was. I reasoned with Basil, but found him besotted with love and convinced that, in some bigoted way, I was deliberately thinking ill of this splendid creature.

Just as my arguments ran finally into a blind alley, the girl herself suddenly quit the Republic for Berlin in the company of a high-ranking officer of the International Brigade who proved also to be an agent of the enemy. Although I was naturally careful not to belabor Basil with I-told-you-sos, he fell into a deep melancholy both at the loss of the loved one and the disclosure of her political vileness.

Soon after, wandering bitterly disconsolate along the quays of Valencia’s harbor, he saw a tiny street menagerie of the kind that in those days was a common form of popular entertainment in Spain. The little group included an ape. And this ape, Basil said, was the first living creature that—since the defection of the Nazi agent—had looked at him with friendly sympathy. He bought the ape and took it with him to the Victoria Hotel, which was the hotel housing all visiting VIPs.

The next I knew, I received a call from the management of the Victoria, who said furiously that they had already strained themselves to the limit by putting up all the foreign visitors I had recommended, and that now, by God, my latest protégé was demanding a room for an ape. After I had pointed out that there were apes enough already living in the hotel, so that one more would hardly be noticed, it was agreed that Basil be moved to a room with a large bathroom, in which the ape might be accommodated.

This arrangement worked well enough for a matter of forty-eight hours. Then Basil, still disconsolate despite the friendly eyes of the ape, drank heavily and fell asleep naked on his bed in the fierce humid heat of a Valencia afternoon. He had locked the ape in the bathroom, but the ingenious and friendly animal became bored with this isolation and longed for the company of its new master. Somehow it picked the lock of the bathroom door and came into the bedroom looking for a game or frolic. Finding the new master disappointingly unresponsive, the ape made vigorous efforts to rouse him, biting him over and over again and finally in frustration biting through his jugular vein.

Apart from my personal regret at the loss of my old acquaintance, I was compelled to see that the situation would be politically damaging. One could surmise at once what a hostile British press would make of the news that a brilliant young Englishman of distinguished family had sought to work for the Red Republic, and had, within a very short time, been bitten to death by an ape. It was possible quickly to announce that Basil had died of pneumonia as a result of the treacherous Valencia climate.

It was also arranged that the British government should send a light cruiser or frigate from its Mediterranean fleet for the purpose of carrying Basil back to Britain. A small cortege of suitable officials from the Republican Foreign Office accompanied the remains to the quayside. It was only when the remains were being moved to the cutter for transfer onto the frigate that a member of the cortege noticed that they had been joined by the ape. It sprang into the stern sheets of the cutter. Faithfully, it followed Basil up the companionway. It appeared on the spotless deck and there, in a gesture suitable for solemn occasions (learned, no doubt, from the owner of the menagerie), it raised its fist in the Red Front salute.

A British warrant officer—having doubtless been warned of the dangerous and even bestial character of the Reds and of the necessity for vigilance while the ship was in a Red harbor—reacted swiftly, drew a pistol and shot the ape dead. Its body fell overboard and disappeared into the Mediterranean. Basil, I believe, had a fine funeral in England, and the episode was closed.

But not really. For weeks afterwards I was pestered by the menagerie owner demanding compensation and heart-balm for his grief at the demise of the ape. He said that when he had sold it to Basil he had not at all envisaged the possibility that the creature would be brutally murdered by the forces of British imperialism, shooting down that helpless animal as ruthlessly as they had shot down innumerable people throughout the Empire.

In addition, the British diplomatic mission to Republican Spain immediately spread the story that we, the Republicans, meaning in this case me, had murdered Basil—poison in the wine, one of them said. Anarchists and others suspicious of the coalition government somehow spread a story that through the government's carelessness or connivance, a British agent had been introduced, and then killed when on the verge of damaging exposure. Enemies of the Murray family, and those disgusted that Basil should have worked for the Republic, spread in England the story that Basil had had improper relations with the ape. They even, I found later, substituted a bear.

As late as the 1950s a close and loving relative of Basil's was delighted to hear from me the true story, which confirmed the genuineness of Basil's determination to do something constructive with his life—however grotesque the actual outcome.

April 15

As one who regards Jerry Ford as our greatest President (least time served, least damage done, husband of Betty, plus Stevens as his contribution to the Supreme Court), I'd always imagined the man from Grand Rapids would never be surpassed in sheer slowness of thought.

But I think Bush has Ford beat. Had he ever made a mistake, the reporter asked at that White House press conference. The President's face remained composed, masking the turmoil and terror raging within, as neuro-electronic networks went into gridlock. It should have been easy for him. Broad avenues of homely humility beckoned him on. "John, no man can stand before his Creator as I do each day and say he is without error ..." Reagan would have hit the ball out of the park. But the President froze. He said he'd have to think it over.

August 10

No alien penetration, or treachery of double agents, have ever done nearly as much damage to the CIA as the infighting consequent upon the arrival of each new director, charged by his White House master with cleaning house and settling accounts with the bad guys installed by the previous White House incumbent.

Bush's new director, former Republican Florida Rep. Porter Goss and his team of enforcers, now rampage through the corridors of CIA HQ at Langley. Goss was once an undercover CIA officer so there's probably a personal edge to his mission of revenge, as he strikes back at the dolts who nixed his expense accounts or poured scorn on his heroic endeavors in the field.

But Goss's most pressing task is to exact retribution for the stories emanating from the CIA in the months before the election suggesting that the Agency's measured assessments of the supposed WMD presence in Iraq were perverted by the war faction headed by (Vice) President Cheney.

Goss and his hit team have acted swiftly. In early November the CIA's number 2, John McLaughlin, resigned, followed days later by the Agency's top man on the clandestine side, Stephen Kappes, and his number 2, Michael Sulick. And, no surprise, into retirement goes Mr. "Anonymous," Michael Scheuer, leader of the CIA unit hunting Osama bin Laden. I'm with Goss on that one. Scheuer probably spent most of each day hunting down his next book advance and kibbitizing about royalties from Imperial Hubris with his true "Controls" at Brassey's Inc., owned by shadowy Books International.

So Goss will exact vengeance, spill blood, leak to favored journalists, and deliver Bush daily intelligence briefings tailored to meet the expectations of his patron.

Of course there's a portentous uproar and wringing of pious hands as the cry goes up that the abilities of the Agency to collect and analyze useful intelligence are being compromised by what Jason Vest in the *Nation* was pleased to call "unparalleled" political partisanship. "We need a director," cries Jay Rockefeller, ranking Democrat on the Senate Intelligence Committee, "who is not only knowledgeable and capable, but unquestionably independent."

There's nothing new in all this. Permit me to take you on a brisk tour of CIA directors. Before Goss we had George Tenet, a former Congressional staffer so eager to please Bush that he uttered the imperishable words "slam dunk" about the supposed ease of making a case for Saddam's WMD.

Tenet, whose political agility is advertised in the fact that he was one of the longer serving DCIs, supplanted John Deutch, an MIT prof who divided his brief sojourn as Director between downloads of the Agency's darkest secrets onto his personal laptop, business ventures with a revolving doorman from DoD, William Perry, and excursions to town meetings in Los Angeles, claiming to black audiences that the CIA had no role in funneling cocaine into the nation's ghettoes. Among the few secret files Deutch apparently failed to download onto his laptop were materials later excavated by the CIA's own inspector general, Fred Hitz, establishing CIA complicity in the cocaine trade.

Deutch's predecessor was Jim Woolsey, unusual for someone in the Clinton-Gore milieu in having no conspicuous record of marijuana consumption, hence a security clearance, thus qualifying him as the nation's top spy. Clinton and Gore mostly liked Woolsey for political reasons, because he had street cred with the neocons (who used to sail under the flag of "Jackson Democrats"). Woolsey later became a prime lobbyist for attacking Iraq.

DCI before Woolsey was Robert Gates, a cat torturer/drowner in his youth, creature of Bush Sr.'s administration, in trouble for lying to Congress; before him William Webster, brought in as air freshener after William Casey, one of the most consummate scoundrels ever to run any government agency in the entire history of the United States. Casey was Reagan's campaign bag man, then given the CIA with the prime function of misrepresenting the threat posed by the Soviet Union and, nearer at hand, Nicaragua.

Casey dislodged Jimmy Carter's man, Admiral Stansfield Turner, a relatively honest fellow. Turner, roasted for firing many in the CIA "old guard" of that era, took over as CIA chief from Bush Sr., who, like JFK, sanctioned a Murder Inc. in the Caribbean, and who wilted under pressure from the Jackson Democrats, aka the Military

Industrial Complex. It was Bush who appointed the notorious "Team B" to contradict previous in-house CIA analyses suggesting the Soviet threat was not as fearsome as that depicted on the cartoon (aka editorial) page of the *Wall Street Journal*.

Bush's predecessor as DCI was William Colby, a CIA careerman mostly famous for running the Phoenix assassination program in Vietnam, battling with the CIA's crazed counter-intelligence czar, James Angleton, and testifying with undue frankness in the Church congressional hearings into the CIA. In retirement Colby continued his career as a conspiracy buff, probing the suicide of Clinton's counsel Vince Foster for his newsletter. Colby finally stepped into his canoe on Maryland's eastern shore after a dinner of clams and white wine and turned up drowned a few days later.

Colby replaced James Schlesinger who ran the Agency for a few months in the midst of the Watergate scandal. Ray McGovern, a twenty-seven-year career analyst with the CIA, now retired, remembers how he and his Agency colleagues were taken aback when Schlesinger announced on arrival, "I am here to see that you guys don't screw Richard Nixon!" To underscore his point, McGovern recalls, Schlesinger "told us he would be reporting directly to White House political adviser Bob Haldeman and not to National Security Adviser Henry Kissinger."

We'll stop with Schlesinger, but you get the idea. There's nothing new about the "political" appointment of Porter Goss, who at least has the agreeable distinction of owning an organic farm in Virginia where tiny donkeys run herd alongside hairy sheep from Central Asia, and chickens lay green eggs, thus reduplicating the Agency's most expensive op ever, the Afghan caper, where the CIA supervised the mujahedeen at a cost of $3.5 billion, and launched Osama bin Laden on his chosen path.

Most intelligence is worthless, with the scant truthful stuff rapidly deep-sixed. Whatever makes its way onto the desks of presidents or congressional overseers is 100 percent "political." Anyone who wants to find out what's happening in the world would be better advised to ask a taxi driver.

September 1

Thanksgiving brought us the one-month anniversary of Bill O'Reilly's disclosure on his show that "to protect my family" he had settled with Ms. Andrea Mackris and her lawyer Benedict Morelli, thus cutting off what millions of O'Reilly haters had hoped would be a protracted season of public humiliation for Fox's apex bully. The settlement established that all parties agreed there had been no wrongdoing and as an earnest of good faith O'Reilly (if you believe the *New York Daily News*) had paid anywhere from $2 million to $10 million to Mackris—nice money if true, though not as nice as the $60 million Morelli had originally suggested to O'Reilly as a satisfactorily round figure.

But there remains the mystery of the transmuted loofa, about which I had been hoping for some pleasing courtroom exchanges. Let's pick up the thread in the court document lodged in Nassau County, NJ, by Morelli on behalf of Mackris.

O'Reilly calls Mackris, a thirty-three-year-old innocent, working as a producer on the O'Reilly show. She, poor lamb, says she thought it was about business and told him she'd call him right back. At this point, we surmise Ms. Mackris may have activated a recording device and with the tape rolling, dialed the boss, who promptly got down to business, launching into what the complaint harshly stigmatizes as "a lewd and lascivious, unsolicited and disturbing sexually graphic talk," about how he imagines he would handle personal relations with Ms. Mackris if they were in the West Indies.

First he'd get two wines into Ms. Mackris, "maybe intravenously." Then, "You would basically be in the shower and then I would come in and I'd join you and you would have your back to me and I would take the little loofa thing …"

A loofa! This is no Motel 6, it's not the Ritz either, where loofas would scarcely be "little," though admittedly size doesn't come up in the definition of loofa offered by *The American Heritage Dictionary of the English Language*, Fourth Edition, 2000:

SYLLABICATION: loo·fa
VARIANT FORMS: or loo·fah also luf·fa

NOUN:
1. Any of several Old World tropical vines of the genus *Luffa*, having cylindrical fruit with a fibrous, spongelike interior.
2. The dried, fibrous part of the loofa fruit, used as a washing sponge or as a filter. Also called dishcloth gourd, vegetable sponge.
ETYMOLOGY: Arabic *loof* singulative form of *loofa.*

And what is O'Reilly, so strong, so masterful, planning to do with this thing of Arab origin? "I would take the little loofa thing and kinda' soap your back and rub it all over you, get you to relax, hot water … and um … You know, you'd feel the tension drain out of you and um you still would be with your back to me then I would kinda' put my arms—it's one of those mitts, those loofa mitts you know, so I got my hands in it, and I would put it around front, kinda' rub your tummy with it and then with my other hand I would start to massage your boobs, get your nipples really hard … 'cuz I like that and you have really spectacular boobs."

At this point, in the document filed in the court house in Nassau County, which would indeed appear to be a transcript right down to the ums, there's an ellipse.

"… So anyway I'd be rubbing your big boobs and getting your nipples really hard, kinda kissing your neck from behind … and then the other hand with the falafel thing …"

NOUN: 1. Ground spiced chickpeas shaped into balls and fried.
2. A sandwich filled with such a mixture.

What happened to the loofa? Maybe Abe Foxman called him on the other line to warn about "going Arab on us." And what is O'Reilly planning to do with the falafel?

"… I would take the other hand with the falafel thing [*sic*] and I'd put it on your pussy, but you'd have to do it really light, just kind of a tease business."

According to the courtroom document available for inspection on Smoking Gun the quality of the conversation goes downhill from there on in. It may be that O'Reilly's tour of Arab commodities was proleptic, as he began to shift gears through the vowel sounds.

For an interesting discussion of the processes involved I recommend

Sebastiano Timpanaro's philological investigation, published in translation years ago by Verso, entitled *The Freudian Slip*. From loofa to falafel to what? Let Ms. Mackris and her lawyer tell it their way. O'Reilly "suggested he would perform oral sex" on Ms. Mackris and she would "perform fellatio on his 'big cock' but not complete the act," maybe to conserve his energies for further deployment of the little loofa or the falafel, though the lifespan of a falafel in a shower is surely limited in duration. After the exciting fa-fel-fell monologue and what to Ms. Mackris's "repulsed" ear sounded like the hum of a vibrator and acoustic intimations of satisfactory climax, O'Reilly launched into a discussion concerning how good he was during a recent appearance on *The Today Show*.

Thanks ever so, Ms. Mackris. It must have been just horrible for you, but it was in a good cause. You gave us a bright moment in a dark year.

December 14

Few spectacles in journalism in the mid-1990s were more disgusting than the slagging of Gary Webb in the *New York Times*, *Washington Post* and *Los Angeles Times*. Squadrons of hacks, some of them with career-long ties to the CIA, sprayed thousands of words of vitriol over Webb and his paper, the *San Jose Mercury News*, for besmirching the Agency's fine name by charging it with complicity in the importing of cocaine into the US.

There are certain things you aren't meant to say in public in America. The systematic state-sponsorship of torture by the US used to be a major no-no, but that went by the board this year. A prime no-no is saying that the US government has used assassination down the years as an instrument of national policy; also that the CIA's complicity with drug-dealing criminal gangs stretches from the Afghanistan of today back to the year the Agency was founded in 1947. That last one is the line Webb stepped over. He paid for his presumption by undergoing one of the unfairest batterings in the history of the US press, as *Whiteout*, by Jeffrey St. Clair and myself, attests.

Friday, December 10, Webb died in his Sacramento apartment by his own hand, or so it certainly seems. The notices of his passing in many newspapers were as nasty as ever. The *Los Angeles Times* took care to note that even after the Dark Alliance uproar Webb's career had been "troubled," offering as evidence the fact that "While working for another legislative committee in Sacramento, Webb wrote a report accusing the California Highway Patrol of unofficially condoning and even encouraging racial profiling in its drug interdiction program." The effrontery of the man! "Legislative officials released the report in 1999," the story piously continued, "but cautioned that it was based mainly on assumptions and anecdotes," no doubt meaning that Webb didn't have dozens of CHP officers stating under oath, on the record, that they were picking on blacks and Hispanics.

There were similar fountains of outrage in 1996 that the CIA hadn't been given enough space in Webb's series to solemnly swear that never a gram of cocaine had passed under its nose but that it had been seized and turned over to the DEA or US Customs.

In 1998 Jeffrey St. Clair and I published *Whiteout*, about the relationships between the CIA, drugs and the press since the Agency's founding. We also examined the Webb affair in detail. On a lesser scale, at lower volume, the book elicited the same sort of abuse Webb drew. It was a long book stuffed with well-documented facts, over which the critics lightly vaulted to charge us, as they did Webb, with "conspiracy-mongering" though also, sometimes in the same sentence, with recycling "old news." Jeffrey and I came to the conclusion that what really affronted the critics, some of them nominally left-wing, was that our book portrayed Uncle Sam's true face. Not a "rogue" Agency but one always following the dictates of government, murdering, torturing, poisoning, drugging its own subjects, approving acts of monstrous cruelty, following methods devised and tested by Hitler's men, themselves transported to America after World War II.

One of the CIA's favored modes of self-protection is the "uncover-up." The Agency first denies with passion, then later concedes in muffled tones, the charges leveled against it. Such charges have included the Agency's recruitment of Nazi scientists and SS officers; experiments on unwitting American citizens; efforts to assassinate

Fidel Castro; alliances with opium lords in Burma, Thailand, and Laos; an assassination program in Vietnam; complicity in the toppling of Salvador Allende in Chile; the arming of opium traffickers and religious fanatics in Afghanistan; the training of murderous police in Guatemala and El Salvador; and involvement in drugs-and-arms shuttles between Latin America and the US.

True to form, after Webb's series raised a storm, particularly on black radio, the CIA issued categorical denials. Then came the solemn pledges of an intense and far-reaching investigation by the CIA's Inspector General, Fred Hitz. On December 18, 1997, stories in the *Washington Post* by Walter Pincus and in the *New York Times* by Tim Weiner appeared simultaneously, both saying the same thing: Inspector General Hitz had finished his investigation. He had found "no direct or indirect" links between the CIA and the cocaine traffickers. As both Pincus and Weiner admitted in their stories, neither of the two journalists had actually seen the report.

The actual report itself, so loudly heralded, received almost no examination. But those who took the time to examine the 149-page document—the first of two volumes—found Inspector General Hitz making one damning admission after another including an account of a meeting between a pilot who was making drug/arms runs between San Francisco and Costa Rica with two Contra leaders who were also partners with the San Francisco-based Contra/drug smuggler Norwin Meneses. Present at this encounter in Costa Rica was a curly-haired man who said his name was Ivan Gomez, identified by one of the Contras as the CIA's "man in Costa Rica." The pilot told Hitz that Gomez said he was there to "ensure that the profits from the cocaine went to the Contras and not into someone's pocket." The second volume of CIA Inspector General Fred Hitz's investigation, released in the fall of 1998, buttressed Webb's case even more tightly, as James Risen conceded in a story in the *New York Times*.

So why did the top-tier press savage Webb, and parrot the CIA's denials? It comes back to this matter of Uncle Sam's true face. Another *New York Times* reporter, Keith Schneider, was asked by *In These Times* back in 1987 why he had devoted a three-part series in the *Times* to attacks on the Contra hearings chaired by Senator

John Kerry. Schneider said such a story could "shatter the Republic. I think it is so damaging, the implications are so extraordinary, that for us to run the story, it had better be based on the most solid evidence we could amass." Kerry did uncover mountains of evidence. So did Webb. But neither of them got the only thing that would have satisfied Schneider, Pincus, and all the other critics: a signed confession of CIA complicity by the DCI himself. Short of that, I'm afraid we're left with "innuendo," "conspiracy-mongering" and "old stories." We're also left with the memory of some great work by a very fine journalist who deserved a lot better than he got from the profession he loved.

2005

January 11
These days a very large number of Americans live about 500 dollars from disaster (and often a tenth of that sum) on their monthly budgets. They're mostly not more than fifty miles from a new prison and a couple of percentage points from a boost in their mortgage payments that would spell ruin. They think both major political parties are worthless. Their main enemies are often cops, social workers and family courts.

January 13
Imagine, in the same month as the death of the muse of high camp, Susan Sontag, we have England in an uproar about Prince Harry and his silly swastika armband. All this while *The Producers* is playing to packed houses in London. They're even talking of banning the swastika. That'll be one in the eye for Indian symbols! The airlines will have to start handing out reminders to the Navajo before they land at Heathrow.

The theme of the party where some jerk snapped Harry was Colonialists and Natives. I suppose the lad could have gone as Lord Curzon or Lord Kitchener, but most of Harry's male relatives still have to dress like that anyway for formal military occasions. The Afrika Korps uniform was a nice idea and a lot more original than putting some shoeblack on his face and going as a native.

How bitterly Harry must regret not dressing up as Captain Cook. Then he could have had an enjoyable Tour of Contrition to the Antipodes and the Pacific region, apologizing to the Maoris and Hawaiians for insensitivity to genocide. Who wants to go to Auschwitz at this time of year?

"Where do you stop with the taboos?" wrote David Ball of Milton Keynes to the *Daily Telegraph*. "Do you not dress as a Dominican Friar, whose order was responsible for the persecution and death of thousands of 'Heretics' i.e. people with different views, in the Middle Ages? Do you not dress as a US cavalryman, who assisted in the systematic destruction of the indigenous native population of America, or as a conquistador, who decimated the Inca population? History is full of evil-doers. Do we try and ignore their existence or accept them for what they were? I don't think Harry was going around shouting neo-Nazi slogans and giving Heil Hitler salutes. He was just dressed as a soldier, complete with all the insignia, swastika included, that the uniform entailed. An insensitive choice but probably only youthful indiscretion. To bar him from Sandhurst would be crass. If anything, the training is likely to teach him some values and a better appreciation of the influence his position has got."

I'll buy that, same way as I buy the view of the *Pravda* editorialist who wrote: "Prince Harry turned up in an Afrika Korps uniform—who better to mock than the German colonials under Hitler, the greatest imperialist project of murder in human history since perhaps Genghis Khan? … If this young man was invited to a Colonials and Natives party, what was he supposed to wear? A pink ballet dress, to be accused of being a fairy, a transsexual or a cross-dresser?"

The English have always had a soft spot for Rommel, the Desert Fox, the Good German outgeneraled by Montgomery and then forced to commit suicide by Hitler. Actually Rommel was outgeneraled by the Matrons who ruled over matters of hygiene at the schools attended by the British officer class. How well I remember Matron at my own school, Heatherdown, who used to line us little boys up and then clasp our testicles in her chill hand and demand we cough. I'm never quite sure why; maybe to detect signs of incipient syphilis in case we eight-year-olds had been infected by the girls at Heathfield, the other side of a forbidding wall.

Why those boyish testicles in Matron's chill hand? Here is one answer.

Dear Mr. Cockburn,
The nominal answer is: to detect inguinal hernias. The Freudian analysis is more complex.

Daniel Wirt MD, Houston

February 7
I was prowling the other day through a box of old Communist Party literature belonging to the late Dick Criley, sent me by his niece, Honey Williams. Among predictable pamphlets on Lysenko, Dimitrov, and other celebrities of the period I came across *Fighting Words*, published in 1949, being selections from twenty-five years of the *Daily Worker*.

There were many very fine pieces of reporting, from Abner Berry on a cotton plantation in Alabama; from William Allan in Michigan about 288 black workers "sold" to a canning company for $35, shipped up from Georgia to farm camps, separated from the pigs by straw bales.

On October 16, 1947, there was a proud bulletin, titled "Socko!," about the achievement of the *Worker*'s handicapper, Al. On his second day on the job Al picked "a phenomenal total of six winners in the seven races at Jamaica yesterday." Readers putting $10 on each of Al's picks would have cleared $116. Al's feat on behalf of the toiler-punters reminds me of the services done to party members in the UK in 1949, most of whom probably put their money on Russian Hero, who won the Grand National at Aintree that year against odds of sixty-six to one, the fifth-longest odds in the history of the race since it began in 1837.

Dipping further into *Fighting Words* I found an enthusiastic news lead on May 14, 1948: "The sun is rising on a new nation, a new state in Palestine … history marches on—in Palestine no less than in Greece, China, or Indonesia. In Palestine, it is the Haganah and its allies; in Greece, it is the heroic guerilla movement; in China it is the mighty and victorious People's Army, led by the Communists. In every case, the enemy is the same—the imperialism of London and Wall Street …"

Oh well. Small wonder it was hard, even in the '80s, to get many old Lincoln Brigaders and kindred comrades, to speak up on behalf of the Palestinians.

Further into *Fighting Words* my eye was caught by the title, "A Trotskyite Slumming Trip," published on November 26, 1947. It was by Samuel Sillen, and took the form of a robust attack on Edmund Wilson. Here it is:

> The editors of *The New Yorker*, with grotesque humor, financed a sort of intellectual slumming trip by Edmund Wilson through postwar Europe. He left his Baedeker home, but not his Trotskyism. His report, published in his new book, *Europe Without Baedeker*, unutterably dull, is worth nothing except as a symptom of the moral decay of capitalist apologists.
>
> Wilson felt most at home in a convent cell at the Hospital of the Blue Nuns in Rome, where he discussed with George Santayana his quaint "weakness for Mussolini." Wilson's militant, unabashed hatred of people naturally accompanies a hatred of the democratic upsurge in post-Hitler Europe. The author laments his departed friends Trotsky and Tukhachevsky, waxes homesick for Alexander Barmine, consoles himself that De Gaulle's big brain, André Malraux, is one of "the most valuable forces still alive on this devastated continent."
>
> Then he scoots back to America with a dazzling proposal. He wants us to set up a Board of Breeding. We should not be so "foolish" as to allow Nazi failures to "discourage us with eugenics." Wilson offers this bright vista: "If we can produce, from some cousin of the jackal and the wolf, the dachshund and the Great Dane, the Pekinese and the poodle, what should we not be able to do with man?"
>
> Fortified by this dog-theory of history, Wilson finds a new key to what is "wrong" with Socialist ideas. It is that Karl Marx was a Jew, "and, being a Jew, from a family that had included many rabbis, he identified the situation of the factory worker with the situation of the Jew." Marx, says Wilson, mistakenly assumed that workers released from capitalism would behave in terms of "Jewish tradition." He did not foresee that

> "what happens, when you let down the bars, is that a lot of gross and ignorant people who have been condemned to mean destinies before, go rushing for all they are worth after things that they can eat, drink, sleep on, ride on, preside at and amuse themselves with."
>
> Thus, in one stroke, the Trotskyite tourist for *The New Yorker* combines the Nazi view of Marxism as a peculiarly "Jewish" philosophy, the Bourbons' contempt for the masses as wild animals, and the hoary capitalist warning that we must not "let down the bars" to the working class.
>
> This leads up to the inevitability-of-war thesis. Wilson goes a step further than your run-of-the-mill warmonger. Not only can't we get along with the Soviet leaders, but Americans "will never be able to cooperate as peoples" with the Russians. It is "ridiculous," says Wilson, to think of the Russian people today as "civilized."
>
> Wilson, borrowing a cue from De Gaulle's Malraux, evidently aspires to be a braintruster of the fascist forces. It is not only moral and intellectual rottenness that we find in his book, but the savagery of desperation.

One might have thought that Boards of Breeding would not have been on Wilson's shopping list, only two years after the defeat of Nazism, but eugenic selection—ardently backed by American liberals from the start—was big in the late 1940s. In 1949 Garrett Hardin was writing about America's declining IQ in his biology textbook. Malthus is never far away, nor the sterilizer's toolkit, intellectual and physical.

February 8

Further memories of a Russian Hero. England in the late 1940s was famously grim. As I remember it, London back then was a very dirty place, from coal dust and smoke, from the grit stirred up every day by the jackhammers still clearing out rubble from the Blitz.

No one had any money. Fun for millions was the weekly flutter on racehorses or football teams. "Is the Middle Class Doomed?" asked *Picture Post* in 1949, and answered its question in the affirmative. Labour's National Health Service opened for business on July 5, 1948, and the great race for drugs, false teeth and spectacles was under way. Spending on prescriptions went from £13 million to £41 million in two years, prompting Rep. Paul Ryan's ideological predecessors to howl that the NHS was on the edge of collapse.

My father was edging his way tactfully out of the Communist Party, though he was still spending time at the *Daily Worker*. More than my father's articles in the *Worker*, the NHS helped the masses see more clearly. Hundreds of thousands of poor people previously had recourse only to prescriptionless specs from the tray in Woolworths. Now they perched on their noses prescription lenses in the 422 Panto Oval frame, as did I, though it took John Lennon, fifteen years down the road, to endow it with retro-chic.

At the *Daily Worker*, with or without prescription spectacles, there wasn't much sign of the fabled millions in Moscow gold supposedly sent by Stalin to foment revolution. In practical terms the most important fellow in the office was a scholarly looking Burmese man who toiled away behind a vast pile of books and manuals. My father reckoned he was set to turn in a particularly meaty series on Burma's prospects after independence, won in 1948 from British colonial rule. In fact he was the *Worker*'s racing correspondent, working up forms for the coming season.

The Burman was red-hot as a tipster and soon had a wide following. Once my father found the *Worker*'s manager half-dead from apprehension. He'd put the entire office Friday wage packet on a pick by the Burman, in the hope of getting the comrades something decent to take home to their wives. "Should that animal fail," he said, trembling, "the lads'll about kill me." But the tipster came through, and that week everyone got full pay and even some arrears.

The biggest day in the National Hunt Steeplechase in England is the Grand National, run at Aintree, outside Liverpool, typically in April; four miles, 856 yards, thirty fences, often lethal to horses and devastating to jockeys. In 1928 the winner, Tipperary Tim, ridden by Billy Dutton and carrying odds of 100 to one, was the only horse out of a starting field of forty-two that didn't fall.

Later, in Ireland, my mother bred horses. My father never cared for them, but he was pretty good at studying form and picking the odd winner, which was just as well because freelance earnings were scrawny, particularly if you were a well-known red.

But when it came to Grand National day, March 26, 1949, no laborious toil over the form sheets was necessary. Among the scheduled starters that year was a horse called Russian Hero. Although the cold war was limbering up, Russians were still heroes to many. Not just members of the CPGB but a wider swath of punters in the union movement would be likely to plump for a horse carrying that name, if only as a side bet in honor of Stalingrad, the siege of Leningrad, the Kursk salient.

One of the jockeys riding that day was young Dick Francis, later the immensely popular author of a long string of racing thrillers. Francis was on a great but temperamental horse called Roimond. In the last mile he took the lead. With only eleven horses still in the race, he was set for victory. Then, just short of the finishing line, Roimond got passed by a horse going so fast Francis knew he had no chance to catch up. It was Russian Hero, ridden by Leo McMorrow, carrying starting odds of sixty-six to one. Russian Hero beat Roimond by eight lengths.

As the BBC man calling the race screamed out the finale, my father—who was no longer a party member but who'd staked his well-frayed shirt on Russian Hero—loosed a triumphant roar. So, across Britain, did all readers of the *Daily Worker* following the advice of the Burmese tipster, who'd picked Russian Hero, no doubt partly through rigorous assessment of the horse's genetic profile—contrary though this Mendelian posture was to the doctrines of Lysenko, riding high in Stalin's esteem.

It was by far the largest collective transfer of wealth ever to Communism's stalwarts in Britain. Around that time the party probably had around 50,000 members, and even a wagered half-crown looked pretty good when multiplied by sixty-six.

Dick Francis took second in 1949. Seven years later, a champion jockey in his eighth Grand National, he rode Devon Loch, owned by Elizabeth the Queen Mother. Francis was ten lengths clear, less than fifty yards from winning, when Devon Loch suddenly went down on his belly, tearing muscles in the process. It's one of horse racing's great mysteries, though Francis thinks it was a sudden wave of noise from the crowd that spooked his horse. "That's racing," the Queen Mother said stoically to Francis.

The event got Francis a contract to write a memoir. He retired from the track and took up a hugely successful life of crime writing. But "given the choice," he says, "I'd take winning the National every time. I was a jockey first, writer second. It's good having a book well received, but it doesn't compare to winning a race."

February 25

I guess I can call myself one of the Dylan generation since, at sixty-three, I'm the same age as him, but the prose stylists that allured an Anglo-Irish lad hopelessly strapped into the corsets of Latinate gentility were always those of American rough-housers: first, in the mid-'50s, Jack Kerouac, then Edward Abbey, then Hunter Thompson.

Thank God I never tried to imitate any of them. Thompson probably spawned more bad prose than anyone since Hemingway, but they all taught me that at its most rapturous, its most outraged, its most exultant, American prose can let go and teach you to let go, to embrace the vastness, the richness, the beauty and the grotesqueries of America in all its thousand landscapes.

I tried to re-read Kerouac's *On the Road* a few years ago and put it down soon enough. That's a book for excited teenagers. Abbey at full stretch remains a great writer and he'll stay in the pantheon for all time. Lately sitting in motels along the highway I've been dipping into his diaries, *Confessions of a Barbarian*, and laughing every couple of pages. "Writing for the *National Geographic*," Abbey grumbled, "is like trying to masturbate in ski mitts."

Could Thompson have written that? Probably not. When it came to sex and the stimulation of the synapses by agents other than drugs or booze or violent imagery Thompson was silent, unlike Abbey who loved women. Thompson wrote for the guys, at a pitch so frenzied, so over-the-top in its hyperbolic momentum that often enough it reminded me of the squeakier variant of the same style developed by his *Herald-Trib* stable mate and exponent of the "New Journalism," Tom Wolfe. In their respective stylistic uniforms they always seemed hysterically frightened of normalcy, particularly in the shape of girls, so keenly appreciated by Abbey.

Thompson's best writing was always in the form of flourishes, of pell-mell bluster wrenched from himself for the anxious editors waiting well past deadline at *Scanlans* or *Rolling Stone*, and in his later years often put together from his jottings by the writers and editors aware that a new *Fear and Loathing* on the masthead was a sure-fire multiplier of newstand sales. Overall, Thompson's political perceptions weren't that interesting except for occasional bitter flashes, as in this sour and prescient paragraph written in 1972: "How many more of these goddam elections are we going to have to write off as lame but 'regrettably necessary' holding actions? And how many more of these stinking double-downer sideshows will we have to go through before we can get ourselves straight enough to put together some kind of national election that will give me at least the 20 million people I tend to agree with a chance to vote for something, instead of always being faced with that old familiar choice between the lesser of two evils? I understand, along with a lot of other people, that the big thing, this year, is Beating Nixon. But that was also the big thing, as I recall, twelve years ago in 1960—and as far as I can tell, we've gone from bad to worse to rotten since then, and the outlook is for more of the same."

There's nothing much to the notion of "Gonzo" beyond the delighted projections of Thompson's readers. The introduction of the reporter as roistering first-person narrator? Mark Twain surely did that, albeit sedately, and less sedately we had Henry Miller, another man who loved women. Which of the road books will last longest between Miller's *American Nightmare*, *On the Road* and *Fear and Loathing in Las Vegas*? Kerouac and then Thompson drove faster but they didn't write better. Norman Mailer took the form to the level of genius in *Advertisements for Myself*, with political perceptions acuter and writing sharper by far than anything Thompson ever produced.

"Gonzo" was an act, defined by its beholders, the thought that here was one of Us, fried on drugs, hanging on to the cliff edge of reality only by his fingernails, doing hyperbolic battle with the pomposities and corruptions of Politics as Usual. And no man was ever a more willing captive of the Gonzo myth he created, decked out in its increasingly frayed bunting of "Fear and Loathing …" "The Strange and Terrible …," decorated with Ralph Steadman's graphic counterpoints.

Like Evel Knievel, Thompson's stunts demanded that he arc higher and further with each successive sentence's outrage to propriety, most memorably in his obit for Richard Nixon: "If the right people had been in charge of Nixon's funeral, his casket would have been launched into one of those open-sewage canals that empty into the ocean just south of Los Angeles. He was a swine of a man and a jabbering dupe of a president. Nixon was so crooked that he needed servants to help him screw his pants on every morning. Even his funeral was illegal. He was queer in the deepest way. His body should have been burned in a trash bin."

Kerouac ended sadly at forty-seven. As Abbey nastily put it, "Jack Kerouac, like a sick refrigerator, worked too hard at keeping cool and died on his mama's lap from alcohol and infantilism." Abbey himself passed gloriously at sixty-two, carried from the hospital by his pals to die at his own pace without tubes dripping brief reprieves into his veins, then buried in the desert without the sanction of the state.

How about Thompson? His Boston lawyer George Tobia Jr. told the *Globe* the sixty-seven-year-old author sat in his kitchen Sunday afternoon in his home in Woody Creek, Colo., stuck a .45-caliber handgun in his mouth, and killed himself while his wife listened on the phone and his son and daughter-in-law were in another room of his house. His wife had no idea what had happened until she returned home later.

Seems creepy to me, same way Gary Webb blowing his brains out a while back with a handgun was creepy. Why give the loved ones that as a souvenir? I suppose Thompson's message was: We were together at the end. Webb was truly alone. He lifted the curtain on one little sideshow of the American Empire, and could never quite fathom that when you do that The Man doesn't forget or forgive. Thompson engaged the Empire on his own terms and quit the battlefield on his own terms too, which I guess is what Gonzo is all about.

March 6

Relentlessly, the increased hours Americans have to work, just to squeeze by, is sapping their will to live any sort of pleasant life, at least in terms of the way "pleasant" was parsed half a century ago.

My neighbor Joe Paff says his older brother Bill worked for McDonald Douglas in the 1960s as a blue-collar line inspector, had a $19,000 house in Anaheim, two bedrooms, swimming pool, hardwood floors, new car every year or so, boat and trailer, and time to enjoy them.

There were millions like Bill and his wife. Back then, when the incomes of ordinary working people reached their apex, the average family lived in an affordable house with a couple of late-model cars at reasonable insurance rates. Their kids could go to college either for free or cheaply. The man worked reasonable hours and could even look forward to a decent pension instead of having it looted by Bernie Ebbers. The woman didn't have to work prodigious hours at two thirds of the man's rate of pay so that they could meet the mortgage payments. They might have a little hideaway in the country. They were not so exhausted that they fell asleep over their supper. They stayed up night after night to watch Johnny Carson on "The Tonight Show," having already enjoyed light-hearted commentary on their happy condition from Jackie Gleeson. The whining racism of Archie Bunker was still ahead, in the 1970s, when the fortunes of the white working class began to dip.

As the Economic Policy Institute's State of Working America 2004 Report instructs us, any story of rising income for working families across the past quarter century is, at bottom, a story about rising annual work hours, particularly among women. The extra hours worked by wives in 2000, compared to 1979, translates into additional full-time workweeks as follows: 8 weeks in the bottom 20 percent, 12.9 weeks in the second, 12.5 weeks in the third, 9.2 in the fourth, and 8.3 in the fifth. If women in poor families hadn't gone to work in the years after 1979, their family income would have fallen by almost 14 percent.

It's always eerie how quickly people accept sharply changed circumstances as normalcy, like paying 22 percent interest on a credit card debt and watching payments on all cards get hiked to the fiercest interest rate if you're late on one payment. Twenty years ago those were credit terms the FBI took to be proof of Mafia membership and got prosecutors to file charges of extortion. Now, both parties in Congress leap to obey when the credit card companies—i.e., the banks—issue their commands. Latest to come under the axe is Chapter 7 bankruptcy, where bankrupts could go down and not have repayments through their next ten incarnations, which is what Chapter 11 bankruptcy mandates.

March 25

How many times, amid the carnage of such homicidal sprees, do investigators find a prescription for some anti-depressant at the blood-spattered murder scene? Luvox at Columbine, Prozac at Louisville, where Joseph Wesbecker killed nine including himself. Scroll through the last fifteen years and you'll find plenty such stories.

That's the trouble with time. As Paul Krassner joked about Waldheimer's Disease, you get old and forget you were a Nazi. But it's never too late to go back to the dim distant origins of the Depression Industry in the late 1980s and early '90s, and the saga of what happened after three researchers working for Lilly concocted a potion in the mid-1970s they christened fluoxetine hydrochloride, later known to the world, to Wesbecker and to Jeff Weise, as Prozac.

Long years of rigorous testing? When Fred Gardner and I investigated the selling of depression and of Prozac in the mid-1990s we found that the clinical trials of Prozac excluded suicidal patients, children, and elderly adults—although once FDA approval is granted, the drug can be prescribed for anyone of any age. According to Dr. Peter Breggin, the well-known Bethesda-based psychiatrist who analyzed the FDA's approval of Prozac, it was based, ultimately, on three studies indicating that fluoxetine relieved some symptoms of depression more effectively than a placebo, and in the face of nine studies indicating no positive effect. Only sixty-three patients were on fluoxetine for a period of more than two years.

Psychiatrists—a breed whose adepts, according to a study published in the *Journal of Clinical Psychiatry* in 1980, commit suicide at twice the national rate—have been central to the entire enterprise. The process linking their alchemy to the corporate bottom line has a robust simplicity to it. As Prozac came off Lilly's research bench and headed for the mass production line, psychiatrists, some in receipt of Lilly's money, labored to formulate conditions to be installed in the *Diagnostic and Statistical Manual of Mental Disorders*, whose chief editor in the 1980s was Robert Spitzer MD, an orgone-box survivor and adept copywriter skilled at coining the DSM's arsenal of "disorders" sanctioning treatment, medication, and most crucially of all, reimbursement by insurance companies. When troubling questions were raised about Prozac's possible linkage to violent acts, psychiatrists were there to douse the flames of doubt.

In the US the government is in the pay of the drug companies, and prescriptions for anti-depressants have risen as the call for any collective social action to cure "depression" has long since been taken from any political manifestos. How they must have cheered at Eli Lilly when Congress wiped out Chapter 7 of the Bankruptcy statutes, creating family violence, heightened crime, and a vast new potential market for Prozac and kindred potions at the stroke of a pen.

March 26

Mumbai—Sainath and Priyanka advise me against going out this morning since it's Holi, a day when rowdy fellows pelt you with dye and balloons filled with stones in honor of spring. I wander out at dawn and soon meet people whose faces and clothes are blotched with red and green stains. I retreat for the rest of the morning to the Club, whose guest board showed roughly a 50/50 split between Anglo and Indian names.

I prowl around the Yacht Club's library, mostly full of light fiction, but finally come across *The Indian Field Shikar Book*, compiled by W. S. Burke, sixth edition, published by Thacker, Spink & Co., Calcutta and Simla, 1928. Embossed on the flyleaf is "J. N. Tata," presumably once the owner. The Tatas are probably India's best-known business family, now running a vast business empire, having flourished down the years from their origins as opium concessionaires, just as Jardine and Matthiessen were further east.

I turn to a chapter called "The Game Destroyers." Burke advised that with the "marked decrease" in game in several parts of India, "it has become urgently necessary for sportsmen to turn their attention to the game destroyers of India." Conservation is the order of the day. And who are these "natural foes"? Burke entertains no uncertainty on the matter. "The leopard is one of the greatest foes to the preservation of deer which, largely owing to his depredations, have been almost, if not quite, exterminated in many parts of India … and of all the leopards the Ounce or Snow Leopard (*Felis unca*) is the most inveterate and successful destroyer of the game to be found in the higher elevations of the Himalayas."

Below the leopard, Burke ranges the other game destroyers: wolves, wild dogs ("should be remorselessly destroyed"), civets and mongooses, martins and weasels, crows ("arrant egg thieves and chick destroyers"), owls ("ditto"), eagles, buzzards, falcons ("usually deserving of a cartridge, though we must not forget that their partiality for rats, snakes and other small and noxious animals is a recommendation to mercy which should carry some weight").

Night—Sainath, full of bitter denunciations of Indian food in America, takes me off to a Mughalai restaurant. He has butter chicken. I choose mutton curry. Despite Sainath's acrid dismissal of all Indian restaurants in the US, the food tastes not too different to a decent Indian meal in New York or Los Angeles, though Sainath's butter chicken was over-salted. Indeed, with some diligence you can find passable North Indian food in a few major American cities.

Southern Indian food is another matter. How I will miss southern Indian cafés and restaurants. How I will yearn for the dosais (crepes or pancakes), the idlis (steamed cakes), both made from a mix of rice grits and urad dhal fermented overnight. I will pine too for fish and shrimp curries, for oothappam (onion pancakes) and rasam (thin soups), of which a popular one is the Tamil milagu-thannit (literally, pepper water), rendered as "mulligatawny" by the British and thickened into the brackish brown sludge served in clubs and British Railway hotels in the 1950s. By the time my trip is done I'll have enjoyed Malabar, Chettinad, Mughalai, Gujarati, city Tamilian, Mangalorian and Goan cooking.

Sainath says he puts on two kilos every time he visits Kerala, and I can see why. I miss the thali too, a stainless steel tray about the size of a pizza platter on which the smaller bowls of vegetable curries, curds, deserts and other elements of the thali palette are set and refilled until you're done. Why is there no southern Indian cuisine in America? After all, the motel industry may be 70 percent run by clans from Gujarat, but there are a lot of Indians from other regions here too, including Andhra Pradesh which, says Sainath with the pride of a native son, has the fieriest food of all.

I ask Sainath how he started working in the countryside.

At the start of the '90s Sainath was in his early thirties, born into a distinguished Brahmin family, educated by the Jesuits in Madras (a city renamed Chennai five years ago), then seasoned in the radical flames of Jawaharlal Nehru University in New Delhi. By 1980, he was at United News of India, and three years later working for R. K. Karanjia, a famous journalistic figure of that era and proprietor of the muckraking weekly *Blitz*, which in the early '80s commanded a national circulation of 600,000 and a readership ten times larger.

Karanjia lost no time in making the teetotal and hard-working Sainath deputy chief editor. Soon Khwaja Ahmad Abbas, author of *Blitz*'s "Last Page" column, which he had written for over forty years, willed the column to Sainath, thus trumping from the grave Karanjia's designated inheritor. Abbas, incidentally, was the author of the great novel *Inquilab* (*Revolution*), plus seventy-two other books, plus the scripts of many of India's greatest movies.

A year later Sainath toured nine drought-stricken states in India, and recalls ruefully, "That's when I learned that conventional journalism was above all about the service of power. You always give the last word to authority. I got a couple of prizes which I didn't pick up because I was ashamed."

Ten years later Sainath's moment came. "The economic 'reforms' began. That's when the great intellectual shift took place." Just as the US press romped ever deeper into celebrity journalism as the war on the poor unfurled through the 1980s and '90s, so too the Indian press plunged into full-tilt coverage of India's beautiful people. "I felt that if the Indian press was covering the top 5 percent, I should cover the bottom 5 percent."

He quit *Blitz* and in 1993 applied for a *Times of India* fellowship. At the interview he spoke of his plans to report from rural India—terra incognita to the national Indian press. An editor asked him, "Suppose I tell you my readers aren't interested in this stuff." Sainath, a feisty fellow, riposted, "When did you last meet your readers to make any such claims on their behalf?"

He got the fellowship and took to the back roads in the ten poorest districts of five states. He walked hundreds of miles. The *Times* had said it would carry a few pieces. He had two good editors there who supported what he was doing. In the end the paper ran eighty-four reports by Sainath across eighteen months, many of them subsequently reprinted in his well-known collection, *Everybody Loves a Good Drought*. They made his journalistic name and earned him a bundle of prizes, both national and international. The prizes furnished him credibility and also money to go on freelancing.

In those days, Sainath remembers, the legitimacy of the "neoliberal reforms" that plunged India's peasantry into the inferno "was very great, like religious dogma. But I was getting 300 letters a month from people applauding and ratifying my reports as well as sending money for the people I was writing about. It was very moving. I learned that readers are far ahead of editors. I was saying that poverty is not natural, but a willed infliction. I asked, what are the survival tactics of the poor? I saw that the Indian woman eats last. She feeds her husband, her children, the parents, and then if there's anything left she eats that. I learned how the poor lived off the forests. I did what they did. If they migrated and got up on top of a train, so did I."

For hundreds of millions of poor Indians, the brave new world of the '90s meant globalization of prices, Indianization of incomes. "As we moved to fortify our welfare state for the wealthy, the state turned its back on the poor, investment in agriculture collapsed, and with it, countless millions of lives. As banks wound down rural credit while granting loans for buying Mercedes Benzes in the cities at the lowest imaginable interest rates, rural indebtedness soared. In the '90s, for the first time in independent India the Supreme Court pulled up several state governments over increasing hunger deaths. Welcome to the world so loved by the Friedmans—Thomas and Milton."

From the mid-'90s on, thousands of Indian farmers committed suicide, including over 5,000 in the single southern state of Andhra Pradesh. As employment crashed in the countryside to its lowest ever, distress migrations from the villages—to just about anywhere—increased in tens of millions.

Food grain available per Indian fell almost every year in the 1990s and by 2002–3 was less than it had been at the time of the great Bengal famine of 1942–3. Even as the world hailed the Indian Tiger Economy, the country slipped to rank 127 (from 124) in the United Nations Human Development Index of 2003. It is better to be a poor person in Botswana, or even the occupied territories of Palestine, than one in India.

Few journalists write well about poor people, particularly the rural poor, who have mostly vanished from public description or discussion. Reporters tend to patronize them. The drama is really about the journalist visiting the poor (whose categories include several hundred million Indians, ranging from destitute itinerants to small farmers crucified by debt). Interviewing the poor as they reel off numbers from the balance sheet of their misfortunes takes concentration. The devil, in recent years often meaning suicides, is in details that have to be got right: inputs per acres, sources of irrigation, market price for crops.

These numbers have to be jotted down in the fields, often in temperatures upward of 110F, and even 118F (47.7C) in the fields, at which point all electronic equipment gives up.

It's necessary to keep good records. When we visited the family of a dalit (i.e., an untouchable), Sainath gave me the standard form he has designed and fills out for the 300 or so families he's personally visited after a suicide. Name: T. T. Johny, aged forty-three. Date of suicide: July 9, 2004. Debt: 60,000 rupees. (Exchange rates: in March and April of 2005: $1 US traded for about 42 rupees. In the Mumbai slums a bucket of water sells for 5 rupees, about 12 cents. One thousand rupees exchange for about $24. So T. T. Johny's debt was c. $1,430.) Family members: one wife, one daughter. Land: one acre. Cattle: none. Crop seed changes …, Sources of credit …, Source of irrigation: no well. Input per acre …

Sainath respects the people he writes about. On first encounter, he makes a point of drinking the glass of water they put in front of him, no matter how cloudy or suspect in origin. He cares about them, stays in touch with them, tries to get them money. He doesn't see poverty as a "condition," but as the consequence of decisions by people, businessmen, politicians, World Bank officials, economists ensconced in some distant Institute for Development Studies. He sees poor people as intelligent actors, well aware of the instigators of their misery, marshalling their tiny resources in the daily search for work and food.

Nothing could be further from Oxfam portfolios than Sainath's photographs of his subjects in the Indian countryside, which he recently took with him on a speaking tour in the US and which he is preparing for displays across India. These photographs don't have the slightly stagy drama of, say, a portfolio from Salgado, but they have twenty times more insight and respect. Rural work is hard to photograph. Take California. Have you ever seen a good photograph of a celery cutter in the Pajaro Valley, or a limonero on his ladder picking lemons around Santa Paula near Oxnard, or a palmero, a date picker, near the Salton Sea?

The American documentarists of the '30s opted for cartoon stereotypes, preferring the easier and less seditious task of presenting migrants as inert victims. You can see from her contact sheet that Dorothea Lange chose the most beaten-down image of the famous migrant mother. It was Lange, so the contact sheets show, who herded children around the woman (actually 100 percent Cherokee), to make it look as though she was burdened with a vast brood, and who passed over more animated images of the same woman.

Sainath's subjects always look alive and even cheerful. They are still significant actors in the larger political drama being fought out in India today. In the US most of the Farm Security Administration's photographers of the 1930s preferred despondency to defiance. Were there no Okie camps with laughing children? Of course there were, but Walker Evans didn't circle those images on his contact sheets, though I'm told the Farm Security Administration has a bunch of color photos of migrants on file it would be worth inspecting.

March 27

Off to Agra (250km) and the early palaces and mausoleums of the Mughals. We hurtle along in a small Tata car, with Sainath's friend JP, Jayaprakash, and a driver. Rural roadside Indian flashes by. The north Indian landscape here is flat, with wheat sheaves stacked. Everything looks half built and half ruined. Vespas and small motorbikes carry the male driver, with a woman and one child pillion. There's often another child up front on the handlebars. The saris are like glorious butterflies everywhere one looks. On we go towards Fatehpur Sikri along the narrow road carrying buses and all bound for India's premier tourist attraction.

We get a flat and while we're getting it fixed by a fellow with a compressor at the side of the road, there's a crash as a 2000 Ambassador (India's warhorse diesel sedan, looking a bit like a '54 Pontiac) tries and fails to squeeze through two tractors. We see it forty yards down the road with its side bashed in. It's the only metal carcass I see, which is astounding because Indian driving is entirely terrifying, and I have strong nerves in this department. I have a photograph of our car overtaking a bus in the narrow main street of a small town, and ahead of us, rapidly approaching, another car, overtaking a truck. This is standard.

Akbar's Fatehpur palace is a marvel in sandstone, like a Utah landscape conjured into sixteenth-century Mughal architecture, robust, imperial, yet delicate. It's certainly one of the most beautiful palace complexes I have seen, without the endless dreary frontages of Vienna or Versailles, with graceful little temples and pools and then vast colonnades, with parasol-like pavilion roofs lightening the rooflines.

Off to Agra town for lunch before our visit to the Taj Mahal. We go to a vegetarian restaurant, thali-style. Sainath spots a publisher looking patriarchal with his family. He wrote a style book. I hope he defended the semi-colon and other cherished values of an age now gone.

Over lunch we start talking about the whole acrid debate about the consequences of British rule. Sainath cites the Madras-based economist C. T. Kurien (in *Global Capitalism and the Indian Economy*, 1994) on one consequence of the American Civil War. Later I look it up in Sainath's copy.

> The rapidly growing cotton textile industry of Britain had initially depended upon raw cotton from its colonies in America, but after these colonies declared themselves to be the United States of America, British industry lost the power to get cotton on its terms. Subsequently, the Civil War in the United States resulted in a sudden interruption in the supply of cotton to Britain and a frantic search started for an alternative and more dependable source. Demand for cotton from India suddenly shot up; the export of cotton from India to Britain increased from around 500,000 bales in 1859 to close to 1,400,000 bales in 1864.
>
> From then on the commercialization of agriculture continued to gain momentum: between the last decade of the nineteenth century and the middle of the twentieth, when food production in India declined by 7 percent, production of commercial crops increased by 85 percent. There was, consequently, some increase in overall agricultural production, but a growing population could not use the commercial crops as food. Widespread and recurring famines became a regular feature during this period. However, those who had the land and other facilities to take advantage of the demand for commercial crops must have become much wealthier. Capitalism was performing its role of enriching some and impoverishing many.

In other words, the Civil War helped install recurring starvation on the Indian calendar.

March 28

We head towards the Taj Mahal, built by Shah Jahan for the dearest of his wives, Arjumand Banu Begum, whom he married in 1612 and who died bearing their fourteenth child in 1631. Shah Jahan took it hard, remaining in seclusion for two years and emerging with spectacles and gray hair. He spent twenty years supervising the construction of the Taj Mahal, joining her in the mausoleum thirty-five years later, having been imprisoned for a number of years by his son, Aurangzeb.

There's a split rate for Indians and foreigners, which seems sensible: 15 rupees for the former and 110 (about $2.60) for the latter. The crowds are large, but without the air of sullen resignation, amplified by the gross corpulence, conspicuous in American crowds in Disney World and other attractions. The children are mostly cheerful and the mothers animated. In all my journeys I saw neither a really fat Indian nor a skeletal one, of the sort enshrined in Oxfam posters, even though we later visited several homes with families so poor that the man of the house had killed himself from shame at the inability to pay off his debts to the banks and to moneylenders. As Sainath stresses, though you can see emaciation in the slums of Mumbai, most hunger is invisible and has been swelling since liberalization began in the early '90s. Sixty-seven percent of Indian kids are malnourished.

I've never cared for the Taj Mahal, depicted on the biscuit tins of my childhood. And after seeing Akbar's first palace compound at Fatehpur Sikri, I feel this more strongly. Kitsch is emotional blackmail and the Taj Mahal, blaring Shah Jahan's bereavement, seems to me the very essence of kitsch. Part of the problem is Shah Jahan's snobbery about red sandstone. Both here and a mile up river at the Fort he ordered white marble, and in the case of the Taj Mahal the result is a sort of airless sterility. The manic symmetry amplifies this. Also, the Taj Mahal is just too big.

On the way home Sainath starts reminiscing about Karanjia, the famous owner of *Blitz*. Karanjia was an owner-editor who plied his trade with élan. At the dawn of the Cuban revolution he traveled to Havana where the new government took him to be the new Indian ambassador and, gratified with such diplomatic recognition, gave Karanjia the red carpet, including an interview with Fidel. Finally, after three weeks, Karanjia disclosed that he was not the ambassador but a journalist and there was a momentary chill, soon dispelled.

For Karanjia, said Sainath, impact was everything. *Blitz*'s stories had sizzle and the phones burned with powerful people howling libel threats down the lines. Death threats came too, in such profusion that reporters would solemnly request the callers to postpone their homicidal visits for a day or two owing to the length of the line of people preparing to exact retribution. The Hindu fundamentalists in

Shiv Sena (Shiva's Army) got mad enough one time at a slur in the humor column that they sent a mob from out of town to burn three of *Blitz*'s delivery vehicles and break office windows. Karanjia was away at the time and Sainath, who'd let the humor column through without reading it, quaked at news of his return.

When he saw his burned trucks Karanjia trumpeted his dismay and Sainath, taking full responsibility, was under heavy fire until Karanjia noticed *Blitz*'s business manager, an elderly Parsee, looking undismayed. So, Karanjia asked him, were the trucks insured? No, said the manager, still calm. Then the glorious truth came out. The trucks had been rented from the local Shiv Sena outfit, whose capo soon appeared at *Blitz*'s office distraught at his dilemma. He could not, he told Karanjia, get compensation from the arsonists since they had been sent from out of town by Shiv Sena's supreme commander. Karanjia told him he could offer no satisfaction.

Sometime in the late '60s a guru made the rounds of India, saying that his spiritual powers enabled him to walk on water. And so he could—with the assistance of a German engineer who had designed a tank with a span of fiberglass rope just under the surface, along which the guru would pace, to the amazement of the rubes.

Karanjia announced that *Blitz* would sponsor a demonstration by the water-walking guru in a local auditorium. He ordered an extra big tank to be fabricated. Seeing trouble ahead, the German engineer made a prudent exit. In front of an excited crowd the guru faltered to Karanjia that the commotion was impinging on his powers and diluting the cosmic forces. "You'll walk on water or I'll break your legs," Karanjia shouted. The trembling guru stepped off the edge of the tank and sank like a stone. When he'd dried off, Karanjia told him to try again. Once again the guru stepped and sank, and then fled into the night. Karanjia's staff worried that the crowd would want its money back but Karanjia wouldn't hear of it. "They have had their money's worth," he crowed. "They're happy."

We bowled along, hooting at the antics and impostures of gurus and fakirs, from the Maharaji on. Only months ago, JP and Sainath told me, an up-and-coming swami, Sri-Sri Ravisander, had headed into southern Tamil Nadu, vowing to project his spiritual powers to those afflicted by the tsunami of December 26, 2004, and soothe the cosmic forces. The bigwigs of the local town assembled to greet the great mystic. But as his cavalcade of seventy cars rolled south along the highway down the coast of Coromandel, some subversive wag raised the cry that a second tsunami, even more immense in destructive potential than the first, was just over the horizon. The swami made a quick estimate of his powers versus those of the cosmic forces and ordered his car to turn round. The road was narrow, and the ensuing jam very terrible to behold as Sri-Sri Ravisanker tried to beat a retreat.

March 28

At 9.30 p.m. JP, Sainath, and I head for Jwaharlal Nehru University for my big talk. They drive round the campus reminiscing about the good old days when they hosted Iranian students protesting the Shah's visit and JP managed to get onto the roof of the car behind the Shah's. The next day JP brings a black and white photo and there he is, a blurry, bearded protester. I ask why the police didn't beat him to death with their lathis—bamboo staves—and he said that they circled him and began to whack away, but the staves clashed above his body, as in a cartoon, and he was able to roll away and flee.

The venue is the mess hall of one of the hostels. At ten Sainath gives me a generous intro and I'm off on my scheduled talk, "War on Iraq, War in America." I go at it for about an hour, throwing everything into the pot, from Judith Miller to Abu Ghraib, to the failures of the American left. It goes down well, and questions are vigorous including from a fellow who asks about the neocons and their origins in a Trotskyite groupuscule headed by Shachtman. I confirm the story and the questioner, obviously a Maoist, grins with knowing approval. The Trotskyites furrow their brows.

April 2

After a few more days in Delhi and Mumbai we fly to the southwest, land in Tamil Nadu and drive over the state line into Kerala to visit a Coca-Cola plant blockaded by peasants since it has destroyed their water supplies. Then we head on down into Kerala, ending up in Khozikode, aka Calicut (a few miles from where Vasco da Gama made landfall in 1498), where I give a press conference under the aegis of *Mathrubhumi*, the million-plus circulation newspaper daily, published in Kerala's language, Malayalam (spoken by seventy million).

After a while a fellow stands up and asks me if the CIA is active on American campuses. I allude in my response to recent pieces in *CounterPunch* about the new Roberts program, covertly funding graduates for intelligence work. He persists. Is it not a fact, he asks, that Professor Franke, at the state university at Montclair in New Jersey, is working with the CIA?

Scenting trouble, I immediately respond to the effect that I have absolutely zero knowledge of Franke or of what goes on at Montclair, including any possible CIA activity. The chap nods happily and sits down. A few days later I get an urgent email from Richard Franke in Montclair. Sainath and I and the fellows from *Mathrubhumi*, traveling in Wyanad, have missed a story in the ultra Hindu nationalist paper run by the RSS, stating that "Cockburn confirms CIA presence at Montclair." Franke, apparently an excellent anthropologist, is frantic to know exactly what I said. It turns out this is all part of a long rumor-mongering campaign of sabotage by left sectarians against Franke, who has played a creditable role in Kerala politics, and a local left leader, T. M. Thomas Isaac, State Secretariat member of the Communist Party of India (Marxist), which as likely as not will be leading the government of Kerala after next year's elections.

April 3

To meet India's rural crisis face to face we drive along the lovely wooded roads of Wyanad, a district in northeastern Kerala. To our east rise the Western Ghat mountains. Last night we stayed in Sultan's Battery, so called because it had been the last stand of the local sultan, when the British came three centuries ago.

Along this road the ancient forests have long since logged off and the state-planted young teak trees are usually cut, to judge by the piles at the side of the road, with the trunk at about twelve inches in diameter. Familiar follies of state-sponsored forestry have occurred. Some years ago the clumps of bamboo, often forty feet across and fifty feet high, were taken off the ridges and slopes of the Western Ghats and *Eucalyptus globulus* put in, the same way it was in California in the 1870s. Elephants don't like it because it replaces their natural habitat and drives them out in search of forage. As the old forest was cut, locals claim the weather cycles in Wyanad changed for the worse, putting paid to the orange groves.

We turn off the road through the woods and onto a smaller lane, guided by the area rep of the Communist Party of India (Marxist), whose red flags and local offices are conspicuous throughout the district. Then we walk up a path past pepper vines, bananas, cashew trees, jackfruit and some coffee bushes to a single-story concrete-block house. Here are Dinesan, two of his sisters and two little children. The mother and another sister are away. Dinesan has a job as a projectionist, though Wyanad's farm crisis means few can afford to go to the movies anymore and so the local cinema is failing. The proprietor refuses to screen the skin movies now churning out of Indian studios.

The property is a house on three acres. Livestock: one cow, one goat. Nearly a year ago Dinesan's father, B. M. Kamelasan, took note of the collapsing price of pepper, vanilla, and coffee, set the sums he'd borrowed from the banks and the moneylenders against the expected yields, and decided to end it all with the one agent he could get for free, a pesticide called monocrotophos made by Ciba-Geigy. It's a horrible way to die.

This is no tableau of beleaguered sharecroppers in a tar-paper shanty in West Virginia fifty years ago. The family is trim, the two kids clean and nicely dressed. A farmer's desperation and suicide do not require the backdrop of a rural slum, even though, after the collapse in agricultural prices, Dinesan and his family have their backs against the wall, with a mudslide of debt (tiny by Western standards) engulfing them. Amid the terrible crisis of the small family farmers in the American Midwest in the past thirty years there have been plenty of suicides or, to put it more tactfully, higher than expected deaths, in trim ranch houses, where the suicide might be reported as accidental death so the survivors get the insurance money.

Kerala has near 100 percent literacy and a tradition of voracious newspaper reading. The libraries are stuffed with poor people catching up on local and world events. Young Dinesan talks about the reasons for the crisis, the collapse of subsidies, the role of middlemen, the World Bank's subsidy to Vietnam whose cheap and inferior pepper comes to Sri Lanka, a free port, and then into Kerala whose Malabar pepper is the finest in the world. As with most peasants and farmers across the world, he understands the world picture. He talks about the weakness of the dollar against the euro.

An hour later it's time to go. The little boy climbs a cashew tree and brings me down a fruit with the large cashew shell growing out of its top. The fruit tastes a little like mango. Cashews came from the New World via the Portuguese, along with chili, tapioca, tomatoes, pineapples, cocoa, potatoes, and groundnuts. That was early globalization. It was quicker in those days. The first housewives on the Indian subcontinent got chilies, a basic for what we regard as the eternal Indian diet, in about 1550, and not too long thereafter it was on every household menu in the whole of India.

In 1957, in free elections, the Communists swept to power in Kerala and delivered on their promise of land reform in a decade where US dollars and the CIA leagued with the local land barons and international firms like United Fruit to crush it in Guatemala and Iran. The Communists delivered on land, on education, and on health. By 1959, under US pressure, the central government in New Delhi struck, dismissing Kerala's government. The long counterattack followed, with brief interruptions by left coalitions. Kerala's still the most literate state in India. Its infant mortality rates are the lowest. Its schools are still good.

Last year Sainath wrote about a little girl whose father, working across the state line as a day laborer in Karnataka, scrapes the money together to send her back on the bus each day to get taught by the nuns in Wyanad, a devotion to his daughter's future all the more remarkable because it's a daughter, not a son he's sending back. Millions of Indian parents crave sons, not daughters. When the ultrasound picks up the evidence of a female embryo in utero, the parents all too often avail themselves of choice and abort that embryo.

Wyanad is a district caught in the backwash of "market freedoms." The Christian churches, who brought in thousands of immigrants into Wyanad after World War II are in trouble, with their Sunday collections down to 10 percent of normal. Priests aren't being paid, though bishops surely must be. Movie houses have closed down. There are less Tamil migrant laborers around and those that are can't afford the 10-rupee ticket.

At least the Kerala State Road Transport Corp's buses are doing a booming business, ferrying people looking for work in Karnataka and Tamil Nadu. Thousands cross every day. Back in 1995 there were six buses a day to Kutta, in Karnataka; now there are twenty-four daily. On them are skilled men—masons, carpenters, electricians. These are the people who worked on the half-built houses, many of them substantial villas, one sees mile after mile each side of Wyanad's rural roads, abandoned after farm income slid into the pit.

The state-licensed toddy shops are in trouble too. Toddy is a fermented brew from the sap of the palmyra palm. We visit Uttaman, the toddy man. He's a genial fellow, with the slightly knowing grin, redolent of tolerance for human folly, one often finds in barkeeps and kindred providers. Uttaman pays 48,000 rupees a year for his license, 100,000 rupees for the welfare fund for his six employees. These days they're tapping 120 liters of toddy a day. Five years ago he brewed and sold 250 bottles a day, today only ten or fifteen. He's being ruined by arrack, a spirit distilled from fermented toddy that's illegal in Kerala but for sale just across the Kabini river in Karnataka. It's stronger, and because it's illegal and the distillers don't pay taxes, cheaper.

Uttaman offers me a glass of toddy. It's pleasant. He lets the toddy ferment for twelve hours, to get an alcohol content of 12 percent. If he leaves it to ferment for twenty-four hours, it will go to 24 percent. It's got a shelf life of forty-eight hours. As I sip, Uttaman describes to us the visit from the cops after Sainath's piece on him was published in the *Hindu* in January. Why was he talking to Sainath, they asked him. Sainath was the man who'd personally overthrown Naidu, the chief minister of Andhra Pradesh. Sainath gives a gratified smirk.

April 4

Sainath tells me he's had difficulty sleeping since he covered the suicides in Andhra Pradesh from the late '90s on. All told, he's visited 300 families in which a suicide has occurred. How did it all begin? From the early '90s forward, zero investment and a collapse of credit ravaged Indian agriculture. The landless poor saw working days crash as a result. Crippling rises in the costs of seed, fertilizer, utilities, pesticides, and water crushed small farms. New user fees sent health costs soaring, and such costs have become a huge component of rural family debt. Newly commercialized education destroyed the hopes of hundreds of thousands of women, as families, given the narrowed options, favored sons over daughters. Farm kids simply dropped out.

Ruin metastasized. Sainath showed me an 8×10 picture he'd made of a woman, Aruna, positioning a photograph of her husband Bangaru Ramachari among the implements he made for farmers, getting payment in kind. Amid the slump he'd no customers for two years. He'd died of hunger, too proud to admit, in his last week before he collapsed, that he'd not eaten for five days. The shift from food crops to cash crops, backed by the World Bank, produced another harvest of disaster. New entrepreneurs replacing old government-run networks sold bad seeds that would not germinate.

"The suicides," Sainath says, "are a symptom of vast agrarian distress. For every farmer who has committed suicide there are thousands more facing the same huge crisis who have not taken their lives. In fact, we will never know how many suicides there have been, since there are so many ways of not counting them. We do know that in seven or eight states since '97 and '98 and most particularly since 2000 farmers have taken their lives by the thousand. In the single district of Anantapur, in the state of Andhra Pradesh, so beloved by the neoliberals because of its 'reforms,' over 3,000 farmers have taken their lives between 1997/98 and 2003."

Increasingly, from 1999 to 2000, Sainath and some vigilant local journalists noticed a mismatch between what they were seeing in the fields and the official data. Narasimha Reddy, who works for the biggest Telugu newspaper, *Eenadu* (with a circulation of around one million), started writing about this gap. The government stats were saying that suicides due to "distress" were no more than fifty-four statewide in 2000. This was strange because when Narasimha and Sainath went to villages to investigate suicides they'd routinely find six or seven. That rattled them. Then they started looking more closely at the death statistics, and found out what the bureaucrats were doing, first as conspiracy, then out of habit.

By far the most common method of suicide was drinking the pesticide dumped on farmers by the government. The journalists found that the police had listed these as "suicides due to stomach ache." Sometimes they said that the pain of the stomach ache "had prompted the victims to take pesticide." Other methods of concealment included counting a death as suicide, but not a "distress" suicide. Or as an "accident." Or as a death due to natural causes or accident. Many of those killing themselves were women running small farms in the absence of husbands who were looking for work elsewhere, or who had already taken their own lives. But because these women rarely owned the land themselves, they weren't classified as farmers, so their suicides were not counted as farm-related.

Then there's the stigma of suicide. Many families don't want it, and that's a big factor in suppressing the numbers. Again, legally speaking, post mortems are free, but to prove that a relative committed suicide the police extort money from family members to pay for the autopsy. Officials undercount suicides among dalits and landless laborers or among migrant farmers who've given up, gone to a town and—severed from their social setting—killed themselves.

While these farmers were being driven to suicide by the thousand in Andhra Pradesh, Chandrababu Naidu, the state's chief minister, was being iconized in the Western press as the apex poster-boy for neoliberal "reform." The *Wall Street Journal* hailed him as "a model for fellow state leaders." *Time* crowned him "South Asian of the year." Bill Gates called on Naidu. So did Bill Clinton. So did Paul O'Neill. John Wolfenson, President of the World Bank, tossed him loan upon loan.

The press projected onto Naidu all their fantasies of what a neoliberal modernizer should be, building an IT-based economy in

"Cyberabad." Oppression of women? Naidu's fixed that, crowed the *Financial Times*: "In a country where lower caste women are locked out of decision-making, the government of Andhra Pradesh is sponsoring a social revolution … Women now dominate the village square."

Indeed, World Bank officials clapped their hands as Naidu kicked aside the panchayats—democratically elected village councils—and announced he was empowering women in new local organizations. What could be wrong with that? Plenty. The new outfits usually turned out to be small coteries with the right connections, which got Naidu's patronage and which filched or wasted the money while the genuinely democratic panchayats were sidelined and starved of funding. The collapse of democracy—that is, the framework for collective action to combat disaster—in the countryside contributed to the terrible harvest of death.

On December 27, 2002, Keith Bradsher of the *New York Times* issued a worshipful résumé of Naidu's assets and achievements, selecting for particular mention the asset that Bradsher deemed vital to Naidu's political grip on Andhra Pradesh. "Naidu and his allies," Bradsher breathlessly confided to the NYT's readers, "speak Telugu, a language spoken only in this state and by a few people in two adjacent states." What Bradsher was saying was that Naidu spoke the same language as the other seventy million inhabitants of Andhra Pradesh. It was as though someone ascribed Tony Blair's political successes in the United Kingdom to his command of English.

Apart from Naidu's wondrous fluency in his native tongue, Bradsher fixed upon other achievements likely to excite an American business readership: "Mr. Naidu," he excitedly confides, "has succeeded in raising electricity prices here by 70 percent" and "has enacted a law requiring union leaders to be workers from the factory or office they represent … Andhra Pradesh has also relaxed some of the restrictions on laying off workers."

In the spring of 2004 the Naidu balloon exploded with a gigantic thunderclap. The Indian poor entered his field of vision decisively, even as they shattered the expectations of almost every national political pundit. Rarely has a poster-boy been more humiliatingly peeled from the billboards and tossed in the gutter. Naidu's elected coalition plummeted from 202 seats to a quarter of that number.

The verdict, from the landless poor to farmers to rural women to the denizens of Cyberabad, was well-nigh unanimous: the Naidu model had been a disaster for Andhra Pradesh, as statistics had been inexorably recording even during his glory years. Economic growth was abysmal and other vital statistics equally wretched. The 5,000 suicides remain the prime epitaph for a politician hailed in the West more than any other Indian as the harbinger of neoliberal triumph. Only the Argentinean collapse was as brutal a rebuff to elite opinion.

April 5

My big evening in Calicut, sponsored by the extremely militant Bank Clerks' Union. There's a full house, I'm glad to say, with Muslim clerics front row right, Hindu fundamentalists, secularist leftists, Christians of various stripes. Kerala is a third Muslim, a third Hindu, and a third Christian, the latter faith having been brought to the Malabar coast in 60 AD by Thomas the Doubting Apostle, no doubt plaguing the navigator with anxious questions.

The meeting is chaired by the local member of the federal parliament, Veerendrakumar, an energetic man in his sixties who also controls *Mathrubhumi*. I let fly for an hour on the topic of the war in Iraq. It seems to go down well. Sainath speaks too, reminding the audience that back in 1916, when the British invaded Mesopotamia, their force was mostly Indian soldiers, most of whom were captured by the Turks and died in forced labor building railroads.

April 6

We drive north back to Wyanad, back to St. George's Battery for a last night, winding our way up to 3,000 feet in the Western Ghats. The next day, with Sudhi at the wheel of the Ambassador, we set off north again into the state of Karnataka, northeast through Mysore to Bangalore, hailed by the Friedmans of this world as India's prime rendezvous with the future, where the cyber-coolies toil night and day in the huge call centers.

The *Hindu*'s classifieds tell the story: "Call Center Placement based US/UK, req'd for Chennai and Blr, Sal up to Rs 1800/m, age 17 to 29.) Any degree, walkin." "ACDA of Chennai wants to hire Part-time faculty to teach Accent Neutralisation and American Accent." Later come the matrimonial classifieds: "Hindu Parkaakulam, Moopanaar/ Udayar 23/167, B.A. Fine Arts, doing M.A. MASSCOMM, good-looking, wheatish complexion, girl from well-to-do family in business seeks well settled groom in business. Early marriage. Send horoscope/photo." And on down the packed columns to: "Karkatha Pillai 30/MCA/employed in TNEB seeks employed guy of same caste."

These were all from the Tamil section, with others allocated to Marathi, Bengali, and "Cosmopolitan" where we find "K–, 33/155/ fair MNC innocent divorcee. Brahmin 35–38 preferably Hyd/Abroad without encumbrances," plus an e-address @yahoo and a box address at the *Hindu* in Chennai. Sainath says such references to innocence—frequent in the matrimonial classifieds—are intended to convey the fact that the advertiser is still a virgin. Since some of the male matrimonials also mention innocence in divorce I'd assumed this meant simply that the advertiser was claiming to be the injured party.

These matrimonial ads aren't on the fringe of the national culture, but in its dead center, as is the poor situation of Indian women overall. Most Indian marriages are arranged, from poor up to wealthy families. Of course there are love marriages and these days some Indian women find a way out of the parental pressure to marry via prolonged stints of education abroad in the US, UK or Australia.

Bangalore may be the modern face of India, but it's paralyzed by traffic. Nothing moves. International businesses are having to relocate into the hinterland. There is, so our host Ashwin Mahesh tells us genially, no central traffic authority. Ashwin, ex-NASA researcher, educated at UW, then with a stint at NASA's Goddard Center under his belt, returned to India to run a fine, public-interest website, india-together. From the sixteenth floor of South Tower, where he and his wife live, we are well situated to review the grid-locked traffic.

Ashwin has already modeled some ideas for traffic relief which are under consideration.

April 7

Chennai. Here I am on the coast of Coromandel. At last a city with the feel and pace of an older time. We go to the guesthouse of the Asian College of Journalism. I give a talk to the students. Then off to a terrific Chettinad restaurant, though in my order I foolishly include curried partridge, which is disappointing as all partridges have been for the thirty-four years since I ate a good one, braised in whiskey and cream.

I drive around with Ashwin, who's come from Bangalore to visit his parents. We drive through the Theosophy Canter, the sanctuary of Annie Besant, also of a banyan of international repute, though now dying. Then we pace about on what is officially classified as the third longest beach in the world. There aren't many women, and no one in bathing dress. The great tsunami of last Christmas washed in over this beach and about three-quarters of a kilometer inland, with a total of forty lives or so lost in all of Chennai.

April 8

We go down to a heritage center south of Chennai called Dakshina Chitra, which is really good, with excellent reconstructions of vernacular Indian architecture of an earlier time in Kerala and Tamil Nadu. Looking at the wooden buildings reminds me of how much Indian architecture of the past fifty years is truly awful.

I distinguish architecture here from landscape. Indian landscapes, whether rural or urban are certainly what one might call "thick," just as most American landscapes are "thin." In India, from a foot in front of one's nose to the horizon, there are infinite medleys of planes and perspectives. There is no thin air, no emptiness. There's the street life, the endless small shop displays and signage, the billboards above, the animals, the stalls, the cars and buses overtaking each other at sixty miles an hour.

The overall effect is endlessly inspiriting, with palette after palette of tumultuous greens, blues, yellows, pinks, and reds deployed on saris, racks of clothes, aging advertisements. Anyone tired of an Indian streetscape or country road is truly tired of life. But the architecture itself is mostly drab cinderblock.

April 10

I give a talk at the Asian College of Journalism on the war in Iraq. There's a fine turnout and many questions. N. Ram, the editor in chief of the *Hindu*, which sponsored the event, is unable to attend, with the rather good excuse that he was meeting the Chinese Prime Minister, Wen Jibao, touring Bangalore and Chennai that week.

The *Hindu*, circulation a million plus, and now Sainath's home port, maintains decent standards and reminds me somewhat of the London *Times* thirty years ago, when a salvo from the editorial page could alter the contours of a whole political battlefield. Ram invites Sainath and me to drop by his house in Chennai the next day, and we do so. When we arrive, his charming wife says that he cannot be with us for a few minutes because he is finishing his editorial on Chinese-Indian relations. She says this with a tinge of gravity, of reverence for the solemn rite of editorial composition that takes me back to the distant years in the '60s when the presses at the *Times* would be held while the editor in chief, William Haley, wrestled unrighteousness to the ground in the "first leader," as the prime editorial was called in England in those days. These days editorials count for nothing in the US. Few read them except for press secretaries and lobbyists. They have no weight.

In due course Ram emerges from his editorial labors, looking weighty, and treats us to an interesting disquisition, which I correctly assess to be the burden of his impending editorial, on the evolution of Chinese-Indian relations since the late 1940s. Then he shifts to a description of his shock when he attended the reunion of his class of '68 of the Columbia Journalism School last year: at a meeting to discuss the burning issues of the day he heard not a word of condemnation of the US invasion of Iraq, so rose to his feet and denounced it himself. He said there were several hisses from other J School grads. It was bracing to find a newspaper editor—probably India's premier editor in terms of political clout—talking like that; bracing too to hear later that in his younger days Ram endorsed a strike at the *Hindu* and was promptly exiled from the paper's premises by his father, then the newspaper's boss.

April 11

Back to Mumbai. Sainath's friend Sudarshan invites me to APNE-AAP, a foundation he runs, in Kamathipura, Mumbai's red light district along the Falkland Road. The foundation has some rooms in an old school, and these are now filled with cheerful kids. The idea is to give children of prostitutes a chance to get out of the life, get some education, get a chance. It's the dearest dream of the prostitutes, many of whom haven't much hope of living past thirty-five, taken off by AIDS or TB. The women working at the drop-in house get the prostitutes ration cards, take them to hospital, run savings accounts for them—over 200 when I was there—where they can squirrel away ten rupees (25 cents) or so a day for their kids.

Without such help the prostitutes get turned away by hospitals and kindred bureaucracies. Already there are 150 kids who've graduated, and sixty-five currently in attendance. Only one graduate has gone into her mother's line of business. I like the atmosphere, mercifully free of social worker sanctimony. APNE-AAP's staff, Manju Vyas, Preethi, Diplai, and Bimbla, are all in good spirits and very impressive.

We walk over to a huge old brothel built by the British a hundred years ago for their garrison. Back then the prostitutes were Tibetan or Japanese. These days they're from Nepal or Bangladesh. The middlemen procuring the girls from their parents get 20,000 rupees or more from the madams. The rooms in the brothel are about ten foot by ten foot, with two tiers of beds and families of four or five cooking and chatting. When a customer shows up and forks over his 50 rupees they presumably stand outside. The girls greet us in friendly style and some of them covertly slide over their 10 rupees to the APNE-AAP women, out of sight of husband, or pimp, or madam. It costs residents 50 rupees a day to rent a bed. Five rupees buys you a bucket of water. Electricity costs 150 rupees a month.

After an hour or so I bid them adieu and go off to the Royal Yacht Club to read for an hour or two before Sainath and his wife Sonia throw me a farewell dinner.

As we wait for friends to arrive, Sainath reminds me of the bit in Tacitus's *Annals* where he describes how condemned people were recruited to serve as candles at Nero's parties: "they were doomed to the flames and burnt, to serve as nightly illumination when daylight had expired. Nero offered his gardens for the spectacle." "What sort of sensibility," Sainath broods, "did it require to pop another fig in your mouth as one more human being went up in flames?"

And by the same token, Sainath asks, what sort of indifference has it required for India's rich—and the very rich in India are the among the richest on the planet—to disport while millions starve not far off, and thousands of peasants kill themselves, some of them less than fifty miles from Mumbai where much of India's wealth is concentrated, and where "theme weddings" costing millions have been the rage? Last year an Indian steel billionaire, Lakshmi Mittal, and his wife Usha promised their daughter Vanisha a spectacular wedding. They cashed the promise by renting Vaux le Vicomte and Versailles in France for the nuptials. The six-day-long wedding bash cost over $80 million and was attended by more than 1,200 guests including leading Indian industrialists and celebrities from the Bollywood film scene.

Just as interesting, I remark to Sainath, as the festivities and excesses of the rich is the mindset of the policy makers, the intellectual formulators of neoliberal policies that they well know will cause terrible suffering. What processes of self-exculpation insulate them from a policy (say, the planned shrinkage of India's small farmers by 40 percent), and the execution of that policy, inflicting terrible privations and early death on millions?

April 29
Weather can wipe out cities forever. It's what happened to America's first city, after all, as a visit to Chaco Canyon, northeast of Gallup, NM, attests. At the start of the thirteenth century it got hotter and by the 1230s the Anasazi upped and moved on. As the world now knows, weather need not have done for New Orleans. There are decades' worth of memos from engineers and contractors giving budgets for what it would take to build up those levees to withstand a Force 4 or 5 hurricane. The sum most recently nixed by Bush's OMB—$3 billion or so—is far less than what the Pentagon simply mislays every year, without even taking the trouble to convert the appropriated cash into cruise missiles or boots.

For much of its post–Civil War existence New Orleans was always a pretty desperate city, despite its boast of a few years ago that it had the highest number of millionaires in America's fifty largest cities. I remember that in the year that G. Bush Sr. accepted his party's nomination in the Superdome in 1988 some 26 percent of the inhabitants were below the poverty line and 50 percent could be classified as poor.

The scarcely suppressed class war in New Orleans was what gave the place, and the music, its edge, and why, at least until now, the Disneyfication of the core city could never quite be consummated. Barely had the hurricane passed before Speaker of the House Hastert caught the Republican mood nicely with his remark that the city should be abandoned to the alligators and Barbara Bush followed through with her considered view that for black people the Houston Astrodome represents the ne plus ultra in domestic amenities.

Music and street food are what anchored the city to its history. On any visit, you could hear blues singers whose active careers spanned six decades. Clarence "Gatemouth" Brown finally left us last week at eighty-one. I heard him at Jazzfest this spring, and though the Reaper was at his elbow, Gatemouth Brown still fired up the crowd. "Goodbye, I hate, I hate to leave you now, goodbye. / Wish that I could help somehow. So long, so long, for now so long. / I pray that I return, return to you some day. You pray that it shall be just that way. So long, so long for now, so long."

May 2

A highlight of the New Orleans Jazzfest was the tribute to Sister Rosetta Tharpe, courtesy of Marcia Ball, Tracy Nelson, Mairia Muldaur, Angela Strehli, and special guest Irma Thomas. They were all strong, but Irma Thomas blew everyone away with "Beams of Heaven." Not a dry eye in the Blues tent, including her own.

On a less portentous level, a big moment for me was Ike Turner's set, also in the Blues tent, a day earlier. Ike of course has been in disgrace ever since Tina's descriptions of his violent abuses.

Ike was terrific. Everything was wonderfully tacky, from the one-size-fits-all maroon suits of his band, looking like fugitives from a bad early '60s movie about Billy Haley, to Ike's own sequined, white, purple, and gold jumpsuit like a hand-me down from a late-Elvis wardrobe. His current Tina-like is (though you wouldn't learn this from Ike, sparse with acknowledgement of his fellow musicians) Audrey Madison, gorgeous and with a big voice. Also a Tina-type wig. Some in the crowd thought this tasteless and left. Ike claimed that he'd just discovered her in Memphis three months ago. Jeffrey St. Clair heard him say the same thing in Portland, Oregon, back in 2001.

Ike was a great musician as always, on guitar and piano. Of course he sang "Rocket 88," deemed by many the first rock 'n' roll song, released in 1951 (and immediately covered by Bill Haley). By the end the act had the initially cool crowd roaring. Ms. Audrey, with her big voice, tumultuous bosom and increasing confidence, had a lot to do with it, though you wouldn't know this from the guy in the band who roared into the mike during Audrey's huge finale, "Ike Turner! Ike Turner!"

May 27

Discussing an Iraqi faker touted by the Bush administration, I recently wrote that "In atrocity stories there are some things that don't ring true, even when dealing with such well-credentialed butchers as Saddam and his sons. Take the story, subsequently identified as one concocted by a Western intelligence agency, that Uday had put some of his victims through a wood chipper. Anyone using these chippers knows the damn things jam if inconvenienced by anything with a diameter larger than that of a stick of asparagus, let alone an Iraqi human, however scrawny. Uday's chipper, whose origin can probably be traced to a scene in the movie *Fargo*, just didn't pass muster, same as the incubator story from the first Gulf War, first identified in this column as intrinsically preposterous."

I was being slightly frivolous about the wood chipper, but the letters poured in:

> Mr. Cockburn,
> I imagine this will be but one of many, but what kind of piss ant wood chipper did you train on? I routinely use a medium sized chipper that will take up to 2″ to 3″ branches of green wood, and I don't think it would have much trouble with a person's arm, or even a leg. (And by the way, commercial wood chippers rarely jam.) Now whether you could get a whole human through one, I don't know, but I've heard of really sweet guys putting small animals through them just to watch the spray, so I suspect that if you did a bit of selective drawing and quartering you might eventually be able to do a whole body. But what mess. And what would be the point, even for someone like Uday? You're right, the idea is farcical. But asparagus as an upper limit is off by several orders of magnitude.
> Nicholas Dykema
> Cleveland, Ohio

June 1

I hate surprise parties and now the scientific evidence is in. Surprise parties can kill. To put the matter in scientific terms: Emotional stress can precipitate severe, reversible left ventricular dysfunction in patients without coronary disease. Exaggerated sympathetic stimulation is probably central to the cause of this syndrome. Or, in the words of the press release from Johns Hopkins:

> Researchers at Johns Hopkins have discovered that sudden emotional stress can also result in severe but reversible heart muscle weakness that mimics a classic heart attack. Patients with this condition, called stress cardiomyopathy but known colloquially as "broken heart" syndrome, are often misdiagnosed with a massive heart attack when, indeed, they have

> suffered from a days-long surge in adrenalin (epinephrine) and other stress hormones that temporarily "stun" the heart …
>
> The research team found that some people may respond to sudden, overwhelming emotional stress by releasing large amounts of catecholamines (notably adrenalin and noradrenalin, also called epinephrine and norepinephrine) into the blood stream, along with their breakdown products and small proteins produced by an excited nervous system. These chemicals can be temporarily toxic to the heart, effectively stunning the muscle and producing symptoms similar to a typical heart attack, including chest pain, fluid in the lungs, shortness of breath and heart failure.

Of course, many rituals in our society have a furtive homicidal intent, most notably those fraught sessions known as family reunions. Grandpa and grandma drive to the event, get mildly looped, head for home and are wiped out on the Interstate by a semi when grandpa pulls out of the rest stop. Father keels over when he opens the front door to see a plump faced man vaguely resembling the daughter who left home all those years ago saying in a throaty voice, "Hi, dad."

So please, no surprises.

July 9

The terrorists' desire is to show the enemy precisely that they—the terrorists—are sane, but implacable. When the Conrad-era French anarchist Émile Henry carried a cooking pot filled with explosive and 120 bullets into the café Terminus near the Gare Saint-Lazare in Paris in February, 1894, touched his cigar to a fifteen-second fuse and strolled out, his plan was to kill ordinary, relatively humble people—shopkeepers, clerks and salesgirls—having a beer and listening to the band.

"Not 'innocent,'" he claimed later. "These beer-drinkers, petty bourgeois with a steady salary in their pockets, are the ones that always line themselves up on the side of the powerful, ignoring the problems of the workers. They hate the poor more than the rich do!" Many anarchists promptly repudiated him. "At least have the courage of your crimes, gentlemen of the bourgeoisie," Henry declared to the court that condemned him to the guillotine, "and agree that our reprisals are fully legitimate." Reprisals for what? "Are these not innocent victims? Children dying slowly of anemia in the slums ... Women turning pallid in sweatshops ... Old people turned into machines for production all their lives and then cast on the garbage dump and the workhouse when their strength is exhausted."

July 10

A jury has found against a South Carolina doctor who referred a patient for electro-shock treatment that left her permanently impaired. The patient, Peggy S. Salters, is a sixty-year-old former psychiatric nurse. She was subjected to thirteen electroshocks within the span of nineteen days. The jury awarded her $635,177.

The jury found that her loss of thirty years of memory and cognitive impairment—which are demonstrable symptoms of brain damage—was due to ECT. Maybe this decision will give shrinks pause before they send the next poor soul off to get battered on the head with an electric club. A press release from Linda Andre, President of Committee for Truth in Psychiatry (CTIP) adds that 100,000 patients in the US undergo electroshock annually—many against their will.

As Andre writes, "ECT is dominated by medical cowboys who push the limits of intensity of electric shock as they please. In his deposition (May 24, 2005) in Peggy Salters's case, Dr. Fink defended the administration of thirteen intensive ECT treatments in nineteen days stating: 'There are no absolute limits on the low side or to the high side if you're going to give a patient a treatment ... I have personally treated patients twice a day. And there was a time when I gave patients eight treatments in one sitting, you know, on an experiment [!!] that we did many years ago. So, yes, I have treated patients with eight seizures in a morning ... It was called multiple monitored ECT. It was a government-supported project in an effort to find out if we can speed up the response.'"

Wouldn't you describe Fink's tone here as one of ghoulish glee?

Leonard Frank outlined the economics of ECT succinctly in testimony: "ECT is a money-maker. An in-hospital ECT series can cost anywhere from $50,000–75,000. Using a low figure of 100,000 Americans who are electroshocked annually, most of whom are covered by private or government insurance, ECT brings in $5 billion a year. ECT promoters are its stakeholders—they include device manufacturers, hospitals and practitioners."

The malpractice verdict was against the referring doctor, Eric Lewkowicz. The jury could not return a verdict against the other two doctors because of one holdout vote for acquittal. The hospital settled its liability for an undisclosed sum early in the trial.

Former patients have reported devastating, permanent amnesia and cognitive impairment since ECT was first invented in 1938, but that has not hindered the treatment's popularity with doctors. The first lawsuit for ECT amnesia, *Marilyn Rice v. John Nardini*, was brought exactly thirty years ago, and dozens of suits have followed. While there have been a few settlements, including one for half a million dollars, no former patient has won a case until now.

In fact, defiant ghoulishness seems to be a stock in trade of the ECT lobby. "For forty years," Dr. Milton Greenblatt told a meeting of the American Psychiatric Association in Miami in 1976, "the therapeutic value of convulsive therapy has been recognized. My personal recollections go back to 1939 shortly after the introduction of metrazol when, as a medical student, I was allowed to inject metrazol into chronically ill patients at Worcester State Hospital—against their terrified and frightened resistance, which, I might add, was overpowered by several burly attendants. In those days we required only the approval of next of kin for the procedure, and had few qualms about proceeding against the patient's resistance."

Greenblatt goes on to describe how ECT was initially hailed as a marvelous substitute for metrazol, since there were no "awful preseizure sensations" and patients "were fortunate to have a period of amnesia after the treatment." It's like saying bleeding via leeches was a big step forward from opening a patient's vein and having his blood splash all over the bed.

The 1950s found Dr. Greenblatt overseeing research into LSD, in a program funded by the CIA.

August 24

These are triumphant hours for Pat Robertson. His standing as America's senior ayatollah is becoming firmer as Billy Graham and even Jerry Falwell yield the prime-time pulpit to the smooth-tongued maestro of the Christian Coalition.

A decade ago CNN would sooner have given half an hour's air time to the leader of North Korea, but last week Wolf Blitzer poked a stick through the bars, and nodded respectfully as Robertson raved on about the End Time:

BLITZER: You see what's going on in the world today in Pakistan, in India, Afghanistan, an earthquake, maybe 20,000 people dead, maybe twice that number; we don't have a count. Hurricanes in the United States and around the world, a tsunami a little bit less than a year or so ago in Southeast Asia. What's happening?

ROBERTSON: Wolf, I might say you're very perceptive to pick up the key in this. If you read back in the Bible, the letter of the apostle Paul to the church of Thessalonia, he said that in the latter days before the end of the age that the Earth would be caught up in what he called the birth pangs of a new order. And for anybody who knows what it's like to have a wife going into labor, you know how these labor pains begin to hit.

I don't have any special word that says this is that, but it could be suspiciously like that. These things are starting to hit with amazing regularity.

Blitzer wagged his head like a mental hospital attendant placating a noisy inmate, and then poked his stick through the bars again:

BLITZER: But what does that mean? Explain that in more simplistic terms so I can understand what you're driving at?

ROBERTSON: Well, what was called the blessed hope of the Bible is that one day Jesus Christ would come back again, start a whole new era, that this world order as we know it would change into something that would be wonderful that we'd call the millennium. And before that good time comes there will be some difficult days and they will be likened to what a woman goes through in labor just before she brings forth a child.

More placatory nods from the hospital attendant:

BLITZER: So you think we're at that moment right now perhaps?

ROBERTSON: It's possible, Wolf. I don't have any special revelation to say it is, but the Bible does indicate such a time will happen in the end of time. And could this be it? It might be.

BLITZER: All right. Let's move on to something that we perhaps can understand a little bit better, which would be Harriet Miers.

After chiding James ("Focus on the Family") Dobson for hyperbolic language, Robertson closed out the interview a few minutes later by claiming that Venezuela's President Hugo Chávez, whose assassination he had recently recommended, was building a nuclear arsenal and had sent Osama bin Laden a million dollars after September 11.

The sobering part of all this is that all the same words could have come out the mouth of the President, whose relationship to Jesus and expectations of the End Time are probably more intense than Robertson's, since the latter is a seasoned professional, rather than an inspired amateur.

Reagan used to talk about the End Time equably too, once stressing that it could occur in "our lifetime." Journalists like Blitzer should raise the issue more frequently, both to ayatollahs of the Apocalypse like Robertson and to the President. It would give press conferences a certain gloomy zest.

The only mystery is why, given his Apocalyptic expectations, Robertson fusses about the threat of Chávez and calls for his murder by the CIA. He surely cannot think that the Venezuelan leader will be spared the Lord's coming wrath, when the saved rise up in the great celestial spiral and the damned are consigned to the pit. Why ask the CIA to do what the Almighty will soon take care of?

August 27

Each time some loudmouth calls for the CIA to murder an inconvenient foreign leader, the tut-tuts of the State Department get more and more casual. When Pat Robertson called a few weeks ago for a CIA hit on Venezuela's Chávez, the best the State Department could manage was a softly murmured "inappropriate." Maybe it's finally being acknowledged that, just like torture, assassination has long been standard US policy.

Standard? Start, in the post–World War II era, with the bid on Zhou Enlai's life after the Bandung Conference in 1954. An in-flight bomb blew up the plane scheduled to take him home, but Zhou had switched flights. Now move to the efforts, ultimately successful, to kill the Congo's Patrice Lumumba. The CIA tried several times to kill Iraq's General Kassem. The first such attempt, on October 7, 1959, was botched badly, and one of the assassins, Saddam Hussein, was spirited out by the Egyptian Mukhabarat to an Agency apartment in Cairo. There was a second Agency effort in 1960–1 with a poisoned handkerchief. Finally, they had Kassem shot to death in the coup of February 8–9, 1963, that brought Saddam to the fore.

Kassem was a very impressive man, as Roger Morris recently reminded me: an Arabized Kurd from Kut with a Shia mother and a Sunni father, a practicing Sunni who knelt at the sickbed of the Grand Ayatollah of his mother's faith, in a symbolism every Iraqi understood. Kassem even embraced the Kurds (whom he'd fought as a soldier) until the Brits bought them back to rebellion, as usual. As Morris remarks, "Kassem was just what poor sick GW needs in Baghdad now, of course."

November 11

Did the White House slip Judy Miller money under the table to hype Saddam's weapons of mass destruction? I'm quite sure it didn't and the only money Miller took was her regular *Times* paycheck.

But this doesn't mean that We The Taxpayers weren't ultimately footing the bill for Miller's propaganda. We were, since Miller's stories mostly came from the defectors proffered her by Ahmad Chalabi's group, the Iraqi National Congress, which even as late as the spring of 2004 was getting $350,000 a month from the CIA, said payments made in part for the INC to produce "intelligence" from inside Iraq.

It also doesn't mean that when she was pouring her nonsense into the NYT's news columns Judy Miller (or her editors) didn't know that the INC's defectors were linked to the CIA by a money trail. This same trail was laid out in considerable detail in *Out of the Ashes*, written by my brothers, Andrew and Patrick Cockburn, and published in 1999.

In this fine book, closely studied (and frequently pillaged without acknowledgement) by journalists covering Iraq, the authors described how Chalabi's group was funded by the CIA, with huge amounts of money—$23 million in the first year alone—invested in an anti-Saddam propaganda campaign, subcontracted by the Agency to John Rendon, a Washington PR operator with good CIA connections.

Press manipulation was always a paramount concern of the CIA, as with the Pentagon. In his *Secret History of the CIA*, published in 2001, Joe Trento described how in 1948 CIA man Frank Wisner was appointed Director of the Office of Special Projects, soon renamed the Office of Policy Coordination (OPC). This became the espionage and counter-intelligence branch of the Central Intelligence Agency, and the very first in its list of designated functions was "propaganda."

Later that year Wisner set up an operation codenamed "Mockingbird," to influence the domestic American press. He recruited Philip Graham of the *Washington Post* to run the project within the industry.

Senate Armed Services Chairman John Warner said recently, apropos the stories put into the Iraqi press by the Lincoln Group, that it wasn't clear whether traditionally accepted journalistic practices were violated. Warner can relax. The Pentagon, and the Lincoln Group, were working in a rich tradition, and their only mistake was to get caught.

December 8

I remarked after reading Pinter's Nobel acceptance speech that it's a sign of the inability of the American Empire that its agents didn't manage to kill off his nomination, or—having failed at that—to kill Pinter before he was able to record his remarks.

Consider the CIA's probable poisoning, at a fraught political moment, of Paul Robeson, the black actor, singer, and political radical. As Jeffrey St. Clair and I wrote a few years ago, in the spring of 1961, Robeson planned to visit Havana to meet with Fidel Castro and Che Guevara. The trip never came off because Robeson fell ill in Moscow, where he had gone to give several lectures and concerts. At the time, it was reported that Robeson had suffered a heart attack. But in fact Robeson had slashed his wrists in a suicide attempt after suffering hallucinations and severe depression. The symptoms came on following a surprise party thrown for him at his Moscow hotel.

Robeson's son, Paul Robeson Jr., investigated his father's illness for more than thirty years. He believes that his father was slipped a synthetic hallucinogen called BZ by US intelligence operatives at the party in Moscow. The party was hosted by anti-Soviet dissidents funded by the CIA.

Robeson Jr. visited his father in the hospital the day after the suicide attempt. Robeson told his son that he felt extreme paranoia and thought that the walls of the room were moving. He said he had locked himself in his bedroom and was overcome by a powerful sense of emptiness and depression before he tried to take his own life.

Robeson left Moscow for London, where he was admitted to Priory Hospital. There he was turned over to psychiatrists who forced him to endure fifty-four electro-shock treatments. At the time, electro-shock, in combination with psychoactive drugs, was a favored technique of CIA behavior modification. It turned out that the doctors treating Robeson in London and, later, in New York, were CIA contractors. The timing of Robeson's trip to Cuba was certainly a crucial factor. Three weeks after the Moscow party, the CIA launched its disastrous invasion of Cuba at the Bay of Pigs. It's impossible to underestimate Robeson's threat, as he was perceived by the US government as the most famous black radical in the world. His embrace of Castro in Havana would have seriously undermined US efforts to overthrow the new Cuban government.

Another pressing concern for the US government at the time was Robeson's announced intentions to return to the United States and assume a leading role in the emerging civil rights movement. Like the family of Martin Luther King, Robeson had been under official surveillance for decades. As early as 1935, British intelligence had been looking at Robeson's activities. In 1943, the Office of Strategic Services, the World War II predecessor to the CIA, opened a file on him. In 1947, Robeson was nearly killed in a car crash. It later turned out that the left wheel of the car had been monkey-wrenched. In the 1950s, Robeson was targeted by Senator Joseph McCarthy's anti-communist hearings. The campaign effectively sabotaged his acting and singing career in the States.

Robeson never recovered from the drugging and the follow-up treatments from CIA-linked doctors and shrinks. He died in 1977.

2006

January 3
Sanora Babb died on December 31, aged ninety-eight. Harry Magdoff died on New Year's Day, at ninety-two. Frank Wilkinson died a day later, at ninety-one.

My line has always been that to get really old it pays to have been a Commie or at least a fellow traveler. In younger years they tended to walk a lot, selling the party paper. They talked a lot and, above all, they never stopped thinking. The quickest way to kill someone is to send them off to quasi-solitary, torn from their comfortable nest and thrown into a nursing home or into managed care, where people talk about them at the tops of their voices, referring to them in the third person. You can see them dying before your eyes, their brains turned to mush. It takes about a year to kill them off, unless a "surprise birthday party" wipes them out even earlier.

Trotskyists tend to be more feverish and stressed out, hence less likely to turn the bend into their nineties. As for Maoists (over here), I don't know. As Zhou Enlai answered, when asked what he thought of the French Revolution, "Too soon to tell." The ex-Maoists I know are mostly still in their mid-sixties.

I don't know whether Sweezy and Magdoff ever took a day's exercise. When I used to see them in the editorial offices of the *Monthly Review* they looked as though they'd been marinating in tobacco smoke there for decades. They certainly thought a lot, to great effect. They liked Mao too.

Frank Wilkinson was a feisty soul. He led the fight for public housing in Los Angeles in the late 1930s and '40s, which earned him the savage enmity of the Chandlers and thus of the *Los Angeles Times*. If his plans had gone right, we'd have public housing built by Neutra instead of Dodger Stadium. He did time for refusing to testify before Congress, then went on to be a great campaigner for the First Amendment, just like his friend and fellow Communist, Dick Criley, who died a few years ago up in Carmel Highlands, also in his high nineties. Dick's sister, Cynthia Williams, is still peppy after a tremendous ninetieth (NOT a surprise) birthday party last fall in Carmel Highlands. Her wonderful piece of advice to the partygoers: "It's a great life if you don't weaken."

Sanora Babb obviously didn't weaken, though she endured some zingers in her long span, the worst being the fact that she wrote a novel about migrant workers in 1939 that was to be published by Random House, until Random House's other novelist on migrant workers, John Steinbeck, scored a huge hit with *The Grapes of Wrath*. Bennett Cerf cancelled Babb's novel, *Whose Names Are Unknown*. It had to wait sixty-five years until it was published to great acclaim in 2004. Babb thought she was a better writer than Steinbeck and some smart people agree with her.

March 9

Americans are in a fever about possible "Arab control" of mainland ports along both coasts of the United States. The whole storm is ludicrous. When it comes to America's national security and penetration of the mainland by foreign capital, there are bigger worries. This very week, the week of the Chicago Auto Show, the widely read magazine *Consumer Reports* lists the ten safest cars sold in America this year.

They are all Japanese, mostly Hondas, and mostly made in US-based plants put up after Japanese and other foreign automakers were welcomed in thirty years ago, partly as a way of undercutting the Union of Autoworkers. This same month the headlines here have been full of stories about the collapse of the top two US automakers—General Motors and Ford—in the face of foreign competition. Well over 100,000 American workers are to lose their jobs, thus vastly increasing US insecurity. Hundreds of thousands more US workers have already lost their jobs to India, China, Mexico, and other low-wage nations because that is the way American business, backed by the US government, wants it.

March 15

Milošević's death in his cell from a heart attack spared Del Ponte and the International Criminal Tribunal for the Former Yugoslavia (itself a kangaroo tribunal set up by the United States with no proper foundation under international law or treaty) the ongoing embarrassment of a proceeding where Milošević had made a very strong showing against the phalanx of prosecutors, hearsay witnesses, and prejudiced judges marshaled against him.

There are now charges and countercharges about poisons and self-medications. Milošević's son says his father was murdered. The embarrassed Court has claimed Milošević somehow did himself in by tampering with his medicines. But no one contests the fact that Milošević asked for treatment in Moscow—the Russians promised to return him to The Hague—and the Court refused permission. As the tag from the poet A. H. Clough goes, "Thou shalt not kill; but need'st not strive Officiously to keep alive."

March 21

For the past few weeks a sometimes comic debate has been simmering in the American press, focused on the question of whether there is an Israel lobby, and if so, just how powerful is it?

To ask whether there's an Israel lobby here is a bit like asking whether there's a Statue of Liberty in New York Harbor and a White House located at 1600 Pennsylvania Avenue, Washington, DC. For the past sixty years the lobby has been as fixed a part of the American scene as either of the other two monuments, and not infrequently exercising as much if not more influence on the onward march of history.

The Democratic Party has long been hospitable to, and supported by, rich Zionists. In 2002, for example, Haim Saban, the Israeli-American who funds the Saban Center at the Brooking Institute and is a big contributor to AIPAC, gave $12.3 million to the Democratic Party. In 2001, the magazine *Mother Jones* listed on its website the 400 leading contributors to the 2000 national elections. Seven of the first ten were Jewish, as were twelve of the top twenty and 125 of the top 250.

There have been plenty of well-documented accounts of the activities of the Israel lobby down the years, from Alfred Lilienthal's 1978 study, *The Zionist Connection*, to former US Rep. Paul Findley's 1985 book *They Dare to Speak Out*, to *Dangerous Liaison: The Inside Story of the US-Israeli Covert Relationship*, written by my brother and sister-in-law, Andrew and Leslie Cockburn and published in 1991. Three years ago the present writer and Jeffrey St. Clair published a collection of eighteen essays called *The Politics of Anti-Semitism*, no less than four of which were incisive discussions of the Israel lobby.

So it can scarcely be said that there had been silence here about the lobby until two respectable professors, John J. Mearsheimer and Stephen M. Walt (the former from the University of Chicago and the latter from Harvard) offered their analysis in March of this year, their paper, "The Israel Lobby and US Foreign Policy," being published in longer form by the Kennedy School at Harvard (which has since disowned it) and, after it had been rejected by the *Atlantic Monthly* (which originally commissioned it), in shorter form by the *London Review of Books*.

In fact the significance of this essay rests mostly on timing (three years' worth of public tumult about the neocons and Israel's role in the attack on Iraq) and on the provenance of the authors, from two of the premier academic institutions of the United States. Neither of them has any tincture of radicalism.

After the paper was published in shortened form in the *London Review of Books* there was a brief lull, broken by the howls of America's most manic Zionist, Professor Alan Dershowitz of Harvard, who did Mearsheimer and Walt the great favor of thrusting their paper into the headlines. Dershowitz managed this by his usual eruptions of hysterical invective. The Mearsheimer-Walt essay was Nazi-like, Dershowitz wrote, a classic case of conspiracy-mongering.

In fact, Mearsheimer and Walt's paper is extremely dull. The long version runs to eighty-one pages, no less than forty of which are footnotes. I settled down to read it with eager anticipation but soon found myself looking hopefully for the end. There's nothing in the paper that any moderately well-read student of the topic wouldn't have known long ago, but it does have the merit of stating rather blandly some home truths which are somehow still regarded as too dangerous to state publicly in respectable circles in the United States.

Meanwhile, mostly on the left, there has been an altogether different debate, over the actual weight of the lobby. Here the best known of the debaters is Noam Chomsky, who has reiterated a position he has held for many years, to the general effect that US foreign policy has always hewed to the national self-interest, and that the lobby's power is greatly overestimated.

April 19

One would have thought that after the humiliating self-critiques of last year the *New York Times* would have simply withdrawn its name from contention in the 2006 Pulitzers, but shame was short-lived and the assigned function of the Pulitzer Prize Committee was to winch the paper's name out of the mud.

The Committee's composition made this task easier. On the eighteen-member board sits Thomas Friedman of the *New York Times*, Nicholas Lemann, dean of the Columbia J-school and contributor to the *New York Times* magazine, and Paul Tash, boss of the *St. Petersburg Times*, which has friendly ties to the *New York Times*.

So the *Times* duly reaped two Pulitzers, the first to a couple of journalists, James Risen and Eric Lichtblau, who sat on an explosive story through the election of 2004, and through most of 2005, before finally disclosing the NSA's wiretaps in time to give a boost to Risen's book on US intelligence.

Two prizes were not enough for full rehab so the Committee threw in another for two *Times* reporters for their China coverage.

April 23

I was harsh about Senator Barack Obama of Illinois, and the very next morning his press aide, Tommy Vietor, was on the phone howling about inaccuracies. It was an illuminating conversation.

Obama's man took grave exception to my use of the word "distanced" to describe what his boss had done when Illinois' senior US Senator, Dick Durbin, got into trouble for likening conditions at Guantanamo to those in a Nazi or Stalin-era camp. This was one of Durbin's finer moments and he duly paid the penalty by having to eat crow on the Senate floor.

His fellow Senator, Obama, did not support him in any way. Obama said, "We have a tendency to demonize and jump on and make mockery of each other across the aisle and that is particularly pronounced when we make mistakes. Each and every one of us is going to make a mistake once in a while … and what we hope is that our track record of service, the scope of how we've operated and interacted with people, will override whatever particular mistake we make."

That's three uses of the word "mistake." This isn't distancing?

Nor did Obama's man like my description of Obama's cheerleading for the nuke-Iran crowd. Obama recently declared that when it comes to the US posture on Iran, all options, including military ones, should be on the table. "All options on the table" is standard senatorial tub-thump, meaning We can nuke 'em if we want to. Anybody aiming for high office in America has to be able to swear they're capable of dropping the Big One. Obama knows that. HRC knows it too, but nobody bothers to ask her, since they know the answer anyway. That woman probably uses a bomb sight to target in on her breakfast grapefruit.

If Obama had any sort of guts in such matters he would have said that if Iraq is to teach America's leaders any lesson, it is that reckless recourse to the military "option" carries a dismal long-term price tag. He did nothing of the sort, which is not surprising to anyone who read his speech to the Council of Foreign Relations last November.

Obama is one of those politicians journalists like to decorate with words like "adroit" or "politically adept" because you can actually see him trimming to the wind, the way you see a conjuror of indifferent skill shove the rabbit back up his sleeve. Above all he is concerned with the task of reassuring the masters of the Democratic Party, and beyond that, the politico-corporate establishment, that he is safe.

There are plenty of black people like that in the Congress now. After a decade or so of careful corporate funding, the Black Congressional Caucus is sinking under the weight of DLC clones like Artur Davis of Alabama, Albert Wynn of Maryland, Sanford Bishop and David Scott of Georgia, William Jefferson of Louisiana, Gregory Meeks of New York, all assiduously selling for pottage the interests of the voters who sent them to Washington. Obama is doing exactly the same thing.

April 24
From: Brian Rothgery
To: Alexander Cockburn

Subject: Obama

You are and were right on about Obama. I met the spineless Dem in the summer of 2004, at a private fund-raiser at the home of a wealthy, suburban Chicago attorney. I asked him one question: "I've heard that you call yourself a Democrat but you support NAFTA, the death penalty, and the war on Iraq—is that true?" Regarding the death penalty (George Ryan had recently suspended all pending executions), he proceeded to feed me some bullshit about how he believed that it was the right of the people to express their will, and that he wasn't going to stand in their way (I'm paraphrasing). I said "but the death penalty is RACIST," and he repeated himself. I got the same mish mash about the war and NAFTA. What a joke. Keep up the good work!

May 3
The Left and the Blathersphere. Thank God Karl Rove is not to be indicted, so the left will have to talk about something else for a

change. As a worthy hobbyhorse for the left, the whole Plame scandal has never made any sense. What was it all about? Outing a CIA employee. What's wrong with that? Many years ago a man came into the offices of the *New Left Review* in London where I was manning the portcullis at the time and said his name was Philip Agee and he wanted to write a book about the CIA. Did we call for a special prosecutor to have this fellow hauled over the coals? No we did not. We arranged for a publisher.

Rove has swollen in the left's imagination like a descendant of Père Ubu, Jarry's surreal monster. There is no scheme so deviously diabolical but that the hand of Rove can not be detected at work. Actually the man has always been of middling competence. Under Rove's deft touch Bush has been maneuvered into one catastrophe after another. It was Rove who single-handedly rescued the anti-war movement last July by advising Bush not to give Cindy Sheehan fifteen minutes of face time at his ranch in Crawford.

Rove and Cheney are the White House's answer to Bouvard and Pécuchet, counselors who have driven George W. Bush into the lowest ratings of any American President. Yet the left remains obsessed with their evil powers. Is there any better testimony to the vacuity and impotence of the endlessly touted "blogosphere" which in mid-June had twin deb balls in the form of the yearly *Kos* convention in Las Vegas and the "Take America Back" folkmoot of "progressive" *MoveOn* Democrats in Washington, DC?

In political terms the blogosphere is like white noise, insistent and meaningless, like the wash of Pacific surf I can hear most days. The blogosphere's signature upset came in early 2004, when the Howard Dean balloon, inflated by millions of cubic feet of hot air from the bloggers, went pop at the first poke of political reality amid the cornfields of Iowa. But this fiasco was soon forgotten. *MoveOn* and *Daily Kos* have become hailed as the emergent form of modern politics, the target of excited articles in the *New York Review of Books*.

Beyond raising money swiftly handed over to the gratified veterans of the election industry, both *MoveOn* and *Daily Kos* have had zero political effect, except as a demobilizing force. The effect on writers is horrifying. Talented people feel they have produce 800 words of commentary every day and you can see the lethal consequences on their minds and style, both of which turn rapidly to mush. They glance at the *New York Times* and speed to their laptops to rewrite what they've just read. Hawsers to reality soon fray and they float off, drifting zeppelins of inanity.

May 5

Galbraith died on April 29, at the great age of ninety-seven. I once drove up to Vermont to interview him in his farmhouse. It was dark and I drove uncertainly along a dirt road and up a driveway and knocked on the door, shouting, "Is this the home of Professor Galbraith?" "No," came a testy cry from within. "It's the home of Professor Hook." Sidney Hook, the prototypical neocon, lived on the opposite side of the hill from the Keynesian progressive, Galbraith. By no means for the last time, I reflected how easy it is in America to take the other path, often without noticing, and end up 180 degrees from where you thought you were headed.

When I got to Oxford in 1960 people had Galbraith's 1958 tract, *The Affluent Society*, on their desks, jacket to jacket with the works of such other moral critics of capitalist consumerism as Leavis, Hoggart, and Williams. How we sneered at the image of a car's tailfin on the cover, which as I discovered twenty-five years later in Detroit when I tracked down the designer, was first drawn in the Chrysler studio by young Cliff Voss in 1954 as emblem of the company's "forward look" launched in 1956.

The consumers had it right, however. Labor never was going to get any purchase on the commanding heights of the economy or any putative supervision by Congress of the allocation of credit, and of social investment, so they bought fun baroque cars on the installment plan instead, as thoughtfully arranged by GM's Alfred Sloan decades earlier.

At least Galbraith, in his nineties, could look back to a time when a reformer could not only body forth a social vision, but tentatively identify the agencies whereby that vision could be put into practice. As I read through the *Nation*'s recent special issue on reforming the world's economic arrangements, with fine contributions by Stiglitz, d'Arista, Galbraith's son James, and others, not once, in all the essays, was the question of agency ever raised, or the Democratic Party even alluded to. If there's going to be a fork in the road ahead, the question of agency had better be on the agenda. Galbraith certainly understood that, though he politely underestimated just how roughly capitalism could play to win.

July 13

A few moments after Italy dashed French World Cup hopes with that disappointing coda of penalty kicks, Alya and I took a five-minute stroll to the Piazza San Marco to see the locals celebrate their nation's capture of the World Cup for soccer. As we left, the TV in our hotel was showing Rome, Naples, and Milan exploding in triumph. Alya's niece, staying in Milan, told her the next day that sleep had been impossible. The racket of cheers and honking horns had lasted all night.

In Venice, looking east across the vast expanse of the Piazza San Marco, we could see a knot of maybe 300 people down the far end, near the Basilica. As we drew nearer they turned out to be tourists leveling their digital cameras at a knot of maybe fifty Italians lofting the national flag and dancing round in a circle.

Things weren't much livelier in front of the Doge's palace facing the Grand Canal. On the Ponte della Paglia, opposite the carving of drunken Noah and his sons, an Italian woman commented irritably that she'd been in Rome when Italy beat Ukraine, and it had all been a lot more fun.

We ambled back to the hotel through the warm Venetian evening. Snatches of German, Japanese, English, and even Russian drifted from couples peering at their maps. An American woman showed me a postcard of the Rialto, stabbing it with her finger, and said slowly, in a loud voice, "How … get … there?"

There were almost no cheering Italians because Italians don't live in central Venice any more. Walking around the city for five days, we could see easily enough where ordinary life, as expressed in the form of grocery stores, bakeries, and so forth, ends and the international enclaves begin.

The writer Andrea di Robilant, author of a marvelous chunk of eighteenth-century Venetian romantic history in the form of his bestselling *A Venetian Affair*, confirms this. When he was writing that book three years ago di Robilant and his wife Alessandra lived in the Dorsoduro district, west across the Grand Canal. These days, said Andrea sadly, the Dorsoduro is dying.

When neighborhoods in Venice die it's not because huge vulgar concrete condos replace delicate eighteenth-century facades. The rules protecting Venice's exterior appearance are rigidly enforced. Nor does death merely come in the vulgar form of T-shirt stalls featuring underwear with the genitals of Michelangelo's David painted on them (plentiful this year on the Lista di Spagna).

Death comes respectably, in the form of moneyed quietness. There's no bustle of everyday life, no local kids in the streets, few old folk, no little food stores or wine shops, just the bland, well-maintained exteriors of high-end international homes, part of a portfolio that might include a condo in Mayfair, or Vail or Hana.

The locals have been moving out for quite a while. The city's population is down to 70,000, from a high of around 200,000. Di Robilant now has a delightful apartment on the island of Guidecca, a district of Venice half a mile south towards the Lido from the main part of Venice.

Rich Venetians used to have summer homes there a hundred years ago. Then the island slowly nose-dived and became a dangerous slum. Clean-up began in the 1990s, with artists and writers—as so often—pioneering the rehab.

If the histories of zones like Manhattan's SoHo are any guide, next usually come the fancy restaurants, the art galleries, the clothes stores, the antique stores. The rents soar and the artists and writers become real-estate operators. The locals leave.

In Guidecca's case di Robilant is optimistic. He thinks there are too many modest-income locals who won't quit the island. I hope he's right, but I fear the worst. At the east end of Guidecca there's already the very high-end Cipriani's, and at the west end a consortium including Hilton has just bought the vast old nineteenth-century mill.

July 30

Twenty-three years after one of America's stupidest Presidents announced Star Wars, Reagan's dream has come true. Behind ramparts guarded by a coalition of liars extending from Rupert Murdoch to the *New York Times*, from Bill O'Reilly to PBS, America is totally shielded from truth.

Here we have a Secretary of State, Condoleezza Rice, who gazes at the rubble of Lebanon, 300,000 refugees being strafed with Israel's cluster bombs, and squeaks happily that we are "witnessing the birth pangs of a new Middle East."

Here we have a president, G. Bush, who urges Vladimir Putin to commence in Russia the same "institutional change" that is making Iraq a beacon of freedom and free expression. Not long after Bush extended this ludicrous invitation, the UN relayed from the Iraqi Ministry of Health Iraq's real casualty rate, which was running at least 100 a day, now probably twice that number.

"Crackpot realism" was a concept defined by the great Texan sociologist, C. Wright Mills when he published *The Causes of World War Three* in 1958, also the year that Dwight Eisenhower sent the Marines into Lebanon to bolster local US factotum, Lebanese President Camille Chamoun.

"In crackpot realism," Mills wrote, "a high-flying moral rhetoric is joined with an opportunist crawling among a great scatter of unfocused fears and demands … The expectation of war solves many problems of the crackpot realists … instead of the unknown fear, the anxiety without end, some men of the higher circles prefer the simplification of known catastrophe … They know of no solutions to the paradoxes of the Middle East and Europe, the Far East and Africa except the landing of Marines … they prefer the bright, clear problems of war—as they used to be. For they still believe that 'winning' means something, although they never tell us what …"

September 5

Though the numbers are dwindling, some people still go through their whole adult lives thinking that the next Democrat to hunker down in the Oval Office is going to straighten out the mess, fight for the ordinary folk, face down the rich and powerful. I got off the plane in New York in 1972 at the age of thirty-one with one big advantage over these naive souls. I'd already spent twenty years seeing the same hopes invested in whatever Labour Party candidate was on the way to 10 Downing Street.

By the time I reached my prep school at the age of nine, the first postwar Labour government was already slipping from power. Back in the summer of 1945, if any party was ever given a mandate, it was surely Labour, propelled into office by the millions who had spent the war years awakened by unusual circumstance—a familiar effect of war—to a fresh awareness of the barely inconceivable incompetence and arrogance of the British upper classes and memories of the prewar Depression when the Conservatives ruled the roost. With one voice they said, there must be a better way.

The Tories thought they were going to win. After all, Churchill was presiding over the defeat of the Axis in the war, and the apparatus of gerrymander was still in place, including an electoral register unchanged from 1935, thus rendering those in their twenties as disenfranchised as American felons today. University graduates and businessmen could vote twice. There were predictably archaic methods to undercount the overseas armed forces vote from troops overwhelmingly for Labour. But Clement Attlee's Labour Party swept to tremendous victory.

When the dust settled, Labour had 393 MPs out of a total of 640, the greatest majority in their history, with the Tories limping along with 213 MPs, almost exactly the reverse of what happened thirty-eight years later when Thatcher trounced Foot and got a majority of 143, which she swiftly put to radical use. In 1945, with an invincible majority of 146 and vast popular hunger for radical change, the challenge was great but Labour's leaders—Clement Attlee, Ernest Bevin, Herbert Morrison, and the others—rose and mastered it, managing successfully in the next five years to keep the British class system intact in all essentials. Of course the Conservatives savagely attacked the onset of "socialism," but the "welfare state" had more to do with the wartime command economy than with any attack on the dominion of capital.

Across the channel the French used their Marshall Plan handouts from the US to reorganize their infrastructure and plan the railway network the British now worship as they surge in a few hours from Paris to Marseilles. The British themselves, Miss Muffets of propriety, paid off old debts and rejected new ideas. French-style planning? "We don't do things like that in our country," Bevin scoffed. "We don't have plans, we work things out practically."

My awareness of this first Labour government was limited, though I do remember my father telling me that "we"—this was 1947 when I was six—now owned the railways. I was no early bloomer. A year later the British Special Branch, tapping my father's phone as part of a continuous program of surveillance of the man, lasting from 1934 to 1954, monitored me urging him to come home to read me Christopher Robin, a conversation finally released into the National Archives in 2004 and perused by my brother Patrick, who swiftly reported the Christopher Robin request to me.

Christopher Robin! By the time he was seven John Stuart Mill was already re-reading Aeschylus, although he confessed later he did not know what an emotion was until he was twenty, which shows the downside of intellectual precocity. We went off to live in Ireland, followed by the Special Branch onto the boat where, so the archives now show, they made "a discreet search" of my father's suitcase, prowling through his socks and shirts in search of the Communist Master Plan, while 4,000 drunks heading home for Easter wondered why the ship wasn't getting under way.

Irish politics, as ripe in intricate corruption as those of Naples or Bangkok, had scant relevance to the vices of the Labour Party or the Democrats of the United States. I returned to England for the late 1950s and '60s. Great was the rejoicing when, in 1964, Harold Wilson led the Labour Party to slim victory, ousting the Conservatives after thirteen long years. Years of disappointment immediately followed, with a celerity that had to wait until 1993 to be equaled by the almost instant collapse of the Clinton administration as any kind of reforming force. By 1972 Edward Heath sat in 10 Downing Street.

Now I was nearly thirty and yearned for escape. I could see English politics stretching drearily ahead. After Wilson's return there would be James Callaghan. After Callaghan, Michael Foot. After Foot, Neal Kinnock. After Kinnock ... One day in the late summer of 1972 I had occasion to be in the portion of south London known as Balham. It was hot, and the streets infinitely dreary. I must get away, I muttered to myself, like Razumov talking to Councillor Mikulin in Conrad's *Under Western Eyes*.

I turned in the direction of the subway station. A dingy sign caught my eye, in a sub-basement window. I knocked, and the sibyl, in Indian saree, greeted me. She had Tarot cards and a parrot, a method of divination with an ancient lineage in India. She dealt the cards. The parrot looked at them, then at me, then at the fortune teller. Some current of energy passed between them. The sybil paused, then in a low yet vibrant voice, bodied forth the future to me, disclosing what lay ahead in British public life. Her lips curved around the as yet unfamiliar words "New Labour." Falteringly, raising her hands before her eyes in trembling dismay at the secret message of the cards, she described a man I know now to have been Tony Blair. I paid her double, then triple as, amid the advisory shrieks of the parrot, she poured out the shape of things to come.

Within a week, obeying the promptings of the parrot, I had booked a flight to New York and a new life. Ahead of me lay a vast political landscape, seemingly of infinite richness and possibility. Never for a moment have I regretted my journey westward. That parrot in Balham had read the cards correctly. It is probably still alive, and I'm sure that if I were to return for another consultation, it would cry out, "I could have told you so," and cackle heartily as it described the blasted expectations raised by Democrats stretching from Carter to Clinton.

We approach the midterm elections; soon thereafter the great masquerade of Election 2008 will commence. There will, I can guarantee it, be once again hopes for change, courtesy of a Democrat. I will remain without illusions. Like the Labour Party, the Democrats offer no uplifting alternative and not even the pretense that they differ in essentials from the Republicans in the way they propose to deal with the rest of the world.

I might even offer a maxim here: the greater the hunger for change, the more thunderous the popular cries for decisive, radical action, the more rapid will be the puncturing of all hopes, as though the whole point of the electoral exercise, of 1964 and 1966 in the case of Wilson, and of 1992 in Clinton's, had been to demonstrate to those foolish enough to have thought otherwise the lesson that all hopes and fierce expectations notwithstanding, business will continue as usual.

It's the same lesson European governments now regularly give European voters. The French vote against neoliberalism, despite the stentorian advice of the entire political establishment. The voters prevail, with a thunderous "Non!" The political establishment, as represented in the major parties, pays no attention. Same in Germany, same in Italy, same in Britain. Same in the United States.

As is now widely recognized, most of all by the voters, there is no effective opposition here, any more than there is in the UK. But if the parties are identical in their essential programs, give or take mini-swerves from the norm such as tactical environmentalism by the Democrats to keep Green and Hollywood money flowing in, then why is there such vitriol between them? Much of it is plain stupidity. Many people in middle age keep the prejudices of their youth intact. What we need from the political scientists is a fresh consideration of political constituencies and their material interests. The current maps are useless. The parrot did a much better job.

October 8

I drove into Eureka to speak at an anti-war rally. I asked one of the organizers—one I knew to be keen on the 9/11 conspiracy scenarios—whether this was planned as basically a conspiracists' convocation. The inviter said No. "Maybe one speaker on 9/11." I went along, to the parking lot north of the jail in the middle of town. There were about 200 people. It was a glorious day.

Speaker #1 was the chairperson, many days into a fast. He told the crowd that he was a 9/11 conspiracy convert. The war in Iraq didn't get much of a mention in his address. Speaker #2 was a 9/11 conspiracy advocate. He gave a long, detailed and incomprehensible speech, whose main effect was to cut the crowd by about a third. The only audible bit of his allocution was a savage denunciation of Alexander Cockburn. He also barely mentioned the war in Iraq. Speaker #3, an academic, read a lengthy speech loaded with refined ironies about Bush. I don't know whether he mentioned the war because two young people, one with a button saying "9/11 was an inside job," were beginning to harangue me. Speaker #4 was my neighbor, David Simpson, who announced he was a global warming cultist and spoke briefly on that theme.

I was the final speaker. It had been over two hours, and the crowd was much depleted. I said, "we are united by one common desire: LUNCH." Big applause. I talked about the war, about 9/11/73, the coup against Allende in Chile, as the starting gun for the Empire's counterattack amid defeat in Vietnam. I talked about the current political situation, and even the prime story of the hour—unmentioned hitherto—the Foley scandal, which may well turn the House of Representatives over to the Democrats. Let's hope so. We need gridlock. My speech went down well with the seventy or so survivors in the parking lot (and the prisoners in the jail maybe).

October 22

Tony Judt, the liberal writer for the *New York Review of Books*, has just discovered the realities of criticizing Israel. Here's a message he released in early October:

> I was due to speak this evening, in Manhattan, to a group called Network 20/20 comprising young business leaders, NGOs, academics, etc., from the US and many countries. Topic: the Israel Lobby and US Foreign Policy. The meetings are always held at the Polish Consulate in Manhattan.
>
> I just received a call from the President of Network 20/20. The talk was cancelled because the Polish Consulate had been threatened by the Anti-Defamation League. Serial phone-calls from ADL President Abe

> Foxman warned them off hosting anything involving Tony Judt. If they persisted, he warned, he would smear the charge of Polish collaboration with anti-Israeli anti-Semites all over the front page of every daily paper in the city (an indirect quote). They caved and Network 20/20 were forced to cancel. Whatever your views on the Middle East I hope you find this as serious and frightening as I do. This is, or used to be, the United States of America.

Judt's disclosure elicited a few stories, including one in the *Washington Post* by Michael Powell, who wrote:

> The pattern, Judt says, is unmistakable and chilling. "This is serious and frightening, and only in America—not in Israel—is this a problem," he said. "These are Jewish organizations that believe they should keep people who disagree with them on the Middle East away from anyone who might listen."
>
> The leaders of the Jewish organizations denied asking the consulate to block Judt's speech and accused the professor of retailing "wild conspiracy theories" about their roles. But they applauded the consulate for rescinding Judt's invitation.
>
> "I think they made the right decision," said Abraham H. Foxman, national director of the Anti-Defamation League. "He's taken the position that Israel shouldn't exist. That puts him on our radar."

It's good that Judt is making a fuss about the ghastly Foxman, but I do have to smile wryly at his sudden discovery that criticizing Israel can be an edgy business. Actually, it was far, far riskier twenty or even ten years ago. It's much easier now, as Chomsky indicated in his note to me and as I and Jeffrey St. Clair have found with talks promoting our book *The Politics of Anti-Semitism*.

Not so long ago, when Chomsky went to a town to talk, the ADL would trail him and file minute by minute reports on his movements and statements. Someone once sent him anonymously one such dossier. On the front page of the Xerox was written "for Alan Dershowitz." Chomsky told me long ago that he and Dershowitz were scheduled to have a debate in a week or so, and evidently the file was being sent to Dershowitz, for him to cull the usual slanders and lies.

The ADL had spies everywhere, sending back feverish reports, mostly hysterical fabrications, about what they claimed to have heard in meetings. That was a joke. Not a joke was what happened at UCLA and Cambridge where there were undercover cops at Chomsky's meetings because they'd picked up serious threats. And that was nothing compared what Edward Said had to live with.

Or Norman Finkelstein. What Judt faces isn't a minuscule fraction of what Norman faces regularly—e.g., being condemned by the *Progressive* (*sic*) as a Holocaust denier or by its editor as a "Holocaust minimizer" on the grounds that he accurately quoted Raul Hilberg.

The difference now is that some of these efforts to crush debate get reported. That wouldn't have happened ten or twenty years ago, at least in the *Washington Post* or Reuters.

November 7

Let me direct you to a recent series of polite coughs, reminiscent of a sheep quietly clearing its throat somewhere on a fog-bound hillside in the north of England. The aforementioned coughs emanated at the start of this week from the Financial Services Authority (FSA), a body set up under the purview of the British Treasury a few years ago to monitor financial markets and protect the public interest by raising the alarm about shady practices and any dangerous slide towards instability. In a briefing paper under the chaste title, "Private Equity: A Discussion of Risk and Regulatory Engagement," the FSA raises the alarm:

> Excessive leverage: The amount of credit that lenders are willing to extend on private equity transactions has risen substantially. This lending may not, in some circumstances, be entirely prudent. Given current leverage levels and recent developments in the economic/credit cycle, the default of a large private equity backed company or a cluster of smaller private equity backed companies seems inevitable. This has negative implications for lenders, purchasers of the debt, orderly markets and conceivably, in extreme circumstances, financial stability and elements of the UK economy.

Translation: "It's about to blow!"

> The duration and potential impact of any credit event may be exacerbated by operational issues which make it difficult to identify who ultimately owns the economic risk associated with a leveraged buy out and how these owners will react in a crisis. These operational issues arise out of the extensive use of opaque, complex and time consuming risk transfer practices such as assignment and sub-participation, together with the increased use of credit derivatives. These credit derivatives may not be confirmed in a timely manner and the amount traded may substantially exceed the amount of the underlying assets.

Translation: "The world's credit system is a vast recycling bin of untraceable transactions of wildly inflated value."

November 10

Lame duck—"A White House controlled by an unpopular, highly partisan lame duck ..." Wherever you look, there's lame-duck Bush limping across the White House lawn, or hobbling out to give a press conference.

According to Brewer's ever-useful 1910 *Dictionary of Phrase and Fable* "a lame duck in Stock Exchange parlance means a member of the Stock Exchange who waddles off on settlement day without settling his account. All such defaulters are black boarded and struck off the list. Sometimes it is used for one who cannot pay his debts, one who trades without money."

November 28

There are plenty of real conspiracies in America. Why make up fake ones? Every few years, property czars and city officials in New York conspire to withhold fire company responses, so that enough of a neighborhood burns down for the poor to quit and for profitable gentrification to ensue. That's a conspiracy to commit ethnic cleansing, also murder.

It's happening today in Brooklyn, even as similar ethnic cleansing and gentrification is scheduled in San Francisco. Bayview Hunters Point is the last large black community in the Bay Area, sitting on beautiful bay front property. So now it's time to move the black folks out. As Willie Ratcliff, publisher of *SF Bay View* writes, "If the big developers and their puppets, the mayor [Democrat Gavin Newsom] and his minions win this war, they'll have made what may be the largest urban renewal land grab in the nation's history: some 2,200 acres of San Francisco, the city with the highest priced land on earth."

That's a real conspiracy, even as many in the Bay Area left meander through the blind alleys of 9/11 conspiracism.

Machiavelli points out that every conspirator you add to the plot has less chance of preserving secrecy than the previous one. The 9/11 group in fact did tell people about their plans in various ways but the prevailing belief that Arabs couldn't do it prevented any of the revelations from being taken seriously. The view that a bunch of Arabs with box cutters weren't up to it was precisely the cover they needed.

The conspiracy virus is an old strand: The Russians couldn't possibly build an A bomb without Commie traitors. The Russians are too dumb. Hitler couldn't have been defeated by the Red Army marching across Eastern Europe and half of Germany. Traitors let it happen. JFK couldn't have been shot by Oswald—it had to be the CIA. There are no end to examples seeking to prove that Russians, Arabs, the Viet Cong, the Japanese, etc., etc. couldn't possibly match the brilliance and cunning of secret cabals of white Christians. It's all pathetic but it does save the trouble of reading and thinking.

It's easy enough to proclaim one's readiness "to speak truth to power," as the self-regarding tag line goes. As yet, that's not a very perilous thing to do, here in America, at least on the part of the folks who like to use the phrase. But to speak truth to people overwhelmed with a sense of powerlessness and hence ready to credit Bush and Cheney with supernatural powers of efficient evil—that's one of our functions at *CounterPunch*. There's no point in marching forward under the banner of illusions.

December 8

The slithery junior Senator from Illinois, Barack Obama, is ensuring himself a steady political diet of publicity by refusing to take his name out of consideration as a possible candidate for the Democratic presidential nomination in 2008. We're entering the time frame when all such aspirants have to make up their minds whether they can find the requisite money and political base for a run. Senator Russell Feingold of Wisconsin, the obvious peace and justice candidate, has already decided that he can't, which gives us a pretty revealing insight into the weakness of the left these days.

It's a no-brainer for Obama to excite the political commentators by waving a "maybe" flag. It keeps the spotlight on him, and piles up political capital, whatever he decides to do in the end.

It's depressing to think that we'll have to endure Obamaspeak for months, if not years to come: a pulp of boosterism about the American dream, interspersed with homilies about putting factionalism and party divisions behind us and moving on. I used to think Senator Joe Lieberman was the man whose words I'd least like to be force fed top volume if I was chained next to a loudspeaker in Camp Gitmo, but I think Obama is worse. I've never heard a politician so careful not to offend conventional elite opinion while pretending to be fearless and forthright.

A couple of weeks ago Obama unleashed another cloud of statesmanlike mush about Iraq to an upscale foreign policy crowd in Chicago. Trimming to new realities, he's now talking about a four-to-six-month time frame for beginning withdrawal from Iraq. Don't mistake this for any real agenda. It's a schedule that can be pulled in any direction, like a rubber mask from a Christmas stocking.

December 27

I bid a sad adieu to Gerald Ford. It has always been my view that Gerald Ford was America's greatest President. Transferring the Hippocratic injunction from the medical to the political realm, he did the least possible harm. Under Ford's tranquil hand the nation relaxed after the hectic fevers of the Nixon years. He finally pulled the US out of Vietnam. Now, "not doing harm" for an American President has to be a very forgiving phrase. True, on his watch, with a US green light, Indonesian troops invaded East Timor.

As a visit to the Ford presidential library discloses, the largest military adventure available for display was the foolish US response to the capture of the US container ship *Mayaguez* by the Khmer Rouge on May 12, 1975. As imperial adventures go, and next to the vast graveyards across the planet left by Ford's predecessors and successors, it was small potatoes.

Ford was surrounded by bellicose advisors such as his Secretary of State, Henry Kissinger; his Vice-President, Nelson Rockefeller; his Chief of Staff, and later Secretary of Defense, Donald Rumsfeld; and his presidential assistant, Dick Cheney. The fact that this rabid crew was only able to persuade Ford to give the green light for Indonesia's invasion of East Timor—an appalling decision to be sure—is tribute to Ford's pacific instincts and deft personnel management. Unlike George W. Bush, Ford was of humane temper and could mostly hold in check his bloodthirsty counselors.

Kissinger was part of the furniture when Ford took over, after Nixon's resignation on August 8, 1974. With latitude to choose, Ford made sensible selections, none more fruitful than his Attorney General, Edward Levy, who in turn prompted Ford to nominate John Stevens to the US Supreme Court, where he has long distinguished himself and dignified Ford's choice by being the most humane and progressive justice.

As a percentage of the federal budget, social spending crested in the Ford years. Never should it be forgotten that Jimmy Carter campaigned against Ford as—this is Carter—the prophet of neoliberalism, precursor of the Democratic Leadership Council, touting "zero-based budgeting."

If Ford had beaten back Carter's challenge in 1976, the neocon crusades of the mid to late 1970s would have been blunted by the mere fact of a Republican occupying the White House. Reagan, most likely, would have returned to his slumbers in California after his abortive challenge to Ford for the nomination in Kansas in 1976.

Instead of a weak southern Democratic conservative in agreement with almost every predation by the military industrial complex, we would have had a Midwestern Republican, thus a politician far less vulnerable to the promoters of the new cold war.

Would Ford have rushed to fund the Contras and order their training by Argentinian torturers? Would he have sent the CIA on its most costly covert mission, the $3.5 billion intervention in Afghanistan? The nation would have been spared the disastrous counsels of Carter's foreign policy advisor, Zbigniew Brzezinski.

During Ford's all-too-brief tenure a mood of geniality was the rule. Even the attempted assassinations of the President by Lynette "Squeaky" Fromme and Sara Moore, in September 1975, had a slapdash, light-hearted timbre.

2007

January 11

A make-or-break speech by a beleaguered US President is usually preceded by a demonstration of American might somewhere on the planet, and the run-up to Bush's address last night was no exception.

The AC-130 gunship that massacred a convoy of fleeing Islamists on Somalia's southwestern border, apparently along with dozens of nomads, their families and livestock, was deployed on Sunday to make timely newspaper headlines indicative of Bush's determination to strike at terror wherever it may lurk. Moral to nomads: when the US President schedules a speech, don't herd, don't go to wedding parties, head for the nearest cave.

February 25

The Clintons have always had short fuses. At the best of times, Hillary is taut by disposition, and already her political prospects for winning the Democratic nomination are getting somewhat cloudier. This last week has been a trying one, crowned by the Oscar-night adulation for Al Gore, no favorite of the Clintons.

On the heels of his $1.3m fundraiser for Hillary's rival, Illinois Senator Barack Obama, Hollywood tycoon and Dreamworks co-founder David Geffen planted a carefully improvised explosive device under HRC's candidacy.

He confided to Maureen Dowd of the *New York Times* that Mrs. Clinton was not the candidate to unify the Democratic Party, nor the nation; also that he would never forgive her husband for ignoring his own appeals and those of many other liberals to give a White House pardon to Leonard Peltier, a native American convicted of killing two FBI agents back in the 1970s. But while leaving Peltier to rot in prison, Clinton *did* pardon financier Marc Rich.

This, and the Oscar triumph for Gore, have left Mrs. Clinton distinctly frayed. But she is defiant. Asked about her vote for the war at a New Hampshire town hall, she said: "If the most important thing to any of you is choosing someone who did not cast that vote or said his vote was a mistake, then there are others to choose from."

February 28

Which scion of which well-known newspaper dynasty assembled a squadron of bulldozers in May of 2005, mounted the lead bulldozer and led this rumbling squadron into a ferocious assault on the house his mother left him on her death in 2001? When it was over, a house that had seen visits from President William Jefferson Clinton and First Lady Nancy Reagan lay in splinters and rubble.

Mohu? It was the name of Katharine Graham's large house, which roosted on over 235 acres on Lambert's Cove Road on the north shore of Martha's Vineyard. When the chairman of the *Washington Post* company died in 2001 she willed it to her second son, Billy. A couple of years ago Billy got into an increasingly acrimonious series of battles with the local township of West Tisbury at the property taxes he had to pay each year, challenging his assessments from fiscal years 2003 and 2004, when he paid the town more than half a million dollars in property taxes. The fight matured into the longest tax-appeal case in the history of the Commonwealth.

Early 2005 the owner of Mohu evidently felt the need to express his feelings of profound loathing for … for whom? Start, obviously, with the tax assessors. End, maybe, with the person who hung the curse of Mohu round his neck. Take in also the people who used to run over from their nearby homes to use Mohu's tennis court. In fact the very first bit of real property on the estate Billy's bulldozer scraped into oblivion was indeed that same tennis court. Then it was the house's turn.

To me the oddest thing about this piece of demolition is that it happened in early May of 2005. Here we are at the end of February, 2007, and there's barely been a whisper, beyond a tiny reference to Mohu having been demolished, in the *Vineyard Gazette*. Did all interest in the Graham publishing clan die with Katharine?

It certainly seems that way. I checked last year to see how many articles there'd been about the role in the *Washington Post*'s editorial policy being played by her oldest son, Donnie. He's the one who got the paper. Month after month, as the *Post* ran one pro-war story and editorial after another, I kept waiting for one of those insiderish stories to appear in *Vanity Fair* or some kindred publication about Donnie pushing the *Post* into a hard pro-war stance. Nothing.

Suppose that when G.W.H. and Barbara Bush finally depart this world, they leave Kennebunkport to G.W. and Laura, who promptly whistle up the demolition crew and tell them to level the place. Will the local press content itself with paeans to W's selfless act of homage to the poor of Maine and Natural Beauty Restored?

Maybe, in the not too distant future, low income structures in Martha's Vineyard will be enhanced by Mohu's vertical grain doug fir flooring, thick canyon red quarry tiles, yellow pine bead board, plus lighting fixtures and hardware. John Abrams, the man who supervised the leveling, says that's the way it's going to be. It seems unlikely to me, though I can imagine this salvage stock being sold off to rich people restoring their homes and the proceeds donated to a housing charity.

March 12

Since there undoubtedly will be a next time, after these latest campus killings at Virginia Tech, what useful counsel on preventative measures can we offer faculties across America? There have been the usual howls from the anti-gun lobby, but it's all hot air. America is not about to dump the Second Amendment giving people the right to bear arms.

A better idea would be for appropriately screened teachers and maybe student monitors to carry weapons. This is not as outré as it may sound to European ears. A quarter of a century ago students doing military ROTC training regularly carried rifles around campus.

Five years ago Peter Odighizuwa, a forty-three-year-old Nigerian student, killed three faculty members at Appalachian Law School with a handgun, but before he could wreak further carnage two students fetched weapons from their cars, challenged the murderer with guns leveled, and disarmed him. The stupidity of the campus cops at Virginia Tech will undoubtedly cost the college hefty damages.

There was plenty of evidence that Cho Seung-hui was a time bomb waiting to explode. Students talked about him as a possible shooter and refused to take classes with him. His essays so disturbed one of his teachers with their violent ravings that she arranged a secret signal in case she needed security during her tutorials.

When the mass murder session began in the engineering building the police cowered behind their cruisers until Cho-Seung Hui finished off the last batch of his thirty-two victims, then killed himself. Then the police bravely rushed in and started sticking their guns in the faces of the traumatized students, screaming at them to freeze or be shot.

More than one teacher felt Cho was scarily nuts. They recommended counseling, then didn't bother to review the conclusions. And it has emerged that Cho was actually institutionalized as a psychotic and suicide risk in 2005. Yet when he returned to campus the administrators didn't even tip off his roommate.

College administrators live in constant fear of declining students enrollment. At the first sign of trouble they cover up. So, there's a double killing in a Virginia Tech dorm at 7.15 a.m., after which Cho has time to go home, make his final home video, walk to the post office, mail his package to NBC and then head off to the engineering building with his guns.

The college's first email to students goes out more than two hours after the first killings were discovered. The ineffable Warren Steger, college president, says later: "You can only make decisions based on the information you have at the time. You don't have hours to reflect on it." Two dead bodies, a killer somewhere on campus, and Steger makes his big decision to do nothing.

May 3

By far the best performance at the recent Democratic candidates' debate organized by MSNBC was by a very distant outsider, Mike Gravel, a seventy-seven-year-old former US Senator from Alaska, well known nearly forty years ago for his opposition to the war in Vietnam. In some electrifying tirades, he flayed Clinton, Obama, Edwards, and the others as two-faced on the absolute imperative of getting out of the war in Iraq and not getting into one in Iran. "They frighten me," Gravel shouted, gesturing at his rivals. "You know what's worse than one US soldier dying in vain in Iraq. It's two soldiers dying in vain. In Vietnam they all died in vain."

June 12

These are troubling times for evangelical Christians. The born-again President they helped elect is in the autumn of his tenure, the bold promises of Christian revival now tarnished or cast aside. Their great champion, Jerry Falwell, has gone to the Judgment, leaving only the Reverend Pat Robertson as their national champion. Mitt Romney, the front-running Republican contender to be Bush's successor, is a Mormon, and although leading evangelical Christians have given him the nod, many foot soldiers in the service of Christ entertain doubts. "The world needs Jesus, the REAL JESUS, not Jesus the half-brother of Lucifer," cries Kevin Stilley on his Christian site.

Then, there's the never-ending struggle with the Evil One in the arena of sexual temptation where, as a one evangelical put it, "Satan and his demons more aggressively attack and tempt those in Christian leadership because they know that a scandal involving a leader can have devastating results, on both Christians and non-Christians." Still fresh in the ears of the righteous are the chortles of unbelievers over the tribulations of Pastor Ted Haggard, leader of the New Life Church and one of the nation's most prominent and politically connected evangelicals. He was outed last year in Colorado by a former male prostitute declaring that Pastor Ted had enjoyed sex with him, their monthly interactions enhanced by crystal meth. In February of this year Pastor Ted had crash counseling across three weeks, overseen by four ministers, to give, as one put it, "Ted the tools to help embrace his heterosexual side," but there have been doubts, even among evangelicals, as to whether Satan and his demons have in this instance been decisively routed after so brief an engagement.

And now evangelicals face fresh evidence that the Darker Forces miss no opportunity to make further ravages among the righteous. Earlier this week ChristiaNet.com, "the world's most visited Christian website," disclosed the results of a survey it has just concluded, asking site visitors questions about their personal sexual conduct. A thousand Christians answered, and ChristiaNet has now evaluated these responses with the analytic assistance of Second Glance Ministries ("a second glance at God's plan for sex"), led by Clay Jones, founder and President of SGM.

"The poll results indicate that 50 percent of all Christian men and 20 percent of all Christian women are addicted to pornography," Jones reports bleakly. It seems that 60 percent of the women who answered the survey admitted to having "significant struggles with lust," 40 percent admitted to "being involved in sexual sin in the past year," and 20 percent of the church-going female participants struggle with looking at pornography on an ongoing basis.

"There have been dynamic paradigm shifts in the behavior of Christians over the last four years," Jones declares. "Technology [i.e., the internet] has allowed pornography to flood the market place beyond a controllable level." The phones at Second Glance Ministries are ringing off the hook with calls for counseling from porn addicts. ChristiaNet.com's President Bill Cooper reports that "we directed over 100,000 inquiries to Second Glance Ministries in one year," and that "we are seeing an escalation of the problem in both men and women who regularly attend church."

Sex surveys regularly conducted by the University of Chicago suggest why Satan and his legions are finding it easy to beguile these evangelical Christians. Their sex lives are more vital than those paddling in the tepid mainstream, and hence they are more easily led into temptation. One such Chicago survey I have claims that Americans are almost entirely straight (maybe 2 or 3 percent gay at most), and the vast majority revel in the loyal married state and have sparse sex. Evangelicals do better. Among women, conservative Christian evangelicals have the highest rates of orgasm.

June 20

In 1938, three years before the first death camps of the Final Solution, Nazi chemist Dr. Gerhard Peters published a full account, in the German science journal *Anzeiger fur Sahahlinskund*, of the El Paso "disinfection" plant. He included two photos and diagrams of the machinery that sprayed Zyklon B on railroad cars. (Peters went on to acquire Zyklon B's German patent.)

As David Dorado Romo describes it in his *Ringside Seat to a Revolution: An Underground History of El Paso and Juarez, 1893–1923* (available from Cinco Puntos Press, El Paso), Zyklon B had become available in the US in the early 1920s when fears of alien infection had been inflamed by the alarums of the eugenicists, most of them from the "progressive" end of the political spectrum.

It should be noted that while the Americans sprayed their victims with toxic chemicals, they restricted use of Zyklon B to freight and clothes. As the Nazis understood, spraying it directly on a human caused almost immediate death. We can only guess what effect it had on the thousands of Mexican men, women, and children who, after a "bath" in DDT or gasoline, were sent away in clothes drenched with Zyklon B.

Romo's book comes at a time when Mexican immigration is at the top of the list of US political issues. There are twelve million illegals in the United States by official count, and certainly twice that unofficially. Among the solutions is the right-wing's vociferous call to build a "Berlin wall" 2,000 miles long across the entire Rio Grande border.

Unsurprisingly, Mexican Americans hate this idea. Their memories—the emerging truth of Mexican-American history—and their votes seem certain to undermine it.

Zyklon B came to El Paso in the 1920s. In 1917 the US Congress passed the Immigration Law and the United States Public Health Service simultaneously published its *Manual for the Physical Inspection of Aliens*. The *Manual* had its list of excludable aliens, a ripe representation of the obsessions of the eugenicists: "imbeciles, idiots, feeble-minded persons, persons of constitutional psychopathic inferiority (homosexuals), vagrants, physical defectives, chronic alcoholics, polygamists, anarchists, persons afflicted with loathsome or dangerous contagious diseases, prostitutes, contract laborers, all aliens over 16 who cannot read."

In that same year US Public Health Service Agents "bathed and deloused" 127,123 Mexicans at the Santa Fe International Bridge between Juarez and El Paso. The mayor of El Paso at the time, Tom Lea Sr., represented, in Romo's words, "the new type of Anglo politician in the 'Progressive Era.' Progressive didn't necessarily mean liberal back then. In Lea's case, 'progress' meant he would clean up the city."

As part of his clean-up operations Lea made his city the first in the US to ban hemp, aka marijuana, as an alien Mexican substance. He had a visceral fear of contamination and, so his son later disclosed, wore silk underwear because his pal, Dr. Kluttz, had told him typhus lice didn't stick to silk. His loins thus protected, Lea battered the US government with demands for a full quarantine camp on the border where all immigrants could be held for up to fourteen days. Local health officer B. J. Lloyd thought this outlandish, telling the US Surgeon General that typhus fever "is not now, and probably never will be, a serious menace to our civilian population."

Lloyd was right about this. Lea forced health inspectors to descend on Chihuahuita, the Mexican quarter of El Paso, forcing inhabitants suspected of harboring lice to take kerosene and vinegar baths, have their heads shaved and clothes incinerated. Inspection of 5,000 rooms did not stigmatize Chihuahuita as a plague zone. The inspectors found two cases of typhus, one of rheumatism, one of TB and one of chicken pox. Ironically, Kluttz, presumably wearing silk underwear, contracted typhus while supervising these operations and died.

But Lloyd did recommend delousing plants, saying he was willing to "bathe and disinfect all the dirty, lousy people coming into this country from Mexico." The plant was ready for business right when the Immigration Act became law. Soon Mexicans were having their bodies checked, daubed with kerosene where deemed necessary, and their clothes fumigated with gasoline, kerosene, sodium cyanide, cyanogens, sulfuric acid and Zyklon B. The El Paso Herald wrote respectfully in 1920, "hydrocyanic acid gas, the most poisonous known, more deadly even than that used on the battlefields of Europe, is employed in the fumigation process."

The delousing operations provoked fury and resistance among Mexicans still boiling with indignation after a lethal gasoline blaze in the El Paso city jail. As part of Mayor Lea's citywide disinfection campaign, prisoners in the jail were ordered to strip naked. Their clothes were dumped in one bath filled with a mixture of gasoline, creosote, and formaldehyde. Then they were forced to step into a second bath filled with "a bucket of gasoline, a bucket of coal oil and a bucket of vinegar." At around 3.30 p.m., March 5, 1916, someone struck a match. The jail went up like a torch. The *El Paso Herald* reported that about fifty "naked prisoners from whose bodies the fumes of gasoline were arising," many of them locked in their cells, caught fire. Twenty-seven prisoners died. In late January, 1917, 200 Mexican women rebelled at the border and prompted a major riot, putting to flight both police and troops both sides of the border.

The use of Zyklon B swiftly became habitual. How many Mexicans suffered agonies or died, when they put on those garments? As Romo recently told the El Paso–based journalist Paul Spike, "This is a huge black hole in history. Unfortunately, I only have oral histories and other anecdotal evidence about the harmful effects of the noxious chemicals used to disinfect and delouse the Mexican border crossers—including deaths, birth defects, cancer, etc. It may well go into the tens of thousands. It's incredible that absolutely no one, after all these years, has ever attempted to document this."

The use of Zyklon B on the US–Mexican border was a matter of keen interest to the firm of DEGESCH. In 1938 Dr. Gerhard Peters called for its use in German *Desinfektionskammern*. Romo has tracked down an article Peters wrote in a German pest science journal, *Anzeiger fur Sahahlinskund*, which featured two photographs of El Paso delousing chambers. Peters went on to become the managing director of DEGESCH, which handled the supply of Zyklon B for the Nazi death camps. He was tried and convicted at Nuremberg. Hilberg reports that he got five years, then won a retrial that netted him six years. He was retried in 1955 and found not guilty.

In the US the eugenicists rolled on to their great triumph, the Immigration Restriction Act of 1924, which doomed millions in Europe to their final rendezvous with Zyklon B twenty years later. By the 1930s the eugenicists were mostly discredited, though many—particularly in the environmental movement—remained true to those racist protocols much longer. The Restriction Act, that monument to bad science married to unscrupulous politicians and zealous public policy, stayed on the books unchanged for forty years.

June 21

Summer's hot breath draws closer and the psychoanalysts of New York and Boston prepare their patients for the difficult two or three weeks of holiday separation. Undoubtedly beach chat among both analysts and analysands will focus on the end of the *Soprano* series which, across the past eight years, courtesy of Lorraine Bracco's Jennifer Melfi—Tony Soprano's analyst—has been the biggest boost to the shrink business since Lee J. Cobb starred in *The Three Faces of Eve*.

Truly comical has been the solemnity with which psychoanalysts across the United States have been deploring the "breach of professional ethics" at a shrinks' dinner party in one of the concluding *Soprano* episodes in which the identity of Dr. Melfi's patient as Mobster Tony was disclosed. The rare moments when shrinks aren't seducing their female patients (seventy percent, in an informal New York survey some years ago) are usually consumed by such indiscretions, a tradition stretching all the way back to the notoriety of the patients trotting up the stairs of Berggasse 19, Freud's chambers in Vienna.

It's true that some psychoanalysts were indignant at the way Melfi, chided by her colleagues for enabling a sociopath, promptly dumped the Mafia boss as a patient, the climax of a process identified back in 1999 in the *British Medical Journal* by Dr. Tony David as the collision of "the superego of Melfi's civilised values and the intellect … with the murky id that is Soprano's stock in trade." "The strict ethical principles established by the American Psychological Association," wrote one APA member furiously, "do not allow for the arbitrary dismissal of a client even if they are sociopathic in nature (unless there is danger to the therapist)."

It so happens that these same "strict ethical principles" of the APA have been the topic of unsparing rebuke that probably won't be cited much on those holiday beaches. A recent report by the Pentagon's Inspector General confirms what has been detailed in a number of news stories since 2005 concerning the starring role played by American psychologists and psychoanalysts in devising and supervising torture techniques as administered by the US military in Guantanamo, Iraq, and Afghanistan, as well as other secret interrogation centers run by the CIA.

The APA leadership has piously maintained that "psychologists have a critical role in keeping interrogations safe, legal, ethical and effective." The Pentagon Inspector General's Report makes clear this claim is ludicrous. So here we have shrinks refining Tony Soprano's brutish violence, draping his id with the national flag.

August 4

Was there ever a luckier clan than the Bancrofts, whose elders okayed the $5 billion sale of the *Wall Street Journal* to Rupert Murdoch's News Corp. on Tuesday? There's been some solemn talk about the Bancrofts' "stewardship of this national institution" since they acquired the Dow Jones company a century ago. In fact the *Journal* was an undistinguished little sheet till a journalistic genius called Barney Kilgore—to whose daughter Kathryn I had the pleasure of being married for a few years in the 1980s—decided in the years after World War II that a businessman in San Francisco should be able to read the same paper as one in Chicago or New York. Kilgore devised the technology to do this, along with the paper's reportorial stance, serious but often humorous, in the style of the Midwest where Kilgore—a Hoosier—was from.

Kilgore made the Bancrofts, though not himself, really rich and they continued in that state for almost half a century though their stewardship was either indifferent or inept, beyond the pleasant chore of raking in the money. Now they can trouser Murdoch's gold and trot off into the sunset, mumbling that they have extracted all the usual pledges from Rupert Murdoch that he will respect the *Journal*'s editorial independence.

The *Journal*'s editorial stance of fanatic neoconnery was established by the late Robert Bartley from the mid-1970s onward, and his pages bulged with every mad fantasy of the cold war lobby. Bartley led the charge against effete liberalism, and since by the late '70s American liberalism had thoroughly lost its nerve, he carried the day, becoming by far the most influential editorial page editor in American journalism. More than its sometimes excellent reporting, Bartley gave the *Journal* its high profile in Washington as well as on Wall Street.

August 7

Right now they're hosing down Barack Obama after he said in the YouTube debate in South Carolina that he would be prepared to meet with Kim Jong Il, Hugo Chávez, Mahmoud Ahmadinejad, and Fidel Castro to hash over problems face to face. The pundits promptly whacked him for demonstrating "inexperience." Experienced leaders order the CIA to murder such men.

Then Obama drew even fiercer fire by saying he would not use nuclear weapons to fight terrorism in Afghanistan and Pakistan. "I think it would be a profound mistake for us to use nuclear weapons in any circumstance," Obama told AP on August 2, adding after a pause, "involving civilians." Then he quickly added, "Let me scratch that. There's been no discussion of nuclear weapons. That's not on the table."

I'm beginning to respect this man. He displays sagacity well beyond the norm for candidates seeking the Oval Office. He comprehends, if only in mid-sentence, that when you drop a nuclear bomb, it will kill civilians. He also realizes that strafing Waziristan with thermonuclear devices in the hopes of nailing Osama Bin Laden is a foolish way to proceed.

So Obama is being flayed for his "inexperience," first and foremost by Hillary Clinton, who permits no table setting which does not include a couple of nuclear weapons next to the salt and pepper.

September 1

Larry Craig of Idaho was a three-term Senator. On June 11, Craig, co-chair of the Mitt Romney presidential campaign, used a stop-over at Minneapolis-St. Paul airport to prowl through a lavatory in the Lindbergh terminal. He spotted under a stall door lower extremities belonging to a man we now know to have been undercover cop Dave Karsnia, who—patient as any spider—had been sitting on the john for thirteen minutes for prey that he could entrap.

Americans following the case have been learning with fascination how easily some innocent action in a public convenience—known in the argot of gay patrons as "tearooms"—can be misconstrued. Don't put your bag in front of the door. That's what Craig did and Karsnia, a youthful-looking blonde decoy, says in his report, "My experience has shown that individuals engaging in lewd conduct use their bags to block the view from the front of their stall." Keep your feet still. "At 12:16 hours," Karsnia relates, "Craig tapped his right foot. I recognized this as a signal used by persons wishing to engage in lewd conduct. Craig tapped his toes several times and moves his foot closer to my foot. I moved my foot up and down slowly. The presence of others did not seem to deter Craig as he moved his right foot so that it touched the side of my left foot which was within my stall area."

Craig then swiped his hand under the stall divider several times. That did it. Karsnia put down his police ID for Craig to check out. Craig quickly pleaded guilty to disorderly conduct and "peeping," which is defined in Minnesotan statutory lingo as "interference with privacy by surreptitiously gazing, staring or peeping in the window, or other aperture of a sleeping room in a hotel, a tanning booth"—this is Minnesota, after all—"or other place where a reasonable person would have an expectation of privacy and has exposed or is likely to expose their intimate parts, as defined in Sec. 609. 341, subd 5, or the clothing covering the immediate area of the intimate parts and doing so with the intent to intrude upon or interfere with the privacy of the occupant. A Gross Misdemeanor."

At some level Craig obviously wanted to get caught, just as compulsive gamblers at some level want to lose.

September 11

Leftists used to think that, at least as a general axiom if not by a precise deadline, capitalism was doomed. But today most of these same leftists deem capitalism invincible and fearfully lob copious documentation at each other detailing the efficient devilry of the executives of the system. The internet serves to amplify this pervasive funk into a catastrophist mindset. It imbues most of the English-speaking left after seven years of Bush and Cheney, and frames Naomi Klein's new book, *The Shock Doctrine*, subtitled *The Rise of Disaster Capitalism*.

At the outset Klein permits herself a robust trumpet blast as intrepid pioneer: "This book is a challenge to the central and most cherished claim in the official story—that the triumph of deregulated capitalism has been born of freedom, that unfettered free markets go hand in hand with democracy." The arc of triumph to which Klein alludes is the half century from the Eisenhower administration's onslaughts on political and economic nationalism in Iran and Guatemala in the early 1950s, to the US attack on Iraq in 2003 and its subsequent occupation.

These are not decades where official apologetics have been entirely without challenge until Ms. Klein embarked on her researches. There are shelves' worth of books on the ghastly consequences of the covert interventions and massacres organized or connived at by the United States in the name of freedom and the capitalist way. Klein's own bibliography attests that there has plenty of detailed work on the neoliberal onslaught that gathered strength from the mid-1970s on, marching under the intellectual colors of one of her arch villains, the late Milton Friedman, the Chicago School economist.

Where Klein would presumably claim originality is in identifying and describing the taxonomy of what she terms "shock capitalism"; the shock of a sudden attack, whether the overthrow of Salvador Allende in Chile in 1973 or the bombing of Baghdad in 2003; the shock of torturers using sensory deprivation techniques and crude electrodes to instill fear and acquiescence; Friedman's economic "shock treatment." Methodically combined and elaborated, these onslaughts now amount, on Klein's account, to a new and frightful chapter in the history of capitalist predation.

Klein begins with a chapter on the CIA-sponsored psychic "de-patterning" experiments of that apex monster, Dr. Ewen Cameron of McGill University's Allan Memorial Institute, and states explicitly that torture, aside from being a tool, is "a metaphor of the shock doctrine's underlying logic." To use shock literary tactics to focus attention on the deliberate and sadistic engineering of collective social trauma is certainly no crime. But, as often happens after a shock, one eventually retrieves a sense of proportion, one that is not entirely flattering to Klein's larger ambitions for her book.

Capitalism, after all, has always been a shock doctrine of selfish predation, as one can discover from Hobbes and Locke, Marx and Weber, none of whom is mentioned by Klein. Read the vivid accounts of the Hammonds about the English enclosures of the eighteenth century, when villagers would find nailed to the door of the parish church an announcement that their common lands had been privatized. Protesters may not have been "de-patterned," Cameron-style, but were briskly hanged or relocated to Botany Bay.

Friedman's Chicago Boys laid waste the southern cone of Latin America in the name of unfettered private enterprise, but 125 years earlier a million Irish peasants starved to death while Irish grain was exported onto ships flying the flag of economic liberalism. Klein writes about "the bloody birth of counter-revolution" in the 1960s and 1970s, but any page from the histories of Presidents Jackson,

Polk or Roosevelt discloses a bleak and blood-stained continuity with the past.

De-patterning? Indian children were taken from their families and punished for every word spoken in their own language, even as African slaves were given Christian names and forbidden to use their own, or to drum. Amid the shock of the Civil War the Republicans deferred by several years the freeing of slaves, while hastening to use the crisis to arrange a banking and monetary system to their liking.

Just as there is continuity in capitalist predation, there is continuity in resistance. Here's where Klein's catastrophism distorts the picture. Her controlling metaphor for the attack on Iraq is the initial "shock and awe" bombardment, designed to numb Saddam's forces and the overall civilian population into instant surrender and long-term submission. But the "shock and awe" tactic was a bust. Having sensibly decided not to fight or die on an American timetable, many of Iraq's soldiers regrouped to commence an effective resistance.

Capitalists try to use social and economic dislocation to advantage, but so do those they oppress. War has been the mother of many a positive social revolution, as have natural disasters. The incompetence of the Mexican police and emergency forces after the huge earthquake of 1985 prompted a huge popular upheaval. In Latin America there have been shock attacks and shock doctrines for 500 years. Right now, in Latin America, the pendulum is swinging away from the years of darkness, of the death squads and Friedman's doctrines.

Klein's outrage is admirable as are her specific accusations across six decades of infamy. But in her larger ambitions her metaphors betray her. From the anti-capitalist point of view she's too gloomy by half. A capitalism that thrives best on the abnormal, on disasters, is by definition in decline. As Cassius put it, "The fault, dear Brutus, is not in our stars, / But in ourselves, that we are underlings."

September 18

Orlando Figes's *The Whisperers: Private Life in Stalin's Russia* is in its most literal sense an act of collective memory, and the only quibble I have with the author's tremendous achievement is that the homage to those he rightly calls "the heroes" of his book comes not at the beginning but at the end, in his "Afterword and Acknowledgements" where he scrupulously describes how *The Whisperers* came to be written.

The project really began as a series of interviews by Figes when he was a graduate student in Moscow in the mid-1980s. Ultimately, after Figes began work in earnest on this book in 2002, he had several teams in the former Soviet Union searching through previously closed archives (some of which have now gone back under lock and key) locating notebooks, albums, diaries—assembling the vast cast of characters, over a thousand of them, who contribute their memories. Masterfully composed and controlled as a narrative by Figes, this is a collective testimony in which you can hear voices through a doorway open at last, the hopes, fears, and numberless awful tragedies of the Soviet era. As Figes himself says of the families who gave him his book, "These people are the heroes of *Whisperers*. In a real sense this is their book. For us these are stories, for them it is their lives."

As overture, we hear from the children of 1917 and memories of the idealism of those early years. Even then it had a sinisterly prophetic cast.

When Sonia Laskin was rejected by the Komsomol—the Communist youth organization—in 1927, the three girls in this Jewish family formed a reading circle with their cousin Mark and other little friends and would "discuss politics and hold 'show trials' of characters from literature. Once they held a trial of the Old Testament." Even as the kids held their trials, the Bolsheviks were methodically destroying the livelihood of Sonia's father, Samuil, who owned a herring stall on Botnaia Square, not far from the Kremlin.

Taking from the theories of the Montessoris, Soviet educators invented improving games such as "Search and Requisition," with the boys playing the role of Red Army units looking for hidden grain in the countryside and the girls acting as the "bourgeois speculators" or "kulak" peasants hiding it. Fantasy melted into reality with horrible speed and Figes soon plunges us into the horrors of forced collectivization of the Russian peasantry, seen centrally through the experiences of the Golovin family.

We meet them amid pastoral contentment: "On 2 August 1930, the villagers of Obukhovo celebrated Ilin Day, an old religious holiday to mark the end of high summer when the Russian peasants held a feast and said their prayers for a good harvest." They all went off to the house of the Golovins, the biggest family in the village, headed by Nikolai, an excellent farmer. The Golovins were not rich. Their net assets add up to two barns, several pieces of machinery, three horses, seven cows, a few dozen sheep and pigs, iron bedsteads and a samovar. Alas for the Golovins, such modest possessions doomed them as "kulaks," a word originally used by peasants to designate usurers and wheeler dealers. The Bolsheviks transmuted it into the absurd designation—a death sentence to millions—of "peasant capitalist," and ultimately a term dooming any peasant opposing forced collectivization.

The pleasant supper in Obukhovo notwithstanding, the destruction of rural Russia had already begun. In two months at the start 1930 half the Soviet peasantry—sixty million people in 100,000 villages—were herded into collective farms. The specific ruin of the Golovins commenced, courtesy of Kolia Kuzmin, a loutish eighteen-year-old son of a failed farmer and local drunk. At the head of a posse of twelve armed teenagers, he becomes the local agent of the Komsomol.

By September Obukhovo, in existence since 1522, was gone. And the kolkhoz (i.e., collective farm) "New Life" was in its place. The peasants had lost their land. Kuzmin, drunk, violent, and incompetent, was chairman of the kolkhoz. The first winter saw half the horses dead and the peasants paid fifty grams of bread a day each. Nikolai Golovin was in a distant prison, with one son in the Gulag, working on the White Sea Canal. Nikolai's wife Yevdokiia and two daughters were still in "New Life," in a hovel with one cow, which Kuzmin a few months later confiscated along with everything else, leaving them one iron bedstead.

They were deported on May 4, 1931, given one hour to prepare. Kuzmin confiscated the eight-year-old Antonina's shawl. "No one hugged us or said a parting word," Antonina recalls. "They were afraid of the soldiers."

Figes correctly calls his chapter on forced collectivization "The Great Break," and writes that Stalin's destruction of the kulaks was not only an appalling human tragedy, but "an economic catastrophe" for the Soviet Union, from which Soviet agriculture never recovered. In the ensuing famine of the early 1930s anywhere from four to eight million died.

The strength of *The Whisperers* is the range of the individual testimonies. On the one hand, "Dmitry Streleys who was 13 in 1930 remembers Serkov, chairman of his village Soviet in the Kurgan region of Siberia, telling his father that he'd been designated a kulak and was being sent into exile: 'I formed a committee of the poor and we sat through the night to choose the families. There is no one in the village who is rich enough to qualify, and not many old people, so we simply chose the 17 families. You were chosen. Please don't take it personally. What else could I do?' "

On the other, we also hear one of the requisitioning Red Army men, Lev Kopelev, a young Communist, remembering the screams of children and the glare of the peasants, and telling himself "I mustn't give in to debilitating pity. We were realizing historical necessity."

The family sagas in this vast canvas are of scarcely believable tenacity and endurance. No novelist would dare invent such feats and such coincidences. Take the Ozemblovskys, a family of six, in the Minsk region. They were exiled to the north, 3,000 kilometers from their home. While Aleksandr stayed to look after the two boys, Serafima and the two girls, nine and five, escaped and hiked south through the forest. Serafima had several gold teeth and periodically would pull one of them to buy a lift in a cart.

They made it home, where Serafima left her daughters and hiked 3,000 km north again, only to find that her husband had been arrested and one of her sons was now working as a police informer. She herself is arrested, escapes again, returns south, where she finally collects her daughters and sets up a new home, where the whole family is finally united.

Terror is vivid on page after page, particularly in the dreadful year of 1937. Maria Drozdova, from a strictly religious peasant family, remembers how her mother Anna became demented with terror after her husband, a church warden, was arrested. "She would not leave the house. She became afraid of talking in the room, in case the neighbors overheard. In the evenings she was terrified of switching on the lamp, in case it drew the attention of the police. She was even afraid to go to the toilet, in case she wiped herself with a piece of newspaper which contained an article with Stalin's name."

Another girl got home late from a party in 1939 and found she had lost her key. She knocked on the door at 1 a.m. There was a long pause. Then her father opened it, dressed as if ready to leave on a journey. He had thought the knock heralded the NKVD. In his mind he had already been tortured and shot. He gazed at her as though in a trance and then, for the first and last time in her life, slapped her across the face.

From every walk of life, from high party people like the Stalinist writer Konstantin Simonov, to peasants like the Golovins, the Soviet tragedy offers itself up, unforgettable in its heroism, villainy, cowardices large and small, endurance.

Take Ignatii Maksimov, from the Novgorod region. He is arrested and sentenced to work in the Gulag, on the murderous White Sea Canal where 25,000 workers died—in the first winter, many simply froze to death. Ignatii's wife Maria gets a job as a cook on the Leningrad to Murmansk railway that ran at one point along the northern sector of the Canal. She wrote notes to her husband on scraps of paper which she threw out the window of the train. Eventually she got an answer from her husband. One of the scraps has reached him, though he was working fifty miles north of where she thought he was. They were finally reunited in Archangelsk.

Here is the whole arc of Soviet history. In its amazing testimonies to the strength of the Russian family in the Soviet Union, as well as the awful fissures the system imposed on those families, *The Whisperers* is like a rainbow over a graveyard.

October 26

In America awareness never sleeps and has been on particularly active duty this October, designated as Breast Cancer Awareness Month (proclamation of President George Bush); as Domestic Violence Awareness Month (proclamation of President George Bush); as Energy Awareness Month (proclamation of President George Bush and the Environmental Protection Agency); and—we speak here specifically of October 22–29—Islamo-Fascism Awareness Week (proclamation of David Horowitz, a fat and hairy ex-Trot living in Los Angeles).

When I first saw Horowitz he was neither fat nor hairy nor apparently aware of Islamo-Fascism. This was in the late 1960s in London and he was working for the Bertrand Russell Peace Foundation, studying at the feet of Isaac Deutscher and Ralph Miliband. About a decade later I saw him again, this time in Washington, DC, presiding over a well-publicized "Second Thoughts" conference, announcing his departure from the left. He spoke harshly of his parents' decision to make him watch uplifting features about the Soviet Union and to forbid any Doris Day movies, a common blunder in child-brain-washing techniques among the comrades at that time.

Since then, like other Trotskyist vets, such as Christopher Hitchens, Horowitz has thrown his energies into crusading on behalf of the American right, fuelled in his efforts by copious annual disbursements from the richer denizens of that well-populated sector. Richard Mellon Scaife—apex demon in the "vast right-wing conspiracy" identified by Hillary Clinton amid the Lewinsky scandal—has poured millions into Horowitz's organizations, as have other well-heeled conservative foundations. Every now and again Horowitz will raise some spectacularly nutty alarum, like the *Los Angeles Times* being taken over by pinkos, and I always assume that Horowitz must be filling out his annual grant applications, and reminding Scaife that others may snooze and idle, but he, Horowitz, is unceasing in his vigilance against sedition.

In Horowitz's bestiary, sedition comes in all the traditional forms, from Commies on campus to Commies in the press, and he's churned out endless bulletins charting their insidious reach. Some of his specific accusations have no doubt been useful to fearful school administrations eager to harry and expel the few radical teachers able to find employment in these bleak times.

But the problem for Horowitz is one of supply. The left in America is really in very poor shape: near zero Commies, and really only a sprinkling of radical black profs, militant lesbians, and kindred antinomians to beat up on. The notion of pinkos in the media is laughable to all except the fearful imaginations of millionaires like Scaife. Hence the spotlight on Islamo-Fascism, a gloriously vague term whose origin is the topic of a tussle between Malise Ruthven, who used the term in 1980 to describe all authoritarian Islamic governments, and Stephen Schwartz, yet another fat, bearded former Trotskyist who says he was the first to use it in its specific application in 2000, eventually receiving a tap on the shoulder for so doing from Christopher Hitchens and John Sullivan. Arise, Sir Stephen!

Islamo-Fascism Awareness Week has been featuring Horowitz and big-name ranters of the right like Anne Coulter and Fox's Sean Hannity, plus former US Senator Rick Santorum, and noted Islamophobe Daniel Pipes. They descended on various college campuses to be received by Christian-Fascists and the curious while they hurled imprecations at the left for being soft on sons of the Prophet stoning women to death for adultery.

The reaction of the left has been mixed. In some ways it always takes Horowitz's antics far too seriously, though the latter's effect on timid college administrations cannot be entirely gainsaid. On the other hand, Awareness Week is having a galvanizing effect. Coalitions have formed to combat Horowitz's version of Awareness with a superior Progressive Awareness about what is good or not so good about Islam. Since Santorum and others have ripe records of intolerance for women, the air is usefully thick with shouts of "hypocrite." Horowitz is probably the best organizer the left has these days.

November 7

Paris in Brumaire—late October and early November in the French revolutionary calendar devised by d'Eglantine—should be mellow and the vegetable stalls full of bolete mushrooms. But this Brumaire has been inhospitable, with a wind as sharp as the knife that sliced through d'Eglantine's neck—though conditions are tolerable when the sun is up.

The plus side held gloriously clear skies and beautiful light, filling Suger's great cathedral at St. Denis. At the Pompidou there is an immense exhibition of Giacometti, in which profusion has a reverse effect. Two or three Giacometti sculptures by themselves look great, but hundreds tell you the guy ran out of steam some time in the late '30s. His studio became a mecca for top level photographers doing "the sculptor at work." Cartier Bresson, Brassai, Arnold Newman, and Irving Penn were all in attendance. Giacometti was a manly looking Swiss-Italian, and played the "artist at work" part well. Annette G. looked less happy as the decades passed and there are odd times when he spends three or four years sculpting and drawing a couple of Japanese men, at least one of whom was Annette's lover. Giacometti chose his fans well too. Genet did a big essay on him and Sartre wrote the catalogue intro for his first New York show.

The Modern Art collection at the Pompidou is really good and reminds one—if reminders are necessary—just how awful "modern art" collections are in US. There was room after room of great and interesting things: ravishing Kandinskys, a fantastic room of Picabias, one with two naked women in '40s movie poster style with a bulldog, plus a really frightening Golden Calf. Then on the next floor a whole late-modern collection with excellent acquisitions from 1950s, 1960s, and on.

Among them was "Manhattan Real Estate Holdings, A Real-Time Social System as of May 1, 1971," the series by Hans Haacke that got his one-man show axed at the last minute by the Guggenheim in the 1970s. The work consists of 146 photographs of buildings, many of them slums, acquired between 1951 and 1971 by Harry Shapolsky, named at the time as the city's top slumlord. Haacke included in each photo the info given in the Real Estate Directory of Manhattan. They make ironic reading now. Back then, to take a couple of examples, Shapolsky had 219 E. 94th, a five-story building with an assessed land value of $25,000 and a total value of $47,000. A six-story walk-up, 346 East 13th St., had an assessed land value of $22,000 and a total value of $57,000.

The best pieces on this floor of the Pompidou were an immense robe made from bottle tinfoil and bottle caps, maybe fifty feet by fifty feet, looking like a Klimt, by a Ghanaian artist, El Anatsui; and a fifty-foot sperm whale or plane, depending on one's point of view, made from bamboo, with about 10,000 scissors, knives, etc., confiscated by security at Sao Paulo airport. The artist is Cai Guo Qiang, about whom one story I found begins with the promising words that he is best known "for his magnanimous works using gunpowder."

The greatest delight of the Pompidou's modern collection is that not one Warhol—as profuse in American institutions of culture as dinosaurs—was on display.

December 11

Overheard by the SF cab driver:

Twenty-something female passenger: How are you feeling?
Twenty-something male passenger: Like I'm about to pass out.
Female passenger: Awesome. Passing out is awesome.

2008

January 2

It's time to take stock of the landscape. The American political system, as conditioned by corporate cash, legal obstructions to independent candidacies, and the corporate press, is designed to eliminate any substantive threat to business as usual. In the case of the Democrats, the winnowing process is working well. Mike Gravel, by far the most vivacious and radical of the party's candidates on the substantive matters of the war and empire, was swiftly marginalized. I've seen very few Gravel buttons.

Dennis Kucinich seems to have a lock on those Democrats prepared to stay true to a hopeless outsider. I don't understand this loyalty to the Ohio congressman. The point of hopeless outsiders is to give us hope. It's a dialectical thing. They convince us that their cause is not hopeless, but his signs and buttons and tickers already look as though they're collectibles on eBay.

The three major Democratic contenders for the nomination are all unalluring. John Edwards is offering us a populist package, with homilies on fair trade, gaps between rich and poor, corporate greed and so forth. Decent people including many labor organizers are working for him. I don't believe a word he says. His substantive record on war and empire is bad. He has poor judgment. Why spend $400 to have a hairdo that makes you look like a slick lawyer with a fancy haircut?

Barack Obama? I can't remember a single substantive statement he's made. In terms of political philosophy and pragmatic intention his platform is like the Anglican clergyman's answer, when asked for his conception of God: an oblong blur. When pressed, Obama's positions on war and empire are usually very bad. Talk about "moving beyond partisan differences" invariably ends with the Establishment's long-term goal of abolishing Social Security.

Hillary Clinton is the candidate for corporate power at home, and empire abroad. She argued passionately in the White House for the NATO bombing of Belgrade. Five days after September 11, 2001, she was calling for a broad war on terror. She voted for the Patriot Act. When it came time for Mrs. Clinton to deliver her speech in support of the war, she reiterated some of the most outlandish claims made by Dick Cheney.

On the Republican side I've liked Mike Huckabee. He had a decent record as governor of Arkansas and deserves support if only for his moral and political courage in his pardoning or sentence commutations of some 1,200 convicted criminals. These acts of mercy and faith in rehabilitation have been predictably attacked by many liberals because one of those he released may well have subsequently killed someone. This is an unavoidable risk unless you achieve certainty by execution or a sentence of life without the possibility of parole—which will be the trend if states continue to abandon the death penalty. The release on New Year's Eve of the seventy-seven-year-old Sara Jane Moore after thirty-two years prison for trying to kill our greatest President since Warren Harding is, alas, scarcely a precedent.

But Huckabee, particularly since he took on board a big-name political strategist, Ed Rollins, has made bad mistakes, flip-flopping on his enlightened position on immigration and taking on the awful John Bolton as a foreign policy counselor. Nonetheless I have a soft spot for the guy, if only because he has real populist character and has panicked the Establishment into regrouping round John McCain as the Republican match to HRC, as the bipartisan candidate of choice.

But my favorite remains Ron Paul, rock solid against war and empire and the neoliberal corporate state. He's a principled fellow who's won passionate support (and millions in modest cash contributions) from ordinary Americans. I recently drove down I-5 from Washington through Oregon to northern California and "Ron Paul" signs were almost the only ones I saw. I like the look of the people behind them.

All great seasons in politics begin with excitement. Right now there's none.

January 3

For the party establishments—Democratic and Republican—it was a bad night, as their favored candidates went down to severe defeat.

With Barack Obama's crushing victory over Hillary Clinton, the campaign scenario of the Democratic elite is now in the trash bin. Their calculation had been that Obama would never be able to match the Clintons' fund-raising. Wrong. Obama raised huge sums from small contributors, who can continue their support. A lot of Hillary's big financial backers have already reached their legal limits.

They thought Obama was another Howard Dean, headed for deflation as soon as the voters faced the moment of decision. Wrong again.

Mrs. Clinton had the big feminist organizations in her corner and a good chunk of organized labor. They didn't deliver, any more than the Democratic machine supervised by campaign chairman Terry McAuliffe and superpollster Mark Penn. They thought they could sink Obama with December's slurs about drug use, Islamic heritage, and color. They backfired.

The only age bracket Hillary scored well in was that of women sixty-five and up. However, Obama was able to expand the electorate, an unprecedented feat in the history of Iowa caucuses. Students currently on winter break went back to Ames, Iowa City and Des Moines to vote for him.

The three main issues on voters' minds were, in descending order, the war, the economy, and health care. Obama led in all three. Overall, he beat Hillary among both men and women. He took the five biggest cities and most of the counties in every quarter of the state. Young people simply don't care for Hillary. Young voters see Obama as a break with the past, and he skillfully manages to avoid any substantive positioning that might disabuse them of this belief. As much as the press tried to say that the war is no longer an issue, it turned out to be the top concern of the voters, and Obama's record features opposition to the war in his Senate campaign in 2004. Clinton and Edwards both voted for the war. Edwards apologized for that vote. Clinton never did.

It's hard to see any future for the Edwards campaign, unless as some kind of Hillary surrogate to siphon votes away from Obama in New Hampshire and South Carolina. There's no evidence that economic populism doesn't sell in Iowa. It's simply that this time around Democrats and Independents didn't see Edwards as a persuasive salesman.

January 16

Terrorism flourishes brazenly at Ground Zero in the new 7 World Trade Center building. Here can be found a secretive entity of fabulous wealth and power. Kingdoms and corporations alike tremble at its shadow and make haste to pay it tribute. I refer to Moody's Investor Services, wholly owned subsidiary of Moody's Corporation, which reported $2.3 billion in revenues in 2006.

On January 10 Moody's, in concert with the other main bond-rating firm, Standard and Poor's, gave the United States its top AAA credit rating. The terrorist blackmail threat came in the form of a demand by Moody's that the US government "reform" Social Security and Medicare. "In the very long term, the rating could come under pressure if reform of Medicare and Social Security is not carried out as these two programs are the largest threats to the long-term financial health of the United States and to the government's AAA rating."

Steven Hess, Moody's top analyst for the US economy, spelled it out more explicitly to the London *Financial Times*: "If no policy changes are made, in 10 years from now we would have to look very seriously at whether the US is still a triple-A credit … The US rating is the anchor of the world's financial system. If you have a downgrade, you have a problem." Thus does Moody's man calmly threaten to plant the financial equivalent of a thermonuclear device under the Statue of Liberty.

Right now the US deficit is around $200 billion, 1.5 percent of GDP, which is not large by recent historical measure and which presents no danger in itself to US financial soundness. But as Professor Robert Pollin of U Mass/Amherst adds, if Moody's analysts want to discuss the causes of fiscal laxity, "Why not look at the Iraq war? The defense budget for 2006 was $617 billion. That is 4.8 percent of a $13 trillion GDP. Before the Iraq war, the defense budget was about 3.0 percent of GDP. So Iraq alone is costing about $150 billion annually, about 1.1 percent of GDP. And what has it accomplished? Social Security and Medicare combined were about $900 billion in 2006. Why assume we first have to attack our minimal welfare state, and leave the imperial budget intact?"

In fact, it's almost entirely Medicare, not Social Security, that accounts for the projected rising costs in our shriveled welfare state. The culprit here is not the swelling ranks of older people but the insurance and drug companies' grip on our health system. Conversion to single payer would mean huge savings.

The US pays around 15 percent of its gross domestic product for health care, about 70 percent more than the outlay of other advanced industrial countries. Shift to single payer and quit shoving money—4.8 percent of GDP—down the imperial sinkhole and there's no fiscal crisis of any sort, short or long term, for Moody's or anyone else to fret about. And in the even shorter term, if Moody's sees a fiscal crisis looming, why don't its overpaid executives for once put the national interest first and call for a tax hike on the rich? Pollin tells me that just going back to Clinton, as opposed to Bush 2, on taxes for those making over $200,000 a year would generate $60 billion a year. Do this and end the war in Iraq and you wipe out almost the whole deficit at a stroke.

Let a real war on terror commence.

March 1

Was there a medium-size right-wing conspiracy to nail Gov. Eliot Spitzer, above and beyond Governor Spitzer's own diligent efforts in the same cause? It certainly looks like it. It's clear that the Feds started with Spitzer whose wire transfers led them to the Emperors Club, a prostitution business efficiently administered by a twenty-three-year-old Blair Academy grad, Cecil Suwal, on behalf of her sixty-two-year-old boyfriend, Mark Brener, from the high rise in Cliffside Park, NJ, with fine views of Manhattan.

The official story is that it was Spitzer's efforts to break down a $10,000 transfer to an account fronting for Emperors Club that alerted clerks at his Manhattan branch of Capital One's North Fork bank. A similar transaction at another bank where Spitzer had an account also supposedly twitched a red flag. Banks have to report deposits of $10,000 and up to the Treasury Department. People not wanting to have their bank snitch to the Feds about their transactions routinely keep the sums below the red-light figure, and the Feds have told the banks to adjust their mandatory snooping to report $8,000-plus sums, or sums that add up to $10,000.

Like innumerable other affronts to privacy, this reporting requirement began as a tool in the "war on drugs," and now is part of the furniture of our lives. All the same, it strains credulity to believe that North Fork's "suspicious activity report" on a well-known and presumably valued client immediately aroused the interest of the IRS employee scrutinizing the hundreds of thousands of SARs churning through his computer in the IRS watchpost in Long Island. The official version has the IRS man noting Spitzer's name, then passing the information up the food chain to the Justice Department, and the US Attorney's office in Manhattan.

Instead of the banks being curious on their own, what if the Feds told the banks to report all of Spitzer's wire transfers to them? It seems likely, and if so, we have here in outline a sting operation which raises another pressing question: who exactly was it that put Spitzer in touch with Emperors Club in the first place?

Once the wheels were set in motion we had the unedifying spectacle of the full resources of the state devoted to exposing Spitzer's various rendezvous with consenting adults, primarily the comely twenty-two-year-old "Kristen." Spitzer's role as the sole target in this recruitment of investigative and prosecutorial manpower since July 2007 is evidenced by the malicious insertion in the prosecutor's indictment of a quote from the phone taps about his sexual preferences (reminiscent of Kenneth Starr's detailed disclosures about the minutiae of physical transactions between Bill Clinton and Monica Lewinsky), which Heidi Fliess, the Hollywood madam, insisted was most certainly a demand for unprotected anal sex.

It's hard to root for Spitzer with much enthusiasm, beyond mandatory support for anyone facing political ruin and possible criminal charges for having sex with a consenting adult. It was extraordinary to hear the Mann Act, ancient weapon of racist bigotry against blacks, being brandished as a possible sanction against Spitzer for having paid for a prostitute to travel from New York to Washington, DC.

Obviously a stewpot of psychic contradictions, Spitzer was brimful of prosecutorial zeal himself, against prostitutes as well as convicted sex offenders. It was Gov. Spitzer who pushed civil commitment into law in March 2007, legalizing possible lifetime incarceration for sex offenders, no matter what their original prison sentences may have been. But Spitzer also frightened Wall Street. There were plenty of very powerful financial institutions that craved his downfall and whose employees cheered wildly when that downfall appeared imminent.

Powerful people on Wall Street didn't like Gov. Eliot Spitzer, and Wall Street plays dirty. Relevant here are remarks on the evening of Spitzer's resignation by Ken Langone. The billionaire venture capitalist was a New York Stock Exchange board member whom Spitzer had gone after when he was Attorney General. Langone was an ally of Richard Grasso, chairman and CEO of the New York Stock Exchange. Attorney General Spitzer sued Grasso in 2004, seeking repayment of most of a $140 million pay package. According to the suit, Grasso, along with former NYSE Director Kenneth Langone, misled the NYSE board about the details of his pay package, beyond that of comparable chief executives. Langone later proclaimed he was launching "a holy war" against Spitzer, when the latter ran for governor.

CNBC: Would you say that you were surprised by this news?

LANGONE: Not at all. I had no doubt about his lack of character and integrity. It would only be a matter of time, I didn't think he would do it this soon or the way he did it. But I know for sure he went himself to a post office and bought $2,800 worth of mail orders to send to the hooker.

CNBC: How do you know that?

LANGONE: I know it. I know somebody who was standing in back of him in line … We all have our own private hells. I hope his private hell is hotter than anybody else's.

In other words, the vindictive billionaire Langone heard about the $2,800 in money orders from a private investigator he or his associates had retained to follow Spitzer. As one Wall Street veteran remarked, "I know this to be standard operating procedure against Wall Street enemies."

How is this not selective prosecution when the members of law enforcement are trying the case in the media? Furthermore, how is this a matter for the Department of Justice's Public Integrity office? Spitzer has income of over a million a year. That would put his assets in the tens of millions. It's not as though he couldn't afford to pay for the prostitutes out of his own pocket. And it's also not like he was guarding the location of nuclear subs.

Now consider the larger context of Wall Street's apprehensions about Governor Spitzer. Pam Martens outlined them eloquently as she described the motivations big Wall Street players had for pumping money into Barack Obama's campaign:

> In March of 2000, the Nasdaq stock market, hyped with spurious claims for startup tech and dot.com companies, reached a peak of over 5,000. Eight years later, it's trading in the 2,300 range and most of those companies no longer exist. From peak to trough, Nasdaq transferred over $4 trillion from the pockets of small mania-gripped investors to the wealthy and elite market manipulators …
>
> Mr. Greenspan was the wind beneath the wings of a carefully orchestrated wealth transfer system known as "pump and dump" on Wall Street.

> As hundreds of court cases, internal emails, and insider testimony now confirm, this bubble was no naturally occurring phenomenon any more than the Obama bubble is …
>
> The current housing bubble bust is just a freshly minted version of Wall Street's real estate limited partnership frauds of the '80s, but on a grander scale … Wall Street created an artificial demand for housing (a bubble) by soliciting high interest rate mortgages (subprime) because they could be bundled and quickly resold for big fees to yield-hungry hedge funds and institutions. A major underpinning of this scheme was that Wall Street secured an artificial rating of AAA from rating agencies that were paid by Wall Street to provide the rating. When demand from institutions was saturated, Wall Street kept the scheme going by hiding the debt off its balance sheets and stuffed this long-term product into mom-and-pop money markets, notwithstanding that money markets are required by law to hold only short-term investments. To further perpetuate the bubble as long as possible, Wall Street prevented pricing transparency by keeping the trading off regulated exchanges and used unregulated over-the-counter contracts instead. (All of this required lots of lobbyist hours in Washington.)

Wall Street has nothing to fear for its subprime frauds from the SEC. The Commission cannot initiate criminal prosecutions. But New York State has the Martin Act, the most powerful criminal enforcement weapon in the country. Now look at why Wall Street was extremely nervous of what New York Attorney General Andrew Cuomo, backed by Gov. Spitzer, might have been planning to do with the Martin Act. News reports in January said Cuomo was preparing such suits.

Later the NAACP and lead counsel Brian Kabateck filed papers seeking to fast track their federal class-action lawsuit against Washington Mutual, Citi, GMAC, and fifteen other mortgage firms who systematically steered African-American borrowers into predatory loans.

> The defendants in this case are CitiMortgage, Suntrust Mortgage, GMAC Rescap, JP Morgan, National City, First Horizon, Ameriquest Mortgage Company, Fremont Investment & Loan, Option One Mortgage Corporation, WMC Mortgage Corporation, Long Beach Mortgage Company, BNC Mortgage, Accredited Home Lenders, Bear

> Stearns Residential Mortgage Corporation, Encore Credit, First Franklin Financial Corporation, HSBC Finance Corporation, and Washington Mutual, Inc. This suit is the first to have ever charged so many major mortgage lenders with racial discrimination.
>
> The suit is supported by a wealth of government and other research: a 2008 study by United for a Fair Economy cites federal data showing people of color are more than three times more likely to have subprime loans. The study estimated losses of between $164 billion and $213 billion for subprime loans taken by people of color during the past eight years. This is thought to be "the greatest loss of wealth for people of color in modern US history." A July 2007 report by Freddie Mac showed that minority borrowers pay higher annual percentage rates on mortgage loans than non-minorities with equal income and credit risk.

There are reasons not to be entirely confident of the defense team retained by Spitzer. The former governor has retained three lawyers from the law firm Paul, Weiss, Rifkind, Wharton and Garrison. This is, according to one seasoned observer, "one of the dirtiest law firms and a huge part of its income comes from Wall Street. It's known as the place that both the US government and Wall Street hire to cover up big crimes." The way things usually work is that Paul Weiss is on board to make sure Wall Street's and the government's dirty secrets remain secret.

The public is pretty much in the dark about the fact that our government is not just wiretapping and email snooping, but it's also going through our mail. Judging from what Langone said about the postal money orders and what the complaint says about the phone calls with Spitzer about the package arriving, it seems Spitzer was mailing his checks and/or postal money orders. So, it seems likely the Feds were snooping in his mail. Opening this window to public scrutiny might disclose that millions of pieces of our mail have been opened without good cause.

March 1

The vast slum projects on Chicago's South Side known as the Robert Taylor Homes, setting for Sudhir Venkatesh's *Gang Leader for a Day*, no longer exist. The bulldozers started rolling in the early 1990s, only thirty years after the mini-city of twenty-eight high rises went up. It was constructed on French modernist principles, a two-mile by two-block concrete desert in which the Chicago Housing Authority had very loose authority over 27,000 people: 99.9 percent black, 95 percent jobless and on welfare, over 40 percent of the heads of household being single mothers.

Venkatesh's colorful and sympathetic memoir is a snapshot, like those you see stuck on posts alongside American highways where a car or truck took its human cargo into the hereafter. Born in Madras and raised in comfortable middle-class academic circumstances in southern California, Venkatesh embarked on his Ph.D. in sociology at the University of Chicago in 1989. The dominant figure in the department at that time was William Julius Wilson, famous for arguing in such books as *When Work Disappears* and *The Truly Disadvantaged* that, contrary to depictions of ghetto blacks in right-wing bestiaries, which spoke of psychological, intellectual, and even genetic deficits, the core problem was work. Without stable, well-paid jobs, any community will slide downhill, with blacks at the bottom of the heap.

Venkatesh soon got bored poring over data sets and yearned to scrutinize actual poor people. Fortunately, Wilson was embarking on a big new study of poverty and told Venkatesh to put together a questionnaire and start interviewing. To the homeboys lounging about in the stairwells of the Projects, selling crack and fending off the competition, Venkatesh must have been an odd sight: a tall, dark-skinned fellow with a pony-tail and a tie-dye shirt, memento of his Deadhead cultural affiliations, flourishing a researcher's clipboard and asking, "How does it feel to be black and poor?"

They figure him as a member of a Mexican gang, or an Arab, and hold him till the gang leader, J.T., a college dropout with a talent for organizing, assays Venkatesh's academic credentials and origins, and in short order says he can stay around—thus setting Venkatesh on a path that would eventually lead him to Harvard and then to Columbia University.

Venkatesh does little more than gesture in a sentence or two about how exactly he earned the trust of J.T. and other powerful people in the Projects, such as the tenant leader, Ms. Bailey. In keeping with his laconic, understated mode—one has the sense now and then of a book written in something of a hurry—he does not broach the subject of his own ethnic origins, but it obviously helped that he is not white. At all events, the laid-back personality that led J.T. and others to trust young Sudhir emerges clearly from his descriptions—at once sympathetic and detached—of slum life and the endless battles of the very poor to make it to the end of the day in one piece. His dry Indian eye allows him to sketch in vivid detail the entrepreneurial hive at the Robert Taylor Homes.

The Projects come alive in Venkatesh's glancing descriptions: urine-soaked stairwells inhabited by squatters and cruised by hookers; the sixteen-story buildings' bleak outside corridors savaged by Chicago's winter winds; welcoming apartments in which heroic mothers raise their kids and cram Sudhir's plate with soul food as he writes up his notes. His posture is genuinely one of respect. The gang members are not the "superpredators" demonized by the right-wing criminologists who dominated discussions of the ghetto and of the justice system's stance toward gangs in the late 1980s and '90s. They are humans given scant choices. "You want to understand how black folks live in the Projects," Ms. Bailey tells Venkatesh. "Why we are poor. Why we have so much crime. Why we can't feed our families. Why our kids can't get work when they grow up. So will you be studying white people?"

Declining a pose of moral affront, Venkatesh's particular talent is to have figured out how the buildings function as a collective business enterprise; how the truly desperate squeeze a hundred dollars a month out of recycling trash; how the hookers rate their services. He had one huge stroke of good fortune in the form of a secret gift of the gang's business accounts, conscientiously maintained by J.T.'s bookkeeper, T-Bone. Using T-Bone's notebook, he established exactly what the junior drug vendors in J.T.'s army—the Black Kings—were making: minimum wage, hence the need to live with their moms. J.T. himself was pulling down from $30,000 a year up to as much as $100,000 at his apex. The books methodically recorded the levies extorted by the gang from local shopkeepers, from the squatters, from the hookers. Venkatesh explains how a vast urban slum was actually governed by innumerable *quid pro quos* and intricate contracts which, being unwritten and with the rule of law not accessible to its inhabitants, were enforced by the threat or the direct exercise of violence.

Adopting a modified Candidean posture as the West Coast naïf in darkest Chicago, Venkatesh lets the reader know early on that, yes, he witnessed more or less mutely some bad stuff, initially when J.T. beats up an elderly squatter called C-Note who refuses to quit working on a car in an area the gang want to use for basketball: "'I told you, nigger,' J.T. said, his face barely an inch away from C-Note's, 'but you just don't listen, do you?' He sounded exasperated but there was also a sinister tone to his voice I'd never heard before. 'Why are you making this harder?' He started slapping C-Note on the side of the head, grunting with each slap, C-Note's head flopping back and forth like a toy … then J.T.'s henchmen pushed him to the ground. They took turns kicking him, one in the back and the other in the stomach …"

It takes C-Note two months to recover from the beating. Venkatesh writes a few pages later: "J.T. and I resumed our normal relationship … I kept my questions to myself … While I was by no means comfortable watching drug addicts smoke crack, the C-Note affair gave me greater pause. He was an old man in poor health; he could hardly be expected to defend himself against men twice his size and half his age, men who also happened to carry guns … But I didn't do anything. I'm ashamed to say I didn't confront J.T. about it until some six months later, and even then I did so tentatively."

This observer/participant theme weaves its way uncertainly through the book. Venkatesh's academic advisors remind him that witness of criminal activities renders him liable to subpoenas and even charges of criminal conspiracy. More experienced ethnographers caution him against excessive involvement with his subjects. Venkatesh's own entrepreneurial instincts prompt him to assert too shrilly the originality of his research methods (i.e., directly observing poor people), and also to contrive the signally unconvincing chapter that gives the book its title, *Gang Leader for a Day*. It is plain enough that Venkatesh was nothing of the sort. Under the careful eye of J.T.

and his lieutenants, he is allowed to make a few inconsequential decisions before surrendering the imaginary role.

It is as a participant that Venkatesh makes the astounding move of revealing to J.T. and Ms. Bailey the actual earnings disclosed to him by the small-time hustlers, hookers, and marginal players, whose confidence he has fostered down the years. Furious at the news of tiny profits undeclared to them, J.T. and Ms. Bailey promptly exact retribution, thus earning Venkatesh the well-merited suspicion of his erstwhile informants. Remorseful across several pages, he never really explains his shameful conduct, and one can only conclude that it was the pride of the business analyst that led him on. He could not resist strutting his stuff to J.T. and Ms. Bailey.

History sidles briefly into the book. Old black men muse nostalgically about the days of the Black Panthers, who offered the ghetto social services along with incendiary politics. An older woman, Cordella Levy, recalls how women used to run social life in the Projects before the possibility of decent local employment disappeared and the drug gangs came in, establishing the cash nexus and rule of force as the motor of social relations. "It was a time for women," Levy says, "a place for women. The men ruined everything."

This brings us back to young men like J.T., who beats up C-Note. Eventually Venkatesh asks him why, and J.T. answers: "C-Note was challenging my authority … I had niggers watching me, and I had to do what I had to do." The sense of insecurity and impermanence—in jobs, relationships, lodging, life itself—that so imbues the lives of poor people takes over Venkatesh's book in its final chapters. The Robert Taylor Homes are now demolished, and amid the rubble lies J.T.'s empire, as a federal onslaught puts many of the Black Kings behind bars.

T-Bone got ten years for drug trafficking and died in prison. J.T. got out of the gang business, but his barbershop failed. He thought he was going to be the hero of Venkatesh's book, but presumably by now has realized that this was a role the author had reserved for himself, crowing on the last page that he was "a rogue sociologist, breaking conventions and flouting the rules." Of course, the roguery has done him no end of good, and *Gang Leader for a Day* will probably end up as a movie. And the moral is ... But no, there is no moral of the sort Venkatesh's supervisor William Julius Wilson might have written about how to fight poverty.

March 26

Suddenly everyone is having a "conversation." The word has come of age. I see it bowing and scraping on the opinion pages and TV talk shows three or four times a day.

Barack Obama's speech in Philadelphia about race stuck pretty carefully to the unwritten rules of a national conversation, in marked contrast to the sermons of the Rev. Josiah Wright whose stimulating rhetoric has caused such extraordinary affront—if you will—to the conversing classes.

The junior Senator from Illinois is a master at drowning the floundering swimmer he purports to rescue, while earning credit for extending a manly hand in human solidarity. Obama's fake-rescue technique is reminiscent of Alexander Pope's eighteenth-century lines about Joseph Addison: "Damn with faint praise, assent with civil leer / And without sneering, teach the rest to sneer."

Our tragedy is that we have three neoliberals left in the presidential race, at a time when neoliberalism has collapsed and life-giving divisiveness is top of the Wanted list. I suppose, out of the three of them, I prefer Obama. McCain is an idiot and HRC wants Volcker, Rubin, and Greenspan to lead a "high-level emergency working group" to recommend ways to restructure at-risk mortgages to help avert more foreclosures. But I don't think Obama is a real fighter. He's too pretty, and he doesn't want to get his looks messed up.

May 3

Every few years New York City cops hear the growl of clear and present danger and subdue the threat with powerful volleys of lead. With Sean Bell, an African-American, in November 2006 the fusillade rose to fifty shots, deemed necessary by the men in blue to lay low Bell outside a nightclub in November 2006.

In Queens last week a judge ruled that the cops who turned young Bell into a sieve on his wedding day had been filled with a most understandable apprehension, even though Bell turned out to be unarmed. As usual the cops walk and sometime later the victim's family may get a settlement from the city. The important thing is that justice is seen *not* to have been done. Power needs the periodic buttress of irrational, uniformed violence.

The crowds protesting in Queens after Judge Anthony Cooperman let Bell's killers go free a week ago were orderly, as instructed by an African American. "We're a nation of laws, so we respect the verdict that came down," Barack Obama said when asked about the case by reporters in Indiana. "Resorting to violence to express displeasure over a verdict is something that is completely unacceptable and is counterproductive."

Spoken like a president of the *Harvard Law Review*. In fact Obama's white rival for the Democratic nomination, Hillary Clinton, put more juice into her press release: "This tragedy has deeply saddened New Yorkers—and all Americans. My thoughts are with Nicole and her children and the rest of Sean's family during this difficult time. The court has given its verdict, and now we await the conclusion of a Department of Justice civil rights investigation."

Obama is now well advanced along the path of reassurance, where each candidate nearing the White House makes clear their fidelity to the standard of irrational violence. As with McCain and Mrs. Clinton, this year he has affirmed his willingness to wipe out America's enemies with nuclear bombs and missiles, though he drew some rebukes for saying he was not in favor of nuking the Hindu Kush, thus casting a disquieting flicker of reason across the path of reassurance.

Since he is, though half white, black in appearance—and in such matters appearance counts for everything—Obama has dealt with the pigmentation problem by declaring that race is no longer a troubling factor in America, and should be low on the fix-it list of any incoming President. In Selma, Alabama, he declared that blacks "have already come 90 percent of the way" to equality. Indeed he's already issued white America a loss damage waiver. "If I lose, it would not be because of race. It would be because of mistakes I made along the campaign trail."

June 7

Obama inspires young people who flock to his rallies. He promises not only to "create a new kind of politics" but to "transform this country," "change the world," "create a Kingdom right here on earth." Comingled with these doses of uplift are the familiar coarse pledges to crucial interest groups, such as the Miami Cubans. Obama's speech to them on May 25 was a dismal exercise in right-wing demagoguery.

Take his speech to the Cuban American National Foundation in Miami on May 23: "Throughout my entire life, there has been injustice and repression in Cuba. Never, in my lifetime, have the people of Cuba known freedom ... This is the terrible and tragic status quo that we have known for half a century—of elections that are anything but free or fair ... I won't stand for this injustice, you won't stand for this injustice, and together we will stand up for freedom in Cuba ... I will maintain the embargo."

Obama also had words of specific comfort for the Uribe regime in Colombia: "When I am President, we will continue the Andean Counter-Drug Program, and update it to meet evolving challenges. We will fully support Colombia's fight against the FARC. We'll work with the government to end the reign of terror from right-wing paramilitaries. We will support Colombia's right to strike terrorists who seek safe-haven across its borders." Note the endorsement of Columbia's foray into Ecuador to assassinate a FARC leader.

After invoking hope and change in St. Paul, Obama rushed the next day to Washington for some ritual groveling to the AIPAC: "We will also use all elements of American power to pressure Iran. I will do everything in my power to prevent Iran from obtaining a nuclear weapon. Everything in my power. Everything and I mean everything." Israel should get whatever it wants and an undivided Jerusalem should be its capital.

We can look ahead to months of Obama deflecting McCain's onslaughts on him as a starry-eyed peacenik by insisting that what the beleaguered Empire above all needs is efficiency, ruthless if necessary. "The [US] generals are light-years ahead of the civilians," he reassured one of his fans, the neoconservative *New York Times* columnist, David Brooks. "They are trying to get the job done rather than look tough."

Can a black man get elected President in 2008? Hillary Clinton said No. In the last weeks she ran up some impressive totals of white voters agreeing with her, as in West Virginia where Obama scarcely campaigned, just as he remained invisible to voters in Kentucky, Colorado, Nebraska, Kansas, and Wisconsin.

Obama right now has an edge in electoral college votes, though this somewhat depends which faction of number crunchers you believe. By almost every yardstick, except the wild card of his skin color, he'll win. It should be inconceivable for a Republican to capture the White House for the third time in a row when the price of gasoline is headed towards $5 a gallon, food prices are soaring, and most Americans reckon things are going to get a lot worse.

At least for now, the Clinton dynasty is headed for the retirement home. None too soon, I say, however Obama turns out.

June 22

The delirium in the press at Tim Russert's passing has been strange. As a broadcaster he was not much better than average, which is saying very little. He could be a sharp questioner, but not when it really counted and when courage was required. He was tough with George Bush in a February interview in 2004. He taxed with him with faking the reasons to attack Iraq. But in the years before the 2003 attack, I used to hear him being merciless with those questioning whether Saddam Hussein had the nukes and bio-weapons alleged by the Bush administration and its conspirators in the press, prominent among them Russert himself.

If Russert had rocked the boat in any serious way he'd have had more enemies. The right-wingers didn't care for Walter Cronkite, but they had no problem with Russert. Rush Limbaugh nuzzled him respectfully on the air and so did Don Imus. Russert was always there with his watering can to fertilize myths useful to the system.

Russert spent many years working for Daniel Patrick Moynihan, who played the greasiest cards in the political deck, whoring for the Israel lobby, and race-baiting for Nixon. Few were more zealous than Russert in shredding anyone with the temerity to criticize Israel. Obama, now shuffling Moynihan's greasy deck with his Father's Day sermon about black responsibility, himself got a dose of Russert's own race-baiting earlier this year, with a ridiculous volley of questions about Farrakhan and Wright in the February 26 debate. Any white telly pundit can make hay with Farrakhan, but when it came to high gasoline prices Russert was meek as a shoeshine boy, lining up the oil execs and tugging his forelock.

After his death the TV played over and over the clip with Russert's interview of Dick Cheney, where the latter said US troops will be greeted as liberators. Russert didn't say, "What do you mean Mr. VP? People historically despise occupying armies. Bombing historically does not win people to your side." It was a softball moment for Cheney. Russert was part of the Amen chorus.

July 9

He went to the big armory in the sky a few years ago, but on the evening of June 26, here in Petrolia, I could almost hear the joyful salvoes that my neighbor, Curly Wright, half a mile down Conklin Creek Road, would have loosed off into the hillside the other side of the Mattole.

June 26? For millions of Americans the political highpoint of 2008 is now behind them. The precise day is forever inscribed in their hearts as one of glorious ratification of America's core freedoms: the day the US Supreme Court for the first time affirmed by a narrow majority of 5–4 the Second Amendment to the US Constitution, "A well regulated Militia being necessary to the security of a free State, the right of the people to keep and bear Arms shall not be infringed."

The last time Joe Paff (co-pilot of the indispensable Goldrush Coffee) and I visited Curly, then in his early eighties, his strict constructionist reading of the Second Amendment was visible in every cranny of his home. Without twisting my head as I sat on the couch I think I counted around thirty long guns disposed about the premises. Tucked between the cushions of the couch itself and in a planter or two there were small handguns available for swift deployment. Curley was an unregulated militia all on his own.

The US Supreme Court's decision was a frightful blow to the gun controllers. "This is a decision that will cost innocent lives, cause immeasurable pain and suffering and turn America into a more dangerous country," wailed the *New York Times* in an editorial. "A frightening decision and a return to the days of the Wild West," said Mayor Richard Daley of Chicago, a city to which gunfire has been street muzak for many decades.

The Court's decision was written by its peppery ultra-conservative, Justice Antonin Scalia, who became positively lyrical in his paean to the handgun: "There are many reasons that a citizen may prefer a handgun for home defense: It is easier to store in a location that is readily accessible in an emergency; it cannot easily be redirected or wrestled away by an attacker; it is easier to use for those without the upper-body strength to lift and aim a long gun; it can be pointed at a burglar with one hand while the other hand dials the police. Whatever the reason, handguns are the most popular weapon chosen by Americans for self-defense in the home, and a complete prohibition of their use is invalid."

Thinking of Curley's well-defended home, I remain astounded by the tiny number of weapons allegedly seized by the Feds in their recent execution of twenty-nine search warrants in Humboldt county, commencing on June 24. *Only thirty firearms seized in SoHum*! Mr. McGregor probably had better home defense against Peter Rabbit.

If that's all that a passel of alleged cultivators can muster in Southern Humboldt, heaven help us when the Chinese declare World War III. They could land at Shelter Cove, and scythe their way through the woods to Garberville with only token resistance from pacifists bunkered down in their plastic greenhouses flourishing watering cans. The red flag would be flapping over Willits by sundown, and

San Francisco right down 101 waiting to drop into the hands of the Commie-Capitalists like a ripe plum.

Europeans, snootily aghast at America's fifty million households holding about 250 million guns, usually miss two important points. "Home defense" is a phrase with profound reverberations. How much it all had to do with killing Indians is for you to decide. And the gun lobby has been successful in anchoring their cause in the notion of a basic "freedom," in an era when Americans correctly feel that freedom—against unreasonable searches and seizures, or to a speedy trial—is being relentlessly eroded by government.

August 23

"Change" and "hope" are not words one associates with Senator Joe Biden, a man so ripely symbolic of everything that is unchanging and hopeless about our political system that a computer simulation of the corporate-political paradigm Senator in Congress would turn out "Biden" in a nano-second.

The first duty of any Senator from Delaware is to do the bidding of the banks and large corporations that use the tiny state as a drop box and legal sanctuary. Biden has never failed his masters in this primary task. Find any bill that sticks it to the ordinary folk on behalf of the Money Power and you'll likely detect Biden's hand at work. The bankruptcy act of 2005 was just one sample. In concert with his fellow corporate serf, Senator Tom Carper, Biden blocked all efforts to hinder bankrupt corporations from fleeing from their real locations to the legal sanctuary of Delaware. Since Obama is himself a corporate serf and from day one in the US Senate has been attentive to the same masters that employ Biden, the ticket is well balanced, the seesaw with Obama at one end and Biden at the other dead-level on the fulcrum of corporate capital.

Another shining moment in Biden's progress in the current presidential term was his conduct in the hearings on Judge Alito's nomination to the US Supreme Court. From the opening moments of the Judiciary Committee's sessions in January 2006, it became clear that Alito faced no serious opposition. On that first ludicrous morning Senator Pat Leahy sank his head into his hands, shaking it in unbelieving despair as Biden blathered out a self-serving and inane monologue lasting a full twenty minutes before he even asked Alito one question. In his allotted half hour Biden managed to pose only five questions, all of them ineptly phrased. He did pose two questions about Alito's membership of a racist society at Princeton, but had already undercut them in his monologue by calling Alito "a man of integrity," not once but twice, and further trivialized the interrogation by reaching under the dais to pull out a Princeton cap and put it on.

A Delaware newspaper made deadly fun of him for his awful performance, eliciting the revealing confession from Biden that "I made a mistake. I should have gone straight to my question. I was trying to put him at ease."

Biden is a notorious flapjaw. His vanity deludes him into believing that every word that drops from his mouth is minted in the golden currency of Pericles. Vanity is the most conspicuous characteristic of US Senators *en bloc*, nourished by deferential acolytes and often expressed in loutish sexual advances to staffers, interns, and the like.

Why did Obama chose Biden? One important constituency pressing for Biden was no doubt the Israel lobby inside the Democratic Party. Obama, no matter how fervent his proclamations of support for Israel, has always been viewed with some suspicion by the lobby. For half the life span of the state of Israel Biden has been its unswerving acolyte in the US Senate.

September 17

Last Monday morning, amid the financial rubble of the weekend disasters, John McCain said he thought the economy was fundamentally sound. Hours later, maybe after a phone call from the Palins, he changed his mind. The man who wants less government now wants a government enquiry. He doesn't know what's wrong but he's bothered.

It would take the pen of Swift to depict a scene more ludicrous than the recent Republican convention, featuring thunderous denunciations of big government a few hours before Treasury Secretary Henry Paulson rushed to bail out Fannie Mae and Freddie Mac in the largest nationalization in history, privatizing the profits and nationalizing the losses, sticking the taxpayers with a $300 billion tab. On Tuesday AIG got the same treatment.

Even Swift could not depict the brazen effrontery of McCain offering himself as the foe of the special interests when his prime, albeit technically unofficial economic adviser is former Senator Phil Gramm. In 1999 John McCain's friend and now his closest economic counselor, then a Senator from Texas, pushed through the Gramm-Leach-Bliley Act. It repealed the old Glass-Steagall Act, passed in the Great Depression, which prohibited a commercial bank from being in the investment and insurance business. President Bill Clinton cheerfully signed it into law.

A year later Gramm, chairman of the Senate Banking Committee, attached a 262-page amendment to an omnibus appropriations bill, voted on by Congress right before a recess. The amendment received no scrutiny and duly became the Commodity Futures Modernization Act which okayed deregulation of investment banks, exempting most over-the-counter derivatives, credit derivatives, credit defaults, and swaps from regulatory scrutiny. Thus were born the scams that produced the debacle of Enron, a company on whose board sat Gramm's wife Wendy. She had served on the Commodity Futures Trading Commission from 1983 to 1993 and devised many of the rules coded into law by her husband in 2000.

Somewhat stained by the Enron debacle, Gramm quit the Senate in 2002 and began to enjoy the fruits of his own deregulatory efforts. He became a vice-chairman of the giant Swiss bank UBS's new investment arm in the US, lobbying Congress, the Federal Reserve, and the Treasury Department about banking and mortgage issues in 2005 and 2006, urging Congress to roll back strong state rules trying to crimp the predatory tactics of the subprime mortgage industry. UBS took a bath of about $20 billion in write-offs from bad real-estate loans this year.

Acknowledged for years as one of the most mean-spirited men ever to reach Congress, utterly charmless (he managed to win only eight delegates in a hugely expensive bid for the Republican nomination in 1996), Gramm kept close contacts with the man dubbed McNasty when he was at the Naval College in Annapolis. Aside from their affinities in viciousness of character Gramm had access to big campaign funders in Texas, necessary for McCain's 2008 bid. He became McCain's campaign chairman and chief economic advisor.

Gramm is exhibit A in any list of the architects of the current economic mess. At the behest of the banking industry he wrote the laws that enabled the huge balloons of funny money debt that exploded this year. His deregulatory statutes prompted Wall Street's looting orgy in the subprime thievery.

After Gramm declared that America was suffering merely a "mental recession," and was becoming "a nation of whiners," McCain had to reposition him as an unofficial economic adviser, but he still remains close to the candidate and has even been touted as a possible Treasury Secretary in a McCain administration. If McCain does win and picks someone else for that job, then maybe Gramm'll chair the commission charged with figuring out what went wrong.

October 7

Election Day is officially November 4. A month earlier voters started mailing in their ballots. We can expect the usual uplifting essays, extolling the spectacle of millions of Americans peaceably exercising their democratic rights, so unlike Cuba or North Korea. Unusually early, the real election day in the United States this year fell on October 3, the day the US House of Representatives finally approved the bailout bill already passed by the US Senate two days earlier.

Real elections mostly come after the symbolic Election Day. They are staged, sometimes protracted events, designed to remind voters that no matter what they may have thought they were voting for when they went to the polls, no matter who the victor or what his pledges, reality is in charge. Examples vivid in my memory include the arrival in Britain of a Labour government in the fall of 1964 after thirteen years of Conservative rule. Prime Minister Harold Wilson had a slim majority of five. Hopes were for sweeping change in accord with Labour's socialist program.

The real election then took place, dragging on for a couple of years. Lord Cromer, governor of the Bank of England, told Wilson that there was a financial emergency: the international integrity of the pound sterling was being compromised in their eyes by the all-important international financial community, known colloquially in those days as "the gnomes of Zurich." Cromer advised the Prime Minister that Labour's plans for economic and social reform must be abandoned forthwith. Wilson told Cromer that this was a challenge to democracy. It was, and across the protracted "real election" it succeeded. Labour's bold promises withered. Cromer and the Gnomes carried the day. Britain was set on the course it has held to this day.

The election of Jimmy Carter in 1977 was also a season of hope, that a new era was dawning, particularly in the arena of foreign policy and the cold war. "If, after the inauguration," Carter's campaign manager, Hamilton Jordan, told the press, "you find Cy Vance as Secretary of State and Zbigniew Brzezinski as Head of National Security, then I would say we failed. And I'd quit." Carter wanted George Ball as Secretary of State but in the backstage maneuverings of the real election the Israel lobby vetoed Ball. Carter was forced pick to pick Vance as Secretary of State and the cold war fanatic Brzezinski as national security advisor. Jordan did not quit. Such "non-resignations" are symbolically important because they indicate that the mandate of the real election is recognized and loyally accepted by all.

The real election in Bill Clinton's case took place across three months after his election. After victory at the polls, he swiftly indicated surrender by making Goldman Sachs Robert Rubin his Treasury Secretary. By March he had announced his total submission to the Wall Street banks and the end of any pretense—thin from the get-go—of economic change or social reform. The left opposition inside his cabinet, headed by Labor Secretary Robert Reich, stayed on board.

This year economic crisis demanded an early real election, designed to fend off the admittedly very remote possibility—Robert Rubin is Obama's close economic advisor—that Barack Obama, victorious in the November 4 election, might arrive in power, claim a reformer's mandate, and seek to prize loose the stranglehold of Wall Street financiers on the economy.

In this real election, dissent dwindled rapidly in the press as the Accredited Commentariat, from George Will on the right to Paul Krugman in the center, declared the bailout odious but necessary. The rebellion of the House Republicans was an unexpected bump in the road and they were stigmatized as "irresponsible" along with the ninety-five Democrats who joined them.

Paulson's draft bill was originally three pages long, a terse classic in the annals of coup d'états, seeking to render the bailout safe from the sanction of any elected body or US court. As it passed to the Senate it swelled to over 700 pages, most of them recording bribes to legislators. The Senate—Obama, Biden, and McCain in the vanguard—duly voted Aye.

At this point the last, best weapon of the Real Electioneers sidled onto the stage. On October 2, Rep. Brad Sherman, a California Democrat and opponent of the bailout, stated in the House that "there would be martial law in America if we voted no." By a pleasing coincidence amid these dramatic events, the *Army Times* had reported on September 30 that the 3rd Infantry Division's 1st Brigade Combat Team, lately in Iraq, would be deployed on October 1 on US soil under the day-to-day control of US Army North, the Army service component of Northern Command. This new mission, wrote the *Times*' Gina Cavallaro, marks "the first time an active unit has been given a dedicated assignment to NorthCom."

As the Senate voted, Obama once again affirmed publicly that he accepted the verdict of the real election. He told reporters in Clearwater, Florida, last Wednesday that "issues like bankruptcy reform, which are very important to Democrats, is [*sic*] probably something that we shouldn't try to do in this piece of legislation." In addition, he said that his own proposed economic stimulus program "is not necessarily something that we should have in this package."

But hold! you cry. Obama may enter office with a secret plan. Even FDR campaigned in 1932 for a balanced budget. And anyway, Obama and Biden will have saved us from Sarah Palin, Alaska's answer to

Eva Peron! My friends, Palin is a distraction from the uncomfortable truth. After the October coup, the November ballot is merely a coda.

October 24

Every politician, good or bad, is an ambitious opportunist. But beneath this topsoil, the ones who make a constructive dent on history have some bedrock of consistency, of fidelity to some central idea. In Obama's case, this "idea" is the ultimate distillation of identity politics: the idea of his blackness. Those who claim that if he were white he would be cantering effortlessly into the White House do not understand that without his most salient physical characteristic Obama would be seen as a second-tier Senator with unimpressive credentials.

As a political organizer of his own advancement, Obama is a wonder. But I have yet to identify a single uplifting intention to which he has remained constant if it has presented the slightest risk to his advancement. Summoning all the optimism at my disposal, I suppose we could say he has not yet had occasion to offend two important constituencies and adjust his relatively decent stances on immigration and labor-law reform. Public funding of his campaign? A commitment made becomes a commitment betrayed, just as on warrantless eavesdropping. His campaign treasury is now a vast hog-swallow that, if it had been amassed by a Republican, would be the topic of thunderous liberal complaint.

In substantive terms Obama's run has been the negation of almost every decent progressive principle, a negation achieved with scarcely a bleat of protest from the progressives seeking to hold him to account. The Michael Moores stay silent. Abroad, Obama stands for imperial renaissance. He has groveled before the Israel lobby and pandered to the sourest reflexes of the cold war era. At home he has crooked the knee to bankers and Wall Street, to the oil companies, the coal companies, the nuclear lobby, the big agricultural combines. He is even more popular with Pentagon contractors than McCain, and has been the most popular of the candidates with K Street lobbyists. He has been fearless in offending progressives, constant in appeasing the powerful.

So no, this is not an exciting or liberating moment in America's politics such as was possible after the Bush years. If you want a memento of what could be exciting, I suggest you go to the website of the Nader-Gonzalez campaign and read its platform, particularly on popular participation and initiative. Or read the portions of Libertarian Bob Barr's platform on foreign policy and constitutional rights. The standard these days for what the left finds tolerable is awfully low. The more the left holds its tongue, the lower the standard will go.

October 30

Over the past two months the entire intellectual superstructure of the "conservative revolution" has collapsed, with conclusive and absolute finality, nicely illustrated by the ludicrous invective lobbed by McCain at Obama. A Republican Treasury Secretary from Goldman Sachs bails out the banks and all McCain and the right-wing talk-show hosts can do is howl that the rather conservative and economically right-centrist Obama is a "socialist."

Nervous liberals are perennially terrified that the Brownshirts will soon be marching down Main Street. Now they worry that economic depression will spark to life a right-wing populist counterattack, headed by Sarah Palin who is already cutting herself loose from McCain and setting herself up as the Jeanne d'Arc of Republican Renaissance in the next four years.

On her current form, she's not up to it. She's just not smart enough to get beyond canned one-liners to the rubes. And how much of a constituency will she really have, beyond the born-agains? In the late 1960s Nixon's speechwriters had the easier task of delighting a solidly confident blue-collar constituency, many of them with good union jobs, with their sallies against pointyhead professors, liberal judges, and unwashed hippy scum. That constituency is long gone, along with the jobs.

The best the Republicans can do at the moment is cling to the rigging, and then hope that President Obama will stick to his campaign promises, launch a wider war in Afghanistan and maybe Iran, sacrifice all his domestic pledges on the altar of imperial maintenance overseas, and see his presidency wither and die, just as Lyndon Johnson did.

When the Republicans have pulled themselves together they'll muster up some new demagogue of the right, to run a right-wing populist campaign of the sort Palin has been too dumb to mount. To counter this, what the Democrats should do, but won't, is run a series of show-trial Senate hearings, with power of subpoena, into the economic meltdown. Get the Wall Street villains up there in the public eye, day after day, and feed with torrents of disgusting facts the huge public appetite for retribution.

November 4

The First 100 Days—Looking back over the record since FDR, the pattern is discernible: declare war on something, or at least kill people; or put a woman in the cabinet.

FDR: Day 1, declares war on fear; nominates Frances Perkins to be Secretary of Labor (the best we ever had).

Truman: Day 5, calls for Unconditional Surrender of Axis powers; Day 113, drops A-bomb on Hiroshima.

Eisenhower: Day 23, refuses clemency to the Rosenbergs; Day 72, appoints Oveta Culp Hobby as head of HEW.

JFK: Day 41, announces Peace Corps and thousands of young Americans duly learn to sit cross-legged on the ground, sowing seeds for bankruptcy of Medicare when knee replacements kick in forty years later. Day 88, launches Bay of Pigs attack on Cuba.

LBJ: Day 8, creates a mass employment program known as the Warren Commission. Within hours tens of thousands of Americans are hard at work, challenging the Commission's proceedings and drawing maps of Dealey Plaza.

Nixon: Day 57, launches secret bombing of Cambodia.

Ford: Day 4, declares war on inflation, "public enemy number one."

Carter: Day 2, pardons Vietnam draft resisters; Day 89, announces National Energy Plan, raising domestic coal production to reduce dependency on foreign oil. Yes, President Obama, we have been here before. Better not start talking about "malaise."

Reagan: Day 66, declares war on corruption and inefficiency in government. This is going too far. Four days later Hinckley tries to kill him.

Bush Sr.: Day 38, goes live on Chinese TV; Day 47, bombs Baghdad.

Clinton: Day 3, allows clinics to offer abortion counseling and abortions; Day 6, appoints Hillary head of his Health Reform task force.

Bush Jr.: Day 3, ends funding of national centers offering abortion counseling and abortions; Day 40, declares big tax cuts for the rich.

November 28

Before Thanksgiving I drove down I-26 and then I-95 from Campobello, in the northwest corner of South Carolina, where a friend of mine owns a small trailer park. By the late summer, as local factories started closing, long-term tenants said goodbye and went on the road in search of work. The vacant trailers were soon filled by families walking away from mountains of mortgage debt and foreclosed homes. They live on budgets so tight my friend says that they can just make the $500 monthly rental, but $550 would put them under.

He pointed to one where an older man had just arrived from Michigan, 650 miles north up Interstate 75, heart of the US auto industry and already in economic ruins long before the major auto companies went begging for bailouts in Washington, DC, in the last couple of weeks. States in the industrial heartlands, like Michigan or Ohio, have been reeling for years as the factory owners redeployed to China, but others like New York or California or Washington and Oregon in the Pacific Northwest now face budgetary implosion and cuts in services of up to 25 percent.

This is the first time since I came to America in 1972 that I've heard almost every day of well-off people sounding somewhat distraught at the money they've lost. From this richer crowd one hears daily stories of portfolios worth half or less of their value three and four months ago, of people losing high salary jobs, often only months shy of long-scheduled retirement on full benefits.

Amid the plunge in the nation's economic fortunes, as in any hospital ward, gloom alternates with determined good cheer. Flying across the country last week I could hear snatches of optimism in airport lounges from the TV sets blaring CNN news bulletins. The market "may have hit bottom." The bounce back after the Citibank bailout was "the quickest two-day climb" up the graphs since the recovery from the crash of '87.

Walking down Las Vegas Boulevard, I watched five huge cranes just south of the Bellagio and Caesar's Palace busy servicing an enormous new hotel-casino complex about halfway to completion. The sponsoring party here is MGM Mirage, the owner of Bellagio, New York-New York and MGM Grand and other properties, and the project is the sixty-eight-acre "CityCenter," scheduled to include more than 6,000 condo and hotel rooms, 165,000 square feet of casino space, and its own power plant based around a sixty-story casino and hotel. Its $7.4 billion budget schedules it to be the single most expensive privately funded project ever in the Western Hemisphere. All told, in Las Vegas right now, there are seven major projects budgeted at a total of $23 billion.

It's hard to tell whether these huge gambles are being staked on economic quicksand. The local housing market certainly has been soft. The man at Dollar Car Rental, an Hispanic fellow, said he'd come to Las Vegas because he couldn't afford the $400,000 or so a decent house in Los Angeles would have cost him. The house in Las Vegas he'd just bought had been advertised at $240,000 and he just signed on the dotted line for $165,000. He was happy.

December 2

Growing up in Ireland and Britain, I gazed with envy at the United States, with its constitutional protections and its Bill of Rights, contrasting with the vast ad hoc tapestry of Britain's repressive laws and "emergency" statutes piled up through the centuries, as successive regimes from the Plantagenet and Tudor periods onwards went about the state's business of enforcing the enclosures, hanging or transporting strikers, criminalizing disrespectful speech, and, of course, abolishing the right to carry even something so innocuous as a penknife.

Instructed by centuries of British occupation, my native Ireland, I have to say, took a slightly more relaxed attitude. My father once asked an Irish minister of justice, back in the 1960s, about the prodigious size and detail of the Irish statute book. "Ah, Claud," said the minister equably, "our laws are mainly for guidance."

We are thankfully near the exit door from the Bush years, after enduring appalling assaults on freedom, built on the sound foundation of kindred assaults in Clinton's time—perhaps most memorably expressed in the screams of parents and children fried by US government forces in the Branch Davidian compound in Waco, and in Bill Clinton's flouting of all constitutional "war powers" inhibitions on his executive decision to wage war and order his commanders to rain bombs on the civilian population of the former Yugoslavia.

Bush has forged resolutely along the path, diligently blazed by Clinton, in asserting uninhibited executive power in the ability to wage war, seize, confine, and torture at will, breaching constitutional laws and international treaties and covenants, concerning treatment of combatants. The Patriot Act took bits of the Justice Department's wish list left over from Clinton's Antiterrorism and Effective Death Penalty Act of 1996, which trashed habeas corpus protections.

The outrages perpetrated on habeas corpus have been innumerable, some of them relatively unpublicized. Take the case of people convicted of sexual felonies, such as molestation of children. Convicted and imprisoned, they reach the end of their stipulated terms and then find that they now face continued imprisonment without any specified terminus, under the rubric of "civil confinement," as fierce as any *letter de cachet* in France's *ancien régime.*

Free speech is no longer a right. Stand alongside the route of a presidential cavalcade with a humble protest sign, and the Secret Service or local law enforcement will hale you off to some remote cage, labeled "Designated protest area." Seek to exercise your right to dispense money for a campaign advertisement or to support a candidate, and you will at once fall under the sanction of McCain/Feingold, otherwise known as the Bipartisan Campaign Reform Act of 2002.

In the case of public expressions of protest, we may expect particular diligence by the Secret Service and other agencies in the Obama years; while, perhaps, Obama's reneging on a campaign promise to accept only public financing has stopped campaign finance reform in its tracks. Liberals, joyously eyeing Obama's amazing $150 million haul in his final weeks, have preserved a tactful silence on this topic, after years of squawking about the power of the corporate dollar to pollute democracy's proceedings.

Worse than in the darkest days of the '50s, when Americans could have their passports revoked by fiat of the State Department, citizens and legal residents no longer have the right to travel freely even inside the nation's borders. Appearance on any of the innumerable watch lists maintained by government agencies means inability to get on a plane and probably even Amtrak, whose unmolested passengers already risk being stranded *sine die* in some remote siding in the southwestern deserts for weeks on end.

Americans no longer have the right to vote, even if of appropriate age. The Indiana statute okayed by the Supreme Court requires under Indiana's voter ID law, that persons lacking "proper" ID can only make a provisional vote, with a bureaucratic apparatus of subsequent verification. In some states, anyone carrying a felony conviction faces a lifetime ban on the right to vote.

Fourth Amendment protections have gone steadily downhill. Warrantless wiretappers had a field day, and Congress re-affirmed their activities in the FISA bill, for which Obama voted, in a turn around from previous pledges. Vice-President-elect, Joe Biden, can claim a significant role here since he has been an ardent prosecutor of the war on drugs, used since the Harrison Act of 1914 (and even before then with the variable penalties attaching to opium, as used by middle-class whites or Chinese) to enhance the right of police to enter, terrorize and prosecute at will. Indeed, the war on drugs, revived by President Nixon and pursued vigorously by all subsequent administrations, has been as powerful a rationale for tearing up the Constitution as the ensuing war on terror. It's like that with all wars. Not far from where I live in northern California, the war on drugs was the excuse for serious inroads in the early 1990s into the Posse Comitatus statutory inhibition on use of the US military in domestic law enforcement—another constitutional disaster of the Bush years.

In the past eight years, Bush Jr. has ravaged the Fourth Amendment with steadfast diligence, starting with his insistence that he could issue arrest warrants if there was reason to believe a non-citizen was suspected of implication in terrorist activity. Seized under this pretext and held within America's borders or in some secret prison overseas, the captive had no recourse to a court of law. Simultaneously, the "probable cause" standard, theoretically disciplining the state's innate propensity to search and to seize, has been systematically abused, as has the FBI's delirious use of the "material witness" statute to arrest and hold their suspects. Good-bye, habeas corpus.

Federalism and the rights of states have been relentlessly eroded, often amidst liberal cheers at such excrescences as the No Child Left Behind law. Government's power to seize property under the canons of "eminent domain" received particularly sinister buttress by the US Supreme Court. Have there been any bright patches in the gloom in Bush time? I salute one: the vindication of the Second Amendment in the Supreme Court's majority decision, vigorously written by Justice Scalia. I've no need to tell you what liberals and leftists thought of that one.

Part 3

2009

January 9

Madoffgate is proof of the old rule: the more elegant the tailoring, the more handsomely silvered the distinguished locks, the more innocently rubicund the visage, the more likely the hand covertly fishing for one's wallet.

Uncle Sam is the biggest Ponzi operator of all. Bernie had to constantly replenish his fund with new deposits; so does Uncle Sam, wheedling more money out of the Chinese, the Indians, the Japanese, and poor Third World nations forced to pony up at the point of a gun. But in the end Uncle Sam has one huge asset denied Madoff, who seems to have stopped short of the straightforward forgery allegedly practiced by Marc Dreier, the Manhattan lawyer arrested in Canada for trying to sell nonexistent bonds to the tune of $380 million. Uncle Sam has the printing press to run off the necessary dollars. He's certainly going to need lots of fresh new bills. You can set your clock now for the alarms scheduled to go off all the way through Obama-time: credit card debt, commercial real-estate implosion, option-ARM financing.

Maybe Madoff, trolling for suckers in the Palm Beach Country Club and the Jewish charitable foundations, will become the sacrificial symbol of Wall Street thievery, sent off to the penitentiary in lieu of the real big-timers.

January 23
So many ghosts crowded the inauguration dais that it's not surprising Chief Justice Roberts flubbed his lines and had to be corrected by the man he was swearing in. Over there on the right! That jowly fellow with the five o'clock shadow and the long upsweeping nose. It's Richard Nixon on January 20, 1973. He'd swept every state in the union in November's election, except for Massachusetts and the District of Columbia. Listen to him: "As we meet here today, we stand on the threshold of a new era of peace in the world." Yet American B-52s were still bombing Cambodia, as they had virtually throughout his administration. One and a half years later he resigned, rather than face impeachment.

Why look! Nixon's smiling. He's just heard Obama call for "a new era of responsibility." He's remembering more lines from his second inaugural in '73: "A person can be expected to act responsibly only if he has responsibility. This is human nature. So let us encourage individuals at home and nations abroad to do more for themselves, to decide more for themselves."

Obama offered a mild version of blood-sweat-and-tears. "We understand that greatness is never a given," he said. "It must be earned. Our journey has never been one of short-cuts or settling for less. It has not been the path for the faint-hearted—for those who prefer leisure over work, or seek only the pleasures of riches and fame." I hope we don't get too much sermonizing about seeking the pleasures of riches. The word "responsibility" from those set in authority over us usually means compulsory belt-tightening and onslaughts on Social Security and Medicare, which Obama more or less promised the *Washington Post* five days before the inauguration.

Each time a new President strides forth, flourishing his inaugural menu of change, one feels the same gloom at these quadrennial displays of leader-lust. Eight years of complaining about George Bush's arrogation of unconstitutional powers under the bizarre doctrine of the "unitary executive" and here we have the national audience enthusiastically applauding yet another incoming President rattling off the I-will-do's as though there was no US Congress and he was Augustus Caesar.

The founders, whom Obama invoked in his opening line, produced a Constitution that gives the President, to quote Dana Nelson's useful new book *Bad for Democracy: How the Presidency Undermines the Power of the People*, "only a thin framework of explicit powers that belong solely to his office: for instance, the power to grant reprieve and pardons, and to fill any government vacancies during any Senate recess. His other enumerated powers are either shared … or secretarial and advisory." Enough of the Commander in Chief! All we need is a decent pardoner and a good secretary.

But credit where credit is due. On his second day in the White House Jimmy Carter amnestied Vietnam draft-dodgers and war resisters. On his second day Obama said Guantanamo and the CIA's secret prisons must close within the year and said that his administration will be on the side of those seeking to end government secrecy rather than those wanting to enforce it.

February 1

There's been no exciting surprise or originality in Obama's opening engagements with the reeling economy. His team is flush with economists and bankers who helped blaze the path to ruin. He's been selling his $819 billion stimulus program on the Hill, with all the actors playing their allotted roles and many a cheering Democrat not entirely confident that the House Republicans may not have had a point when, unanimously, they voted "No" on the package

America's economy may be so hollowed out, its industrial base so eroded by twenty years of job exports to China and other low-wage sanctuaries, that a bailout may not turn the tide. Then the Republicans will have their told-you-so's primed and ready to go in the mid-term elections.

But Obama can scarcely be blamed for putting up his $819 billion pump primer. It was a given, from the moment he got elected, and indeed probably owes, both in its good and bad components, more to Rep. Charlie Rangel, chairman of the House Ways and Means Committee, than to Geithner or Summers.

Obama's timid folly comes with the impending two to four trillion dollar bailout package for the banks, signaled by Treasury Secretary Geithner. If anything can make Wall Street smile bravely through the hail of public ridicule for the way it's been handing out the previous wad of bailout money in the form of bonuses, it's the prospect of getting further truckloads of greenbacks to lend out to Americans already crippled by debt. So Wall Street can feel satisfaction that its investment in Obama seems to be paying off.

February 12

I walk into a local plumbing store, a large place used by building contractors. There's one other man in the store, buying a $5 plastic fitting. One of the owners says there's zero new construction in the area. "We fix a few toilets. The only people actually building are the marijuana growers down in southern Humboldt."

Take out Humboldt's good fortune in being in the Emerald Triangle and multiply by every plumbing store in America. Throw in the idled lumber yards, construction stores, paint suppliers, and building crews. Count in the car lots that are going out of business because the banks won't finance car loans. Go to the lost auto assembly jobs. It tots up to a job loss across America, just in December and January, of 1,175,000. And that's an underestimate. Every President since Reagan, particularly Clinton, has jimmied the unemployment criteria to produce an undercount. The actual number for the two months is nearer one and three quarter million. The actual total unemployment rate by pre-Reagan criteria, according to statistician John Williams, rose to 18 percent in January, from 17.5 percent in December.

These are numbers out of the Great Depression of the 1930s, and it's going to get worse as businesses put up their shutters. The air is whistling out of the American economy. My own state of California—often touted as the eighth largest economy in the world—can't pay its bills. There's a shortfall in revenues and it can't sell enough bonds.

On January 26 the California State Controller John Chiang announced that the state is going to print its own money. If the state owes us money we'll get this scrip as IOUs. Who knows, in happier times maybe we can hawk them on eBay. Student aid and payments to the disabled and needy will also come in the form of IOUs. Governor Schwarzenegger and his aides are negotiating with the banks to get them to accept the IOUs as deposits.

March 13

In town after town across America these days one can physically see the economic mantras of an entire generation turning to boarded-up wasteland before one's eyes. Shopping malls, which changed the American landscape within the course of a generation, are dying week by week.

Take the Bayshore Mall in my own town of Eureka, northern California—a covered, pedestrian arcade opened in the 1980s, owned by the Utah-based General Growth company. Located on the edge of Humboldt Bay, though facing the opposite direction towards Highway 101, our mall was an optimistic place in the early days. People dressed up to go there. A friend of mine who opened a coffee stall wore a tie—purchasing it from Ralph Lauren which opened an outlet. Every pretty girl in Humboldt County wanted to work there, to see and to be seen. People drove for three hours through the Yolly Bolly Wilderness all the way from Redding in the Central Valley to savor its glories. There were stylish concerts in its ample food court.

Today the Bayshore Mall molders, embodying the misfortunes of General Growth—the second largest mall owner in the US—whose stock trades now for 55 cents, down from $44 last May. General Growth has now ousted its CEO, John Bucksbaum.

Some major retailers, like Ralph Lauren's Polo, have long since fled from Bayshore Mall. Walk east along one of the arcades and you come to a wall of plywood, behind which lies the desolation that was Mervyn's, a clothing chain which has now filed for bankruptcy. The little stores nearby have a somber mien, like people compelled to live in the chill shadow of a funeral home. The food court, serviced by six or seven fast-food businesses, is becoming a sanctuary for the poor who sit in the warmth with modest snacks and while away the hours.

Across the past forty years some 200 cities built pedestrian malls. Today, only thirty remain. Drive around any town and one can see strip malls in similar decline, their parking lots nearly empty, boarded stores in the retail frontage like a mouth losing its teeth, as the lights of Circuit City go out and Linens n Things, Zales, Ann Taylor, and Sharper Image retrench or collapse entirely.

Out of crisis comes opportunity, one that's been discussed for some years by movements such as the New Urbanists and crusaders for the refashioning of the American urban landscape such as James Howard Kunstler, author of *The Geography of Nowhere*. A mall can be razed to the ground, like the Belle Promenade, on the west bank of the Mississippi in New Orleans. Eureka's too poor a town to do that. But a mall can be refashioned into a more congenial quartier, one blessed with easier parking.

In the same way that coastal cities like Boston finally realized the asset of nineteenth-century quaysides with their warehouses and customs depots, today's failed or failing malls can be reconfigured, converted to mixed use, with residential housing, public spaces and constructive social uses. In the Bayshore even now I see groups of the mentally ill being brought along for an outing in a place that's sheltered, still physically safe, equipped with bathrooms, and has plenty of space with chairs or benches where they can relax.

In many towns one can imagine that energetic councils and resourceful financing could offer the reeling mall operators terms and take the properties off their hands, reconfiguring the malls as social assets. Opportunity is there, to be seized from the jaws of capitalism's shattering reverses. From the malls to the commanding heights of the economy, let the Reconquest begin.

April 20

On March 18 Bill Richardson, governor of New Mexico, had his opportunity to raise the dead and bring them back to life. This was the day he signed a law, already ratified by the state Senate and House, formally ending New Mexico's death penalty. Did Richardson ennoble this solemn occasion by endorsing the idea that all human life has value, and even those who have fallen into the lowest moral abyss are capable of redemption? Did he cite Holy Scripture as buttress for such thoughts? He did not.

Richardson festooned the signing with language about this being the "most difficult decision" of his political life, arrived at only after he had toured the maximum-security unit where offenders sentenced to life without parole would be held. "My conclusion was those cells are something that may be worse than death," he said. "I believe this is a just punishment."

Lest anyone be under the misapprehension that he was endorsing some quaint notion of the value of a life, the governor was at pains to emphasize that since the new law comes into force only on July 1, the two condemned men currently residing on death row in New Mexico still face execution.

For Richardson the flaw with the death penalty lies in its imperfection. "Faced with the reality that our system for imposing the death penalty can never be perfect, my conscience compels me to replace the death penalty with a solution that keeps society safe." Embalmed in this self-serving verbiage are many pointers to how seriously the whole cause of death-penalty abolition has gone off the rails, fleeing the arduous moral battleground where Revenge tilts against Redemption for the low-lying pastures of Efficiency.

New Mexico's lawmakers were bolstered by this rationale of cost-effectiveness. A cost assessment report pointed to the fact that in one case, *State v. Young*, the public defender's office put up $1.7 million to defend Young. Add in costs for the prosecutors and the courts and the bill soared to nearly $6 million. In that instance, the state Supreme Court barred the state from pursuing the death penalty further because insufficient resources were being provided for the defense.

Bill Clinton did his best to speed up the conveyor belt by signing the Antiterrorism and Effective Death Penalty Act of 1996. But it's still a hugely expensive hassle to line things up so lethal injection can proceed. Against all this, what's brisker than the offer of LWOP as part of a plea bargain? Sign on the dotted line. Pack the prisoner off to a concrete box and throw away the key. As the *Dallas Morning News* editorialized in support of LWOP for Texas, which is considering whether to abandon the costly death penalty in favor of confinement unto death: "It's harsh. It's just. And it's final without being irreversible. Call it a living death."

The pendulum is swinging against the death penalty, however. DNA evidence—posthumously exonerating some, clearing others waiting to die—has been a big factor in waning enthusiasm for the ultimate sanction. The current total of defendants on state and federal death rows is 3,307. Fifteen states don't have the death penalty, New Mexico being the most recent.

Nothing much is going to change in New Mexico, except for the worse. The state has only formally executed one man since 1960: Terry Clark, a child-killer, had his appointment with the lethal needle in 2001 after abandoning further appeals. This number may soon swell to three because of the two men whose situation I noted above. Presumably their chances of commutation have diminished, since no one wants to be accused of giving killers anything resembling a lucky break.

When I drive south to the Bay Area, I pass San Quentin, where 667 prisoners sit on death row. In the very unlikely event they get executed, they will have waited an average of 17.5 years from the moment they were condemned. Thirteen people have been executed in California since the US Supreme Court allowed capital punishment to resume in 1976. When I drive from Crescent City, at the northwest corner of California, with its terrifying supermax Pelican Bay prison, down Highway 101, jog over to Redding and head south on Interstate 5 to Los Angeles, I traverse a Gulag Archipelago in which thousands of prisoners are serving decade upon decade of hard time, with hundreds of them in solitary confinement, often for years on end.

How many prisoners nationally are under sentence of "living death"? The Sentencing Project, a nonprofit organization based in Washington, DC, says there were 33,633 people serving life sentences without parole in the United States in 2003, which is 26.3 percent of the total number of people serving life sentences. The analyst at the Sentencing Project discloses that they have tried to determine how many people are effectively serving life sentences without parole (i.e., life plus extra years), but that it's been a nightmare to do so. They don't even have a ballpark estimate. There are at least seventy-three US inmates—most of them from minorities—who were sentenced to spend the rest of their lives in prison for crimes committed when they were thirteen or fourteen.

It was de Tocqueville who lauded American penology, in the book he wrote with Gustave de Beaumont, *On the Penitentiary System*, and who wrote in a letter in 1836: "Isolate the detainees in prison by means of solitary cells, subject them to absolute silence … prohibit every communication between souls and minds as between their bodies; that is what I would consider the first principle of the science [of prisons]." As Professor Sheldon Wolin writes in his *Tocqueville Between Two Worlds*, this was a theory of "total control … 'pure' power and wholly opposite to the unlimited space, frenzied time and near anarchical subjects of Democracy." The prison that de Tocqueville and Beaumont particularly admired was Auburn, with its system of penitential solitary confinement developed by the Quakers, partly advanced as a substitute for the death penalty, which they opposed on principle.

May 8

Shades of Gogol, who was born 200 years ago this year. The motor of his great novel is the economic use of "dead souls"—deceased serfs listed by the state as assets of the landlords. The novel's central character, Chichikov, goes around buying them up. New York State could take Gogol's hint and start auctioning its "living dead" as income generators to other states in need. Looking at our criminal justice system here, Gogol would surely use the line carved on his gravestone: "And I shall laugh my bitter laugh."

May 15

You could say the '60s began, at least in part, in 1884, when Stiles Hall was founded in Berkeley by some high-minded do-good Christian Protestants. This private, nonprofit institution—a YMCA for much of its existence, though no longer—was never formally part of UC Berkeley, but its premises, which shifted about over the decades as the university expanded unrelentingly, have always been right next to the campus. In the '50s, Stiles Hall was where it is today, at Bancroft and Dana.

On March 14, Stiles Hall celebrated its 125th anniversary. The university chancellor was there. So was the mayor of Berkeley. So were a good many veterans of the '50s and '60s, among them Joe Paff, my friend and neighbor here in Petrolia.

In the '40s, returning GIs had changed the UC Berkeley campus dramatically in terms of dress, style, and new kinds of students. Clearly, fraternity draft-dodgers were not about to haze returning soldiers. By the mid-'50s, they were regaining their "piss and vinegar" (to use the words of UC Vice-Chancellor Alex Sheriff) and reached their zenith in the notorious panty raid of 1956.

By 1957, Middle America was resurging with khaki buckle-in-the-back pants and button-down collar and Oxford cloth. It was, Joe recalls, pretty much a uniform. Compulsory ROTC required males to drill in uniform once a week; fraternity boys at the entrance to campus enforced conformity; the student body elections were considered jokes ("if elected, I will launch Sather Gate into space to compete with sputnik"). Faculty who had opposed the loyalty oath had been purged.

In this climate of conformism, conservatism, and William Whyte's "Organization Man," the campus had decided that students should not talk about "off campus issues" and should be protected from "outside agitators." Hence, Stiles Hall provided a meeting space for a wide variety of groups—socialists, libertarians, single-issue groups, farm workers, African studies, ACLU, SNCC support, student CORE, and so forth.

Stiles Hall had been greatly shaped by the long-term influence of Harry Kingman—who had first worked there in 1916, leaving to fight in World War I, and in its aftermath spending six years in China. In China, Harry was a friend and teacher of some of the students arrested in the famous demonstrations at the international settlement over foreign companies exploiting (and shooting) workers.

He wrote a letter defending the students that was translated and published throughout China, leading to his transfer from Shanghai to Tienstin.

While a pariah to the Westerners in China, he was quite famous with the Chinese. His "China Newsletter" of 1925 and 1926 was circulated worldwide, and letters of praise and requests for more information came from Senator Borah (the Idaho Republican and Senate chair of the Foreign Relations Committee), Mahatma Gandhi, Ramsay MacDonald, H. G. Wells, Lloyd George, and Bertrand Russell. At Tienstin, he met and became friend of then Lt. Col George Marshall.

Kingman finally returned to Stiles Hall in 1928. In the early 1930s, he made it his business to extend a welcoming and helpful hand to the 2,000 new students, many of them poor. All of them were invited to dinner by Stiles people, with Harry's wife, Ruth, cooking dinners for 500. Then Kingman looked around the area for jobs for them, and found just twenty-five available.

A student came to him and said his father had been able to give him $3 for the entire semester, and after six weeks he'd already spent $1.50. This is when Harry organized the housing co-ops, where the students could live and cook. Clark Kerr and Robert McNamara were among those students. Stiles also provided a meeting place for the Social Problems Club—accused by the campus administration of being a haunt of New Yorkers and Communists. Kingman also was active in creating a student minimum wage for employment.

These commitments to the First Amendment, equal housing, and fair and equal wages became permanent principles. During the war, Stiles and Harry Kingman were active and strong opponents of the internment of Japanese—not a common posture on the left, alas—and raised money to help the internees, make legal challenges, and help to relocate released people. Older Japanese men in Joe's era in the late 1950s used to come in and hail Kingman—who retired in 1957—as a great man.

Kingman had to stand up to the Un-American Activities Committee, who were witch-hunting leftists. He fought back triumphantly. In 1946, when Harry was director of the Western Region of the Fair Employment Practices Committee, Ed Rutledge, whom he'd hired, had been called before one of the McCarthy committees. Kingman flew to Washington, stiffened Rutledge's resolve, and turned the tide. "We're going to fight this," he said, and they did.

Kingman retired from Stiles Hall in 1957 and went to Washington to form the Citizens Lobby for Freedom and Fair Play. He and his wife lobbied for thirteen years—never raising more than $5,000 dollars to support this effort—living in one room and entertaining guests with food on paper plates.

An interesting Harry anecdote: when Joe McCarthy died, the flags were flying at half-staff. As Harry walked the streets of Washington, DC, he reached the Supreme Court and saw that above the Court there was no half-staff flag. Harry found Earl Warren to go to lunch and asked about it. A sly smile was the response.

Joe Paff went to Berkeley in 1957, then took eighteen months off to avoid ROTC, came back to Berkeley from Europe and got an apartment in Stiles Hall, with duties that included opening and shutting the building and setting out chairs for meetings, a duty that often required nice judgment. One would not, for example, embarrass the score or so turning up for the Berkeley-Bulgaria Friendship Society by setting out 200 chairs. Sometimes, no one would show up. Norman Thomas drew ten people, and Joe took him out and bought him a piece of pie by way of consolation.

By 1960, Joe was on the student council, running a weekly coffee hour with a speaker: "I invited Dizzy Gillespie twice, Ralph Gleeson, Jean Renoir, the movie director who'd been sitting in his office with nothing to do. His son taught at Cal. I invited Linus Pauling and Martin Luther King Jr. I asked Mrs. Sobel when her husband Morton was in prison as a spy. Anti-communists came and made her cry. Young Caspar Weinberger running for state assembly drew no one to the meeting, so we went and had lunch. John X came from the Open Temple, the first time any Black Muslim spoke in the Bay Area."

Joe invited Gus Hall, general secretary of the CPUSA, and Eric Hoffer. He got into trouble when he invited Vincent Hallinan to discuss the Gary Powers trial, which Vincent had attended in Moscow. Sheldon Wolin had given a lecture on Richard Hooker "coveting eccentricity." A student who'd attended Wolin's lecture accused

Joe of "coveting eccentricity" by inviting Hallinan, and the majority agreed with him.

Malcolm X was supposed to speak on campus in May of 1961, Joe reminisces, "but the University high command rejected him, saying he was a minister who might convert people to Islam. So Stiles Hall offered him a venue at the last minute, with no time for publicity and room for only 160. It was electric, the most extraordinary speaker I have ever heard. He changed everyone's life forever. You'd ask him a question, he'd look you in eye and repeat your question, then really go into it. Pretty soon people got scared of asking dumb questions. All blacks sat together and not one of them acknowledged you when they left. Within a month, half the blacks were giving Malcolm's speech."

The 1960s rolled into motion. Stiles had long had a concept of incubating groups and activities that could soon stand alone and form independent groups. Berkeley's residential co-ops were a good example. Student activists soon followed the same policy. Fired by the gatherings in Stiles Hall, campus meetings became more politically conscious, more boisterous. Protests against bans on collecting money became more vigorous. It was not long before the Free Speech Movement was under way.

Many Stiles members became active in the civil rights movement—going to Mississippi, getting arrested, beaten. Many had been hosed off the steps of the San Francisco City Hall as the House Un-American Activities Committee held hearings. Thelton Henderson went south for the Justice Department—he was the first African American in the Civil Rights division—for two years until he was fired for loaning his car to Martin Luther King Jr. to drive to Selma. Henderson has remained all these years on the Stiles Board and was honored at the 125th anniversary.

At seventy-six, Henderson is senior judge in the federal Northern California division. It was Henderson who, in 2005, found that substandard medical care in the California prison system had violated prisoners' rights. In 2006, he appointed Robert Sillen as receiver to take over the health-care system of the California Department of Corrections and Rehabilitation; he replaced Sillen with J. Clark

Kelso in 2008. The Internal Affairs Division of the Oakland Police Department remains under his supervision.

"One could say that going to lunch at Stiles from 1957 to 1963," Joe concludes, "and going to the events, if combined with going to Pauline Kael's little movie theater and reading her extensive program notes, was a complete education. A carefully chosen small set of classes at UC would do the rest."

In June of 1965, the California Senate Fact-Finding Subcommittee on Un-American Activities released its *Thirteenth Report*. Chairman Hugh Burns was also the President pro tempore of the state Senate. In the section on "Communists on the Campus," it excoriated President Kerr and the regents for removing the Speaker Ban.

> [After] Albert J. Lima ... came the deluge. In came Malcolm X, William Buckley Jr., Mark Lane, Dr. Fred Schwartz—an endless procession of political candidates, folk-singers, and an incredible procession of controversial figures ranging from the extreme right to the extreme left, with heavy emphasis, in our view, on the left. The students no longer had to walk across the street to Stiles Hall, the YMCA facility where Communist speakers had been holding forth for years, because the university was now bringing the Communists to the campus ...
>
> It is difficult for us to understand how a disciplined Communist who addresses a crowd of students for thirty minutes can actually teach them anything worthwhile about Communism. Certainly not anything they could not learn much better from the thousands of books on the subject in the university library. The Communist is obviously there to indoctrinate and recruit, so he benefits. But the student, presumably there to learn, gains nothing except a satisfaction of his morbid curiosity and thirty minutes of entertainment.
>
> If, as a result of several years of exposing students to the propaganda emitted by Communist lecturers, one student is drawn into the Communist conspiracy against his own country, who is really to blame? We conclude it must be the persons who are charged with the high responsibility of caring for and teaching the students entrusted to them. The Communist speaker is clad with the reflected prestige of the university where he is a guest; and we are unable to understand why the people should contribute to their own destruction by making their public institutions available to those who are dedicated to the task of overthrowing our government by any means available ... It is our considered view that

to throw wide the portals to any controversial speaker, who wishes to utilize the opportunity to harangue a college audience, is to put curiosity and entertainment above the educational process, and to appeal to the morbid and emotional rather than to the scholarly and the intellectual.

May 22

How long does it take a mild-mannered, anti-war, black professor of constitutional law, trained as a community organizer on the South Side of Chicago, to become an enthusiastic sponsor of targeted assassinations, "decapitation" strategies, and remote-control bombing of mud houses on the far end of the globe?

Obama campaigned on a pledge to "decapitate" al-Qaida, meaning the assassination of its leaders. It was his short-hand way of advertising that he had the right stuff. And, like Kennedy, he's summoning the exponents of unconventional, short-cut paths to success in that mission. Lt. Gen. Stanley A. McChrystal now replaces General David McKiernan as Commander of US Forces in Afghanistan.

McChrystal's expertise is precisely in assassination and "decapitation." As commander of the military's Joint Special Operations Command (JSOC) for nearly five years starting in 2003, McChrystal was in charge of death squad ops, with its best advertised success being the killing of Abu Musab al-Zarqawi, head of al-Qaida in Iraq. McChrystal, not coincidentally, was involved in the prisoner abuse scandal at Baghdad's Camp Nama. (He also played a sordid role in the cover-up of the friendly fire death of ex-NFL star and Army Ranger Pat Tillman.)

Whatever the technique, a second certainty is the killing of large numbers of civilians in the final "targeted assassination." At one point in the first war on Saddam in the early 1990s, a huge component of US air sorties was devoted each day to bombing places where US intelligence had concluded Saddam might be hiding. Time after time, after the mangled bodies of men, women, and children had been scrutinized, came the crestfallen tidings that Saddam was not among them.

The logic of targeted assassinations was on display in Gaza even as Obama worked on the uplifting phrases of his Inaugural Address.

The Israelis claimed they were targeting only Hamas even as the body counts of women and children methodically refuted these claims and finally extorted from Obama a terse phrase of regret.

It didn't take long. But it's what we've got—for the rest of Obama-time.

May 24

Go to any Tea Party rally and three quite different political components are in evidence. There are the libertarian populists, chaotic in philosophy, strong on the right to bear arms, hostile to all forms of taxation, bankers, and big business. There are the social conservatives massed behind Sarah Palin. And, lurking nervously behind the speaker's rostrum, there are the Republican politicos like former Texas Representative Dick Armey, hoping to harness the Tea Party to the chariots of the Republican Party establishment.

The politicos have now learned with acute dismay that many Tea Party members, particularly the libertarian populists, regard the Republican leadership as a significant part of the problem. Following Rand Paul's shattering upset in Kentucky, one member wrote on his blog, in an idiom which accurately catches the *echt*, slightly nutty Tea Party flavor: "There are now two forces in America—not Democrats and Republicans, but a patriotic pro-American anti-Wall Street faction which cuts across both parties, and a traitor faction that supports the financial parasites, a pro-British column in the US, which also cuts across the two parties."

Scroll through the political positions Paul took in the primary and one can see at once that the Tea Party is firmly lodged in a political lineage in Republicanism that has been muted for decade after decade since Barry Goldwater was crushed in his presidential bid against Lyndon Johnson in 1964. Its ancestry goes back to the Isolationists who fought vainly to keep America out of both World Wars and who saw the American Empire as a betrayal of the Republic's historical destiny.

This brings us to another powerful strain in the genetic coding of the Tea Party as a right-wing populist movement—a strong racist antipathy to blacks and browns, symbolized most vividly for them by Barack Obama, whom many Tea Partiers believe was born in either Kenya or Indonesia and therefore has no right to be lodged in the White House, however many votes he won in 2008.

Kentuckians displayed no particular interest in Paul's deprecation of those bits of the Civil Rights Act forbidding private businesses to put "whites only" notices on their premises. But at the national level it was a different story. Twenty-four hours after his victory, Paul was on national television, carefully explaining to the very liberal Rachel Maddow of MSNBC that while he abhors racism, he does indeed think private businesses have every right to pick and chose the customers they want.

America is a discontented place. Unemployment remains high. Liberals are disappointed in Obama but lack any of the fire that the Tea Partiers have in their bellies. The established parties are widely despised, as is "big government." Rand Paul's victory is the augury of a turbulent time. The demands for "change" are far greater than Obama and the Democratic and Republican leadership ever bargained for.

June 5

As they drafted his speech to the Muslim world, delivered in Cairo on Thursday, President Obama's speech writers strove to suggest that cordiality towards Islam is soundly embedded in America's cultural history. The first Muslim congressman, Obama confided to his vast audience across the Muslim world, was sworn into the House of Representatives with his hand on Thomas Jefferson's copy of the Koran.

Obama reminded the world that Morocco had been the first nation to recognize the infant United States, signing the Treaty of Tripoli in 1796, which declared in its preamble that the United States had no quarrel with the Muslim religion and was in no sense a Christian country. The second US President, John Adams, said that America had no quarrel with Islam. As my father Claud said, Never believe anything till it is officially denied. Adams and Jefferson both saw it as a vital matter of national security to settle accounts with the Muslim world, as represented by the Barbary states.

America needed free access to the Mediterranean and the Barbary "pirates" controlled the sea lanes, and, furthermore, supposedly had some Christian slaves, all no doubt using the opportunity of captivity to imbibe the first principles of algebra, whose invention Obama took the opportunity in Cairo correctly to lay at the feet of the mathematicians of Islam, though ancient India deserves some credit too. He also credited Islam with the invention of printing and navigation, which should surely require the Chinese People's Republic to withdraw its ambassador in Washington, DC, in formal diplomatic protest.

An early version of the "Star-Spangled Banner" by Francis Scott Key, written in 1805 amid the routing of the Barbary states, offered a view of Islam markedly different from Obama's uplifting sentiments in Cairo:

> In conflict resistless each toil they endur'd,
> Till their foes shrunk dismay'd from the war's desolation:
> And pale beamed the Crescent, its splendor obscur'd
> By the light of the star-bangled flag of our nation.
> Where each flaming star gleamed a meteor of war,
> And the turban'd head bowed to the terrible glare.
> Then mixt with the olive the laurel shall wave
> And form a bright wreath for the brow of the brave.

In 1814 Key rehabbed this doggerel into the "Star-Spangled Banner." So America's national anthem began as a gleeful tirade against the Mohammedans. And of course every member of the US Marine Corps regularly bellows out the USMC anthem, beginning "From the halls of Montezuma to the shores of Tripoli."

In short, America's march to Empire was minted in the crucible of anti-Islamic sentiment.

June 12

I came to America in 1972 to the *Village Voice*, which Dan Wolf, Ed Fancher, and Norman Mailer founded in 1955 to bring light to those whole sectors of civic life kept in darkness by the major newspapers of the day, starting with the *New York Times*. As a tot I'd been given bracing tutorials about the paradigms of journalism and class power by my father, Claud, who'd founded his newsletter the *Week* in the 1930s as a counterbalance to the awful mainstream coverage in those years. From Europe, I'd already been writing for Kopkind and Ridgeway's *Hard Times* and also for *Ramparts*, respectively a newsletter and a monthly founded—like much of the old underground press—to compensate for the ghastly mainstream coverage of the upheavals of the '60s and the Vietnam War.

In other words, any exacting assessment of the actual performance of newspapers rated against the twaddle about the role of the Fourth Estate spouted by publishers and editors at their annual conventions would issue a negative verdict in every era. Of course there have been moments when a newspaper or a reporter could make fair claims to have done a decent job, inevitably eradicated by a panicky proprietor, a change in ownership, advertiser pressure, eviction of some protective editor, or summary firing of the enterprising reporter. By and large, down the decades, the mainstream newspapers have—often rabidly—obstructed and sabotaged efforts to improve our social and political condition.

In an earlier time writers like Mencken and Hecht and Liebling loved their newspapers, but the portentous claims for their indispensable role would have made them hoot with derision, as they did the columnist Bernard Levin, decrying in the London *Times* at the start of the 1980s the notion of a "responsible press": "we are, and must remain, vagabonds and outlaws, for only by so remaining shall we be able to keep the faith by which we live, which is the pursuit of knowledge that others would like unpursued and the making of comment that others would prefer unmade."

But of course most publishers and journalists are not vagabonds and outlaws, any more than are the professors at journalism schools or the jurors and "boards" servicing the racket known as the Pulitzer industry. What the publishers were after was a 20 percent rate of return, a desire that prompts great respect for "the rule of law," if such laws assist in the achievement of that goal. In 1970 this meant coercing Congress to pass the Newspaper Preservation Act of 1970, exempting newspapers from antitrust sanctions against price-fixing in a given market. Nixon signed the law and was duly rewarded with profuse editorial endorsements in 1972.

South of me in Mendocino County, California, is the *Anderson Valley Advertiser*, a weekly edited by my friend Bruce Anderson. I've written a column for it for over twenty years. The AVA does everything a newspaper should do. It covers the county board of supervisors, the court system, the cops, water issues, the marijuana industry. It's fun to read and reminds people of what a real newspaper should be, which is why half its circulation is outside the county, often the other end of the United States. The AVA lives resolutely up to the injunction by Joseph Pulitzer it carries on its masthead, "A newspaper should have no friends."

I asked Bruce about proposed bailouts of the mainstream press: "Do you like these bailout ideas?" "No I don't. I don't even want them to rest in peace. I want them to twist and turn in their graves eternally. Why? They don't do any local reporting and haven't for about twenty-five years. I'm talking here about the Santa Rosa *Press Democrat*, owned by the New York Times Company, and the *San Francisco Chronicle*."

Does this remind you of a paper near you? Weep not for yesterday's papers, for the old Fourth Estate. At every critical hour, in every decade, it failed us. And yet they do weep. It's like the dogs in Konrad Lorenz's book running up and down either side of the fence, barking at each other. One day they take the fence down and after a moment's bewilderment the dogs continue as before. The other night I watched Bill Ayers at some bookstore being filmed by C-SPAN. He was asked what he thought about the press. Ha! I said to myself, here's a fine opportunity for the Terrorist Ayers to throw some bombs, hail the rise of the internet. Come on, Bill, greet the new day. But no, Ayers said that he liked to settle down at the breakfast table with the *New York Times* and the *Nation* and have his daily little bicker with them.

Bark, bark, bark. It adds up to what Mark Ames just referred in an email to me as that "inexplicable cowardice that everyone here in print is infected with. Jesus, they don't even shoot or club people here like they do in Russia [where Ames founded the splendid *Exile*] and still they exercise more freedom, take more risks there in print than they do here."

Comrade Ayers, that's not your lifelong partner the *New York Times* on the other side of the fence; that's the graveyard. So much for the so-called left. Without the *New York Times*, the Federal Reserve, the public school system, the fundamentalists, and the IRS to yap at, they'd be lost.

In the David v. Goliath struggle of the left pamphleteers battling the vast print combines of the news barons the tide has turned. On a laptop's twelve-inch screen we stand as high as Punch Sulzberger, or Rupert Murdoch. Twenty years ago the *Los Angeles Times* was a mighty power. The owners of the Knight Ridder chain complacently counted on a 20 percent-plus rate of return on their properties.

Today the *LA Times* totters from one cost-cut and forced employee retirement to the next. Knight Ridder's papers of high reputation went on the auction block. Will the broadsheets and tabloids vanish entirely? Not in the foreseeable future, any more than trains disappeared at the end of the railway age. A mature industry will yield income and attract investors interested in money or power long after its glory days are over. But it's a world in decline, and a propaganda system in decline.

The left is so used to being underdogged that it is often incapable of looking a gift horse, meaning a dead horse, in the mouth and greeting good fortune when it knocks on the door. Thirty years ago, to find out what was happening in Gaza, you would have to have had a decent short-wave radio, a fax machine, or access to those great newsstands in Times Square and North Hollywood that carried the world's press. Not anymore. We can get a news story from a CounterPuncher in Gaza or Ramallah or Oaxaca or Vidharba and have it out to a world audience in a matter of hours.

June 19

I have taken the first necessary step in my own quest for the White House by becoming a citizen of the United States at approximately 10 a.m., Pacific time, last Wednesday, June 17, in the Paramount Theater in Oakland, California.

To my immediate left in the vast and splendid deco theater was a Moroccan, to my right a Salvadoran, and around us 956 other candidates for citizenship from ninety-eight countries, each holding a small specimen of the flag that was about to become our standard. All of us had sworn early that day that since our final, successful interview with immigration officials we had not become prostitutes or members of the Communist Party. Inductees to US nationhood were downstairs; relatives and friends were up in the balcony, including CounterPuncher and friend Scott Handleman, attorney at law. I was determined to start out on the right path. What is more American than to have a lawyer nearby?

Master of ceremonies was US Citizenship and Immigration Service agent Randy Ricks. The amiable Ricks actually conducted my final interview in USCIS's San Francisco HQ. At the Paramount he pulled off the rather showy feat of making short welcoming speeches to the cheerful throng in French, Spanish, Chinese, Tagalog, Russian, and I think Hindi. After various preliminaries, including uplifting videos about Ellis Island that tactfully omitted the darker moments in the island's past, Ricks issued instructions. Each time, starting with Afghanistan, he announced a country, the cohort from that nation stood up and it was easy to see that China, India, the Philippines, and Salvador were very strongly represented.

A handful of Zambians brought us to the end of the roster and we were all on our feet. We raised our right hands and collectively swore that we "absolutely and entirely renounce and abjure all allegiance and fidelity to any foreign prince, potentate, state, or sovereignty" and that that we would "bear arms on behalf of the United States," or perform "work of national importance under civilian direction when required by the law." The phrase rang a bell. During World War II in Britain, so my mother Patricia would recall from time to time, cats patrolling warehouses where food was stored would get extra rations for performing work of national importance.

Minutes later I was outside on the sidewalk, registering to vote, albeit declining to state which party I would favor.

My own path to citizenship began with a green card in 1973, allowing me to work for the *Village Voice* in New York and to be a legal resident. The man who helped me get that card was Ed Koch, at that time a supposedly liberal US congressman living, then as now, in Greenwich Village. A few years later, in 1977, he ran for mayor of New York City and I wrote about him harshly.

Koch was heavily backed by Rupert Murdoch and the *New York Post*, running on a law and order platform. Ed was always a petty man, and this trait was well displayed the night he won. A PBS interviewer asked him what his "worst moment" in the race had been and he promptly said in his trademark squeaky whine, "the attack by ALEXANDER COCKBURN in the *Voice* … To think I got him his green card!" In that race there had been slurs a lot nastier than any I made. If you walked around Queens in that campaign you'd see "Vote for Cuomo, not the homo," scrawled on plenty of walls.

There were others with thin skins. In my *Voice* column I made fun of a *New Yorker* writer, a woman dispensing lethal does of tedium on an almost weekly basis. I didn't know that her lover was a New Jersey congressman powerful on the Immigration and Naturalization subcommittee. Within days I was the object of a probe by the INS. That New Jersey congressman could have pressured the INS to put me on the watch list, meaning the next time I returned to the US I could have found the door slammed in my face.

In the mid-1980s a nutball colonel called Oliver North, working in the White House for Ronald Reagan, began to re-activate a national system of prison camps for lefties from a blueprint that had sat in government filing cabinets ever since the Palmer raids in the Red Scare following World War I. Dick Cheney most certainly dusted it off after 2001. On North's plan, as with Cheney's, it was safe to assume that potentially troublesome legal residents would have been locked up, then kicked out.

These are negative reasons, of the sort that guided me in earlier years to elect to be Irish when I got my first passport. I had the choice between the UK and Eire, as it was then called. I was pondering this when our school radios announced in 1956 that the RAF had bombed Ismailia as a first blow in the Suez invasion. The lads in our Patchell's house room in Glenalmond rose to their feet cheering. My sympathies were with the Egyptians. I remained seated and listened to a heated debate as to whether I should be tried and hanged as a traitor.

Plenty of my schoolfellows in this Scotch school had fathers serving in the British armed forces and the mood in Patchell's was very ugly. Looking at the choleric supporters of the Union Jack it seemed better to be Irish. My brothers Andrew and Patrick made the same decision about Irish citizenship a few years later. Patrick was vindicated in 2005 when Shia fighters at a road block in southern Iraq asked to look at his papers and when they saw his passport was Irish let him pass. Patrick reckons that if he had been carrying a UK passport they would have shot him on the spot.

So much for the negative reasons. But I have plenty of positive thoughts about America and am very happy to be stepping aboard a sinking ship. After three and a half decades, why be a non-voting (albeit tax-paying) visitor, particularly if you've been dispensing measured counsel for many years on how the country should be run? I've lived in every quadrant of the United States and driven across it maybe forty times—not hard when you live in the west and buy old cars from a friend in the southeast. I know the place as well if not better than many.

August 19

LIFE'S TOO SHORT …

Dear Editor,
I have been enjoying the AVA for the past year and deeply appreciate the good writing of yourself and your staffers. I probably disagree as least as much as I agree but it's intellectually stimulating in any case.

On Alex's latest on the way overpublicized Gates saga I just have to laugh. He gives white America another pompous lecture on our racism but the nearest group of blacks to him is at the supermax prison at Pelican Bay. Since Gates's verbal abuse of the officer is on tape it really doesn't matter what Alex believes. He didn't believe that the Soviets killed tens of millions and Mao even more but these facts are well documented by R. J. Rumnel and other historians. Alex didn't believe the stories of Castro's torturers but of course all the Pinochet atrocity tales are solid gold. Whew!

Then Alex drags out local "talent" Ismael [*sic*] Reed as the objective authority on Uncle Toms. I guess the black officer present at the Gates arrest is a Tom too because he supported the arrest.

I love it when Alex refers to an Oakland cop shooting a black man as if blacks don't shoot other blacks and sometimes whites far more often than the very occasional police shooting. But Alex has a schizoid side to him because he endorses libertarian books like Robert Higgs's *Against Leviathan* which explicitly attacks all legislation of the New Deal–Great Society era including government laws outlawing non-governmental discrimination. Maybe he can't make up his mind whether he wants to be a libertarian or Stalinist when he grows up. Sort of like poor Lyndon LaRouche, who couldn't decide whether he was a Communist or National Socialist. He now labels himself a FDR New Deal Democrat which combines both above concepts.

I think the real reason for Cockburn's transparent blackophilism is to make up for being widely hated in US Jewish circles, a venomous hatred that matches what Ismael Reed and white feminists feel for each other. As a frontier Tennessee housewife said while watching a brawl, "Go husband, go bear!"

On the recent school teacher case I agree that the guy reads like a real pervert but I don't agree with any prison sentence unless it was actually rape. In more rational places like Ontario the legal age of consent is fourteen. There's something deeply sick about America as it has always related to sex. Goes back to our fundamentalist communist Puritan heritage and the fact that we have the largest group of Christ-Cult nuts in the Western world. We are split between the good Athenian part of our intellectual heritage and the bad

Jerusalem part. As Nietzsche said, Christianity is the Jews' revenge on the Gentiles.

Well I've been living here since 1973 and the only good public policy I've seen here in that time is Prop 13. We still pay way too much taxes but if we were in some rathole like New Jersey it would be triple.

Best Regards,
Mike Hardesty, Oakland

Alexander Cockburn replies: Among the Rules for Life to which I cling is a commitment not to read anything to which the name Hardesty is appended. I concluded long ago that reading his unique brand of ignorant venom was a worthless and degrading activity.

October 14

Of the four US Presidents who have been given a Nobel Prize—Teddy Roosevelt, Woodrow Wilson, Jimmy Carter, and Barack Obama—the one who's shown the cleanest pair of heels when it comes to escaping the world's guffaws for the absurdity of the award is Jimmy Carter.

It's easy to throw mud at TR. The excuse for his prize, awarded in 1906, was his role in ending the Russo-Japanese War. But what the committee of those worthy Norwegians was actually saying was that when it comes to giving a US President the peace prize, the bar has to be set awfully low. After all, TR was fresh from sponsorship of the Spanish-American War and ardent bloodletting in the Philippines.

He accepted the prize not long after he'd displayed his boundless compassion for humanity by sponsoring an exhibition of Filipino "monkey men" in the 1904 St. Louis World's Fair as "the missing link" in the evolution of man from ape to Aryan, and thus in sore need of assimilation, forcible if necessary, to the American way. On receipt of the prize, Roosevelt promptly began planning the dispatch of the Great White Fleet (sixteen Navy battleships of the Atlantic Fleet) on a worldwide tour to display Uncle Sam's imperial credentials.

Wilson, the liberal imperialist with whom Obama bears some marked affinities, won the Nobel Peace Prize for 1919. The rationale was his effort to establish the League of Nations. His substantive achievement was to have brought America into the carnage of World War I and to have refined the language and ideology of liberal interventionism. Between TR and Wilson, it's hard to say who was the more fervent racist. Probably Wilson. As governor of New Jersey he was a fanatical proponent of the confinement and sterilization of "imbeciles," a eugenic crusade that culminated in the US Immigration Act of 1924, which barred Jews and other suspect genetic material from entering the United States. Much against their will, many of these excluded Jews made their way to Palestine. Others involuntarily stayed in place in Russia and Eastern Europe and were murdered by the Nazis. Above all, Wilson at Versailles was the sponsor of ethnic nationalism, the motive force for the Final Solution. And they say Obama's award has brought the Peace Prize into disrepute!

Carter got his prize in 2002 as reward for conspicuous good works. But there again, the message of the Nobel committee was—Take the rough with the smooth. It was Carter, after all, who amped up the new cold war, got Argentinian torturers to train the Contras, and above all dragged the United States into Afghanistan. It was in 1978 that a progressive secular government seized power in Afghanistan, decreeing universal education for women and banning child marriage. By early 1979 Carter was hatching plans with Pakistan, Saudi Arabia, and China to arm mujahedeen and warlords in Afghanistan to overthrow the government and attempt to lure the Soviet Union into combat. In December 1979, after repeated requests from the government in Afghanistan, the Soviet Union sent forces to fight against the rebellion by the fundamentalists. The CIA launched the most expensive operation in its history to train and equip these fundamentalists and allied warlords.

The Nobel Peace Prize committee loves paradox, which is why I tend to believe that it toyed with the idea of giving Hitler the award in 1939, before the Führer's sponsor withdrew the name. But it remained adamant about denying the prize to another nominee in 1939—Mahatma Gandhi—as it had done in 1937 and 1938, and would again in 1947 and 1948. When it came to the man Churchill described as a "half-naked fakir," the committee lost the forgiving appreciation of realpolitik it had evinced in the cases of men like Roosevelt and Wilson and became inflexibly high-minded. Jacob Worm-Müller, a Norwegian history professor who wrote a briefing memo for the committee, remarked censoriously that Gandhi "is frequently a Christ, but then, suddenly, an ordinary politician." Year after year the committee found reasons to reject him.

The chairman of this year's committee, a ductile social democrat called Thorbjørn Jagland, was refreshingly frank about the selection of Obama. They could not, year after year, simply honor peace workers without marquee appeal. He didn't mention it, but last year's recipient, Martti Ahtisaari, the former Finnish President, drew a collective world yawn except among those fuming at his disgusting record as a broker in the dismemberment of the former Yugoslavia. So they decided to shop for the headlines.

People marvel at the idiocy of these Nobel awards, but there's method in the madness, since in the end they train people to accept without demur or protest absurdity as part and parcel of the human condition, which they should accept as representing the considered opinion of rational men. It's a twist on the Alger myth, inspiring to youth: you too can get to murder Filipinos, or Palestinians, or Vietnamese, or Afghans and still win a Peace Prize. That's the audacity of hope at full stretch.

So one shouldn't take these prizes too seriously but simply cheer when a prize committee somewhere does the right thing. What do Paul Robeson, Bertolt Brecht, and Pablo Neruda all have in common? They won the International Stalin Prize for Strengthening Peace Among Peoples, which was in business from 1950 to 1955. Then it became the International Lenin Prize, honoring many estimable toilers for human betterment, such as W.E.B. Du Bois, Salvador Allende, Sean MacBride, and Angela Davis. Read that list and you rapidly get a fix on the outer limits of the Nobel committee's range of political sympathy. Obama's award was a gift dispensed from the battlements of capital, recognizing that empire is in a safe pair of hands.

October 17

The transition from the Tennessee chunk of Interstate 40 to the Arkansas section always makes me laugh. On I-40 you start in Wilmington, NC, and ahead of you lie 2,555.4 miles of road, running through eight states, all the way to Barstow, California. Through Tennessee you roll for a day and half on smooth tarmac, often three lanes each way—tribute to the state's wealth and the patronage powers of Senator Albert Gore Sr., father of the portly Warmist.

It was Gore Sr., along with a crafty Irish Rep. from Maryland called George Fallon, who was responsible for the bill enabling the financing of the Interstate system, appropriating $25 billion in 1956, sucking in a generous whack of the money for his own state, already engorged with federal pork for the Oakridge nuclear complex and the TVA. In honor of these achievements all Interstates entering Tennessee are labeled the "Albert Gore, Sr. Memorial Highway." It's no doubt why, out of forlorn hopes for emulation, Al Jr. preposterously claimed he'd invented the internet. The unimpressed citizens of Tennessee duly doomed Al Jr.'s presidential bid by voting for George Bush in 2000.

I rolled through Memphis, battleground for a very significant victory for We the People. The blueprint for I-40 had the Interstate slicing through Overton Park on the east side of town. There's an old-growth arboretum here, also the famous band shell, one of twenty-seven built by the WPA in the 1930s. Elvis Presley gave his first paid concert there, opening for Slim Whitman on July 30, 1954. Since the shell was a graceful piece of architecture the forces of darkness yearned to bulldoze it flat and put in something useful like a parking lot. Lovers of the shell beat back two such onslaughts, and the shell survives, gussied up. The I-40 builders neared Memphis at a bad moment, in 1969. For a decade after World War II the freeway lobby crushed all before them. The downtowns of city after city were destroyed or menaced by rapidly advancing glaciers of concrete. *Si monumentum requiris*, go to downtown Buffalo and weep.

October 27

Across the country last weekend there were anti-war demonstrations, modest in turnout, but hopefully a warning to Obama that war without end or reason in Afghanistan, plus 40,000 more troops to Kabul, is not why people voted for him.

I spoke at our own little rally in my local town of Eureka, California. My neighbor Ellen Taylor decided to spice up the proceedings by having a guillotine on the platform, right beside the Eureka Courthouse steps. It's in the genes. Her father was Telford Taylor, chief US prosecutor at Nuremberg.

When she told me about the plan for the guillotine, I wasn't sure it was a good idea. But Ellen said she wanted to reach out to new constituencies beyond the committed left, and what better siren call than the swoosh of the "Avenging Blade"?

A hundred years ago people liked to stress the similarities of the American and French Revolutions. Mark Twain composed the most passionate defense of the Terror ever written, in *A Connecticut Yankee in King Arthur's Court*. But then, after 1917, the French Revolution was seen as the harbinger of Bolshevik excess and it grew less popular.

Up on the platform I took the guillotine issue head on. Only 666 aristocrats had been topped in Paris in what is now the Place de la Concorde; 1,543 throughout France. The reward: a decisive smack on the snout of the land-holding aristocracy; durable popular power for peasants, workers, and the petit-bourgeois: *M. le patron* and *M. le proprietaire* stepped into history.

There's no sign of populism in any energetic form. The anger is formulaic.

October 28

Just how funny was that story of the man in Fairfax County, Virginia, who got up early on the morning of October 19 and walked naked into his own kitchen to make himself a cup of coffee? The next significant thing that happened to twenty-nine-year-old Eric Williamson was the local cops arriving to charge him with indecent exposure. It turns out that while he was brewing the coffee, a mother who was taking her seven-year-old son along a path beside Williamson's house espied the naked Williamson and called the local precinct, or more likely her husband, who happens to be a cop.

"Yes, I wasn't wearing any clothes," Williamson said later, "but I was alone, in my own home and just got out of bed. It was dark and I had no idea anyone was outside looking in at me."

The story ended up on TV, starting with Fox, and in the opening rounds the newscasters and network blogs had merciless sport with the Fairfax police for their absurd behavior. Hasn't a man the right to walk around his own home (or, in this case, rented accommodation) dressed according to his fancy? Answer, obvious to anyone familiar with relevant case law: absolutely not.

Peeved by public ridicule, the Fairfax cops turned up the heat. The cop's wife started to maintain that she first saw Williamson by a glass kitchen door, then through the kitchen window. Mary Ann Jennings, a Fairfax County Police spokeswoman, stirred the pot of innuendo: "We've heard there may have been other people who had a similar incident." The cops are asking anyone who may have seen an unclothed Williamson through his windows to come forward, even if it was at a different time. They've also been papering the neighborhood with fliers, asking for reports on any other questionable activities by anyone resembling Williamson—a white guy who's a commercial diver and who has a five-year-old daughter, not living with him.

I'd say that if the cops keep it up, and some prosecutor scents opportunity, Williamson will be pretty lucky if they don't throw some cobbled-up indictment at him. Toss in a jailhouse snitch making his own plea deal, a faked police lineup, maybe an artist's impression of the Fairfax Flasher, and Williamson could end up losing his visitation rights and, worse comes to worst, getting ten years plus being posted for life on some sex-offender site.

You think we're living in the twenty-first century, in the clinical fantasy world of *CSI*? Wrong. So far as forensic evidence is concerned, we remain planted in the seventeenth century with trial by ordeal, such as when they killed women as witches if they floated when thrown into a pond.

Let's head north from Fairfax County to Massachusetts, home of the witch trials. How about if you're white in Boston (wise decision), weigh yourself in your own bedroom with no clothes on and … But let my Boston friend pick up the story, because it happened to him:

> It was the early '90s. Early on Xmas eve two burly cops pushed into our house and invaded our bedroom—no warrant. They only backed off after they realized that the scale in our bedroom where I weighed myself was in front of a window. To see me there the born-agains who moved in next door (actually on the far side of a vacant lot separating us) had to keep a tight watch since it does not take long to weigh oneself.
>
> My girlfriend was dressing in the bedroom and my mom and step-daughter were visiting. By the time the cops understood that I had been weighing myself every morning, the paddy wagon was there ready to take me away.
>
> I would have sued them but I was running for Congress at the time. The cops liked my opponent, a right-wing pro-lifer, and I have always thought that had something to do with their moral diligence that day. One of the cops, the chief, later resigned in a corruption scandal.

November 24

No one told us it would be boring, but it is—the Obama presidency. Having an adulterer and a moron at 1600 Pennsylvania Avenue for eight years apiece, plus Dick Cheney down the corridor, spoiled us. Which side of Bill's head did Hillary hit with the lamp? Would George fight his way to the end of the sentence in his daily battles with the English language?

These days tranquility reigns—or seems to—in the Obamas' private quarters. Senior White House staffers remain loyal and tight-lipped. Small wonder Jay Leno's nightly show is sagging. There was nothing to make jokes about, at least until Sarah Palin went on her book tour.

Politics is getting duller by the day, too, as the idealists watch their expectations trickling all too swiftly through the hourglass. What's left? Enforcing private coverage and savaging the Medicare Advantage plans of low-income seniors. Obama has dipped below 50 percent in public approval, which—so the pollsters tell us—is nothing particularly unusual for a new President at this stage of the game. What's going to stop him sliding down more?

But lo! There's light a little way up the tunnel: the upcoming trial in the shadow of Ground Zero of Khalid Shaikh Mohammed and four alleged co-conspirators, the best news for the print press since Monica Lewinsky. Ahead lie months of searing headlines and blood-curdling editorial howls for vengeance in the *New York Post* and the *Daily News*.

The scenario envisaged by Obama, Emanuel and Attorney General Eric Holder is presumably that sometime before the election of 2012, KSM will be ushered into an execution chamber, thus vindicating Obama's oft-advertised commitment to track down the perps of 9/11 and kill them. So eager was Obama to underline this point that while in Asia he declared that those offended by the trial will not find it "offensive at all when he's convicted and when the death penalty is applied to him." This remark came after his assertion that the trial would be "subject to the most exacting demands of justice." Realizing that the latter remark might be construed by some pettifogging civil libertarians as prejudicial to a fair trial, Obama then added piously that he was "not going to be in that courtroom. That's the job of the prosecutors, the judge and the jury."

It's certain that the legal team mustered to defend KSM and the other four will be reviewing mountains of documents amassed by the prosecution, setting forth the evidentiary chain that led to the indictments of the Ground Zero Five. Of course, most of these will no doubt be classified top secret, to be reviewed by defense lawyers only under conditions of stringent security; but it's a safe bet that enough will be leaked to portray the Bush administration and Republicans in general in a harshly unflattering light, with Bush and Cheney ignoring profuse indications of the unfolding conspiracy.

There are those who gravely lament the impending spectacle, ranging from pinkos raising wussy concerns about secret witnesses and confessions extorted under torture, to the right blaring that KSM and the others will defile the Foley courtroom with their filthy Muslim diatribes. Bring them on, say I. The show trial is as American as cherry pie, as the former Black Panther H. Rap Brown—currently serving life without the possibility of parole in the supermax in Florence, Colorado—famously said about violence.

American political life is at its most vivid amid show trials. Their glare discloses the larger political system in all its pretensions. At the very least we need the drama to help us get through what is looking more and more like the bland, respectable corporate rule of the Eisenhower years.

2010

January 8

Connoisseurs of the ritual known as "accepting full responsibility" will surely grade Obama a mere B for his performance Thursday at his White House press conference. "Ultimately, the buck stops with me," Obama said, apropos Terror's near Christmas Day miss on Northwest Flight 253. "As President, I have a solemn responsibility to protect our nation and our people, and when the system fails, it is my responsibility."

First strike against Obama's speech writer is the weasel-use of "ultimately," not to mention the mawkish use of "solemn." Second strike is his habitual dive into "systemic failure," as he termed it earlier in the week. Everyone knows that systemic failure spells out as "No one is to blame. This is bigger than all of us." That's the phrase's singular beauty.

I give John Brennan low marks too. "I told the President today I let him down," said Obama's top counterterrorism aide, who followed his boss at the press briefing. Okay so far. Exciting, even. In medieval Japan he would have stuck a sword in his stomach at this point. Not Brennan. "I am the President's assistant for homeland security and counterterrorism and I told him I will do better and we will do better as a team."

February 5
If you want to draw a line to indicate when history took a great leap forward, it could be February 1, 1960, when four black students from the Agricultural and Technical College of North Carolina sat down at a segregated lunch counter in Woolworth's department store in Greensboro, North Carolina. Three months later, the city of Raleigh, NC, eighty miles east of Greensboro, saw the founding of the Student Non-Violent Coordinating Committee (SNCC), seeking to widen the lunch-counter demonstrations into a broad, militant movement. SNCC's first field director was Bob Moses, who said that he was drawn by the "sullen, angry and determined look" of the protesters, qualitatively different from the "defensive, cringing" expression common to most photos of protesters in the South.

In contrast to that time, here are two important reminders about political phenomena peculiar to America today, which help explain the decline of the left: the first is the financial clout of the "nonprofit" foundations, tax-exempt bodies formed by rich people to dispense their wealth according to political taste. Much of the "progressive sector" in America now owes its financial survival—salaries, office accommodation, etc.—to the annual disbursements of these foundations which cease abruptly at the first manifestation of radical heterodoxy. In other words, most of the progressive sector is an extrusion of the dominant corporate world, just as are the academies, similarly dependent on corporate endowments.

A second important reminder concerns the steady collapse of the organized Leninist or Trotskyite left which used to provide a training ground for young people who could learn the rudiments of political economy and organizational discipline, find suitable mates, and play their role in reproducing the left, red diaper upon red diaper, tomorrow's radicals, nourished on the Marxist classics. Somewhere in the late 1980s and early '90s, coinciding with collapses further East, this genetic strain shriveled into insignificance.

An adolescent soul not inoculated by sectarian debate, not enriched by the *Eighteenth Brumaire* and study groups of *Capital*, is open to any infection, such as 9/11 conspiracism and junk-science climate catastrophism substituting for analysis of political economy at the national or global level.

February 10

There used to be a time when the CIA would go berserk at the merest suggestion that its executive actions included torture and assassination. This modesty has long gone but even so, it was astonishing to hear the Director of National Intelligence, Dennis Blair, blithely tell a Senate committee this week that "Being a US citizen will not spare an American from getting assassinated by military or intelligence operatives overseas if the individual is working with terrorists and planning to attack fellow Americans." Blair added helpfully that "If we think direct action will involve killing an American, we get specific permission to do that."

Does that mean the President or one of his cabinet members issued an okay for the FBI to riddle Detroit Imam Luqman Ameen Abdullah on October 28, 2009, with twenty-one bullets, some of them aimed at his testicles and at least one in his back? They say the Imam was handcuffed after this lethal fusillade.

February 22

Thirty years ago, driving across the hill country in the South, every fifty miles I'd pick up a new Pentecostal radio station with the preacher screaming in tongues in a torrent of ecstatic drivel—"Miki taki meka keena ko-o-ola ka"—the harsh consonants rattling the speakers on my Newport station wagon. I had a friend, a "shouter," whose trailer featured by way of cultural uplift only the Bible and a big TV set tuned to the Christian Broadcasting Network, on which Pat Robertson used to denounce New Age paganism on an hourly basis.

Last time I visited, a few months ago, my friend's nice home still featured the Bible. Next to it was a thick manual of astrological guidance—could Geminis pair up with Scorpios with any hope of success, and kindred counsel—and he and his wife surfed through a big menu of channels. Out on the highway my radio picked up Glenn Beck spouting drivel, but the old Pentecostalists had vanished from the dial. These days, my friend told me, he and his wife didn't tithe to any particular church and pastor. "All crooks," he said dryly. They stay home and hold their own Sunday service there.

James Cameron gives us *Avatar* and the planet Pandora, which is Gaia brought to life in the most savage denunciation of imperial exploitation, explicitly American, ever brought to screen. Now a huge hit, *Avatar* is the most expensive anti-war film ever made (at $200 million, about half the cost of a single F-22). "It is nature which today no longer exists anywhere," a peppery German called Marx wrote in 1845. But Rousseau is having his revenge on Karl.

The night I went to *Avatar* the audience cheered when Pandora, as a single Gaian organism, puts Earth's predatory onslaught to flight and man's war machines are crushed by natural forces. Against Genesis and the Judeo-Christian tradition, pagan mysticism is carrying the day, at the level of fantasy, as it is in those astrological manuals down in the Bible belt.

March 4

Joe Stack wrote: "I saw it written once that the definition of insanity is repeating the same process over and over and expecting the outcome to suddenly be different. I am finally ready to stop this insanity. Well, Mr. Big Brother IRS man, let's try something different; take my pound of flesh and sleep well."

Stack was now thirty words from the end of his life. He continued: "The communist creed: From each according to his ability, to each according to his need. The capitalist creed: From each according to his gullibility, to each according to his greed. Joe Stack (1956–2010)."

Then, on February 18 this year, the computer software engineer climbed into a Piper Cherokee plane and flew it into the IRS building in Austin, Texas. When the smoke cleared and the fires had been put out, the IRS counted many injured and one dead, Vernon Hunter, a sixty-eight-year-old Vietnam veteran on the edge of retirement.

Later that day, Stack's thirty-six-paragraph suicide note surfaced on the internet. Though opaque in its recitation of his precise personal grudges with the tax man, as a farewell blast at the system it was eloquent on the essentials of the American Way: "When the wealthy fuck up, the poor get to die for the mistakes."

Such a system, Stack correctly emphasized, is predicated on "two interpretations for every law; one for the very rich, and one for the rest of us …" What to do? "Violence not only is the answer, it is the only answer." From several Republican politicians, hoping to harness the huge head of political steam building up in a society facing mass unemployment for years to come, Stack's last flight got astonishing respect. "It's sad the incident in Texas happened," said Representative Steve King, Republican of Iowa, "but by the same token, it's an agency that is unnecessary. And when the day comes when that is over and we abolish the IRS, it's going to be a happy day for America."

March 31

Marijuana was by no means the first boom crop to delight my home county of Humboldt, here in Northern California, five hours' drive from San Francisco up Route 101. Leaving aside the boom of appropriating land from the Indians, there was the timber boom, which crested in the 1950s when Douglas fir in the Mattole Valley went south to frame the housing tracts of Los Angeles.

In the early 1970s new settlers—fugitives from the '60s and city life—would tell visiting friends, "Bring marijuana," and then disconsolately try to get high from the male leaves. Growers here would spend nine months coaxing their plants, only to watch, amid the mists and rains of fall, hated mold destroy the flowers.

By the end of the decade the cultivators were learning how to grow. There was an enormous variety of seeds—Afghan, Thai, Burmese. The price crept up to $400 a pound, and the grateful settlers, mostly dirt poor, rushed out to buy a washing machine, a propane fridge, a used VW, a solar panel, a 12-volt battery. Even a three-pound sale was a relatively big deal.

The 1980s brought further advances in productivity through the old Hispanic/Mexican technique of ensuring that female buds are not pollinated, hence the name *sin semilla*—without seeds. By 1981 the price for the grower was up around $1,600 a pound. The $100 bill was becoming a familiar local unit of cash transactions. In 1982 a celebrated grow in the Mattole Valley yielded its organizer, an Ivy League grad, a harvest of a thousand pounds of processed marijuana, an amazing logistical triumph. Fifteen miles up the valley from where I write, tiny Honeydew became fabled as the marijuana capital of California, if not America.

That same year, the "war on drugs" rolled into action, executed in Humboldt County by platoons of sheriff's deputies, DEA agents, roadblocks by the California Highway Patrol. The National Guard combed the King Range. Schoolchildren gazed up at helicopters hovering over the valley scanning for gardens. War in this case brought relatively few casualties and many beneficiaries into the local economy: federal and state assistance for local law enforcement; more prosecutors in the DA's office; a commensurately expanding phalanx of defense lawyers; a buoyant housing market for growers washing their money into legality; $200 a day and more for women trimming the dried plants. A bust meant at least a year of angst for the defendant and at least $25,000 in legal fees, though rarely any significant jail time. It did produce a felony conviction, several years of probation and all the restrictions of being an ex-felon. There are thirty-two people serving life sentences in California on a third-strike marijuana conviction. In 2008, 1,499 were in prison on marijuana convictions; in 2007, 4,925 in county jails.

By now the cattle ranchers were growing too. Where once you'd see a battered old pickup, now late-model stretch-cab Fords, Chevys, and Dodges would thunder by. Ranch yards sported new dump trucks and backhoes. Dealerships were selling big trucks and Toyota 4Runners, purchased with cash. By the mid-'90s the price of bud was up around $2,400 a pound.

Best of all, the war was a sturdy price support in our thinly populated, remote Emerald Triangle of Humboldt, Mendocino, and Trinity counties. Marijuana remained an outlaw crop. Then in 1996 came California's Compassionate Use Act, the brainchild of Dennis Peron, who returned from Vietnam in 1969 with two pounds of marijuana in his duffel bag and became a dealer in San Francisco. In 1990, when his companion was dying of AIDS, Peron began his drive for the legal medical use of marijuana.

It was the launch point for greenhouses big enough to spot on Google Earth, plus diesel generators in the hills cycling 24/7 and lists of customers in the clubs down south. By 2005, with increasingly skilled production, the price was cresting between $2,500 and even $3,000 a pound for the grower. These days, in San Francisco and LA (the latter still fractious legal terrain), perfectly grown and nicely packaged indoor pot—four grams for $60, i.e., $6,700 a pound—can be inspected with magnifying glasses in tastefully appointed salesrooms.

The age of Obama saw Attorney General Eric Holder tell the DEA to give low priority to harassment of valid medical marijuana clubs in states—fourteen so far, plus Washington, DC—that give marijuana some form of legality. On March 25, California officials announced that 523,531 signatures—almost 100,000 more than required—had been validated in support of an initiative to legalize marijuana and allow it to be sold and taxed, no small fiscal allurement in this budget-stricken state. The initiative will be on the November ballot. Various polls last year indicated such a measure enjoyed a 55 percent approval rating.

People reckon legalization is not far off and spells the end of the thirty-year marijuana boom. The local weekly, the *North Coast Journal*, has made a somewhat comic effort to construct a silver lining for the county. It talks hopefully of branding the Humboldt "terroir," of tours of "marijuanaries." Dream on. Down south there's more sun, more water, and very capable Mexicans ready to tend and trim for $15 an hour. The smarter growers reckon they have two years at most. Here on the North Coast the price of marijuana will drop, the price of land will drop, the trucks will stop being late-model. There'll be less money floating around.

The New Deal began with an end to prohibition of the sale of alcohol across the United States. The individual small producers of bourbon—some good, a lot awful or downright poison—shut down, and the big liquor producers took over, successfully pushing for illegalization of marijuana in 1937. How long will the small producers of gourmet marijuana last before the big companies run them off, pushing through the sort of regulatory "standards" that are now punishing small organic farmers?

April 9

The seventeen-minute video recording the US military's massacre from the air in Baghdad is utterly damning. The visual and audio record reveal the two Apache helicopter pilots and the US Army intelligence personnel monitoring the real-time footage falling over themselves to make the snap judgment that the civilians roughly a thousand feet below are armed insurgents and that one of them, peeking round a corner, was carrying an RPG, that is, a rocket-propelled antitank grenade launcher.

The dialogue is particularly chilling, revealing gleeful pilots gloating over the effect of their initial machine-gun salvoes. "Look at those dead bastards," one pilot says. "Nice," answers the other. Then, as a wounded man painfully writhes toward the curb, the pilots eagerly wait for an excuse to finish him off. "All you gotta do is pick up a weapon," one pilot says yearningly.

Defense analyst Pierre Sprey, who led the design teams for the F-16 and A-10 and who spent many years in the Pentagon, stresses two particularly damning features of the footage. The first is the claim that Noor-Eldeen's telephoto lens could be mistaken for an RPG. "A big telephoto for a 35mm camera is under a foot and half at most. An RPG, unloaded, is 3 feet long and loaded, 4 foot long. These guys were breathing hard to kill someone."

May 7

Oil drilling is one of the dirtiest of all businesses, physically and politically. In recent years BP has spent many millions in the US, trying to winch its reputation out of the mud with bright advertising paeans to its green commitment. Along with its green washing ad campaigns it's staked $500 million on a biofuel research center at the University of California's Berkeley campus. Every gallon gushing from the holes in the ocean floor in the Gulf of Mexico sinks the company's reputation back in the primal ooze of a reputation permanently disfigured by environmental havoc, political bribes, and ruthless campaigns against those courageous enough to blow the whistle on the company.

Obama now wags his finger at BP and vows that it will pay for every penny of the clean-up. He actually took more campaign money from BP than did his Republican opponent in 2008, Senator John McCain.

June 4

Israel regrets? But no! Israel doesn't regret. It preens and boasts and demands approval, which it duly gets from its prime sponsor, the United States government, and most of the press. The attack on the Mavi Marmara was carefully planned.

Israel is plunging into deeper darkness. As the Israeli journalist Gideon Levy recently told one interviewer: "In the last year there have been real cracks in the democratic system of Israel. It's systematic, it's not here and there. Things are becoming much harder." And Levy also wrote in *Ha'aretz*, "When Israel closes its gates to anyone who doesn't fall in line with our official positions, we are quickly becoming similar to North Korea. When right-wing parties increase their number of anti-democratic bills, and from all sides there are calls to make certain groups illegal, we must worry, of course. But when all this is engulfed in silence, and when even academia is increasingly falling in line with dangerous and dark views, the situation is apparently far beyond desperate."

June 11

Aggrieved British politicians denounce the Obama administration for throwing heavy emphasis on the formally discarded "British" in BP. What do they expect? Here in Petrolia, California (site of spec oil drilling back in 1864) someone asked me at the post office yesterday was it true the Queen owned BP.

What goes around comes around. One of the greatest bailouts in history came in 1953, when the Eisenhower administration authorized a CIA-backed coup in Iran. The Anglo-Iranian Oil Company, owned by the British government, had been expropriated and nationalized in 1951 by unanimous vote of Iran's parliament. The '53 coup evicted Prime Minister Mohammed Mossadeq and installed Shah Reza Pahlevi, the creature of the West's oil companies, with full tyrannical powers. The AIOC got back 40 percent of its old concession and became an internationally owned consortium, renamed? British Petroleum.

July 2

There's been ripe chortling about the spy network run in the US by the Russian SVR, successor to the KGB in the area of foreign intelligence. The eleven accused were supposedly a bunch of bumblers so deficient in remitting secrets to Moscow across nearly a decade that the FBI can't even muster the evidence to charge them with espionage.

All of the defendants who appeared in the New York court except one, the fetching Anna Chapman, are also charged with conspiracy to commit money laundering, which carries a maximum penalty of twenty years of prison. Assuming their lawyers don't get them off, a doubtful proposition, we can assume the Russians will round up eleven Americans, accuse them of spying and then do a trade.

Then both sides will start again, the Russians training fresh sets of agents to spout American baseball records, burn hamburgers over the backyard grill, jog and do other all-American things like have negative equity on their houses and owe the IRS money. Meanwhile the Americans are forcing their agents to read Dostoevsky.

July 9

It's the worst of times. America is plunging back into Depression. Only one out of every two Americans of working age has a job. Across the last two months, more than a million Americans simply gave up seeking employment, even as benefits are running out.

Somewhere near ten million Americans without work aren't getting any kind of check. One in every five children is living below the poverty line, sometimes by as much as 50 percent, classed as "extreme poverty."

The stimulus has failed. The housing market is in free fall. A couple of months ago market analysts predicted there would be five million more foreclosures between now and 2011 and it looks like they're on target. Forty percent of delinquent homeowners have already loaded up the SUV, thrown the plastic chairs in the swimming pool and tossed the house keys back at the bank.

For tens of millions of Americans the house is as central and crucial a financial asset as a pig was for an Irish peasant family in the nineteenth century. The pig, as the old Irish saying goes, was "the man beside the fire." It had the place of honor. The pig died, the family starved.

People are down. I meet young people every day who say they've simply given up watching the news. It's all too depressing.

August 6

It took a gay Republican judge with libertarian leanings to issue from the bench, in a US District courthouse in San Francisco, one of the warmest testimonials to the married state since Erasmus. Last Wednesday Vaughan R. Walker struck down California's ban on gay marriage, prompting ecstatic rejoicing among a mostly gay crowd outside the courthouse. His ruling was the first in the country to strike down a marriage ban on federal constitutional grounds.

A final judicial verdict is years away, because appeals will now wend their way slowly through the system until they reach the US Supreme Court, six of whose nine current members are Catholics.

Judge Walker marshals the testimony mustered by the plaintiffs, those challenging Prop 8, into a veritable thesaurus of the miracles wrought by the marriage ceremony. At the mere overture of "Wilt thou take" it seems that anxieties about self-worth, the burdens of low self esteem, the shadows of social ostracism, dissipate in the warm glow of the marriage contract.

In fact the drive for gay marriage is against the trend of the times, which is the single state, or people increasingly united—depending on the state they live in—by some form of civil union for the purpose of benefits, pensions, health care, wills, inheritances and so forth. Across America, on the last Census, there were 100 million unmarried employees, consumers, taxpayers, and voters who headed up a majority of households in twenty-two states, more than 380 cities.

Gays are crowding to board a sinking ship. Married couples with kids, who filled about 90 percent of residences a century ago, now total about 20 percent. Nearly 30 percent of homes are inhabited by someone who lives alone—no doubt awaiting foreclosure.

August 18

I went to get my hair cut the other day in the town of Fortuna and waited ten minutes while the elderly barber finished buzz-cutting a young Mexican American. After the young man had exited under his thin skullcap of black stubble, Don the barber sighed and said, "That's the third boy I've cut today who's headed into the Marines. They all say the same thing. 'There's no work around here and I've got a family to support.' When I tell them to hold off, they say the same thing: 'Too late. I've signed up.'"

Millions are plummeting into total destitution, having reached the end of their ninety-nine weeks of unemployment benefits. Their only option then is the soup line at a church and getting on the waiting list for a homeless shelter.

The nearest big city north of me is Portland, Oregon, where the downtown area is filled with homeless people, napping on steps, bedding down on cardboard in doorways. Along the Willamette one can see colonies of the destitute all along the river bank, from the shipyards to Willamette Falls, sleeping under thin plastic and gray skies.

Frank Bardacke, who lives in the farm town of Watsonville, a couple of hours south of San Francisco, recently described a bank robbery by one young, desperate immigrant:

> Several months ago Jario took his father's pickup truck, drove 20 miles to the upscale tourist playpen Carmel by the Sea, and walked into the local branch of the Bank of America. He waited in line to see a teller, and, when his turn came, he pretended to have a gun under his shirt and quietly demanded that the teller give him her cash. As she was passing out the money, he apologized for frightening her; meanwhile, she was hiding a GPS device among the bills.
>
> He left the bank, his crime apparently unnoticed, and returned to the truck for the drive home. On the way, he got confused and took a wrong turn through Monterey before he got back on the right road home. Twenty police cars from four different police jurisdictions followed the GPS signal and stopped him 45 minutes after he left the bank. He immediately confessed, explaining that he needed the money to help his dad pay the family mortgage. When his case came to trial, the DA pressed for two years in State Prison. The judge decided that six months in the county jail and five years probation would be enough.

In Texas or anywhere in the South the fellow would probably have got twenty-five years. But in desperate times one can expect people to do desperate, stupid things, and this decent judge showed compassion and understanding.

We can probably expect more laid-off workers going postal. On August 3, at 7 a.m., Omar Thornton showed up for a disciplinary hearing at the Hartford Distributors, a Budweiser distribution warehouse in Manchester, Connecticut. Thornton had been caught on video pinching some beer. They asked him whether he wanted to be fired, or just quit. Thornton pulled out a handgun and killed seven fellow employees before shooting himself dead. Before he loosed off his last shot into his head, Thornton, a black man, called a friend on his cellphone and said he'd taken care of some racists who'd been giving him a hard time. Unemployment means fear and fear nourishes racism, all the more because we have a black President. Racism is drifting across America like mustard gas in the trenches of World War I.

And, final token of hard times, we have Bonnie and Clyde on the run. In their latest guise the duo consists of John McCluskey and his cousin and fiancée, Casslyn Welch, who's no Faye Dunaway. She threw some wire cutters over the fence of her man's Arizona prison. Cops suspect them of killing a couple of retirees, then stealing their truck and heading north up to the Canadian line through Glacier National Park. That's the last sanctuary in America of *Ursus horribilis*, the American grizzly.

Behind them the cops, ahead the bears. It could be the first movie of a new era.

August 29

If the attack on Iraq was a "war for oil," it scarcely went well for the United States.

Run your eye down the list of contracts the Iraqi government awarded in June and December 2009. Prominent is Russia's Lukoil, which, in partnership with Norway's Statoil, won the rights to West Qurna Phase Two, a 12.9 billion-barrel supergiant oilfield. Other successful bidders for fixed-term contracts included Russia's Gazprom and Malaysia's Petronas. Only two US-based oil companies came away with contracts: ExxonMobil partnered with Royal Dutch Shell on a contract for West Qurna Phase One (8.7 billion barrels in reserves); and Occidental shares a contract in the Zubair field (4 billion barrels), in company with Italy's ENI and South Korea's Kogas. The huge Rumaila field (17 billion barrels) yielded a contract for BP and the China National Petroleum Company, and Royal Dutch Shell split the 12.6 billion-barrel Majnoon field with Petronas, 60–40.

Throughout the two auctions there were frequent bleats from the oil companies at the harsh terms imposed by the auctioneers representing Iraq, as this vignette from Reuters about the bidding on the northern Najmah field suggests: "Sonangol also won the nearby 900-million-barrel Najmah oilfield in Nineveh. Again, the Angolan firm had to cut its price and accept a fee of $6 per barrel, less than the $8.50 it had sought. 'We are expecting a little bit higher. Can you go a little bit higher?' Sonangol's exploration manager Paulino Jeronimo asked Iraqi Oil Minister Hussain al-Shahristani to spontaneous applause from other oil executives. Shahristani said, 'No.'"

So either the all powerful US government was unable to fix the auctions to its liking, or the all powerful US-based oil companies mostly decided the profit margins weren't sufficiently tempting. Either way, "the war for oil" doesn't look in very good shape.

The left—or a substantial slice of it—snatches defeat from the jaws of a victory over America's plans for Iraq by proclaiming that America has successfully established what Milne calls "a new form of outsourced semi-colonial regime to maintain its grip on the country and region." Iraq is in ruins—always the default consequence of American imperial endeavors. The left should report this, but also hammer home the message that in terms of its proclaimed objectives the US onslaught on Iraq was a strategic and military disaster. That's the lesson to bring home.

September 3

This weekend brings us the August 28 anniversary of the March on Washington back in 1963. It was when Martin Luther King delivered his famous "I have a dream" speech from the Lincoln Memorial.

This year the anniversary celebration has been hijacked by the right-wing commentator, Glenn Beck. The prime speaker will be Sarah Palin, the Tea Party's pinup girl and as unlikely as any woman in Alaska ever to have had a pinup of MLK on her dorm wall. To have the March on Washington honored by Beck and Palin is as shocking to liberal America as installing Jefferson Davis, President of the Southern slave states in the Civil War, next to Lincoln in the Memorial.

Beck admits that when he scheduled a rally in Washington on August 28 to boost his new book, *The Plan*, and strut his stuff to the Tea Party masses, he had no idea it was the anniversary of the March. But he swiftly turned ignorance into opportunity. He's now saying that's he is working "to finish the job" that was at the heart of the 1963 March on Washington and King's vision. Beck claims the ideas of Dr. King have been corrupted and that he will resurrect the true King. As part of this mission, Beck is trying to separate Dr. King from social justice and limit King to advocacy of individual Christian salvation.

If Beck's hijacking provokes some honesty among the left in general about King and about black leadership today, then Beck will have performed a useful service. Too late now to organize the obvious, a huge counter-demonstration to call Beck to accounts and run him and Palin off. The left is too weak for that, having now given up gluten that has given us leavened bread for 5,000 years.

September 24

There was a memorial for Ben Sonnenberg last week. Ben died on June 26 at the age of seventy-three—and a substantial crowd of the people who knew and loved him were invited by his widow, Dorothy Gallagher, to muster at the Century Club, on West 43rd Street in New York, on September 15 and honor his memory. Speakers included two of his daughters, Susannah and Saidee, Dan Menaker, Michael Train, Anne Carson, Rebecca Okrent, Susan Minot, James Salter.

The world has lost a true humanist, in the Renaissance heft of that word, one in whom refinement of taste and wideness of culture mingled with political passion. I mourn a very close friend. His greatest literary achievement was *Grand Street*, the quarterly he founded in 1981 and edited till 1990, when multiple sclerosis was far advanced and his fortune somewhat depleted. His friend Jean Stein took the magazine over and it ran till 2004. As he put it laconically, "I printed only what I liked; never once did I publish an editorial statement; I offered no writers' guidelines; and I stopped when I couldn't turn the pages anymore." As another great editor, Bruce Anderson, of the Anderson Valley Advertiser, wrote after Ben's death, "*Grand Street* under Sonnenberg was the best literary magazine ever produced in this doomed country. His *Grand Street* was readable front-to-back. If you've never seen a *Grand Street*, the last literary quarterly we're going to have, hustle out to the last bookstore and get yourself one and lament what is gone."

When I first came to New York in 1972 I went to a couple of parties thrown by Ben's father, Ben Sr., one of the trailblazers in public relations who gave elaborately staged parties to advance the interests of his various clients, at 19 Gramercy Park. He looked a bit like a comfortably retired Edwardian bookie in 1890s London, with enough knowingness in his glance to deliver "fair warning" to the unwary. Though he publicly prided himself on never have taken a dime from either Howard Hughes or the Kennedys, Ben Sr. certainly milked big clients like General Motors of plenty of moolah, a satisfactory chunk of which he left to Ben.

Ben Jr. detailed his somewhat raffish and caddish youth in his 1991 memoir, *Lost Property*, but I had already known for almost a decade the tastes that he listed on the first page and that endeared me to him: "My favorite autobiographers in this century are Vladimir Nabokov, Theodor Adorno and Walter Benjamin." A paragraph later he cited "my friend Edward Said," whose savage essay "Michael Walzer's 'Exodus and Revolution'—a Canaanite Reading" Ben had published in *Grand Street* in 1986.

There was no other cultural periodical at that time that would have given the finger so vigorously to polite New York intellectual opinion. The finger could be puckish. In January of 1989 he sent me a copy of his offer—which I published in the *Nation*—on behalf of himself, me and others, to Marty Peretz: "Dear Mr. Peretz: Do you wish to sell the *New Republic*? May I know your terms? I am one of a small group whose members are eager to buy the *New Republic* and restore its credit as a liberal journal. We suspect you may be ready to sell from the vacancy and desperation of recent articles, which I at least associate with the moral and material bankruptcy of the state of Israel. I am the editor of *Grand Street*, but none of my associates is in the magazine publishing business."

Ben's decent obit in the *New York Times* by William Grimes mentioned many of the writers he published: Ted Hughes, Alice Munro, James Salter, Susan Minot, John Hollander, Northrop Frye, W. S. Merwin, Christopher Hitchens, Amy Wilentz, and the present writer. But not Edward Said. Their relationship was very close and among my warmest memories are dinners, with Ben and his wife, Dorothy Gallagher, in their apartment at 50 Riverside Drive, listening as Edward thunders to the company about some fresh outrage of his enemies, some new libel lavished upon him, the Canaanite—"a mere black man"—and hearing Ben's delighted laugh, raspy and soon spent because there was not much puff power in his body, imprisoned in the wheelchair or propped up in bed.

Ben was just such a physical captive for over a quarter of a century, ultimately unable to move anything but his head, but I never saw him dull of eye or wit, amid what a similarly spry and creatively indomitable Alexander Pope, crippled from the age of twelve, half blind and afflicted with asthma, in the "Epistle to Dr. Arbuthnot," ruefully called "this long Disease, my life." Great though the editorial achievement of *Grand Street* was, the resilience that carried him onward through the two decades that followed was what seized me. Ben's late style was a marvelously warm and inspiring achievement.

I first met him in 1982, when I conducted negotiations on behalf of my father Claud, whom Ben wanted to write a memoir about spies and the Spanish Civil War. I reported to my father the large sum Ben had agreed without much demur to pony up, and Claud duly turned in a very funny essay, full of astute observations about Guy Burgess and spy mania, but also with a wonderfully tragicomic memoir about the strange death of Basil Murray and his ape in Valencia.

Soon I was writing for Ben myself, and it was always agreeable. He was good at soft-edged editorial blackmail, designed to propel one past the finishing post. The substantial checks spurred creativity, too, and by 1985 I managed a very long memoir about my childhood, "Heatherdown," which was well received. I never would have written it if it hadn't been for Ben. When, to his irritation, I quit New York for Key West in the early 1980s, and ultimately settled here in northern California, he would refer to my location as though it was in Kamchatka, filled with metropolitan wonderment that we could even communicate past the barrier of the Rocky Mountains, the wastes of the Great Basin, the Sierra, even unto a northern Pacific shore on which he had never, would never, set eyes. But we spoke on the phone constantly, and I like to think these hundreds of parleys—interspersed with occasional visits—brought us far closer than if I had been trudging down the West Side from my old roost on Central Park West and 94th Street.

He had been a young *flâneur* in London in the 1960s and, no doubt, we passed each other unwittingly from time to time on the Kings Road: I in the long, dark navy velour overcoat, velvet trousers, borsalino hat, chiffon scarf I affected at that time, Ben in the tweed suits made for him by Huntsman on Savile Row and shoes hand-stitched by Cleverly, "bespoke shoemaker" in the Burlington Arcade.

Not long after I moved to Petrolia, Ben, probably worried I wasn't warm enough, nor adequately shod, in this Kamchatka-in-the-Pacific-Northwest, sent me two of his exquisite old tweed suits and brown walking shoes and, since we are the same build, I wear the herringbone Scotch tweeds and the brown brogues often amid the winter chills of Petrolia, sometimes wondering that if I keel over in the road and some stranger finds me and looks at the label on the inside pocket, he'll see "Huntsman & Sons Ltd. B. Sonnenberg 5.6.69" and launch off into some surreal farce of confused identity of the sort Ben loved. Earlier this year he sent me no less than six pairs of black shoes, of minutely varied design, supplied by the diligent and extremely expensive Mr. Cleverly. At least physically, I can stand in Ben's shoes and when he was alive could feel that at least I was doing his walking for him.

But the alumnus of Savile Row and Wilton's, of the Boulevard Haussmann, of Malaga back in the day, was no whimsical dabbler. He was that best mix—serious and radical about politics and art in a fashion that never forfeited lightness of touch (though, to my chagrin, he had no feeling for Wodehouse).

This spring I felt I hadn't seen him for too long. We seemed to be talking less. I feared for his health and jumped on a plane and spent a long weekend in New York. I entered that bedroom in which I had spent so many delightful hours, its paintings and prints in their familiar spots, and here was Ben, not sinking at all but in good voice, his eyes agleam. A dinner with him and Dorothy, Mariam Said and JoAnn Wypijewski was a tumult of laughter and political sallies and disputes. And then, three months later, he was gone—taken off by an infection he was too weak to battle. His hundreds of friends were unprepared when he slipped away, surrounded by Dorothy and his daughters. Of course, I comfort myself with the thought of that last trip. I look fondly and sadly at his suits, the books he gave me along with the autograph letter from Zola on my wall.

Privileged is the person who has had such a friend. He was so loyal, and when he was being loyal about people I didn't care for, I comforted myself with the thought that when someone was confiding to Ben some reservations, animosities even, concerning yours truly, Ben would be reliably loyal about me too, though he never shirked his exacting critical standards.

At the memorial James Salter recalled that when Ben was editing *Grand Street*, Harold Brodkey, a close friend, sent him a very long poem. Ben didn't care for it. He wrote to Brodkey to say that at best he might publish a few pages of it. Brodkey withdrew the poem. Then later Brodkey sent Ben a short story. Ben didn't like that either, and declined to publish it. Brodkey severed their friendship. Then, sometime later, Brodkey wrote to Ben saying he would like to put the friendship back on its feet. Ben declined, writing to Brodkey that he didn't relish the prospect of the "watchful cordiality" that a resumption of relations would now require.

Ben always makes me think of Proust, because of his cultivation, because they both spent so much time in bed (in Proust's case a surprisingly small one, now ensconced in the Carnavalet Museum in Paris, not much wider than Ben's), because so many chats sent us off down the boulevards of common memory. He was like Proust in cultivation, stylishness, humor, and, as regards his physical afflictions, the way he bore them with such fortitude and grace.

October 8

George Soros announced a few weeks ago that he is giving $100 million to Human Rights Watch, conditional on the organization finding a matching $100 million a year from other donors for ten years. He's been rewarded with ringing cheers for his disinterested munificence.

With Soros's extra money, HRW will be dangling big funds at its non-American recruits. Regarding the hefty salaries that will surely follow, it's worth raising the experience of Eritrea, which immediately got into trouble with the NGO system after independence in 1991. Eritrea-based journalist Tom Mountain tells me, "For one, Eritrea won't allow the NGOs to pay above civil service salaries. Why? NGOs come into a country and find the best and brightest and give them salaries ten or twenty times the local rate, buying their allegiance and often turning them against their country. Two, Eritrea has implemented a 10 percent overhead policy, and all the NGOs that couldn't or wouldn't comply with the documentation were kicked out, about the same time Eritrea kicked out the UN 'peacekeepers' here."

NGOs endowed by the rich are instinctively hostile to radical social change, at least in any terms that a left-winger of the 1950s or '60s would understand. The US environmental movement is now strategically supervised and thus neutered as a radical force by the Pew Charitable Trusts, the lead dispenser of patronage and money.

Back at the dawn of the twentieth century, Lenin and Martov were organizing their international congresses and looking for grant money to this end. Martov, the Menshevik, told Lenin he must absolutely stop paying for the hotels and halls with money hijacked by Stalin from Georgian banks in Tblisi. Lenin reassured Martov, and then asked Stalin to knock over another bank, which he did, Europe's record bank heist up till that time. It was one way, perhaps the only way, past the grip of cautious millionaires. Then as now.

October 29

The sun will rise next Wednesday on a new American landscape, the same way it rose on a new American landscape almost exactly two years ago. That was the dawn of Obama-time. Millions of Americans had dined delightedly on Obama's rhetoric of dreams and preened at his homilies about the inherent moral greatness of the American people.

Obama and the Democrats triumphed at the polls. The pundits hailed a "tectonic shift" in our national politics, perhaps even a registration of the possibility that we had entered a "post-racial" era.

The realities of American politics don't change much from year to year. The "politics of division" which Obama denounced are the faithful reflection of national divisions of wealth and resources wider today than they have been at any time since the late 1920s. In fact the "dream" died even before Obama was elected in November 2008. Already in September that year Senator Obama, like his opponent, Senator McCain, had voted, at the behest of Treasury Secretary Hank Paulson (formerly of Goldman Sachs) and of Fed chairman Ben Bernanke, for the bailout of the banks. Whatever the election result, there was to be no change in the architecture of financial power in America.

Contrary to a thousand contemptuous diatribes by the left, the Tea Party is a genuine political movement, channeling the fury and frustration of a huge slab of white Americans running small businesses—what used to be called the petit-bourgeoisie.

The World Socialist Web Site snootily cites a *Washington Post* survey finding the Tea Party to be a "disparate band of vaguely connected gatherings." The WSW sneers that the *Post* was able to make contact with only 647 groups linked to the Tea Party, some of which involve only a handful of people. "The findings suggest that the breadth of the tea party may be inflated," the WSW chortles, quoting the *Post*. You think the socialist left across America can boast of 647 groups, or of any single group consisting of more than a handful of people?

Who says these days that, in the last analysis, the only way to change the status quo and challenge the Money Power of Wall Street is to overthrow the government by force? That isn't some old Trotskyist lag like Louis Proyect, dozing on the dungheap of history like Odysseus' lice-ridden hound Argos, woofing with alarm as the shadow of a new idea darkens the threshold.

Who really, genuinely wants to abolish the Fed, to whose destruction the left pledges ever more tepid support? Sixty percent of Tea Party members would like to send Ben Bernanke off to the penitentiary, the same way I used to hear the late great Wright Patman vow to do to Fed chairman Arthur Burns, back in the mid-'70s.

November 19

As Obama reviews his options, which way will he head? He's already supplied the answer. He'll try to broker deals to reach "common ground" with the Republicans, the strategy that destroyed those first two years of opportunity. Even many of Obama's diehard fans are beginning to say that the guy hasn't a backbone, no capacity to stand and fight.

The left must abandon the doomed ritual of squeaking timid reproaches to Obama, only to have the counselors at Obama's elbow contemptuously dismiss them, as did Rahm Emanuel, who correctly divined their near-zero capacity for effective challenge. Two more years of the same downward slide, courtesy of bipartisanship and "working together"? No way. Enough of dreary predictability. Let's have a real mutiny against the Obamian rightward drift. The time is not six months or a year down the road. The time is now.

The White House deserves the menace of a convincing threat now, not some desperate intra-Democratic Party challenge late next year. There has to be an independent challenge.

We have a champion in the wings.

This champion of the left with sound appeal to the populist or libertarian right was felled on November 2, and he should rise again before his reputation fades. His name is Russ Feingold, currently a Democrat and the junior Senator from Wisconsin. I urge him to decline any job proffered by the Obama administration and not to consider running as a challenger inside the Democratic Party. I urge him, not too long after he leaves the Senate, to raise—if only not to categorically reject—the possibility of a presidential run as an independent; then, not too far into 2011, to embark on such a course.

Why would he be running? Feingold would have a swift answer. To fight against the Republicans and the White House in defense of the causes he has publicly supported across a lifetime. He has opposed the wars in Iraq and Afghanistan. His was the single Senate vote against the Patriot Act; his was a consistent vote against the constitutional abuses of both the Bush and Obama administrations. He opposed NAFTA and the bank bailouts. He is for economic justice and full employment. He is the implacable foe of corporate control of the electoral process. The Supreme Court's Citizens United decision in January was aimed in part at his landmark campaign finance reform bill. He broke with his party in Senate votes ninety-three times. At the end, he voted against Obama's "compromise" on extending the Bush tax cuts.

Run, Russ, run.

December 10
To: Patrick Cockburn; Jeffrey St. Clair
Subject: Put it on the wall (or front door)

COVER: A drawing of the cuneiform transcription of a debt cancellation (amargi law) by Enmetena, ruler of the Sumerian city-state of Lagash, c. 2400 BC, the first known legal proclamation.

December 24
The prime constant factor in American politics across the past six decades has been a counterattack by the rich against the social reforms of the 1930s.

Twenty years ago the supreme prize of the Social Security trust funds—the government pensions that changed the face of America in the mid-'30s—seemed far beyond Wall Street's grasp. No Republican President could possibly prevail in such an enterprise. It would have to be an inside job by a Democrat. Clinton tried it, but the Lewinsky sex scandal narrowly aborted his bid.

If Obama can be identified with one historic mission on behalf of capital it is this, and though success is by no means guaranteed, it is closer than it has ever been.

As with Clinton, we have an opportunistic, neoliberal President without a shred of intellectual or moral principle. We have disconsolate liberals, and a press saying that Obama is showing admirable maturity in understanding what bipartisanship really means. Like Clinton, Obama is fortunate in having pwogs to his left only too happy to hail him. The landscape doesn't change much, as evidenced by the fact that Jeb Bush, former governor of Florida and George W.'s brother, looks as though he's ready to make a bid for the Republican nomination.

December 29

Unlike the French or the Italians, for whom conspiracies are an integral part of government activity, acknowledged by all, Americans have been temperamentally prone to discount them. Reflecting its audience, the press follows suit. Editors and reporters like to offer themselves as hardened cynics, following the old maxim "Never believe anything till it is officially denied," but in truth, they are touchingly credulous, ever inclined to trust the official version, at least until irrefutable evidence—say, the failure to discover a single WMD in Iraq—compels them finally to a darker view.

Once or twice a decade some official deception simply cannot be sedately circumnavigated. Even in the 1950s, when the lid of government secrecy was more firmly bolted down, the grim health consequences of atmospheric testing of nuclear weapons in the South Pacific, Utah, and Nevada finally surfaced. In the late 1960s, it was the turn of the CIA, some of its activities first exposed in relatively marginal publications like the *Nation* and *Ramparts*, then finally given wider circulation.

Even then the mainstream press exhibited extreme trepidation in running any story presuming to discredit the moral credentials of the US government. Take assassination as an instrument of national policy. In these post–September 11 days, when Dennis Blair, the Director of National Intelligence, publicly declares, as he did before the House Intelligence Committee, that the government has the right to kill Americans abroad, it is easy to forget that nothing used to more rapidly elicit furious denials from the CIA than allegations about its efforts, stretching back to the late 1940s, to kill inconvenient foreign leaders. Charges by the Cubans through the 1960s and early '70s about the Agency's serial attempts to murder Fidel Castro were routinely ignored, until finally the Senate hearings conducted in

1976 by Senator Frank Church elicited a conclusive record of about twenty separate efforts.

Indeed, there was a brief window in the early '70s, amid revulsion over the Vietnam War and the excitement of the Watergate hearings, when the press exhibited a certain unwonted bravado, in part because investigative committees of Congress, enlivened by Watergate, made good use of subpoena power and immunity from threats of libel. Hence the famous Lockheed bribery hearings.

Decorum soon returned, however. Just over twenty years later, in 1996, the *Washington Post* fired off a six-part series, concocted with the help of Harvard profs, decked out with doleful front-page headlines such as "In America, Loss of Confidence Seeps into Institutions." The *Post*'s earnest message was that mistrust is bad and that it is better for social stability and contentment to trust government, as in the golden '50s, which, the older crowd may recall, was a time when government told soldiers it was safe to march into atomic test sites and when government-backed doctors offered radioactive oatmeal to disabled kids without their parents' knowledge.

The mainstream press—what's left of it—sees an important duty to foster confidence in public institutions. On May 6, right after disclosure of Goldman Sachs's double dealing, came the plummet in the stock market that for a brief moment sliced 998 points off the Dow, prompting serious losses to small investors who had placed stop-loss orders on individual stocks. On Comedy Central, Jon Stewart showed a stream of news anchors characterizing everything from the GM bailout to the mortgage crisis to the rescue of AIG as caused by a "perfect storm." Stewart said, "I'm beginning to think these are not perfect storms. I'm beginning to think these are regular storms and we have a s—ty boat." But the mainstream press zealously steered clear of suggestions that market manipulators might have engineered a killing.

The integration of journalists into Washington's policy apparatus—with its luxuriant jungle of lobby shops thinly disguised as nonprofits, with their seminars, "scholars in residence," and fellowships—has led to a decorous tendency to ignore the grime of politics at the level of corruption, blackmail, and bribery—mostly inaccessible anyway without the power of subpoena. There's an interesting genre of books, some written by political fixers in the aftermath of exposure or incarceration—Bobby Baker's *Wheeling and Dealing* is a good example—that usefully describe the grime, but these are rarely reviewed in respectable journals.

Sometimes a cover-up does surface, propelled into the light of day by a tenacious journalist. Then there's the outraged counterattack. Are you suggesting, sir, that the CIA connived to smuggle cocaine into America's inner cities? Gary Webb's career at the *San Jose Mercury News* was efficiently destroyed. Those who took the trouble to read the subsequent full report of CIA Inspector General Fred Hitz found corroboration of Webb's charges. But by then the caravan had moved on. A jury issued its verdict, but the press box was empty.

Maybe now the decline in power of the established corporate press, the greater availability of dissenting versions of politics and history, and the exposure of the methods used to coerce public support for the attack on Iraq have engendered a greater sense of realism on the part of Americans about what their government can do. Perhaps the press will be more receptive to discomfiting stories about what Washington is capable of in the pursuit of what it deems to be the national interest. Hopefully, in this more fertile soil, Syd Schanberg's pertinacity will be vindicated at last, and those still active in politics who connived at this abandonment of principles will be forced to give an account.

When it comes to journalistic achievements in 2010, the elephant in the room is WikiLeaks. The alleged leaker of the WikiLeaks files, Army Private Bradley Manning, currently being held in solitary confinement in sadistic conditions, should be vigorously applauded and defended for doing his sworn duty by exposing such crimes as the murder of civilians in Baghdad by US Apache helicopters. Assange and his colleagues should similarly be honored and defended. They have acted in the best traditions of the journalistic vocation.

2011

January 6

For the past seven months, twenty-two-year-old US Army Private Bradley Manning, first in an Army prison in Kuwait, now in the brig in Quantico, Virginia, has been held twenty-three hours out of twenty-four in solitary confinement in his cell, under constant harassment. If his eyes close between 5 a.m. and 8 p.m. he is jolted awake. In daylight hours he has to respond "yes" to guards every five minutes. For an hour a day he is taken to another cell where he walks figures of eight. If he stops he is taken back to his other cell.

Manning is accused of giving documents to Julian Assange at WikiLeaks. He has not been tried or convicted. Visitors report that Manning is going downhill mentally as well as physically. His lawyer's efforts to improve his condition have been rebuffed by the Army.

Accusations that his treatment amounts to torture have been indignantly denounced by prominent conservatives calling for him to be summarily executed. After the columnist Glenn Greenwald publicised Manning's treatment in mid-December, there was a moderate commotion. The UN's top monitor of torture is investigating his case. Meanwhile Manning faces months, if not years, of the same. Torture is now solidly installed in America's repressive arsenal. Not in the shadows where it used to lurk, but up front and central, vigorously applauded by prominent politicians. Coercion and humiliation seep through the culture.

On his second full day in office, President Obama signed a series of executive orders to close the Guantanamo detention center within a year, ban the harshest interrogation methods, and review military war crimes trials. In his first State of the Union address a week later, Obama declared to the joint session of Congress: "I can stand here tonight and say without exception or equivocation that the United States of America does not torture. We can make that commitment here tonight."

Nonetheless, the torture system is flourishing, and the boundaries of the American Empire are marked by overseas torture centers such as Bagram. There are still detainees in Guantanamo—as of November last year, 174 of them. They are supposedly destined for a supermax in Illinois. Manning fights for his sanity in Quantico.

January 13

Tucson is a schizoid town, pleasantly laid back but also with heavy enforcement under- and over-tones. The last time I spoke at a public meeting down there, a couple of years ago, the decidedly counter-cultural audience looked like a throwback to the late '70s in New York, which is probably where many in the crowd originally hailed from.

It's an informal place, which is why it was not surprising for Rep. Giffords to set up her table in a Safeway grocery store's parking lot, chatting with locals. This is what she was doing on Saturday. So Jared Loughner, twenty-two, with his newly purchased 9mm Glock with extended magazine, was able to stride up to within a yard of the congresswoman and shoot her in the head, then spray the small area with an extended salvo.

With this twenty-second fusillade Loughner killed US District Judge John Roll, sixty-three; Dorothy Murray, seventy-six; Dorwin Stoddard, seventy-six; Phyllis Scheck, seventy-nine; Gabriel Zimmerman, thirty; and Christina Green, nine. Zimmerman was Giffords's; director of community outreach and had helped organize the event. Christina Green, born on September 11, 2001, was taken along to see Giffords by a relative, because the nine-year-old was interested in public affairs. Federal judge Roll had just dropped by to say hello to Giffords, who shared his liberal opposition to Arizona's fierce stance on illegal immigrants.

Sarah Palin had played to her base all through the last four months of 2010 with website pictures of select Democratic candidates' districts—where there was a Tea Party challenger—with crosshair gun sights over them. Giffords got this treatment and stated publicly that Palin should know this sort of rhetoric could have consequences. Palin pulled the image from her site only after the shooting, just after TLC cancelled her Alaska show and will not be bringing it back for a second season. The cancellation didn't have anything to do with the shooting in Tucson. The show was fairly solid in the ratings at 3.2 million viewers and it seems TLC's worry was that if Palin runs for the Republican presidential nomination, they'd have to give her opponents equal access time.

But will Palin now be pilloried as Loughner's motivator? She'll certainly get flak, but it will be from people who loathe her anyway. Her base will construe her as a martyr to the Commie conspiracy led by Obama and will turn out for her in even greater numbers. They'll quote Jefferson even more fervently: "And what country can preserve its liberties, if its rulers are not warned from time to time, that this people preserve the spirit of resistance? Let them take arms. The remedy is to set them right as to the facts, pardon and pacify them. What signify a few lives lost in a century or two? The tree of liberty must be refreshed from time to time, with the blood of patriots and tyrants. It is its natural manure."

January 15

Editor,

Alex Cockburn has been bashing the "Truthers" for many years now. He finds it OK to attack those who seek the truth of what really happened on 9-11-01. Now, he ridicules those who ask why the CIA "missed" the underpants bomber, even though they had plenty of warning.

"The Truthers reject the obvious answers—caution, bureaucratic inertia, buck-passing, turf fights—and say it was a plot." Oh really Mr. Cockburn, do we? We don't know one way or another, and you are now the spokesperson for the Truthers? What's obvious is your "strawman" attacks are very misplaced. Like, why spend so much time attacking truth seekers? Especially when these "failures" keep benefiting certain countries and military-industrial-corporations.

"The Israeli firm, ICTS, and two of its subsidiaries are at the crux of an international investigation in recent days, as experts try to pinpoint the reasons for the security failure that enabled Umar F. Abdulmutallab to board Northwest flight 253 and attempt to set alight explosives hidden in his underwear."

A *Ha'aretz* investigation has learned that the security officers and their supervisor should have suspected the passenger, even without having early intelligence available to them. The failure was a twin flop: An intelligence failure, which US President Barack Obama has already stated, in the poor handling of information that arrived at the State Department and probably also the CIA from both the father of the would-be bomber and the British security service; and a failure within the security system, "including that of the Israeli firm ICTS." Nothing to see here, move along Truther scumbags!

So, the US is relying on Israeli security, and we are to believe that everyone just messed up, again? Mr. Cockburn wants us all to fall in line with his theory, the Official US Government Incompetence Theory. OUSGIT. OUSGIT! OUSGIT!! OUSGIT!!! OUSGIT!!!! Over and over, again and again, just plain dumb goy? For how long? How many more times to fall for lies? As many as it takes. As one commenter wrote online, "If the plane went down, maybe Israel could of fed us intelligence saying it was Iran." But, that'd NEVER happen, that's a CRAZY conspiracy theory, false flag operations NEVER happen. I'm sure Mr. Cockburn would be glad to agree.

Cheers,

Rob Mahon, Covelo

P.S. I'd rather be a Truthseeker, than a Denialist.

Alexander Cockburn replies: From this it's impossible to discern what Mahon's version of events is. I'd prefer to stay within the ambit of buck-passing, bureaucratic rivalries, and incompetence, starting with the fact that Umar Farouk Abdulmutallab didn't show up on the Watch List because someone had entered his name wrong. As for denialism, Rob, go preach Warming in Western Europe or Beijing, as temps plunge to new lows. The world has been cooling since 1998 and that's da cold truth. Petrolia.

February 6

The career profiles of the man Obama picked to send to Egypt to talk to Mubarak give a useful mini-portrait of US-Egyptian realities, shorn of happy talk about democracy and the will of the people.

The seventy-two-year-old Frank Wisner is a former US ambassador to Egypt and a senior fixer in Washington. He has secure footholds in government and corporate America. Until recently he was vice chairman of AIG, which he left to become a foreign policy adviser at the politically powerful law firm and lobby shop, Patton Boggs. Wisner's father, Frank Sr., ran the CIA's covert arm, went mad after the failure of the Hungarian rising of 1956, and committed suicide in odd circumstances in a CIA secure house outside Washington, DC, in 1967.

As ambassador to Egypt, Wisner formed a close relationship with Mubarak and long after leaving Cairo continued to nourish it. In 2005 he celebrated the Egyptian election (Mubarak "won" with 88.6 percent of the vote) as a "historic day." Wisner promptly headed further into egregious falsehood: "There were no instances of repression; there wasn't heavy police presence on the streets. The atmosphere was not one of police intimidation."

Mubarak is despised, as he has been throughout his entire career. These days, mutilated by neoliberal policies forced on it by the usual international agencies, Egypt is an economic disaster zone, able to feed its exploding population for only nine months in the year. The current political explosion has sharply aggravated the economic crisis.

The custodians of the American Empire are right to be perturbed. Those crowds in Tunis and in Cairo, facing projectiles "made in America," know well enough the ultimate sponsor of the tyrannies against which they have risen. A belated chirp for "democracy" from Obama or Secretary of State Clinton will not purge that record.

February 11

We need good news. When was the last time we had some, here in this country? The Seattle riots against the WTO? That was back in 1999. Around the world? Hard to remember—it's been a long dry spell. It reminds me of the old Jacobin shivering in the chill night of Bourbon restoration, and crying out, "Oh, sun of '93, when shall I feel thy warmth again!"

We raise our glass to the Egyptian people.

The brave Egyptian demonstrators did it. Conscripts ready to mutiny if ordered to fire on the crowds did it. Immensely courageous Egyptian union organizers active for years did it. Look at the numbers of striking workers enumerated by Esam al-Amin today; this was close to a general strike. It reminds me of France, its economy paralyzed in the uprising in the spring of 1968. That was when President de Gaulle, displaying a good deal more energy and sangfroid than Mubarak, flew to meetings with senior French military commanders to get pledges of loyalty and received requisite assurance.

And next for Egypt? These chapters are unwritten, but the world is bracingly different this week than what it was a month ago. Rulers and tyrants everywhere know that. They know bad news when they see it, same way we know good news when we hear its welcome knock on the door of history.

February 14

The Reagan cult celebrates the centenary of their idol's birth this month, and the airwaves have been tumid with homage to the thirty-eighth President, who held office for two terms, 1981–1988, and who died in 2004. The script of these recurring homages is unchanging: with his straightforward, sunny disposition and aw-shucks can-do style the manly Reagan gave America back its confidence. In less flattering terms he and his PR crew catered expertly to the demands of the American national fantasy: that homely common sense could return America to the vigor of its youth and the economy of the 1950s.

When he took over the Oval Office at the age of sixty-six whatever powers of concentration he might have once had were failing. The Joint Chiefs of Staff mounted their traditional show-and-tell briefings for him, replete with simple charts and a senior general explicating them in simple terms. Reagan found these briefings way too complicated and dozed off.

The Joint Chiefs then set up a secret unit, staffed by cartoonists. The balance of forces were set forth in easily accessible caricature, with Soviet missiles the size of upended Zeppelins, pulsing on their launch pads, with the miniscule US ICBMs shriveled in their bunkers. Little cartoon bubbles would contain the points the Joint Chiefs wanted to hammer into Reagan's brain, most of them to the effect that "we need more money." The President really enjoyed the shows and sometimes even asked for repeats.

March 11

The inhibitions that prompted his stutter extended to other regions of the King's body, as Kitty Kelley narrates in her fine book *The Royals*. Sexual dysfunction plagued poor George VI. Allegedly, Elizabeth and Margaret were conceived (respectively in 1926 and 1930) with the help of artificial insemination, donor undisclosed.

My maternal grandfather, Jack Arbuthnot of the Scots Guards, could be a candidate as the mystery donor for the future Queen. In terms of physiognomy Margaret is less likely. When he was commanding the guard detail at Balmoral, Elizabeth Bowes-Lyon, later George VI's consort, would visit from Glamis castle as a young girl. The high-spirited Elizabeth used to insist that Major Jack play "Horse," carrying her about on his shoulders. Perhaps in 1926 the Duchess, as she then was, remembered that early, fairly intimate proximity and sent him a royal request.

The popularity of the Royal family after the war should not be overestimated. In his excellent history *Austerity Britain*, David Kynaston quotes James Lees-Milne as recording in his diary for November 18, 1947—apropos the announcement of the engagement of Princess Elizabeth to Prince Philip of Greece—a disturbing dinner with Simon Mosley of the Coldstream Guards: "Says that 50 percent of the guardsmen in his company refused to contribute towards a present for Princess Elizabeth. The dissentients came to him in a body and, quite pleasantly, gave him their reasons. One, the Royal Family did nothing for anybody, and two, the Royal Family would not contribute towards a present for their weddings." Moreover, "when Simon Mosley said that without the Royal Family the Brigade of Guards, with its privileges and traditions, would cease to exist, they replied, 'Good! Let them both cease to exist.'"

March 17

Last Sunday my phone rang a couple of times from people watching *60 Minutes* reporting that in a segment on Christopher Hitchens, the following exchange occurred:

INTERVIEWER (Steve Kroft): Alexander Cockburn, a former friend of yours, called you a "self-serving, fat-ass, chain-smoking, drunken, opportunistic, cynical contrarian."

HITCHENS: Well, I don't see what's wrong with that … though he should see my ass now.

I was puzzled. It's not my argot of abuse, and besides, I haven't written anything recently about Hitchens. Why, unless occasion absolutely requires it, publicly kick a man in as tough a spot as he's evidently in?

It seems that *60 Minutes*, an immensely popular and profitable adornment of CBS News, can't afford to hire conscientious or experienced researchers and checkers. The phrase is taken from the headline of a torrent of measured abuse of Hitchens written by Jack McCarthy for *CounterPunch* in 2002, a year when emotions were running high, amid the work-up to the attack on Iraq. Any moderately seasoned checker knows headlines are no-nos for specific attribution without detailed inquiry, which certainly did not occur in this case.

March 18

Americans read the increasingly panic-stricken reports of deepening catastrophe at Fukushima Daiichi, speed to the pharmacy to look for iodine and ask, "It's happened there; can it happen here?" They already know it can, and almost certainly will.

President Obama took plenty of money from the nuclear industry for his presidential campaign and in his State of the Union address last January reaffirmed his commitment to "clean, safe" nuclear power, as insane a statement as pledging commitment to a nice clean form of syphilis. This week Obama's press spokesman confirmed that nuclear energy "remains a part of the President's overall energy plan." As Will Parrish reports, Obama was flacking for boosted plutonium production even as Fukushima Daiichi went into meltdown.

The United States produces more nuclear energy than any other nation. It has 104 nuclear plants, many of them old, many prone to endless leaks and kindred malfunctions, all of them dangerous.

Perhaps the news that Japanese nuclear reactors have been damaged and that clouds of official deception are already rising above them will cool the revival of enthusiasm for building new nuclear plants here in the US, spearheaded politically by President Obama and okayed by major Green groups using the cover of alleged anthropogenic global warming, as long ago planned by the nuclear industry.

April 4

In 2009 the New York Academy of Sciences published *Chernobyl: Consequences of the Catastrophe for People and the Environment*, a 327-page volume by three scientists, Alexey Yablokov and Vassily and Alexey Nesterenko, the definitive study to date. The book stresses that the cover-up began immediately. Official secrecy imposed by the Soviet government lasted three years, during which time an unknown number of people died from early leukosis. There were 830,000 "liquidators," as the clean-up workers were somewhat bizarrely termed, and for three years "it was officially forbidden to associate the diseases they were suffering from with radiation."

Set the desperate efforts to avoid apocalypse at the Tokyo Electric

Power Company's Fukushima plant next to Chernobyl and its ongoing lethal aftermath. Compare the hundreds of square miles of abandoned land in Ukraine next to the evacuated zone, already twenty kilometers in radius on Japan's northeast coast. Think of southern California or North Carolina or … The United States has 104 nuclear plants.

Nuclear expert Robert Alvarez writes that a single spent fuel rod pool—as in Fukushima or Shearon Harris—holds more cesium-137 than was deposited by all atmospheric nuclear weapons tests in the Northern Hemisphere combined, and an explosion in that pool could blast "perhaps three to nine times as much of these materials into the air as was released by the Chernobyl reactor disaster."

Significant sections of the environmental movement here, impelled by monomaniacal concern over the hypothesis of anthropogenic global warming, have made their shameful pact with the nuclear industry. It's over. Look at Chernobyl, look at Fukushima. There's no middle ground.

April 9

Fox News says Glenn Beck's daily program will "transition" off the network show some time before the end of this year. Beck cosigned the statement and confirmed this on his show on Wednesday, April 6, speaking vaguely of sustaining the two-year relationship with Fox by "developing things." He sounded shell-shocked, like a man who'd been shown the door.

I've always had a soft spot for Beck, partly because of his deep roots in the mulch of American nutdom, fertilized by the powerful psychic idiom of rebirth and redemption. "Progressives," today's milquetoast substitute for old-line radicals, have trembled at his ravings about the left's conspiracies against freedom. Personally, I found them heartening. Respect at last! Who but Beck could turn a conservative African-American Harvard grad, an errand boy for corporate America, into a latter-day re-creation of W. E. B. DuBois and Malcolm X, now installed in the White House?

A fairly typical reaction from the pwog sector was that of Michael

Keegan, President of People For the American Way, who swiftly proclaimed that "It's encouraging to know that it is no longer economically viable for a major television network to support the demagogic rantings of its most unhinged conspiracy theorist." But from Keegan's point of view, aren't demagogic and unhinged rantings exactly what he and his liberal fellows should want from Fox? Isn't it good to have a clownish ideologue bringing the Republican Party into disrepute?

Give me Beck any day.

April 14

What began in Britain in 2005 as "a third-rate burglary" of voicemails, supposedly limited to a criminal invasion of privacy by a *News of the World* reporter and a private investigator, has flowered beautifully into a Level 7 scandal that threatens the careers of two of Rupert Murdoch's top executives, not to mention the heir apparent to the News Corp. empire, James Murdoch. It even laps at the ankles of the eighty-year-old magnate, threatening the final financial triumph that was scheduled to usher him into Valhalla.

Will Rupert himself be enmeshed? Bruce Page, author of a fine book on Murdoch, suggests to me that what could drag the dirty digger into the swamp would be the disclosure of any deal he may have made to stem the scandal when Gordon Brown was still PM. Brown won't confirm or deny that Murdoch approached him.

April 20

It looks as though eastern Libya will slide into the Mediterranean under the sheer weight of Western journalists assembled in Benghazi and Misrata. A tsunami of breathless reports suggests that Misrata is enduring travails not far short of the siege of Leningrad in World War II. The reports have been seized on by President Obama, British Prime Minister Cameron and French Prime Minister Sarkozy to raise the ante on Mission Odyssey Dawn. In their joint newspaper column published on both sides of the Atlantic they now say that to leave Gaddafi in power would be an "unconscionable betrayal" and speak of Misrata as enduring "a medieval siege."

Not yet, surely. A medieval siege was something that usually lasted at least a year, in which the city's inhabitants were reduced to eating rats, then each other, and the besiegers all succumbed to plague.

Maybe it will turn out that way, with reporters eying each other from a gastronomic perspective and wiring Ferran Adrià, seeking recipes for preparing Haunch of Hack sous vide. "So long as Gaddafi is in power, NATO and its coalition partners must maintain their operations so that civilians remain protected and the pressure on the regime builds," write the three leaders. This is not Mission Creep but, once again, Mission Leap, way beyond the UN mandate.

It seems that the rebels might actually be under the overall supervision of the international banking industry, rather than the oil majors. On March 19 they announced the "designation of the Central Bank of Benghazi as a monetary authority competent in monetary policies in Libya and appointment of a Governor to the Central Bank of Libya, with a temporary headquarters in Benghazi."

CNBC senior editor John Carney asked, "Is this the first time a revolutionary group has created a central bank while it is still in the midst of fighting the entrenched political power? It certainly seems to indicate how extraordinarily powerful central bankers have become in our era." Ellen Brown, author of the terrific *Web of Debt: The Shocking Truth About Our Money System and How We Can Break Free*, wrote recently about the rebels' sophisticated financial operations in the following terms:

> According to a Russian article titled "Bombing of Lybia—Punishment for Gaddafi for His Attempt to Refuse US Dollar," Gaddafi made a similarly bold move: he initiated a movement to refuse the dollar and the euro, and called on Arab and African nations to use a new currency instead: the gold dinar. Gaddafi suggested establishing a united African continent, with its 200 million people using this single currency. During the past year, the idea was approved by many Arab countries and most African countries.
>
> The only opponents were the Republic of South Africa and the head of the League of Arab States. The initiative was viewed negatively by the

> USA and the European Union, with French President Nicolas Sarkozy calling Libya a threat to the financial security of mankind; but Gaddafi was not swayed and continued his push for the creation of a united Africa.
>
> And that brings us back to the puzzle of the Libyan central bank. In an article posted on the Market Oracle, Eric Encina observed: "One seldom mentioned fact by Western politicians and media pundits: the Central Bank of Libya is 100% State Owned … Currently, the Libyan government creates its own money, the Libyan Dinar, through the facilities of its own central bank. Few can argue that Libya is a sovereign nation with its own great resources, able to sustain its own economic destiny. One major problem for globalist banking cartels is that in order to do business with Libya, they must go through the Libyan Central Bank and its national currency, a place where they have absolutely zero dominion or power-broking ability. Hence, taking down the Central Bank of Libya (CBL) may not appear in the speeches of Obama, Cameron and Sarkozy but this is certainly at the top of the globalist agenda for absorbing Libya into its hive of compliant nations."

I'd really like to see an objective account of Gaddafi's allocation of oil revenues versus the United States', in terms of social improvement.

April 22

For a nation that loves anniversaries, the 150th anniversary of the outbreak of the American Civil War—April 12, 1861—crept by on tiptoe, like a burglar slipping through a darkened house. The reason for this eerie semi-silence is not hard to find. The Civil War is contested political terrain, particularly in the racist backwash after the 1960s and the civil rights movement which naturally looked back on the Civil War as one in which tens of thousands of Americans gave their lives for the principle that all are born free and slavery is a shameful blot on any society.

These days we live in the shadow of Nixon's southern strategy, which became Reagan's southern strategy and is now standard issue campaign politics for the Republican Party: Play the racist card, throw money at think-tanks to churn out papers delivering an onslaught on quotas, deride all attempts to level the racial playing field. Speak "frankly" about the supposed pathologies of the black family.

Meanwhile, up north, the forthright honoring of a war waged for honorable principles has faded amid revisionist histories of what the war was really about. Add to this a general wan feeling that the fruits of a terrible conflict were the appalling racism of the Reconstruction Period after the Civil War, when the Ku Klux Klan began to burn and lynch, and the migration of southern slaves and their descendants from the Deep South to the slums of Chicago and other northern cities. Ahead lay decades of poverty and oppression that prompted the riots of the 1960s.

So the Civil War is a dangerous football to start kicking around on network TV, bad for the advertising business, except for the deadened hand of Ken Burns. The arrival of a black man to the White House has naturally intensified these divisions.

April 28

Americans were offered closure Wednesday to one of the multifarious strands of our national dementias. It took the drab guise of the "long-form" birth certificate, signed and filed in Hawaii on August 8, 1961, indicating that the President is a legitimate occupant of the Oval Office. But will the White House's release of the certificate finish off the "birther" movement? Certainly not.

Harold Camping, President of Family Stations Ministry, has been preaching for some time now to a vast and devoted national audience that God's plan is to inaugurate the Second Coming and end the world by flooding on May 21, 2011 (thus achieving a Judeo-Christian planetary closure before the prime current pagan rival, the end of the Mayan calendar, scheduled for December 21, 2012).

It's a safe bet that Camping and his disciples will be saying on May 22 that his math was merely a year or two off, and the end is still nigh. His congregation will have its faith fortified. Membership will probably increase, as it did after the failure of Camping's last prediction of the Second Coming, which he scheduled for September 6, 1994.

Sociologists call the phenomenon of increased commitment to a batty theory, at the very hour of its destruction by external evidence, "cognitive dissonance."

May 6

Peering briefly at the royal nuptials in a house high up in the mountains above Malibu, I was surprised to see how spectacularly tacky the British upper classes have become. They looked very vulgar. The appalling cuteness of the Aston Martin supplied the coup de grace. The groom didn't know how to stand up properly. Contrary to effusive comparisons, the bride's much touted dress from the atelier of the wildly overpraised late Alexander McQueen was a far cry from Grace Kelly's, designed by Helen Rose, who had dressed her in *High Society* and *The Swan*. The bride's headdress hung like a dishrag.

The only vestments borne with confidence and aplomb were those of the churchmen. The Archbishop of Canterbury, with his emphatic beard and specs, had a splendid cape. His voice was confident. I'd like to see him in debate with one of Tehran's ayatollahs. But the Anglo actresses watching the event on our mountain were ecstatic. My daughter Daisy, returning to London two days later, reported that the young women she was encountering were all swept away by the event and eager for marriage.

May 11

Has there ever been such a chilling launch to a re-election campaign? I take the kickoff to be April 27, when Obama produces his long birth certificate at a White House press conference. He says it's time to abandon such idle distractions and face the big, serious issues. He knows something we don't—that serious issue number one is a killing.

The Navy SEALs are on standby, primed with Obama's orders for the summary assassination of Osama bin Laden. There's cloud cover over Abbottabad, so bin Laden gets an extra couple of days puttering around the house listening to his old speeches. William and Kate won't have to share Saturday's headlines with the head of Osama.

Had all gone well, Sunday's newspapers would have been freighted with the news that Muammar Gaddafi had been killed in the course of a NATO bombing strike on a "command and control" site in Tripoli. It had been on the cards from day one; indeed, on April 29 the Russian Foreign Intelligence Service leaked an accurate forecast to *Rex*, a Russian online news agency, whose Kirill Svetitsky quoted an anonymous source within the intelligence service: "There will be an attempt to kill Muammar Gaddafi on or before May 2. The governments of France, Britain and the US decided on it, for the warfare in Libya does not proceed well for the anti-Libyan alliance."

The April 30, 2011, bombing attack, made in the direct aftermath of Gaddafi's call for a cease-fire, was not burdened with fancy talk about Article 51. UN Resolution 1973, which simply established a no-fly zone, was the sole legal pretext for targeted assassination.

Obama is certainly not the first US President to have taken a keen interest in assassinations. We could start with the bid on Zhou Enlai's life just before the Bandung Conference in 1955. Then we could move on to the assassination of the Congo's Patrice Lumumba in 1961. The Kennedy years saw the first of many well-attested CIA efforts to assassinate Fidel Castro.

In his *Killing Hope: US Military and CIA Interventions Since World War II*, Bill Blum—one of Osama's favorite authors—has an interesting list of US targets, starting in 1949 with Korean opposition leader Kim Koo and going on to Indonesian President Sukarno, Kim Il-sung of North Korea, Mohammed Mossadegh, Philippines opposition leader Claro Recto, Jawaharlal Nehru, Gamal Abdel Nasser, Norodom Sihanouk, José Figueres Ferrer, François "Papa Doc" Duvalier, Gen. Rafael Trujillo, Charles de Gaulle, Salvador Allende, Michael Manley, Ayatollah Khomeini, the nine *comandantes* of the Sandinista National Directorate, prominent Somali clan leader Mohamed Farah Aidid, Slobodan Milošević …

In sum, assassination has always been an arm of US foreign policy, just as in periods of turbulence, like the '60s, it has always been an arm of domestic repression as well. This is true on either side of the executive order President Gerald Ford issued in 1976 banning assassinations. "No employee of the United States Government shall engage in, or conspire to engage in, political assassination," stated Executive Order 11905, now inoperative.

May 13

Pinko terror-symps and the "rule of law" gang may cavil and whine at the lack of legal propriety in the execution of Osama, but it's not cutting much ice with liberal America. For long years what might be called the "progressive" segment of American voters have chafed at Republican gibes that their guy Obama is a wimp, all the more irritably because deep down many of them thought the charge had some merit.

It's wondrous what two expanding bullets to the head of an unarmed man will do. The chorus of approval for the SEALs covers the liberal spectrum. The *Nation*'s Jeremy Scahill exulted, as did Gary Wills on the *New York Review of Books* site, with an ecstatic paean, "The President's Crack Team," concluding, "we should keep in mind what superb things can be done by our Navy Seals. And we should keep somewhere in the back of our minds a remembrance that the one ultimately pulling the trigger … was the President of the United States."

May 20

The French are for the millionaire. The Americans are for the maid. Among the French, three out of five think the IMF's former managing director, Dominique Strauss-Kahn, has been framed. Here in the US there's not been a reliable poll, but public sentiment is clearly against Strauss-Kahn, amplified by self-congratulation that America is a nation of laws, a maid's word as potent as that of a millionaire, in contrast to the moral decay and deference to the rich prevalent in France.

The French, for their part, stigmatize America as a puritanical, omnipotent imperial police state, whose intelligence agencies are efficiently capable of any infamy. But even as they charge that Strauss-Kahn was set up, the French press is rather weak on identifying or even suggesting the precise mastermind or group working to destroy a man who might have been the French Socialist Party's candidate, evicting Sarkozy from the Élysée Palace.

May 27

Was there ever a nation so marinated in hypocrisy as America? At home and abroad President Barack Obama trumpets Uncle Sam's virtues and dispenses patronizing homilies to other nations on how to behave themselves and honor freedom and democracy. This last week it's been Europe's turn to hear these self-righteous preachments.

A couple of weeks ago Secretary of State Clinton attacked China, contrasting untiring efforts by the US to encourage human rights around the world, at a time when the Chinese "are trying to stop history, which is a fool's errand. They cannot do it. But they're going to hold it off as long as possible."

A week earlier Obama signed an expanded trade pact with Colombia where in 2010 fifty-one Colombian labor organizers were murdered, many of them by government-sponsored death squads. As Richard Trumka, head of the AFL-CIO remarked, he doubted the trade agreement would be moving forward if fifty-one CEOs had been killed.

If there's one state in the Middle East where the US surely has clout it's Bahrain, which just happens to be the base for the US Fifth Fleet. While Clinton was wagging her finger at China, details were surfacing of the ferocious repression of Bahrain's Shia majority by Bahrain's Sunni rulers, backed by Saudi troops.

Masked squads raid Shia villages at night. At least twenty-seven Shia mosques and religious meeting places have so far been wrecked or bulldozed flat. If this was Libya, Clinton would trumpeting the repression as further justification for NATO's onslaught. Not so in Bahrain. Peter Lee recently described the repression in the country: "In one sequence, a Human Rights Watch representative directs the reporter's attention to a crime scene that has come to symbolize the worst excesses of Bahrain's riot police: the place where a young man, Hani Jumah, was beaten. Apparently, he was not a demonstrator; he was just in the wrong place at the wrong time as riot police swept the area. The camera pans on the bloodstained floor of a deserted construction site as the HRW staffer relates with forensic detachment: 'We found fragments of his kneecap … we also found one of his teeth.' And you're left to wonder: how does someone get beaten so severely a piece of his kneecap is dislodged from his body? The young man was taken to the hospital for treatment, then got disappeared from the hospital. His family was summoned to retrieve his body four days later."

Amid Obama's grandiose eloquence about freedom, he has effectively excluded Palestinians from his supportive embrace and, amid meaningless verbal froth, collapsed yet again in the face of Israeli intransigence, and the lobby. US diplomacy, supervised by Obama and Clinton, will of course be dedicated to efforts to hold back history while strong-arming the UN into attempting to do the same.

June 16

Here's Trotsky on Céline—"Louis-Ferdinand Céline walked into great literature as other men walk into their own homes. A mature man, with a colossal stock of observations as physician and artist, with a sovereign indifference toward academicism, with an extraordinary instinct for intonations of life and language, Céline has written a book which will survive, independently of whether he writes other books, and whether they attain the level of his first. *Journey to the End of the Night* is a novel of pessimism, a book dedicated by terror in the face of life, and weariness of it, rather than by indignation. Active indignation is linked up with hope. In Céline's book there is no hope … Decay hits not only parties in power, but schools of art as well. The creative methods become hollow and cease to react upon human sensibilities—an infallible sign that the school has become ripe enough for the cemetery of exhausted possibilities—that is to say, for the Academy … Céline will not write a second book with such an aversion for the lie and such a disbelief in the truth. The dissonance must resolve itself. Either the artist will make his peace with the darkness or he will perceive the dawn."

I like the cemetery of exhausted possibilities. Put it next to Robert Browning's lines in "Bishop Blougram's Apology":

> What's the vague good o' the world, for which you dare
> With comfort to yourself blow millions up?
> We neither of us see it! we do see
> The blown-up millions—spatter of their brains
> And writhing of their bowels and so forth,
> In that bewildering entanglement
> Of horrible eventualities
> Past calculation to the end of time!

Round out the funeral bouquet with this, from Adorno: "The injunction to practice intellectual honesty usually amounts to sabotage of thought. The writer is urged to show explicitly all the steps that have led him to his conclusion, so enabling the reader to follow the process through and, where possible—in the academic industry—to duplicate it. This demand not only invokes the liberal fiction of the universal communicability of each and every thought and so inhibits their objectively appropriate expression, but is also wrong in itself as a principle of representation. For the value of a thought is measured by its distance from the continuity of the familiar."

From *Minima Moralia*—and as succinct a critique of the culture of the internet as one can find.

June 29

How many nails does it require to whack down forever the coffin lid on European social democracy? Lenin, outraged in 1914 at the sight of Social Democratic parties across Europe rallying behind their national flags and voting war credits to unleash the horrors of World War I, would have been caustically unsurprised just over a century later at the current spectacle in Athens.

Here, last Wednesday, Greek Prime Minister George Papandreou won a no-confidence vote for what Michael Hudson describes as a program for national suicide, which can only be thwarted by a national referendum. The confidence vote was to ram through an austerity package, amounting to over €78 billion, against the furious protests and resistance of the Greek people. Around €28 billion of the total is to be raised through spending cuts and increased revenue, while €50 billion will be raised through the privatization of state enterprises.

It really is a bit rich to hear preachments from Germany about the importance of paying debts. Ninety percent of all Germans oppose a bailout for Greece on the grounds of the latter's aversion to paying reparations for its supposed profligacy. Never has a country flourished more mightily than Germany from flouting reparations and debts.

Albrecht Ritschl, a professor at the London School of Economics, points out in an interview in *Der Spiegel* that Germany welshed on loans from the US to pay the reparations levied by the Allies after World War I. After World War II, a divided Germany was excused reparations to countries such as Greece that it had invaded. Under a 1953 treaty, the issue of reparations was on the table after reunification in 1990. But, Ritschl says, "With the exception of compensation paid out to forced laborers, Germany did not pay any reparations after 1990—and neither did it pay off the loans and occupation costs it pressed out of the countries it had occupied during World War II. Not to the Greeks, either." Ritschl reckons Germany was "the biggest debt transgressor of the twentieth century."

July 18

On August 2, the United States could start defaulting on its obligations as the Tea Party crowd in the House of Representatives refuse to raise the debt ceiling.

America is in love with Apocalypse. It always has been. Every couple of years someone says the End Is Nigh. When I came to America's shores in 1972 Hal Lindsey's *The Late Great Planet Earth* had just been published and sold thirty million copies over the next twenty years. Lindsey wrote, rather presciently, that the Antichrist would rule over a ten-nation European Community through the 1970s until the Rapture—scheduled for the 1980s—and the Second Coming.

Not many people here really think the US government will shut down on August 3. The fight over the deficit is one of those American ceremonies, as embalmed in ritual speech and gesture as an English coronation.

August 4

Of course he blew it. Whether by artful design or by sheer timidity is immaterial. He blew it. Two days before the United States was officially set to default on its debts on August 2, Barack Obama had the Republicans where he wanted them: All he had to do was announce that he'd trudged the last half mile towards a deal but that there's no pleasing fanatics who reject all possibility of compromise, who are ready and eager to shut down the government, to see seniors starve and veterans denied their benefits. So, Obama could proclaim, he was invoking the Fourteenth Amendment to the US Constitution that states that the "validity of the public debt of the United States … shall not be questioned."

Obama could have done that, but he didn't. At the eleventh hour and the fifty-fifth minute he threw in the towel, and allowed the Republicans to exult that they'd got 95 percent of what they wanted: cuts in social programs, a bipartisan congressional panel to shred at its leisure what remains of the social safety net, no tax hikes for the rich, no serious slice in the military budget.

August 10

What's a riot without looting? We want it, they've got it! You'd think from the press that looting was alien to British tradition, imported by immigrants more recent than the Normans. Not so. Gavin Mortimer, author of *The Blitz*, had an amusing piece in the *First Post* about the conduct of Britons at the time of Their Finest Hour:

> It didn't take long for a hardcore of opportunists to realise there were rich pickings available in the immediate aftermath of a raid—and the looting wasn't limited to civilians.

> The looting was often carried out by gangs of children organized by a Fagin figure; he would send them into bombed-out houses the morning after a raid with orders to target coins from gas meters and display cases containing World War I medals. In April 1941 Lambeth juvenile court dealt with 42 children in one day, from teenage girls caught stripping clothes from dead bodies to a seven-year-old boy who had stolen five shillings from the gas meter of a damaged house. In total, juvenile crime accounted for 48 percent of all arrests in the nine months between September 1940 and May 1941 and there were 4,584 cases of looting.
>
> Perhaps the most shameful episode of the whole Blitz occurred on the evening of March 8, 1941 when the Café de Paris in Piccadilly was hit by a German bomb. The cafe was one of the most glamorous night spots in London, the venue for off-duty officers to bring their wives and girlfriends, and within minutes of its destruction the looters moved in.
>
> "Some of the looters in the Café de Paris cut off the people's fingers to get the rings," recalled Ballard Berkeley, a policeman during the Blitz who later found fame as the "Major" in *Fawlty Towers*. Even the wounded in the Café de Paris were robbed of their jewellery amid the confusion and carnage.

The riots in London last week started in Tottenham, an area with the highest unemployment in London, in response to the police shooting a young black man, in a country where black people are twenty-six times more likely to stopped and searched by the cops than whites. As the *Daily Mash* puts it: "Many of these kids are less than two miles away from people who get multi-million pound bonuses for catastrophic failure and live in a culture where the material excess of people who are famous for nothing is rammed relentlessly into their faces by middle-brow tabloid newspapers. And of course later today the looters will be condemned in Parliament by a bunch of people who stole money by accident."

September 7

The protesters outside the White House have furled their banners and headed home. Now the Obama administration will decide whether to issue a presidential permit for the 1,700-mile Keystone XL pipeline extension—a $7 billion project to bring heavy, "sour" crude oil extracted from tar sands in Alberta, Canada, down through Montana and the Plains states to refineries on the Gulf Coast, notably in Port Arthur, Texas.

Even as the protesters savaged the scheme as a fearsome environmental disaster, the State Department issued its final environmental impact statement on August 26. Not surprisingly, it was favorable to the project, furnishing such nuggets of encouragement as "analysis of previous large pipeline oil spills suggests that the depth and distance that the oil would migrate would likely be limited unless it reaches an active river, stream, a steeply sloped area, or another migration pathway such as a drainage ditch."

There's no national need for the Keystone XL extension. But money talks, of course. Obama received $884,000 from the oil and gas industry during the 2008 campaign, more than any other lawmaker except John McCain.

September 8

America's problems are huge: fourteen million Americans officially looking for jobs—about four job seekers for every job vacancy; 8.8 million part-time workers since the recession began; roughly 2.6 million people too discouraged even to look for a job: total—about twenty-five million people needing work or more work and an economy that is creating no new jobs.

As the economists Randall Wrey and Stephanie Kelton point out, "Business will not hire more workers until it has more sales. Consumers will not spend more until they've got more jobs."

You can find America's future in blueprints minted in business-funded think-tanks thirty to forty years ago at the dawn of the neoliberal age: destruction of organized labor; attrition of the social safety net; attrition of government regulation; a war on the poor, fought without mercy at every level. Last year the New York police stopped and questioned 601,055 people, predominantly blacks and Hispanics, and the numbers were up 13 percent for the first six months of this year.

September 22

First, a simple rule for killers: If you are going to murder someone in the United States, don't try to get the job done in Texas. Keep your captive alive in the car till New Mexico, which recently banned the death penalty, or press on to California, which retains the death penalty but makes available very large sums of state money—potentially, hundreds of thousands of dollars—for a capable death penalty defense.

Business is correspondingly brisk in the lethal injection chamber in Huntsville, Texas. There are currently 413 on death row, and at the time of writing, 475 have been executed since 1976, 235 of them during Rick Perry's decade-long stint as governor.

It turned out Thursday we won't have to adjust the numbers yet. On September 15, the scheduled execution day for Duane Edward Buck, the US Supreme Court granted a stay of execution for Buck (who on September 12 had his clemency request turned down by the Texas Board of Pardons and Paroles) while it reviews the case.

No one claims that Buck, forty-eight, didn't shoot to death his former girlfriend and her male companion and wound a third in Houston in 1995. He himself admits his crimes. At issue is what an expert witness told the court during the sentencing hearing, where the jury decides whether the convicted murderer should go to prison for a life term or get lodgings on death row. To get Buck lined up for the lethal needle, his prosecutors needed to prove "future dangerousness." How might Buck behave in the event he ever got out of prison?

Dr. Walter Quijano, a psychologist practicing in Conroe, a town just south of Huntsville, had actually been called by the defense, who hoped he would testify that Buck's killing spree was an act of rage unlikely to be repeated. Under cross-examination, however, the prosecutors asked Quijano: "The race factor, black, increases the future dangerousness for various complicated reasons; is that correct?"

"Yes," Quijano answered, probably out of sheer force of habit, because usually he was the prosecution's expert, and he had testified in similar fashion for the prosecution in six other cases, racially profiling the defendants into the Huntsville death house. His "yes" was enough for the jury, which cut smartly through all uncertainty about Buck's future decisions by saying he should die, thus rendering speculation unnecessary.

In 2000, then-Texas Attorney General John Cornyn (now a Republican US Senator), recognizing the constitutional abuse for what it was, called for Buck and the other six to receive a retrial. Buck is the only condemned man who hasn't gotten one. On September 13, Linda Geffin, one of Buck's prosecutors in 1995, joined the chorus of voices calling on Gov. Perry to stay his execution.

Of course, it doesn't help anyone on death row, headed for the injection chamber and amid last-ditch appeals, that we're in campaign mode and right after Perry issued a fervent endorsement of the death penalty, earning him hearty cheers in the auditorium of the Ronald Reagan Presidential Library, when he stressed that imposing it has never lost him a moment's sleep.

October 12

Even by the forgiving standards of American credulity, the supposed Iranian plot to assassinate the Saudi ambassador to the US is spectacularly ludicrous. Why would Iran want to kill the Saudi envoy—the mild-mannered functionary, Adel al-Jubeir? I could understand an inclination to dispose of the irksome Prince Bandar who held the job for twenty-two years, from 1983 to 2005—simply in the spirit of "change." But to kill any ambassador—particularly a Saudi ambassador—is to invite lethal retaliation, even war. Iran doesn't want war with the US.

Suppose the CIA leaks a secret national security review concluding that the moon is actually made of cheese, and the Chinese are planning to send up a pair of gigantic bio-engineered rats to breed in numbers sufficient to eat the cheese and thus sabotage US plans for Missile Defense radar deployment on the moon's dark side.

The headlines will initially proclaim "Doubts on Chinese Rat Threat Widespread. Many scoff." The lead paragraphs in news stories in the *New York Times*, *Washington Post* and *Wall Street Journal* will quote the scoffers, but then "balance" will mandate respectful quotation from "intelligence sources," faculty professors, think-tank "experts" and the like, all eager to dance to the government's tune: "Many say rat scenario 'plausible,'" etc., etc.

Lo and behold, by the end of a couple of days of such news stories, the Chinese rat plot is firmly ensconced as a credible proposition. News reports then turn to respectful discussion of the US government's options in confronting and routing the Chinese rat threat: "Vice President says 'all options are on the table,'" etc.

October 28

Denied post-mortem imagery of Osama bin Laden and Anwar al-Awlaki, the world now has at its disposal photographs of Muammar Gaddafi, dispatched with a bullet to the head after being wounded by NATO's ground troops outside Sirte. Did the terminal command, Finish Him Off, come via cell phone from the US State Department, whose Secretary, Hillary Clinton, had earlier called for his death, or by dint of local initiative? At all events, since Gaddafi was a prisoner at the time of his execution, it was a war crime, and I trust that in the years of her retirement Mrs. Clinton will be detained amid some foreign vacation and handed a subpoena.

My friend and neighbor in Petrolia, Joe Paff, wrote a response to a dreadful story about Gaddafi's killing on Yahoo's site, commenting "This kind of gloating is bound to come back and bite your butt. Imagine how many people in the world would like to see Netanyahu or Obama dragged from their hiding holes and tortured. It will take about six months for everyone to regret the 'new' Libyan 'democrats.'"

Yahoo's initial electronic response was to write to Joe, "Oops! Try again." So he checked "post" a second time. Yahoo then rewrote his comment, complete with misspellings, stripped of any mention of Netanyahu or Obama, and "posted" it as: "This is the kind of gloating that comes back and bites you on the butt. Just imagine how many peopel in the world would like to see Americans dragged through the streets and tortured to death." As Joe wrote me, "Just another small episode in artificial intelligence and the present taboos."

October 29

Remember Tilikum, kidnapped by whale-slavers off Iceland at the age of two in 1983? Deliberately starved as part of his "training" in a Sealand tank in Victoria, Canada, Tilikum has spent the past nineteen years at the SeaWorld marine park in Orlando, Florida. The whale has been involved in three lethal onslaughts on his captors, the most recent being an attack on Dawn Brancheau, a trainer he dragged into his tank and drowned in February 2010.

Why was Tilikum spared? Big whale, big money.

There's a lot riding on the slave orcas toiling away, giving as many as eight performances per day, 365 days a year, as the star attractions in these marine parks. Tilikum's asset value is enhanced by his duties as a sperm donor. He's a breeding "stud" often kept in solitary, away from the other orcas, and has fathered thirteen killer whales.

Earlier this week, People for the Ethical Treatment of Animals (PETA) filed a lawsuit against SeaWorld for "enslaving" five orcas. Tilikum is one of the plaintiffs. PETA's suit invokes the Thirteenth Amendment, abolishing and prohibiting slavery, and demands the orcas' release under the Amendment's terms. "All five of these orcas were violently seized from the ocean and taken from their families as babies," says PETA's President Ingrid Newkirk, echoed by PETA's lawyer, Jeff Kerr, who told AP: "By any definition, these orcas are slaves—kidnapped from their homes, kept confined, denied everything that's natural to them and forced to perform tricks for SeaWorld's profit."

Will the orcas get legal standing?

Animals currently have no rights recognized in US law, but many groups of lawyers are working to strengthen laws that protect animals and many individuals have successfully brought lawsuits to protect the welfare of animals. Animal rights, or animal liberation, are one of the oldest forms of Animal Law.

Three years ago the *DC Bar* journal ran a very useful survey by Kathryn Alfisi who pointed out that it was the Michael Vick case "that allowed for just the right atmosphere to push for state and federal legislation that would strengthen dog-fighting and animal cruelty laws." Vick was the Atlanta Falcons quarterback who pulled a twenty-three-month sentence after pleading guilty to conspiring to run a dog-fighting ring on his property in Surry County, Virginia.

Some animal lawyers flee the term "animal rights" while others question the whole concept of legal boundaries between animals and humans. Several state bars have animal law sections or committees. In 2005 the American Bar Association's (ABA) Tort Trial and Insurance Practice Section created its Animal Law Committee. More than 100 animal law courses are being taught at law schools across the States.

The legal system, Alfisi reckons, is beginning "to reflect the increasingly complex relationship between people and their pets in our society."

The phrase "increasingly complex" does the Middle Ages a grave injustice. Just read my *CounterPunch* co-editor Jeffrey St. Clair's marvelous introduction to Jason Hribal's *Fear of the Animal Planet: The Hidden Story of Animal Resistance*: "In medieval Europe (and even colonial America) thousands of animals were summoned to court and put on trial for a variety of offences, ranging from trespassing, thievery and vandalism to rape, assault, and murder. The defendants included cats, dogs, cows, sheep, goats, slugs, swallows, oxen, horses, mules, donkeys, pigs, wolves, bears, bees, weevils, and termites. These tribunals were not show trials or strange festivals like Fools Day. The tribunals were taken seriously by both the courts and the community."

Humans and animals often ended up in the same courtroom as co-conspirators, especially in cases of bestiality. The animals were given their own lawyers at public expense. "Sometimes, particularly in cases involving pigs," St. Clair writes, "the animal defendants were dressed in human clothes during court proceedings and at executions."

The animal trials peaked in the late sixteenth and early seventeenth centuries, then faded away, done in by the Enlightenment and by René Descartes, who argued that animals were mere physical automatons. They lacked the power of cognition, the ability to think and reason. At Port Royal the Cartesians cut up living creatures with fervor, and in the words of one of Descartes' biographers, "kicked about their dogs and dissected their cats without mercy, laughing at any compassion for them and calling their screams the noise of breaking machinery."

Across the Channel, Francis Bacon declared in his *Novum Organum* that the proper aim of science was to restore the divinely ordained dominance of man over nature, "to extend more widely the limits of the power and greatness of man" and so to endow him with "infinite commodities." Bacon's doctor, William Harvey, was a diligent vivisector of living animals.

Thus, at the dawn of capitalism, the materialistic view of history left no room for either the souls or consciousness of animals. They were no longer our fellow beings. They had been rendered, philosophically and literally, resources for guiltless exploitation, turned into objects of commerce, labor, food—and entertainment. Tilikum should get his day in court.

November 2

I have to admit, writing these lines at the start of November, that after digesting the daily reports from our national battlefield (Zuccotti Park, Oscar Grant Plaza, Austin, Philadelphia, Atlanta, Nashville, Portland ...), my eyes flicker across the world map to Greece, and my heart beats a lot faster. Now *there*, surely, we can savor the whiff of a pre-revolutionary situation!

It must be the dratted Leninist in me, even after years of therapy. Surfeited with somewhat turgid paeans to the democratic gentility of the OWSers, I clamber up to the dusty top shelf, furtively haul down Vladimir Ilyich's "April Theses" of 1917 and dip in: end the war, confiscate the big estates, immediately merge all the banks into one general national bank ... The blood flows back into my cheeks, my eyes sparkle. Then, hearing my daughter's footfall outside the library, I shove Lenin back into place, scuttle back down the ladder and pluck a copy of E. F. Schumacher, even though I'm not at all sure what is on the OWSers' reading lists or Twitter menus.

Now take an arc of Greek history, as evoked in a photo that landed in my inbox at the end of October, featuring a group of Greek demonstrators in front of the Parthenon holding a white banner with

"OXI 1940–2011" written on it in red and black letters. In Greek "OXI" means "no." The email reminded me that the "no" of 1940 was the answer, given on October 28, to the Italian ambassador relaying Mussolini's demand that Greece open its borders to the Italian army. The "no" thus marked Greece's entry into World War II. Annual ceremonies have officially commemorated this response to fascism.

This year, on the morning of October 28, a group of artists, authors, and academics smuggled a big OXI sign onto the Acropolis, "wrapped up around the body of an excellent theater actress under a very large coat. And we managed to demonstrate for more than half an hour on the Acropolis itself!" The group could do this because "all policemen were at the parades' battlegrounds at Syntagma and everywhere in Attiki [district] and none managed to climb the Acropolis in time."

OXI in 1940 to Mussolini. OXI in 2011 to the bankers seeking to plant their neoliberal jackboots on the neck of the Greek people. OXI to the bankers' local collaborators.

Like Greece, the strength of the OWS movement lies in the simplicity and truth of its basic message: the few are rich, the many are poor. In terms of its pretensions the capitalist system has failed. Nearly six million manufacturing jobs in the United States have disappeared since 2000, and more than 40,000 factories have closed. African Americans have endured what has been described as the greatest loss of collective assets in their history. Hispanics have seen their net worth drop by two-thirds. Millions of whites have been pitchforked into penury and desperation.

But for all its simplicity and truth, how much staying power does the OWS message have as presently deployed? In terms of its powers of repression, the system has not failed. To date, the OWS movement has not even confronted the moneyed elite with a threat on the scale of the 1999 protests in Seattle. There are many options lying ahead for the OWSers to ponder, though they should remember Lenin: there is never a final collapse of capitalism unless there is an alternative.

Having briefly tasted batons and pepper spray, OWSers should know that when capital feels it is being pushed to the wall, it will stop at nothing to crush any serious challenge. The cop puts away his smile. The indulgent mayor imposes a curfew. "Exemplary" sentences are handed down. The prisons fill up. Organized repression can be defeated only by organized resistance, nationwide. How to mount this is the OWSers' urgent, immediate challenge.

November 8

As he prepares to follow Gov. Rick Perry into the oubliette of campaign history, Herman Cain can at least console himself that as an alleged harasser of women, his was certainly a classier act than that of a man who not only got elected President in 1992 but was triumphantly reelected in 1996, each time by about forty-five million Americans armed with the knowledge that if you left your wife at the table next to Gov. Bill Clinton of Arkansas in McDonald's, by the time you got back from ordering more fries Bill would be ensconced in your seat, his hand already hovering above your wife's thigh.

So Obama's opponent in 2012 will surely be Mitt Romney, a Mormon millionaire reminiscent in style, and utter lack of any fixed political conviction beyond knee-jerk conservatism, to George Bush Sr. There's no point in trying to sketch in "the real Mitt Romney," because there isn't one. He's been campaigning for the Republican nomination for eight solid years, and his brain has been washed clean years ago of anything approaching an original or useful thought about America's condition.

November 16

What next? Thus far the OWS movement has mostly been evoked by its participants in terms of self-education and consciousness-raising about the nature of America's political economy. There's been a lot of talk about a brave new world being born. One fellow chided me for not writing more about the movement which he hailed as "the most militant upsurge from the Left since the Vietnam War, the most frontal assault on the worst features of capitalism since the Great Depression." This is a vast overstatement. In terms of substantive achievements, OWS has a long way to go, which is scarcely a reason for reproof since it only really got going in September. "The most frontal assault on the worst features of capitalism since the Great Depression?" Scarcely.

Today, the OWSers have registered a presence and won considerable public support, which should not be surprising because America is in poor shape, the rich unpopular, and politicians despised. But, as yet, there is no sign of any material political consequence deriving from this popularity.

November 24

It's Thanksgiving here in America, a day of infamy for turkeys. At my place in Humboldt County, northern California, turkeys learned their lesson a few years ago, when five fine specimens of *Meleagris gallopavo*—wild turkey to you—wandered onto my property. I assume they forgot to check the calendar. Under California fish and game regulations, you can shoot them legally for two weeks around Thanksgiving.

Out came my 12-gauge, and I loosed off a shot that at some 100 feet did no discernible damage, and after a brief bout of what-the-hell-was-that the turkeys continued to forage. A fusillade of two more shots finally brought down a fourteen-pounder. I hung him for four days, plucked him and by Thanksgiving's end he was history.

Wild turkeys hadn't been seen in California since earlier in the Cenozoic era, but in recent years two ranchers in my valley imported a few and now they've begun to appear in our neighborhood in substantial numbers. I've heard reports of flocks of up to 100 wild turkeys fifteen miles up the Mattole River around Honeydew, an impressive quantity though still far short of the thousand birds counted in one day by two hunters in New England in the 1630s. The taste of wild turkey? Between you, me, the drumstick and my dog Jasper, it was markedly similar to farm-raised turkeys, though of course superior to the flanges of blotting paper consequent upon the familiar over-roasting of store-bought turkey at low temperatures for ten hours. I'm for high heat and about three-and-a-half hours for a turkey of average size, though not for the dirigibles they use to raise on a farm in Loleta, near here, which turned the scales at forty pounds.

Globalism has its alluring sides. It was good that turkeys, potatoes, and peppers got to Europe (though I have my doubts about the squashes, which evoke the bland horrors of pumpkin pie). That was early globalism. It was much more rapid in those days. The speed with which New World foods spread across Europe and Asia is astounding. The first Indian housewife got the basics for what we regard as part of the eternal Indian diet—curry—in about 1550, and within five years it was on every household menu in India.

The Spanish brought turkeys back to Europe from Mexico, and by the 1530s they were well-known in Germany and England, hailed at the festive board as part of tradition immemorial. The Puritans had domestic turkeys with them in New England, gazing out at their wild relatives, offered by the Indians who regarded them as somewhat second-rate as food. Of course, wild turkeys have many enemies aside from the Beast called Man. There are swaths of Humboldt and Mendocino counties where coyotes and mountain lions now hold near-exclusive sway.

Ranchers running sheep used to hold off the coyotes with M-80 poison-gas canisters that exploded at muzzle touch, but these are now illegal, and the alternatives are either trapping, which is a difficult and time-consuming job, or getting Great Pyrenees dogs to guard the flock. But the coyotes are crafty and wait till the sheep have scattered, then prey on the unguarded half.

And not all Great Pyrenees have that essential sense of "vocation." My neighbors down the river, the Smiths, who raise sheep, had a fine Great Pyrenees, Esme, partnered with the idle Tofu. Esme would rush about protecting sheep while Tofu lounged under the trees near the homestead, reading the paper and barking importantly whenever cars drove up.

Before she died in childbirth, Esme produced Baxter, taken by my neighbors up the river, the Weaver-Wrens. Baxter grew bored at the Weaver-Wrens. I would see him trotting down the road, then up every driveway to gossip with the locals. Jasper would run him off, and Baxter would never make a fight of it but collapse instantly like a vast white eiderdown, paws in the air and throat exposed.

It's ended well for Baxter. He rapidly ingratiated himself with a new couple on the road, implanting in their minds the notion that he would be a good match for another vast white dog, Grendel, already in their possession. He correctly perceived they were from Berkeley, where he knew that at last he would be able to get a decent shampoo. They commute to the Bay Area and I hear that Baxter is now a familiar *flâneur* on Shattuck, pausing to review the menu outside Chez Panisse before crossing the road to greet the pizza crowd next to the Cheese Board.

I'll have to check with Baxter, but doubtless turkey is on the menu at Chez Panisse for Thanksgiving. Most Americans, even the stylish crowd at that fabled restaurant, won't eat anything else on the big day.

December 8

When in doubt, wheel on Teddy Roosevelt. It's in every Democratic President's playbook. TR was President from 1901 to 1909. He was manly, ranching in North Dakota, exploring the Amazon and nearly expiring on the River of Doubt. He was an imperialist *con amore*, charging up San Juan Hill, sending the Great White Fleet round the world, proclaiming America's destiny as an enforcer on the world stage. He loved wilderness, mostly through the sights of a big-game hunter's rifle—a wilderness suitably cleansed of Indians. "I don't go so far as to think that the only good Indians are dead Indians," he wrote in *The Winning of the West*, "but I believe nine out of ten are, and I shouldn't like to inquire too closely into the case of the tenth."

When necessary he could play the populist rabble-rouser's card, flaying the trusts, railing against "the malefactors of great wealth." But on TR's watch the modern, centralized corporate American state came of age. LBJ loved TR for his "toughness." Draft-dodging Bill Clinton invoked TR as his ideal. At least Johnson and Clinton had elements in them of TR's most admirable trait—gusto, something of which Obama is dismally devoid.

December 10

Editor,

According to petroleum expert Alexander Cockburn we have an oil surplus. This surplus is caused by excessive production from fields in North Dakota. If we're suffering such a surplus, how come (according to the CIA website) more than half the oil we use is imported? Seems like this glut problem is easy to fix.

Best regards,

Bart Boyer, San Diego

Alexander Cockburn replies: Yes, these days the US consumes about nineteen million barrels of oil every twenty-four hours, about half of them imported. At 25 percent, Canada is the lead supplier. Second comes Saudi Arabia with 12 percent. Third comes Mexico. But supply of crude oil to the US is only half the story. Saudi Arabia controls OPEC's oil price and adjusts it carefully with US priorities in the front of their minds. If Alaska oil was not exported to the Far East, contrary to the US Congress's original mandate for the North Slope oil only to be used in the Lower 48, and if US oil companies weren't exporting diesel to Europe and Latin America because they can make more money that way, the US would be floating in even more of a glut than it is now.

The amazing feature of the subdivision of moronic humanity known as the Peak Oilers is that they dwell in a moral stratosphere so pure that they forget entirely that oil companies, now and always, want to make money, as much as possible, and to this end rig supply, markets, and prices to that end. It's sad that some of the best journalism on this theme ever produced in America, right down to James Blair and Robert Sherrill, is too coarse for the POs' delicate sensibilities.

December 18

The great historian Gabriel Kolko makes a persuasive case that in the end the euro zone, indeed the EU, will go into meltdown. This is just fine in my book. The sooner we get back to francs, lire, punts, drachmas, and the rest of the old sovereign currencies, the better in the long run. It used to be as much a part of going to France as choking on Gauloise smoke to change money and be handed a bundle of notes featuring the devious Cardinal Richelieu, instead of the characterless but somehow always expensive euros.

The EU "project" is in potential outline a totalitarian nightmare. Down with federalism! Remember Simone Weil's hatred of the Roman Empire and what it did to Europe's cultural richness and diversity: "If we consider the long centuries and the vast area of the Roman Empire and compare these centuries with the ones that preceded it and the ones that followed the barbarian invasions, we perceive to what extent the Mediterranean basin was reduced to spiritual sterility by the totalitarian State."

As Weil's biographer, Simone Pétrement, comments, "The Roman peace was soon the peace of the desert, a world from which had vanished, together with political liberty and diversity, the creative inspiration that produces great art, great literary works, science, and philosophy. Many centuries had to pass before the superior forms of human life were reborn."

December 21

I can't count the times, down the years, that after some new outrage friends would call me and ask, "What happened to Christopher Hitchens?"—the inquiry premised on some supposed change in Hitchens, often presumed to have started in the period he tried to put his close friend Blumenthal behind bars for imputed perjury. My answer was that Christopher had been pretty much the same package since the beginning—always allowing for the ravages of entropy as the years passed.

As so often with friends and former friends, it's a matter of what you're prepared to put up with and for how long. I met him in New York in the early 1980s and all the long-term political and indeed personal traits were visible enough. I never thought of him as at all radical. He craved to be an insider, a trait which achieved ripest expression when he elected to be sworn in as a US citizen by Bush's Director of

Homeland Security, Michael Chertoff. In basic philosophical take he always seemed to me to hold as his central premise a profound belief in the therapeutic properties of capitalism and empire. He was an instinctive flagwagger and remained so. He wrote some really awful stuff in the early '90s about how indigenous peoples—Indians in the Americas—were inevitably going to be rolled over by the wheels of Progress and should not be mourned.

On the plane of weekly columns in the late 1980s and '90s it mostly seemed to be a matter of what was currently obsessing him: for years in the '80s he wrote scores of columns for the *Nation*, charging that the Republicans had stolen the 1980 election by the "October surprise," denying Carter the advantage of a hostage release. He got rather boring. Then in the '90s he got a bee in his bonnet about Clinton which developed into full-blown obsessive megalomania: the dream that he, Hitchens, would be the one to seize the time and finish off Bill. Why did Bill—a zealous and fairly efficient executive of Empire—bother Hitchens so much? I'm not sure. He used to hint that Clinton had behaved abominably to some woman he, Hitchens, knew.

Actually I think he'd got to that moment in life when he was asking himself if he could make a difference. He obviously thought he could, and so he sloshed his way across his own personal Rubicon and tried to topple Clinton via betrayal of his close friendship with Sid Blumenthal, whom he did his best to ruin financially (lawyers' fees) and get sent to prison for perjury.

Since then it was all pretty predictable, down to his role as flagwagger for Bush. I guess the lowest of a number of low points was when he went to the White House to give a cheerleading speech on the eve of the 2003 invasion of Iraq. I think he knew long, long before that this is where he would end up, as a right-wing codger.

He used to go on, back in the '80s, about sodden old wrecks like John Braine, who'd ended up more or less where Hitchens got to, trumpeting away about "Islamo-fascism" like a Cheltenham colonel in some ancient Punch cartoon. I used to warn my friends at the *New Left Review* and Verso in the early '90s, who were happy to make money off Hitchens's books on Mother Teresa and the like, that they should watch out, but they didn't and then kept asking ten years later, What happened? Between the two of them, my sympathies were always with Mother Teresa.

One awful piece of opportunism on Hitchens's part was his decision to attack Edward Said just before his death, and then for good measure again in his obituary. With his attacks on Edward, especially the final postmortem, Hitchens couldn't even claim the pretense of despising a corrupt presidency, a rapist and liar or any of the other things he called Clinton. That final attack on Said was purely for attention—which fueled his other attacks but this one most starkly because of the absence of any high principle to invoke. Here he decided both to bask in his former friend's fame, recalling the little moments that made it clear he was intimate with the man, and to put himself at the center of the spotlight by taking his old friend down a few notches. In a career of awful moves, that was one of the worst.

He courted the label "contrarian," but if the word is to have any muscle, it surely must imply the expression of dangerous opinions. Hitchens never wrote anything truly discommoding to respectable opinion and if he had he would never have enjoyed so long a billet at *Vanity Fair*. Attacking God? The big battles on that issue were fought one, two, even five hundred years ago when they burned Giordano Bruno at the stake in the Campo de' Fiore. A contrarian these days would be someone who staunchly argued for the existence of a Supreme Being.

He was for America's wars. I thought he was relatively solid on Israel/Palestine, but there too he trimmed. The Jewish Telegraphic Agency put out a friendly obit, noting that "despite his rejection of religious precepts, Hitchens would make a point of telling interviewers that according to halacha, he was Jewish," and noting his suggestion that Walt and Mearsheimer might be anti-Semitic, also his sliming of a boatload of pro-Palestinian activists aiming to breach Israel's blockade of the Gaza Strip. (His brother Peter and other researchers used to say that in terms of blood lineage, the Hitchens boys' Jewishness was pretty slim and fell far outside the definitions of the Nuremberg laws.) I always liked Noam Chomsky's crack to me when Christopher announced in *Grand Street* that he was a Jew: "From anti-Semite to self-hating Jew, all in one day."

As a writer his prose was limited in range. In extempore speeches and arguments he was quick on his feet. I remember affectionately many jovial sessions from years ago, in his early days at the *Nation*, but I found the Hitchens cult of recent years entirely mystifying. He endured his final ordeal with pluck, sustained indomitably by his wife Carol.

December 22

A couple of months ago came a mile marker in America's steady slide downhill towards the status of a Banana Republic, with Obama's assertion that he has the right as President to order secretly the assassination, without trial, of a US citizen he deems to be working with terrorists. This followed his betrayal in 2009 of his pledge to end the indefinite imprisonment without charges or trial of prisoners in Guantanamo.

Now, after months of declaring that he would veto such legislation, Obama has crumbled and will soon sign a monstrosity called the Levin/McCain detention bill, named for its two senatorial sponsors, Carl Levin and John McCain. It's snugged into the 2012 National Defense Authorization Act. The detention bill *mandates*—don't glide too easily past that word—that all accused terrorists be indefinitely imprisoned by the military rather than in the civilian court system; this includes US citizens within the borders of the United States.

Simultaneous to the looming shadow of indefinite internment by the military for naysayers, we have what appears to be immunity from prosecution for private military contractors retained by the US government, another extremely sinister development. The corporations involved are now arguing in court that they should be exempt from any investigation into the allegations against them because, among other reasons, the US government's interests in executing wars would be at stake if corporate contractors can be sued. They are also invoking a new, sweeping defense. The new rule is termed "battlefield preemption" and aims to eliminate any civil lawsuits against contractors that take place on any "battlefield."

You've guessed it. As with "associated forces," an elastic concept discussed above, in the Great War on Terror the entire world is a "battlefield."

2012

January 6

Rumor is running rife. Prosecutor Fouquier-Tinville has agreed that there are certain words that have counter-revolutionary potential, in the sense they have the power, as Fouquier put it, to debase and coarsen common speech by repeated and thoughtless use.

There's a grinding noise, a squeaking of axle, and round the corner from its long journey from the Conciergerie comes the first load of the condemned.

First up: "sustainable." It's been at least a decade since this earnest word was drained of all energy, having become the prime unit of exchange in the argot of purposeful uplift. As the final indication of its degraded status, I found it in President Obama's "signing statement" which accompanied the whisper of his pen, as on New Year's Eve—a very quiet day when news editors were all asleep—he signed into law the National Defense Authorization Act (NDAA) for 2012 which handed $662 billion to the Pentagon, and for good measure ratified by legal statute the exposure of US citizens to arbitrary arrest without subsequent benefit of counsel, and to possible torture and imprisonment sine die, abolishing habeas corpus. Don't bother asking what happens to non-US citizens.

As he set his name to this repugnant legislation the President issued a "signing statement" in which I came upon the following passage: "Over the last several years, my Administration has developed an effective, sustainable framework for the detention, interrogation and trial of suspected terrorists …"

So much for "sustainable." Into the tumbrils with it.

Next up: "iconic." I trip over this golly-gee epithet thirty times a day. No warrant for its arrest is necessary, nor benefit of counsel or trial in a US court. Off to the tumbrils, arm in arm with "narrative." These days everyone has a narrative, an earnest word originally recruited, I believe, by anthropologists. So we read "according to the Pentagon's narrative …" Why not use some more energetic formulation, like, "According to the patent nonsense minted by the Pentagon's press office …"? Suddenly we're surrounded by "narratives," all endowed with equal status. Into the tumbrils with it.

I think "parse" has almost run its course, though occasionally this shooting star of 2011 is to be spotted panting along in some peloton of waffle from the Commentariat. Off with its head, along with "meme," an exhausted little word that deserves the long dark rest of oblivion.

January 13

The world's press is chocabloc with "if" questions about Iran and war. Will Israel attack? Is Obama, coerced by domestic politics in an election year, being dragged into war by the Israel lobby? Will he launch the bombers? Is the strategy to force Iran into a corner, methodically demolishing its economy by embargoes and sanctions so that in the end a desperate Iran strikes back?

As with sanctions and covert military onslaughts on Iraq in the run up to 2003, the first point to underline is that the US *is* waging war on Iran. But well aware of the US public's aversion to yet another war in the Middle East, the onslaught is an undeclared one.

As for the embargo of Iranian oil, Obama is most certainly doing the oil industry a big favor. There have been industry-wide fears of recession-fueled falling demand and a collapse of oil prices. That has led to industry-wide enthusiasm (aided by heavy pressure from the majors) for strongly cutting total world oil production (and enjoying the bonuses flowing from the subsequent world price rise), with all the cuts to be taken out of the hide of the Iranians. The *Financial*

Times made clear the need to shrink world production in the following key paragraph in a report last week: "Oil prices have risen above $110 a barrel since Iran threatened to shut down the Strait of Hormuz, the world's most important oil chokepoint, accounting for about a third of all seaborne traded oil. Oil fell to a low of $99 in October amid global economic growth worries."

As Pierre Sprey remarked to me, "Note also that this is one of those rare but dangerous moments in history when Big Oil and the Israelis are pushing the White House in the same direction. The last such moment was quickly followed by Dubya's invasion of Iraq."

January 20

Newt Gingrich is a one-man, made-in-America melting pot. Here's a committed devotee of tooth-and-claw capitalism, vultures perched on both shoulders, advocate of eight-year-old black children working as janitors—campaigning with a pro-worker film of which John Reed or Ken Loach would be proud, paid for by a rabidly anti-union billionaire who thinks Israel should bomb Iran and drive the Palestinians into the sea.

Gingrich burned for revenge for his rough treatment in New Hampshire by Romney's campaign commercials. But how, on a tight timeline, to acquaint South Carolina Republicans with Romney's infamies? He needed money, lots of it, double-quick. *Occupy Las Vegas!*

Some things don't change in American politics, and rich people sitting in Las Vegas with pots of cash is one of them. Joel McCleary, a friend, remembers fund-raising in Las Vegas when he was working for the Jimmy Carter campaign in 1976. The crucial Pennsylvania primary was coming up and the Carter people (their chief fund-raiser was Morris Dees) needed a big wad of cash for the final push against Henry "Scoop" Jackson of Washington, known as "the Senator from Boeing," also running for the Democratic nomination and favored by powerful labor chieftains in Pennsylvania.

Joel was told the go-to guy for untraceable campaign cash was Hank Greenspun, publisher of the *Las Vegas Sun*. Greenspun was a notoriously tough egg, a former gun-runner for the Haganah, the man who, in the midst of the cold war witch-hunts, outed Senator Joe McCarthy in the *Sun* as a homosexual. Joel was told to act manly. Greenspun duly received him in his office. "Why the hell should I get money for Jimmy Carter?" he asked. "Because Jimmy Carter is going to be President," Joel answered boldly, "and if you don't support his campaign he'll fuck you."

Greenspun told Joel to come back in two hours. He returned to find Greenspan sitting at a table surrounded by other toughs. In the middle of the table was a paper bag. "So the Baptist fuck wants money," Greenspun growled, as he pushed the bag over to Joel. "Remember, this comes from the State of Israel. Don't you ever forget it."

Enter seventy-eight-year-old Sheldon Adelson, the world's sixteenth richest man, a bit dented by the property crash in Nevada but still with $23 billion at his disposal. The sun rises on his empire in Las Vegas, sets on it in the east in Macao, with its zenith over the State of Israel, whence his second wife hails. On Israel Adelson entertains very harsh views about the advisability of negotiations of any sort with Palestinians and lately has been lobbying fiercely—he owns the free weekday *Israel Hayom*, the largest circulation newspaper in Israel—for an attack on Iran.

When Newt Gingrich, fishing for Zionist money, abandoned his previous, relatively temperate, posture on the Israel/Palestine issue, and declared that Palestinians were an "invented people," he was directing his remarks to an audience of one.

Adelson was exceedingly pleased and expressed his gratification in material terms, with a further $5 million, now staking Gingrich's campaign ads in South Carolina. To date Adelson has donated about $13 million to Gingrich's campaign—a US record.

January 27

Last week revolutionary Prosecutor Fouquier-Tinville announced the capture and imminent trial of "grow," long sought in its counterrevolutionary mutation as a transitive verb governing an abstraction, as in "grow the economy," a formulation popular among the

Girondin faction. "Grow," said the Prosecutor, was being held in the Conciergerie, under constant surveillance.

I've no doubt that the Tribunal will not long delay in sending "grow" in this usage to a well-deserved rendezvous with the fatal blade. I associate the usage with the 1992 Clinton campaign, where talk about "growing the economy" was at gale force. My friends and neighbors here in Petrolia, Karen and Joe Paff, tell me that when they were starting up their coffee business, Goldrush, at the start of the 1980s, the local bank officials were already hard at it, talking about "growing the business." I hate the usage, with its smarmy implication of virtuous horticultural effort. As CounterPuncher Michael Greenberg writes, "It sounds phony, aggressive, and even grammatically incorrect, not the nurturing 'grow' that one associates with living things."

Joining "grow" in the tumbril will, I trust, be "blood and treasure," used with great solemnity by opinion formers to describe the cost, often the supposedly worthy sacrifice, attached to America's wars. The usage apparently goes back to Jefferson, but that's no excuse. The catchphrase seeks to turn slaughter and the shoveling of money to arms manufacturers into a noble, almost mythic expenditure.

Shackled to "blood and treasure" should be its co-conspirator, "in harm's way." Jack Flannigan writes from Kerala, "Mr. Cockburn, Somebody might have beat me to it but my candidate for the squeaky old tumbril is 'in harm's way.' It has, especially in the last ten years, acquired a treacly red, white, and blue patina about it that is overwhelmingly connected to the military and police. Someone sailing on a Gaza flotilla or staring down a line of sneering, rabid cops is not very likely to be referred by our political/media elites as 'in harm's way.'"

Last week, dispatching the phrase to the tumbrils, I said the G. H. Bush campaign of 1979 for the Republican nomination hefted "It's not over till the fat lady sings" to national prominence. Jeremy Pikser writes to say the phrase "was actually first popularized by the coach (or owner?) of the Baltimore Bullets basketball team in 1978. As usual G. H. Bush was only capable of feeble imitation when he used it, hoping to sound like a 'real guy.'" Further research discloses its use in sports journalism has been attributed to writer/broadcaster Dan Cook around the same time, and in the mid-'70s by a Texas Tech sports official.

From: Kevin Rath
Mr. Cockburn,
Recently I have been accosted with the phrase "reaching out to you" by sales people. While it may be inappropriate since your focus is the news, this stupid phrase people from marketing use in their email subject titles and language is really annoying.

Reaching out to your tumbril cart,
Kevin Rath, a CP member

January 31
Why do American jobs end up in China? The supposed answer in an anecdote: the late Steve Jobs summons his senior lieutenants and holds up the iPhone prototype. It's due to be shipped to stores in not much more than a month. He points out that the plastic screen has been scratched by his keys. "I won't sell a product that gets scratched," he says, according to a recent *New York Times* story. "I want a glass screen, and I want it perfect in six weeks."

"After one executive left that meeting, he booked a flight to Shenzhen, China," the *Times* reports. "If Mr. Jobs wanted perfect, there was nowhere else to go." The next sequence reads like a montage in some 1920s film about industrial production. Within days, a Corning Glass plant in China is turning out big sheets of toughened glass, which are shipped to a nearby Chinese plant to be cut into iPhone panes. The small panes are trucked to a Foxconn factory complex eight hours away.

The first truckloads arrived in the dead of night, according to a former Apple executive. Managers rousted thousands of workers out of their beds, lined them up, gave each of them a biscuit and a cup of tea and launched them on a twelve-hour shift. In ninety-six hours, the plant was producing more than 10,000 iPhones a day. Within three months, Apple had sold one million of them; since then

Foxconn has assembled more than 200 million units. The suicide rate among its workers was, Jobs insisted, below the overall Chinese rate.

Of course, typical *Times* readers nod their heads. No, cohorts of American workers aren't available to be kicked out of bed in their communal dorms and put to work in half an hour. There's no China-subsidized factory space. And pulsing just below the surface of the text: no tiny, skillful Oriental fingers ("flexibility, diligence and industrial skills of foreign workers"), not to mention tiny Oriental wages, for the uniformed assemblers.

When President Obama dined with the kings of Silicon Valley last year and asked, "Why can't that work come home?" Jobs's reply was "unambiguous": "Those jobs aren't coming back."

Apple is spiritually offshore. "We sell iPhones in over a hundred countries," an Apple executive told the *Times*. "We don't have an obligation to solve America's problems. Our only obligation is making the best product possible."

It was the phrase about having no obligation that riled up Clyde Prestowitz, one of the US government's top trade negotiators in the Reagan years. In an acrid posting on the *Foreign Policy* website and in a chat over the phone with me from his winter quarters in Maui, Prestowitz efficiently dismembered Apple's "no obligation" pretensions and its rationale for why it and kindred companies had no alternative to offshoring.

In the 1981–86 period, Prestowitz says, Jobs and his executives "had the funny notion that the US government had an obligation to help them … We did all we could, and in doing so came to learn that virtually everything Apple had for sale, from the memory chips to the cute pointer mouse, had had its origins in some program wholly or partially supported by US government money … The heart of the computer is the microprocessor, and Apple's derived from Motorola's 680X0, which was developed with much assistance, direct and indirect, from the Defense Department, as were the DRAM memory chips. The pointer mouse came from Xerox's PARC center near Stanford (which also enjoyed government funding). In addition, most computer software at that time derived from work with government backing."

Prestowitz points out that Apple also assumes the US government is obligated to stop foreign pirating of Apple's intellectual property and, should supply chains in the Far East be disrupted, to offer the comforting support of the Seventh Fleet. "And those supply chains—are they the natural product of good old free market capitalism, or does that scalability and flexibility and capacity to mobilize large numbers of workers on a moment's notice have something to do with government subsidies and the interventionist industrial policies of most Asian economies?"

What about those jobs that "aren't coming back"? We're not talking about simple assembly that costs a bundle per unit in America and mere cents in China. In the mid-'90s, at the Apple plant in Elk Grove, California, the cost of building a computer was $22 a machine, compared with as little as $5 at a factory in Taiwan. This is not a dominant factor when the machine sells for $1,500 and you have costs like transport to figure in. Furthermore, stricken America is actually becoming a low-wage magnet.

The high-wage, more complicated manufacturing jobs are in microprocessors, memory chips, displays, circuitry, chip sets and so forth. This is where America is supposed to have a comparative advantage. So why are Asian countries supplying the memory chips and microprocessors and displays instead of the United States? Prestowitz points to government subsidies and protection for Asian producers, currency manipulation and bureaucratic pressure on US corporations by Beijing to make the product in China.

So there's nothing irrevocable about the job loss. US workers, taught the necessary skills, can put things together properly. But if the jobs keep going away, why would any American lay out the money to learn those skills? Obama's recent State of the Union speech was a step in the right direction: calling on business leaders to "ask what you can do to bring the jobs back." Specifically, he proposed ending tax breaks for US corporations operating overseas, rewarding US-based production and turning the unemployment sinkhole into a re-employment system. "These jobs could and would come back to America," says Prestowitz, "if Washington were to begin to respond tit for tat to the mercantilist game … It wouldn't be difficult to make a lot more of the iPhone in America and to make it competitively if either Apple or the US government really wanted that to happen."

February 8
"Civilian deaths due to drones are not many, Obama says." So that's okay then. This was a headline in the *New York Times* for January 31, accurately reflecting Obama's expressed views. It was back in the mid-1920s that my father Claud, then working as a night editor at the London *Times*, won a prize for writing the dullest headline actually printed in the *Times* for the following day. Headline: "Small earthquake in Chile. Not many dead."

February 10
Back in the 1960s Herbert Marcuse pointed out in one of his books that the Pentagon had given up on verbs. Pentagonese consisted of clotted groups of nouns, marching along in groups of three or four. Verbs, which connected nouns in purposive thrust, were regarded as unreliable and probably subversive. They talked too much, gave too much away.

Despite the Pentagon's best efforts, linguistically the '60s were a noisy and exhilarating era: "bitching." The '70s gave us the argots of feminism and queerdom and then suddenly we were in the wastelands of Political Correctness, where non-white people were described as being "of color," cripples became "less-abled," and sexual preference (non-heterosexual) became LGBTQ, though another capital letter may have been added while my back was turned.

Where are we now? Irritating words and terms spread across the internet like plague through a European town in 1348. There's something very passive about the overall argot and a look through one's daily inbox is like walking along a beach piled with decayed words and terms. There's much more ill-written prose than there was thirty years ago.

The following words and phrases are under severe scrutiny by Prosecutor Fouquier-Tinville, renowned for his implacable fairness:

"Reach out," "discourse," "the Other," "massive" and its associate "whopping."

Next week I shall report on the decisions of the Prosecutor on the accused.

From: Thomas Naylor
"Have a nice one..."

Nice what? Cheese, mushroom, and pepperoni pizza? Hearty dump? Damn good f...? Well, you know. Probably the first—since most of those robotic sales types uttering that apogee of inanity have cheesy smiles on their faces and are programmed to masticate only sound-bite-sized slices.

From: N. Haiduck
I wonder if there is room on the tumbril cart for on (or off) the table? I seem to remember Obama saying that prosecuting Bush and Cheney were off the table. I'm sure I've seen it a number of times in the last few years.

From: Stuart Newman
... with "on the ground," notwithstanding all the insights garnered there by guests of The PBS NewsHour and Charlie Rose.

Here, http://www.pbs.org/newshour/bb/politics/jan-june12/nevada_02-03.html, at 3:02, Judy Woodruff asks a reporter what he has learned on the ground about Mitt Romney's popularity among Nevada voters, and the reporter responds in kind (3:13), despite the fact that he is 100 feet above a fake cityscape of Las Vegas.

From: Bruce Anderson
Not much in circulation yet but spotted twice now in edu-prose: "... a search firm dedicated to SURFACING (my emphasis) appropriate candidates for school district leadership positions." I also nominate "appropriate" as now applied to everything from mass murder to bad table manners.

From: Ed Szewczyk
I have some nominations for the tumbrils: 1. "Robust," as in robust interrogation techniques, or robust Article II powers. Seems always to be used as a euphemism for the unconstitutional and/or illegal abuse of something …

From: Troy Nichols
Another proposition, let's just permanently dispose of an entire class of obnoxious business speech: the made-up business gerund (examples: "decisioning," "bootstrapping," "costing," "tumbrilling?" New ones are being invented every day). These clunky mutations are often close to meaningless, and the rest of the world surely laughs when they hear us talking like that. At present these words are highly concentrated in corporate memos and various official statements, but they'll soon leak into the public discourse if left unchecked. You see it every once in a while already. Proliferation is certain. Let's preempt this danger and send them all to the tumbrils now. If there's any doubt about a certain word, say it in its infinitive form ("to decision," "to cost"). If it sounds ridiculous, off it goes …

February 17
Few spectacles have been more surreal than that of senior US officials—starting with the President, the Secretary of State and the US ambassador to the UN—solemnly lecturing Assad and his beleaguered Syrian government on the need to accommodate rebel forces whose GCC sponsors are intent on slaughtering the ruling Alawite minority or driving them into the sea.

At one grimly hilarious moment last Friday, these worthy sermons were buttressed by a message from Ayman al-Zawahiri, the head of al-Qaida, therefore presumably the number one target on President Obama's hit list, similarly praising the "Lions of Syria" for rising up against the Assad regime. Al-Qaida and the White House in sync!

March 7

Suddenly the right has gone truly crazy. It must be sunspots. We're three years into sunspot cycle number twenty-four and it crests in activity with fifty-nine sunspots in early 2013, the weakest sunspot cycle in a hundred years, therefore not much help in the earth's current cooling phase, during which—contrary to warmist doctrine—CO_2 levels have been rising. Overall there has been a fairly steady warming trend of 0.5°C per century since 1680, which is when that notorious playboy Charles II of England began racing his Ferrari at Silverstone.

If you're into sunspot theory, increased negative ionization during sunspot maximum periods increases human excitability.

The sunspot-sodden American right—in this instance the male right—is imploding under the sheer pressure of its repressions, always nearer the surface than in the more decorous psychic plumbing of the liberal legions. It feels like we're back in 1960 when the pill first came on line and predictions of moral collapse were selling by the gross at every convenience store.

March 23

"In the twenty-first century, the best anti-poverty program around is a first-class education," President Obama famously declared in his 2010 State of the Union Address, just as millions of high schoolers across the nation were embarking on the annual ritual of picking their preferred colleges and preparing the grand tour of the prospects, with parents in tow, gazing ashen faced at the prospective fees.

The image is of the toiling students springing from lecture room to well-paying jobs demanding advanced skills in all the arts that can make America great again—out-thinking, out-knowing the Chinese, Japanese, Indians, South Koreans, and Germans in the cutting edge, cut-throat high-tech economies of tomorrow.

Start with the raw material in this epic knowledge battle. As a dose of cold water over all this high-minded talk it's worth looking at Josipa Roksa and Richard Arum's recently published *Academically Adrift: Limited Learning on College Campuses*. The two profs followed more than 2,300 undergraduates at twenty-nine universities, selected to represent the range of America's 2,000-plus four-year college institutions. As summarized by Steven Kent in *Daily Finance*:

> Among the authors' findings: 32 percent of the students whom they followed in an average semester did not take any courses that assigned more than 40 pages of reading per week. Half did not take any courses in which more than 20 pages of writing were assigned throughout the entire term. Furthermore, 35 percent of the students sampled spent five hours or less a week studying alone.
>
> Typical students spent about 16 percent of their time on academic pursuits, and were "academically engaged," write the authors, less than 30 hours a week. After two years in college, 45 percent of students showed no significant gains in learning; after four years, 36 percent showed little change. And the students who did show improvement only logged very modest gains. Students spent 50 percent less time studying compared with students a few decades ago.
>
> Students who majored in traditional liberal arts fields like philosophy, history and English showed "significantly higher gains in critical thinking, complex reasoning and writing skills over time than students in other fields of study." But of course these are the courses and instructors being ruthlessly pruned back.
>
> One of the study's authors, Richard Arum, says college governing boards, shoveling out colossal sums to their presidents, athletic coaches and senior administrative staff, demand that the focus be "student retention," also known as trying very hard not to kick anyone out for not doing any measurable work. As Arum put it to *Money College*, "Students are much more likely to drop out of school when they are not socially engaged, and colleges and universities increasingly view students as consumers and clients. Unfortunately, there is no guarantee that all students want to be exposed to a rigorous academic program."

The US government's Bureau of Labor Statistics (BLS) reports that in 2010 only 20 percent of jobs required a bachelor's degree, whereas 26 percent of jobs did not even require a high-school diploma, and another 43 percent required only a high-school diploma or equivalent.

Please note that the latter 69 percent were therefore free of the one debt in America that's even more certain than taxes—a student loan. At least if you're provably broke the IRS will countenance an "offer in compromise." In fact they recently made the process slightly easier.

No such luck with student loans. The banks are in your pocket till the last dime of loan plus interest has been extorted.

Now for the next dose of cold water. The BLS reckons that by 2020 the overwhelming majority of jobs will still require only a high-school diploma or less and that nearly three quarters of "job openings due to growth and replacement needs" over the next ten years will pay a median wage of less than $35,000 a year, with nearly 30 percent paying a median of about $20,000 a year (in 2010 dollars).

As Jack Metzgar, emeritus professor of humanities at Roosevelt University, correctly remarks, "Put these two sets of numbers together, and it is hard to avoid the conclusion that Americans are over educated for the jobs that we have and are going to have. It's hard to imagine why anybody would call us 'a knowledge economy.'" In other words, millions of Americans are over-educated, servicing endless debt to the banks and boosting the bottom lines of Red Bull and the breweries.

The snobbery, as Metzgar points out, stems from the fact that America's endless, mostly arid debates about education are conducted by the roughly one-third who are college-educated and have okay jobs and a decent income. The "knowledge economy" in the US now needs more than six million people with master's or doctoral degrees, with another 1.3 million needed by 2020. But this will still be less than 5 percent of the overall economy.

Even if we expand the definition to include jobs requiring any education beyond high school, the "knowledge economy"—now and a decade from now—will still represent less than one-third of all available jobs. This is a lot of jobs, about forty-four million now, and if you work and live in this one-third, especially in its upper reaches, more education can seem like the answer to everything. Indeed, according to the BLS, having a bachelor's degree should yield a person nearly $30,000 a year more in wages than a high-school graduate. But most of the American economy is not like this.

The BLS's three largest occupational categories by themselves accounted for more than one-third of the workforce in 2010 (forty-nine million jobs), and they will make an outsized contribution to the new jobs projected for 2020. They are: office and administrative support occupations (median wage of $30,710); sales and related occupations ($24,370); food preparation and serving occupations ($18,770). Other occupations projected to provide the largest number of new jobs in the next decade include childcare workers ($19,300), personal care aides ($19,640), home health aides ($20,560), janitors and cleaners ($22,210), teacher assistants ($23,220), non-construction laborers ($23,460), security guards ($23,920), and construction laborers ($29,280).

So what is the best anti-poverty program? Higher wages for the jobs that are out there, currently yielding impossibly low annual incomes. The current American minimum wage ranges between $7.25 and $8.67 per hour. From time to time senior executives of Walmart call for a rise in the minimum wage since, in the words of one former CEO, Lee Scott, "our customers simply don't have the money to buy basic necessities between pay checks." The minimum wage in Ontario, Canada, is currently well over $10 per hour, while in France it now stands at nearly $13. Australia recently raised its minimum wage to over $16 per hour, and nonetheless has an unemployment rate of just 5 percent.

March 23

From: Michael Dawson, Portland, OR

In Harm's Way: This one was apparently used by our friend Staff Sgt. Robert Bales in a 2009 Pentagon-published discourse on how to distinguish "good guys" from "bad guys": "We discriminated between the bad guys and the noncombatants, and then afterward we ended up helping the people that three or four hours before were trying to kill us. I think that's the real difference between being an American as opposed to being a bad guy, someone who puts his family in harm's way like that."

In harm's way. It dehumanizes and dehistoricizes all enemies. It flatters the speaker as somebody who chooses to stop Evil, presumably also suggesting the notion that, once one gains that status, one has the right to go shoot up a village.

April 5

I'd say the chances of George Zimmerman spending time behind bars for killing Trayvon Martin are about the same as Sgt. Robert Bales doing time for killing those sixteen Afghan villagers the night of March 11. Zero.

Like most things that happen in America these days, the Trayvon Martin case is turning into yet another hearse trundling the Republican Party to its doom in November.

Zimmerman stakes his defense on Chapter 776.013 of the Florida criminal statute on home protection and the use of deadly force. Paragraph 3 states, "A person who is not engaged in an unlawful activity and who is attacked in any other place where he or she has a right to be has no duty to retreat and has the right to stand his or her ground and meet force with force, including deadly force if he or she reasonably believes it is necessary to do so to prevent death or great bodily harm to himself or herself or another or to prevent the commission of a forcible felony." This is what's colloquially known as the Stand Your Ground Law.

Outrage about the case built across the first two weeks of March. By the third week it was a national scandal. Black columnists described how they warn their sons not to run in any crisis situation, always be polite to the cops no matter how provoked. The Rev. Al Sharpton covers the case full volume on MSNBC. The usual litter of deadly cop shootings of blacks are exhumed from recent Florida police records. Protest demonstrations are held in Sanford.

There are the obvious questions. If Martin had wrestled the gun away from Zimmerman and shot him, would he have been allowed to walk away free? No, Sir. Political pressure forces the appointment of Special Prosecutor Angela Corey, to determine whether to charge Zimmerman. If she does so, it will probably be for second-degree manslaughter.

President Obama speaks on March 23 about the killing of Trayvon, saying, "If I had a son, he would look like Trayvon … I think [Trayvon's parents] are right to expect that all of us as Americans are going to take this with the seriousness it deserves, and we are going to get to the bottom of exactly what happened."

Two Republican candidates for their party's nomination to the presidency promptly bring out the hearse, most recently deployed to freight denunciations of women's right to birth control. Newt Gingrich states that Obama's comments are "disgraceful" and that "Any young American of any ethnic background should be safe, period. We should all be horrified, no matter what the ethnic background. Is the President suggesting that, if it had been a white who'd been shot, that would be OK, because it wouldn't look like him? That's just nonsense."

Then Rick Santorum chimes in, stating that Obama should "not use these types of horrible and tragic individual cases to try to drive a wedge in America." This unleashes Rush Limbaugh who says that Obama is using the case as a "political opportunity." Geraldo Rivera suggests Martin brought it on himself by wearing a hoodie. At which point the conservative columnist William Tucker has had enough. In the hard-right *American Spectator*, under the headline: "Count Me Out on Trayvon Martin: Why Gingrich, Santorum, and Many Conservatives Are Dead Wrong on This One," Tucker writes, "Republicans have no reason to intervene in this fight. Seventy-five percent of the public thinks Zimmerman should be charged with something … Personally, I can't wait until Newt Gingrich and Rick Santorum get offstage so we can start running a presidential campaign that isn't based on trying to alienate the vast majority of Americans over irrelevant issues."

What is it that prompts Republicans to try so hard to alienate women, blacks, Hispanics, independents, and all those millions and millions of Americans to the left of the Tea Party they'll need to beat Obama? Maybe they feel it's their last throw. All the demographics look unfavorable for any future Republican majority. So there is a desperate effort to get everything they can right now. Conning working-class whites with racism, sexism, anti-gay/anti-immigrant rhetoric, etc., has worked so well since Nixon that it's become an addiction.

April 18

This has been a bad year for grand restaurants in the three- to four-star range. The clang of their closing doors raises the question—is the whole gastro-frenzy that stirred into life in the mid-1970s finally lurching towards closure? Goodbye Iron Chefs, sayonara "molecular gastronomy" in the style of Ferran Adrià, farewell those overcooked paragraphs of fine restaurant writing that became the hottest reading in the *New York Times*.

On March 7 the high society eatery La Côte Basque (used as a chapter heading in habitué Truman Capote's *Answered Prayers*) closed its doors. This last Wednesday the *New York Times* mourned at length the Chicago restaurant Charlie Trotter's, slated for extinction in August. According to the *Times*, Trotter's "had a huge and lasting impact on Chicago's culinary landscape, if not the nation's."

Okay, a couple of big time restaurants bite the dust in the great recession. So?

For several years one of the *New York Times*' most avidly read writers was Sam Sifton. Sifton approached his job con amore. Not from him any cavils about price, let alone high-end gastro flim flam. His prose had the confident lilt of a man writing for Wall Streeters for whom a couple of thousand dollars dropped on a dinner for four was absolutely no problem, and indeed almost an emblem of parsimony.

In early October last year he published an emotional eulogy to Per Se, "the best restaurant in New York City," located in the Time-Life building at Lincoln Center. A photo disclosed no less than six Per Se employees mustered round a dish being plated for some expectant customer.

"Per Se's signature starter course is Oysters and Pearls," wrote Sifton. "It combines a sabayon of pearl tapioca with Island Creek oysters (small, marble-shaped, from Duxbury, south of Boston, fantastic) and a fat clump of sturgeon caviar from Northern California. These arrive in a bowl of the finest porcelain from Limoges. Paired with a glass of golden semillon from Elderton, they make a fine argument for the metaphor of transubstantiation."

After this rather laconic reference to the Eucharist, an editorial note disclosed that this was Sifton's last review. I've no idea whether

Sifton's liver couldn't take the pace any more ("I have eaten in restaurants five or more nights a week for the last two years") or whether the *Times* simply felt things were getting a little out of hand, and the paper was becoming a stand-in for *Gourmet* magazine. Either way it seemed we'd got to the end of an era. The day it announced the closing of Charlie Trotter's, an article counseled *Times* readers on how to use leftovers.

The readers seemed to be getting testy too, though they are by nature on food sites, saving for the post mortem all the things they didn't dare tell the waiter. Oliver Gardener from Florida wrote: "Ate there one time in 2006. Was awful. Paid $400 for a bottle of wine that retailed for $60. Ridiculous mark up. A couple of the courses were very good, but each consisted of about two bites of food. It was over before you knew it. Attitude like I've never seen. Snooty snooty snooty. Would not return. Better meal, by far, at Momofuku Noodle Shop."

When I first came to New York in 1972 the high-end gastro-porn industry was barely in motion. If you wanted to have a fancy French meal, you went to Lutèce, which closed down in 2004. Domestic kitchens were wreathed in smoke from burned offerings to Julia Child. Fiery Hunan cooking was all the rage, followed by a pallid style of cooking known as cuisine minceur, where tasteful dollops of steamed chard held sway.

Then, in 1975, Craig Claiborne reported on the front page of the *New York Times* that he and Pierre Franey had blown $4,000 on a thirty-one-course, nine-wine dinner at Chez Denis in Paris, a feast offered by American Express at a charity auction.

In those post-Vietnam days, columnists kept whole stables of moral high horses pawing the ground in their stalls. Espying the $4,000 binge, Harriet Van Horne stabbed furiously at her typewriter: "This calculated evening of high-class piggery offends an average American's sense of decency. It seems wrong, morally, esthetically and in every other way." Above the column I remember an editor ran the head "Edunt et Vomant" (they eat and they vomit).

People were shocked but Claiborne had put down a marker. Thirty years later, you didn't need to eat your way through thirty-one courses to run up a tab of $4,000. The wine alone could cost that. These days several restaurants offer food clad in gold. New York's Serendipity, for example, advertises "the Golden Opulence Sundae, a chocolate sundae covered in 23-karat gold leaf, suffused with gold dragets, and served with an 18-karat gold spoon that diners can keep." The price? $1,000. (Don't eat the spoon. Any gold of less than 23 karats may contain other, possibly harmful, metals.)

Mannerism began to creep onto the food pages. In 2010 bugs were suddenly all the rage. "A five-course Mexican feast at the Brooklyn Kitchen in Williamsburg last Saturday night [was] engineered to introduce New Yorkers to the succulent wonders of edible insects," the *New York Times* reported. "The first couple of courses [offered] yucca frites dotted with mealworms, a smoked corn custard sprinkled with crispy moth larvae ... at some point during dinner a bowl of squirming wax moth larvae was passed around."

Good restaurants are still cooking excellent food. Restaurants establishing direct relationships with small farm suppliers is surely a good thing, though often the menu in such places begins to look like a gazetteer, and one does ask oneself, is the "Niman ranch" really all that it claims to be? Overall the standard, domestic as well as professional, of American cuisine has never been higher. It's just that one doesn't pick up that crackle of excitement, that rush to get a table at that new place down the block.

Also, there have been unpleasing stories of the darker side of the profession, with the owners or managers of restaurants, such as Mario Battali, stealing the tip income of their miserably underpaid waiters. In a recent story in the *Guardian* by Moira Herbst, three Manhattan bartenders accuse the owners of downtown wine/tapas spots Bar Veloce and Bar Carrera of skimming up to 30 percent of their tips, along with failing to pay proper wages and overtime.

Lists of America's best restaurants these days have a somewhat haphazard look, which may be no bad thing. One site, *The Daily Meal*, lists Le Bernardin in New York as its top pick. Le Bernardin is indeed a very fine restaurant, but scarcely evidence of exciting novelty. My brother Andrew and I went there in the early 1980s, pockets stuffed with expense money from *House and Garden* with which to track down America's best of that era. We had plates of flaked salt cod followed by oxtail stew—just about the simplest, cheapest ingredients money could buy. Both were unbeatable, with faddism kept at bay by Italian cooking at its simple best.

April 20

SCENE ONE

Antechamber to Heaven, a large reception room in the Baroque style. A door opens and an angel ushers in Christopher Hitchens, dressed in hospital clothing. The angel gestures for CH to take a seat. He is about to do so when he espies a familiar figure reading some newspapers.

CH: Dr. Kissinger! The very last person I would have expected to encounter here. All the more so, since I don't recall any recent reports of your demise.

HK: You will no doubt be cast down by the news that I am indeed alive. This is a secret trip, to spy out the terrain diplomatically, assess the odds.

CH: You think you have the slightest chance of entering the celestial sphere?

HK: Everything is open to negotiation.

CH: Have you threatened to bomb Heaven—secretly of course?

HK: Very funny. As a matter of fact, Wojtyla—Pope John Paul II, I should say—has kindly offered to intercede at the highest level. And talking of negotiation, perhaps we could have a quiet word.

CH: What about?

HK: That worthless book you wrote about me—*The Trial of Henry Kissinger*. John Paul says that the prosecutors here have been using it in drawing up preliminary drafts of their case against me. Now, he also says it would be extraordinarily helpful if you would sign this affidavit—my lawyers have already prepared it—saying that you unconditionally withdraw the slurs and allegations, the baseless charges of war criminality, and attest under eternal pain of perjury that these were forced on you by your *Harper's* editors.

CH: Dr Kissinger! Your idea is outrageous. I stand behind every word I wrote!

HK: Hmm. Too bad. After all, you certainly have experience in, how shall we say, adjusting sworn affidavits to changing circumstance. I believe Mr. Sidney Blumenthal could comment harshly on the matter.

CH: Dr. Kissinger, let me reiterate—

HK: My dear fellow, spare me your protestations. Let us consider the matter as mature adults—both of us, if I may say, now in potentially challenging circumstances.

CH: Speak for yourself, Dr. Kissinger. I do not recognize this as Heaven's gate, or you as a genuine physical presence. I do not believe in the afterlife and therefore regard this as some last-second hallucination engendered in my brain in my room in M.D. Anderson hospital in Houston, Texas. I may be dying, but I am not dead yet. I have not dropped off the perch.

HK: Off the perch … How very English. You will dismiss these as a mere last-second hallucination, a terminal orgy of self-flattery on your part, but (*flourishes bundle of newspapers*) the *New York Times* certainly thinks you're dead. The *Washington Post* thinks you're dead.

CH: Let me look at those … (*snatches the papers from HK's hand; skims them intently*)

HK: Rather too flattering, if I may be frank. But, of course, as you say, all fantasy.

CH: They're very concrete. Far more amiable than I would have dared to imagine … I … I … (*passes hand over brow*). Is it possible to get a drink in this anteroom?

HK: Ah, after the soaring eagle of certainty, the fluttering magpie of doubt. I think we can bend the sumptuary laws a little (*pulls a large flask from his pocket*). Some schnapps?

CH: I would have preferred Johnnie Walker Black, but any port in a storm (*drinks*).

HK: Bishop Berkeley, a philosopher, claimed, like you, that the world could be all in one's imagination. It was your Doctor Samuel Johnson who sought to rebut Berkeley's idealist theories by kicking a stone. And what did Dr. Johnson say when he kicked that stone?

CH: He said, "Sir, I refute it thus."

HK: Precisely. Let the schnapps be your empirical stone. Now, if I may, let me continue with my proposition. As you know, you wrote another pamphlet, equally stuffed with lies and foul abuse, called *The Missionary Position*.

CH: Yes, a fine piece of work about that old slag, Mother Teresa.

HK: The "old slag," as you ungallantly term the woman, is now part of an extremely influential faction in Heaven, including Pope John Paul II. Mother Teresa remains vexed by your portrait. She says it is in libraries and all over the internet. She, like me, would dearly love to see you make an unqualified retraction of your slurs.

CH: And that, of course, I will not do!

HK: You're aware of the fate of Giordano Bruno?

CH: Certainly. One of reason's noblest martyrs. Burned at the stake in the Campo de' Fiore in Rome in 1600 for heresy. He insisted, with Copernicus, that the earth revolves around the sun and that the universe is infinite.

HK: Quite so. A noble end, but an extremely painful one. Perhaps, with Satanic assistance, I can remind you of it.

He claps his hands, and two fallen angels in black robes draw open a pair of heavy red velvet curtains at the far end of the room. HK makes a theatrical bow and motions CH forward. The latter edges near the space are now suffused with leaping flames. For a brief moment there's a ghastly wailing, and CH leaps back into the room.

CH: Great God!

HK: You seem to have reverted to religious belief with startling speed.

CH: No, no. It was purely a *façon de parler*. Not a pretty sight.

HK: But in your view, a pure hallucination, nein? No need to kick the stone, like Dr. Johnson.

Before CH can answer, the fallen angels seize him and start dragging him toward the open curtains. They are about to hurl him into the pit, when—

ST. MICHAEL (*suddenly appearing through the gates of Heaven*): Stop!

He hands CH and HK tickets.

These are one-day passes to Heaven. In Mr. Hitchens's case, for purposes of interrogation by the Board of Inquiry and Final Judgment.

Exeunt St. Michael, HK, and CH through ornate gilded doors to Heaven.

SCENE TWO

Heaven. A vast baroque gallery, in which an animated throng is enjoying itself in something closely resembling a cocktail party.

ST. MICHAEL: We've just remodeled. Before, we had something in the Gothic style, but the feeling was that in keeping with the times there should be more gold, more sense of extravagant illusion. And that of course brought us to the baroque. You will no doubt detect many echoes of the Palazzo Colonna in Rome.

HK: I think I see His Holiness John Paul II, over there. With your permission, I might have a word?

ST. MICHAEL: Of course. And Mr. Hitchens, before we get to the

Board of Inquiry, I'm sure there are some immortals you'd like to tip your hat to.

CH: The hat is all very well, but—

ST. MICHAEL: How forgetful of me! In general we're an abstemious crowd here, but there's no ban on moderate enjoyment.

A cherub swoops down, proffering a well-stocked tray.

CH (*gulping down one glass quickly and taking another*): Angel!

POPE PIUS V (*joining the group*): Michael, I couldn't help overhearing your reference to the Palazzo Colonna, built in the late seventeenth century, and of course memorable for the marvelous depictions on the ceiling of its Grand Gallery of the Battle of Lepanto in 1571, our Holy League's historic defeat of the Ottomans.

CH: Ha! The wily Turk, lurking like a cobra 'midst the fairest flowers of God's creation, lies ever ready to pounce upon the unsuspecting traveler and bugg—

PIUS V: I don't believe I've had the honor.

ST. MICHAEL: This is Mr. Hitchens, a British-American writer here on a possibly brief visit. And (*to CH*) this is St. Pius V, who indeed occupied the Holy See at the time of Lepanto.

CH (*theatrical bow*): The honor is mine.

PIUS V: Those were the days, when the wind was truly at our backs! Two hundred and ten ships of the Ottoman armada—almost their entire fleet—sent to the bottom of the Gulf of Patras; the Counter Reformation in full spate; the Council of Trent a magnificent success; heresy confronted and extirpated by our Inquisitors.

CH: The screams of their victims no doubt inaudible amid the general brays of triumph.

PIUS V: Speaking as a former Inquisitor, let me say that by modern standards of bloodshed consequent upon religious or ideological conflicts, the number of those who perished by reason of their adamant heresy was startlingly small. Have you kept up with recent scholarship on the topic? I thought not. Out of 62,000 cases judged by the Inquisition in Italy after 1542, only 1,250 ended with death sentences. The Spanish Inquisition held an average of 350 trials a year between 1560 and 1700 and executed between 3,000 and 5,000 people.

CH (*snatching two more glasses from the tray of a passing cherub*): I do not propose to stand silently here, your so-called Holiness, and endure from a dotard in a white petticoat filthy apologias for atrocious barbarism in the name of his so-called God.

ST. MICHAEL: Mr. Hitchens! I suggest you moderate your language immediately.

PIUS V (*walking away*): Brutto insolente, ignorante, ubriacone pieno di merda!

MOTHER TERESA (*approaching, with Pope John Paul II; HK lurking discreetly*): Brutto insolente, indeed! Mr. Hitchens, I understand from Dr. Kissinger that you are prepared to repudiate your libels upon me.

CH: Certainly not.

JOHN PAUL II: But why not? After all, your arguments against the Blessed Teresa were either trivial or absurd, and in all instances morally odious. To focus on the latter: by 1996, the Blessed Teresa was operating 517 missions in more than 100 countries. And you, what were you doing for the poor? Would a starving person near death be more likely to get a bowl of soup or shelter from the Blessed Teresa or from Christopher Hitchens?

CH: I have never had pretensions to be in the professional charity business.

MALCOLM MUGGERIDGE: If I may intrude. Of course, as a great admirer of Mother Teresa, I was in receipt of Mr. Hitchens's barbs, so I do speak as a biased witness. I regard it as truly extraordinary that while Mr. Hitchens was blithely ladling his sewage over our heads, he was—as a sometime US correspondent, I have followed these matters closely from here in Heaven—a fierce and influential advocate of one of the most violent onslaughts on the poor in recent historical memory: first, the sanctions on Iraq, which caused untold misery to Iraq's poorest citizens; then the actual attack of 2003, which eventually prompted the deaths of over a million Iraqis and a crisis that still virtually paralyses that wretched nation.

CH: I would not change a syllable of what I wrote.

MM: Worse still—I speak also as someone who reported from the Soviet Union during Stalin's rule—Mr. Hitchens displayed himself as a craven apparatchik of the Bush White House, actually going to 1600 Pennsylvania Avenue the night before the invasion to give a pep talk to the President's staff about their noble mission.

Since Beatrice Webb was my wife's aunt, I am intimately familiar with the follies of socialists. You, in your contempt for "lesser" cultures, remind me of the German social democrat Eduard Bernstein, who argued that to oppose Rhodes's suppression of the Matabele uprising was to oppose "the spread of civilization," and that "the higher culture always has the greater right on its side over the lower; if necessary it has the historical right, yea, the duty, to subjugate it."

CH: The mission to Baghdad *was* noble: the eviction of a filthy tyrant—

MM: … was worth the denial of medicine and medical equipment for babies, the forcing of hundreds of thousands of poor Iraqis into near starvation, the creation of millions of internal refugees plus those who managed to flee the country, the unleashing of sectarian bloodshed on an unparalleled scale? Just so that your hero, Tony Blair, and your supreme leader, Mr. Bush, could boast "Mission Accomplished"?

CH: Since His Holiness St. Pius V, who has departed the field of disputation, was invoking the Battle of Lepanto, I'm surprised not to hear any parallels drawn between that engagement and the Crusade against Islam, of which the war in Iraq—and the terror axis of Hussein and Osama—was a significant element.

MM: You mean your precious crusade against so-called "Islamofascism," the bizarre coinage of a Trotskyite, such as you once were? Lepanto at least saw the Ottoman armada, and the unfortunate slaves who rowed their galleys, sent to the bottom of the sea. Your crusade in Iraq saw the triumph of the Shia, and a significant victory for Iran. With Vice-President Cheney you must be the last two men alive who believe in the Hussein/Osama axis.

JOHN PAUL II: The Holy See strongly opposed the war. Before it began, I sent Cardinal Pio Laghi to tell Bush it would be a disaster and would destroy human life. The war was useless, served no purpose and was a defeat for humanity. Such was my view, which was the recorded opinion of the Holy See.

MM: Surely, a more humane posture than your own hosannas to cluster bombs: "Those steel pellets will go straight through somebody and out the other side and through somebody else. So they won't be able to say, 'Ah, I was bearing a Koran over my heart and, guess what, the missile stopped halfway through.' No way, 'cause it'll go straight through that as well. They'll be dead, in other words."

CH: Rather well put, if I say so myself.

MM: You are impervious to rebuke, which is not surprising, since if one rebuke is let in the door, it can usher in another, and then some serious inner reflection may become unavoidable. As Cardinal Newman put it, "To live is to change, and to be perfect is to have changed often."

CH: Newman, that old queen!

MM: Like St. Pius, I'll quit the field now, but let me return to something His Holiness John Paul II said. "Would a starving person near death be more likely to get a bowl of soup or shelter from the Blessed Teresa or from Christopher Hitchens?"

What has constantly struck me is the desolate sterility of your atheism. We had atheists in our generation, of course, but they lived in a world and consorted with people for whom religion had profound meaning, often inspiring them to acts of nobility and extraordinary self-sacrifice. In your book, religious people are stupid. But they weren't stupid, and the atheists—I'm thinking of my dear friend, a man you profess to have admired, Claud Cockburn—didn't deride them, but cheerfully swapped quotations from the Sermon on the Mount. The context was one of respect and mutual striving for a better world.

What sort of moral leadership did you, the great and ultimately rather wealthy exponent of atheism, display? Extreme disloyalty to close friends, constant public drunkenness and brutish rudeness, particularly to women, and a life, if I may say so, of almost psychotic self-centeredness and exhibitionism. You had your claque—Messrs Amis, Fenton, and the others—and their energies in promoting you as a major intellectual and stylist were unceasing, and in their somewhat homoerotic loyalty, rather touching, but I don't think the verdict of history will be quite so kind.

SCENE THREE

Antechamber to Heaven. CH is sitting on a bench. Door opens and St. Michael bids HK a cheerful goodbye.

HK: Mr. Hitchens. You seem somewhat subdued. (*Proffering flask*) A little schnapps?

CH: My dear fellow! (*Drinks deeply*) You arranged your affairs successfully?

HK: Entirely so. In large part owing to you. Pope John Paul II and Mother Teresa, not to mention St. Pius V, were so shocked by your views and by your language that they entirely discounted the charges you leveled against me, and believe me to have been vilely traduced.

CH: I suppose I should be glad to have been of service. But let me ask a question: since you are Jewish, why would you be taking such trouble to build up contacts in what is clearly a Christian Heaven?

HK: Between ourselves, I am preparing for a final conversion and absolution. Jews are vague about heaven and, after a lifetime's observation, I am inclined to think that the atmosphere in Gehenna would be extremely acrimonious. Your plans?

CH: Once again, I feel it necessary to insist that I do not recognize myself as being in Heaven, or disputing with a sixteenth-century pope, or indeed being reprimanded by St. Michael and Malcolm Muggeridge. Or talking affably with Henry Kissinger. So, please, regard this as ongoing cerebral activity on the part of C. E. Hitchens, patient at M. D. Anderson.

HK: As you wish. But here, (*slips him the flask*) just remember Dr. Johnson's stone. Farewell, my friend.

Lights fade to a dark red.

END

April 27
Alex,
During last week's tumbril break, while the blade was re-sharpened and the cart wheels greased, Fouquier-Tinville's agents—ever vigilant—fingered another enemy of the revolution, an expression that has managed to evade tribunal scrutiny and a well-deserved turn in the tumbril: "the new normal."

"The new normal" is the new vexing news-speak for matters that are rotten. Mark how "the new normal" only refers to degeneration and deterioration—political, economic, social, cultural, environmental and so on. That our kids are graduating from college with no job prospects and debts approaching a home mortgage is the new normal. That millions of skilled factory workers and trades people can only find work flipping burgers or emptying bedpans in nursing homes is the new normal.

That the NSA now vacuums up and stores all of our electronic communications is the new normal. That grannies and toddlers are "groped or scoped" at airports is the new normal. That our legal system has become two-tiered—no accountability for political and economic elites while the rest of us face strip searches and isolation cells for petty infractions—is the new normal.

Perhaps I missed one, but I can't recall any usage of "the new normal" in reference to a situation that is better now than it was a decade or a generation ago—unless it was used in a corporate board room.

If I may reword a statement by the late philosopher and teacher J. Krishnamurti: "There's nothing 'normal' about being well adjusted to a sick society."

Off with it!

Best regards,

Bill Allen, Philo, CA

Bill, your denunciation carries no small measure of the passion of the great Maximilien. The "new normal" has trundled on its last journey to the Place de la Revolution, shoulder to shoulder with "nuanced," a wormy little term that has crept into popular usage in the press in recent months. Its function seems to be one of flattery by the writer for sentiments which, if set forth in straightforward English, would excite derision, as in "In his nuanced arguments for reforms in Social Security and Medicare ..."

Two weeks ago I wrote "Fouquier-Tinville is preparing for a major trial, having announced the arrest and incarceration in the Conciergerie of 'telling truth to power'—a hugely annoying phrase, simultaneously exaggerating the courage required to tell the truth and underestimating power's own resourcefulness in adjusting truth to its own requirements ..."

The preparations continue.

April 28

In September 2004, Merck, one of America's largest pharmaceutical companies, issued a sudden recall of Vioxx, its anti-pain medication widely used to treat arthritis-related ailments. There was a fair amount of news coverage after the recall, but pretty slim considering the alleged 55,000 death toll. A big class-action lawsuit dragged its way through the courts for years, eventually being settled for $4.85 billion in 2007.

Senior FDA officials apologized for their lack of effective oversight and promised to do better in the future. The Vioxx scandal began to sink into the vast marsh of semi-forgotten international pharmaceutical scandals.

The year after Vioxx was pulled from the market, the *New York Times* and other media outlets ran minor news items, usually down column, noting that American death rates had undergone a striking and completely unexpected decline.

Typical was the headline on a short article that ran in the April 19, 2005, edition of *USA Today*: "USA Records Largest Drop in Annual Deaths in at Least 60 Years." During that one year, American deaths fell by 50,000 despite the growth in both the size and the age of the nation's population. Government health experts were quoted as being greatly "surprised" and "scratching [their] heads" over this strange anomaly, which was led by a sharp drop in fatal heart attacks.

May 18

The news is in. White births are no longer a majority in the United States. The Bureau of the Census confirms that non-Hispanic whites accounted for 49.6 percent of all births in the year ending July 2011, while minorities including Hispanics, blacks, Asians, and those of mixed race reached 50.4 percent.

Is whitey ready for a fresh start? Face it, we may be a minority, but we got the firepower. Where did we go wrong? Too much atonal music, maybe. Richard Pryor probably put his finger on it. Pryor to a white audience: "What the matter, y'all stop fuckin'? There will be no shortage of niggers. Niggers is fuckin'."

The news is not good. At almost exactly the moment we yielded majority status, we—not the people to be sure, but our President and our Congress—were putting the finishing touches to our modern system of government, known as fascism.

The mobs who flooded into the streets to revel in the execution of Osama bin Laden were not exulting in America, land of the free and of constitutional propriety. They were lauding brute, lawless, lethal force. In this year of political conventions we'll be hearing a lot of tub-thumping about American freedoms, but if there's any nation in the world that is well on the way to meriting the admittedly vague label of "fascist," surely it's the United States.

May 20

In the dock is "anecdotal," long sought by the force of revolutionary vigilance. Prosecutor Fouquier-Tinville says he can do no better than read from the denunciation filed with his office by Patrick Cockburn:

> A telling example of how undervaluing evidence as "anecdotal" gives a free pass to misrepresentation, fraud and crime came last week in a report in Britain over unsafe breast implants. It had emerged that 47,000 British women had French manufactured implants made out of mattress gel using industrial grade silicon, never intended for medical use, that can burst and swell in the body. The "deliberate fraud" by the French company was unmasked by French investigators in 2010.
>
> In Britain, it emerged, surgeons had warned that the implants were rupturing during demonstrations as long ago as 2006, one demanding the implants no longer be used. Two other surgeons had experience of the "catastrophic disintegration" of implants. But the British government medical devices watchdog, MHRA, decided to do nothing because, so the report says, the evidence was "anecdotal." Furthermore the official watchdog, discounting the evidence of three surgeons, felt that to issue a warning would lead to an "unwanted scare which could have serious commercial implications."

There were lively outbursts of emotion during the unfolding of this outrage to morals and upright conduct and it was clear to "anecdotal" in the dock that this was not its lucky day and that a rendezvous with the fatal blade would not be long postponed. Sentence was duly pronounced, without a single dissenting voice.

May 30

A heart in love will decipher every squiggle in the letter as a kiss. In the final days of the 2008 campaign and in the opening ones of his administration, Barack Obama and his top legal aides seemed to the eager ears of marijuana legalizers on the West Coast and around the country to be opening the door to a new, more sensible era.

Drug activists exulted in a big win. "Today's comments clearly represent a change in policy out of Washington," Ethan Nadelmann of the Drug Policy Alliance said to the *Los Angeles Times*. Attorney General Eric Holder, Nadelmann added in the *New York Times*, had sent a clear message to the DEA that the Feds now recognize state medical marijuana laws as "kosher."

On January 22 (two days after Obama's inauguration) DEA agents raided a South Lake Tahoe dispensary run by Ken Estes, a wheelchair-bound entrepreneur. In a typical "rip-and-run," they seized about five pounds of cannabis and a few thousand dollars but made no arrests. Less than two weeks later, the DEA raided four dispensaries in the LA area. Eight days after that came a bust on the Mendo-Healing Cooperative farm in Fort Bragg, California.

The love-lost Obamians had forgotten how to read political declarations with a close and cynical eye, and to bear in mind the eternal power struggle between federal prosecutors and enforcers—e.g., the DEA and equivalent state bodies. The Feds wanted to make it completely clear that, whatever Obama might hint at, they weren't going to be hogtied by wussy state laws. Bust a guy in a wheelchair, bust a dispensary, make your point: I'm the man.

Meanwhile, what has been happening out in the fields, dells, plastic greenhouses, and indoor grows in the counties of Mendocino, Humboldt, and Trinity? The timeless rhythms of agriculture: overproduction, plummeting prices, the remorseless toll of costly inputs like soil and fertilizers. Back in the early 1990s, the price to grower per pound was around $5,000. A couple of years ago, the average had dropped to about $2,000—more for really skilled growers who "black box" their greenhouses, darkening them earlier each day to trick the plants into putting out an early crop. Right now, it's down to maybe $1,000 a pound in the fall, $600 in the Christmas rush. Do these prices bear any relation to the prices in the fancy dispensaries in Southern California? Guess.

Bruce Anderson, editor of the weekly *Anderson Valley Advertiser*, says that in recent weeks, "raids were conducted on two homes—one in Eureka, one in Redwood Valley—where better than $400,000 cash was confiscated by the forces of law and order. Every time the cops make big cash hauls, more people are convinced that they, too, should get into the pot business. Looked at objectively, and all things considered, the nebulous legal status of marijuana is perfect for Mendocino County's financial well-being: every year the cops take off just enough dope to keep pot prices at at least $1,000 a pound. Legalization would further depress the Mendocino County economy, and depress it big-time. Short of legalization, nothing is going to stop any kind of grow, indoors or outdoors."

But legalization is not a realistic prospect, and so the status of the herb will inevitably remain cloudy. For its part, the DEA is announcing big impending raids in Mendocino County, some targeting the vast stretches of the (federally controlled) Mendocino National Forest and the growers drawing on the waters of the Middle Eel.

This is all happening under the aegis of a president who cozily disclosed his marijuana habit as a young man. One bust and Obama would still be organizing communities on the South Side of Chicago. But his sense of self-righteousness is too distended to be deflated by any sense of hypocrisy. The war on marijuana has nothing to do with medical properties and so forth. US drug policy is about social control. That's the name of the game.

June 1

Never trust a president who claims he reads himself to sleep with the help of Marcus Aurelius. That was Bill Clinton, who claimed this thundering imperial bore never strayed far from his hand. Most certainly view with profound suspicion a president who professes to be guided in his conduct in grave moral matters by Augustine and Aquinas.

The excellent, astounding *New York Times* story by Jo Becker and Scot Shane, published on May 29, reports that Obama decided to take personal control of the White House's secret and unconstitutional death list after reading Augustine and Aquinas. "A student of writings on war by Augustine and Thomas Aquinas, he believes that he should take moral responsibility for such actions. And he knows that bad strikes can tarnish America's image and derail diplomacy." Notice how the paragraph devolves rapidly from moral duty to PR.

June 3

With rare emotion Prosecutor Fouquier-Tinville announced that "play by the rules" had been captured by revolutionary vigilance, and faced the supreme penalty. This pious phrase, he said, is the tribute power pays to the oppressed. Yes, he cried, the feudal peasants whose daughters were raped by Monsieur Le Vicomte "played by the rules," even as they groaned under the extra taxes levied by the Vicomte. "Our glorious revolution says No, we do not play by the rules." A stormy ovation accompanied the condemned to his final night in the Conciergerie.

The keen blade of justice must fall swiftly on the word "tsunami" which has turned into a cliché through overuse with astonishing speed. This happened rapidly after the 2004 Indian Ocean tsunami and its use reached epidemic proportions after the tsunami in Japan in 2011. Its use is mainly to add verbal spice and drama to usually mundane events by suggesting that what is happening is massive, devastating, and unstoppable.

Users of the word can often hope to see their use of the phrase "a tsunami of ..." promoted into a headline. Take, for instance, the case of identity theft tax fraud in southern Florida. Whatever else this is doing it is not, unlike Sri Lanka in 2004 or Fukushima in 2011, killing a lot of people. But the chief federal prosecutor for the Southern District of Florida, Wilfredo A. Ferrer, first described it as an "epidemic" and then added "the IRS is doing what they can to prevent this, but this is like a tsunami of fraud."

And sure enough "Tsunami of Fraud" was in the headline in the *International Herald Tribune* version of the *New York Times* story.

June 4
To: Patrick Cockburn
Subject: Directions

After reviewing our intended restaurants in what aides emphasized was *an unusual personal initiative*, it seems to me much better you come directly to the apartment, leave your bags, and then we can walk the 100m or so to a restaurant reconnoitered by Daisy.

Tell your taxi driver to cross on to the Ile St. Louis from the right bank (i.e. Gare du Nord side) across the Pont Marie, debouching—on the Ile itself—into the Rue Des Deux Ponts.

Cross straight over the Quais Bourbon/d'Anjoi running on the northern edge of the Ile. Then, take a RIGHT, onto the Rue St. Louis en L'Ile (which is the street running up the middle of the Ile). Then take the first RIGHT on the Rue Regrattier, go about 20 m. Number 24 is on the right hand side and an antique shop on the left. We'll be able to spot you.

NB I think there's some mysterious Ile St. Louis elsewhere in their search engines. Just thunder Ile St. Louis, next to Notre Dame island.

June 15
I'd never realized, until reading Neil Schaeffer's biography, how close Sade came to being guillotined by the Committee of Public Safety.

His trial, which would also have been his death sentence followed by instant decapitation, was scheduled for July 27, 1794. But the bailiff never came for him at his prison at Picpus. There's no clear explanation why. Bribery of the bailiff by Sade's faithful friend Mme. Quesnet may have been Sade's salvation. That same day, July 27, spelled Robespierre's own doom, on 9 Thermidor, in the revolutionary calendar. The next day Robespierre was executed and Sade was safe. He was freed on October 15, 1794. This was not the end of his experience in prison. By the end of 1801 Sade was in Charenton, dying there in 1814, his final liaison being with Magdeleine LeClerc, a seventeen-year-old. He was seventy-four and there seems to have been affection on both sides. He recorded her visits to the prison meticulously, as was his habit. The last embrace was their ninety-fourth.

Poor Mme. de Sade. She had to run around Paris looking for glass test tubes that would serve as dildos for her husband, the Marquis, to use in auto-erotic stimulation in his prison in Vincennes. She had to order them from a glass-blowing factory, where the sales folk would ogle respectable Renee, indicating their view that these glass flasks—Sade wanted some of them 9.5 inches in circumference—were intended for her own gratification. In twenty-seven months, Sade noted, he used such flasks a total of 6,536 times, an average of eight a day.

Names Sade called his wife in one letter sent from Vincennes in the late fall of 1783 included "Mohammed's delight," "heavenly pussy," "fresh pork of my thoughts," "shining paintbox of my eyes," "mirror of beauty," "spur of my nerves," "violet of the Garden of Eden," "seventeenth planet of space," "discharge of angelic spirit," "rose fallen from the bosom of Graces," "my baby doll."

June 22

The predictable word is in from Rio: failure. The conference twenty years on from the huge Earth Summit, Rio '92, has been unable to produce even the pretense of an energetic verbal commitment of the world's community to "sustainable principles."

The reason? These conferences have always been pretty fraudulent affairs, lofted on excited green rhetoric and larded with ominous advisories that "this time we cannot afford to fail" and that "the tipping point" is finally here. But failure has been a loyal companion, and many a tipping point has tipped without amiss. There is no such thing as a world "community." There are rich nations and poor nations, all with differing national interests and the former will never accede willingly to the agendas of the latter, however intricate the language of the final windy "declaration." Since Gro Brundtland lofted it to glory in 1987, the word "sustainable" has long been drained of all meaning.

The general absurdity of these earth summits—Rio, Kyoto, Copenhagen, Durban, and now Rio again—is summed up in what the green forces hoped this time would be a concluding declaration to which enough nations could fix their name and declare Victory for the planet. Originally it was to be the commitment to a "Green World," but not enough nations cared for that so the fall-back face-saver was a plan for a UN treaty to protect the international high seas.

To the greens' utter astonishment, early on Tuesday it turned out that the US and Venezuela were vetoing this plan. Whatever Hugo Chàvez's motives, the reason for the US veto was obvious and should have been so from the moment the plan was mooted. The Brazilians threw in the towel, insisting on a spineless final declaration. "Sustainability" was suddenly thrust forward as a face-saver.

Like some Trollopian parson, somehow surviving the bureaucratic infighting was the Commission on Sustainable Development, which had been leading a quiet and unassuming life in some UN back office. Now the hitherto toothless Commission will be elevated into a high-level body charged with monitoring and enforcing "sustainable development goals" (SDGs) and will report to the UN General Assembly. Among its possible areas of concern: food security and sustainable agriculture; sustainable energy for all; water access and efficiency; sustainable cities; green jobs, decent work, and something called social inclusion.

By the time the actual world leaders settled into their suites—US President Barack Obama, Britain's David Cameron, and German leader Angela Merkel were all no-shows—there was absolutely nothing to do: no rousing declarations, just muted jawboning about how the mere fact that these sessions were taking place was important for the planet.

These and other conferences sustain, year by year, a kind of fiscal stimulus for NGOs and the hospitality industry. Ban Ki-Moon himself admits nothing useful will be agreed in Rio but says calling such conferences "junkets" is irresponsible. He says: "If you can find any alternative, please let me know."

July 11

Hardly had the boyish visage of JPMorgan Chase's Jamie Dimon quit CNN screens than it was succeeded by that of Bob Diamond, former chief executive of Barclays, accused of masterminding the greatest financial scandal in the history of Britain. Columnists shook with rage at the "reeking cesspool" being disclosed—disclosed, mind you, four long years after the *Wall Street Journal* broke the story that the Libor was being fixed. Libor, which stands for "London interbank offered rate," is supposed to be based on the average rate of interest banks charge to borrow from one another. The rate is set every morning by a panel of banks. Each bank "submits" the rates at which it believes it can borrow from the collective money pool, from overnight to twelve months.

Libor is the benchmark for investments all over the world—the *Financial Times* estimates that $350 trillion worth of contracts have been pegged to it. It is also considered a barometer of a bank's health. Just as customers with bad credit records have to pay higher interest rates, banks deemed in financial distress have to pay more to borrow. In October 2008, a doomsday month for the world banking industry, it looked like Barclays was next in line for a rescue after taxpayers bailed out the Royal Bank of Scotland and Lloyds/HBOS on October 13. One big warning flare was that beleaguered Barclays could borrow from the common money pool only at a very high rate of interest. The answer was to fix the rate, with Barclays traders secretly winching it down. It was all completely illegal.

Next thing we knew, there was Diamond being reprimanded by a Select Committee of the House of Commons for being nothing better than a common thief. But then into the hurly-burly suddenly intruded a new actor, actually one in the form of a savior: Paul Tucker, deputy governor of the Bank of England. It turned out that Diamond and Tucker had had a conversation of considerable moment, one prudently recorded by Barclays, on October 29, 2008.

Diamond said Tucker had relayed concerns from "senior Whitehall figures" that Barclays's Libor was consistently higher than that of other banks. Tucker is alleged to have conveyed the view from Westminster that the bank's rate did not "always need to appear as high as it had recently." In other words, Westminster wanted Barclays to massage its rate to a lower level.

But all with full deniability. According to Barclays, "Bob Diamond did not believe he received an instruction from Paul Tucker or that he gave an instruction to [former top Barclays deputy] Jerry del Missier. However, Jerry del Missier concluded that an instruction had been passed down from the Bank of England not to keep Libors so high and he therefore passed down a direction to that effect to the submitters."

Barclays said there was no allegation by the authorities that this instruction was intended to manipulate the Libor. And when he was questioned by Tory MP David Ruffley on July 9, Tucker testified that "a bell did not go off in my head" that banks were lowering their Libor submissions.

Marvelous: the join between civil society and state was tactfully seamless, with deniability all round.

So first there are the "senior Whitehall figures" (one turned out to be Cabinet Secretary Sir Jeremy Heywood)—i.e., the permanent government running Britain. When a senior Whitehall figure urges the commission of a serious crime, he merely murmurs that the bank's Libor did not "always need to appear as high as it had recently." There then follows a flurry of talk about misunderstandings but, Lord save us, certainly *not* an order to fix the Libor. Then, unmistakably, there is a huge plunge in Barclays's rate. The government's concern—that Barclays might appear to be on the brink—is averted.

But we live in a capitalist world, duly furnished with its rewards and penalties. Barclays has agreed to a $450 million settlement, and Diamond and del Missier have resigned. On his way out the door, Diamond said he'd been promised £18 million ($28 million) as a golden handshake. The standing committee had a good jeer, but Diamond stuck to his guns, and there the matter rested until July 10, when Barclays announced that Diamond will forfeit up to £20 million ($30 million) in bonuses and incentives but will retain one year's salary, pension, and other benefits worth £2 million ($3 million).

Of course, there have been furious calls for further punishment and reform. Labour leader Ed Miliband says, "We should break the dominance of the big five banks … and strike off those whose conduct lets this country down and prosecute those who break the law." He also wants to increase competition by forcing the big banks to sell off up to 1,000 of their branches. In the current culture of rabid criminality in the banking system, that would surely be unwise, unleashing 1,000 small-time banksters.

People calling for banking reform on either side of the Atlantic are underestimating the problems of enforcement. A writer on the financial news blog Zero Hedge recently remarked that "the Libor scandal seems to be waking people up to manipulation and fraud by the big banks." Of course, there are tools at the ready: sanctions, tribunals, a ban for life for crooked traders. But Libor was meant to be the prime glittering advertisement for the free market. Now it turns out that the whole thing is a fix—a grimy hand all too visible. It's like the spy in Conrad's *Secret Agent* vowing to destroy the first meridian.

Is it possible to reform the banking system? There are the usual nostrums—tighter regulations, savage penalties for misbehavior, a ban from financial markets for life. But I have to say I'm dubious. I think the system will collapse, but not through our agency.

July 13

Two years after he was sacked by President Obama as the top commander in Afghanistan for suggesting to *Rolling Stone* magazine that the real enemy were "the wimps in the White House," General Stanley A. McChrystal has recycled a perennial chestnut: Bring back the draft—i.e., a conscripted army, not the volunteer army of today. These days McChrystal teaches at Yale with what must be a protection unique in the annals of academic freedom. Everything he tells his students is by contractual agreement off the record.

But he made his proposal about the draft in a public venue. McChrystal claimed: "One of the few good legacies of Vietnam is that after years of abuses we finally learned how to run the draft fairly. A strictly impartial lottery, with no deferments, can ensure that the draft intake matches military needs. Chance, not connections or clever manipulation, would determine who serves."

It's certainly true that the volunteer army is a mess. Suicides are surging among the troops. According to AP, the 154 suicides for active duty troops in the first 155 days of the year far outdistance the US forces killed in Afghanistan. The volunteer army also struggles with increased sexual assaults, alcohol abuse, and domestic violence. Liberals like the idea of a draft army because they think it would curb any President's eagerness to go to war. There are indeed sound arguments for a draft. They were put eloquently not so long ago by Bill Broyles, a Vietnam vet: "In spite of the President's insistence that our very civilization is at stake, the privileged aren't flocking to the flag."

The war, Broyles wrote, is being fought by Other People's Children. If the children of the nation's elites were facing enemy fire without body armor, riding through gauntlets of bombs in unarmored Humvees, fighting desperately in an increasingly hostile environment because of arrogant and incompetent leadership, then those problems might well find faster solutions. The truth is that despite all these fine words, a draft is never going to happen. The military-industrial complex needs the money—it's why they're cutting back troops right now.

When Obama introduced "the new strategy" last year, he emphasized that the Pentagon will be getting more money not less. In the past five years the US has spent $2.59 trillion on defense. The new plans call for an allocation of $2.725 trillion between 2013 and 2017. So much for any peace dividend when the troops come home from Afghanistan.

As my brother Andrew Cockburn recently predicted, the budget will grow but the military will shrink. There will be no more "nation building" with its long and expensive occupations. Overall, troop levels will be cut by about 100,000 soldiers and marines. Fewer new planes will be built. America will no longer be equipped to fight two full-scale wars at the same time—an official requirement for decades.

Such was the military-cultural context for calls for the draft: huge ground forces stocked with draftees. What we have now is precisely the opposite—robot/drone wars, with no need for suicidal soldiers or politically awkward draftee casualties. The money all goes to Lockheed and the other big aerospace companies. Remember there's a good reason why they abolished the conscript army. It mutinied in Vietnam and thus was a prime factor in America's defeat.

Afterword

In one of the many diverting episodes in *A Colossal Wreck* my father describes an evening in his house in Petrolia, when, as a storm blows outside and friends are over, he recounts adventures with *7 Days*, a weekly newspaper he worked on in London in the sixties: "By dawn we had the pages made up and then it was a rush to the train station, then an hour down to the printers. So different now; so much easier, so much cheaper. Who says there isn't progress in human affairs, though I do miss the inky excitement of those old hot type days."

My father embodied a kind of inky excitement. It wasn't just that his clothes often bore the traces of his involvement with leaking pens, old cars, gardening tools, or blackened saucepans, but also that he contained the energy and strength of a team of nineteenth-century revolutionary printers working to a deadline.

I remember how, on childhood trips with my father, I tried to keep up with his lean galloping figure as he sped through airports and car parks laden with the tools of his trade. In the age before laptops and mobiles, he'd think nothing of carrying a fax machine and a typewriter along with his favored fiberglass suitcases heavy with books, a leather (ink-stained) sack-like bag of old cameras and lenses, Turkish coffee decanters and an electric ring for motel breakfast enhancement, as well as an array of colorful scarves to put over the motel lamps to create a more convivial atmosphere. On arrival at any new place his suitcases exploded with useful and charming items, which he'd immediately deploy. At the bottom of his pockets languished all sorts of objects. To his amazement his favorite penknife was once confiscated in De Gaulle airport.

He could write anywhere, and he did. Throughout the last three months of his illness in Spring 2012 he wrote in the crowded Wi-Fi lounge of the hospital where we resided, his back to a piano from which often thundered grotesquely sentimental tunes played by a fellow patient. Always a deadline looming, he dictated his last column to me for the UK site *The First Post*. One word came back by email from the editor, Nigel Horne: "*Brilliant*."

Nigel was not the only one who had no inkling my father was ill. He wanted to keep his illness to himself, out of his writing, out of the press and out of many of his close friendships. He didn't want the distraction of death talk, and he wanted to be seen as he had always been—engaged, interested, unambivalently alive. He would keep writing to the end, in the manner that he always had. And, as he points out in the first entry of this book, he didn't go in for death much, preferring things more "bushy-tailed."

His energy was such that he was assumed invincible. Friends felt they would forever call on him for his take on world events, or for a gossip, or advice on anything from heartbreak to the best kind of glue for fixing broken china. Neighbors dropped by to discuss all manner of things. Young local artists knew him as a patron and came by to see their work up on his walls. Master craftsmen called in to go over plans for the next building project. The cider house, Greek temple, redwood tower, still room, dark room, stables and library were just some of the additions resulting from these collaborations. At home the phone rang constantly and I admired his habit of picking it up every time, if only to say he was on a deadline and could he call them back in ten minutes …

Friends took it for granted that they would one day see his ninety-five-year-old figure behind the wheel of the 1959 Chrysler Imperial as he roared past the ordinary Subarus on the road out of Petrolia. His cars were more than just vehicles. Repeated breakdowns, though exasperating, perhaps provided adventure that might otherwise be missing. Each time one of his various cars failed last year, he was miraculously rescued, by a really nice Marine for example, or an engaging nurse, and in the most unlikely or dangerous of spots. He would report on these encounters when he got home. He was always interested in people. A few days before he died, when a doctor asked him, "How are you feeling, Mr. Cockburn?" he replied, "I'm good. And how are you?"

When I was a teenager my father used to suggest I read the dictionary when I had a spare minute, or if I was feeling a bit down. His own father, Claud, had recommended a dip into Marx if darkness descended. The point being made was a reminder not to collapse, to find meaning, counter chaos with spirited punches—get to the root of things and then improvise, blow your trumpet from there.

"Beat the Devil," "Fanning the Flames of Discontent"—these phrases were at one point in the '80s darned into colorful patches onto his jacket and baseball cap. And more recently *CounterPunch* designed a badge featuring the slogan "Dogs Against Romney" above an image of our dog Jasper (who wouldn't forget Seamus's ordeal on the roof of Mitt's car).

His death came as an impossible blow, not only to those closest to him, but to the thousands that depended upon his voice week after week. That voice remains, and is at its constant best, in *A Colossal Wreck*.

Daisy Cockburn
Petrolia, March 2013

Index

On the Typeface

This book is set in Minion, a typeface designed by Robert Slimbach for Adobe Systems in 1990, which has become one of the few contemporary book faces to rival the classic types of Caslon, Bembo, and Garamond. Though it has no obvious precursor, it retains a calligraphic sentiment that Robert Bringhurst dubs "neohumanist" in his *Elements of Typographic Style*.

Telltale features of Minion include the subtle cant in the bar of the "e," the angular bowl of the "a," and the tapered bulbs that terminate the head of the "a" and the tails of the "y" and "j."

Minion's restrained personality and even color have made it a popular workhorse type, the narrow set width of which provides economy yet does not detract from its suitability for book settings.